W9-BTG-690

Regis College Library
15 ST. MARY STREET
TORONTO, ONTARIO, CANADA
M4Y 2R5

FUNDAMENTALISMS
COMPREHENDED

THE FUNDAMENTALISM PROJECT

————————— VOLUME —————————
5

FUNDAMENTALISMS COMPREHENDED

BL
238
F83
1991
v. 5

EDITED BY
Martin E. Marty and R. Scott Appleby

Sponsored by
The American Academy of Arts and Sciences

Regis College Library
15 ST. MARY STREET
TORONTO, ONTARIO, CANADA
M4Y 2R5

WITHDRAWN

The University of Chicago Press
Chicago and London

MARTIN E. MARTY and R. SCOTT APPLEBY direct the Fundamentalism Project. Marty, the Fairfax M. Cone Distinguished Service Professor of the History of Modern Christianity at the University of Chicago, is senior editor of *The Christian Century* and the author of numerous books, including the multivolume *Modern American Religion,* also published by the Univeristy of Chicago Press. Appleby, associate professor of history and director of the Cushwa Center for the Study of American Catholicism at the University of Notre Dame, is the author of *"Church and Age Unite!" The Modernist Impulse in American Catholicism.*

The collection of essays in this volume is based on a project conducted under the auspices of the American Academy of Arts and Sciences and supported by a grant from the John D. and Catherine T. MacArthur Foundation. The opinions expressed are those of the individual authors only, and do not necessarily reflect the views of the American Academy or the supporting foundation.

The University of Chicago Press, Chicago 60637
The University of Chicago Press, Ltd., London
© 1995 by The University of Chicago
All rights reserved. Published 1995
Printed in the United States of America

04 03 02 01 00 99 98 97 96 95 5 4 3 2 1

ISBN (cloth): 0-226-50887-0

Library of Congress Cataloging-in-Publication Data

Fundamentalisms comprehended / edited by Martin E. Marty and R. Scott Appleby.
      p.   cm. — (The Fundamentalism project ; v. 5)
    "Sponsored by the American Academy of Arts and Sciences."
    Includes bibliographical references and index.
    1. Religious fundamentalism. 2. Religion and sociology. 3. Religions. I. Marty, Martin E., 1928– . II. Appleby, R. Scott, 1956– . III. American Academy of Arts and Sciences. IV. Series.
BL238.F83   1991   vol. 5
291′.09′04 s—dc20   94-45338
[291′.09′04]   CIP

∞ The paper used in this publication meets the minimum requirements of the American National Standard for Information Sciences—Permanence of Paper for Printed Library Materials, ANSI Z39.48—1984.

CONTENTS

Part 3 Fundamentalisms Compared within Traditions

Part 4 New Disciplinary Approaches and Interpretations

Part 5 Fundamentalisms Comprehended

ACKNOWLEDGMENTS

We thank first the advisers who began planning and conceptualizing this volume in meetings at the House of the American Academy of Arts and Sciences in Cambridge, Massachusetts. Gabriel A. Almond, Nancy T. Ammerman, T. N. Madan, Stephen Graubard, Samuel C. Heilman, Emmanuel Sivan, Marvin Zonis, and Tu Wei-Ming participated in those sessions on May 10 and 11, 1992.

Also contributing significantly to discussions in Cambridge and Chicago were Walter Andersen, Leonard Binder, Walter Capps, José Casanova, Francis Deng, Charles Dunbar, Hugh Roberts, David Rapoport, John Garvey, R. Kent Greenawalt, Elaine Pagels, Douglas Johnston, David Little, Martha Olcott, Hilal Khashan, Susan Rose, S. N. Eisenstadt, William Pfaff, Sadik Al-Azm, and Martin Kramer. Professors Almond, Appleby, and Sivan owe a special thanks to Raymond Grew, who challenged and thereby improved our early formulations of the concluding essay of this volume. Many other scholars contributed to this volume through written responses and criticisms of particular essays after they were presented during a public conference in March 1993; those not mentioned here by name are acknowledged by the authors in the endnotes.

One of the most gratifying aspects of directing an interdisciplinary, crosscultural project was the experience of working closely with a core team of scholars who also became good friends. For their insight, dedication, and fellowship we thank Mumtaz Ahmad, Gabriel A. Almond, Nancy T. Ammerman, Robert E. Frykenberg, Samuel C. Heilman, Timur Kuran, Bruce B. Lawrence, Daniel H. Levine, T. N. Madan, Robert McKinley, Harjot Oberoi, and Emmanuel Sivan.

Joel Orlen, executive officer of the American Academy of Arts and Sciences, provided leadership and encouragement during the six years of the project. We appreciate his various efforts on behalf of the project, and his prudent counsel at key moments in its development.

Alan Thomas of the University of Chicago Press committed significant resources and time to a project that has produced five handsome (and large) multi-authored volumes in five years. Anyone familiar with academic publishing will recognize the extraordinary service Alan performed in directing these manuscripts through the publication process as efficiently and quickly as he did. That he was able to offer substantive recommendations and criticisms along the way is doubly impressive, given his many other responsibilities. He was ably assisted in this work by Randolph M. Petilos. We also thank Jean Eckenfels and Joann M. Hoy, who contributed to the editorial process for the present volume in significant ways.

The University of Chicago professors W. Clark Gilpin, dean of the Divinity School, and Frank Reynolds, director of the Institute for the Advanced Study of Religion, granted coveted office space to the project and invited our colleagues to participate in the stimulating intellectual life of Swift Hall. We thank them for fostering the spirit of collegiality and collaboration that characterized our experience at the Divinity School these years.

Later stages of the editorial work, proofreading, and technical preparation of the volume took place at the University of Notre Dame. There John H. Haas and Angela Appleby-Purcell contributed many long hours, for which we are most grateful. Duane G. Jundt skillfully prepared the index.

For their many sacrifices in support of this work, Harriet Marty and Peggy Appleby each deserve a medal of valor in addition to our love, admiration and thanks.

During the six-shading-into-seven years of the project Barbara Lockwood logged hundreds of hours of overtime managing the office, responding to correspondence, planning conferences, hosting international travelers, and bearing the pressures of working with two men whose personalities may politely be described as "driven." Few people could have endured the intensity of demands with the competence and grace that Barbara exhibited daily. We owe our deepest appreciation to her.

INTRODUCTION

Martin E. Marty and R. Scott Appleby

F*undamentalisms Comprehended* is the fifth and final volume in a series examining contemporary militant and political religious movements which have organized in reaction to the prevailing patterns of modernization in their respective societies.

The first volume in the series, *Fundamentalisms Observed* (1991), presented fourteen detailed studies of movements within Christianity, Judaism, Islam, Hinduism, Sikhism, Buddhism, and Confucianism, which, despite the substantive differences among them in terms of doctrine, cosmology, social composition, size, organization, and scope of influence, share certain general traits. In those studies, fundamentalism, the term used to refer to these shared traits, was described as, among other things, a tendency of some members of traditional religious communities to separate from fellow believers and to redefine the sacred community in terms of its disciplined opposition to nonbelievers and "lukewarm" believers alike. "Fundamentalists" within these historic religious traditions, convinced of the conspiratorial nature of secularists and liberal religionists, adopted a set of strategies for fighting back against what is perceived as a concerted effort by secular states or elements within them to push people of religious consciousness and conscience to the margins of society. Male charismatic or authoritarian leaders emerged from each religious tradition, often in defiance of the conventions and conventional leadership of the tradition in its nineteenth- or twentieth-century incarnations. Acting strategically, these new fundamentalist leaders ransacked the tradition's past, retrieving and restoring neglected or soft-pedaled doctrines and practices, and creating others, in a largely successful effort to construct a religiopolitical ideology capable of mobilizing disgruntled youth into militant cadres or into grass-roots political organizations. The religious ideologues established new boundaries between "insiders" and "outsiders" and imposed a strict discipline on their followers; in many if not all cases, they were able to elevate their mission to a spiritual plane in which eschatological expectation and apocalyptic urgency informed even the most mundane world-building tasks of the group.

All of this unfolded in the name of defending and preserving a hallowed identity rooted in religious tradition but now under assault. *Fundamentalisms Observed* demonstrated, however, that radical Shi'ite Muslims in Lebanon and Iran, militant Sikhs in Punjab, Jewish extremists on the West Bank, Hindu nationalists at Ayodhya, and Christian cultural warriors in the United States—despite being worlds apart from one another geographically, historically, and in the specific content of their beliefs and practices—were establishing "progressive," world-creating and world-conquering movements that looked to the past for inspiration rather than for a blue-print. Direction, and models, would come not only from a selective interpretation of the sacred past, but also from a shrewd (or sometimes awkward) mimesis of what works in the present. Thus fundamentalists are important players in local, regional and even national politics not as a result of their nostalgia or "backwardness," by which their underestimators often know them, but for their ability to adapt to modern organ-fjizational imperatives, political strategies, communications advances, and economic theories.

The second and third volumes in the series were published simultaneously in 1993 as companion pieces, for they explored the extent of influence of fundamentalist move-ments in six "zones" or spheres of human existence. *Fundamentalisms and Society* measured the impact of Islamic, Christian, and Jewish fundamentalisms on scientific research and the application of technology in societies in North America and the Middle East. Contributors to the volume also explored a fundamentalist "family trait"—the defense and consolidation of patriarchy as the divine plan for the moral ordering of society—by surveying the role of women and children in fundamentalist movements of the United States, Latin America, Egypt, Iran, Pakistan and Japan. Fi-nally, other contributors analyzed fundamentalist educational systems and communi-cations networks in the United States, Guatemala, Israel, Iran, and India.

Because the state regulates many aspects of social existence and establishes the basic political and cultural conditions within which social life occurs, fundamentalists inevi-tably become involved not only in science, education, and domestic reform, but also in modern political life. Even when fundamentalists attempt to preserve their separate-ness from secular society, they find themselves participating in a common discourse about modernization, development, political structures, and economic planning. *Fun-damentalisms and the State* chronicled fundamentalists' participation in politics, law-making, and economics up to 1992. Case studies included Christian anti-abortion activists in the United States and militants in Northern Ireland; Muslim radicals in Iran, Egypt, Pakistan, Saudi Arabia, Sudan, and Turkey; Jewish settlers in Israel; and Hindu, Sikh, and Buddhist extremists in South Asia. The volume also compared a variety of militant fundamentalists in their use of violence as a political tool.

In some states—Iran, Pakistan, India, and the United States, to name a few—reli-gious fundamentalists have influenced the terms of political and social discourse, but they have also found the construction of an Islamic or Christian or Jewish polity to be well out of reach. This appears to be the case even in contemporary, postrevolutionary Iran, the premier late-twentieth-century "fundamentalist" state, where economic exigencies and international politics, among other forces, have conspired to dissipate Islamic revolutionary energies and have undermined the principles of Khomeinism as the litmus test for practical political decisions.[1] When fundamentalists play politics to influence the policies of the state, in other words, they are necessarily involved in compromise and accommodation. Political involvement may alter the exclusivist, dogmatic, confrontational mode of the fundamentalist to such a degree that the word *fundamentalism* or its cognate is no longer appropriate.

Indeed, how may we account for the various attitudes, ideologies, and behaviors of fundamentalist movements toward the outside world? Drawing upon the same religious tradition, why do certain fundamentalist movements act aggressively against outsiders, while others are integrationist or accommodationist, still others passive or separatist in relation to the surrounding communities and cultures? *Accounting for Fundamentalisms* (1994), the fourth volume in the University of Chicago Press series, explores the dynamic character of religious radicalism as it moves into or away from a fundamentalist mode of relating to the outside world. What "causes" a modern religious movement to become militant and exclusivist or, by contrast, to join coalitions and lower its defenses? The twenty-eight contributors to the volume explore the conditions under which fundamentalist movements around the world change their ideological and behavioral patterns, resulting in either a greater or lesser engagement with people and forces outside the group or movement. Each author charted the relationship, over time, between the *organizational characteristics* of a particular fundamentalist movement (its structure, size and social composition, recruitment process, mode of governance or decision making, and means of retaining members and mobilizing resources) and its *changing worldviews, ideologies, and programs* (the "fields of discourse" fundamentalist leaders construct through the reinterpretation of symbols and ethical traditions, through the stories they tell of themselves, of the world, and of their aims, etc.). As with the preceding volumes in the series, examples were drawn from several major religious traditions, including Judaism (e.g., the Lubavitcher Hasidim, the Gush Emunim, and the world of Torah studies), Hinduism (e.g., the Vishwa Hindu Parishad and the Bharatiya Janata Party), Christianity (e.g., South Asian Pentecostals, and the Italian Catholics of Comunione e Liberazione), and Islam (e.g., Iraqi Shi'ites and Algerian Sunnis of the Islamic Salvation Front [FIS]).

Together these four volumes of essays provide the "database" for *Fundamentalisms Comprehended,* the culmination of the series. *Webster's Encyclopedic Dictionary* offers two definitions for the verb *to comprehend:* "1. to understand the nature or meaning of; grasp with the mind; perceive. . . . 2. to take in or embrace; include; comprise."[2] In choosing the present volume's title we did not intend to proclaim victory in our seven-year quest "to grasp with the mind" the "nature and meaning of" global fundamentalisms; rather, we entertain the more modest goal of taking in or embracing a variety of movements in one inclusive analytical statement.

The capstone statement of the Fundamentalism Project takes the form of a four-part, collaborative, monograph-length essay comprising chapters 16–19 of this volume. Authored by Fundamentalism Project veterans Gabriel Almond, Emmanuel Sivan, and Scott Appleby, the essay, in chapter 16, examines the "genus and species" of fundamentalism by presenting five ideological and four organizational properties of the "family," as these properties have been observed in various configurations during the fieldwork and empirical research of the project. Basing their judgments on the findings reported in the previous volumes and on their own independent research, the authors differentiate among religious movements around the world on the basis of their manifestation, or lack thereof, of these properties. Almond, Sivan, and Appleby thus make the necessary distinction between fundamentalist movements, on the one hand, and "fundamentalist-like" movements that behave somewhat differently; they also indicate that certain movements or groups clustered previously under the comparative rubric "fundamentalism" do not properly belong there.

Chapter 17 describes four patterns of fundamentalist behavior toward the world outside the religious enclave; these patterns are the world conqueror, the world transformer, the world creator, and the world renouncer. The chapter also presents a model for explaining the origins, emergence, growth, strategies, and decline of fundamentalist and fundamentalist-like movements. In developing the model, the authors proceeded on the theoretical principle established in *Accounting for Fundamentalisms*: the explanation of a particular fundamentalist movement is found in the interaction between its external environment (i.e., the society's political order, economic patterns, religious culture, and so on), and its organizational characteristics, worldview, and historical experience. In accord with this principle, Almond, Sivan, and Appleby provide a grid of three interlocking levels of analysis—the long-term economic, social, religious, and political structures that provide the conditions in which fundamentalisms operate; the short-term crises or "triggers" that inspire movements or affect their fate; and the internal dynamics of the movements themselves. This chapter theorizes about the ways these levels interact in the emergence of fundamentalist movements and in determining whether a given movement at a given time will follow a world-conquering or world-transforming or world-creating or world-renouncing pattern of relation to outsiders.

Chapter 18 tests the theory in action, as the authors run the case studies through the grid, organizing the material according to the four patterns of relation to the world. The chapter explains why some movements attempt to "conquer" outsiders, while others seek to transform society gradually, and still others withdraw from society to create a world of their own. This analytical process yields insightful narratives about the patterns of origin, growth, and decline of fundamentalist movements in the late twentieth century. Chapter 19 focuses more narrowly on the political and ethnic aspects of fundamentalism, zeroing in on the political strategies adopted by different movements in different cultural and political settings.

This concluding essay (chapters 16–19) should be read in tandem with the opening chapter of the volume, Sivan's compelling portrait of "The Enclave Culture," which offers a rich, detailed, phenomenological description of the lifeworld of Jewish, Christian, and Muslim fundamentalist communities. What Sivan's opening essay implies about the dynamics of fundamentalisms' worldviews, practices, and internal organization, the collaborative essay makes explicit by positing the four patterns by which fundamentalist movements relate to the outside world. In two of these patterns, the world renouncer and world creator, readers will discover resonances to the literature on "expressive" sects; in another pattern, the world transformer, the analogy to "transformative" sects is clear. In the world conqueror model, we see fundamentalisms in their hegemonic trajectory, in their attempt to break the bonds of "sect" as well as church or synagogue or mosque. Students of Max Weber, H. Richard Niebuhr, and other typologists of religiopolitical communities will find these categories familiar but not confining, we hope, as they are here employed.

Thus the volume is framed, so to speak, by two major essays that reflect, to some degree at least, the understandings of the core members of The Fundamentalism Project on matters of phenomenology, definition, theory, and comparative analysis. "To some degree": Marty, Appleby, Almond, and Sivan are hardly the only "core members" of the project; several other scholars have participated in our common inquiry from the beginning, and frequently along the way. These scholars do not agree on every detail of interpretation—who would expect that they would?—and one can readily suppose that the other seventy-five or so contributors have their own qualms about and modifications of our common comparative and definitional enterprise. As with every stage of this project, we directors and editors welcome the diversity of perspective and interpretation; the present "conclusive" volume, being no exception, is appropriately "inclusive."

Thus the authors of the "middle chapters" of the volume—chapters 2 through 15, a vast middle indeed—take a synoptic view of the previous scholarly and journalistic research on various aspects of fundamentalism, in order to draw direct comparisons within and across religious traditions. In so doing, these authors test the project directors' original characterization of fundamentalism as a reactive, selective, absolutist, comprehensive mode of anti-secular religious activism. Various essays focus on different aspects of that preliminary conceptualization of fundamentalism. Ernest Gellner (chapter 11), for example, examines the notion that fundamentalism is a "comprehensive" utopian system, demonstrating that the strength of Islamic fundamentalism lies in its hesitancy to present itself as an all-encompassing guide for economic and political as well as personal and social behavior; this is more clearly seen, Gellner argues, when Islam's reform program is analyzed in comparison with Soviet Marxism's stifling comprehensiveness. Similarly, T. N. Madan's historical survey of Islam in South Asia (chapter 12) challenges the Fundamentalism Project axiom that fundamentalism is uniquely a modern, indeed a twentieth century, phenomenon.

Other middle chapters, while accepting the Marty-Appleby-Almond-Sivan consensus on fundamentalism, take issue with certain aspects of it and contribute further specificity to its presentation. Samuel Heilman's comparative analysis of scholastic enclaves within ultra-Orthodox Judaism and Shi'ite Islam (chapter 2) develops a nuanced distinction between traditionalism and fundamentalism that bears significantly on the volume's definitional enterprise. Said Arjomand (chapter 7) performs a similar service by constructing categorical descriptions of the diverse kinds of fundamentalist movements within Islam. Emile Sahliyeh (chapter 5) looks at three very different groups— militant Sikhs in Punjab, Hizbullah guerrillas in Lebanon, and Hamas activists in Palestine—in order to illustrate some of the comparable environmental conditions that give rise to fundamentalism. Harjot Oberoi (chapter 3) considers Indic fundamentalisms and nationalism in light of Hegel's criteria of modernity, while S. N. Eisenstadt (chapter 10) compares axial-age religion-based civilizations with contemporary "neofundamentalism," seen as a type of modern utopian movement.

May the term *fundamentalism,* employed as a comparative construct rather than as a clumping and clustering device, properly be applied to a variety of movements without introducing serious distortions into the analysis of these autochthonous movements? Daniel Levine (chapter 6) and Gananath Obeyesekere (chapter 9) assess the practice of applying the conceptual lens of "comparative fundamentalism" to the "candidates" in Latin American Pentecostalism and Sri Lankan Buddhism, respectively. Each author explores the usefulness of the term in these settings; each examines both the methodological and conceptual problems with the term, and explains how the reality is often more complex and subtle than any ideal type will allow.

Among these middle chapters is a section devoted to "new" interpretations of, and approaches to, comparative fundamentalism. Not by design or intent but by sheer force of momentum and material available, social scientists have dominated this five-volume survey of fundamentalisms. Regrettably, the humanities have been less in evidence in a project that purports to be interdisciplinary. Literary theorists and social psychologists in particular seem potentially valuable contributors who have made few appearances in these pages. The present volume suggests reasons for this deficiency by exploring, and partially attempting to overcome, the methodological difficulties in drawing a psychosocial profile of fundamentalists (Valerie Hoffman, chapter 8) and in employing literary criticism of fundamentalist "fiction" (Wayne Booth, chapter 15). Focusing on conversion narratives, James Peacock and Tim Pettyjohn (chapter 4) explore the differences between fundamentalisms and mystical or spiritualist reform movements. In this way they begin to comprehend the personal, interior, visionary, and expressive manifestations of fundamentalist, as compared to nonfundamentalist, religious fervor. Gideon Aran's discussion of fundamentalist "humor" (chapter 13) suggests an anthropological approach to the same set of questions.

Comparativists and theorists—and polemicists on both sides of the question—will continue to review the various usages of the word *fundamentalism* and continue to debate whether or not one (Western, originally Protestant Christian) term, even when emptied of its original connotations and used as a broad comparative construct, is sufficient to encompass the "family resemblances" noted by scholars studying these phenomena. As some scholars argue, the term *fundamentalism* may be too laden with pejorative or imperialist connotations to be employed by responsible commentators; in chapter 14, Mark Juergensmeyer carries this argument further by reviewing media representations of "fundamentalism" in the early 1990s. He also notes that the accusation of "fundamentalism" is used to justify human-rights abuses by government authorities in India, Algeria, and elsewhere.

The misuse and vagueness of the term *fundamentalism* is one reason that the American Academy of Arts and Sciences applied a portion of a public policy grant from the MacArthur Foundation to study the varied phenomena to which the term has been applied, and to detail and reinforce the kinds of distinctions made in the present volume. The central substantive similarity among the various movements we identify as fundamentalist is a process of selective retrieval, embellishment, and construction of "essentials" or "fundamentals" of a religious tradition for the purposes of halting the erosion of traditional society and fighting back against the encroachments of secular modernity. The fundamentalizing process, shared by otherwise quite different religiously inspired protest movements, will continue to exist; and a knowledge of its dynamics will continue to be essential to informed discussion of global religiopolitical resurgence, even if the term *fundamentalism* itself fades from the discourse of journalists, scholars, and diplomats.

Notes

1. Elaine Sciolino, "Iran's Problems Raising Doubts of Peril to U.S.," *New York Times,* 5 July 1994, pp. A1, A5.

2. *Webster's Encyclopedic Unabridged Dictionary of the English Language* (Avenel, N.J.: Gramercy Books, 1989), s.v. "comprehend."

1

Fundamentalism as Enclave

The Enclave Culture

Emmanuel Sivan

[T]his is an age of demons and amoral angels and all sorts of deep fears.
Like the first centuries of the Christian era, it's an age of extreme
solutions.
Iris Murdoch, The Message to the Planet

In Exile

Just after World War I, Dr. Nathan Birnbaum, formerly a Jewish secularist thinker (Zionist, then cultural autonomist) who had recently returned to the faith, took stock of the state of Judaism. It was almost a century after the early proponents of ultra-Orthodoxy such as the Hatam Sofer (d. 1839) had been alarmed to discover an "unheard of phenomenon: the father being still God-fearing and knowledgeable in the Talmud while the son desecrates the Sabbath." Birnbaum assessed the impact of fourteen decades of Jewish enlightenment and produced a gloomy diagnosis: most Western European Jews have ceased altogether to be *mitzvot* (precepts) observant and are indifferent to divine Providence; the mass immigration from Eastern Europe to the United States brings hundreds of thousands to a land of greed and licentiousness; and they are bound to lose their religion in this *treifene medina* (defiled country), as it was commonly dubbed by Orthodox rabbis. In Eastern Europe, Birnbaum thought, most Jews still observed the halakha in both ritual and social relations, but there was no mistaking the fact that the curve was on the decline and defections from the faith were on the upswing. The observant, or haredim, live "in exile among Jews" (*in Galus bei Yidn*), that is, among nominal Jews, Jews by birth only.[1]

Even this diagnosis may have been too sanguine. The great halakhic authorities of the day—the Hafetz Haim (Rabbi I. M. HaCohen), and Rabbi E. Wasserman—expressed grave doubts as to the quality of observance and belief among Eastern Europe's Jewish plain folk.[2]

In the post–World War II era, with these masses having been annihilated in the Holocaust, Birnbaum's diagnostic formula seemed to haredi activists more poignant than ever. As Rabbi E. Dessler, who had escaped to England (and then to Israel), put it in an incisive pun, virtually all Jews replace the injunction "thou should be *qdoshim* [sacred]" by a newly concocted one, "thou should be qaddishniks," thus reducing their Judaism to the act of saying the prayer for the dead (*qaddish*) on the memorial days of deceased family members.[3] Small wonder that "in exile among Jews" is indeed one of the most common terms the haredim use, in sermons as much as in informal conversation, in order to denote their sense of being a tiny minority, marginal and alienated.

In the fall of 1990 an ultra-Orthodox weekly, *Ha-Mahane ha-Haredi,* was sentenced by an Israeli court to pay heavy punitive damages for calling a left-wing member of Knesset, a long-time critic of the haredim, a Nazi. The haredi press saw this libel verdict as further proof that "we live in exile among Jews," and, irony of ironies, in the Holy Land.[4] The demographic growth of the ultra-Orthodox community in the 1980s, and its political clout, barely mitigated the gloomy, defensive gloss they tended to put on reality.

At about the same time that Birnbaum coined this term, Rashid Rida, a Syrian-born thinker living in Cairo, pondered the question, "How fares Islam?" He found most so-called believers to be mere "geographical Muslims" (*muslimun jughrafi-yyun*), people who belong to the faith merely by virtue of living in an Islamic land and performing certain rituals. Their belief is tepid, and, worse still, they acquiesce to the European-inspired laws introduced by their ostensibly Muslim rulers who "forsake what was enjoined upon the believers by Allah. . . . They abolish allegedly distasteful penalties such as cutting off the hands of thieves or stoning adulterers and prostitutes. They replace them by man-made laws and penalties."[5]

Terms like the "eclipse of Islam" were already frequent in Rida's day and age, especially after the breakup of the Ottoman Empire, the abolition of the Caliphate (1924), and the imposition of atheistic Communist rule upon Muslim Central Asia. Coining a powerful metaphor to depict this decline was a task left to an Indian Muslim, Maulana Maududi, in the late 1930s, and to an Egyptian, Sayyid Qutb, a decade or so later. They saw a relapse of Islam to a state of *jahiliyya,* that is, to that of pre-Islamic pagan Arabia. Mid-twentieth-century Muslims, like their ancestors thirteen centuries earlier, were a tiny and harassed minority, surrounded by idolators and the groupies of modernity cults, as well as by nominal and hypocritical "believers."[6]

Jahiliyya was an emotion-laden metaphor, redolent of historical connotations. The present day idols—such as nationalism—were Western-imported, but rendered all the more insidious for being cloaked in indigenous garb. In the 1980s another metaphor emerged: "Islam is in exile [*ghurba*] in its own lands," much like it was in Arabia when Muhammad had to flee pagan and hostile Mecca for Medina. As the Hadith has it: "Islam began in exile and will return in exile in the [end of history]. Blessed are the exiled."[7]

Idols more openly inspired by European culture also made blatant inroads. By the late 1950s the Iraqi mullah Muhammad Baqir al-Sadr would voice grave concern over the lure that communism and the Ba'th Party held for youth, including Shi'ite madrasa students. Such jeremiads would soon be echoed in Morocco and Egypt, and were no different in a way than those of al-Sadr's Roman Catholic contemporary, Luigi Giussani, also a theology professor. Giussani, the future founder of the Italian Catholic movement Communione e Liberazione, worried that the nominally Catholic students in Italian high schools and universities were signs of the ultimate victory of the Enlightenment in an increasingly dechristianized and individualistic Italian society, in which some Catholic rituals still subsisted but were increasingly devoid of any real significance. The upshot of this mass defection, Giussani felt, was the marginalization of religiosity. Even a good many of the church's adepts—following theologians like Jacques Maritain and Pierre Teilhard de Chardin—had made their peace with modernity and accepted the autonomy of the world vis-à-vis the faith.[8]

As for those who remained loyal to Islam, their state of mind was expressed by al-Sadr as well as by his Lebanese counterpart, Shaykh Muhammad Husayn Fadlallah. Faced with this seemingly unstoppable decline and defection, Muslims felt despair and humiliation, impotence and disgrace.[9]

After three decades as a missionary in Africa, Archbishop Marcel Lefebvre returned to France in 1962, at the time of decolonization. He discovered to his dismay a similar mood in French Catholic circles. This he attributed to a substantial dwindling of attendance at Mass, a steep decline in new priestly and monastic vocations, and the growing republican liberalism of Catholic political groupings. (These were phenomena no different in nature, yet wider in scope, than those deplored by Giussani in Italy, which had not known the ravages of the French Revolution.) Troubled by this crisis, Lefebvre was soon to suffer a shock when the Second Vatican Council introduced what he considered the wrong type of response to the crisis. Instead of greater discipline, a closing of the ranks, stronger hierarchy, and a more aggressive stance, the council seemed to be moving toward "a conversion of the Church to the World [of modernity]." Lefebvre deplored the accommodative attitude of the council, an attitude based upon the "heretical" principles of collegiality (power-sharing among the bishops), liberty of conscience, and ecumenical dialogue. This was not, he thundered, the remedy needed for an ailing church operating in a "society governed by a liberal and hedonistic mentality."[10]

Even before Birnbaum and Rida wrote their own pessimistic diagnoses of Judaism and Islam, Protestant America was already deeply worried by the late-nineteenth-century expansion of Romanism (a euphemism for "garlic-eating" Catholic immigrants from south and southeast Europe). Protestants experienced their own doubts as to the solidity of the Bible-believing bloc early in the twentieth century. The faithful, who took the name Fundamentalists (ca. 1910), detected a takeover of this bloc (especially of its Baptist and Presbyterian parts) from within by liberal modernism. They saw everywhere the hidden hand of modernist Protestants with their devotion to the higher criticism of the Bible, to German philosophy of the Enlightenment, to the progress-oriented social gospel ("that Godless social-service nonsense"), to accommodation with secularism, and, not least, to the discoveries of science.

By the 1960s the heirs to Protestant fundamentalism began to view the danger as much broader, as coming from a more alluring and external force—secularism, later called secular humanism (or scientific humanism), a full-fledged alternative to religion per se. This social force, said to be predicated upon the twin doctrines of atheism and evolution as well as upon an amoral way of life appealing to humanity's baser instincts (permissiveness, promiscuity, pornography, feminism, etc.), seemed to have usurped cultural hegemony. By controlling the media and the educational establishment and wielding influence upon the intrusive federal government, secular humanism was spreading its facile credo into every nook and cranny and drawing in the naive masses.[11]

Die-hard American Bible believers confronted with this "disintegration of our social order," in Jerry Falwell's terms, came to see themselves as outsiders, aliens in their own land. In the words of the popular revival hymn, they were "stranger[s] here, within a foreign land" or, in the words of reconstructionist thinker Gary North, prisoners of a "new Babylonian captivity." The same metaphors recurred among Catholic Pentecostalists in the United States, who lamented that "[w]e are in a post-Catholic society and in some ways we are Christian exiles in it." The similarity of these statements to Birnbaum's diagnosis of Judaism is evident, as is the adage of Muslim militants: "We are in one ravine [*wadi*] and life is in another." The diagnosis was also shared by European Catholic theologians in the mid-sixties such as Henri de Lubac and Hans Urs von Balthasar (who inspired Giussani), and who noted the marginalization of the old faith by the hegemony of the "atheistic humanism" bred by the Enlightenment.[12]

It is true that at certain moments, after investing in a huge countercultural endeavor, American fundamentalists saw a glimmer of hope: we have reversed the tide, we grow and expand, perhaps we are on the way to restoring our hegemony. This hope fueled the Moral Majority movement when it was launched in 1979. Tim LaHaye, among its other spokesmen, even performed intricate computations to prove that most Americans are not actually lost, being either silent believers or unwitting hostages of the devious secularist forces of moral decay. Once activated and regenerated, they would provide the troops of the coming majority and remake America into a City on the Hill. Some six years later, however, all hopes had evaporated. A mood of doom and despair returned.

Shi'ite radicalism followed the same curve in a shorter span. Fervent visions of Khomeinist insurrections across the Middle East were deflated in a matter of three years following the Iranian revolution. Sunni radicals proved to be lukewarm, if not hostile, to Khomeini's appeal; even Arab Shi'ite communities, whether cowed by repression or depressed by the peripeties of the revolution, were not ready to follow Iran's deed.

Haredim, who comprise 6 percent of Israeli Jews, also indulge sometimes in day-dreaming about becoming a majority—or at least the second largest political bloc—due to their high birthrate and the "growing numbers" (actually no more than several thousand) of secular Jews who make their return (*teshuva*) to the Orthodox fold. For the shorter term, the haredi Jews fantasize that, thanks to the swing votes they control in the Knesset enabling them to make or break government coalitions, they may overhaul legislation and make Israel Jewish again.[13] More often than not, however, they exceed the limits of their clout and find themselves rebuffed, as when Israeli prime minister Yitzhak Shamir balked at the prospect of having to pass the "who is a Jew" bill. Rather than run the risk of incurring the wrath of American Jewry, Shamir broke off negotiations with the Agudat Yisrael and established a national unity coalition in December 1988. The "projects" of Orthodox political control having proved to be chimeric, the deep-lying fear once again came to the fore. A haredi newspaper editorialized:

> Some of us tended to forget that we are in Exile and pretended that we may become kingmakers in this secularist so-called kingdom. We rather have to be afraid of the resurgence of an anti-Orthodox consensus. If we do not close ranks and fight back, antireligious laws will, God forbid, be enacted, and the status quo [in religious matters] disappear. We will be thrown into a rearguard battle for our very survival as Haredi Jews in a "religious autonomy," lest our own educational system, our sacred yeshivas, may not be immune from the claws of the powers-that-be.[14]

This combination of loss of hegemony and mass defection represent, in Protestant parlance, "the worst danger to the church since Luther." Archbishop Lefebvre dubbed it a catastrophe more intimidating than the persecution of Catholics under the French Revolution's Cult of Reason. Haredi rabbis such as the Hazon Ish (d. 1953) and E. M. Schach (b. 1897) consider it the worst calamity in two millennia of life in exile. Sunni and Shi'ite Muslims see it as analogous to the infidels of Mecca falling upon Muhammad's tiny host, and, in the Shi'ite case, as reminiscent of the encirclement of Imam Hussein and his few followers by the Umayyad army, ending in the infamous massacre of the late seventh century. Archbishop Lefebvre compared his tiny flock (perhaps seventy to one hundred thousand worldwide) to the seven thousand disciples of the Prophet Elijah in his fight against the prophets of the Baal.[15]

What makes the danger all the graver is its lure and insidiousness.

Alluring the alternative, secular way of life certainly is. It appeals to the instincts, promising instant gratification, better material conditions, and the experience of "marrying one's own times" in terms of scientific and technological achievement. How easy it is, and how common, to be addicted to it. Religious tradition is likely to be shed lightheartedly, often unwittingly. Tradition succumbs to a pleasant infatuation and dies a sort of sweet death, a painless euthanasia, if you will.

Images of addiction and infatuation crop up incessantly in the fundamentalist diagnosis. Nathan Birnbaum wrote of the "assimilation mania" (*Assimilationgesucht*) from which fellow Jews, especially the enlightened intelligentsia (*maskilim*), "these Jewish rebels," suffered. The Iranian Jalal Al-e Ahmad (d. 1969) coined the term *West-mania,* or rather *Westoxication* (*gharbzadagi*) to explain the predicament of intellectual elites drawn to modern culture. The Westernized (*faranji-ma'ab*) are in fact West-infatuated (the Arabic equivalent, in Sunni parlance, is *mustaghribun*). The secularists had fallen prey to a fit of insanity, said Jonathan Blanchard, while other Protestant polemicists identified the sexual obsession unleashed by permissiveness as the most enticing facet of the secular-hegemonic way of life. Marcel Lefebvre used the metaphor of AIDS—an insidious malady contracted due to permissive behavior—as an apt description of the syndrome afflicting both society and the postconciliar church—a syndrome of pleasurable self-destruction.[16]

The insidiousness of the danger proceeds from its being not only an overt, well-articulated, intellectual challenge, but one that operates on a broader front, in every walk of life, appealing to instinct, to the subconscious, to mimetic action. It unwittingly subverts norms of behavior well before consciousness follows suit, molding social and ritual practice even among people who still consider themselves true believers. "The trouble is that the secularized are wholeheartedly secularized, while the orthodox are no more completely orthodox. Their Jewishness is rather mediocre, tepid, operating by rote," remarks a recent pamphlet of self-styled Concerned Yeshiva Students. This holds true not just for the masses, they add, but for the beliefs of many yeshiva students as well.[17] The result is a state of limbo, the blurring of distinctions (*bilbul tishtush* or *tishtush ha-tehumim*), so frequently deplored in writings of the twentieth-century rabbis or in synagogue sermons.[18] In the Yinglish (Yiddish-English) dialect common to the ultra-Orthodox in the United States one speaks of *mish-mash,* a term that can be found even among Protestant fundamentalists (when they wish, for instance, to excoriate liberal modernists for indifference to the true and crystal-clear instructions of the Gospel). A commonly cited example is the blurring of God-ordained gender distinctions by liberals and humanists alike.[19]

Lack of clarity has many shades and is hence difficult to detect and to pinpoint. No wonder that the Hafetz Haim's halakhic magnum opus, designed to stem the tide, was entitled *Mishna Berura* (The clear code). The same malady he wanted to combat, confusion and disorientation, is often cited by Protestant Bible believers and by Muslim preachers who see it as the upshot of the eclecticism and contrivance (*talfiq* and *iltiqat*) so typical of reformist apologetics, which tried hard to accommodate every modern fad within the tradition.[20]

The Enclave

"The number of defectors is on the rise, while the distinction maintained in the past between apostates and those faithful [to the Covenant] has gotten blurred."[21] This diagnosis of pre–World War II Eastern European Jewry could be borrowed by the proponents of Islamic and Protestant fundamentalism. Fear of losing many members of a traditional religious community seems to be the essential impulse (at least at the leadership level) for the creation and maintenance of fundamentalist movements. This impulse may also be an interesting indicator for the social and cultural dynamics involved in such movements. To grasp its full significance we have to turn to cultural theory, a hermeneutic device developed by the anthropologist Mary Douglas.[22]

Briefly put, cultural theory proposes that in any social context shared cultural ideas (about time and space, human and physical nature, ethics, etc.) will be structured in such a way that individuals within that social context can negotiate their way through the constraints they experience in daily life in order to make sense of the world in which they live.

Social contexts are determined by two sorts of constraints (or claims). *Group* constraints determine the extent to which people are restricted in their social relations by their commitment to a human group. *Grid* constraints restrict how (rather than with whom) people interact by virtue of their category (gender, color, age, formal rank, etc.).

By combining the group and grid dimensions, Douglas developed a typology designed to facilitate comparative analysis. This typology consists of three major (and two minor) social contexts. Each carries with it, as posited above, its own "cultural package" that, together with its prescribed mode of behavior (and organization), makes it into a way of life.

The three major types of social contexts are the *hierarchy,* the *market,* and the *enclave.* The hierarchy is more or less assured of its outer group boundary and invests most of its energy in controlling its various and separate compartments and keeping them in smooth interaction. The market consists of individually negotiated social networks with little interference of group or grid.[23]

The enclave is usually the response to a community's problem with its boundary. Its future seems to be at the mercy of members likely to slip away. For some reason, usually the appeal of the neighboring central community, it cannot stop its members from deserting. Devoid of coercive powers over the members, it cannot punish them; lacking sufficient resources, it cannot reward them. The only control to be deployed in order to shore up the boundary is moral persuasion. The interpretation developed by this type of community thus stands in opposition to outside society. (This is of course easier to achieve when an enclave is created not by pull but by push, that is, by exclusion from the central community, as was the case of the Jews in pre-Emancipation Europe.) In other words, the defining relations for the enclave are "inside-outside" (relations between the enclave and what exists beyond its boundary) rather than "upside-downside" (relations between the hierarchy of social categories within the given community).

At first glance the description seems to fit the primordial problem of the fundamentalist movement, as presented in the preceding section of this essay. Let us now examine in greater detail the culture fundamentalists evolve so as to enable their loyal members to steer their way under the constraints of a way of life designed to seal a porous group boundary.

Wall of Virtue

An enclave's outer boundary is leaky, due above all to the material and social temptations of the central community, which enjoys prestige, cultural hegemony, and access to governmental sanctions as well as to resources (whether the state's or wealthy individuals'). Virtually the only thing the beleaguered enclave can offer from its own authority is moral rewards.

In some instances moral rewards may be accompanied and complemented by social or economic benefits. Access to welfare state emoluments, for example, as in the case of the haredim in the United States and in Israel, may reduce this dependence upon moral suasion, as may charity contributions—by the Saudis to Islamic *jama'at* (associations) in Egypt and North Africa, for example, or by ultra-Orthodox benefactors to students in yeshivot and *kollelim.* Dependence on moral suasion alone is also mitigated by the employment of haredi and Baptist women by the community (as teachers, for instance); by the establishment of cooperatives by the Italian Catholic movement Communione e Liberazione; by the tutoring of student members in Muslim jama'at, and by the granting of soft loans by Islamic banks. Nonetheless, most sanctions are moral in nature, even in these cases.

How does one come to wield such a suasion? Cultural theory posits that the enclave must stress the voluntary character of its members, who are specially chosen (in religious enclaves, elected to salvation by God), and how much the community relies upon their commitment to the "holy cause." The value of each member is highlighted, and distinctions (at least overt and formal ones) between them are minimized as much as possible, a strategy that, as we shall see, shapes the nature of the enclave's authority. Last but not least, the enclave must place the oppressive and morally defiled outside society in sharp contrast to the community of virtuous insiders. A sort of "wall of virtue" is thereby constructed, separating the saved, free, equal (before God or before history), and morally superior enclave from the hitherto-tempting central community. Who but the depraved would desire to cross such a boundary and join the defectors and the evil outsiders?

The wall in question may at times be physical as well (as in the case of the fence surrounding Bob Jones University in South Carolina), but even then its significance is primarily moral. It is quite typical that the organ of the Neturei Karta haredi sect is called "The Wall" (*Ha-Homah*).

The most obvious bricks of the wall of virtue are the shorthand terms used within fundamentalist communities, in a matter-of-fact fashion, in everyday conversation, in sermons, and in their press to designate fellow members: Christians, Muslimun (Muslims), Mu'minun (believers), Yidn (Jews), Reb Yisroel (the Jew as an individual). The sense is unmistakable: the real, the true-blue, full-fledged Christians, Muslims, or Jews. All the rest are cut from an inferior cloth; they are lesser affiliates of the same tradition if not outright rejects—apostates and disbelievers. One also speaks of a "Christian home (or attitude)," an "Islamic solution," "Jewish Jews." The adjective is invariably positive, signifying the sole type in full accordance with the tradition. References to the scriptural basis of that tradition crop up in synonyms: "Bible believers," "Biblical standard," a "Qur'anic way of life," "Torah-true."

The tradition—as could be expected from the above diagnosis—is presented as shrunken and under siege, nay, even persecuted. The faithful, the Believing Remnant, the Last Outpost, Covenant Keepers are some of the most common self-descriptions in fundamentalist writings in the United States.[24] Anxiety as to the fate of the tradition is interlaced with praise for the virtuous who stick with it. And as all these terms have Old Testament roots, it is no wonder that one finds their Hebrew analogues (and, often, original) among haredim: She'rit Yisrael, Shlumei Emunei, Sridim. An exact analogue of the first of these terms, "the remnant of Israel," is used by Lefebvre's and Giussani's disciples to describe their respective movements.[25] That amalgam, anxiety cum virtue, is evident in the very term *haredi* (based on Isaiah 66:5 and Ezra 10:3), which refers to those anxious to obey the Lord's word.[26] The ultranationalist rivals of the haredim plume themselves the Bloc of the Faithful (Gush Emunim) who remain loyal to the Great Israel idea; their settlement branch is called Covenant (*Omana*).

Shi'ites (and, to a lesser degree, Sunnis) prefer to express this through the Qur'anic term for Muhammad's disciples, "the Oppressed" (*mustad'fun,* and some of its synonyms).[27] When the Islamic Republican Party refers to present-day Iranian territory as the "liberated part of the lands of Islam" (*qesmat-e azad shoday-ye mamlekat-e Eslam*), it may be adding a dash of hope.[28] Evident is the sense of being just a segment in a perverted sphere (that used to pertain to one's own tradition).

The righteous character of the enclave is brought forth even more sharply by the common Protestant terms of self-reference such as "the saved," "the saints," and "the defenders of the faith," as well as in some less common but quite telling titles such as "salt of the earth," "the leaven in the dough," "the zealots."[29] *Zealots* (*qana'im*) is indeed an epithet the haredim take great pride in, though their secularist opponents hurl it as a slur.[30] Marcel Lefebvre, as we have seen, used the same term, "zealots of Elijah," to refer to his supporters, whom he also dubbed "the leaven of the dough."

Terms like *saved* would, of course, make no sense in a Jewish, or for that matter Islamic, context (and the "redeemed" the Gush Emunim speaks about is the land, not the individuals). One should not look for exact equivalents. Each dissident community molds its worldview from the symbolic capital available in its own tradition. Even zealots is a much more powerful metaphor in Jewish lore, based as it is not only on the story of the prophet Elijah (1 Kings 19:10) but also on the Great Revolt against the Romans (A.D. 67–70).[31] The Muslim militants, who do not share in the reverence for the Old Testament, dub themselves, as a matter of course, the righteous (al-Salihun, al-Rashidun).

What imports, though, is the virtuous significance attached thereto, as well as the implicit notion that it behooves the insiders to keep apart from the defiled outside and to fight it in order to save souls, to win them to obedience to halakha and Shari'a. (Hence the common usage, in all three traditions, of holy-war terminology, interspersed, in the American case, with sports metaphors.)

In effect, the outside casts a heavy shadow on the dissidents inside. Dichotomy is the thread running through much of the terminology: light is opposed to darkness (in Hebrew *bnei or* versus *bnei Hosekh;* in Arabic *daw'* versus *zulumat*), truth to falsehood (in Arabic *haqq* versus *batil*), the party of God to the forces of the Great Satan (in Arabic *hizb Allah* versus *a'da' Allah, hizb al-Shaytan;* in Hebrew *ne'emanei ha-Shem* versus *shluhei ha-satan ha-madi'ah*), the wholesome to the unwholesome (in Hebrew *shalem* versus *pagum, qatu'a;* in Arabic *salim* versus *marid*). One could stretch the list on and on, but there is no point in boring the reader. These few illustrations are a small sample of a manichean vocabulary that would make sense in all three traditions.[32]

There is no mistaking the leitmotiv: the outside is polluted, contagious, dangerous. The outside is all the more harmful as it may look as though it partakes of the same tradition as the inside, while being in essence its very negation. In fact the raison d'être of the outside lies in subverting the enclave.

The notion of an ever-lurking risk goes some way toward accounting for the prevalence of conspiracy theories in fundamentalist thinking. Leaders as much as rank and file tend to see everywhere the infiltration of some fifth column. This is a sort of mortar joining the bricks of self-image and the image of the outside. For the enclave, nothing is ever as it appears (hence also the predilection for allegorical hermeneutics). The enemy—modernity in its myriad forms—is a wolf in sheep's clothing and a charming one at that. Islamic radicals warn above all against the danger of *munafiqun* (hypocrites), alleged Muslims who conspire to subvert the faith from within. Their danger is graver than that of outside, imperialist plots. In the case of the Lefebvre movement, for instance, such an argument—"the liberal plot of Satan against Church and Papacy alike," carried out at the Second Vatican Council—became the juridical justification for not obeying pope and council, despite the doctrine of infallibility. The so-called sedevacantists carried this thesis to its logical extreme: as Paul VI, who presided over the council, was not a true pope, its resolutions are null and void and the throne of St. Peter remains vacant until the election of a truly traditionalist pope.[33] The ineluctable consequence of this obsession with conspiracies is the need for constant vigilance.

But, of course, if the righteous are said to be weak this is *peccatis nostris*—due to the sins and imperfections of the enclave itself (though these may be to some extent inspired by the evil outside). The dual result is thus the call for further exertion in self-chastisement and improvement, existing in tandem, at times, with purges of the unworthy.

The Nature of the Beast

Modernity is the common denominator of the outside forces. These may operate from within the given tradition, as in the case of liberal churches (for Christian fundamentalists); of Reform, Conservative, and even modern Orthodox Jews (for the haredim); of dovish religious Zionists (for Gush Emunim); or of liberal Muslims and most of the conservative Islamic establishment and its religiously tepid adherents (for Sunni and Shi'ite radicals). Modernity is also an external threat, as in the cases of the secularist majority in the United States or in Israel; or of the Arab, Iranian, and Pakistani secular intelligentsia and parts of the middle class.[34] The raw nerve of all these forces—implicitly in U.S. and in Israel, openly in the Islamic world—resides in their being human-centered. The modernity-suffused outside assumes human autonomy as the ultimate end. *Khod-bonyadi* is the Persian term for such a stance, whether as ideology or as lifestyle geared to serve human self-realization, even if by transgressing (or adapting and subverting) God-prescribed (*shari'a*) rules of conduct.

One may draw a parallel with North American fundamentalists' attacks on the social-service, self-help, "me generation" notions of the secular humanists, with their reliance upon human judgment and "anything goes" cultural pluralism. The fundamentalists scoff at the humanist argument that one becomes thereby "totally free." Haredim designate secular Jews as "free" (or freethinker, *hofshi, hofshim be-de'ot*) because they "threw off the yoke of Torah and mitzvot." And again one finds analogous terms of opprobrium among North American fundamentalists, with "yoked" ("yoked together") as the ultimate praise for insiders, for the saved.[35]

In the United States Hugh Hefner, Gloria Steinem, and Jane Fonda are the supreme examples of this ethos of false freedom. Muslim and Jewish pamphleteers take aim at popular entertainers and sports figures—the embodiments of the cult of anthropocentric hedonism. Even Gush Emunim, with its quite modern ethos of (Zionist) settlement and stress on military efficacy, dub their dovish-secular opponents 'Akhshavists, that is, proponents of instant gratification (a mocking allusion to Peace Now, Shalom 'Akhshav).

The latent significance of modernity is humanity's revolt against God. The outside is predicated, for Shi'ite radicals, upon *istikbar,* a Qur'anic notion originally singling out "those who haughty with pride refuse to accept the Qur'an." It is often employed in tandem, and in pun, with "servants of *isti'mar*" (imperialism). The Sunnis prefer a modern term, *ghatrasa,* or arrogance, which consists of rejecting the sovereignty (*hakimiyya*) of Allah by replacing his laws with ones made by man—a notion much like that proposed by, among others, Protestant Reconstructionists and their dominion theologians. And haredi thinkers speak, in the same context, of the *hutzpa* (arrogance) typical of the worst (and latest) periods of exile. The arrogant ones are *yiddische rebellen* who are in fact "Jewish heathens." Islamic and Christian polemics against modernity also employ the metaphor of paganism: the contemporary condition of Islam is jahiliyya; the Christian church faces today a paganism reminiscent of the first century as Darwinism, materialism, and other human-centered paradigms loom as idols.[36]

The arrogant rebels who are the quintessential (though not the sole) manifestation of the outside are, let us remember, affiliated with a monotheistic tradition, however formal and tenuous are their links with it. Even secular humanists pay a kind of homage to the Judeo-Christian roots of the American experience. They are usually not believers of, or converts to, another faith (or to outright atheism). Few are the cases—Hamas in the occupied territories, the Mujahidin in Afghanistan, the Kach movement of Meir Kahane, perhaps also Pentecostal Christians in India—in which the outside, or center community, is composed of infidels, old and new. In those cases the enclave would take different forms that are beyond the scope of the present essay. (For a treatment of these cases, see chapter 17 in this volume).[37]

Shades of Black and Gray

In principle, the outside is black. Yet, as one takes a closer look, this manichean worldview appears more complex. Time and space, as well as the impact of the specific tradition, produce many shades of black and gray. (The enclave, however, remains a priori and metaphorically white, although a constant effort is required to keep it lily-white.)[38]

In Judaism, an enclave social context existed throughout medieval and early modern times, albeit by push—exclusion by the dominant Gentile community in the lands of the Diaspora—rather than by pull. Jewish pre-Enlightenment enclaves adhered to the halakhic principle "A Jew remains a Jew even if he sins," in order to keep as many members as possible within the fold (including, in theory, Jews who converted of their own free will). The guiding principle was the group's responsibility for individual believers, as slack as they might become in the dire straits of Exile. Even in a worse-case scenario, they remain part and parcel of *klal Yisrael* (the community of the Jews).

With the nineteenth century the perception of danger changed. Exclusion diminished, and conversion was less often the issue (intermarriage was). Yet Jews tended to slip away in droves. Some embraced new ideals (liberalism, socialism, indigenous nationalisms) without necessarily denying their faith; they often merely became indifferent to it. Others tried to modify age-old religious norms completely, thereby virtually "Protestantizing" the faith, as in the case of Reform Judaism. (Marcel Lefebvre made an analogous argument in reacting against the newfangled Catholic ritual in the 1960s.)

The worst part of this new syndrome (*neliza* was the term the Hazon Ish coined for it) [39] was a third deviation, this one in the quality and regularity of mitzvot observance due to changing material conditions. The uprooted life of immigrants in North America, Western Europe, and Australia made the halakhic precepts harder to follow, as did the requirements of the big-city capitalistic economy into which formerly shtetl Jews were now increasingly integrated in Eastern and Central Europe.

While the emergent ultra-Orthodox were busy shoring up the boundary around the separatist *kehillah* (local community) pioneered by the Hatam Sofer, the Hasidic court, and the transnational politicocultural organization (e.g., Agudat Yisrael, founded 1912), the principle "a Jew remains a Jew" was too ingrained to be abandoned. Not merely because of its halakhic authority and long pedigree, but also for its affective value, klal Yisrael is oft assimilated to *ahavat Yisrael,* love of the Jews and, thence, responsibility for their fate.[40] One did not easily despair of getting the deserters to return to the fold.

The lenses that this notion offered were now focused differently, however, in order to account for new conditions. Rabbinical authorities endeavored to introduce distinctions. Some of these distinctions were homespun in style, such as the Hafetz Haim speaking—in a manner reminding one of Bob Jones, Sr., decades later—of warm, lukewarm, and cold Jews,[41] the first type being within the enclave, the second in its immediate periphery and likely perhaps to be recuperated, the third being hard-core modernists. Other rabbis, employing a more halakhic lingo, viewed the "cold Jews" as more variegated: there were both *kofrim le-hach'is* (disbelievers out of spite) and the less aggressive *epikoirsim,* and neither forfeited their Jewishness by (maternal) origin. Alongside these Jews, one distinguished shades of gray: *frumer epikoiros* (observant of many mitzvot but not believing in some essential values), *yehudim beinonim* (of mediocre observance and belief), *amei ha-aratzvot* (observant, yet often transgressing norms out of sheer ignorance), and so forth.[42]

Perceptions fluctuated incessantly with the changing times. Until the late 1950s, Zionism and socialism were tarred the darkest black. In the early days of the State of Israel many haredim feared that even baking matzo or carrying phylacteries in public might be prohibited. Irate rabbis had to contend with the overconfident declarations of Israeli politicians (mostly left of center) that Zionism had definitely replaced traditional Judaism, with the Knesset being a sort of Third Temple.[43] Toward the end of the decade, some authorities observed that the Zionist zeal was fizzling out, and most unbelievers were so not "out of spite" but "out of appetite" (*kofrim le-te'avon,* i.e., hedonistic). Most second-generation Israelis, it was argued, are actually "captive children in the hands of unbelievers" (*tinokot she-nishbu*). That is, they are gray more than black, indifferent and ignorant rather than hostile, typical products of the irreligious education they received at the hands of the first generation. This was said to be even truer of Oriental Jews, who were still suffused by tradition when they migrated, but were transformed by schooling or by the temptations of the Israeli city, that modern Babylon.[44]

The above description represents mainline ultra-Orthodoxy and does not do justice to minor variants. There are, for example, extreme separatists such as the Neturei Karta, who view all secular Jews as evil-doers (*resha'im*, i.e., black). By contrast, others, whether inspired by the Lubavitcher rebbe or, in the case of Gush Emunim, by Rabbi A. I. Kook, see a sort of kabbalistic "spark of sanctity" in any Jewish soul, and thus consider virtually all Jews as recuperable.[45]

Roughly the same trajectory can be charted for Islam. Due to the traumatic shock it suffered during the civil wars of its first century, Islam tended to define very narrowly the conditions making one an outright apostate (*murtadd*) and hence punishable by execution. To fall into this category a Muslim would have to explicitly reject the credo ("There is no God but Allah and Muhammad is his messenger"). Prior to the twentieth century, and in a way even today, such cases were few and far between.

The arguments of a modern agnostic like Salman Rushdie—that he cannot be penalized as he is not a Muslim but a secular pluralist, and that what one has not affirmed one cannot apostatize[46]—would have sounded as bizarre to a medieval Muslim as they do to present-day radicals of Tehran, Cairo, or Bradford, England. In their eyes, Rushdie is Muslim by (paternal) origin, and having slandered the Prophet in *The Satanic Verses,* he thereby denied the credo (*shahada*).

Yet the modern challenge to Islam was rarely as blatant as that. Even Communists in Muslim lands learned fast to play down their atheism. The implicit or half-concealed secularism of other modern ideologies represented an uncanny and insidious challenge precisely because it was indirect and conceived in terms hallowed in Islamic history. Radical Muslim thinkers, from the 1930s on, thus had to develop finer heuristic tools and denounce major modern creeds as latently (but not ineluctably) opposed to the shahada. Topping the list, after communism, was nationalism, be it pan-Arab (*qawmiyya*) or of the nation-state variety (*wataniyya*). Nationalism, for the radicals, was a new type of polytheism (*shirk*), in that it attaches a modern idol, the nation, to Allah, whom the nationalists profess they do not reject. Shirk, of course, equals apostasy. To add confusion to sacrilege the nationalists used for the national community the same term, *umma,* reserved for the "community of the believers."[47] (Such a "polytheism argument," interestingly enough, was likewise employed by haredim against Zionism.)[48]

As in the case of Judaism it was soon discovered that the polluting danger operated on a broader front. The state disregards the Shari'a and introduces laws borrowed from Europe; it also limits the scope of Shari'a courts in sensitive domains such as personal status. Due to secularized education and fewer, or inefficient, state sanctions, the believers neglect rituals and Islamic social precepts. As Islam, much like Judaism, is predicated upon orthopraxis rather than orthodoxy—molding behavior rather than belief—this was a frightening diagnosis. Moreover, the transgressions took place, frequently and with impunity, in the public eye and not just behind the closed doors of hearth and home. Their contagious threat was thereby multiplied.[49]

The diagnosis led Muslim radicals to reinterpret a minor strand of the tradition, the neo-Hanbali legal school, which already in the fourteenth century posited that application of the Shari'a, and not just professing the credo, was the test of the true Muslim ruler. The neo-Hanbali doctrine was carried, however, well beyond its typically medieval self-imposed boundaries (which excluded armed revolt against a nominally Muslim ruler). According to the revamped doctrine, "outside" (that is, *ridda,* apostasy) was now wherever the Shari'a is not applied.[50] From the early 1960s this new principle determined for most radical circles the shades of black. The top echelons of the state, its repressive apparatus, and the official media are to be found at the darker end of the gamut; so is a part of Westoxicated intelligentsia. This end consists of apostates (*murtaddun*), polytheists (*mushrikun*), or plain infidels (*kuffar*). The latter term (with its plethora of synonyms, such as *pharaohs*), was reserved primarily for political leaders such as Anwar Sadat, the shah of Iran, Hafiz al-Asad, and Saddam Hussein. These leaders and their henchmen persecuted Muslim radicals and initiated or presided over the massive introduction of non-Shari'a law and irreligious indoctrination. By virtue of the reinterpreted neo-Hanbali doctrine it was now legitimate to take up arms against these leaders. This was a daring novelty, for the leaders still professed Islam.[51]

Secondarily, one would include some dubiously Muslim pre-twentieth-century sects, such as the Ahmadiyya in India and Pakistan, or the Baha'is in Iran and Egypt, that not only survived but even flourished through adjustment to the modern economy. Their value was mostly as whipping boys and as means for drawing the boundary. In the campaigns against these sects, the vindication of the principles of tradition and resentment of those who were both strange and successful commingled.

The black shades off into various hues of gray. Most Muslim radicals do not consider the bulk of society to be apostate, as it just drifts away, out of hedonistic appetite, the victim of brainwashing by the elites. The man on the street is still Muslim, albeit a bad one, not up to the standards of the enclave. Such bad Muslims must be admonished and, if possible, even coerced by vigilante action, in conformity with the hallowed precept of "command that which is good and prohibit that which is abominable" (*al-amr bi-l-ma'ruf wa-l-nahy 'an-i-l-munkar*).[52] By no means can they be the targets of violent action with extreme prejudice. Rarely would the effort exerted in this direction be defined as jihad.

As one proceeds down the social ladder, toward the "ignorant masses" (*al-'amma al-jahila*), the Muslim activists become more comprehending, at times indulgent, though never resigned. The ignorant, those of slack practice and shallow belief, are the most obvious target of outreach work, which can take two major forms. Outreach is either combined with vigilantism or appears as a strategy per se, designed to reprimand but also to educate, emphasizing a more regular observance of rituals as the path leading back into the faith. The latter form, as developed by the Tablighi missionary movement, is roughly the Islamic equivalent of the Lubavitcher sect (though without the mystical elements typical of this Hasidic group).[53] Nevertheless, the "ignorant masses" are not taken to be part of the enclave. Be it Tablighi or Lubavitcher, they remain, at best, at its periphery.

This perception of a many-shaded outside may account for the fact that many Muslim and Jewish enclaves, although jealous of their separate entity, make frequent sallies out of their bounds in order to impose their behavioral norms. The tactics are manifold, dictated both by ideological bent and by circumstances; they include "creeping" into neighboring areas, recourse to lobbying and to local (or statewide) ad hoc coalitions, and vigilante-type militancy. This is essentially a defensive action, aimed at creating a sort of cordon sanitaire (e.g., banning "licentious" advertising posters as an eyesore or as a potential tempting object for yeshiva students and jama'at members). Yet in many cases it also expresses sincere concern for the fate of lukewarm (or indifferent) individuals who make up the vast majority of so-called Muslims and Jews in this day and age. The sermons of the Egyptian Shaykh Kishk, distributed commercially in tape cassettes all over the Arab world, are the most eloquent expression of such concern. So too, at a more basic level, are the tapes of Rabbi Nissim Yagen of Jerusalem or the famous televised address of Rabbi E. M. Schach to "pork-guzzling kibbutzniks," which decided the fate of the Israeli government coalition in March 1990.

The Jewish (or Muslim) street is thus not merely a defensive perimeter. To create it is also the performance of a religious duty, although how important a duty is a question answered differently by various groups (and even by the same group at various points in time). The underlying notion common to most enclaves is that the boorish masses must be made to conform to norms, albeit without comprehending them. In so conforming they are at least somewhat improved, and may even end up by perceiving the significance of the norms and returning to the fold.[54]

Extreme separatist enclaves (e.g., Neturei Karta and 'Eda Haredit; Jama'at al-Takfir wa-l-Hijra) are important exceptions to this pattern. For them, "in our days darkness covers the whole earth";[55] the whole of society is renegade. The extreme separatists would make such sallies only rarely, and then only for immediate and defensive aims. They may, for example, desecrate "paganlike" tombs of alleged "holy men" that have been placed in a mosque; or impose norms of "modest" dress and licit music in quarters in which they live; or forbid the driving of cars on Shabbat in their vicinity. There is no concern for the klal or umma of the so-called believers, for one is faced with an "infidel society" (in Arabic *al-mujtama' al-kafir*), an "evil kingdom" (in Hebrew *malchut ha-resha'a be-Yisrael shultanut zola*). Doomed to damnation, it can be saved, if at all, either by messianic intervention or by imposing the Divine Law upon one and all once the elect take power by force.[56] The extremist critique of the less separatist group is not predicated upon the diagnosis of the ills of the center community. The extremists also point out, quite plausibly, that a dangerous feedback relationship is set up by too frequent sallies into the central domain: the more you deal with the surrounding society, the more you tend to perceive it as variegated and develop some empathy toward it. (That very logic, that it is better not to have any commerce with the wicked, crops up among Protestant separatists of the Bob Jones variety, who refuse, for instance, to accept federal grants.)

Lest the qualifications create a skewed picture, one should stress that even enclaves that engage in day-to-day sallies for the sake of a Muslim or Jewish street—and even intervene on questions related to the private domain (e.g., abortion, pork eating, homosexuality)—never essentially modify the sharp distinction between inside and outside (even though the latter may not be taken to be uniformly black). It strikes one that mainline haredim in the 1990s no longer use the slur the "evil kingdom" in referring to the State of Israel (and may refer to "our state," "our army").[57] Yet never do they call it a "kingdom of grace" (*malchut shel hesed,* a fair-minded state). That title is reserved for the United States, a goyish and hence by definition alien entity. And it was applied to the United States only after the 1960s when the evolution of the welfare state, combined with notions of cultural pluralism, gave the ultra-Orthodox access to federal and state funding. The "in exile among Jews" diagnosis is, of course, not challenged in such a situation, for the haredim are still a minority within a minority. Obviously, when Israeli haredim perceive that the conditions for "sallies" are not favorable (as in the late 1980s), they retreat into the cocoon of their enclave. Its survival takes priority over all other concerns.

One would expect Protestant fundamentalists, especially independent Baptist churches, to constitute a totally different case. Shouldn't their insistence upon personal faith and individual salvation predispose them to indifference about the fate of the vast majority of un-Christian Americans? Why care about those not destined to be saved at the moment of rapture? The saved, who are "called to be winners for God's glory,"[58] are indeed a group apart—a notion quite at odds with the traditional Islamic and Jewish positions as well as with the Catholic doctrine of the community of the baptized, the communion of saints (who remain Christian as long as they are not excommunicated). Such a doctrine makes the Italian movement Communione e Liberazione strive so mightily in the milieu of tepid Christian Democrats or indifferent Socialists. And Archbishop Lefebvre, for all his anti-establishment vituperations, considered the bulk of baptized Catholics as "sheep of the flock of Our Lord Jesus Christ delivered defenseless to the ravishing wolves [of the conciliar church]."[59]

But even our generalization with regard to the Protestants is true only up to a point. It disregards the fundamentalists' vision of America as a nation elected by God, a shining City on the Hill, a Beacon of Light unto the Nations. This mission accounts for its success in its age of pristine purity, the seventeenth century, and its decline in more recent times (especially since the late nineteenth century, when old-time religion last held sway). Despite current moral decay and disarray, America—that linchpin of Christian civilization—can still be "turned around," its moral decline reversed and "made great again," provided that "the Bible [gets] back into American schools," and "Biblical standards" once again dictate social mores.[60]

This upbeat American patriotism is often xenophobic (anti-German in the early twentieth century, anti-Soviet since World War II) and saturated with the rhetoric of manifest destiny. Further, it relies heavily on military and sports metaphors ("marines for Christ," "be a champion for Jesus")[61] redolent of U.S. popular culture. Xenophobic patriotism may lead to the drawing of a populist distinction between perverted individuals on the one hand, and the somewhat wholesome, perhaps still redeemable, mass of ordinary Americans on the other. Hence also the respect for the flag, the "I love America" rallies. Hence the teaching of "American church history" as a time perspective that sets a sort of road map charting present and future.

Combined with a posttribulationist twist on the premillennial vision, this implicit sense of some responsibility for America's fate was a prime mover in the direction of fundamentalist political activism in the early eighties.[62] Yet the fact that the essential rhetoric remained the same from the sixties to the present suggests that, while fundamentalist empathy toward the mass of unsaved Americans may be dubious, America as an entity is a cherished object of concern. In such a context a "revolutionary defeatism"—let the United States go down the drain like the Roman Empire of yore—can hardly be envisaged.[63]

Space: Symbolic and Social

"God's greatest call is separation," claimed A. C. Gaebelein in the prophetic Bible conference of 1914.[64] The slogan would have made sense for the founders of Agudat Yisrael (in Katowice, 1912) who gave a Europe-wide organizational expression to Hatam Sofer's pioneering effort at the local level. The enemy from whom one should separate was the liberal Methodist church in the former case, Zionists and Reform Jews in the latter; in both cases, the logic was the same. That logic also presided over Hasan al-Banna's initiative in setting up the Muslim Brotherhood in 1928; he put flesh on the bones of Rashid Rida's alarmist theories. Al-Banna, an Egyptian, sought separation from the Islamic establishment with its addiction to apologetics designed to make religion conform to the requirements of modernity.

But how to separate? Not merely by formal, doctrinal boundary making. When religion is a way of life (in Arabic *nizam shamil, manhaj hayat;* in Hebrew *orah hayim*),[65] it behooves one, in the lingo of American fundamentalists, not just to believe in the Bible (or another authoritative text) but to live it. It is interesting to note that Luigi Giussani, though Catholic, quotes in such a context none other than Puritan theologian Jonathan Edwards: theological study is valueless unless affirmed through concrete commitment, that is, by molding behavior.

Behavior is indeed paramount in enclaves—including Christian ones where orthodoxy is supposed to have precedence over praxis, but in fact they are at least *ex aequo*. Behavior endows belief with a mimetic and affective dimension.[66] A viable enclave wields efficient group constraints and should thus be able to have its individual members conform to homogeneous public norms. And their most immediate product is a separate space.

Space is, to begin with, symbolic, as one could deduce from the distinct Islamic and Jewish terminology surveyed above. But a quick checklist of Protestant terms attests that these fundamentalists do not fall behind: "bear witness," "walk with the Lord," "surrender one's life to the Lord," "soul harvest" (recruiting new members), "sacrifice" (contributing money or leisure time), "salvational plan (or work)," "faith promises" (contribution to missions), "excise the cancer" (of deviation, sexual or otherwise). Such metaphors, not to mention those referring to holy war (or crusade) bestow a special, sacred significance upon behavior approved for members of the enclave.

The language one has recourse to, immersed as it is in scriptures—in the above passage, the King James Bible with its Scofield premillennialist exegesis—is, in itself, an act of self-assertion.[67] It also provides members with lenses to view and select reality.

Obviously cosmology, in the sense of assumptions about history, nature, and so forth, would likewise express itself through language and other symbolic means. Vocabulary is not the sole linguistic aspect involved. One notes Talmudic-Aramaic and/or Yiddish terms among haredim even when modern Hebrew or English syntax is employed; in the Islamic case, flamboyant Qur'anic rhetoric, Hadith idiom. Of equal significance is the linguistic stratum mined: one finds Yiddish or posttalmudic legal commentary, Yinglish; classical rather than modern or colloquial Arabic; the classical Arabic component in Persian; and so on.

Which brings us to the music preferred in the enclave, albeit not necessarily enjoined by an authoritative text: late-nineteenth-century hymns among American fundamentalists; eighteenth- and nineteenth-century hasidic chants; Qur'anic psalmodies, traditional Muslim folk music; Gregorian chants in the Lefebvre movement's rites. All provide clues to the golden age placed on a pedestal, but they particularly imply rejection of the present, namely the texture of contemporary pop music, especially rock.[68] The audial space thereby created at home, at the place of worship and/or assembly, at the homogeneous residential quarter (if there is one) reinforces the impact of language.

The same holds true for other distinguishing marks such as body language (compare the bent posture of the haredim and the erect one of Gush activists); vestmental code (white galabia and headgear for Muslim males, veil for females; pioneering-military style in Gush Emunim, black *streiml* and distinct headgear for haredi males, wig and long-sleeved dress for females; reintroduction of the cassock for priests of the Lefebvre obedience); and hairstyle (compare the shaggy haredi beard and the trimmed one of Islamic militants; in all enclave communities including Protestant, long hair is banned for males). Dress, in particular, seems to be a further indicator as to the historical period held as the model, as do names given to offspring (compare, again, the traditional Jewish ones among haredim, the rare biblical or sabra-nationalist names in Gush settlements).

Behavior consists, first and foremost, of strict observance of norms of conduct derived from the tenets of the faith. The observance is strict, if not punctilious, because of the gravity of the outside danger. The norms are, of course, voluntarily assumed, as befits a posttraditional world in which age-old rules of conduct (many of which had been rather lenient) dissolved with the demise of solid, territorially anchored communities due to the constant migration typical of our century.[69] The voluntary nature of membership is legitimated by the notion of the elect who throw their lot in with a dissident—that is, a materially and socially unrewarding—community. In turn the community represents, as we have seen, a deliberate effort to preserve the essence (or fundamentals) of the tradition in an alien, posttraditional setting (within the limits set by an understanding as to what this essence is). This serves as an incentive for conformity predicated on moral suasion.

As a contribution to a sacred group effort, the duties of members of the enclave are frequently depicted in holy-war terms. To wit: the slogan "wage a battle royal for the fundamentals" in the United States of the 1920s; the "crusader passport" distributed by Jerry Falwell to his supporters; the terms *jihad,* or *jihad al-nafs* (against the evil in one's soul) applied by Muslim militants to activities as varied as fasting and super-erogatory prayers or the banning of TV viewing; the term *milhemet qodesh* (holy war, or *milhamta shel Torah*) applied by haredim to the fight for a modest dress code as much as for (or against, as the case may be) participation in elections. The sacralization of the enclave implies, then, the sacrality of all actions, including "sallies" in which it is involved. That may include, of course, the sacralization of politics in general, as in the rhetoric of the Moral Majority in the 1980s as well as for Gush Emunim in Israel.

At the root of it all, strictness is the product of the need for clarity in an age of ambiguity and confusion. Strict behavior is, again, made possible by the fact that so much traditional (and by necessity local) practice had been lost as a result of migration and other demographic dislocations.

The imposition of a set of rules, preferably hypernomian, is thus in part a new creation—it is the enclave's attempt to dictate a semblance of order. This new order, in turn, is in a way quite out of sync with the myriad coexisting forms of the tradition as it had once been practiced. And this is a modern set of rules, the strictness of which is understandable, given that it is geared to fighting the prevailing tendency in the center community—be it in allegedly religious segments thereof—to compromise with modernity, that is, to the bending of some age-old rules.

This would account for the pivotal position enjoyed in Sunni militancy by the neo-Hanbali legal school. During its seven-hundred-year history neo-Hanbalism made the extirpation of novelties (*bid'a*) and of looseness of morals (*fasad*) its guiding principles. The modern interpreters of neo-Hanbalism—some of them converts from other, more accommodationist schools—perceived the arsenal of arguments and stratagems it provides to those who would opt for *'aqd* (tying the knot, holding the line) rather than *hall* (untying the knot, rendering licit). 'Aqd is required, more often than not, by the insidious dangers lurking everywhere.[70]

The same dynamics can be observed in halakhic norms. If "bar innovations" was the watchword in nineteenth- and early-twentieth-century ultra-Orthodoxy (encapsulated in the Hatam Sofer's adage "Novelty is prohibited by the Torah"), from the time of the Hazon Ish it came to share pride of place with *humra* (extra stringency, *diqduq, hiddur*). Wherever possible, and even with regard to old customs or matters where no open modern challenge is involved, there is a sort of built-in moral superiority for the stricter alternative. *Frumkeit* (stricter than thou) is made the object of competition among halakhic authorities and their groupies, especially the yeshiva youth who have become the accepted role models (or core) for the haredi plethora of communities.[71]

One should note in passing that antinomian tendencies—arguably the structural counterpart of the hypernomian—are rare in enclaves. Among Jews this may be due to the enduring lessons of the nihilistic offshoots of the seventeenth-century Shabbatean movement (which ended up embracing Islam or Christianity), although some such tendencies have lately been evident in fringe underground groups in Jerusalem. Among American fundamentalists a powerful brake operating in this direction may be the gut reaction against the permissiveness of the 1960s, which underlies much of the resurgence of independent Baptist churches. In Islam, neo-Hanbalism, present from the very inception of the movement under Rashid Rida, set ironclad limits which few groups dare transgress. Prominent among them was Jama'at al-Takfir, the Sunni group that rejected the Shari'a wholesale, as the product of time-serving ulama and demanded that communal life be regulated on the basis of the Qur'an alone. Because of the paucity of laws in the Islamic holy book, this would have left enormous leeway for this sect's leader, a self-styled caliph cum messiah.[72]

The stringency and the antinovelty stance are not, however, as all-embracing as they may first seem. Strict observance focuses just on certain aspects deemed crucial (or "fundamental") for the time and place. Gush Emunim would make the precept of the settlement of the Land of Israel, as well as other precepts related to this land, the end-all of the 613 mitzvot, for this land is the center both of the universe and of "wholesome, untruncated Judaism." Their extreme messianic fringe would add some of those 292 precepts related to ritual in the Temple, held in abeyance since A.D. 70; others, the majority, tend to be haredi-inspired and put almost equal emphasis on some rituals. The haredim pay particular attention to family and dietary law rituals (mostly in public, and in Hebrew)—as the basis for group solidarity—leaving aside, for instance, civil law. Writing around 1930 the Hazon Ish set forth seven conditions for the survival of the ultra-Orthodox: in each town they should have their own primary school (*talmud Torah*), kosher slaughterhouse, ritual bath, observance of Shabbat, a synagogue, and autonomy of the community from control by impious Jews. Sixty-odd years later this formula (education and dietary matters and ritual and organizational autonomy) still serves as the basis for haredi communities. Leniency, if not slackness, in legal matters related to the above is the gravest sin the ultra-Orthodox impute to modern Orthodox, Conservative, and Reform Jews, and at times to some of their own persuasion.[73]

Strictness in Shari'a observance relates emphatically to matters of personal status that had been throughout history the de facto core of Islamic law and immune from state intervention. From the 1950s, however, even this core was invaded by legislative initiatives of the regimes in Egypt, Iran, Syria, Tunisia, Iraq, and Algeria, and brought under the control of civil courts. The implications seemed to Muslim radicals alarming. Threatened were a gender-based division of labor and status, the traditional means of defining "who is a Muslim," and the role of the family as the major socializing agent (especially given the pervasive irruption of the state media and education into the domestic sphere). Lagging behind as objects of the radicals' concern are ritual affairs, but they are important particularly for novices' self-expression. Here an effort is exerted, in tune with neo-Hanbalism, to "decontaminate" practice from "pagan," anthropomorphic (often Sufi) "insidious accretions."[74]

Control of behavior should perhaps have lesser salience in Protestant enclaves due to the stress upon inner belief. But in fact it seems about the same. What the Protestants lack, of course, is the firm textual authority of an elaborate jurisprudence like that provided by the Shari'a for Muslims, the halakha for Jews, and canon law for Roman Catholics—that is, a sort of formal, objective anchor. Neither do Protestants invest a huge intellectual effort in its study and further development. In practice, however, members of independent Baptist churches are subject to rigorous controls in some key areas. There are bans on drinking, on profanity, on abortion, and on certain sexual behavior (premarital, extramarital, and homosexual relations). Strong parental authority over children is stressed, as is attendance at prayer and certain other church activities. Censorship of reading, listening, and viewing material is common. Needless to say, at fundamentalist institutions of higher education such as Liberty University in Virginia and Bob Jones University in South Carolina, controls are stricter on the above issues and apply even to dating, mate selection, and so forth.[75]

Novelty is frowned upon in principle, yet monotheistic radicals have proven themselves quite ingenious in accommodating modern realities whenever they deem it vital for the survival of the enclave. This was naturally easier in issues unrelated to "fundamentals" of religious law, but feasible in the core domain as well. Sunni radicals elaborated this attitude into a full-fledged doctrine by subscribing to the concept of "opening up the gates of *ijtihad*" (independent legal judgment by jurists), gates closed since the tenth century A.D. This is, significantly enough, the sole idea they borrowed from the Muslim reformists, although they refuse to open the gates as wide as the latter would. Nonetheless, they have regular recourse to this tool on matters as diverse as interest taking, new technologies, and civil disobedience.[76]

Shi'ite radicals, in whose tradition this ijtihad had never been banned, had a lighter task, further facilitated by the fact that a good part of the Islamic establishment (the *mujtahidun*, madrasa graduates trained in jurisprudence) joined their ranks, often in leadership positions. This is something quite rare in the Sunni milieu, where radical leaders are self-taught laypeople. The learned and self-confident Shi'ite mujtahid is more likely to take innovative risks, in cases considered to be of dire necessity, than the Sunni autodidact with his rather narrow vision of jurisprudence. The Hizbullah mentor, Shaykh Muhammad Husayn Fadlallah, went so far as to permit birth control (though not abortion) in the name of the supreme interest (*maslaha*) of the umma, suffering as it does from overpopulation. He likewise prohibited as "pagan and tribal" the killing of daughters for "crimes of honor," and banned the imposition of a spouse upon women by their male guardian.[77]

The halakhic case is quite similar to the Shi'ite. Throughout posttalmudic times innovation was licit, albeit subject to strict rules. The spate of innovations introduced by the Reform-minded in the nineteenth century elicited a principled stance against novelty per se. Yet at the hands of the right authorities—whose doctrinal standing was actually bolstered in the twentieth century—"the right kind" of innovation was always possible. Present-day haredi dispensers of responsa follow here the lead shown by the Hafetz Haim,[78] who allowed more lenient practice for Jewish recruits in the tsarist army or immigrants in the United States, as well as the Hazon Ish, who solved the problems of the first ultra-Orthodox kibbutz. Certainly Gush Emunim rabbis would issue permits for work on Shabbat in case of "manifest necessity" for furthering the settlement of the Land of Israel and, for self-defense, against Palestinian terrorism.

Stringency in observance, and supererogatory endeavors (minor Jewish fasts, extra prayers on Muslim feast days) are deemed virtuous in both traditions. But not when carried to extremes. Conspicuous and extreme display is frowned upon. Innovations introduced in such a spirit are often flatly rejected. Haredim denounce confirmation rites (*bar mitzvot*) held at the Western Wall as smacking of the "anthropomorphic paganism" of Gush Emunim (and the kindred National Religious Party) circles. Lefebvrists fulminate against the laxity of the clergy with regard to access to sacraments (e.g., in condoning baptism of babies of nonbelieving parents). Egyptian radicals, for all their commitment to the jihad against Israel and for the liberation of Jerusalem, anathemize jama'at who turn in prayer toward Jerusalem (*qiblat al-quds*), instead of Mecca.[79]

Claims on Time/Space

Let us not forget that enclaves are usually people living in close physical proximity, face to face. The end product of the imposition of fundamentalist norms is a strong claim on individual members' "operational time"[80] as lived, as a group (not individual) resource. There is no distinction between sacred and profane, work-bound and free. Claims are most evident in the way the religious calendar regiments and punctuates the cadence of members' lives in a way sharply divergent from that of the surrounding society. Suffice it to look at the way the week is organized around Sunday, the Shabbat (beginning Friday evening), or Friday (especially the noon prayer). Moreover, as Nancy Ammerman has shown in her study of a Connecticut fundamentalist congregation, between attending prayer, study and hymnal groups, outreach and committee activity, and so forth, most of the members' after-work time is invested in the group and subject to its controls. (And this includes even "private dates" such as spiritual birthdays, celebrating one's conversion.)[81]

Located in sprawling suburbia, with many members commuting to work, such a Protestant community does not enjoy a condensed "operational space" (i.e., space as lived) of its own. Because they have to live within walking distance of the synagogue in order not to desecrate the Shabbat, the haredim have such operational space, as does a Gush Emunim settlement. The haredi definition of a "good environment" hinges first and foremost upon space near a synagogue of haredi persuasion.[82] Nevertheless, there are some heavily fundamentalist residential areas where some analogous Christian rules are introduced, municipal politics permitting, as well as brand new spatial guarantees such as "Christian shopping malls" (where blue movies and "adult" bookshops are forbidden, and homosexual vendors are prohibited).

But even in regular fundamentalist communities the church (or the Scuola di Communità in the Italian Communione e Liberazione) is the focus of social life for the majority of members. Its role in their lives is no different in essence from that of the *ahli* (not subject to government control) mosque under the auspices of a *jama'a* (religious association), or even a state mosque that a Muslim association has succeeded in gaining control of, bribing, or subverting the imam of prayer.[83] This is also the long-term perspective, on top of the immediate effect, that accounts for forceful "occupation" of churches in France by Lefebvre disciples in communities where they had been minorities. Space, much like time, becomes a group resource, an object of the enclave's claims.

Thus welded, the enclave becomes an arena of sociability. Individual members—who may have been anyhow, in all three traditions, recruited through existing networks of friends and acquaintances—find that the bulk of their social interaction is with fellow members. This is, of course, even more easily the case with haredim who constitute multigenerational communities, existing for decades.

Cutting off some of one's former friendships, due to divergent lifestyles or new enclave responsibilities, is a leitmotiv in life histories of converts to U.S. Baptist churches, to Communione e Liberazione in Italy, to students joining jama'at in the dorms of colleges in Gaza, Cairo, and Amman, and to kibbutznik returnees to the faith in Jerusalem. The theme of the "friendly church," or its equivalents—a warm and safe haven in an atomized and anonymous world—is typical not only of Ammerman's interviewees,[84] but of Muslim, haredim, and Communione e Liberazione members I talked to as well. The Talmud after-work study society called *khavrusa* (fellowship, companionship), a fixture of the ultra-Orthodox enclave, provides just such a haven. "Fellowship" is also a secondary meaning of the term *jama'a* used for Islamic radical associations.

Enclave solidarity in action is both positive and negative, uniting and confrontational. Human warmth, generated within, compensates for the tough norms and tight schedules imposed by the group. A powerful agent of enclave sociability is endogamy, effectively practiced by the haredim, often for a number of generations,[85] as well as by some of the extreme Islamic groups like Jama'at al-Takfir wa-l-Hijra. Elsewhere this is done by nudging and other indirect pressures rather than by direct injunction as, for instance, in the way mate selection is encouraged at Liberty University or at the annual festival of Communione e Liberazione, an organization that caters mostly to singles in their twenties. Marriage is, however, quite often a sore spot: Baptists complain of "unequally yoked" marriages, those in which one spouse is not saved. Indeed, dominion theologian Gary North has pointed to haredi in-group marriage strategy as the model for Protestants if they wish to survive.[86] One wonders whether this would be easily applicable, for the haredi endogamy tends to exclude even ba'alei teshuva (the equivalent of the "recently saved") for fear of contamination by their secularist families; the "returnees" are exhorted to marry fellow "returnees."

A structural problem, and one plaguing all three traditions, consists of the fact that the burden of claims (on time, space, behavior) may be too heavy. How to keep up standards without condemning the enclave to be a minuscule sect? After all, members wish to ensure, in principle, that as many as possible will persist in the faith, and beyond sheer survival, perhaps even create an alternative society.

The solution adopted by some enclaves is to divide the community into concentric circles: an inner one of ascetic "religious virtuosi" who observe to the letter a maximum number of norms; one or several outer circles where a lesser number of precepts are observed with the same measure of stringency and where less time or effort is invested in other norms. The haredim, who possess an explicit doctrine on degrees (*madregot*) in the fulfillment of mitzvot, maintain as inner circles the yeshiva and kollelim students and their rabbis, dedicated to the study of "Torah for its own sake" (and by association also the wives of postgraduate kollelim students who contribute to their upkeep by their work, usually in ultra-Orthodox schools). Sustained in large part by scholarships financed by state allocations and grants from benefactors, the students—usually young males between the ages of sixteen and thirty—live in decent genteel poverty, spending most of their waking hours in the study of Talmud and its exegesis. The purity of their monasticlike effort is supposed to impress and set a role model for the bulk of laypeople (*ba'ale batim*) of the community. The latter are gainfully employed, but are expected to observe "fundamentals" of law and ritual (e.g., major fasts but not necessarily all minor fasts, all dietary laws but not with the same punctiliousness); they also engage daily in some evening study (e.g., a daily page of the Talmud).[87] In Gush Emunim circles one can distinguish between the "inner sanctum" of settlement members along with a close periphery of "national-haredi" yeshiva students who contribute some time on a regular basis to the settlement effort, and an outer periphery of supporters in urban centers.

A somewhat analogous grading is found in the St. Pius X Fraternity, the legal-cum-organizational framework of the Lefebvre movement. The nucleus was the seminary in Econe, Switzerland, together with four "missionary" seminaries (in Germany, Italy, the United Kingdom, and the United States), in which students were subject to the near-ascetic controls. The next layer comprised 260 priests, members of the fraternity in like-minded communities worldwide, assisted by individual monks, nuns, and lay auxiliaries. Loosely affiliated with the fraternity were seven nunneries, free-floating dissident priests and monks, and at the outermost periphery, associations of lay sympathizers, subject to lesser controls, yet providing valuable moral and financial support.

In a more diffuse fashion this is the function of Scuola di Communità, Compagnia delle Opere, and Movimento Popolare, the three organizational layers of Communione e Liberazione. And the same pattern holds for the distinction developed among Pentecostalists between, on the one hand, a sectarian nucleus (covenant communities, ministry teams) held to ideals such as monastic celibacy, and, on the other, a cultlike periphery.[88] A certain evolution in the same organizational direction can be observed after the mid-1980s among jama'at in Egypt, Tunisia, and the Gaza Strip: a core group supported by an outreach periphery that sends its children to the group's kindergartens (a novelty in Arab lands) and schools, frequents its mosques (invariably on Friday noon but also on some weekdays), participates in evening study groups, applies for counselling (shar'i, but also familial) to the group's ulama or to self-taught lay authorities. In technical doctrinal jargon, the core's work for the holy war is *fard 'ayn* (individual obligation) and the periphery's work is *fard kifaya* (group obligation).

In a way, both the Muslim Tablighi movement, and its Jewish analogue, the Habad, resort to this very principle, although with a much broader, at times differentiated, periphery.

The importance of the core/peripheries mode of organization lies, first, in maintaining an equality of effort (and status) at each level, while enlarging the scope of the movement. Equality is crucial, for in enclaves the grid (i.e., constraints due to formal distinctions) has to be minimal, almost zero, in order to preserve its voluntary character. Second, the peripheries mediate between the core and the surrounding society, serving as a defensive envelope and allowing the movement to operate in society without polluting the core, in belief or in action.[89]

Cosmology

In their own eyes, the fundamentalists are reasonable people. It is just that, committed to the revelation, they are pitted in a fight against the outside. "Zealots but not extremists" is an adage common to haredi rabbis; it is echoed by Muslim radicals: "We are partisans of a median way [*hall wasat*], we are devoted to it, not to extremism." Rational yet embattled, it is a self-perception no doubt as sincere as it is deep.[90]

For a type of rationality to survive in its social context requires cognitive anchors—notions about historical space and time, physical and human nature, knowledge—in a word, a cosmology. Such anchors provide it with indicators as to its place in a wider scheme of things. Cosmology thus sustains and fashions, in a sort of feedback loop, the culture of the enclave, its mode of behavior, authority, and organization. The underlying assumption is that some sort of balance (or consonance) between cosmology and the social context—in this case, the enclave—must be maintained for the enclave to endure.

Historical time is the cosmological element most readily accessible to the analyst, in that it relates directly to that primal impulse—the diagnosis—which the enclave feeds on. Its time perspective tends to be somewhat shrunken, collapsed, and condensed. The past is reduced to a few key eras, closely related to the enclave's notion as to what accounts for the glory and decline of the tradition; it is hence intensely relevant for the present. The future perspective is likewise rather short; the more radical the enclave, the shorter it is. Its overall bent is pessimistic if not doom-laden.

The specific content, vocabulary, and significance of the time perspective are determined, yet again, by the tradition in question. One should emphasize here that what is meant by "tradition" is neither desiccated book lore nor some marginal past component (or set of long-forgotten precedents). It is a matter of a living tradition, transmitted from generation to generation by clergy, scholars, mystics, and other activists, and one that is part and parcel of the mainstream of that religion. It is not the case of an age-old heresy suddenly raising its head. American fundamentalism is heir to the Calvinist postmillennialism, to John Nelson Darby's premillennialism and, at the root of it all, to Puritan concepts of the City on the Hill, the Beacon of Light.

Sunni and Shi'ite radicalism was born out of an antiaccommodative attitude toward political power which had always existed within these two strands of Islam. This attitude was much more important in Shi'ite Islam, given its persecuted stance throughout history. But even among Sunnis, who are, on the whole, more accommodative, there has always been a legitimate, vigilante-type alternative that was definitely antiaccommodative and was perceived as being within the pale, an integral part of Sunni political lore. Some of this vigilante lore has been covered by historical dust (e.g., the writings of the school of Ibn Hazm in Muslim Spain), but other variants continue to exist to this day (namely, the neo-Hanbali school founded by Ibn Taymiyya in the fourteenth century). When modern Sunni radicals looked in the 1950s for a tradition to build upon, they naturally turned to Ibn Taymiyya. Neither here nor in Shi'ite Islam does the phenomenon in any way represent a case of heresies raising their heads, outside the pale of the legitimate religious discourse. All attempts made by the Egyptian regime to brand radicals as heretics (for example, as Kharijites in the seventh century A.D. or Qarmats in the tenth century A.D.) inevitably failed.

Heresy is likewise definitely not what Jewish radicalism consists of. The ultra-Orthodoxy of the haredim and the Neturei Karta is a successor to a long tradition of Jewish exclusionary life in the Diaspora, a tradition that until the age of enlightenment and secular nationalism (nay, even up to the Holocaust) was the major living tradition of Judaism, resigned to life outside of history (and outside of politics) as long as God had not performed the miracle of messianic redemption. As for Gush Emunim, they build upon the minor but legitimate tradition of Jewish activist messianism—exerting oneself to hasten the arrival of the Messiah and not just passively waiting for him—a tradition that has played a key role in certain historical moments as late as the seventeenth century (with the mass movement of Shabtai Zvi with its deep roots in the kabbala). These medieval kabbalistic concepts were revamped by Rabbi Zvi Yehuda Kook in the 1950s in order to answer questions raised by the establishment of the State of Israel, in a manner no different in essence from the one used by Sunni thinker Sayyid Qutb to reinterpret the Ibn Taymiyya political theory for the needs of the twentieth century. In a slightly different fashion, this is also what Khomeini did to the Usuli notion of ulama hierarchy and social responsibility.

Finally, the Lefebvre movement is an outgrowth of the so-called traditionalist trend in Catholicism. It is dedicated to the very notion of tradition, as laid down in the sixteenth century at the Council of Trent (and reaffirmed at the First Vatican Council). Facing the challenge of Luther's principle of *sola scriptura,* the council consecrated tradition, that is, the doctrinal developments recognized by the church throughout history. The Latin Mass is a vivid symbol of what has been lost in the post–Vatican II era. Fighting for it proceeds from an overall approach to Catholicism that reflects, in Archbishop Lefebvre's words, "an instinctive horror of novelty under any pretext."[91] These movements' strong base in the religious tradition goes far to explain the initial appeal they have for "true believers." That base is also what makes the believers' task of transcending the living tradition, while remaining true to it, so complex and daunting.

This excursus on tradition may help us to better understand the historical perceptions, to which we now return.

Common to most enclaves is a special perspective on the past: members consider themselves to be living at the end of an era drawing to a close. American Protestants, who are usually of a dispensationalist conviction, would see it as a late stage of the church age (which began with Christ's resurrection), a stage when apostasy and heresy threaten Christian civilization with collapse. Some would even suggest an analogy of their situation to that of the underground church of the first century.[92] Haredim would view it as that tail end of the Exile when, in the words of the Mishna, "insolence will increase . . . the kingdom will become heretical . . . the study hall of scholars will become a state of licentiousness."[93] Shi'ites saw Islam about to revert to the paganism of the Iranian kings of 2,500 years ago (celebrated with pomp and circumstance in Persepolis, 1972) or to the persecution of the partisans of true Islam under the apostate Umayyad caliphs (661–750). The same twin-pronged fear reverberates in the Sunni belief that one witnesses the return of the jahiliyya, which forced Muhammad into exile.

A certain cyclical perception of time is often implied: the tradition had known such dangers in the past. The Muslims refer to the Crusaders and their native collaborators in the twelfth and thirteenth centuries or the Arab and Persian adepts of Greek philosophy in the tenth century; haredim refer to the Hellenized Jews of the second century B.C. or the Shabbateans in the seventeenth century A.D. Yet time is also, and above all, linear: in crucial respects the present danger is unheard of, worse than anything that has happened since the combative early days of the tradition.

The combined effect of the cyclical and the linear has a distinct pessimistic flavor to it. Enclaves tend indeed to be obsessed with binary formulations, revolving around a before/after axis. The watershed mark is the historical moment when decline and decay set in. Some thinkers, more philosophically minded, place it at the Renaissance, Humanism, and the European Enlightenment,[94] but the majority (followed by the rank and file) locate it closer to the present: middle (or late) nineteenth century for Protestants and Jews (and the Communione e Liberazione); early (or post–World War I) twentieth century for Muslims. Lefebvre's disciples refer to the separation of church and state in France.

This is no idle speculation. If one wishes to do something about it and not just wax nostalgic about bygone glory, an imminent danger of decline concentrates the mind, condenses the past. Relevant are periods that account for the present menace and/or may provide an ideal to strive for, a model to be reconstituted (allowing, of course, for some adaptation to technological and economic realities). American Protestants speak with great intensity and longing about the United States before industrialization and mass immigration, with its small-town life and traditional family structure. The very architecture of their churches and topics of their posters bespeak attachment to this era, privileged at the expense of all others, preceding or following. A minority of Calvinist-inspired dominion theologians add to it seventeenth-century Puritan colonies, a society controlled by Christianity, before the disastrous separation of church and state.[95]

For the Catholics, the golden age is either the thirteenth century, with the rise of the religious orders, the consolidation of scholasticism and Thomism in particular, and the high-water mark of the medieval papacy; or it is the Counter-Reformation, with the Council of Trent representing the right type of response—tradition-bound, disciplinarian—to a major crisis within both church and society. The council inaugurated the last "wholesome" era in the church's history, an era that would end with the disaster of the French Revolution. It is no coincidence that the two popes the Lefebvrists revere are Pius V, a paragon of the Counter-Reformation (whose rite they vindicate for the Latin Mass), and Pius X, after whom they name their fraternity, who combatted the separation of church and state in France (1905)—the culmination of the revolutionary anticlericalism—and theological modernism. Communione e Liberazione likewise cherishes Pius X together with his predecessor Leo XIII, as models of social Catholicism, committed to changing the modern outlying society without accommodating it; they show how "to be in the world without being of the world."

In Islam, much like in Protestantism, one finds a divergence between majority and minority versions, both legitimately ensconced within the tradition. Sunnis are focused upon Muhammad and the first four caliphs (al-Rashidun), supposed to be of the era when divine law was effectively applied by the state and its norms reigned supreme in civil society. (The Ottoman caliphate, a secondary object of nostalgia, is not held up as a model to which to return, perhaps because for most Sunnis, who are Arabic-speaking, it meant alien rule.) Shi'ites shrink the scope of the relevant past to the times of Muhammad and of his sole legitimate heir, Caliph 'Ali (656–60), when the true version of the Law commanded obedience.

The haredi "foundation myth" is, as one could expect, the eighteenth-century shtetl of east Europe, an emblematic expression of a Diasporic, close-knit, halakha-governed, autonomous community. This is assumed to be the maximum available to Jews under the conditions of exile, created in the first century A.D. "because of our sins," and bound to endure as long as the Lord sees fit. In contradistinction, Gush Emunim are heirs to a minority strand within Judaism that looked for ways to bring about the end of Exile through human agency and reestablish a sovereign entity in the Holy Land.[96] No wonder that the past enthroned by the Gush is the First Commonwealth (thirteenth to sixth century B.C.) and Second Commonwealth (second century B.C. to second century A.D.). Dress codes and topics for children's literature or for sermons vary accordingly between ultra-Orthodox and the Gush.

This "highlighted" past is experienced with utmost contemporaneity, spoken about in the same way that one talks about figures and events appearing in the major text, the product of the revelation, which carries authority in the enclave. Chronological distance is abolished, as is clear to any observer watching haredim on the ninth of Av as they lament the A.D. 70 destruction of the Temple and the onset of Exile, or Shi'ites weeping in self-flagellation for the murder of Imam Husayn, 'Ali's grandson, on the tenth of Ramadan ('Ashura).

As we shall see, the past has its counterpart in the future, for history is, as fundamentalists put it, "purposeful," governed by an omniscient Providence. The intersection of past and future grants the believer a secret road map, enabling him to comprehend from whence he comes and where he or she is headed—a "plan of salvation," in Protestant parlance.

The major cognitive function of the plan is to make sense of the Decline, which consists of the spread of man-centered, progress-minded cosmologies from elites to popular culture, with the backing of a new, interventionist state. A prominent landmark in this context is said to be World War I. The war led to the demise of the Ottoman Empire and the abolition of the Caliphate (1924), along with the enforced assimilation of Russian Jews under Soviet rule and elsewhere, the disruption of shtetl life, and the decline of the community rabbinate. In a hitherto optimistic, postmillennialist

American Protestantism, the mass slaughter on the battlefields and the subsequent materialism of the Roaring Twenties bred a profound cultural pessimism. The sole dissenting note in interpreting this cataclysmic event can be found in the theology of Rabbi A. I. Kook, which inspires Gush Emunim. There the British conquest of Palestine and the Balfour Declaration (1917) were viewed as a hopeful sign of the times, heralding the Age of Redemption (*athalta di-ge'ula*)—a transitory phase from end of Exile to the messianic era.

Subject to divine control and "purposeful," history must produce miracles—and not only at the formative, sacred periods of the faith, as depicted in the Scriptures, but also in later periods up to and including the recent past. In a similar vein haredim celebrate the Allied victory over the Nazis and the escape of leading halakhic authorities and Hasidic rabbis from Europe during World War II. The Gush as well as many American fundamentalists celebrate the establishment of the State of Israel and the Six Day War. Islamic radicals impute miraculous qualities to the demise of Nasser (1967–70).

The cognitive function of the past is inextricably entwined with its behavioral consequences: the past is a spur to action, especially when past and present action are situated in conjunction with the future. This is true because the present is viewed as the end of a historical age. Here the symbolic capital provided by the tradition, and room for variations deemed legitimate within its mainstream, play perhaps even greater a role than in times past, when the long-term perspective was seen as a continuation of present realities, more or less in the same manner.

The dominant strand in American fundamentalism is premillennial and pretribulationist—a tradition imported from England in the mid-nineteenth century and coming to prominence in the second decade of the twentieth century. Its message of messianic redemption following an imminent worldwide catastrophe (from which only the saved, "raptured" Christians would escape) reflected and responded to the downbeat, beleaguered mood in the independent Baptist churches. Their bleak diagnosis of the state of the world gained credibility when war in Europe dealt a heavy blow to the illusions of progress. The older and more optimistic postmillennialist tradition lost its hegemony but persisted in certain pockets such as the Reconstructionists. It still saw Redemption about to dawn, culminating eventually in the Second Coming, and called not just to wait for the messianic breakthrough to happen but to help in bringing it about.

Premillennialism is a strong incentive for focusing on personal salvation in the context of the coming Rapture, with the independent church serving as the support group. This theological outlook sets limits on sallies to the outside, which are geared to recruit new members (who may be among the raptured), and to improve the Christian quality of life in the immediate vicinity of the enclave, a sort of protective perimeter. Transforming the entire society tends to be viewed as an impossibility in this day and age. It can only come after the Tribulation is over; but there is no telling when this will be, even though this is definitely the last stage of the church age. Both the Rapture and the subsequent seven years of Tribulation are expected to take place at some indeterminate date. Such notions are hotly contested by the postmillennialists and denounced as passive and defeatist. They take an interest in collective, not just personal, salvation. Imposing Christian norms (i.e., banning abortion) on the whole of society through influence upon (and perhaps ultimately control of) government is, for them, quite feasible. Moreover, it carries the United States farther on the road to redemption.[97] But as we shall see, even premillennialists can sometimes be jolted into social action, like Falwell, by the fear that there will be no future generation of Christians to wait for the Lord if secular humanism continues its ravage.

The haredim, although they view themselves as living toward the end of the Age of Exile (*seifa de-galuta*) and within an indeterminate range of the footsteps of the Messiah, stick with the major, passive strand of Jewish messianism: one should always wait for the Messiah as if he were around the corner, yet expect him to come through divine agency alone (*it'aruta dl'eila*). The haredi is, in consequence, resigned to live outside history (and outside politics), for Jewish sovereignty can only be established when God performs the miracle of redemption and dispatches the Messiah. For all the tribulations characteristic of the end of the Age of Exile, including the Holocaust, they detect no signs that redemption is imminent. Seifa de-galuta may be rather protracted.[98] Only the Lubavitchers set forth a different cosmic calendar: the final moments of the Age of Exile are approaching, the sole condition that must still be fulfilled being a massive return to the faith (*teshuva*). Human agency may help prompt the divine.

The pessimistic messianism of the haredim accounts for their denial of any theological significance for the State of Israel. In turn this denial has deep roots in their sense of alienation from its secularist lifestyle—another example of the "feedback loop." The denial likewise implies that it is vain to strive to impose halakha upon all walks of life; the "state of the Jews" can become a "Jewish state" only when the Messiah comes. The optimistic counterpart in the Jewish context is represented by the Gush Emunim, who build upon a minor (yet legitimate) tradition of Jewish activist messianism, suffused with kabbalistic elements: one should exert oneself to hasten the arrival of the Messiah. In its more extreme variations, like the Jewish underground of the early 1980s, this leads to virulent denunciations of passive messianism as sheepish and quietistic, a typical product of the Diasporic way of life; there is no place for such a mode in the great Land of Israel.

Divergence of diagnosis is involved here as much as theological controversy. For the Gush, inspired by the revamping of the activist mode by Rabbi Z. Y. Kook, the establishment of the State of Israel signifies the dawn of redemption. But in order to prove this assessment they had to resort to a theological innovation: there is a transitory phase between the end of Exile and the actual coming of the Messiah. This transitory stage, begun with the Zionist settlement of Palestine and consolidated in 1948, is already situated outside history. As an integral part of the redemption it is sacred, even though secular Jews are in charge (and halakha is not implemented).

Different road maps make for different readings of unfolding events. The haredim saw the 1973 war, not without Schadenfreude, as a punishing blow to Zionist "idolatry" of military might. For the Gush this was a setback on the way to redemption, after the huge step forward taken in 1967; it was accounted for by the insufficient effort made toward the settlement of the recently "liberated" parts of the Holy Land. The founding and rise of the Gush is closely linked with this "setback" and with what they saw as the defeatism prevalent in Israeli society in the wake of the Yom Kippur War. This conforms to a pattern discussed above: a bleak evaluation of the present spurs the development of an enclave. In Gush terms (and in line with their theological optimism) this was an *it'aruta dilteta,* an act catalyzing the process of redemption through human agency.

The fact that the place of messianism is much less prominent in Islamic living tradition endows the future time perspective, among Sunnis and Shi'ites, with a different texture. The messianic element is held in abeyance in almost all Sunni groups (much as it is in Catholicism). The only exception is the Takfir wa'l-Hijra sect in Egypt, which declared its leader, who was later executed, *Mahdi* (messiah). (This is the only case in all three traditions where a messiah is specifically designated. Even among the Lubavitchers the late rebbe was just rumored to be Him). This idiosyncratic group, unlike the Reconstructionists or Gush Emunim, was furthermore antinomian, rejecting most of the Shari'a as evil. In any case, it is an exception that just proves the rule. The messianic element is on the whole quite irrelevant to the Sunni discourse on delegitimation as well as to the reading of current events (and this is, again, equally true of Catholic radicals). Sunni radicals hold that the present order must be toppled in "normal" (nonmessianic) historical time and a new legitimate order—ushering in the application of the Shari'a—without awaiting the new messiah (or mahdi).[99]

In this stance Sunni radicals are true heirs to the Sunni tradition, where there is indeed a belief in a messiah who would come at the end of time, and after a struggle with the Antichrist will establish the realm of justice upon earth. But not only was this belief quite secondary, it has become in the course of the centuries virtually marginal. The great eleventh-century theologian al-Ghazali passed over it in silence, while the famous philosopher of history Ibn Khaldun (fourteenth century) subjected it to a scathing critique.

Belief in the apocalypse was typical, though by no means prominent, among Sufis (mystics), and even there the context was in general quietistic—knowing that the Messiah was due to come enabled one to forbear suffering and injustice, sit tight, and do nothing but pray. While in the first two centuries of Islam there were Sunni apocalyptic revolts, this tradition was soon taken over and almost completely monopolized by the Shi'ites (or to be more precise: by the Isma'ili and Imamite branches). The few such Sunni revolts in later times erupted in peripheral Islamic countries (Algeria, Sudan) in an anticolonialist context, and were the product of a subculture of marginal mystics and preachers. Such a subculture was soon to be completely erased by modernization, and with it died much of the spirit of apocalyptic activism.[100] Contrary to what the Arab left expected, messianism did not become the mainstay of a revolutionary tradition in the lands of Islam.[101]

Messianism is more important for the Shi'ites, especially the majority Imamite sect with its belief in a Hidden (twelfth) Imam "in occultation" since 941 and due to come back upon earth on judgment day and reestablish the rule of the House of 'Ali as well as the perfect application of Islamic law, and, hence, the rule of justice. This is seen as the coming vindication of Shi'ite suffering throughout history.[102]

This is a major Shi'ite myth, whereas the precept of *raj'a* (return to earth) of the Hidden Imam is accepted by most Shi'ites—with the exception of a few ecumenical thinkers[103] who wish not to hurt Sunni sensibilities—as a fundamental tenet. Yet the notion of a Hidden Imam operated from the early tenth century above all in a quietistic context. After all, the very use of this idea among Twelver (Imamite) Shi'ites was associated with the time of the worst Abbasid persecutions and tended to thwart Shi'ites from virtually suicidal insurrections, recommending them to suffer in silence and bide their time. This was its major function throughout most of Imamite history. Indeed, most of the important Shi'ite revolutionary movements came from the Isma'ili branch (e.g., the Qarmats, for whom the Mahdi was always steeped in an activistic lore with antinomian overtones).

Khomeini did not try his hand at infusing activism into Iranian beliefs in the Mahdi, judging, quite sensibly, that there was no great apocalyptic tension to be energized among the masses. In his major work, *Islamic Government* (1971), he criticizes the many Shi'ites who collaborate with the authorities based upon the premise that man must strive to achieve justice in the here and now, in this world from which the Imam is absent, and not wait "hundreds and perhaps even thousands of years" for the establishment of absolute justice by the Imam upon his return to earth. However, even if Khomeini did not stress the concept of Imam (or the Mahdi), his teaching repeatedly implies the principle that forms the boundary of the time frame in which he worked. (The fifth article of the Iranian constitution states that it will be valid "as long as the Twelfth Imam is absent.") Furthermore, Khomeini served as a *marja' al-taqlid* (source of imitation; highest religious authority) since the early 1960s, and his authority as such was defined as stemming from a delegation of authority for the sake of guardianship (*wilaya 'amma*) on behalf of the Hidden Imam. Only in this way could Khomeini transform the institution of marja' from a strictly religious function into one that is political as well. Some of his adepts who were inclined to literal interpretations would even claim that Khomeini was a mystical emanation issuing directly from the Mahdi and serving as vanguard for the Mahdi's return. It is this concept from which the title applied to Khomeini—but not yet to his successor Ali Khamanei—*na'ib al-imam* (vicar of the [Hidden] Imam)—is derived. Khomeini did try to emphasize that he was not imbued with the Hidden Imam's spiritual powers (especially not with *'isma,* infallibility), and that since in essence he was not different from other mortals, his rule was strictly functional (*wilaya i'tibariyya*). Nonetheless, the frame of reference and the basis for comparison is the Mahdi: the regime was measured against him, and the time allotted for it to rule was delimited by his eventual return. This was an important pillar of Khomeini's worldview, though not as crucial as *wilayat al-faqih* (guardianship of the jurist). It should therefore come as no surprise that the Hidden Imam's birthday (which falls on the fifteenth of Sha'ban) has always been one of the four major religious holidays in Iran (along with the 'Ashura and the birthdays of 'Ali and Husayn, each of which relate to the "foundation myth"). During this holiday, Khomeini used to extol the "return of the Imam-Mahdi in the End of the Days" in fervid speeches that received wide media coverage.

Eschatology is thus present in Shi'ite mythology but in a different fashion than among dominion theologians or Gush activists: no fervent expectation of an imminent End of Days, no computations of the expected date based on signs and miracles, no reading of any crisis (such as the Intifada) as part and parcel of the "pangs of redemption," no temptation "to force God's hand" and hasten the Redemption (as in the case of the Jewish underground). It is true that at the affective level the Shi'ites do retain an eschatological undercurrent, although even in Iran a certain decline can be observed since Khomeini's death. It is mostly in embattled Shi'ite enclaves, such as among the Hizbullah in Lebanon, that one notes from time to time eruptions of messianic rhetoric, followed by computations of the frequency of lunar eclipses as signs of the times (*akhbar al-sa'ah*). Yet on the whole, much like with the Sunnis, the myth of the Shari'a, with its clear-cut orientation toward the past, as the panacea for all social ills definitely reigns supreme among the Shi'ites, especially as the interpreters of the law, the ulama, lead the Shi'ite radicals and, in fact, constitute the revolutionary cadre.

Possessing the secret road map for the future is likely to empower the enclave member, fill him with a sense of orientation, enable him to "decipher" oncoming events. One can identify players in the world (or national) scene by their biblical codes: Russia, for American premillennialists, is the Kingdom of the North (or Gog), Libya is the Kingdom of the South (or Magog).[104] Similar attempts can be heard in "national-haredi" yeshivot close to the Gush. Code names are pointers to the ultimate behavior and fate of the players. Deciphering them is evidently helpful for decision making in conditions of uncertainty, that is, in molding risk perception and risk management strategies. As risk is a cultural construct, moral commitments do enter in its evaluation and in the lessons drawn therefrom.

The enclave tends to see itself as inherently fragile, given the ever-lurking outside. Its future is expected to be different from the present, most probably—in the short run, at least—for the worse (or worse preceding change for the better). The enclave must, hence, fear irreversible, involuntary, and hidden changes, about which there is imperfect knowledge and little or no control. An enclave rarely discounts a piece of bad news about future events. And this explains its propensity to indulge in conspiracy theories, as well as the shrill tone of its press in reporting current events.

Obsession with risk underlies the haredi view that Jews in the Exilic Age are eternally persecuted by hateful goyish nations, "a lamb surrounded by seventy wolves," harassed (at times oppressed) by obtuse if not hostile "apostate" Jews.[105] Both evil forces are powerful and have already brought catastrophes on the faithful (Holocaust, assimilation) and may perpetrate worse. The strategy must consist of risk avoidance (or risk minimization). There must be as little confrontation as possible (limiting, at times, the scope of the "sallies") and no provocation of the type that had cost the Jews the destruction of the Second Temple and the loss of sovereignty, ushering in the Exilic Age. This concept (a.k.a. the Three Oaths) makes the haredi parties, on the whole, adopt dovish attitudes to the Arab-Israeli conflict, and denounce the Gush-affiliated underground and the Temple Mount Faithful. Their prominent rabbis severely condemned their own hotheads, yeshiva students who in the early 1950s dynamited and set fire to shops and restaurants that broke the Shabbat, sold pork, and so forth. Nor is this a recent attitude. The concept of the Three Oaths is embedded in talmudic literature (Tractate Ketuboth) and represents a major strand of Jewish thought and action all through the medieval and modern periods. It underlies the rejection of Zionism by Hasidic rabbis in the interwar era as a movement that breaks the commitment not to "take off the yoke of exile." Zionism's activism bothered them no less than its secularism. The passivity of these rabbis and their adepts vis-à-vis the Holocaust is to be accounted for, in part, by this same stance.

This is not to say that the haredim today renounce the hope that the Messiah may come at any moment and change this state of affairs (this is why they oppose the custom of the double tombstone, as it is uncertain that the living spouse will die before the Resurrection, which follows the Coming). Yet all that is in principle only. In actual fact, they do not bank on it and are not filled with intimations of the Messiah's approaching arrival.

The Lubavitchers, who do have such intimations, are the exceptions to this rule. Their future perspective is not just shorter, it is optimistic. Risks are of small magnitude or are to be compensated for by a redemption that is just around the corner. Risk taking is justified. Goyish threats are pooh-poohed. The Lubavitcher rebbe is rigidly hawkish on holding on to Judea and Samaria, the sacred arena of redemption (and that although he recognizes the State of Israel only de facto).

The imminent messianism of Gush Emunim is placed at the service of sacred entities: the Land of Israel and the State of Israel. What results is a total sacralization of politics, which reminds one of dominion theologians or of Shi'ite thinkers in postrevolutionary Iran (the state has become sanctified now that it is in the hands of virtuous mullahs). Such a view is alien to haredi thought, where politics is a realm apart (Sunnis and most Protestant fundamentalists would concur). As the Gush is certain of the sanctity of its tools (arms, settlement), assured of oncoming success if only sufficient help from down below would be given to divine Providence, it is consequently quite cavalier about risk taking. All the more so as the alternative is nothing short of catastrophic: loss of the historical opportunity to hold on forever to core areas of Eretz Yisrael, postponement of the Redemption for lack of determined human prodding. Such doom-laden arguments in the mouths of optimists are not bizarre; they are quite typical to enclaves that, fragile, tend to fluctuate between extremes. But what about incurring the wrath of the United States or Arab retaliation? The Gush responds that this is a reasonable price to pay for avoiding the catastrophe. Hence its opposition to the evacuation of part of Sinai and Golan (1974–75), evacuation of the whole of Sinai (1979–82) and, above all, its insistence on the massive settlement of Judea and Samaria.

The hegemonic eschatology in U.S. fundamentalism—premillennial, pretribulationist—is pessimistic as to what awaits humankind, holding hope just for those individuals (144,000, by a literalist biblical accounting) who will be saved by the Rapture on the eve of the seven years of Tribulation preceding the Second Coming. Recruiting more people to the contingent of the saved and keeping them in an unpolluted milieu until the hour comes—this is the prime goal for the meantime, that short-range future that, in typical enclave fashion, is all they care for. Survival is not an easy task given the temptations, conspiracies, and ever-insidious immoralities of modern society. Reducing contact with the latter—except for self-defensive sallies—helps diminish, maybe avoid, irreversible risks: defections, damage to the purity of the enclave. In short, this is a haredi-type strategy predicated upon a different symbolic capital.

The Reconstructionists, with their postmillennialism, evidently present the obverse of the coin: the sole way to avoid the greater risks of de-Christianizing, profane modernity consists of taking some risks: to launch a bid for power. This is just a short-term risk, much smaller than any damages that are bound to evolve if the current situation persists over the long haul. After all, victory for such a bid for dominion is practically certain: the time is ripe for miraculous divine intervention, redemption is about to unfold the thousand-year reign.

The type of messianism involved is not, however, the only perceptual context that determines the enclave's attitude toward risk taking. Consider the Islamic case. There is no doubt that some Shi'ite groups, such as the Iranian-Lebanese-Tunisian terrorist network brought to trial in France in 1990, as well as segments of the Hizbullah are immersed in "Mahdi now" cosmology, seeing everywhere the tell-tale signs of "growing debauchery and chaos"; ready, much like Gush militants, to take risks in order to forestall graver dangers (i.e., "arrogant imperialist dominance"), hoping for help from the Mahdi. Yet on the whole Sunni and Shi'ite activists live in a world where the Last Days are not taken as an operative eventuality during the course of their own lives. Those who resort to violent acts (the Jihad Organization, assassins of Sadat and, more recently, of the president of the Egyptian parliament) do so impelled by fear that the cancerous jahiliyya is spreading fast and is at the point of becoming irreversible. Emergency surgery is thus imperative. No reference to the End of Days is necessary here. (This also seems to be the logic motivating the majority in Hizbullah, logic shaped by anxieties bred out of the jungle life of Lebanon, where state and public order disappeared.) Nevertheless, the same jahiliyya diagnosis, coupled with a hard-nosed assessment of the resilience and repressive ingenuity of the state, drives most Sunni radicals to consider the risks of "holy violence" to be too great, leading to a head-on collision with a ruthless government. Jahiliyya, rather than being smashed, might win an even greater victory. Caught between a rock and a hard place, the radicals opt for retreat into the enclave community, shoring up their social and physical boundaries, and from there branching out, as circumstances permit, into educational and welfare extensions and local political work (all based on the mosque as "immune space"). Perhaps later—as in the case of the Algerian Front Islamique du Salut—into national politics. We arrive, once again, at a haredi-type strategy, but with messianism not even secondary but marginal.

This supple, fluctuating kaleidoscope calls for some caution in the use of labels such as pre- or postmillennial, "messiah now" or "messiah in his own good time," and so forth. None of these labels is ineluctably entwined with a specific diagnosis (optimistic or pessimistic, for instance); none leads inexorably to just one type of risk perception, or to a specific course of action. Feedback from reality—be it interpreted allegorically or factually—may elicit varying responses within the same enclave. Thus while most haredim conclude that until the Messiah comes there is no point in striving toward imposition of halakha as state law in Israel, there are those, perhaps among the impatient young, who argue that given their growing political clout they should do it and thus improve life of klal Yisrael at the End of Exile.[106]

Moreover, feedback from reality may even modify the doctrinal stance regarding the future, albeit within certain parameters deemed by the enclave to be sacred. The growing conviction of Jerry Falwell, Pat Robertson, Randall Terry, and Tim LaHaye in the late seventies as to the possible emergence of a Moral Majority, likely to acquire hegemony in American politics and culture, made them introduce a "postmillennial window"[107] into their premillennialism. They assumed that the arrival of the millennium depends upon their activism for fear that there will be no believers left when the millennium comes. Tribulation will precede Rapture, not follow it. In consequence, one should act immediately in order to better American society, otherwise devastation would be so comprehensive as to hit the saved as well, and, anyhow, it might be so cataclysmic as to render reconstruction extremely difficult. Only a daring bid for power—till then thought to be an un-Christian course of action—could save the day.

It is, of course, their scriptural and charismatic authority that empowered Falwell and his consorts to operate this exegetical legerdemain. The same goes for Gush Emunim, shaken as it was in the mid-1980s by its failure to stop through mass protest the evacuation of Yamit in Sinai (1982) and by the dismantling of the underground (1984), an autonomous outgrowth of the Gush that sought to hasten redemption and block further territorial concessions by murdering Palestinian mayors and plotting to blow up the mosque on the Temple Mount. The ensuing soul-searching in the Gush was intense: was it not presumptuous to assume that we know for certain God's messianic timetable? Was it not to commit the sin of arrogance to claim that we can prod him to perform the miracle of redemption when we deem it most urgent?

Some of the Gush mentors, such as Rabbi Shlomo Aviner, while maintaining allegiance to the Kook cosmology, reacted to this quandary by introducing new (or, they would claim, hitherto neglected) distinctions. These distinctions were based, of course, as in Falwell's case, on proof texts—in this case, mostly midrashic and kabbalistic ones. Aviner argues that Redemption is on the way, the Messiah will eventually come "even though he may tarry," but man can neither know the timing nor can he hasten it significantly by initiatives from below. All he can do is help prepare the terrain by settlement in Judea and Samaria and immersion in the study of the Torah (hence enhancing the role of the yeshivot), particularly the study of portions of the Talmud related to the 292 precepts effective in messianic times. (Aviner's yeshiva, 'Ateret Cohanim, in the Old City of Jerusalem, specializes in Temple service procedures.) Prepare the terrain so that all will be ready when the hour cometh, but without alleging one can force God's hand or fathom his plan. The doctrine is essentially preserved, yet the order of priorities for action is reshuffled.

In much the same way, but requiring no modification in its theological premises, Communione e Liberazione has passed recently from direct involvement in the internal politics of the Christian Democratic Party to an emphasis on welfare and educational work. The risks involved in the former strategy (loss of members unhappy with their too-conservative positions, especially during the referenda on divorce and abortion) were enough to justify the switch from "dominion"-type activity to "sallies." As Catholics invest relatively little in eschatology, Communione e Liberazione did not need an adjustment on this score. Past models (the Counter-Reformation, the church's struggle in late nineteenth century) were supple enough to remain.

So much for cosmological time. It is more arduous to examine attitudes related to cosmological space. By that I mean space as learned, not as directly experienced (the latter dubbed "operational"). In such a context, physical realities crucial for operational space—for example, contiguous areas around mosque/synagogue/church creating a "sacred environment"—lose much of their value. Areas physically distant may be perceived as structurally near. Children in afternoon classes held in a Cairo mosque declared Bosnia-Herzegovina, the Philippines, and Burma as "lands close to our heart" because of Muslim minorities persecuted there. Other than that they knew nothing about these countries, not even what their majority religion was. Haredi school children in B'nai B'rak easily tackled Poland and the Soviet Union on a globe, pinpointing towns in which major Hasidic sects originated. But they were otherwise quite ignorant as to the geography of these states.[108] Jerry Falwell's moral (or imaginary) space refers above all to the two-hundred-odd churches whose pastors are graduates of Liberty University—the saved enclave in pagan America.[109] The Lefebvrists analogue is the network of more than two hundred like-minded communities in France, Germany, Switzerland, Austria, the United Kingdom, the United States, Argentina, and Brazil. The rest of the world gets barely a mention in the movement's press.

Cosmological space is not linear. One may not actually care for "apostate" neighbors, yet feel intense affinity with members of like-minded enclaves. The common model is that of concentric circles in diminishing status of spatial importance. "Egypt for me is this [al-Nur] mosque with its afternoon and evening school, its preschool and outpatient facilities," says a radical shaykh in northern Cairo. "This working-class area [al-Abbasiyya] where most of our members live is our immediate buffer. Beyond, I look at Egypt as a map studded by those private mosques engaged in the same sacred work of changing Egyptian society from within. And beyond that? I do care for our long-suffering brethren in Palestine and in Algeria. And beyond that, well, the whole dar al-Islam [abode of Islam, countries where Islam is the majority religion], at least in as much as it is populated by Muslims enraged by the jahiliyya and resolved to combat it."[110]

What strikes one in this telling interview is that, despite the shaykh's repugnance for the nation-state ideology of Sadat and Mubarak (a "polytheistic idolatry"),[111] Egypt is the outer circle he cares for most. Transforming Egyptian society (not dar al-Islam in general) is the maximum he can hope for. The division of dar al-Islam into territorial states is deplored but accepted as a fait accompli. It certainly helped that the radicals' cherished theologian, Ibn Taymiyya (d. 1328), had attempted to come to terms with the fact that dar al-Islam had been divided since the tenth century into territorial states. Yet even revolutionary Iran—which is not beholden to Ibn Taymiyya and has pan-Islamic aspirations—is suffused with commitment to Iranian patrimony.

Defense of the independence and territorial integrity of Iran is a basic tenet of the 1979 constitution (article 9) as well as the program of the governing Islamic Republican Party. This conviction was certainly invigorated by the war with Iraq but was also directed against centrifugal tendencies among minorities (Azeris, Kurds). At gut level, it is the expression of a powerful politicocultural tradition, rooted in territory and closely entwined, since the sixteenth century, with Shi'ism.[112] Even the Hizbullah, for all their admiration for Iran, have drawn up several scenarios describing their future as bounded by a Lebanese framework, and that despite the fact that this is a land where the state is in poor shape. Hizbullah spiritual leader Fadlallah takes great care to point out that even in doctrinal matters the Iranian writ does not run in Lebanon (e.g., with regard to the interpretation of wilayat al-faqih).[113]

American fundamentalists see the United States as the third concentric circle of their "moral landscape," beyond their own independent church and the loose network of churches to which they belong (Baptist Convention, Liberty University graduates, etc.). America is of course endowed here with a theological dimension (as the City on the Hill), a dimension usually irrelevant for Muslim movements (except for the Palestinian case; see below). The fourth concentric circle is the Middle East, with the Holy Land as its hub and the war theater of the Apocalypse, preceding the Second Coming. The prophetic landscape depicted in the Books of Ezekiel, Daniel, and Revelation saw its veracity confirmed by the strategic role of the Middle East in the international arena over the last quarter century. Cosmology has suddenly been endowed with a down-to-earth significance.[114]

When both theological time and space enter into close interplay, the affective dimension is greatly intensified. For Gush Emunim not only is Eretz Yisrael sacred and the center of creation, but Judea and Samaria are its backbone, with Jerusalem and, in it, the Temple Mount, at its very core. Small wonder that the extreme fringes of the Gush, the terrorist underground, with its exalted messianism, highlighted the attachment to the core, even at the expense of settlement in the West Bank. Hence their 1984 plot to blow up the al-Aqsa and Umar mosques in order to "clear up" the terrain and prepare it for the building of the Third Temple when the Messiah comes, a plot predicated upon a kabbalistic critique of the attitudes of the mainstream Gush, which were said to prefer the "peel" (*klippa,* external dimension, in kabbalistic lingo), that is, the Western Wall, over the "inner core" (*toch*), that is, the Temple Mount. The Gush, it was argued, pays homage to the wall as a religio-national symbol (accepted also by Zionist doves), while tolerating that the mount is "sullied" by the Islamic presence.[115] Not for the first time in Jewish history, such mystical views had practical consequences.

By a "mimetic desire effect," of the sort René Girard speaks about,[116] Gush Emunim cosmology and behavior produced its counterpart among the Palestinians. First came the renewed emphasis on Jerusalem (following the 1967 conquest by Israel) as a third holy city of Islam, a position based on the story of Muhammad's night journey and ascension (*isra' wa-mi'raj*). By the mid-1970s—in a mode replicating developments during the Counter-Crusade of the twelfth to thirteenth century[117]—the city became essentially the focus of the sanctity of the whole of Palestine (the Blessed Land,

Land of the Prophets, Land of the Night Journey). Later on, with the Intifada and the rise of the Hamas movement, an innovative concept was hatched out of this medieval framework: Palestine in its entirety is the *waqf* (religious endowment) of the Islamic umma and, in consequence, no part of it can be ceded to non-Muslims. The analogy, willy-nilly, with the idea of Great Israel—without which Judaism is "truncated" (*qetu'a*)—is evident.[118]

Finally, what about the human agent operating within the confines of time and space? The Hafetz Haim seems to have said it all for his Christian and Muslim counterparts: "The whole world is topsy-turvy, our religion suffers persecutions, is vilified by infidels, ridiculed by apostates, *let alone that each and everyone of us suffers from his own Evil Will*" (my emphasis).[119] Human nature is bad—though perfectible—and subject to constant infiltration of outside impurity. Of course female nature is weaker, enticing males and prone to be ensnared by consumerism—so runs the lament in enclaves in all three religions. The advice to the faithful is clear: always be on your guard, strive hard to bolster defenses against temptations, clean up your act by meditation and strict behavior. Any visitor listening to tapes played by taxi drivers in Cairo and Jerusalem is likely to hear Shaykh 'Abd al-Hamid Kishk or Rabbi Nissim Yagen dispensing such counsel. The visitor will not fail to detect in these sermons—alternately florid and homespun—the prevalence of terms like *yetzer, ta'va* (Hebrew: desire, passion), *hawa'* (Arabic synonym of *ta'va*). Before bracing oneself for the small jihad (*jihad asghar*) against disbelievers (i.e., Israel), the Arabic tape intimates, one should throw oneself into the great jihad, the holy war against evil in one's own heart (*jihad akbar, jihad al-nafs*). Israel cannot be ready for the Messiah, says the Hebrew tape, before the licentious imprint of Zionism is erased from Jewish hearts. All this reminds the listener of hellfire-and-brimstone sermons heard over the car radio in the American northeast and south. The Jim and Tammy Faye Bakker and Jimmy Swaggart cases were even used there to illustrate the point.

The underlying assumption is always the same: there is a strong correlation—set and controlled by divine Providence—between the macro- and microspheres, the state of physical nature and human nature, society and morality. Social disorder is but a symptom of the individual's moral transgressions on the inside as well as on the outside (e.g., the decline of the traditional family in the United States, the spread of homosexuality and abortion, higher criminality, AIDS, lower economic performance, and lesser clout in world politics).[120] "Our problems are neither economic nor political, our problems are moral," chanted the Islamic demonstrators in Algeria during the Couscous Riots (fall 1988). Their firebrand preacher, 'Ali Belhadj, claimed later that the consecutive droughts in recent years were the result of sexual permissiveness, mixed education, soccer fever, and the video craze. Belhadj would be surprised to hear that the Gush-affiliated radio, Channel Seven, made that very claim for the Israeli drought in fall and winter 1990. The haredim, for their part, argue that the Intifada is the end product of "promiscuous" norms of secular schools. How different is this from Jim Bakker's groupies a year earlier in Charlotte, North Carolina, depicting hurricane Hugo hitting their town as the Lord's punishment for the unjustified persecution of their minister?[121]

Yet human nature is capable of improvement. Both haredim and independent Baptists point as a guideline to the Proverbs verse "He who spares the rod spoils the child," acting upon this at home. By extension, they seek to impose stringent regulations on behavior in schools, streets, swimming beaches, and malls subject to municipalities they control, as do mayors associated with the Algerian Front Islamique du Salut, brought to power in the landslide elections of June 1990. Some harmony between nature and society, society and the individual may be restored, provided the rotten inside is purged, outside influence barred, boundaries reimposed.

Authority and Empowerment

While the enclave can be expected to be quite rigid in defense of its boundaries,[122] I have noted above several cases where there is suppleness and room for innovation in legal matters as well as eschatology. In all such cases it was not enough that this was done for a good cause, the better to ensure the survival (or flourishing) of the group. They always required that initiatives be taken on behalf of the leadership and assumed unquestioned authority of the latter.

What is this authority? To what extent is it a throwback to the past or an adjustment to modern challenges?

The enclave, to repeat, is predicated upon voluntary membership and upon the equality of the virtuous insiders (circumscribed by grids of gender and age). Yet these characteristics, combined, produce an unintended consequence: they hamper decision making and render authority ambiguous. This is all the more acute, as formal ranking and differentiated remuneration tend to be shunned (or minimized) for fear of defection. Who is, then, to constrain whom? How will virtue be maintained and strife avoided?

The solution to this quandary lies, in part, in the doctrine of the inerrancy of the authoritative text (and its approved commentaries), which takes pride of place in all the religious enclaves discussed in this essay: the Scofield Bible; papal encyclicals and conciliar resolutions; the Talmud (and the codes based on it, notably the Shulkhan 'Arukh); the Qur'an, Hadith (oral tradition), and Shari'a. So central are these texts even to everyday life that enclave members resort to "bringing out the word," that is, random selection of a page in order to deduce instructions or omens for mundane choices and actions. The term is Protestant, but the custom appears in Jewish and Muslim enclaves as well. Of course, the major use of the texts is to set boundaries between virtue and vice, inside and outside. To function well they require some flesh-and-blood authority, preferably alive, to interpret them. For without interpretation—whether literal, allegorical, or otherwise—how can the text be applied to rapidly changing realities of our time?[123] Still, this has to be done in a manner that will introduce as little institutional hierarchy as possible into the enclave and thus disrupt that cherished asset, the intrinsic equality of the insiders.

In no area is the modern nature of the enclave more evident than with regard to authority, fashioned as it is in quite a novel way. Authority is usually vested there in a small number of individuals (preferably one, at least for each local community of the enclave). Scholarship and formal training may play a role in the selection of the leader(s), but the crucial factor is charisma: that special heavenly grace (in Arabic *baraka;* in Hebrew *hesed elohi*) that sets one man (virtually never is it a woman) apart from the rest of the enclave members. That man is to combine virtue, decision-making ability, and mastery of the tradition. It's interesting that although Sayyid Qutb, the founder of Sunni radicalism, had considerable renown as a Qur'anic scholar (the selections from his commentary, *Signposts on the Road,* is still a best-seller in Egypt), memoirs written by his disciples set in relief his personality traits (simplicity, stringency, courage) to be crowned by martyrdom at the gallows. The Sunni movement Jama'at Tabligh resorts less to the Qur'an proper than to the manual *The Garden of Pious Believers,* an anthology of Qur'anic verses assembled by the nephew of the movement's founder, Muhammad Zakariya, and hadiths telling about the Prophet Muhammad's life as models for behavior on matters, large and small, from garb to the treatment of lapsed Muslims. Khomeini, despite his long career as scholar and teacher in a Qom madrasa, was never considered to possess towering intellectual acumen before he entered the political arena in 1962–63. His most popular book, *Islamic Government,* is based on lectures to theology students and retains a conversational style. His most effective medium, before and after the revolution, was sermons and talks (distributed on tape cassettes, later on television), delivered in a homespun style. These talks were reminiscent of the fables for which Hafetz Haim was famous in that they utilized an old-fashioned, rural-provincial vocabulary. And while the founder of Communione e Liberazione, Luigi Giussani, is the author of a number of theological treatises, the handbook of the movement is his *Conversations* (long interviews with a journalist). Members explain that his "luminosity" comes across better there. American Protestantism is, of course, an even more clear-cut case, given the role of televangelism (followed, at a distant second, by pamphlets and books, some of which, like Hal Lindsey's best-seller *The Late Great Planet Earth,* are written in science-fiction style).

It goes without saying that the Lefebvre movement is due almost entirely to the initiative of its founder and the verve of his sermons (taken to be the sole valid interpretation of the inerrant texts), as well as to his leadership style and organizational skills. Following his death (March 1991) supporters and observers alike were keen to know whether the successor he had groomed for nine years, Father Franz Schmidberger, would be able to carry his mantle. The very survival of the movement may depend on it. Similar questions are raised today in Habad, and with lesser acuity in haredi circles in Israel, by the imminent demise of the Lubavitcher rebbe and of Rabbi Schach.

Charismatic authority was upgraded to the level of full-fledged (and new) doctrine in haredi and Shi'ite circles. Faced with the decline of the authority of the local community's rabbi (*mara de-atra*) throughout the nineteenth century, the haredim developed, especially during the second quarter of the twentieth, the concept of da'at Torah: the authority of the great Torah scholar (*gadol ba-Torah*), by virtue of his total immersion in the scriptural-exegetical tradition as well as his model lifestyle and character, to issue binding rulings, not just on purely halakhic matters but likewise on mundane issues of the day, including politics.[124] Each autonomous haredi grouping (*khug,* i.e., circle) constituted around a major yeshiva or Hasidic court has such a gadol at its head. The structure of the haredi world, which leaves sufficient leeway for the various "circles," is, in consequence, a sort of loose confederation of enclaves—not entirely unlike a network of independent Baptist churches (those grouped around the Southern Baptist Convention, Operation Rescue, Christian Voice, the Religious Round Table; or churches shepherded by graduates of Liberty University) or Sunni jama'at subscribing more or less to the same ideological variant (e.g., Tanzim al-Jihad).[125] The major haredi confederation was institutionalized by Agudat Yisrael in the 1930s with the establishment of the Council of Torah Sages, comprising half a dozen or so yeshiva heads or Hasidic rabbis set forth by the principal "circles" (with future changes decided by cooptation).[126] In 1992 there were in fact three such coordinating councils, mirroring the split of the haredim into three large "confederations," each with its own political party and educational system. Habad, who consider themselves a world apart with claims to superiority over the rest (they used to dub their rabbi President of the Generation), constitute a fourth such confederal structure, with the 'Eda Haredit, who reject da'at Torah as a heretical innovation, being a fifth.[127] Within each council there may be one gadol whose da'at Torah holds sway over the rest (for example, Rabbi E. M. Schach).

Within both the khug and the "confederation" the rabbi's authority is not just a matter of erudition. What makes his immersion in the Talmud so effective and awesome is the insights he has been endowed with by Providence (helping him evaluate current situations, future events, human nature), insights made all the more credible by his noble personality traits. Hagiography, whether written or oral, referring to dead or living rabbis is the staple of haredi life, especially in social gatherings and off-the-cuff conversations.

Observers rightly point out that the yeshiva world has undergone a process of admorization (*Admor* is the honorific title of the Hasidic rabbi). And when one looks at the Muslim jama'at one notes likewise how closely the members' dependency upon their authority figure, the emir, resembles that of the *muridun* (groupies of a Sufi fraternity) and the *murshid* (mystical leader). Hagiography, again, is a major feature, as are rituals like the kissing of the emir's hand, touching the train of his mantle. All the more so as various jama'at have their origins in a Sufi milieu (e.g., the Naqshbandis in Turkey, Syria, and Egypt). Many are the jama'at that are indeed called after their emirs (Samawiyya, Shawqiyya, etc.), in the manner of the Sufi fraternity.

To come back to the yeshiva heads: as men who control the core ascetic groups who serve as models for the whole khug, they have transferred into their own hands decision-making powers (on matters political, economic, etc.) that since the Middle Ages had been in the hands of the prominent laity (ba'ale batim).[128] The charismatic dimension of their power is best encapsulated in the doctrine of *emunat hakhamim*—belief in the sages without daring to question their rulings, or as it is sometimes dubbed, the Fifth Shulkhan 'Arukh (the Shulkhan, the major halakhic code, has four parts).[129]

This doctrine was crystallized in these far-reaching terms in response to the Holocaust, which raised tough questions as to the perspicacity of the *gedolim* in prewar Eastern Europe who had resisted migration (especially to Palestine), and many of whom had escaped during the war (thanks to affidavits sent by American disciples), leaving their local communities behind.[130] And no wonder. For charismatic leadership finds it more arduous than any other type to weather the crisis, as a result of which it appears as a manifest failure. Its very grace—the divine insight—is called in question. To bolster such a shaken authority, a sort of "escape route forward" was taken: da'at Torah was elevated to the stature of a fifth pillar of the faith, so to speak.

In actual fact, however, decision making is heavily influenced by khug or 'asqanim (party organizers) who may not have any formal position but who carry weight either as wealthy laity or as shrewd manipulators and mediators with the outside.[131] Because the gadol depends on the organizer for his information as well as upon his uncanny assessment of the "world," the latter's input may be crucial. The gadol is shielded, in part, by the fact that his governing—much like in the Shi'ite case—is not hands-on governing. He tries to intervene selectively and rarely.

Laity carries some weight even in the Lefebvre movement, where priests reign supreme. The archbishop's decision, in May 1988, to renege on the just-signed compromise agreement with the papal delegates—a decision that meant full-blown schism—was due to backlash from the lay associations that could not understand how one could retreat from some ardently defended positions, even in the face of a more conservative pope than the one they had rebelled against. The Communione e Liberazione, on the other hand, had risen in revolt against the collaboration of the Italian Catholic establishment, through the Christian Democrat Party, with the secularized state; therefore, laymen have always been paramount at all levels—laymen who enjoy, much like Giussani, considerable charisma.

In having developed by the mid-nineteenth century a hierarchy, the Shi'ites have the advantage over the haredim and the Sunnis. It was not, however, a Catholic-type hierarchy, for it was constituted of ulama (mullahs) graded by scholarly achievement, not by access to Grace. At the pinnacle of the hierarchy were located the "models of emulation" (Maraji' al-taqlid). The maraji' possessed the authority to operate the ijtihad and overrule the lower levels. In principle, but not always in practice, they should be headed by a "supreme model" (*marja' a'la*); since 1962 this post has been unoccupied.

The authority wielded by this hierarchy—including the higher ranks (from mujtahid to marja')—extended solely to legal affairs. In matters political, they could at most advise and admonish the ruler, which in fact they did quite often as they were less dependent economically than their Sunni counterparts upon the government: they enjoyed a steady income from tithes donated by the believers (as a sort of material acknowledgment of their holiness) and from lands held in mortmain.

Khomeini's revolutionary contribution to Shi'ite thought consisted of the doctrine of wilayat al-faqih. He claimed that in the absence of the Twelfth Imam governing powers lie in the hands of the mullahs who are the inheritors from this descendent of 'Ali of his political and legal—but not spiritual—authority. In a situation where it is possible to reach some understanding with the ruler, the task of the mullahs is to castigate his aberrations so as to return him to the right path. Yet when the aberrations reach such proportions that accommodation is no longer possible—as was the case, said Khomeini, under the Pahlavi dynasty—the mullahs must take the reins of government into their own hands. This duty falls in particular upon mujtahidun (authorities in matters of jurisprudence) and the maraji'. One of the latter, the virtuous jurist (*fa-qih*) would serve as apex: in him would be vested not merely religious authority but also political rule (wilaya 'amma, a concept that originally referred to the authority of the Hidden Imam). The ulama were thus supposed to constitute the nucleus of the revolutionary vanguard to be led by the mujtahidun (ayatollahs), with the virtuous faqih at their head. The faqih mantle devolved upon Khomeini's shoulders almost as a matter of course, although he was just one of six maraji': first, because he conceived the whole doctrine, and, second, because his disciples (mostly mullahs who had been his students in Qom, or later in Najaf, his place of exile) formed a sort of circle or nebula that was to constitute the revolutionary cadre (later, the Islamic Republican Party).[132]

In 1979 Khomeini was elected faqih by the Council of Experts, set up by the new Iranian constitution, and placed above the president of the republic. In actual fact, much like the haredi sages', his was not a hands-on government. He would intervene in matters deemed crucial (certain appointments and demotions, the decree against Rushdie) or in order to break the stalemate within the ayatollah-dominated political elite (on nationalization of land, right to strike, cease-fire with Iraq, etc.). Nevertheless, toward the end of his life (January 1988) he extended the scope of the doctrine, claiming for the faqih the absolute governance of the Prophet (*wilayat al-faqih al-mutlaqa*), that is, the right to overrule or suspend the Shari'a itself on matters judged vital to the survival of the Islamic Republic, that "liberated portion of dar-al-Islam," survival that will determine the fate of this religion.[133]

The wilayat al-faqih doctrine is accepted, though not necessarily in its latest version, by most Shi'ite militants in Arab lands as well. The blueprint for a Lebanese Islamic republic drawn up by Hizbullah sees it, for instance, headed by a council of ulama.[134]

Yet there is no mistaking it: Khomeini's death dealt a heavy blow to the charismatic facet of the faqih institution, due to the paler personality of his successor, Ali Khamenei, who can likewise be faulted for his scholarly record (he has not presented the *risala* [book-length thesis] required for the award of great ayatollah, the rank just under marja'). Significantly enough, Khamenei is dubbed commander (*qa'id*) of the revolution, as distinguished from Khomeini, who is still called leader (*za'im*) of the revolution. Khamenei's personal relationship to his predecessor is part of his legitimacy: he is defined a "brother (or successor) of Ruh Allah [Khomeini]."[135] The latter's rulings (and political testament) are to this day amply discussed in sections headlined the "Method [or Line] of the Imam." Indeed the popular title vicar of the [Hidden] Imam (na'ib al-imam) was not transferred to Khamenei, and troops on parade swear allegiance both to the present faqih and to the tomb of his predecessor.

This is reminiscent of the Habad rebbe manifestly sharing his authority with the former one by referring to his rulings and to messages relayed to his tomb.[136] In Gush Emunim in the absence of any mechanism of succession, the charismatic authority of Rabbi Kook the Younger dissipated after his death. A collective and rather split leadership took his place. Since the crisis of the underground in 1983/84, the leadership is virtually eclipsed by various settlement bodies and their elected officials.

Without the benefit of a doctrinal innovation U.S. fundamentalists responded to the authority challenge by raising the status of the pastor at the expense of lay leaders. His is, however, a hands-on government (including finances), assisted by lay appointees. The ingredients of authority are much the same as those referred to above: a shepherd elected by the Lord to lead the flock, virtuous personality traits, biblical scholarship.[137] All three come together in his touted ability to make the right ruling out of a page of Scriptures opened at random. The pastor's unquestioned authority—if and when called in question this would lead (as among the haredim) to strife and splits—is rendered manifest by symbols: the "sacred desk" (pulpit), the nonparticipatory nature of the sermon itself. Charismatic authority among the Sunnis is cut from a different cloth. Their ulama have never enjoyed any spiritual status except that which their erudition confers upon them; they have had throughout history nothing to match the affiliation of Shi'ite ulama to the Hidden (Twelfth) Imam. The very hadith, "The ulama are the heirs of the prophets," interpreted by the Shi'ites to represent this affiliation, meant in Sunni gloss just the ulama duty to provide moral guidance for the community. Furthermore, the ulama have never enjoyed the status accorded their Shi'ite counterparts and have thus been more reluctant to be audacious toward the powers that be. The Sunni sages have actually been instilled with a feeling of subservience with regard to the state, an attitude shaped by the traumatic events of the civil war of early Islam (644–750). The conclusion drawn by the ulama was that it was incumbent to avoid anarchy at almost any cost. As far as they were concerned even a bad Muslim ruler (and the latter had always been Sunni, like the ulama) was preferable to chaos.[138]

It is no wonder that Sunni radicalism did not spring from the midst of the ulama and that radicals tend to loathe the whole ulama stratum for legitimating the powers that be even when they trample over religious injunctions; this accusation was of particular salience as the interventionist character of the modern Muslim state was seen as reducing the scope of civil society where Islam had held sway.

Sunni radical leaders tend, in consequence, to be recruited from the ranks of the laity, and, even among activists, shaykhs are a rarity.[139] Some of these laypeople were intellectuals of high caliber (for example, the Egyptian Sayyid Qutb, the Indian Maududi) suffused with modern and traditional culture. It was they who transformed Sunni political theory from an accommodationist to a revolutionary orientation, ready to confront the "apostate" regimes and, if need be, topple them and seize power. Other lay intellectuals, such as the Moroccan Abd al-Salam Yasin, contributed a reasoned critique of modern ideologies—in the manner of Jewish "returnees to the faith" like Nathan Birnbaum and Moshe Scheinfeld—and helped fight for the hearts and minds of youth lured by Marxism and existentialism.

Inevitably this makes for a much more decentralized organizational framework, for there is no hierarchy of mullahs available, devoted to a particular grand ayatollah or marja'. What one gets is a nebula of jama'at. The *amir al-jama'a* (lay leader) in Arab lands, Turkey, and Pakistan tends to be an autodidact in matters religious, with no great intellectual acumen. Trained more often than not as engineer, doctor, or agronomist,[140] he may still have a definite advantage over his quite ignorant disciples—usually students in scientific disciplines—who depend on him for those scraps of religious knowledge they have acquired. (In the loose and fluid Tabligh movements even this type of intellectual dimension of leadership is irrelevant, for, much like the Pentecostalists, they favor "heart knowledge" over "head knowledge.")

The upshot is leadership that relies heavily on power of personality and rhetorical skills, thus explaining why Sunni groups are characterized by a Sufi-style murshid/murid relationship. Splits result here more often from a personal challenge to the leadership than from an ideological controversy.

In a way splits are the staple of life within an enclave. Addicted as it is to homogeneity and to equality in purity, a "loyal opposition" has no place there. Any opposition is bound to be accused of treachery and become the object of witch-hunts and ostracism, liable ultimately to be "excised" (the latter term, borrowed from the King James Bible, is in Protestant usage but has analogues among Sunnis, Shi'ites, and haredim). The sequels of splits, whether recent or long-standing, are the vituperation between "confederations" (disciples of Schach against Lubavitchers, Takfir against other jama'at). These consume a lot of energy, generate much heat, and are sometimes more poisonous than invectives directed at secularists. Yet splits are ultimately functional, for they help preserve equality and assure that decision making can take place.

Even without internal squabbles over authority, life inside the enclave is not all sweetness and light, as its denizens would like the outside to believe. Grumbling, bickering, and envious calumny are the price one pays for the ideal of equality in virtue, as they serve too as means for enforcing conformity and for nipping in the bud any formal distinctions.[141] It is not in vain that the Hafetz Haim, fully aware of the claustrophobic, hothouse atmosphere of the enclave and influenced by the late-nineteenth-century Mussar (ethics) movement, dedicated a major essay to slanderous gossip (*leshon ha-ra'*), tagged as an insidious vice of the kehillah. That this essay has been, and still is, a best-seller and provides the topic for many a sermon and adult education class indicates its relevancy.[142] One encounters the same concern in talking to members of jama'at, perusing their press, and listening to tapes of preachers such as Kishk, al-Mahalawi, al-Qattan.

An air of conflict and ambiguity envelops relations of authority within the enclaves. But this is compensated to some extent by the empowerment of its members. Members possess a secret road map with regard to past and future, they know where they are located in space (operational and cosmological), and they hold firm answers on questions related to nature (human and physical). Their behavior is regulated, but in an equitable manner with other enclave members and not just for the benefit of other human beings (as happens, they claim, in other forms of organization). All this is, rather, for a higher entity. Within the face-to-face structures that form the hub of life, members are thus kept virtuous, on a par with other insiders, superior to all outsiders. They have no human master except for one (at most several) gurulike figure, whose unique, virtually out-of-this-world, qualities legitimate his position.

One may hazard a guess that this may account for the particular appeal such movements have for people who find themselves in a social context that is, structurally, the very opposite of an enclave—subordination. Individuals living in such a context are severely constrained, in an inegalitarian manner, as to how they behave, usually in terms of the category (or rank) they are assigned to; yet they do not enjoy the protection and privileges of group membership. They are manipulated, are peripheral to all decisions that may determine their destiny, and have a limited scope for forming alliances. Consequently they are isolated, passive, and conformist. Such people are perhaps not blatantly oppressed or deprived, but certainly alienated.[143] Examples abound. American suburbanite commuters feel stuck at midlevel in large corporate organizations. Recent migrants, from small town to urban sprawl in the American south, from villages to the shantytowns of Tehran or Cairo, from the Italian south to Milan or Turin, feel the strain of displacement, as do Holocaust survivors and Moroccan immigrants in Israel, whose old reference groups have been disrupted. Other examples include students in huge, anonymous, congested, and understaffed universities in Italy, Algeria, Iran, and Egypt, who on top of their atomized predicament suffer anxiety as to the likely future awaiting them—as members of the lumpenproletariat of diploma holders. What they also have in common is that they figure prominently among recruits to the enclaves discussed in this essay.

The reason may be that a major strategy for extricating oneself from the manipulated/alienated context is to move into one diametrically opposed: you shed your worst constraint—isolation and subordination to a large and impersonal structure—and you gain what you lacked most, group identity and insertion in a sociability network. Isolates—that is, high grid/low group individuals—have restricted choices. It follows that they have nothing to lose by joining the enclave.

When U.S. fundamentalists fulminate against the bankruptcy of the federally controlled welfare state; or when members of the Communione e Liberazione decry the inept government bureaucracy, captive to political clientelism and big business vested interests; when Islamic jama'at decry the alliance of the all-intrusive state and the economic-opening profiteers linked to multinationals—their message falls on ready ears.[144] Ears are particularly attentive among the multitude of people trapped within the lower ranks of huge, impersonal modern institutions (or dependent upon the benefits thereof). The ideal of comunione, fellowship, khavrusa, or jama'a may mean here not just human warmth, face-to-face interaction, and equality in virtue; it may signify the lessening of outside constraints and a measure of self-determination. Human solidarity becomes, as in the Communione e Liberazione vision, both the social ideal one hopes to implement one day for society at large, and a mode of life actually achieved within the group (or countersociety), a mode that satisfies intrinsic needs of the members.[145]

The antistate, anti–big structures message gains in credibility to the extent that there is a growing consciousness in the society at large that these institutions function badly. Yet the message, couched as it is in lingo and concepts building upon a certain monotheistic tradition, requires that its target population be somewhat familiar with this tradition. This sets no significant limits in Muslim countries where in-depth secularization (and the resulting profanization) is still rather circumscribed. In other traditions this would mean that, among people trapped in the atomized social context, a prime target would be U.S. evangelicals, Catholic traditionalists in France and

Germany, the Israeli national religious milieu, recent transplants from the Italian south, and so on. Would it be justified to speak of "black-diaper babies"?

The above is suggested as a sort of speculative coda and would require empirical research. Still, as long as large, impersonal modern institutions endure (with their attendant dysfunctions), that residual category—the isolated and the manipulated—is likely to grow.

May this indeed create a huge pool of potential recruits for enclaves of all kinds, including fundamentalist ones?

In Flux

A culture is in process of constant negotiation, *within* its membership and *between* its members and the outside. The enclave should not be viewed as static but rather as a shifting pattern that tends, if successful, toward low constraints of grid (category, rank, function) and high constraints of group imposed upon members' behavior and perceptions. As it is shifting and almost never static, both grid and group are in danger of moving each in the opposite direction (high and low, respectively).

The group dimension risks being lowered due to the difficulty of maintaining the boundary in the gray area discussed above. Separating oneself from a blatant secularist, be he atheist or agnostic, is relatively easy. Much more arduous is to distinguish oneself from the lukewarm traditionalist. All the more so as many enclave members have relatives, neighbors, and friends among the latter. Behavioral requirements may be useful. Avoiding eating and praying with nonrigorist family members, or visiting them, or playing with their children, is a protective measure.

A hostile hegemonic society further facilitates separation, yet when that society turns more accommodating, when religion becomes "in" (as happened in Israel from the late sixties), the boundary is harder to maintain. An outside that goes out of its way to establish a dialogue, to be considerate, suffocates the dissenter with kindness. Dependence upon federal and state subsidies made fundamentalist schools in the United States more amenable to pressure and more mindful (and understanding) of the concerns of the authorities. The total refusal of any subsidy, as practiced by Bob Jones University, may be the only way out, but one not easily taken. Enduring persecution is a better guarantee of purity (though not of size). Such persecution barely exists in the West, but in the Third World it may be lethal, leading to the physical elimination of the enclave (as happened to the Syrian Muslim Brotherhood in 1982, and to the Iraqi Shi'ite militants in 1980 and again in 1991). A situation of simmering ethnoreligious conflict, however, is a boon for the enclave (as in Israel/Palestine, India, Afghanistan). The Other, at least, is an infidel, hence clearly demarcated; all the more so if he is uniform. He can generate a powerful and lasting hostility.

The nature of the modern, open-market society further complicates matters. Unlike premodern groups, such as the Amish, the fundamentalist enclaves are located in urban surroundings or in suburban sprawls and are thus rarely self-sufficient. They establish certain economic niches which facilitate group cohesion, (e.g., the New York diamond trade, electronics retail), but more often than not many members (usually male) work in various sectors and locations. Not only may they be easily "tempted," given human nature as posited by the enclave, but behavioral requirements are harder to keep to and are less subject to social control. Outside norms (in consumption, entertainment) creep in casually. Vestmental distinguishing marks may help, but just up to a point. Even residential separation can be difficult to keep. The guards on the "wall of virtue" are lowered, as is the group dimension.

The grid dimension is likewise the hostage of the material success of the enclave. Economic achievements imperil the austerity and genteel poverty upon which the enclave prides itself. Furthermore, material success creates grids or ranks by wealth and positions in the society at large, which might eclipse the internal equality the group aspires to. Wealthy laypeople may get some sway over the pastor. As contacts with a more benevolent outside develop, members of the enclave more conversant with outside discourse acquire a special rank as mediators (Egyptian Islamic bankers or members of parliament, for instance). Envy, the deadly sin most typical of an enclave, has thus a fertile ground to thrive on, fed by flesh-and-blood discrepancies with the egalitarian ideal—discrepancies that have nothing to do with "legitimate" ranking created by ultrapiety or meritocratic achievement in studying the Scriptures or in fighting the evil outside. Gossip, envy's poisonous weapon, has a field day. Splits and squabbles (inter- and intragroup) become more frequent and more venomous than ever, as materialistic factors interlock with (or masquerade behind) ideological arguments. Beyond a certain threshold, intragroup splits become dysfunctional.

When a prophecy comes true—with the enclave's success—the dangers of instability and decline lurk. When a prophecy fails—the Messiah does not arrive (for Habad in 1992)—a situation almost as potentially deleterious occurs. Or when victory, predicted on the basis of the divine road map, eludes the enclave, decline may threaten to set in. When the electoral triumph of the Front Islamique du Salut was canceled by the Algerian army in 1991/92, the enclave was smashed and splintered into mindlessly violent fragments.

Moreover, as the enclaves become richer or more powerful, they tend to rely less on moral suasion and more upon the manipulation of members' dependency through material rewards, such as scholarships for yeshiva students, which the group gets from rich benefactors or from the state. The group thus moves downgrid, that is, toward a loosening up of those constraints related to how people interact by virtue of their social category. It may slide even farther when membership grows, either due to mass recruitment or to success in retaining members, be it through conviction or dependency (as in the case of haredi students offered draft deferral as long as they are in school and who are not taught any modern subjects or given vocational training). A large membership requires a more differentiated governance body, such as a hierarchy.

Mindful of the need to arrest slippage, enclaves strive to keep hierarchies as small as possible. They even develop new organizational strategies like the nebula or confederation—that is, a decentralized network of enclaves coordinated by a bureaucracy.

The latter may sometimes be headed by a charismatic figure, capable of cutting through layers of the bureaucracy and serving as a focal point for the rank and file. This is the case with certain Islamic jama'at, in haredi circles, and in Falwell's and Robertson's networks (but not in the Southern Baptist Convention). Islamic militants like to describe this structure as resembling "a bunch of grapes."

The nebula is based on a fragile compromise, however, for it introduces the hierarchic mode. Try as they may to trim the bureaucracy down to size, the fundamentalists always run the risk of seeing this body take over the autonomous cells, and thus they also risk dealing a heavy blow to members' motivation. The peril grows in proportion to the expansion of the hierarchy's control over material resources and social rewards. In an insurgency movement such as Hamas, of course, grids and compartmentalization are necessarily tighter.

Depending upon a charismatic authority is a tricky proposition. A leader may die with no successor cut from the same cloth. Kahane's death indeed dealt a heavy blow to Kach; the Lubavitcher rebbe's demise haunts his disciples, as he was childless. A leader may be replaced by a pallid bureaucrat or by one eclipsed by a powerful bureaucracy. Opposition to the successor may bring about splits, which inevitably involve loss of membership and/or waste of time and energy in fights with other "illegitimate" enclaves and their leaders. This is often the case in Islamic jama'at.

The charismatic figure may likewise be eclipsed by the rise of entrepreneurial, competitive market-type success within the enclave (e.g., rich entrepreneurs gaining power over Agudah-haredi rabbis). Such success might confer upon rising individualists (who are, by definition, low group) a measure of authority. Obviously, this may rarely happen when an enclave is subject to persecution—a situation that encourages austerity, decentralization, and compartmentalization. Adversity has its advantages.

An enclave subject to either or both of these developments—downgroup and upgrid—is likely to lose its religious specificity, become less of an enclave, decline, and even die out. It may introduce outside norms and perceptions accommodating the hegemonic society, as in the case of some haredim becoming a-Zionist rather than anti-Zionist; or Muslim Brothers diluting their opposition to the Jordanian "secularist-minded" state as they are sucked into its political process; or as in the case of corruption and conspicuous consumption spreading through Islamic or haredi banks and enterprises. The enclave may also lose members: they may drift into an outside society as separation landmarks get blurred; or they may defect, as former isolates are disappointed by not finding in the enclave that absence of grid controls, and/or solidarity, they desired.

The fiery Algerian preacher, 'Ali Belhadj—now under house arrest but still enjoying enormous popularity through audiocassettes of his sermons—never tired of repeating this theme: maintaining the cohesion and purity of the jama'a (enclave) is an arduous and everyday task. To phrase this in his Islamic lingo, one would say that before setting upon the small jihad against society at large, one must engage in a great jihad to cleanse one's own heart and group. Jihad, comments Belhadj, means effort, or struggle, and a constant one at that. It is a full-time job.[146]

Notes

1. Nathan Birnbaum, *Gottesvolk* (Vienna, 1919); Hebrew trans., *'Am ha-Shem* (B'nai B'rak, 1977), pp. 62–63, 117–22; idem, *Ktavim Nivharim* (Tel Aviv, 1943), pp. 17–25. Cf. Hazon Ish (Rabbi Abraham Karlitz), *Igrot* (B'nai B'rak, 1955), 1:102–3.

2. Hafetz Haim, *Yalqut Meshalim* (Tel Aviv, 1952), p. 31; Moshe Yoshor, *Ha-Hafetz Hayyim* (Tel Aviv, 1959), 2:525, and cf. 1:202, 260, 438; Elhanan Wasserman, quoted in *Be-'Ein Hazon* (Haifa, 1976), p. 93, and see pp. 12–13, 94. Cf. memoirs of Shlomo Lorincz in *Diglenu,* November 1990.

3. Arieh Surasky, *Marbitzei Torah u-Musar* (B'nai B'rak, 1973), 3:68, and see p. 158. Cf. Moshe Scheinfeld, "In Exile among Brothers," *Diglenu,* October 1951, and his articles in *Diglenu,* October 1948 and April 1966.

4. E.g., *Yated Ne'eman,* 8 October 1990. Cf. Ya'acob Kanievsky, *Qarayna de-igreta* (Jerusalem, 1990), 3:40, 191; Moshe Scherer, *Bi-Shtei 'Einayim* (New York, 1988), p. 275.

5. *Tafsir al-Manar* (Cairo, 1906–34), to Qur'an V, 44–48.

6. Maulana Maududi, *Islam and Jahiliyya* (Lahore, 1939); Sayyid Qutb, *Ma'alim fi-l-Tariq* (Cairo, 1964); Muhammad Mahdi Shams al-Din, *Bayna-l-Jahiliyya wa-l-Islam* (Beirut, 1975).

7. 'Ali Belhadj, *Ghurbat al-Islam al-Haditha,* audiocassette no. 11; Ra'id Salah, mayor of Umm al-Fahm, Israel, *Fada'il al-Quds,* audiocassette; 'Ali Khamenei, Friday sermon in Keyhan (Tehran), 3 November 1982; Shaykh Yazdi, sermon in *Ettela'at,* 10 January 1981.

8. Luigi Giussani, *Le mouvement communion et libération* (Paris, 1988), pp. 15 ff., 82; Luigi Amicone, *In nome del niente* (Milan, 1982), p. 21. Sadr articles, in *Al-Adwa'* (Iraq, 1958–59). Cf. also Abd al-Salam Yasin, *La révolution à l'heure de l'Islam* (Paris, 1981); Wa'il 'Uthman, *Hizb Allah fi Muwajahat Hizb al-Shaytan* (Cairo, 1976).

9. E.g., Muhammad Husayn Fadlallah, *Al-Islam wa-Mantiq al-Quwwa* (Beirut, 1976); and *Qadiyat al-'Izz wa-l-Dhull fi-l-Islam* (Beirut, 1979).

10. Selection of speeches and articles from this period in Marcel Lefebvre, *Un évêque parle* (Jarze, 1974), vol. 1; and *La Fraternité St. Pie X: Une oeuvre d'église* (Martigny, 1982).

11. Frances Fitzgerald, "A Disciplined, Charging Army," *New Yorker,* 18 May 1972, esp. p. 64; Tim LaHaye, *The Battle for the Mind* (Old Tappan, N.J., 1980); Steve Bruce, *The Rise and Fall of the New Christian Right* (Oxford, 1988), p. 77; Hal Lindsey, *The Late Great Planet Earth* (New York, 1973), pp. 38, 91, 171; Gary North, *Unconditional Surrender* (Tyler, Tex., 1988), pp. 182, 213, 228–29.

12. Fitzgerald, "Disciplined, Charging Army," pp. 70, 73, 108, 110; H. Rodeheaver and B. P. Ackley, eds., *Great Revival Hymns* (New York, 1911), hymn by E. T. Cassel; Mary Beth McGuire, *Pentecostal Catholics* (Philadelphia, 1982), pp. 190, 56–58, 89, 91; North, *Unconditional Surrender,* pp. 103, 112, 122. For Catholic theologians: Henri de Lubac, *Le mystère du surnaturel* (Paris, 1965); Hans Urs von Balthasar, *Cordula ou l'épreuve décisive* (Paris, 1968); Luigi Giussani, *Il senso religioso* (Milan, 1968).

13. Shmuel Cohen, ed., *Pe'er ha-Dor* (B'nai B'rak, 1973), 2:291; interview with a yeshiva student in *'Emda* (June 1987); *Ha-Modi'a,* 17 January 1990.

14. Yisrael Eichler in *Ha-Mahane ha-Haredi,* 10 January 1990.

15. George M. Marsden, *Reforming Fundamentalism* (Grand Rapids, Mich., 1987), p. 193; L. L. King, "Bob Jones University," *Harper's Magazine,* June 1966, pp. 52–53, 56, 58; Hazon Ish, *Igrot,* 1:111, 125; Eliezer Menachem Schach, *Mikhtavim u-Ma'marim* (B'nai B'rak, 1986), 2:4, 12,

41–42, 84; Elhanan Wasserman, *'Iqveta di-Meshiha,* 2d ed. (B'nai B'rak, 1969), pp. 40, 145, 150; Yoel Teitelbaum, *Divrei Yoel* (New York, 1980), p. 91; M. al-Hakim, *Thawrat al-Husayn* (Tehran, 1982); Raghib Harb, *Al-Minbar al-Muqawim* (Beirut, 1986).

16. Birnbaum, *'Am ha-Shem,* p. 127; Jalal Al-e Ahmad, *Gharbzadagi* (Tehran, 1962); Moshe Feinstein, *Bastion of the Faith* (New York, 1973), p. 250; George M. Marsden, *Fundamentalism and American Culture* (New York, 1980), p. 219; LaHaye, *Battle for the Mind,* p. 64 ff.; Marcel Lefebvre, *Ils l'ont découronné* (Escurolles, 1987), p. 235.

17. *Be-'Ein Hazon,* pp. 93, 65. Cf. Natan Wolpin, ed., *Seasons of the Soul* (New York, 1983).

18. Kol Yisrael (Aguda, Jerusalem), 17 July 1930; Agudat Yisrael, *The Struggle and the Splendour* (New York, 1982), chap. 1; Moshe Scherer in *Jewish Week,* 28 July 1970; Hazon Ish, *Igrot,* 1:31, 43, 111; Moshe Scheinfeld in *Diglenu,* August 1974.

19. Marsden, *Reforming Fundamentalism,* p. 162; LaHaye, *Battle for the Mind.*

20. Nancy T. Ammerman, *Bible Believers* (New Brunswick, N.J., 1987), p. 62. On *idtirab* (confusion), see Bassam Jarrar (Hamas), Al-Sakina, audiocassette; Shaykh Kishk, *Sermons,* audiocassettes nos. 206, 419; 'Ali Sorush, *Danesh va Arzesh* (Tehran, 1979).

21. Birnbaum, *'Am ha-Shem,* p. 131. Cf. Scheinfeld in *Diglenu,* October 1958.

22. Mary Douglas, *Cultural Bias* (London, 1978); idem, ed., *Essays in the Sociology of Perception* (London, 1982); Mary Douglas and Aron Wildavsky, *Risk and Culture* (Berkeley, 1982); Mary Douglas, *How Institutions Think* (Syracuse, N.Y., 1986); Michael Schwarz and Michael Thompson, *Divided We Stand* (London, 1990); Michael Thompson, Aron Wildavsky, and Richard Ellis, *Cultural Theory* (Boulder, Colo., 1990); Mary Douglas, *In the Wilderness* (Sheffield, United Kingdom, 1993).

23. In the jargon of cultural theory, the enclave is low grid/high group.

24. E.g., Marsden, *Reforming Funda-mentalism,* p. 241; Lindsey, *Late Great Planet Earth,* pp. 163, 174; North, *Unconditional Surrender,* pp. 287, 329.

25. E.g, Reuven Grusovsky, *Ba'yot ha-Zeman* (B'nai B'rak, 1960), pp. 10, 17, 20–21, 41; Kanievsky, *Qarayna de-Igreta;* Scherer, *Bi-Shei 'Einayim,* pp. 109, 246; Schach, *Mikhtavin u-Ma'marim; Milhamta shel Torah* (B'nai B'rak, 1977); *Kovetz mikhtavim . . . me't Rabotenu* (B'nai B'rak, 1975).

26. Or *yere'im* (those afraid of God). Other significant synonyms: *shomrei Torah, sridei helqa tovah.*

27. Synonyms (mostly Qur'anic): *mutakhadhilun, mutdahadun, mahrumun, mazlumun.* These terms were given a Fanon-inspired, Third World twist by 'Ali Shari'ati (d. 1977). See the concept *mardon e-khofteh* (oppressed people), as in a sermon reproduced in *Ettela'at* (Tehran), 10 January 1981; 'Ali Belhadj, audiocassettes nos. 10, 2, 7. For examples of usage by Sunnis, see Yasin, *La révolution à l'heure de l'Islam.* Cf. Said Amir Arjomand, *The Turban for the Crown* (New York: Oxford University Press, 1988), p. 136.

28. In Islamic Republican Party organ *Jomhuri-e Eslami.*

29. Ammerman, *Bible Believers.* For the less common terms see King, "Bob Jones University," p. 54; North, *Unconditional Surrender,* pp. 315, 336.

30. Hazon Ish, *Igrot,* 1:109, 111, 2:80.

31. In the Islamic case: *murtaddun* (apostates), *zandaqa, mushrikun* (polytheists), *taghut* (false god), *fir'awn* (pharaoh), *yazid* (Shi'ite term for oppressor); the Sunni equivalent, *nimrud.* In the Jewish case: *Qara'im* (Qara'ites), *Shabta'im* (Shabbateans), *Kna'anim* (Canaanites), *sone'i Yisrael* (enemies of the Jews), *rodfim* (persecutors).

32. For the same reason, tradition-specific vituperative terms, such as the Christian "religion of the beast," and "allies of Antichrist," are best consigned to a footnote. This is usually a Christian metaphor (King, "Bob Jones University," p. 56). Muslims prefer *mu'amara* or *ta'amuriyya,* and the Jews, *horshei mezimot.*

33. Lefebvre, *Ils l'ont découronné*, p. 217; cf. Muhammad 'Ata, *Sifat al-Nifaq* (Beirut, 1985).

34. I do not deal here with the few cases where the enemy is an infidel affiliated with another, long-established tradition (e.g., in Gaza and the West Bank, in Afghanistan). On the conspiratorial vision in Iran, see Ervand Abrahamian, *Khomeinism* (Berkeley: University of California Press, 1993), chap. 5; cf. 'Ali Belhadj, audiocassettes nos. 40, 41.

35. Ahmad Fardid seems to be the thinker who coined *khod-bonyadi;* cf. Birnbaum, *'Am ha-Shem*, p. 242 ff.; LaHaye, *Battle for the Mind*, p. 117 ff.; Ammerman, *Bible Believers*, p. 135; *Ettela'at* (Tehran), 11 October 1980, 28 February 1981, 21 October 1981 (on hypocrites).

36. Toshihiko Isutsu, *Ethico-Religious Concepts in the Koran* (Montreal, 1966); North, *Unconditional Surrender*, pp. 131, 255, 287; Lindsey, *Late Great Planet Earth*, pp. 170–72; *Kovetz mikhtavim*, introduction; Wasserman, *'Iqveta di-Meshiha;* Birnbaum, *'Am ha-Shem;* Yoshor, *Hafetz Hayyim*, p. 11; 'Ali Belhadj, audiocassette no. 5; N. Yagen, *Ason ha-Me'a*, audiocassette.

37. A competing (but not dominant) infidel community, such as the Copts in Egypt, may also help set up the boundary; so do old-type heresies from within the tradition (e.g., the Ahmadiya in India and Pakistan, the Baha'is in Iran).

38. Only among Protestant reconstructionists does the term *white* also have a racial connotation, i.e., Caucasian.

39. Hazon Ish *Igrot*, 1:43, 113. *Neliza*, a geometric term, is borrowed from Maimonides and given a theological twist.

40. In the United States, outreach activity is called by the ultra-Orthodox "klal work."

41. Yoshor, *Hafetz Hayyim*, p. 591; King, "Bob Jones University," p. 52; Marsden, "Unity and Diversity," pp. 66–69.

42. Kanievsky, *Qarayna de-Igreta*, 1: 125–26; Cohen, *Pe'er ha-Dor*, 1:128, 2: 246 ff.; *Be-'Ein Hazon*, pp. 65, 93–94; Hazon Ish, *Igrot*, 1:36, 102, 108.

43. Cohen, *Pe'er ha-Dor*, 4:245–47; Grusovsky, *Ba'yot ha-Zeman*, pp. 26–36; Moshe Scheinfeld, *Beyn Medinat Yisrael ve-'Am Yisrael* (B'nai B'rak, 1975), esp. articles from 1951, 1952, 1964. The most militant haredim, the Toldot Aharon yeshiva, have this slogan: "May the State of Israel perish but so that no Jew is harmed."

44. The best expression is Rabbi E. M. Schach's televised sermon of 26 March 1990. But see already in Hazon Ish, *Yoreh De'ah* (Jerusalem, 1951), chaps. 2, 5, 16, 25; and Yequtiel Yehuda Halbestamm in *Diglenu* (March 1960). The greater the integration of the haredim into Israeli politics, the stronger this trend. See also the jocular cassettes of Rabbi Shabtai Yudelevitch (on tape) poking fun at secularist "bestiality."

45. Cf. Gideon Aran, "Jewish Zionist Fundamentalism: The Bloc of the Faithful in Israel (Gush Emunim)," in Martin E. Marty and R. Scott Appleby, eds., *Fundamentalisms Observed* (Chicago: University of Chicago Press, 1991), pp. 265–344; Ravitsky (vol. 3); Teitelbaum, *Divrei Yoel*.

46. Salman Rushdie, *In Good Faith* (London, 1990).

47. Sati' al-Husri, *Ara' wa-Ahadith fi-l Wataniyya wa-l-Qawmiyya* (Beirut, 1944); Sayyid Qutb in *Al-Risala*, 5 January 1953, p. 16; idem, *Ma'alim fi-l-Tariq*, pp. 30–31, 194–97; Muhammad al-Ghazali, *Haqiqat al-Qawmiyya* (Beirut, 1961); Salah Jawhar, *Al-Mawta Yatakalamun* (Cairo, 1977), pp. 33–38, 86–87, 129, 135. Cf. Yann Richard, "Du nationalisme à l'islamisme," in *Le fait ethnique en Iran et en Afghanistan* (Paris, 1988), p. 267 ff.

48. Scheinfeld, *Beyn Medinat Yisrael;* Grusovsky, *Ba'yot ha-Zeman*, pp. 7–11, 46–47.

49. Muhammad al-Sawwaf, *Al-Mukhattat al-Isti'mariyya* (Beirut, 1979); Fathi Yakan, *Mushkilat al-Da'wa wa-l-Da'iya* (Beirut, 1967); Anwar al-Jundi, *Sukut al-'Ilmaniyya* (Beirut, 1973); 'Ali Jarisha, *Shari'at Allah Hadima* (Cairo, 1973); Muhammad al-Bahi, *Mustaqbal al-Islam* (Cairo, 1978); Yusuf al-Qardawi, *Al-Hall al-Islami* (Cairo, 1974); Muhammad Mahdi Shams al-Din, *Al-Ilmaniyya* (Beirut, 1980); Muhammad Dandawi, *Kubra a-Haraqat al-Islami-*

yya (Tunis, 1978); Rashid Ghannushi, *Maqalat* (Paris, 1984).

50. Qutb, *Ma'alim fi-l-Tariq;* Sa'id Hawwa, *Durus fi-l-Amal-Islami* (Amman, 1981); idem, *Min Ajl Khutwa ila-l-Amam* (Beirut, 1979); 'Ali Uways, *Al-Muslimun fi-Ma'rakat al-Baqa* (Cairo, 1979). For the neo-Hanbali doctrine, see Ibn Taymiyya, *Fatawa* (Cairo, 1909), 4:198, 280–81.

51. Muhammad 'Imara, ed., *Al-Farida al-Gha'iba* (Cairo, 1982); Abdallah Abu-l-Khayr, *Dhikriyati ma'a Jama'at al-Muslimin* (Kuwait, 1980); Hassan Hassan, *Muwajahat al-Fikr al-Mutatrif* (Cairo, 1978); Bayan al-Thawra, *Al-Islamiyya fi Suriya* (Damascus, 1980). Note that radical Jewish fundamentalists do not envisage the use of violence against lapsed coreligionists, perhaps due to a Diasporic tradition where Jews did not control tools of violence. The lapsed are to be excommunicated.

52. Cf. Michael Cook, "Ibn Hanbal and al-Amr bi-l-Ma'ruf," paper presented to the fifth colloquium, "From Jahili'yya to Islam," Jerusalem, July 1990. In revolutionary Iran this precept would be given an institutional embodiment in Bonyad-e Monkarat, a sort of morality militia.

53. Cf. Mumtaz Ahmad, "Islamic Fundamentalism in South Asia: The Jamaat-i-Islami and the Tablighi Jamaat of South Asia," in Marty and Appleby, *Fundamentalisms Observed,* pp. 457–530.

54. This is based, in Judaism, upon the adage "mitoch she-lo li-shma bali-shma."

55. In the words of the Satmar rabbi (Yoel Teitelbaum) in *Der Yid* (New York), 5 Av 5681/1981.

56. The second scenario is envisaged only by Islamic radicals; their Jewish counterparts do not expect to have political power before the advent of the Messiah.

57. Editorials in *Yated Ne'eman, Ha Modi'a, Ha-Mahane ha-Haredi;* Schach, *Mikhtavim u-Ma'marim.*

58. Jerry Falwell, *Listen America!* (Garden City, N.Y., 1980), pp. 6, 18–19, 205; Pat Robertson, *America's Dates with Destiny* (Nashville, 1986), p. 191 ff.; Frances Fitzgerald, *The Battle for the Public Schools* (Old Tappan, N.J., 1980), p. 72 ff.; Lindsey, *Late Great Planet Earth,* pp. 150, 171, 173; Marsden, *Reforming Fundamentalism,* pp. 96–98, 125–27, 173.

59. Luigi Giussani, *Communion et Libération* (Paris, 1988). But perhaps not Communists; see Lefebvre, *Ils l'ont découronné,* p. 235.

60. Fitzgerald, "Disciplined, Charging Army," pp. 78, 107; Falwell, *Listen America!;* Ammerman, *Bible Believers,* p. 199 ff.

61. Cf. the title "soldiers of the House of David" for Lubavitcher militants.

62. This cluster of ideas, which hark back to the church fathers, was developed in a full-fledged manner in the early nineteenth century by E. Irving in Scotland, then by John Nelson Darby in Ireland.

63. Could this defeatism be the case, implicitly, with separatists of the Bob Jones hue? It is certainly not the case for the reconstructionists (see North, *Unconditional Surrender,* pp. 120, 370, 374).

64. A. C. Gaebelein, "The Present Day Apostasy," in *The Coming and the Kingdom of Christ* (Chicago, 1914), p. 154. Cf. Lindsey, *Late Great Planet Earth,* pp. 119, 171.

65. Orah hayyim is also the name of one of the four parts of the Shulkhan 'Arukh, the authoritative halakhic compendium (dating from the sixteenth century).

66. See Haym Soloveitchik, "The Role of Texts in the Haredi World," in Martin E. Marty and R. Scott Appleby, eds., *Accounting for Fundamentalisms* (Chicago: University of Chicago Press, 1993); and P. Connerton, *How Societies Remember* (Cambridge University Press, 1990).

67. For the haredim the major text is the Babylonian Talmud (A.D. 500) and its commentaries. For the Muslims it is the Qur'an (and to a lesser extent, the hadith, or oral tradition; shar'i treatises are more rarely used).

68. Or rock's local equivalent, such as the *rai* in Algeria, a hodge-podge of rock and Maghrebi folk chants; town councils taken over by the Front Islamique du Salut in the June 1990 elections in effect hastened to ban rai. An exception is Communione e Liberazione, which has ample recourse to gospel and jazz music (but not to rock).

69. From small town to big city or to sub-urban sprawl in the United States; the rural exodus in Islamic lands; Maghrebi and Turkish workers moving to Europe; Jewish Eastern Europe to the United States or to Israel. In the Jewish case one should also add the impact of the annihilation of six million Eastern and Central European Jews, most of whom were still observant to some extent. Another demographic phenomenon, not yet studied sufficiently, is the spiralling birthrate in Islamic countries, where about two-thirds of the population is under twenty-five and thus has no memory of what life may have been like before the onslaught of modernity.

70. Cf. Yusuf al-Qardawi, *Fatawa Mu'asira* (Qatar, 1984); 'Abdallah 'Ulwan, *Hukm al-Islam fi Wasa'il al-I'lam* (Hama, 1978); 'Ali Jarisha, *'Indama Yahkumu al-Islam* (Cairo, 1975); Ahmad 'Abduh, *Wad' al-Riba* (Cairo, 1977); Muhammad 'A. Khamis, *Al-Mar'a bi-l-Taswwur al-Islami* (Cairo, 1975).

71. Shlomo Min ha-Har, *Shi'urei ha-Torah* (Jerusalem, 1966); Hazon Ish, *Igrot,* 1:115, 2:47; Kanievsky, *Qarayna de-Igreta,* 1:129–31, 182, 2:10, 95; Shlomo Elberg, "Bnai Brakism," *Ha-Pardes* 38, no. 3 (December 1963); M. Scheinfeld, ed., *Yalqut Da'at Torah* (Tel Aviv, 1962); editorial in *Jewish Observer,* October 1990.

72. 'Abdallah Abu-l-Khayr, *Dhikriyati ma'a Jama'at al-Muslimin;* (Kuwait, 1982) Hassan, *Muwajahat al-Fikr al-Mutatarif.*

73. Hazon Ish, *Igrot,* 2:82–83. The letter was written in Lithuania, but he did not change his prescription when he moved to Palestine three years later.

74. See my "Islamic Resurgence: Civil Society Strikes Back," *Journal of Contemporary History* 25 (June 1990) 353–364; "The Islamic Republic of Egypt," *Orbis,* 31 April 1987, 43–54.

75. Ammerman, *Bible Believers;* King, "Bob Jones University"; Fitzgerald, "Disciplined, Charging Army."

76. 'Ali Jarisha, *Din wa-Dawla* (Cairo, 1979); Qardawi, *Fatawa Mu'asira; Al-Liwa al Islami* (Cairo), 17 June 1982; *Mayo* (Cairo), 24 December 1982; *Al-Siyasa* (Kuwait), 27 October 1979.

77. Muhammad Husayn Fadlallah, *Mafahim Islamiyya* (Beirut, 1982) 2:54–56, 74–75, 77.

78. E.g., Moshe Feinstein, *Igrot Moshe: Yoreh De'ah,* 2 vols. (New York, 1973).

79. Jerusalem served as the direction of prayer for eighteen months between A.D. 622 and 624 during Muhammad's pact with the Jews, but was then replaced by Mecca.

80. On this concept as well as "operational space," see Steve Rayner's article in Douglas, *Essays in the Sociology of Perception.*

81. Ammerman, *Bible Believers,* p. 34 ff.

82. A "good environment" may be further bolstered by proximity to a ritual bath (and—especially in Israel—application of rules of modesty of dress in public, no transport on Shabbat).

83. Ahmad Rouadjia, *Les Frères et la mosquée* (Paris, 1990).

84. Ammerman, *Bible Believers,* chap. 8.

85. And with some of the genetic risks involved.

86. Ammerman, *Bible Believers,* p. 135; North, *Unconditional Surrender,* p. 193.

87. Yoshor, *Hafetz Hayyim,* pp. 426–27; Cohen, *Pe'er ha-Dor,* 2:113 (Hazon Ish: "The yeshivas are the deserts and caves of our times"); Kanievsky, *Qarayna de-Igreta,* 1:37, 67, 2:12–13. Dietary law also creates a market relationship, consolidating that of residence, marriage, and social control (by gossip, street posters).

88. McGuire, *Pentecostal Catholics,* chap. 8.

89. For such a model in other social contexts, see Gerald Mars, "Hidden Hierarchies in Israeli Kibbutzim," in James Flanagan and Steve Rayner, eds., *Rules, Decisions, and Inequality in Egalitarian Societies* (Aldershot, United Kingdom, 1988), p. 98 ff.; and Rayner's own essay in the same volume.

90. Cohen, *Pe'er ha-Dor,* 4:240 n. 15; Hazon Ish, *Igrot,* 1:109–11; Baruch Hirsch in *Yated Ne'eman,* 15 July 1990; Moshe Gifter, *Pirkei Emuna* (Jerusalem, 1969). For the Muslim formula see sermons of Shaykh Kishk, audiocassettes nos. 206, 386, 418, 425; 'Ali Belhadj, audiocassettes nos. 2, 35, 43.

91. Marcel Lefebvre, *J'accuse le concile* (Martigues, 1976).

92. Lindsey and North are typical of this approach.

93. Tractate Sota. The term coined by the Hazon Ish for the decay was *neliza*.

94. Typical of this approach are Tim LaHaye, Luigi Giussani, Ahmad Fardid, Abd al-Salam Yasin, Shmuel Rafael Hirsch, and Ya'akov Rosenheim. The major organ of this persuasion in Catholicism is *L'ANTI-89*, published by pro-Lefebvrists.

95. Ammerman, *Bible Believers*, chap. 8; Jeffrey K. Hadden and Anson Shupe, *Televangelism: Power and Politics in God's Frontier* (New York, 1988), pp. 99–105; Razelle Frankl, *Televangelism* (Carbondale, Ill.: Southern Illinois University Press, 1987), pp. 99, 114.

96. Ya'akov Katz, *Halakha ve-Kabbalah* (Jerusalem, 1986), pp. 226–29.

97. North, *Unconditional Surrender*, pp. 307, 325, 354, 367, 385.

98. Cf. Wasserman, *'Iqveta di-Meshiha*.

99. See the sermon appended to *Be-'Ein Hazon*, pp. 97–104. Cf. Schach, *Mikhtavim u-Ma'amarim*, 1:41, 86.

100. See Hussein Ahmad Amin's article on radical scenarios for the future, *Al-Musawwar*, 26 September 1986.

101. Peter Von Sivers, "The Realm of Justice," *Humaniora Islamica* vol. 1 (1973).

102. Muhammad Amin al-Alim, *Dirasat fi-l-Islam* (Beirut, 1981). Some messianic rhetoric can be detected among Hamas in Gaza and in the Front Islamique du Salut in Algeria as evidenced by audiocassettes (Shaykh As'ad al-Tamimi, Bassam Jarrar, 'Ali Belhadj). The same was true of the Abu Kurus messianic Sufi order active in Numeiri's Sudan (1983).

103. Ethan Kohlberg, "From Imamiya to Ithna-Ashariyya," *Bulletin of the School of Oriental and African Studies* (1975): 521 ff.; Abdulaziz A. Sachedina, *Islamic Messianism* (Albany: State University of New York, 1981). An eschatological format is, for instance, absent from Shi'ite writings in Baghdad at the time of the fall of the Abbasid caliphate (A.D. 1258), where one would have

expected it to surface (Muhammad Kashif al-Ghita', *Asl al-Shi'a wa-Usuliha*, 10th ed. [Beirut, 1958], p. 128). A good summary of the Sunni position is Shaykh Kishk's audiocassette *Al-Mahdi al Muntazar*.

104. Lindsey, *Late Great Planet Earth*, pp. 52–57; cf. Cohen, *Pe'er ha-Dor*, 2:121–22.

105. Schach, *Mikhtavin u-Ma'marim*, 1:13–15, 33.

106. Interview with yeshiva student in *'Emda*, June 1987; polemic against such views in Scheinfeld, *Beyn Medinat Yisrael*, p. 22 ff. The Gulf War (1991) saw a surge of messianism not only among Sunnis but also among haredim; see Rabbi Moshe Hayyim Sofer, audiocassette on the lessons of this war.

107. Harding article in *Accounting for Fundamentalism*. Cf. S. Abruzzesse, *Communione e Liberazione* (Paris, 1990).

108. Note the similarities in contents between "In Dar al-Islam" and "In the Jewish World" sections in the Muslim and haredi press.

109. This space is not too imaginary. These churches constitute a loose network bound by doctrine, information exchange, and educational material dispatched from Falwell's headquarters. The network also influences the selection of pastors by providing an approved list of candidates.

110. Sheikh Salameh, in interview with the author (Cairo, June 1987).

111. *Al-Mukhtar al-Islami* (Cairo), September–October 1985, pp. 37–38; *Al-I'tisam* (Cairo), April–May 1986, pp. 10–12. So is Egypt for preachers (on tape) such as Kishk, Ahmad al-Mahalawi, Muhammad Hassan, Walid Ghunayim, and Hassan Ayyub.

112. Richard, "Du nationalisme à l'islamisme."

113. Hizballah, *Risala Maftuha*, 16 February 1986; *Al-Safir* (Beirut), 17 February 1986; *Al-Siyasa* (Kuwait), 26 March 1986. Cf. *Al-Anba'* (Kuwait), 4 March 1987; Muhammad Husayn Fadlallah's article in *Al-Muntalaq* (Beirut), October 1986.

114. Lindsey, *Late Great Planet Earth*,

chaps. 5–6; North, *Unconditional Surrender,* pp. 121, 370, 384.

115. Haggai Segal, *Ahim Yekarim* (Jerusalem, 1987); Gideon Aran, *Eretz Yisrael: Between Politics and Religion: Jerusalem,* Institute for Israel Studies, no. 18 (1985).

116. René Girard, *La violence et le sacré* (Paris, 1972).

117. See "The Sanctity of Jerusalem," in my *Interpretations of Islam* (Princeton, 1985).

118. Hamas Covenant (in Arabic), December 1988, articles 11, 31; *Al-Dustur* (Amman), 2 November 1988; 'Abdallah 'Azzam, *Al-Difa' 'an Aradi al-Muslimin ahamm Fara'id al-A'yan* (Jedda, 1987), pp. 29–49. At times there is even an apocalyptic undertone to the argument: As'ad al-Tamimi, *Zawal Isra'il Hatmiyya Qur'aniyya* (Cairo, 1982).

119. Yoshor, *Hafetz Hayyim,* p. 525. Cf. Hafetz Haim, *Yalqut Meshalim.* A similar argument in an audiocassette by the Palestinian 'Abdallah 'Azzam, *Al-Hubb fi Allah;* and in 'Ali Belhadj audiocassettes nos. 6, 12, 27, 46. This is a recurrent theme among haredi preachers (on tape) such as Shabtai Yudelevitch, David Sicherman, Yoel Schwarz, and Mordechai Neugerschal.

120. McGuire, *Pentecostal Catholics,* pp. 30, 87–89, 103, 111, 169 ff.; North, *Unconditional Surrender,* pp. 166, 239, 255, 382; Falwell, *Listen America!,* pp. 12–16. Shaykh Kishk thundered in October 1992 that the Cairo earthquake was an omen of God's wrath about Egypt's sins (audiocassette, *al-Zilzal*). Note the argument made by Rafsanjani after the Iranian earthquake (sermon, Radio Tehran, 29 June 1990).

121. *Toda'a-'Alon le-Shabbat Qodesh,* 2 November 1990; *Le Monde,* 3 November 1990. Cf. Eliyahu Dessler, *Mikhtav me-Eliyahu,* 2d ed. (Jerusalem, 1963), 1:183, 278; Frances Fitzgerald, "Jim and Tammy," *New Yorker,* 23 April 1990, pp. 45–47. This correlation is likewise a frequently invoked argument in audiocassettes of haredi preachers like Nissim Yagen, Emmanuel Tehila, Amnon Yitzhak, Reuven Elbaz, and Mordechai Ifargan. Gush Emunim rabbis argued in fall and winter 1993 that the recent rise in road accidents in Israel was the upshot of the "defeatist" Israel-PLO agreement.

122. A typical anti-innovation case is the polemics over the banning of Rabbi Steinsalz's books; see the opposing views of Rabbis Elias and Greenblatt (*Jewish Observer,* November 1990).

123. The type of interpretation involved is never automatically literal. See the shocked reaction of haredi Knesset members when a left-wing member, combatting their antipornography bill, read passages from the Song of Songs, literally presented as an erotic work (Knesset Proceedings, 26 November 1990).

124. Scherer, *Bi-Shtei 'Einayim,* pp. 246–49; Abraham Wolf, *Ha-Tequfa Ba'yoteha* (B'nai B'rak, 1965), pp. 90–101; Abraham Diskin in *Diglenu,* May–June 1990.

125. On Tanzim al-Jihad's mentor, 'Abd al-Salam Faraj, see above.

126. Two of the most prominent authorities, the Hazon Ish and the Rabbi of Brisk, never took part.

127. Yeshayhu Tuviya Director, *Da'at Torah* (New York, 1983), 2:30, 4:20–27, 58–65; Nissim Yagen, *Da'at Torah,* audiocassette.

128. Local notables and wealthy individuals, as distinct from the masses (*hamoyn*).

129. Dessler, *Mikhtav me-Eliyahu,* 1:75–77. Cf. Yoshor, *Hafetz Hayyim,* p. 685.

130. Menachem Friedman, "The Haredim and the Holocaust," *Jerusalem Quarterly* 53 (1990): 86–114. See Frances Fitzgerald's remarks in "Jim and Tammy" on how difficult it was for Bakker's groupies to acknowledge the Bakker's guilt.

131. See the memoirs of Shlomo Lorincz in *Diglenu,* October, November 1990.

132. Khomeini, *Al-Hukuma al-Islamiyya* (Najaf, 1971; Arabic ed., Beirut, 1979). See the special issue on his thought, *Al-Tawhid* (Beirut) 47 (July 1990): 21–34, 59–68, 98–107.

133. *Kayhan al-'Arabi,* 16 January 1988. Due to his successor's, Khamenei's, lower stature, this doctrine (which had never been implemented by Khomeini) has been held in abeyance till now. Cf. *Keyhan* (Tehran), 24

November 1990; *Resalat* (Tehran), 31 May 1990.

134. *Al-Safir* (Beirut), 17 April 1986; *Al-Siyasa* (Kuwait), 26 March 1986; Muhammad Baqir al-Sadr, *Lumha Tamhidiyya* (Beirut, 1979); Muhsin al-Hakim, *Bayan bi-Munasabat Khulul Muharram* (Tehran, 1982). Note that the Lebanese "council" was not supposed to be subject to Khomeini's authority and its mentor, Fadlallah, was rather linked with the marja' Kho'i in Najaf. After the latter's death, Fadlallah declared that this post can no more be filled by feeble nonagenarians, for it requires an activist political acumen.

135. *Kayhan al-'Arabi,* 29 July 1989, 23 September 1989. Cf. Abrahamian, *Khomeinism,* epilogue. The family-planning campaign launched in October 1991 is an example of an innovation launched after Khomeini's death.

136. Ravitzky in *Accounting for Fundamentalism.*

137. Ammerman, *Bible Believers,* chap. 7; idem, *Baptist Battles* (1990), pp. 171–79. Cf. Luigi Giussani's interview on the importance of charisma in *Trente jours dans l'église et dans le monde* (1987), p. 8.

138. See the writings of a Syrian radical, 'Abdallah 'Ulwan, *Warathat al- Anbiya'* (Beirut, 1983).

139. With a few notable exceptions: Shaykhs Abbasi Madani and 'Ali Belhadj in Algeria; Sa'id Sha'ban in Lebanon; 'Umar 'Abd al-Rahman in Egypt; Sa'id Hawwa in Syria.

140. Notable cases: Shukri Mustafa, 'Abd al-Salam Faraj in Egypt; Shaykh Ahmed Yassin in Gaza; Marwan Hadid in Syria.

141. Haredim refer to the Israelites grumbling or revolting against Moses (a classic case of charismatic leadership), especially Deuteronomy 1:27 and Numbers 16:3.

Sunnis and Shi'ites speak, inter alia, of munafiqun (see above).

142. Hafetz Haim, *Shmirat ha-Lashon* (Warsaw, 1914); *Hovat ha-Shmira* (Warsaw, 1921).

143. In the jargon of cultural theory, high grid/low group. The enclave is low grid/high group. The relationship between these two is dubbed "negative diagonal." The best descriptions of fundamentalist groups in terms of empowerment can be found in Ammerman, *Bible Believers,* chap. 11; Abbruzzesse, *Communione e Liberazione,* chaps. 3–4.

144. E.g., Falwell, *Listen America!* p. 12 ff; Giussani, *Il senso religioso* (Giussani is here, as on other issues, largely indebted to the thought of Cardinal Joseph Ratzinger); the jama'at argument can be read in almost any monthly issue of the Egyptian *Al-I'tisam* and *Al-Mukhtar al-Islami.* Even among Pentecostalists the right to individual interpretation is never pushed to an extreme (low group/low grid). Groups maintain a common manner of interpretation, preferring gemeinschaft over individualism.

145. Amicone, *In nome del niente,* pp. 74–75; Abruzzesse, *Communione e Liberazione,* p. 169 ff. This is not to underestimate the tangible services rendered by Communione e Liberazione to its supporters (employment in its cooperatives, student canteens, help for students in their studies, etc.). Yet the most crucial dependency link is in the realm of group solidarity. The same is true of Muslim student jama'at, and to a lesser extent (because the material dependency is bigger, especially for yeshiva students who are married with children) with regard to haredim.

146. 'Ali Belhadj, audiocassette no. 43; his four-part cassette series *Silsilat al-Jihad;* and the seven-part cassette series *Al-Amr bi-l-Ma'ruf wa-l-Nahy 'ani-l-Munkar.*

2

Fundamentalisms Compared
across Traditions and Cultures

The Vision from the Madrasa and Bes Medrash: Some Parallels between Islam and Judaism

Samuel C. Heilman

I begin these comparative considerations of resemblances between the transmission of traditional learning in Judaism and Islam with a shared misgiving about the applicability of the term *fundamentalist* to the Jewish and Islamic settings with which I am familiar and to which I refer in what follows. There are at least two reasons for this. First, in both the Jewish and Islamic populations I consider, members do not generally refer to themselves as fundamentalists. On the contrary, haredi Jews (the Orthodox most associated with traditional textual study) and those who sit in the yeshiva over holy books simply call themselves *Yidn*, Jews; and those who are identified with Gush Emunim, the so-called bloc of the faithful, also generally refer to themselves only as Jews, and finally the "people referred to as 'Muslim fundamentalists' in the West . . . usually speak of themselves either as 'Muslims' . . . or, more recently, as 'Islamists' (*Islamiyyun* in Arabic)."[1] The implications that follow from this are that *fundamentalist* is a characterization attached to these people by outsiders. Implicit as well is the notion that, to these people, those who do not share their views and patterns of behavior, who do not recognize the sovereignty of religion and its masters, are not truly Jews or Muslims. To be sure, this latter attitude certainly does set them apart from their more liberal-minded or pluralist coreligionists, but it does not automatically make them fundamentalists.

Second, while there are surely important affinities between the traditional Jewish *bes medrash*, the study hall of the yeshiva, and the Islamic *madrasa* (along with their associated practices and functionaries) as indeed there are common elements in these religious traditions, traditionalism and fundamentalism are not identical. Often the key element that turns an orthodox attachment to tradition into a form of fundamentalism is the context in which it occurs. To be insistently traditional when others all around are not is to transform that tradition into something more than a simple handing on of the old ways to another generation. More specifically, to dress in the old ways, to teach according to ancient rules, to practice scrupulously rituals in a manner that connects one with another time, to guard customs so rigorously that even minor changes do not occur, to see the past as the greatest teacher when most others embrace the novelties of today and tomorrow, to hallow scripture with a sense of its inerrancy, to review endlessly set texts according to ritualized rules of exegesis that run against the norms of contemporary critical interpretation, effectively transforms traditionalism into fundamentalism. In effect, "to defend the comprehensiveness of religion" as the people whom we are considering here do, at a time when religion is viewed as either marginal or outdated, becomes itself a resolute and fundamental "act of faith."[2] Even under these conditions, the term "fundamentalist" is problematic. In the context of Shi'ite Iran, in which the majority of the population still accepts the "comprehensiveness of the religion," such attitudes among the clergy cannot, for example, so clearly be labeled fundamentalist.

Yet what seems fundamentalist to observers may to the practitioners seem nothing more than a fidelity to the tradition. Where their traditionalism slides over into something akin to if not identical with fundamentalism is perhaps in the ardor of the countermovement of this religious culture, its reluctance to change the core of its scholastic or legal tradition.

Four other caveats are in order before any consideration of resemblances between religious traditions. First, Judaism and Islam are great religious traditions with many common themes.[3] Both these "Peoples of the Book" echo one another. Not only does Islam draw many of its heroes and some of its narratives from Jewish tradition, but because both have roots in the Middle East (even though they have attracted adherents beyond it), there is also much overlap in attachment to geography, and cultural outlook. Thus, at the most general level there are parallels between these two great religious traditions that act as a basis for comparison. Some of the common elements that are discussed below flow from this basic connection.

Second, to suggest that correspondences and resemblances exist is not to gainsay important differences. And the definition of "important differences" is both subjective and internal to the believers' culture. Religious schisms and wars have after all been stimulated by what from external perspectives seem like petty differences but from the outlook of the believers are contrasts of the boldest sort and distinctions of profound meaning.

Third comes a reminder of the importance of perspective. As Georg Simmel long ago pointed out, the distance, both physical and cultural, an observer stands from the object of his observations ineluctably affects his perceptions. While some might argue only a close-up, insider's view of a religion can give a true picture of it, others might argue that only greater remoteness provides an objective sense of what is involved in it. Moreover, purpose plays a crucial role in the perspective the observer chooses. That is, some might argue that if one goes deliberately in search of parallels one will find them. To each of these objections and to those who argue that the resemblances suggested in this paper come from the particular perspectives and distance of the observers, I plead guilty but add, quoting Simmel, that "[a]ll we can say is that a view gained at any distance whatever has its own justification. It cannot be replaced or corrected by any other view emerging at another distance."[4]

Finally, to point to resemblances between Islam and Judaism is not to suggest that what is common to both is necessarily so *only* for these two traditions. On the contrary, in some cases, parallels between the two are suggestive of similarities with Christianity, the third great religion that traces a common heritage with these two. Moreover, to presuppose that either Islam or Judaism is monolithic and can therefore be posited as having set characteristics that can be compared or contrasted is to ignore the important variations that exist not only between, for example, the Shi'ite and Sunni in Islam, the Hasidim and Misnagdim, or haredi and modern Orthodox in Judaism but also to disregard important ethnic differences among Muslims in places like Iraq, Pakistan, Malaysia, Indonesia, or Syria and among Jews in Israel, America, or other places in the Diaspora.

With all these qualifications in mind, I would nevertheless like to suggest resemblances between Judaism and Islam, particularly in its Shi'ite orientation, as suggested by an examination of the yeshiva bes medrash and the madrasa. Both bes medrash and madrasa are locales in which those immersed in the religion are to be found and where believers communicate, perpetuate, and develop their knowledge about, and attitudes toward, life through the medium of their religion. They are thus places that both express the character of the religion and shape it. Where better, therefore, to examine it?

Any consideration of parallels must begin with the elements of a common Weltanschauung or ideological underpinning for Judaism and Islam as expressed in these schools. These worldviews both underlie, inform, and shape much of the substance of the learning and the character of the students and teachers. The first of these is a particular view of history that appears to be common to both traditions.

The Paradox of History

Like moderns, both these traditions do not look upon history as a series of unrelated episodes, the origins and results of each being as widely separated as their localities, but rather see it as an organic whole with vicissitudes and events necessarily related to one another. Moreover, that relationship, as is clear to the faithful, tends to point in directions governed by religious belief.[5] Hence, as explained or interpreted by the prophet(s), religious virtuosi, or even simple believers, the events of history are perceived as related to one another in that they demonstrate the truth of the belief or some divine revelation. Nothing just happens; religion contextualizes everything: past, present, and future.

Crucial, if not paramount, in this reading of history is a sense that there was a glorious or at least better time in the past, some occasion of revelation or collective effervescence, a moment when, unlike today, humanity was in harmony with the divine. "Our forebears were the *zaddikim,*" the righteous ones, say the Jews in question; a Sunni Muslim tells V. S. Naipaul that "good Muslims believe that the best time in the world was the time of the Prophet and the first four, good caliphs."[6]

Since then, however, things have grown worse. "We are experiencing the greatest level of spiritual impurity the Jews have ever lived through," say the haredi Jews; there has been a decline in the ideals of the Jewish nation and a "sagging morale" say the Gush Emunim; many among both the Sunni and Shi'ites in question "view all history since the death of 'Ali in 661 as a long process of decay from the pristine Islam of the prophet Muhammad and his closest companions, and with the Shi'is generally also viewing the rule of the first three caliphs from 632 to 656 as a period of corruption."[7] To some interpreters, this attitude is essential to fundamentalism: "In the fundamentalist scheme," in V. S. Naipaul's words, "the world constantly decays and has constantly to be recreated."[8] Indeed, some even go so far as to argue that a decline and descent is an historical necessity as a prologue to amelioration and ascent. In Judaism—and especially Hasidic mysticism—this is often referred to as *yerida l'tsorech aliya*, decline for the purpose of ascension. Or, again as the Shi'ites have traditionally believed, the Dajjal or Antichrist must come before the Messiah will come or universal conversion to Islam will occur. In his study of religion and politics in Iran, Roy Mottahedeh quotes a mullah who explains, "Removing Pharaoh was only the first step; we may have to wander for a time until God's promise is fulfilled."[9] These are the trials and tribulations inherent in the encounter with contemporary civilization. But throughout there remains the hope, in the words of Jewish liturgical refrain, to "renew our days as of old" (Lamentations 5:21).

The Rejection of the West

Related to this view of history is a notion (common to both traditional Judaism and some versions of Islamic fundamentalism) that considers Western civilization and all it represents to be responsible for the corruption of what is good in the world. Not only is the West judged decadent and bankrupt in its values, its "vice and lust, alcohol and women, wild parties and tempting surroundings," as well as its moral anomie are emotionally rejected.[10]

To the Muslims this is articulated in terms of *jahiliyya* (ignorance of God, the Prophet, and the law), a condition in which one subordinates oneself to ephemeral contemporary concerns, to man rather than to the perceived will of Allah. To the Jews, the analogue is *borut* and *chiloniyut* (ignorance of the law and secularity); and its adherents, who are none other than a version of the Gentile, the proverbial goy. To the fundamentalists, there can be no compromise either with jahiliyya or the ways of the goy; only an "all-out offensive" is in order.[11]

V. S. Naipaul captures this attitude in a statement from a Malaysian Muslim who asserts, "Whatever is yes in America is no to us in Malaysia, and whatever is no in America with us is yes."[12] And in my book *Defenders of the Faith,* I document a teacher in a third-grade class for haredi boys explaining to his students that "America embodie[s] *goyim* . . . [it is] a place where there is no honor for elders, a place where the young run amuck," a world ruled by base appetite and immorality, and that America is an evil empire, and one can speak evil about it.[13] In short, both Islamic and Jewish fundamentalists share a confidence in their traditions and "perceive that the imported

Western models for creating social institutions and social ethic have failed to respond to their aspirations."[14] They therefore reject the contemporary West, its values, and its ethics.

Even the Orthodox Jews who are not haredim, but rather make up the Gush Emunim share this attitude. Although many appear to align themselves with contemporary culture, they may dress and look a bit more like members of general Western culture, but their religious Zionism—particularly as it is taught in the yeshivot—rejects much that comes from non-Jewish sources. Moreover their reference to the Bible and prophets as their certificate of title to the Promised Land, and their devotion to the Jewish Law as their ultimate constitution, also inexorably moves them away from ideals that are rooted in Western liberalism or concepts of universalism. In the end they, too, reject Western models in favor of a return to their religious and biblical roots in the Land of Israel, what they call "Torah Zionism."[15] "Gush Emunim is in its entirety a movement of religious return," wrote Moshe Shapiro, head of Machon Shuvah, a school in the settlement of Ofra whose purpose is to enhance the religious life of its students and bring them back to tradition.[16] To be sure, this is a change from the status quo, but for the believers the change that comes about from such struggle is often conceived as "resurgence" or "return"—something that makes the new Zionism turn out to be essentially old faith.[17]

In this sort of return to the fundamentals both Jews and Muslims express a kind of ethnic pride, a refusal to justify their beliefs and practices in terms that outsiders choose. "We do not need the Gentiles. We have better sources, thank God," as Rabbi Shlomo Aviner, head of the 'Ateret Cohanim yeshiva in Jerusalem and resident rabbi of Bet El, a settlement in the conquered territories, put it. "I have a right to live my life my way," as Yisrael Eichler, editor of a haredi newspaper, expressed it; or in the words of Sayyid Qutb of the Muslim Brotherhood in Egypt: "There is nothing in Islam for us to be ashamed or defensive about."[18] And, beyond this, they often proclaim the decline and imminent collapse of the West, seeing evidence of it in their own revival.

Indeed, those who have fallen short of an all-out offensive, whose modern Orthodox Judaism or modernist Islam has tried to find a middle road, lack the energy of the revival. Their way of life is no less repugnant than that of those who have been completely assimilated by the decadent West. The argument that "many major elements of Islam are compatible with modernity (at least if cleverly or 'creatively' interpreted)" or that in Judaism it is possible to hold an "equally firm commitment to Torah on the one hand, and to the values of World Culture on the other" is rejected by the world of the bes medrash and the madrasa.[19] To those in them the assumption that compromise is possible is perhaps the greatest sin of all. One rosh [head of a] yeshiva put it this way: "Some people say that the people you call the modern Orthodox are worse than the secular Jews. A secular Jew knows he is secular, but a modern Orthodox thinks he is religious and can do all sorts of things and not lose faith—and that is the error."[20]

In a similar vein, Sayyid Qutb characterizes the modernist Muslims as apostates who "pretend that they accept the domination of Allah and merely need expert jurist advice on how to put it into practice, in presumed conformity with the dictates of modernity."[21] In both cases, those who claim to be true to both worlds are viewed as counterfeit at best and perfidious at worst.

But of course the alternative rejection of the West is ambiguous at best, for both these Jews and Muslims realize that in some ways the West "is needed, for its machines, goods, medicines, warplanes," the technology, and even the "remittances" that some of its people send back to the faithful.[22] This ambivalent bond makes both groups particularly wary of the threat to them, their way of life, and values that the West embodies. That is another reason they are so threatened by and antagonistic toward the compromisers, whose life choices are conceivable and at times even latently attractive.

Ironically, as some of the more reflective recognize, Westernization—if only by negation—is precisely what "fostered a return to older and more deeply rooted values" by engendering a reaction in those who experienced its breakdown.[23] It threw into bold relief the contrasting character of the religious traditions that run so much in a counterdirection. If there were not an America and its ways to rail against, they would have had to invent one. Both traditionalism and fundamentalism are in great measure attractive as an antidote to "Westoxication," the overindulgence in and consequent poison intoxication believed to derive from Western culture. Furthermore, the West also had to serve as "witness" to the great revival, a witnessing from which the faithful "took encouragement."[24]

Religious Revival

As noted, an expression of the rejection of Western values is often formulated in terms of a perception of the West's decline along with a simultaneous conviction among both the Jewish and Islamic believers and the truly pious, that they can stem the erosion it engenders, cleanse or purify their world, and—if not bring about the new millennium or messianic age—at the very least prepare the road for the return to a renewed and revived religion. This is the underlying agenda of the houses of study, especially among those catering to students whose interest in religion is a product of the recent atmosphere of revival. Here efforts to guide one's life based on a shared and active belief in the imminence of a messianic age are more than an idea; they are a program for action.

All this requires vigilance, a capacity to interpret properly the meaning of history, and a steadfast belief in the principles of faith as well as a punctiliousness in ritual practice and a knowledge of the law of God that will serve to alert the world and encourage the faithful. This is a prerequisite for moral leadership. As Yisrael Eichler, disciple of the Hasidic Belzer rebbe and editor of a prominent Israeli newspaper written by and for haredi Jews, expresses it: "What will happen if, to our distress, among the haredim as well as among the secular and orthodox Jews a spiritual erosion continues? We must raise the alarm to trumpet a warning about the dangers that surround us."[25] For believers, the answer to that trumpet call is, in terms that 'Ali Shari'ati uses in the title to his book, *The Return to Ourselves,* a return that undoes the damage of contemporary culture and civilization,[26] a cultural detoxification.

Among inward-looking groups there are essentially three strategies used for assuring this revival: expanding the scope, detail, and strictness of religious law, especially through an ambitious program of religious education; disdainful rejection of the surrounding, poisoning, apposite culture; and social isolation when the surrounding culture appears to the faithful beyond their capacity to change it. All these are part of a general Kulturkampf and moral rearmament, which at its most extreme fights back and seeks to make changes that will bring back what are perceived to be the "better" old ways.[27] All these strategies have been used both by Islamic and Jewish revivalists.

To some, the revival requires an accompanying activist quest for authenticity and an effort to substitute the "true religion" for the false messiahs or corrupt and corrupting contemporary civilization. This means going beyond quietistic endurance or simple insulation from the tides of contemporary secular culture. To Shi'ite Muslims this is a move from the passivity and acquiescence to the activism and mobilization now reinterpretively understood to be exemplified by Imam Husayn.[28] It means challenging the rotten values and degenerate behavior of the contemporary world with an alternative and revivified tradition that draws inspiration from the past but strength from the struggle in the present. "When there are no struggles, naturally most of the youth remain passive," writes Benny Katzover, one of the leaders of Gush Emunim.[29]

Such activism, however, is often carried out in the clear knowledge and acceptance of the fact that it may lead to martyrdom and temporary defeat. This is a repeated theme in the ideological reading of history in many a bes medrash and madrasa. For Jews, particularly the haredim, who trace their roots to the Jewish communities decimated by exile, crusade, pogrom, and finally Holocaust, this possibility of defeat is simply part of the pattern of Jewish life, not unexpected. Jewish history is, after all, viewed as replete with suffering, martyrdom, and waiting for the Redeemer. Similarly, "Shi'ism developed and drew upon an identity rooted in a sense of a communal suffering and passion in anticipation of that day when God would send the Imam to deliver the community."[30]

Yet, among both Jews and Muslims, this tendency for a revolutionary revival and activist response is often counterbalanced by a reluctance to engage the other, lest one be caught up in an antithetical way of life that will ultimately undermine adherence to the traditional orthodoxies. That is, the greater risk is perceived to be not the suffering but rather the possible absorption in the ways of the adversaries. Hence, both the Jews and Muslims in question, while sometimes activist and militant, are in their revival "essentially defensive," their way of life acting as a kind of "holding operation" against all they view as corrosive.[31] Thus, many of the so-called b'nai yeshiva, those who sit in the bes medrash reviewing sacred texts, have been predisposed toward a quietistic, conservative, isolationist, and more passive reaction to the dominant host cultures among which they have found themselves (including the secular and assimilated Jewish ones).[32] Similarly among inward-looking Muslims, "the refrain of all fundamentalist litanies is 'Islam is isolated from life.'"[33] While Shi'ites tend toward the relatively more revolutionary and activist and the Sunnis less so, the lines have at times become blurred.[34] Historically, both Shi'ism and Sunnism have at periods been relatively more or less revolutionary and activist according to circumstance and shifts in ideology.

In a sense, the life that revolves around study—whether in the bes medrash or madrasa—is a key element of this holding operation, for it maintains a cadre of experts who can, when called upon and energized by activists, assist in the moral rearmament. Hence, Rabbi Yitzhak Shilat, lamenting the overconcern with settlement activity among the Gush Emunim, issued a call to "invest more in education." [35] And the haredim spend their time awaiting the Messiah while poring over holy books in the yeshiva. In the end, the holy men/scholars wish activists of all stripes would turn to them for guidance or legitimation.

The Dangers of Material Life and the Risks of Technology

Often the wariness about the West takes the form of misgivings about what many see as a creeping materialism that threatens to suck even the most pious into both the market economy of the West and the lifestyle and values that the quest for these creature comforts fosters. With improving economic conditions and rising material expectations, with the wealth that allows many to acquire everything from T-shirts to televisions that come from the West, many of the leaders of the faithful feel themselves in danger of being swallowed up by materialism and possessed by their possessions, a scourge that they believe they have caught from contemporary culture. This has often led to an emphasis on dressing in traditional clothes—caftan and fur cap, *kippah* (skull cap) and *tzitzit* (fringes), or the chador and other forms of the *hijab*—that act as markers that inhibit the wearer from being assimilated into other cultures. [36]

In addition there is an ideological devaluation of the very material concerns that absorb so many. A well-to-do faithful Muslim in Jakarta says: "I have an office on the ninth floor of one of these big new buildings. It is centrally air-conditioned. I go to the office in an air-conditioned car. . . . I look at television." And from all this he concludes "I feel in Jakarta I have lost my sensitivity." [37] He needs to rid himself of his material comforts, though he says this within his luxurious office. Similar sentiments are voiced by Gush Emunim settlers who leave Jerusalem and Tel Aviv for caravans in the West Bank wilderness of Mount Hebron. And in the yeshiva this is often articulated in *mussar* that stresses the disciplined abnegation of selfish instincts through meditation, exhortation, study, spiritual exercise, and attachment to the dictates of law "until the teachings of the Torah would become . . . second nature." If not asceticism, this often meant embracing austerity, in emulation of the Mussar movement's founder Yisrael Salanter's "rejection of material comforts and possessions." [38] Translating this attitude into contemporary folk wisdom, one haredi, speaking from the comfort of a new and well-appointed apartment in a Jerusalem suburb, asserts: "You look at the material improvements we have made in our lives and you think how successful we have become. But I know that all this can be our ruin. A person who has fewer material possessions needs far less to busy himself with the work necessary to acquire these possessions. We would be better off just sitting and learning Torah." [39]

All this is not to say that there is a rush toward asceticism and a throwing off of material pleasures; on the contrary, the creature comforts are maintained. Those caravans in the Jewish settlers' wilderness are air-conditioned and electrified, and they are soon exchanged for comfortable, well-appointed cottages with lush backyards.[40] Moreover both rebbes and mullahs have their limousines and cellular phones. Yet there is an abiding ideological wariness of these comforts along with an ontological devaluation of them.

Similarly technology—perhaps the quintessential expression of the comforts that the Western world has created and made available—is for these people not an end, whose development takes up their energy and gives purpose to their lives. Rather the technology, like the world that created it, is a means for their own ends; it has only to be inherited—never seen as an end in itself. But this inheritance is not without risks. Radios, televisions, cassette recorders, and most recently video players—machines that can appeal to everyone, even illiterates—have catapulted the outside world into the heretofore protected region of the home. They jump past the sheltering walls of the bes medrash and madrasa, invading the private domain without going through the mediation of the sectarian society and the cultural gatekeepers who rule on what is acceptable for sectarian society. To the latter, such instruments, whose availability expanded beyond all imagination in the last half of this century, became the prime battleground because of their potential power to corrupt. The technology had to be controlled; the goodness of the medium became inextricably tied to the message.

Both Jewish and Islamic fundamentalists share a distrust of and desire to regulate these media. Whether it is the haredim calling television "the great satan" or the Muslim Brotherhood seeing in it an "anti-Islamic" force, the uneasiness about this technology has infiltrated the atmosphere of the yeshiva and the madrasa.[41]

At the same time the Lubavitcher Hasidim beamed cable broadcasts by their rebbe to his followers and prepare tapes of his talks, yeshiva rabbis distribute cassettes of their teachings, and Hasidim circulate their melodies on tape, while the supporters of Khomeini used his taped exhortations and later televised speeches to nurture the Islamic revolution. These believers have no intention of putting the genie of technology back into the bottle and one better learn to make it do one's bidding. Indeed, the cassette tape and increasingly the video have become among the most ubiquitous tools of transmitting the holy word to followers in both the Jewish and Islamic world.[42] The same technology that breached the school walls can also become the instrument of a school without walls. Accordingly, both the Jews and Muslims in question approach this technology of communication with distrust but a keen recognition that its power can and must be harnessed and controlled lest it allow the raw outside world unmediated into the sanctum sanctorum.

The Society of Scholars

The comments "we would be better off just sitting and learning Torah," and "we must invest more in education" are suggestive and emblematic. According to many of the faithful, the first steps toward religious revival and return to the better times have already been taken, especially in the houses of learning where people have remained closest to the tradition. Among both Jews and Muslims who embrace the tradition, this has lead to an ideological emphasis not only on plumbing the texts but also on the importance of a society guided by scholars, or at the very least by those who emerge out of the bes medrash or madrasa. For the learned, be they mullahs or rabbis, ayatollahs or roshey yeshiva, have the authority and the power to lead the faithful back to the glory or forward to the eschaton or messianic age. Generally, in both the yeshiva bes medrash and Shiʻite madrasa, "religious achievement is at the same time social achievement," and hence doing well in one's studies can lead to a position of influence and power.[43]

This has also led in both groups to an increased motivation to send sons (in both groups women are largely excluded from this) to such houses of learning for some extended period.[44] And here, together with their study partners, they become socialized to a way of life that integrates learning with identity and peer-group experience. They become part of a group with a common worldview and shared attitudes. To be sure, in the academic haven there is a tendency to exchange the ideal for the real, demanding a greater purity of motive and morals than is sometimes possible in the outside world.

The madrasa and the yeshiva bes medrash represent an effort at some sort of professionalization of the learned. Both have evolved into institutions where students are usually separated from their families and home communities and thus resocialized. Both are institutions that create an elite cadre of graduates who see themselves as moral leaders of the religious (which may account for the Islamic and Jewish cases having had governments that have tried to affect curriculum and through it the nature of the religious leadership).[45] Both separate their students from the community, yet both are dependent on it (and particularly the merchant classes) for pecuniary support and for a supply of students. Such support, moreover, is not only for the institutions but also for the scholars and teachers. In Islam this is the *sahm-e* (share of the) Imam or *haq al-imama* (one-fifth of the earnings of a Shiʻite), and among the haredi Jews this is the *nedava* (pledge) or *chalukah* (distribution) that the rabbi/scholar receives to enable him to spend his time totally absorbed in his sacred task of studying and teaching. It also may explain why both the ayatollahs and many of the leading rabbis have intermarried with the well-to-do among the merchant classes. The former gain material support for their learning and expression of piety while the latter gain religious respectability and a vicarious connection to the precincts of the sacred and its authority.

Often the legitimating instruments of the challenge to contemporary decadence, these scholars, while waiting for the End of Days, "guide the community in their mundane as well as spiritual affairs."[46] In both institutions, these teachers, who represent moral and intellectual ideals, stand in place of the parents. The ulama and ayatollahs in Islam, the b'nai Torah and rabbinic roshey yeshiva in Judaism, become the social, political, and cultural elite. Both serve as guardians of the community pending the final redemption. Not only do these leaders offer "divine guidance in a wide range of daily transactions including dress, food, drink, mating, . . . and a host of other things," but they also offer a comprehensive picture of the meaning of life and the value orientations of those who remain true defenders of the faith.[47]

The Endless Review and Authority of the Texts and Their Interpreters

Although the particular texts reviewed in the Islamic and Jewish institutions differ, both Islam and traditional Judaism share the conviction that all wisdom is contained in the book; or more precisely, the wisdom of that book as interpreted by those who truly understand it is all one needs to navigate through life. Indeed, as Bernard Lewis points out, "among Muslim theologians there is as yet no . . . liberal or modernist approach to the Qur'an, and all Muslims, in their attitude to the text of the Qur'an, are in principle at least fundamentalists."[48] Much the same could be said about yeshiva students. Although some variations in approach to the texts studied exist, they by and large support a view of the inerrancy of the holy books and their rabbinic commentaries.

In Emmanuel Sivan's felicitous articulation, both groups demonstrate through their study that in "their ferocious attention to detail in these . . . texts" they affirm that the past from which the texts come and in which they seem embedded is "a living reality for them, capable of guiding the perplexed in the later thirds of the twentieth century in all realms."[49] To both these Jews and Muslims, learning is an endless review of the sacred texts whose sense is up-to-date even though it must be uncovered through a series of increasingly complex set of explanations and exegeses that come from within the normative view of the indigenous culture and, according to the more traditional, have no need "to be inspired by exogenous criteria."[50] For such strict traditionalists, those who master the texts and the traditional forms of exegesis become the knowledgeable: ulama among the Muslims, *talmidei hachamim* among the Jews.

"Strictly speaking, there are no clerics in Islam. That is to say, there are no men with an essential mediating role between the believer and God."[51] The ulama are simply people who by virtue of their time studying Islamic doctrine and law are therefore judged to possess a special knowledge. The same is true in Judaism. In the original meaning of the term, a rabbi is not a cleric but simply a recognized Torah scholar. Moreover, the term *laity* is "a meaningless expression in the context of Islam," as it is in Judaism.[52] Every man is expected to expose himself to an endless review of the sacred texts and acquire the knowledge that comes from this. Life exists for the sake of learning. However, in Judaism as well as Islam, those who dedicate their lives to this serve as judges and teachers: mullahs in Islam, rabbis in Judaism.

A clergy has emerged de facto out of both these traditions. And it is they who are entrusted with the task of education and religious leadership. This does not mean that everyone who becomes a rabbi or mullah necessarily comprehends the texts in exactly the same way. Indeed, among Jews, *poskim* or rabbis who provide judgments of law, and among Muslims the ulama, or the mullahs who serve as religious guides, represent a spectrum of opinions, interpretations, and understandings of what the religion demands. Some tend to be more demanding and critical of the West than others.

Closely related to this emphasis is a common reliance on the notion of *the authority of past interpreters,* above all interpreters who lived in golden and/or formative ages. While both traditions legitimate much of their interpretation of what is required for life in the present by an ideological reliance on precedent—"we are agents of the ancients," they might say—they nevertheless often reinterpret the past in such a way that what might not appear to be past authority turns out to be one. I have called this process elsewhere "traditioning and contemporizing," where the basic idea is respectively that there is nothing so new that it cannot be understood as somehow being in continuity with the tradition, and there is nothing so old that it cannot be understood as being in tune with the times. Neither is the new absolutely novel nor is the old really archaic.

Yet to establish this conviction, both Jewish and Islamic learning and teaching must invest a great deal of energy in the process of reinterpreting history and the present. Both are forced to refract all vision, toward the past, present, and future, through the lens of their ideology and belief. One must learn how to see what has happened, is happening, and will happen *from those who have sufficiently absorbed the lessons.* Among the strict traditionalists, there is no free interpretation that carries any ultimate authority by the individual who stands outside the tradition. Yeshiva Jews consult rabbis; devout Muslims consult mullahs to find out how to make sense of events. And all are bonded to a set of fundamentally inerrant texts.

What happens if the law does not make sense? In both groups, the commitment to the Halakha or Shari'a, the one right path, is such that there is an a priori "willingness to conform to . . . law, even in the face of doubt, spiritual aridity, and dark nights of the soul," this being the sign of a serious and true believer.[53] This steadfast persistence in the face of obstacles remains a hallmark of both traditions, and it is a stance that is inculcated in both groups' educational institutions, often by statements and moral lessons that impress the student that he must do what is demanded of him even if it seems to run counter to his desire or understanding. The emphasis on authority here has a very practical meaning; it restricts independence, the bane of all traditionalism and fundamentalism.

Charismatic Authority and Religious Virtuosi

While for the most part authority in both Judaism and Islam comes from the text or those who through their scholarship have become mediators of those texts, there is a growing tendency in both these religions, particularly among those who appear to fit the activist fundamentalist mold, to venerate and even glorify some of these scholars or mediators, to endow them with charismatic authority, and even to model themselves on them. Among haredi Jews these inclinations were at first associated with Hasidism and its focus on the person of the zaddik or rebbe, who was viewed as being endowed with miraculous power to intercede with Heaven. His lifestyle dictates the precepts for religious action. Among Muslims, "the Shi'i mujtahids [fully authorized interpreters of the Shari'a] of recent centuries have been charismatic leaders venerated" by the masses.[54]

The matter of religious virtuosi also recalls striking parallels between the two traditions in the domain of practical knowledge of what the religious codes demand. Islam has its mullahs who, serve as "jurisconsults," and in like fashion Judaism has its rabbis who are *poskim*. Both possess a capacity to translate for the believers the divine demands embedded in the sacred texts into concrete requirements and behavior guidelines. Often this calls for not only an accurate knowledge and reading of the law but also a capacity to read *into* the law in order to extrapolate an interpretation that gets to its motives. In this way both posek and jurisconsult guide believers through the as yet uncharted waters of contemporary existence, extending sacred texts into new domains. Various poskim or jurisconsults will not necessarily arrive at the same conclusion in response to the same question. Each arrives at what for Muslims Mottahedeh calls his "best guess" of what should be done, a capacity to fathom the will of the Qur'an.[55] For the posek this means a capacity to comprehend the intention of the Torah, the *da'as Torah*. This is a move from the textual to the esoteric.

Originally, da'as Torah was something *talmidei hachamim,* rabbinic scholars, had. It was their ability "to interpret day-to-day events in a proper Torah light," discern what the tradition had in mind, and thereby deduce its intention, thus being able "to anticipate the ramifications of events . . . in the future."[56] With da'as Torah rabbis could deliver guidance beyond the judicial. As modern life threw into the basket of human experience all sorts of unprecedented new realities that seemed to go beyond the boundaries of the Torah, traditionalists turned to the concept and bearers of da'as Torah to fill the vacuum created by the seeming silence of the time-honored texts on many of these matters. From being deciders of the law or teachers, these men became something more.

In Judaism, while the scholars of the yeshiva world emphasized a sober study of texts and an austerity in spirituality, the popular will transformed the yeshiva rabbi into a rebbe, gave him charismatic authority that flowed even beyond his textual expertise. "For the *talmid chacham* is like the Torah itself and he is in its image, and therefore it is certain that for this reason the Torah also commanded us to 'not depart from all he will instruct you,' for the *hachamim* are the Torah itself, and as the Holy One, may He be blessed, decreed and gave the Torah to all of Israel, so he gave us the *hachamim* and they are also the essence of the Torah."[57] "My will," as Hasidic rabbi Avraham Mordecai Alter of Gur put it even more starkly in a 1922 letter to his followers, "is the will of Heaven."[58] As Fuad Khuri notes, "unlike the exoteric and the explicit, which can be standardized, the esoteric and the implicit must remain fluid and elusive."[59] The possessor of da'as Torah became not just one who could fathom the meaning of texts but one endowed with charisma, who could shape an understanding of life that emerged out of the text and went beyond it. He understood the religious significance of social and political behavior.[60]

As da'as Torah evolved into charisma, it merged the scholar rabbi with the Hasidic rebbe. In spite of the efforts of the yeshiva world, particularly in its Lithuanian tradition, to remove these associations, the rebbe-ization of the scholars continued. Scholars became saints, or at least saintly rabbis. Thus rabbis Zvi Yehuda Kook, head of the Merkaz Harav yeshiva in Jerusalem, and Rabbi Eliezer Schach, yeshiva head at Ponovezh in B'nai B'rak, became for their students no less charismatic figures than the

Lubavitcher rebbe or the Belzer rebbe were for their Hasidic disciples. Among the Gush Emunim, some of this has transformed yeshiva heads and scholars into partisan commanders.

In Islam, "religious leadership has always received greater attention in Shi'ism than in Sunnism."[61] While the Shi'ites in the early period were concerned with the role of leaders and mediators with the divine, Sunnis embraced a more this-worldly, noncharismatic approach—like those in the yeshiva world. In time, however, like the yeshiva world, "popular Sunni Islam [also came to] emphasize the role of mediators," and worshippers from both streams went to imams to beseech their help in gaining divine favor.[62] These leaders, like the rebbes and others possessing da'as Torah, drew authority from their "ability to interpret divine revelation infallibly," something they got from their juridical and textual expertise.[63] They became more than scholars. Accordingly, in Shi'ite Islam, there emerged ayatollahs (literally, miraculous signs of God) who alone had the authority to give decisive interpretations of the law.[64] Among these were the supreme leaders, grand ayatollahs, those who actually had the mass following necessary to have their opinions set the behavior of thousands and even millions. Clearly, such figures had considerable charisma.

"For Muslim jurists," Mottahedeh writes, "the law existed in its full form in the mind of the Divine Legislator, but on the human plane positive law was whatever the jurist said it was by applying his training in the law to the situation before him."[65] As Ayatollah Khaza'ali explained, "The Jurist is the lieutenant of God, and his command is God's command."[66] As situations continued to change, and as the jurisconsults found themselves to be the defenders of God, the applications of the law expanded in sometimes radical ways.

In both traditions, these authorities were also seen as someone to emulate: a *mu-qallad,* or "imitable model," for Muslims and a rebbe among Hasidim or a *rav* in the yeshiva world.[67] Whether they were the *marja' al-taqlid* (greatest scholar) of Islam or the *gadol ha'dor* (giant of the age) of Judaism, these authorities (infallible de facto if not de jure) and the tremendous influence that they had on their followers represented a revolutionary and threatening force.

In the contemporary world with its rapidly shifting realities, such religious virtuosi become indispensable for helping to determine what is or is not acceptable. That is, in the face of a novel situation where "common practice" does not yet exist and therefore has "lost its independent validity," life must increasingly "be squared with the written word."[68] And those who are expert in the written word thus gain a greater importance than ever before. For both the Muslims and Jews in question, "traditional conduct no matter how venerable, how elementary, or how closely remembered, yields to the demands of theoretical knowledge"; and that is when the jurisconsult and posek become paramount leaders.[69] For them, "long-term educational effort" both through the books and the review of them is "destined to bring about popular pressure" to bring this reinstitution to reality.[70]

Over the centuries the process has evolved from being authority personally passed from master to disciple; today one becomes a rabbi after an extended period of study in a yeshiva. While the formal procedure of ordination is something that emerged in the Middle Ages and became even more standardized in modern times, the essential mechanism for making someone rabbi consists of his acquiring his title from a rabbinic mentor who precedes him. The term *smicha,* which is used to refer to the ordination, literally means a laying on of hands. Thus rabbis make other rabbis by imparting them with a tradition. Among the Orthodox, this happens when the student has mastered the various codes of law: Orach Chayim and Yoreh De'ah, which he can now interpret and teach. So, too, in Islam, "the teacher, after giving a full course, personally [gives] a certificate (*ijaza*) to the student," who thereafter is "allowed to teach [the text or subject in question]."[71] In both cases, the new virtuosi often distinguish themselves by the names of their teachers who have ordained them and vouchsafed their juridical expertise.

Not only experts in the codes have their parallels, but also preachers whose role is to elicit moral and spiritual lessons from the sacred texts. The Islamic *rowzeh-khans,* whose task is to give recitations from the sacred canon that are meant to elicit weeping and to raise the spiritual level, passion, and emotional attachment to the religion of believers, play a role that is very much like that of the *maggid,* whose aim is to retell the narratives of the tradition in such a way as to make them parables and moral models. In both cases, the characters and events of the text become exemplary and serve as a kind of moral template for the present. Both the rowzeh readers and the maggidim are supposed to be able to lift their listeners out of their mundane existence and onto the spiritual plane of the stories they tell while they also enhance the drama of the stories. The Shi'ite rowzeh-khan does this through a variety of retellings of the martyrdom of Husayn that will encourage in the listeners a conviction that "only a return to a strictly Islamic way of life will induce God to free the faithful from the faithless."[72] The successful maggid always presents biblical characters and narratives in a way that connects them with the life of the listener, no matter how far apart that life might seem from the original text. Thus in one striking example a maggid was able to turn Samson, normally a character associated with brute strength and high hubris, into a model of the suffering Jew, humbled and crippled by persecution, who in a final act of piety, self-abnegation, and prayer was enabled to bring down the Philistines who had imprisoned and blinded him.[73]

In both the Islamic and Jewish cases distinctions are drawn between the religious leaders who operate within the community—the town mullah or rabbi—and those who are religious models in the school. In the contemporary situation where observance has become more and more a matter of keeping a precept rather than simply replicating an action, the models have increasingly become those yeshiva rabbis who have published a basic code book or religious commentary on precepts as drawn from the sacred canon.[74] Thus authority flows from what is perceived to be their superior scholarship, as demonstrated in both religious traditions not only by their having endlessly and painstakingly reviewed the holy books but also by their having written their own exegetical treatises. No posek or jurisconsult can claim authority in the absence of such a text, which forms an important foundation of his legitimacy. And these books often become best-sellers among the students of the madrasas and yeshivot. To their readers and authors they often serve as the basis of the debate about reinstituting sacred laws as the law of the land.

While there is often considerable ingenuity buried in these commentaries, they eschew originality in subject. Nevertheless, in spite of the limited intellectual innovation of commentaries, those who write them have become the elite. This has led to diminished prestige for the town rabbi when compared to the rosh yeshiva and made the latter the ideal model, the *gadol*. In Islam there are similarly two sorts of *talabehs,* one in the madrasa who has higher prestige and can better serve as a model, and one who serves in the village as a local cleric.

Isolated in the ivory tower of the madrasa or yeshiva, these scholars are likely to exert absolute authority that can ignore the realities of life in the outside world. This has led to a tendency for the school-based religious virtuosi to be more stringent in their interpretations of what the religion demands, while the local clerics, forced by the realities of community life, often interpret the law more leniently. This is true in both Islam and Judaism. However, since both the Jews and their Islamic counterparts increasingly view the school-based religious leader as the ideal model, they are forced to embrace the stringent interpretations of the religious code as more authoritative.

The dislocations of contemporary civilization have moreover made the texts and their most scholarly interpreters more important than ever before. In times of turmoil, going by the book is the best refuge for those who would maintain tradition. And that has made religious education and educators more than simply vehicles for pedagogic instruction; it has made an attachment to or dependence upon them a propaedeutic to being a true believer. Among the Orthodox Jews this means that everyone not only goes to a yeshiva but also has a personal rav or rebbe, while among their Islamic counterparts it means that the madrasa has expanded its boundaries. Thus the mullah may sit in a holy city, but his word goes forth to every village and town where he has superseded the local mullah. The yeshiva rabbi and the ayatollah are now mass leaders, even as they claim still to be wedded to the educational institutions in which they are based. Thus the ayatollah in the madrasa in Qom speaks directly to the believers all over the world, and the rosh yeshiva in the bes medrash in B'nai B'rak or the rebbe in Crown Heights is heard far beyond the borders of his neighborhood and institution.

The Search for Wholeness

In contradistinction to the compartmentalized and segmented character of contemporary society, fundamentalist-like Jews and Muslims refuse to be "divided" between their social and religious selves. They seek, as one modern Jewish woman put it, describing her experience of Jewish learning in a yeshiva for women, "to shed . . . the multiple 'personas' of my everyday life" in favor of a single identity.[75] They retain a hope that they will overcome "the frustrating compartmentalization" that characterizes life for those who seek to inhabit the two worlds of contemporary secular culture and the traditional Jewish one.[76] For the religious Zionists this has meant turning their texts and tradition into a political program as well as a master plan for quotidian existence. For haredi Jews this means a rejection of the acculturative model of the Jewish enlightenment or *haskalah* that urged people to be "a man in the street and a Jew in the home" (or in its even more restrictive statement in America, "to be a man in the street and a Jew in the synagogue"). Haredim and religious Zionists seek publicly and privately to be Jews and nothing but Jews. Their state must be governed by Halakha.

The same might be said about those who have revived their attachments to Islam. They seek to be *kamal,* complete, and reject the idea of having several faces. They impress upon their followers and students the idea that they must not abandon for even a moment their total attachment to the demands and boundaries of the tradition. In this there is a pressure to arrive at consistency and harmony in one's life, so that everything one does to which Islam might speak is, in fact, Islamic. Their state must be governed by Shari'a.

Sovereignty

Among the haredim sovereignty is something that cannot be achieved without divine intervention. Until then, exile—both in its theological sense as an absence of redemption and in its existential meaning as an absence of a homeland—is the ineluctable Jewish condition.[77] This is true even in the secular State of Israel, which the haredim refuse to recognize as the true end to their Diaspora (even when they reside there). It is a land where for them God's promises are not yet fulfilled.

But not all Orthodox Jews of the yeshiva world see things this way. For many of the Zionist Orthodox, contemporary Israel is the answer to their religious hopes and waiting.[78] Political Zionism is a tool toward this end, but religion is its motive force. To these Jews, exegesis of old texts often becomes a response to contemporary problems, and the bes medrash is the place where the proof texts can be found in which to ground religious motives that are woven into the fabric of a quite modern life. Here parallels between past, present, and future are drawn. To the religious Zionists, these parallels point to the need to take an active part in the redemption, something the haredim are not willing to do. A key to the activity in behalf of the faith is, for the radical religious Zionists, Jewish return to and sovereignty over the Promised Land, all of which is considered holy. For them, many of the events of recent Jewish history are evidence of the imminence of redemption, *atchalta d'geula,* while others are recipes for action.[79] Thus a reading of a portion of the Bible chanted in the synagogue on a Sabbath in July in which God promises "you shall take possession of the land and dwell therein for unto you have I given the land to possess it" (Numbers 33:53), and follows that with the injunction, "But if you will not drive out the inhabitants of the land from before you, then those you allow to remain shall be as thorns in your eyes and as pricks in your sides and they shall harass you in the land that you dwell therein" (Numbers 33:55), is seen as a religious motive and sacred source for contemporary political action. This has merged sociopolitical goals with religious ones.

Many rabbis and roshey yeshiva, to say nothing of their willing students, including most prominently graduates of the Merkaz Harav yeshiva in Jerusalem and disciples of its late head, Zvi Yehuda Kook, have moved easily from the text to the real world, from religion to politics and social action.[80] As such they have called for Jewish (i.e., Orthodox) alternatives to the secular and socialist Zionist models. The Bible—in some ways even more important for them than the Talmud (even though the latter is the text with which they spend the most time)—is more than heritage, as it was for all Zionists; it is a Jewish template in which time makes no difference. Thus, as Benny Katzover, a leader of the Jewish settlers in Samaria, explains in *Nekuda,* a settlers' magazine, "If we establish a settlement in Samaria this is essentially because we see ourselves in continuity with that ancient nation returning to its land."[81]

To be sure, a merger of politics and religion is not limited to the yeshiva world. Thus the current Belzer rebbe, leader of the second largest Hasidic sect in Israel, traditionally gathers his followers at a *tish,* or festive table, on the evening after the holy day of Simchat Torah, the occasion of completing the annual cycle of weekly readings of the Five Books of Moses, and offers a lecture that mixes da'as Torah and politics.

And where the political process does not yield success, God's intervention is enlisted. To take a recent example, in the face of political defeat in the 1992 Israeli elections, one prominent rosh yeshiva, Rabbi Shaul Yisraeli, head of the Merkaz Harav yeshiva, questioned "whether the prayer for the welfare of the [Israeli] state and its leaders recited in many synagogues on the Sabbath should continue to be said in its present form." He explained that he wondered "whether the verse entreating God to give of His wisdom to the country's leaders should be said about ministers who do not observe halakha, and who do not take into consideration the sentiments of the religious."[82]

Haredim differ with these Zionist Orthodox Jews in that they believe that nationalism (even when religiously motivated) loosens religious solidarity and ends up replacing it, something viewed as sacrilege.[83] Accordingly, they differ with the religious Zionists about when and politically how Jews must begin to act to bring about the redemption. Yet *both* groups are convinced that, if Jews are to regain the blessings of Heaven and the Promise of the Land, as well as the redemption of the Messiah, they must restore the strict practices of Jewish law (halakha) and the society that holds it to be supreme. And both believe that once the halakha is dominant and universally applied among Jews, this will not only bring about great changes in the character of Jewish life but will also conquer the many social, political, and moral problems confronting the Jewish people.

In this there are important parallels with the teaching of many Islamic religious leaders who oppose "Westoxication," and "Euromania" and have sought to challenge the Western and European patterns of culture with a revitalized Islam that governs life according to the Qu'ran and the words and example of the Prophet.[84] Having sought "to prevent further internal deterioration of Islamic religious life" while simultaneously "protesting and resisting alien domination in any form over the Islamic character of Muslim societies," these believers affirm that "if the Muslims want to regain their early positions of power and prestige, they must fashion their practice, including the government, on the ideals prescribed by the Qu'ran and by the pristine community."[85] They seek "inspiration in its ever-living values, its eternal ideals."[86] These last words come from the Cairo Muslim Students' Association booklet entitled "Contemporary Reflections on Our Heritage," but it echoes Jewish sentiments of both the Gush Emunim and the haredim. Once having done this, they too trust that this "will effect dramatic change and vanquish manifold sociopolitical problems afflicting the Muslim peoples."[87] But this ultimately demands sovereignty; "the Islamic *umma* [community of the faithful] is not that which simply implements the *shari'a* [command of God for man], but that which does so under Islamic sovereignty."[88] This, as Fuad Khuri argues, "explains why some Muslim Arabs would rather live under Israeli occupation while rejecting the state of Israel than live independently in peace with the Zionist state."[89] And it helps us understand why Ayatollah Khomeini saw the defeat of Israel and Zionism as an ineluctable religious goal.

In both cases, the convictions are absolute, always confirmed by the events of history and supported by proof texts that serve as legitimation for radical reorientations of society and activism on behalf of the divine Word. And all this is worked out in the academies of learning.

Hay'at and Shiur

Augmenting the madrasa and the yeshiva bes medrash are those community associations that mix the social with the religious, where the review of sacred texts and the accompanying religiocultural indoctrination become the frame around or pretext for gathering. For Iranian Shi'ite Muslims this is the *hay'at,* and for the Jews it is the *shiur.* More than simply a study group, neighborhood organization, or social gathering—although clearly sharing some of their character—these associations serve as a forum for discovering what it is that the religion requires of the true believer and how it can provide meaning through its texts, codes, and rituals.[90] Lead by a religious virtuoso eminent for his knowledge of the text or the demands of the faith, these associations are often opportunities to receive some basic knowledge about what the religion demands of one and how it responds to the challenges of everyday existence. Many use the hay'at or shiur as a means for integrating religion into their otherwise profane daily lives and of bonding the students to the tradition and one another.[91] They also offer opportunities for indoctrination and radicalization in that they serve as important vehicles for keeping the community within the reach of religion and religious virtuosi. As such these religious study groups (like certain Christian Sunday Bible classes) act as a particularly important counterforce in a world seen as an implacable adversary to the demands and expectations of religion.

Spiritual Parallels

There are also resemblances that point to a spiritual parallel in the inner life of believers. They may seem minor, for they are part of the practical reality of everyday religious behavior, by-products of larger ideological or structural parallels. Yet they are crucial, for they are what give the different religious traditions a similar feel, particularly when experienced from the inside. Included here are such elements as the emphasis on holy places, and in particular a focus on some sort of axis mundi. For the Jews this is Jerusalem and the site of the remains of the Holy Temple; for the Muslims, it is Mecca and the Ka'ba.

Yet another parallel is in the emphasis, particularly in the haredi yeshivot at the primary school level, on memory work and rote learning. Indeed, much of the sound one hears emanating from the bes medrash is of text and commentary chanted aloud.[92] This too is something that, according to Fazlur Rahman, has for centuries been a characteristic of madrasa learning.[93]

Another common element of praxis is the importance attached to the regularity of prayer, and in particular prayer with others. For both haredim and devout Muslims, the day is oriented around the rhythm of repeated gatherings for prayer, before which ritual ablutions must be made. And the longer one's prayers last, the better.[94]

But prayer is simply one such benchmark. Standing behind it is an inherent nomism that asserts that law is the guiding principle of life. There is no assumption that a person is free to do as he pleases. To be a devout Jew/Muslim is always to have distinctive things to do, to be forever directed by rules. In the moral sense this means—to quote Jean-Marie Guyau, the nineteenth-century student of religion—an unwillingness to "take a step without consulting their gods and carrying their images before them to show the way," an attitude that informs every lesson and remains part of the taken-for-granted reality that justifies the need to learn what the Divine Legislator has commanded those who follow his precepts.[95]

Conclusion

For each of these resemblances, the case could persuasively be made for drawing distinctions. That is, after all, at the heart of religious diversity. But religion does not exist in some sort of cultural vacuum. On the contrary, as already suggested, context—social, political, practical, or ideological—frames it and determines what is highlighted and what overshadowed. In the context of contemporary Western civilization, the civilization that marks religions and religious practitioners as "fundamentalist," these resemblances appear to be salient. Whether they really are or whether our perspective here is what makes the reality is a matter of debate.

Finally, one might wonder about the long-term consequences of a relatively narrow and rigid educational system that focuses much of the learning of its students on orthodox tradition. Will it allow for intellectual growth or will its emphasis on a ritualized relearning of the tradition lead instead to narrowness and stagnation? No one can, of course, predict the future with any certainty. We can, however, learn from the past. According to the late Fazlur Rahman, an Islamic modernist, between the tenth and twelfth centuries an orthodox system of Muslim education became "so effective that the movement of religious rationalism," the development of intellectuality that expanded Muslim thinking to a variety of fields and yielded a creative reformulation of such fields as geography, general history, and belles lettres, "lost all its strength." In its place came a "restricted curriculum" that took "the place of the entire field of knowledge." From this he concludes the "relative narrowness and rigidity of education in the madrasas was, indeed, mainly responsible for the subsequent intellectual stagnation of Islam."[96] This situation where thinking is "passive and receptive rather than creative and positive" came about because of the madrasas' "isolation from the life of lay intellectualism."[97] The dates offered by Rahman are open to question, the strength of many branches of culture both inside and outside the madrasa are an incontestable fact, and some new trends of interpretation in the world of the madrasa have on occasion occurred.[98] Nevertheless, the madrasa curriculum has remained remarkably stable for the last six hundred years, and its near monopoly of higher learning until the last century gave higher learning an undeniably centripetal character.

A somewhat similar process has occurred more recently in Judaism. After centuries of intellectual development, where the great Torah academies produced scholars whose thinking touched on philosophy, history, mysticism, and "a new flowering of Biblical scholarship," the yeshivot that arose in the contemporary period have devolved into academies that, separating themselves from the laity, in reaction to the intellectual explorations and perceived heresies of the period of Jewish enlightenment and emancipation that blossomed in the nineteenth century, restricted the curriculum to the study of Talmud almost to the exclusion of everything else. Such study filled not only the day in the bes medrash but replaced all other knowledge (except codes that were essentially extracted from Talmud). Moreover, the study of these texts was carried on in a ritualized fashion where the traditional pathways of exegesis were seen as the only avenue to thinking. Here knowledge was something to be acquired and not expanded. Here in the Orthodox bes medrash where the best questions to ask are those that have been asked before rather than something new, where intellectual trailblazing is discouraged because of its iconoclasm, where reason is in subordination to religion and study is a kind of imitation of the ancients, the results have also often been narrowness and rigidity.[99] Here religious thinking developed in isolation from any external challenge and opposition. Even in the yeshivot of the Gush Emunim, much the same occurred: "a deliberate isolation from and gradual decay of secular intellectualism."[100] In this, all yeshivot were the same.

To be sure, like the madrasa, the yeshiva bes medrash occasionally allowed new trends of interpretation to develop, particularly in the intellectual turbulence of the nineteenth and early twentieth centuries, but it, too, ultimately assimilated these new interpretive trends into a pattern of learning that has allowed the study that goes on inside the yeshiva to remain generally centripetal in character.

As had been the case in the madrasas, so too in the bes medrash of the yeshiva; besides Talmud, codes, and their related commentaries, "all other knowledge was superfluous if not utterly condemnable."[101] Although the Gush Emunim yeshivot that emerged out of the Merkaz Harav model added the consideration of nontalmudic texts (often in an extracurricular context), these became a mere subtext for sustaining a political program of territorial expansion and settlement. The pursuit of all knowledge not related to this program of action or to the traditional yeshiva study of Talmud was discouraged or inhibited. Talmud remained absolutely dominant.

Writing of the madrasas, Rahman suggests that they "have, almost from the beginning of their organized existence, aimed at merely imparting a system of ideas, not at creating newer systems; and therefore they have not been interested in inculcating the spirit of enquiry and independent thought." [102] While this statement neglects the important element of disputation in the madrasa system, which sometimes drove skeptical students to leave the madrasa, and neglects the role of some teachers of intellectual originality, it remains true for very many madrasas at very many points. Much the same could be said about the yeshivot, especially in the last half of this century when—in spite of some important teachers of original thinking, like Joseph Dov Soloveitchik—they have likewise become bastions of conservatism and sanctuaries of tradition as well as shelters from the storm of cultural change. If they became anything different, they would no longer fulfill their implicit mission as bulwarks of Orthodoxy. It is no accident that the heads of the yeshiva rail against the university and its kind of thinking.[103] As for the Muslims, many chose the universities as the cultural battleground in the ideological struggle over what should be the true character of learning.[104]

For those who see the maintenance of the status quo or texts in the service of ideology as the highest ideal, the conservatism of the madrasa and the bes medrash will hold great promise for the future. But for those who believe that a narrowing of the intellectual horizon is ultimately dangerous for any religion, these developments may rather arouse anxiety about the days ahead.

Notes

This paper was written with important contributions from Roy Mottahedeh, whom I wish to thank. I, of course, remain responsible for any shortcomings of the final product.

1. Samuel C. Heilman, *Defenders of the Faith* (New York: Schocken, 1992); Henry Munson, Jr., *Islam and Revolution in the Middle East* (New Haven: Yale, 1988), p. 4. It is worthwhile recalling here that the word *Islam* means "surrender to the will of God."

2. Fuad I. Khuri, *Imams and Emirs: State, Religion, and Sects in Islam* (London: Saqi Books, 1990), p. 32.

3. "That, theologically speaking, there is Judaic content in the Qur'an, far from surprising anyone, is insistently confirmed by the Qur'an itself from first to last" (Fazlur Rahman, *Islam,* 2d ed. [Chicago: University of Chicago Press, 1979], p. 27).

4. Georg Simmel, *The Sociology of Georg Simmel,* trans. and ed. Kurt Wolff (New York: Free Press, 1950), pp. 7–8.

5. To be sure, this is not unique to Islam and Judaism. "All religions have *sacred histories*—that is, stories about primordial beginnings that are understood by the believer to

explain the human condition" (Munson, *Islam and Revolution,* p. 7).

6. V. S. Naipaul, *Among the Believers: An Islamic Journey* (New York: Vintage, 1982), p. 379.

7. See Heilman, *Defenders of the Faith,* pp. 94–107, 260–76; Gideon Aran, "Jewish Zionist Fundamentalism: The Bloc of the Faithful in Israel (Gush Emunim)," in Martin E. Marty and R. Scott Appleby, eds., *Fundamentalisms Observed* (Chicago: University of Chicago Press, 1991), p. 277; and Munson, *Islam and Revolution,* p. 18.

8. Naipaul, *Among the Believers,* p. 167.

9. Roy Mottahedeh, *The Mantle of the Prophet* (New York: Pantheon, 1985), p. 16.

10. Naipaul, *Among the Believers,* p. 288.

11. See Emmanuel Sivan, *Radical Islam,* enlarged ed. (New Haven: Yale University Press, 1990), pp. 23–27, 66–67; and *Fi Zilal al Qur'an,* commentary on Sura V, 44–48. See also Aran, "Jewish Zionist Fundamentalism," p. 277.

12. Naipaul, *Among the Believers,* p. 258.

13. Heilman, *Defenders of the Faith,* pp. 193–94.

14. Abdulaziz A. Sachedina, "Activist Shi'ism in Iran, Iraq, and Lebanon," in Marty and Appleby, *Fundamentalisms Observed,* p. 407.

15. See Aran, "Jewish Zionist Fundamentalism," p. 277.

16. Moshe Shapiro, "Gush Emunim Must Repent" (in Hebrew), *Nekuda,* 11 July 1986, p. 41.

17. Cf. Khuri, *Imams and Emirs,* p. 223; Shapiro, "Gush Emunim Must Repent"; and Heilman, *Defenders of the Faith.*

18. Shlomo Aviner, "An Answer to a Question regarding Study of Christian Sources," *Iturey Kohanim,* no. 56 (November 1989): 25; Heilman, *Defenders of the Faith,* p. 104; Sayyid Qutb, *Ma'alim fi-l-Tariq,* p. 214, quoted in Sivan, *Radical Islam,* p. 68.

19. Sivan, *Radical Islam,* p. 67; Chaim Dov Keller, "Modern Orthodoxy: An Analysis and Response," *Jewish Observer,* June 1970, p. 12. Although Keller claims to eschew this position, he perfectly defines it.

20. Heilman, *Defenders of the Faith,* p. 270.

21. Qutb, *Ma'alim fi-l-Tariq,* p. 58, quoted in Sivan, *Radical Islam,* p. 67.

22. Naipaul, *Among the Believers,* p. 168.

23. Mottahedeh, *Mantle of the Prophet,* p. 10.

24. Naipaul, *Among the Believers,* p. 378.

25. Yisrael Eichler, "An Open Eye," in *Ha-Machaneh ha-Haredi,* 3 May 1990, p. 3.

26. See Mottahedeh, *Mantle of the Prophet.*

27. See Charles Liebman, "Extremism as a Religious Norm," *Journal for the Scientific Study of Religion* 22 (March 1983): 75–86.

28. See Khuri, *Imams and Emirs,* p. 124.

29. Benny Katzover, "Not to Institutionalize Too Much" (in Hebrew), *Nekuda,* 11 July 1986, p. 34.

30. Sachedina, "Activist Shi'ism," p. 403.

31. Sivan, *Radical Islam,* p. 3.

32. Some might argue that hasidim—who are also Orthodox Jewish extremists—contradict this pattern, that they are radical rather than quietistic. To understand Hasidism and its revolutionary changes in Judaism, which began in Eastern Europe with Israel ben Eliezer, the so-called Ba'al Shem Tov, and his disciples in the eighteenth century and expanded in the nineteenth to become a mass movement that reinvigorated Jewish life by appealing to the masses, would go beyond this paper. However, one cannot help but note the structural parallels with the earlier movement in Islam: Sufism. Like the Sufis, Hasidim emphasized spirituality. Like the Sufi brotherhoods who carried Islam to new adherents, Hasidic courts focused on charismatic rebbes, carried a revitalized Judaism to people and places whose Judaism had flagged. And just as Sufism as a popular religion challenged the orthodox system of Islam, so too did Hasidism. What al-Ghazali did in the twelfth century, the Maggid of Mezerich, the main disciple of the Ba'al Shem Tov, would do in the eighteenth. In both cases, as a result, "orthodoxy itself experienced a revival and new strength" In time, however, at least in hasidism, radicalism gave way to conservatism. (Rahman, *Islam,* p. 6; Mendel Piekarz, *Ideological Trends of Hasidism in Poland during the Interwar Period and the Holocaust* [Jerusalem: Bialik Institute, 1990], esp. pp. 37–49).

33. Sivan, *Radical Islam,* p. 3.

34. As Sachedina puts it: "The quietist . . . stance became associated with the majority Sunni Muslims. . . . However, following numerous unsuccessful attempts by the Shi'ite leaders at different times in their history to overthrow the ruling power, . . . Shi'ites adopted the quietist attitude rather than the activist one" (Sachedina, "Activist Shi'ism," p. 408). See also Samuel C. Heilman, "Quiescent and Active Fundamentalism," in Martin E. Marty and R. Scott Appleby, eds., *Accounting for Fundamentalisms* (Chicago: University of Chicago Press, 1993). Pp. 173–196.

35. Yitzhak Shilat, "Return to the Straight and Narrow," *Nekuda,* 26 June 1985, 15.

36. See Heilman, *Defenders of the Faith;* and Eliezer Don-Yehiya, "The Book and the Sword," in Marty and Appleby, *Accounting for Fundamentalisms.*

37. Naipaul, *Among the Believers,* pp. 380–81. See also Mottahedeh, *Mantle of the Prophet,* p. 309.

38. Joseph Elias, "Israel Salanter," in Leo Jung, ed., *Jewish Leaders* (Jerusalem: Boys Town, 1953), pp. 203, 208.

39. Interview, 2 March 1989.

40. See the comment by a Jewish settler in the film "This Land Is Our Land," episode 2 in the series *The Glory and the Power,* Quest Productions.

41. See how Mottahedeh takes up the subject and delineates the ambivalence about television and radio among the believers (*Mantle of the Prophet,* p. 343).

42. Ibid., p. 351.

43. Khuri, *Imams and Emirs,* p. 183.

44. I do not mean to suggest that women get no religious learning. Theirs, however, is a concentrated elementary education. Cf. Rahman, *Islam,* p. 181.

45. In one well-known case the Russian government tried to force the Volozhin yeshiva to teach Russian language to its students. In an Islamic case, Mottahedeh describes the Tehranian efforts to revise curriculum (*Mantle of the Prophet,* p. 236).

46. Sachedina, "Active Shi'ism," p. 403.

47. Khuri, *Imans and Emirs,* p. 31.

48. Bernard Lewis, *The Political Language of Islam* (Chicago: University of Chicago Press, 1988), p. 118 n. 3.

49. Sivan, *Radical Islam,* p. x.

50. Ibid., p. 69.

51. Munson, *Islam and Revolution,* p. 29.

52. Lewis, *Political Language of Islam,* p. 3.

53. Mottahedeh, *Mantle of the Prophet,* p. 198. See also Samuel C. Heilman and Steven M. Cohen, *Cosmopolitans and Parochials: Modern Orthodox Jews in America* (Chicago: University of Chicago Press, 1989), pp. 83–87.

54. Munson, *Islam and Revolution,* p. 34.

55. Mottahedeh, *Mantle of the Prophet,* pp. 210, 367.

56. Elya Svei, "Torah: A Source for Guidance in Every Phase of Jewish Activity," *Jewish Observer,* February 1982, p. 7.

57. The Maharal of Prague, quoted in Piekarz, *Ideological Trends,* p. 84.

58. Avraham Mordecai Alter, *Collected Letters,* pp. 51–52, cited in Piekarz, *Ideological Trends,* p. 109.

59. Khuri, *Imams and Emirs,* p. 18.

60. Cf. ibid., p. 20.

61. Sachedina, "Active Shi'ism," p. 424.

62. Munson, *Islam and Revolution,* p. 35.

63. Sachedina, "Active Shi'ism," p. 33.

64. Mottahedeh, *Mantle of the Prophet,* p. 233.

65. Ibid.

66. Said Amir Arjomand, *The Turban for the Crown* (New York: Oxford University Press, 1988), pp. 156–57.

67. Khuri, *Imams and Emirs,* p. 124.

68. Hayim Soloveitchik, "Migration, Acculturation, and the New Role of Texts," in Marty and Appleby, *Accounting for Fundamentalisms,* p. 199.

69. Ibid., p. 200.

70. Sivan, *Radical Islam,* p. 112.

71. Rahman, *Islam,* p. 185.

72. Munson, *Islam and Revolution,* p. 13.

73. Heilman, *Defenders of the Faith,* pp. 246–48.

74. Soloveitchik, "Migration, Acculturation, and the New Role of Texts," pp. 209–11; Mottahedeh, *Mantle of the Prophet,* p. 188.

75. Shoshana Gabbay, "Matan: A Personal Note," *Matan Women's Institute for Torah Studies News,* 1990–91, p. 2. The yeshiva for women is a very recent development and its character only approximates the male's institution (see note 44 above).

76. Aran, "Jewish Zionist Fundamentalism," p. 333.

77. Aviezer Ravitzky, "Exile in the Holy Land: The Dilemma of Haredi Jewry," in P. Medding, ed., *Studies in Contemporary Jewry Annual V* (New York: Oxford University Press, 1989), p. 91.

78. See Aran, "Jewish Zionist Fundamentalism"; and Don-Yehiya, "Book and the Sword."

79. See Ravitzky, "Exile in the Holy Land," p. 101.

80. See Don-Yehiya, "Book and the Sword."

81. Katzover, "Not to Institutionalize Too Much," p. 34.

82. *Jewish Week,* 30 July 1992, p. 8.

83. Sivan describes very similar notions in certain Islamic views. Reading Muhammad al-Bahi in *The Future of Islam and the Fifteenth Century Λ.H.,* he finds a view that "nationalism (be it Arab or Persian) loosens religious solidarity and virtually replaces it," an attitude that gave many of the radicals an antinationalist tilt at the outset of their revival (*Radical Islam,* p. 2).

84. See Mottahedeh, *Mantle of the Prophet,* pp. 296–99; and Sachedina, "Activist Shi'ism," p. 405.

85. Sachedina, "Activist Shi'ism," p. 405.

86. Quoted in Sivan, *Radical Islam,* p. 70.

87. Sachedina, "Activist Shi'ism," p. 406.

88. Khuri, *Imams and Emirs,* p. 33. The bracketed translations are from Rahman, *Islam,* p. 1.

89. Khuri, *Imams and Emirs,* p. 33.

90. See Mottahedeh, *Mantle of the Prophet,* esp. pp. 343–54 passim; and Samuel C. Heilman, *The People of the Book* (Chicago: University of Chicago Press, 1983).

91. See Heilman, *People of the Book,* pp. 202–36, and Arjomand, *The Turban for the Crown,* p. 92.

92. See Heilman, *Defenders of the Faith,* pp. 168–69.

93. Rahman, *Islam,* p. 191.

94. Mottahedeh, *Mantle of the Prophet,* p. 136. See also Samuel C. Heilman, *The Gate behind the Wall* (New York: Penguin Books, 1984), pp. 51–52.

95. Jean-Marie Guyau, *The Non-religion of the Future* (1897; New York: Schocken, 1962), p. 98.

96. Rahman, *Islam,* p. 5. See also pp. 185–86.

97. Ibid., p. 186.

98. Roy Mottahedeh, personal communication.

99. See Heilman, *People of the Book.*

100. Although this phrase comes from Rahman (*Islam,* p. 186) and is meant to describe what happened in the madrasas of the tenth and eleventh centuries, it just as well describes the contemporary bes medrash in the yeshiva world.

101. Ibid., p. 186.

102. Ibid., p. 251.

103. See Heilman, *Defenders of the Faith,* pp. 260–76.

104. See Sivan, *Radical Islam,* p. 60.

Mapping Indic Fundamentalisms through Nationalism and Modernity

Harjot Oberoi

We have to look again at the nature of modernity itself which, for certain
fairly specific reasons, has been poorly grasped in the social sciences hitherto. Rather than entering a period of post-modernity, we are moving into one in which the consequences of modernity are becoming
more radicalised and universalised than before.

Anthony Giddens, The Consequences of Modernity

But now the Hindus are waking up. They are becoming acutely conscious
of how they have been cheated by their own political leaders of their
rightful place in the national life of the country, and of all the tragedies
that have overtaken their society, their culture and their motherland because of the suicidal denial of the genuine spirit of nationalism of Hindus
than by their leaders. They have, more than all, come to realise that it is
high time they close up their ranks, do away with all their internal weakness and stand up as one single, solid, social entity determined to assert
their legitimate rights and uphold their historic national role.

H. V. Seshadri, Hindu Renaissance under Way

Scholars interested in comparing fundamen-
talistlike movements have largely concentrated on Abrahamic religions.[1] Given the
general association of fundamentalism with scriptural inerrancy, some comparisons
have been restricted to religions that affirm the identity of their constituents in relationship to a revealed text. Religions that are devoid of such texts, like Buddhism,
therefore find no place within established frameworks for the comparative study of
fundamentalism. In this essay I move beyond what may be described as Semitic-centric
narratives of fundamentalism by examining two religious traditions indigenous to India: Hinduism and Sikhism. Much like the Abrahamic religions, the two share a great
deal in imagination and doctrines, but starting at the turn of the century many prominent Sikh leaders refused to acknowledge any commonalities. They began to view
Hinduism with great suspicion, insisting that Sikh notions of self, God, and society
have always been distinctive and find no correspondence within Hinduism.[2] The resulting controversies and passions have generated many of the "structures of experience" (Raymond William's phrase) that will in part be of concern in this study. It is
somewhat ironic that, despite the professed differences, many of the Sikh activists have

once again ended up sharing a great deal with Hinduism; I am referring here to how many within the Sikh leadership, much like Hindu militants, presently articulate their personal and collective identities through the modern discourse of fundamentalism. This perception would not be shared by the two communities; their leadership constantly reminds us that what they are battling for has nothing to do with fundamentalism; they seek to establish the rights of Sikh and Hindu nationalism. In the former case they do so, they say, by establishing an independent nation-state called Khalistan; in the latter by making Hindutva the cementing ideology for the highly fragmented Indian society and polity.

Thus it is not surprising that Hew McLeod is of the view that the category fundamentalism does not fit the Sikh case, and similarly Ainslie Embree argues that the main object of the Rashtriya Svayamsevak Sangh (RSS) is to define the *modern* Hindu nation.[3] Peter van der Veer concurs when he states that what we have here, particularly in the case of Vishwa Hindu Parishad (VHP), is not a revolt against modernity but in fact an expression of modernity.[4]

Clearly, we have the making of an interesting theoretical problem here, for if we are going to argue that the counterdiscourse that is at present being formulated in Amritsar and Benares is best understood as part of global fundamentalism—and that is explicitly the position I take—then the precise role of the categories nationalism and modernity must be clarified, especially as applied to organizations like the Damdami Taksal (DT), Bharatiya Janata Party (BJP), RSS, and VHP. While there may be much that overlaps across modernity, nationalism, and fundamentalism, all three are powerful cultural answers to certain human predicaments. For the purpose at hand, however, we cannot simultaneously deploy these concepts as if they described one and the same thing. Epistemology, as much as history, requires that we distinguish among them and see which category best helps deal with the cultural materials currently being generated in India. This is no simple task, for like many other key concepts in the human sciences there are no standard definitions of modernity. Consequently, I will review the writings of a major theorist of modernity (not to be mistaken with developmental modernization, a material manifestation of modernity, by now widely established all over the world) and see how best the Sikh and Hindu data relate to his framework. First, I provide an ethnography of Indic fundamentalisms, as a point of entry for the conceptual debate that follows.

Ethnographies: Two Nationalisms

In the spring of 1984 Jarnail Singh Bhindranwale, the leader of the Sikh fundamentalist forces, moved into the Golden Temple at Amritsar, the holiest of the Sikh shrines. He turned a part of the temple, known as the Akal Takht, into his personal residence. All Sikh devotees, however holy or eminent, were barred from doing this. But no one within the Sikh political leadership dared challenge what Bhindranwale had done. Every morning Bhindranwale would address thousands of Sikh pilgrims. In the afternoon he would hold court, settling conflicts ranging from marital discord to land disputes.

There was nothing that he could not fix, or so his admirers proclaimed. It was almost as if the civil administration of the Indian province of Punjab was being carried out of the Golden Temple by fiat of a religious coterie.[5] Bands of young men would be commissioned to kill anyone—administrators, academics, journalists—thought to be violating the orders of Bhindranwale or criticizing his mission.

With the writ of the state running at an all time low, many of Bhindranwale's men began to fortify the temple. Under the supervision of a cashiered general from the Indian army they smuggled in huge quantities of arms, sandbagged entrances to the shrine, and posted young marksmen around the perimeter of the temple complex. It is hard to say if they were doing all this to proclaim their new status of running a state within a state or because they thought an attack was imminent. Whatever the rationale, they were soon compelled to put their fortifications and weapons to use. On the evening of 2 June 1984, the late Indira Gandhi, then prime minister, announced on the radio and the television that Punjab was being placed under army control. The entire province was put under curfew for three days, and the Indian army launched a massive assault, code-named Operation Blue Star, against Bhindranwale and his followers in the Golden Temple. What happened in that battle from the night of 3 June till the morning of 7 June will always remain a matter of debate among historians. In the end, however, Bhindranwale was killed, the Akal Takht tower that he had turned into his residence was reduced to rubble, and over two thousand people were killed in the Punjab by the time the army operation was completed.[6]

Soon after Operation Blue Star was over, followers of Bhindranwale posed the question, Why was the holiest of the Sikh shrines invaded by the Indian army? They answered, Because India is ruled by chauvinistic Hindus who are bent on destroying the Sikh minority and its culture. In this discourse Delhi becomes an imperial capital and the Gandhis an imperial dynasty. This kind of reasoning reveals a great deal about the cultural logic of Sikh activists. In their eyes the primary building block of Indian society is the religious community. Categories like class, caste, regional identities do not enter their discourse. Religion is viewed as the natural classification for the people of India; all other taxonomies are discarded as worthless. Therefore any conflict that arises in society is bound to be religious in nature, and it is in the order of things, that Hindus seek to establish their hegemony over all other religious communities in India. The demise of Buddhism in India is often cited in support of this reasoning. It is argued that, although Buddhism originated in India, it did not continue to flourish on the subcontinent because of Hindu intolerance and persecution. Sikhs are constantly warned that if they do not fight for their identity and culture they will end up sharing the fate of Buddhism. Thus for many Sikhs their present struggle is a nationalist movement, one that they hope will eventually translate into a sovereign nation-state of their own. As Ganga Singh Dhillon puts it: "We are not just looking for a piece of land. We are looking for a territory where Sikhs can protect their women and children. Where a Sikh can become a master of his own destiny—where our religious shrines are not allowed to be run over by army tanks. You can call it an independent Punjab, a sovereign state, or Khalistan. What we are asking for is a homeland for the Sikh nation."[7]

In this statement of Dhillon and others that may be culled from documents re-leased by the present Sikh leadership there is little talk of inerrancy of scriptures, Mani-chaeanism, subordination of women, millenarianism, or many other elements associ-ated with global fundamentalism. Instead what we hear is the violation of human and cultural rights, the exploitation of natural resources by outsiders, and the rights of a people to be a master of their own land. These are familiar themes in the his-tory of nationalist rhetoric and the making of the modern nation-states. Thus it could be protested that reference to the Sikh struggle as fundamentalist is a ploy to rob it of legitimacy; more fitting terms are freedom struggle, war of independence, or ethnonationalism.[8]

Much like the episode of Sikh resistance, Hindu grievances too have taken shape around a place of worship. The shrine located in the north Indian city of Ayodhya is a mosque that some historians date to the sixteenth century and others to an earlier period; either way the VHP-BJP-RSS and the Bajranj Dal support the claim that the site of the mosque is the exact spot where the Hindu god Ram was born, and, in commemoration of his birth, a temple called Ramjanambhoomi was constructed at the site.[9] This temple and many other places associated with Ram fell into disuse until a Hindu ruler named Vikramaditya in the fifth century C.E., following a divine revela-tion, ordered the reconstruction of 360 temples at Ayodhya, the most important among them the Ramjanambhoomi temple. In March 1528 Babur, the founder of the Mughal dynasty, came to Ayodhya and ordered the Hindu temple demolished, and in its place a mosque was constructed. That came to be known as the Babri Masjid, taking its name from the Mughal ruler. Although almost everything in this story is open to question—the historicity of Ram, the massive temple construction undertaken by Vikramaditya, Babur's coming to Ayodhya—by the mid–nineteenth century what were essentially mythical narratives took on for many the contours of historical fact.

For Hindu fundamentalists the facts were that Ram was born in Ayodhya and the Muslim invaders had despoiled the site of his birth by constructing a mosque atop it. The Muslims deny this and claim that the mosque has always been a place of worship for members of their community living in the city of Ayodhya. What for a hundred years was essentially a local contestation over facts and dispute over proprietorship began to take on an all-India focus in 1985 when the VHP announced its intention to have Hindus conduct regular *puja* (worship) in the mosque. This was quickly achieved by February 1986, and the next demand of the VHP was to replace the mosque with a temple. To rally public support for their cause, L. K. Advani, then president of the BJP, on 25 September 1990 launched his famous *rath yatra* (pilgrimage on a chariot), from Somnath in the province of Gujarat to Ayodhya in the state of Uttar Pradesh, covering a distance of ten thousand kilometers. His arrival in Ayodhya on 30 October was to coincide with launching the construction of the proposed Ramjanambhoomi temple.

Before the party president could finish his much publicized pilgrimage, the Bihar state government had him arrested, and in Uttar Pradesh Hindu activists, named *kar sevaks* by the VHP, were banned from travel to Ayodhya. Despite massive administra-tive efforts to prevent kar sevaks from congregating at Ayodhya, tens of thousands of them made a determined bid on 30 October to reach the grounds of the disputed shrine; in the ensuing melee the security forces started firing at the crowd, leaving twelve dead and thousands injured. When the kar sevaks made a second bid on 3 November to storm the mosque, eighteen more were killed by police firing. Although Advani in his rath yatra failed to achieve his mission of razing the mosque, his widely publicized chariot procession earned his party massive political mileage. In the 1991 general elections the strength of the BJP in the federal parliament went up from a mere 2 members in 1984 to 119 (the party received 23.4 percent of the national vote). Advani became the official leader of the national opposition, and his party came to rule in four of the country's twenty-five states, including Uttar Pradesh, the site of the Ayodhya dispute. Emboldened by the political success of the BJP, party pundits got ready for a final showdown. In their eyes Hindu organizations now had a public mandate to dismantle the Babri Masjid. On the morning of 6 December 1992, over 200,000 Hindus descended on the tiny city of Ayodhya and in less than five hours tore down the over-four-hundred-year-old mosque.

Just as Operation Blue Star earlier gave Sikh activists a chance to challenge all that the postcolonial India state stood for, similarly the Ayodhya agitation, the rath yatra, and the demolition of the Babri Masjid gave Hindu leadership an opportunity to powerfully express their distaste for modern India as constituted by the country's political elites in the postcolonial period. The government rejection of the plan to turn the mosque into a temple became a clear demonstration in their eyes of the fact that there is no place for real Hindus in India. The country is perceived to be ruled by an anglicized elite that has come to disown its own heritage and religion and has taken up the cause of secularism. Harboring a deep sense of betrayal by national leadership, a Hindu intellectual writes:

> My temples have been desecrated, destroyed. Their sacred stones are being trampled under the aggressor's feet. My gods are crying. They are demanding of me for reinstatement in all their original glory. When I speak out my agony, you of the secular tribe condemn me as a threat to our "secular peace." You add insult to my injury. You rub salt into my wounded heart, and still expect me to keep my mouth shut? . . . Anything objected to by the "minorities" as Hindu becomes a cause of intense concern for you. Even the breaking of a coconut or lighting a lamp is taboo. For you, our national life minus every bit of Hindu is secularism. In short, you want me to cease to be myself. . . . Sometimes, I really pity you for your diseased mind. Can you not see the simple glaring fact that I form 85% of this land? And that I have shed my blood and sweat for making this country free? And still you expect that I should continue to be deprived of rights which those who sided with the foreigner and bisected my motherland [the reference here is to the Muslims in the subcontinent] enjoy with impunity? That I should not be permitted to teach my children love for my culture and spiritual heritage; that I should stop speaking of my ancestral heroes? While at the same time elements inimical to all that I hold sacred have a field day in their schools! Do you not see a shocking discrimination in all this? [10]

In the rhetoric of Hindu organizations like the VHP-BJP-RSS and Bajranj Dal, they are fighting for Hindu nationalism, the only authentic form of nationalism possible for India, for all its other local manifestations are tainted by association with secularism and cater to the interests of religious minorities like the Muslims. H. V. Seshadri, the general secretary of the RSS and a leading party ideologue, argues: "For the first time in our post-Independence history, there is a clear-cut polarisation of two forces: one, of the pristine nationalism of the soil and the other, a combination of the pseudo-secularists, fanatic communalists, and splitters of the country's unity and subverters of national identity. Such a polarisation was long overdue and is verily a boon in disguise."[11] In the battle for Hindu nationalism, the mosque complex in Ayodhya was seen as a sign of "Hindu slavery," and tearing it down is viewed as a sign of freedom.[12]

Neither the Sikh nor the Hindu activists admit that they are leading fundamentalist movements. Each claims to represent the true forces of nationalism, and in their public discourse they incessantly speak of injustice, betrayal, exploitation, alterity, territory, cultural heroes, and the inherent rights of a people, themes that have for long been considered part and parcel of nationalism. In a discussion of India's indigenous religions, however, we must go beyond the nationalistic rhetoric of their leaders if we are to characterize the movements they are presently leading. In so doing we must state where they stand in relationship to what Habermas succinctly calls the "project of modernity."[13] In other words nationalism versus fundamentalism is not the real issue. By Ben Anderson's minimalist definition of nationalism as an imagined community, the contemporary struggles of the Sikhs and Hindus could be labeled nationalistic, with one critical reservation.[14] Historically, nationalism in its pure variety, the kind that was spawned in nineteenth-century Europe and over time picked up by the Asian-African liberation movements, generally sought to transcend all parochial identities, like those of religion, region, sect, or tribe, for only by doing so could it forge the new nation-states and promise entitlements based on equal citizenship. Today when Sikh and Hindu leaders speak of their respective nationalisms, they are not interested in pursuing the ideals of a secular nationalism in its pure form; for them the choicest prize in their war against the secular Indian nation-state is a citizenship that is rooted in religious loyalty to Hinduism or Sikhism. Social and cultural entitlements, those often described as fundamental rights of citizenship, will accrue, under Khalistan or Hindutva, to only those who by virtue of their religion are either Sikhs or Hindus; this would be a natural consequence of a nationalism that is defined on the basis of religious affiliation.

Fundamentalism and the "Project of Modernity"

The first major thinker to grapple with the problematic of modernity was Hegel. Historically, he located modernity in the early eighteenth century and saw it as a culmination of the Reformation, the Enlightenment, and the French Revolution. The Reformation established the autonomy of the subject; the Enlightenment freed man from the terror of nature; and the French Revolution gave people rights and morality that were not derived from God but instead from civil society. Philosophically too, modernity for Hegel marked a radical departure from earlier epochs in not having to seek legitimacy from the past but instead establishing its own modes of validity. Based on his historical and philosophical deliberations Hegel proposed four features that characterize modernity: (1) individualism: each person is entitled to his own subjective freedom; (2) the right to criticism: nothing need be taken for granted; (3) autonomy of action: an individual is responsible for his own actions; and (4) philosophy of reflection: the subject can know himself without having to rely on explanations grounded in religion.[15] How do these Hegelian propositions relate to what I am calling Indic fundamentalisms?

Prior to addressing this question, we must consider a preliminary one: Why must Sikh and Hindu social movements be measured according to a Western (Hegelian) paradigm of modernity? After all, both of these religious traditions during their long history have fostered rich cultural resources that grapple at great length with questions of philosophical reflection, the role of the individual in society, the idea of dissent, and so on. Would it not be more appropriate to judge what the Sikhs and Hindus are doing according to their own respective normative traditions, rather than turn to an exogenous construct, particularly given the view that modernity is very much a Western outgrowth? The British social philosopher Anthony Giddens argues that modernity is the result of two institutional clusters—the nation-state and systematic capitalist production—and since both of these are rooted in European geography and history, modernity is "distinctively a western project."[16]

The use of modernity as a heuristic device to evaluate Indic fundamentalisms may be defended on the following grounds. Existing scholarship on Sikh and Hindu religious movements argues persuasively that these movements are expressions of modernity. This claim requires that we understand what is entailed by modernity and how it relates to contemporary events in India. If we apply the category *nationalism,* another Western derivation, to Indian religious movements, intellectual consistency requires that we do not flinch from exploring modernity as well. Most telling, perhaps, is that neither Sikh nor Hindu fundamentalist leaders have proposed any major alternatives to modernity as the paradigm of development. They are deeply troubled by modernity and express profound opposition to aspects of it, but in their everyday lives they rely heavily on its institutional and material manifestations, such as the nation-state and telecommunications, to take two examples.

Hegel's first postulate—individualism—is rejected by both Sikh and Hindu fundamentalists. Individualism in their eyes is a disease from which people require protection. The West has already suffered its debilitating consequences; the people of South Asia need not become its next victims. How are Sikhs and Hindus to save themselves from history repeating itself in their case? The answer is fairly simple: societies must be constituted on the basis of religious community. There ought to be neither singular identities nor idiosyncratic quests for a personal meaning; all individuals must belong to a religious collectivity, and their everyday lives must be governed by the normative traditions of such collectivities. In a tract entitled *Be Proud You Are a Hindu,* G. M. Jagtiani writes: "Hinduism should not divide one Hindu from the other Hindu. It should bind one Hindu with another Hindu."[17] Such thinking is most clearly revealed in the political history of the BJP. After the 1989 general elections the BJP decided to support the minority government of V. P. Singh in the Indian parliament. However, when on 7 August 1990 Singh decided to implement the Mandal commission report that sanctioned job reservations for backward castes, the BJP national executive started to make noises about withdrawing their support for the government and eventually did so in October. This action was taken because acceptance of the Mandal commission report would have implied recognition of caste as the fundamental category of social organization in Indian society, whereas the BJP and its allies have always insisted that the most salient unit of stratification for Indian society is the religious community.

This is why Hindu leadership today constantly intones the corporate ideology of Hindutva, while their counterparts among the Sikhs extol an overarching Panth. So expansive is the idea of Hindutva as first expounded by V. D. Savarkar in 1923 and now vigorously advanced by the BJP and the RSS, that it even encapsulates all religions indigenous to India. Much as individuality is negated within Hindu fundamentalism, similarly its expression is denied within Indian religions. Sikhism, Jainism, and Buddhism are seen to have no separate identity; they are lumped together with Hinduism. Rajendra Singh, general secretary of the RSS, recently stated: "Our society should be homogeneous. Let India be a Hindu commonwealth."[18] Similarly among the Sikhs the idea of the Panth allows for no ethnic or sectarian differences. Every Sikh must belong to the homogeneous community, and all differences, particularly those grounded in individual aspirations, are viewed as enfeebling and dangerous. Thus individuality, the first element in the Hegelian definition of modernity, has no place within the discourse of Sikh and Hindu fundamentalists. To admit such a possibility could potentially undermine their entire project.

The second of Hegel's postulates for modernity, the right to criticism, finds no recognition within the ranks of Sikh and Hindu activists. All those who produce critical knowledge (taking nothing for granted), particularly in the domain of history, religious studies, literature, and journalism, are suspect; and it is not uncommon for them to be subjected to harassment, censorship, and even assassination.

Let me illustrate this with several examples. My first case, popularly known as the textbook controversy, goes back to May 1977 when the Jan Sangh (an earlier incarnation of the BJP) was a major constituent of the multiparty Janata government in New Delhi.[19] Within months of taking over the reins of power, party stalwarts supported an initiative to proscribe four history textbooks used in schools across India. The books at stake were *Ancient India* (1977) by R. S. Sharma, *Medieval India* (1967) by Romila Thapar, *Modern India* (1970) by Bipan Chandra, and *Freedom Struggle* (1972) by Amales Tripathi, Barun De, and Bipan Chandra. These authors are India's leading historians. They had been commissioned to write these textbooks by bodies (National Council for Educational Research and Training and National Book Trust) associated with the education ministry, but now the same ministry was told by the prime minister's office that their works were "biased" and conveyed "a prejudiced view of Indian history."[20] At stake was the representation of some of the most important themes in Indian historiography: the nature of Hindu beliefs, the beginnings of

Muslim expansion in India, the religious perceptions of the leadership that led the Indian struggle for freedom. For the Jan Sangh lobby the only legitimate answers to these issues were those given by the party or historians it favored. Unwilling to accept alternative readings of the Indian past, particularly when these were enunciated within a secular framework, the party launched a concerted campaign to discredit the books, and their authors were subjected to personal harassment. For instance, in October 1977 R. S. Sharma was denied a passport to travel overseas. Given constitutional guarantees for freedom of expression, it would have been hard to ban these books outright. All that could be done immediately was to make their publication and distribution difficult. In July 1978 the Central Board of Secondary Education withdrew Sharma's book from the syllabus of class XI in the 1,100 board-affiliated schools. It is highly likely that the attacks against these books would have continued but for the Jan Sangh–dominated government's losing power in 1980.

Writing critical history is of course only one mode of dissent. There are many other arenas in modern societies where individuals seek to test the liberties given them by those they live among. Perhaps the most privileged of these contestary zones today is literature. This is as much realized by those who produce literature as those who seek to restrict them. In 1988 Vibhuti Narain Rai published a Hindi novel entitled *Shar mein curfew* (Curfew in the city). Its theme was a 1980 Hindu-Muslim riot in the city of Allahabad, and Rai wrote freely about how religious prejudice in the Hindu-dominated police force and provincial administration led to Muslim citizens' being viewed as enemies and thus becoming easy targets of brutality and murder. The VHP readily took offense and denounced the novel for being "anti-Hindu." It now wants a ban imposed on the novel, and when Ashok Singhal, secretary general of the VHP, was told of a producer wanting to turn the story into a film, he threatened to burn down theaters that dared to screen the planned film. All this ire surrounds a project that has still not begun and a work of fiction that at no point directly criticizes any Hindu organization. It is worthwhile to quote here from a recent interview given by the author: "The intolerance of dissent is increasing in our society and the Ayodhya mobilisation has largely contributed to this disturbing trend. The attacks on inconvenient writers and dissenting journalists are in fact motivated by a desire to silence all criticism and all reason, thereby making the very existence of rationally-thinking people redundant to the social and political process. This is extremely distressing."[21]

My third example comes from the Sikh movement. The most important Sikh literary magazine in the Punjab for several decades has been the *Preet Larhi*. Its founding editor was Gurbaksh Singh, who in his lifetime did much to develop modern Punjabi prose and brought his readers into close contact with world literary trends. Outside the Sikh holy city of Amritsar he founded a writers' colony and launched many experimental projects. On his death in 1977, the editorship of the journal passed first to his eldest son, Navtej Singh, and later to his son Sumeet Singh. The rise of Sikh fundamentalism in the early 1980s became a subject of discussion in *Preet Larhi*. Critical reviews were not favorably received by some; on 22 February 1984, Sumeet Singh was gunned down by a squad of hit men in Amritsar.

The three cases are primarily concerned with the fields of history, literature, and journalism; while they serve as good illustrations of how Indic fundamentalist movements seek to cope with critical knowledge, no study of such movements can be complete without examining how their constituents handle the study of scriptural materials. In classic definitions of fundamentalism that register the experience of American Protestantism at the turn of the century, inerrancy of scriptures and a literalist interpretation of sacred texts has for long been taken to be a hallmark of a fundamentalist worldview. Since scriptures are a divine revelation, they are infallible, and any human effort to historicize or provide a hermeneutic understanding of such texts is therefore immediately scoffed at and often denounced as blasphemous.

An ideal illustration of this theme is provided by the reception of a doctoral dissertation by Pashaura Singh, entitled "The Text and Meaning of the Adi Granth" (1991). Before registering as a graduate student at the University of Toronto in 1987, Pashaura Singh was the *granthi* (literally a reader of the book; functionally a ritual officiant of a Sikh shrine) of a Sikh shrine in Calgary; at present he is professor of Sikhism at the University of Michigan, Ann Arbor. Trained in the Punjab as a traditional religious scholar and ritualist, he was able to make a successful transition to the methods of modern textual scholarship. In his thesis he argues that the key Sikh scripture, the Adi Granth (popularly known as the Granth Sahib), resulted from a long historical process that started with the writings of Guru Nanak, the founder of the Sikh tradition, and culminated with the poetry of Guru Arjan, the fifth Sikh master. In order to substantiate his hypothesis, Pashaura Singh rigorously examined manuscripts predating the final text of the Adi Granth, which was completed under the editorial guidance of Guru Arjan in 1604 C.E. His findings are simple and straightforward: the Sikh scripture is the product of a complex human endeavor, and the proof of this is available in heavily edited extant manuscripts that show how verse and content within the Sikh scripture shifted before it was finally canonized. In addition, Pashaura Singh states that the evolution and the content of the scripture was shaped by the constituency of the early Sikh movement and the contemporary sociopolitical environment.

Pashaura Singh did not have to go through the laborious process of revising, polishing, and publishing his dissertation to receive reviews of his work. One of the first to respond was the Chandigarh-based Sikh scholar Gurtej Singh.[22] Writing in the Punjabi daily *Ajit,* he suggested that Western scholars were conspiring to destroy Sikhism and that Pashaura Singh was part of that conspiracy.[23] He recommended that Pashaura Singh be hauled before the Shiromani Gurdwara Prabandhak Committee (SGPC), a Sikh religious body based in Amritsar, and that Sikh leaders award him punishment for suggesting that the Adi Granth is the result of human effort rather than divine revelation. Others in the Punjab and outside soon brought forth further charges.

Sikhism is a revealed religion. The spiritual and religious truths which Guru Nanak preached had been revealed to him "through a direct encounter with God at some level of consciousness" and he preached what he had been told and taught by God himself. He conveyed only those words to the world which God had wished him to give forth as his divine message. . . . As is well known to the students of comparative religion, contents of a revealed religion are conveyed to the people by the Supreme Being through His special messengers either by calling them to his presence, as in the cases [*sic*] of Moses, or by communicating His messages to them, as in the case of Prophet Muhammad. As regards Sikhism, God is stated to have been pleased to use direct ways to convey his words, Laws and Commandments to its founder. . . . The thought contained in the Sri Guru Granth Sahib is not the product of the environment, nor were the Gurus compelled by the circumstances, the conditions of that period to say whatever they said. There was nothing new in the environment to bring about the revolutionary changes in thought made by Guru Nanak. Revelation can never be the product of the circumstances or environment. It is the direct experience of the Truth. The Sikh thought produced history, it is not the product of history. Thought which has the capacity to transform man, to change the circumstances, cannot be the product of environment. The argument and evidence in support of alleged changes in Mulmantar [literally root formula; the basic theological statement of the Sikh faith] and other Shabads [divine Word] is an unholy exercise called Textual Analysis. Pashaura Singh should understand that Sikh Religion is the only religion in the world where revealed Bani [sacred utterance] has been written by a living prophet himself. If you believe in prophets, then Textual Analysis has no meaning in evaluating such revelatory thoughts.[24]

Another reviewer echoes a similar sentiment.

Nothing has been emphasized more in the Guru Granth than the revelatory and authentic character of the Bani in the Adi Granth compiled by the Guru. And nothing is more sacred than the Shabad therein and its truth. What Pashora [*sic*] Singh has repeatedly asserted, we feel, is clearly contrary to the established and recorded authenticity and revelatory and unalterable character of the Bani. We, therefore, believe that his statements are baseless and blasphemous, and need thoughtful and appropriate response from the sangats [Sikh community] and other organizations.[25]

From the vocabulary of Pashaura Singh's detractors it is clear that he has earned their ire because his work does not promise an authoritative reading, certainty, authenticity, revelation, and validation of tradition, features much admired by fundamentalists and a central part of their socioreligious program. Instead, his dissertation is based on critical rationality, rejecting the idea of revelation and literalism; it assumes human origins and subjective meanings, elements that are intrinsically associated with the project of modernity. Ernest Gellner has called this project "Enlightenment Rationalist Fundamentalism": a mode of thinking and social action that

desacralizes, disestablishes, disenchants everything substantive: *no* privileged facts, occasions, individuals, institutions or associations. In other words, no miracles, no divine interventions, and conjuring performances and press conferences, no saviours, no sacred churches or sacramental communities. All hypotheses are subject to scrutiny, all facts open to novel interpretations, and all facts subject to symmetrical laws which preclude the miraculous, the sacred occasion, the intrusion of the Other into the Mundane.[26]

All of this is unacceptable to Sikh fundamentalists, who are easily antagonized by people who apply the axioms of modernity to study Sikh religious texts. In a world constantly in flux, the fundamentalists hold tightly to a sacred text that is beyond history, rationality, and textual deconstruction; the power and mystery of a revealed text ought never to be sullied by scholarship, for it will ensure true identity and manifest destiny in this universe.

Many other instances could be added to the four cases we have examined here, but the underlying logic would remain the same: fundamentalists battle all forms of discourse that implicitly or explicitly question their assumptions and understanding of the universe. This opposition becomes greater when it is perceived that what is being contested is one of the fundamental beliefs or practices of the group. Fundamentalist ideology depends on absolute truth claims; within its framework, unlike the Hegelian paradigm of modernity, there is no scope for refutation by criticism. To do so would undermine fundamentalism.

Much like the first two propositions in Hegel's schema of modernity, the third—that an individual is responsible for his own actions—is absent from both the Hindu and the Sikh case. Given the corporate ideology of Indic fundamentalisms, this is not surprising. Autonomy of action goes hand in hand with individualism. For the BJP or the DT to admit that an individual is free to determine his own actions is to destroy both its legitimacy and constituency. In their eyes the actions of an individual are best determined by the religious community. A Sikh or Hindu on his own has no right to decide what he ought to be doing. This directive comes either directly from divine forces or organizations that are seen to represent the interests of the community. It will be instructive to relate here how the BJP and the VHP came to recognize that it was incumbent upon Hindus to free the birthplace of god Ram from the mosque at Ayodhya that has been at the center of the most serious religious conflict in India since national independence in 1947. According to their official pronouncements on the night of 23 December 1949, god Ram personally became manifest in the form of a child, indicating to the devotees, through a second coming, that the disputed mosque at Ayodhya was indeed the exact spot of his birth. The following testimony attributed to a Muslim guard, charged with the duty of protecting the Babri Masjid, is used by Hindu militants to buttress their claim that the site of the demolished mosque was the birthplace of god Ram:

My name is Abul Barkat. I am assigned for duty at the Sriram Janmabhumi (Babri Masjid), and ever since I was assigned I have regularly reported for duty. Up to the present the Hindus have undertaken no action which could be called unlawful. At roughly 2:00 AM on the night of 22–23 December [1949] when I was at my assigned post, suddenly a gleam as if of moonlight appeared in the

Babri Masjid. I looked carefully in that direction, but in the meantime it seemed to me that a mysterious divine brilliance filled the mosque. Gradually that effulgence became golden, and in the midst of it I saw the face of an extremely beautiful child of four or five years. His hair was curly, his face plump and healthy-looking; in all my life I have never seen such an adorable child. Beholding him, I went into a dream-like state, and I can't say how long I remained in that condition. When I came back to myself, I observed that the lock of the main gate was broken and lying on the ground, and a countless multitude of Hindus had entered the mosque who were worshipping some idol installed on a throne and singing, "The compassionate one became manifest." Well, I immediately sent a report of the matter to my officers. That's all I know about this.[27]

Since the mid-1980s the campaign to have the mosque demolished, involving tens of thousands of people, has been predicated on this miraculous event. The alternative explanation is that a group of Hindu activists erected images in the mosque. But the BJP and VHP are not willing to accept the second account, not just because it suggests an illegal act, but also because it would mean owning up to individual autonomy. Similarly, Jarnail Singh Bhindranwale, the most important Sikh leader in the 1980s, claimed that all he did was based on the will of God. His claims commanded considerable legitimacy because one of the key concepts in Sikh theology is the doctrine of *hukam,* or divine order. According to this principle only an individual deluded by his ego thinks he determines his own actions. Human liberation lies in recognizing the limitations of personal autonomy and following hukam; in the process, an individual may attain liberation.[28] Such theology is ideal for any enterprise wanting to claim divine sanction, a notion that has been repeatedly invoked by Sikh militants.

This brings us to Hegel's final criteria for modernity: an individual has the capacity to know himself independently of any explanations provided by religion. Both Sikh and Hindu fundamentalists would forcefully contest this assertion. A major rationale behind the powerful movements they have launched is to expand the role of religion in society instead of having it reduced or, as in this Hegelian axiom, move toward its complete denial. The lives fundamentalists find exemplary, the causes that fire their imagination, the actions they undertake, the leaders they follow, all hold a close connection with religion. They find what religion has to give them deeply meaningful.

The theoreticians of Hindu fundamentalism like to argue that secularism has badly failed India and its people; it has provided a philosophical-cultural smokescreen to cover up the misdeeds, corruption, brutality, and immorality of the country's power elites. Secularism is blamed for shattering the religious integrity of the common person, preventing him from realizing his self-dignity and true place in an independent nation. For the VHP-BJP-RSS, in order to rectify these terrible wrongs from the past, it is imperative that Hinduism be brought center stage at both the personal and the public level.

With this agenda in mind Hindu fundamentalist groupings, since the early 1980s, have underwritten a powerful campaign to rally Hindus in the name of their religion.[29] A Hindu Unity Conference (Hindu Samajotsav) was held at Shimoga in Karnataka in January 1981. The VHP held similar unity conferences all over India. In October 1981 a Virat Hindu Sammelan was convened in the capital city of Delhi; in January 1982 a Hindu Jagriti Ekta Sammelan was organized in Kanyakumari; in February 1982 a three-day Purbanchal Hindu Conference was held at Gauhati; in March 1983 a three-day Vishal Hindu Sammelan was held in Jammu. The tempo of these conferences was sustained by holding massive Hindu public meetings at Ranchi (1987), Triupati (1988), and Alandi in Maharashtra (1987).

The late Victor Turner taught that religion is all about performance; VHP leaders independently of Turner seem to have arrived at a similar conclusion. To fortify the religious convictions of Hindus they added to the religious unity conferences a repertoire of processions and highly theatrical rath yatras, namely, Jana Jagarani Abhiyans, Vishal Hindi Aikya Yatras, Etatmata Yatras, Ram Rath Yatras. "New bonds of unity," writes Neeladri Bhattacharya, are being "cemented through earth (consecrated bricks), water (Ganga-jal), fire (torch-lights), blood, and ashes of the dead."[30] The consequent stirring of religious emotion eventually led to the demolition of the Babri Masjid in December 1992.

Clearly, Hindu fundamentalists have no wish to emulate the historical trajectory of modernism that Hegel perceptively discerned; in their eyes the only possibility of a self-realization lies in the religious discourse of Hinduism. Religious texts and their interpretations loom large in their lives. A key element in the BJP's campaign for the 1991 general elections was the establishment of Ram Rajya, literally the kingdom of Ram, a concept that goes back to a Hindu religious text and is suggestive of a religious utopia. Similarly, Bhindranwale in his speeches at the Golden Temple never missed an opportunity to quote from the Sikh scriptures.

Having looked at all four of Hegel's postulates of modernity, it is quite striking that neither of our cases of Indic fundamentalism find any correspondence to them whatsoever. The data generated by real life rarely fully match social theory. But in the case of Indic fundamentalisms and the Hegelian paradigm of modernity, the divergence is so great that it cannot be accommodated even if we were to make some minor modifications to the theory, something that is often done to make paradigms more responsive to empirical detail, for it is always hard to find reality replicating abstract models.

Hegel of course was not the last word on modernity. Many thinkers after him, from a variety of perspectives, have continued to take a deep interest in the problematic of modernity. Some like Marx have welcomed it, and others following Weber have warned us of how it will end in the "iron cage" of bureaucratic rationalism; but outside their prognosis of modernity, in conceptualizing its contours they have all returned to Hegel. Habermas summarizes aptly: "Hegel inaugurated the discourse of modernity. He introduced the theme—the self-critical reassurance of modernity. He established the rules within which the theme can be varied—the dialectic of enlightenment."[31]

In conclusion, the "project of modernity" must be built into any discussion of fundamentalism. Any contemporary movement comfortable with Hegel's postulates is not purely fundamentalist. But social movements inspired by defiance of these postulates may be deserving of the label *fundamentalism,* as is the case with contemporary Hindu and Sikh religious movements.

To sharply differentiate between modernity and fundamentalism is not to deny that fundamentalists readily appropriate the products of modernity. It has been widely noted that fundamentalists are fully at home with electronics, missiles, and aircraft, among other gifts of modernity. In 1990 L. K. Advani, then president of the BJP, undertook a pilgrimage from Somnath, a city in western India, to Ayodhya, a town in northern India. He did not travel by foot as has been the custom for pilgrimage among ordinary Hindus. He traveled in a well-equipped Toyota van, but instead of recognizing his mode of transport for what it was, he and his party labeled it a *rath,* or chariot. The Sikh leader Bhindranwale was very fond of publicly displaying his Mauser pistol. But alongside this modern weapon he also always carried an arrow. This ambivalent behavior reveals something crucial about the relationship between modernity and fundamentalism, but it is rather early in the history of global fundamentalism to come up with any final conclusions on what is entailed by this ambivalence.

It may be protested that the argument presented here is too partial to the "project of modernity." For is it not modernity that engendered the unprecedented destruction of the two world wars, the horrors of Nazism, and Stalinist gulags, just to name a few of the evils of this century, not counting the human and ecological toll of modernity since its inception in eighteenth-century western Europe. In rethinking the legacy of Enlightenment, philosophers like Alasdair MacIntyre have proposed that an epistemology that does not help man discriminate between good and bad is doomed to failure from the start.[32] This, however, was not always the case. In the Aristotelian tradition virtue and its practice was at the center of social enterprise, but this ceased once Enlightenment thinking unsuccessfully sought to formulate "rational foundations for an objective morality."[33]

Plagued by the practical and philosophical ills of modernity, many in the world today have come to view the rise and spread of fundamentalism with hope that this reassertion of religion will help create a new moral community by combatting a corrosive culture where individuals are constantly lured by consumerism, promiscuity, drugs, and crime. In short, fundamentalism can instruct humanity on how to live a noble life and provide us all with a renewed moral discourse that will once again distinguish good from bad.[34] While this restorative element within fundamentalism is welcomed, its practical record, at least in India, has not been impressive.

Sikh militants in the Punjab received considerable support from the community during the 1980s because they were supposed to occupy a high moral ground, especially compared to the political leadership the Sikhs had known for much of this century. Men like Jarnail Singh Bhindranwale were admired because they spoke of establishing a new moral world where wisdom, care, compassion, piety, and justice would reign supreme. As the 1980s came to an end, a completely different picture has emerged. Behind the rhetoric of a good life is hidden a long list of activities—extortion, rape, kidnapping, robbery, murder—that have cast Sikh fundamentalist leadership in a worse image than their predecessors within the Sikh community.[35] "Perhaps the most urgent and powerful cluster of demands that we recognize as moral," writes Charles Taylor, "concern the respect for life, integrity, and well-being, even flourishing, of others. These are the ones we infringe when we kill or maim others, steal their property, strike fear into them and rob them of peace, or even refrain from helping them when they are in distress."[36] Sikh fundamentalists have not approached these ethical standards.

The moral record of Hindu organizations like the VHP-BJP-RSS may be reviewed by examining the inner workings of BJP-led state governments in the Indian provinces of Uttar Pradesh, Himachal Pradesh, Madhya Pradesh, and Rajasthan; by documenting the campaign to destroy the Babri Masjid; or by scrutinizing the public record of Hindu leaders like Ashok Singhal.

Or one might assess how radical Hindu leaders have come to view Indian Muslims, for it is by how societies recognize the rights of their diverse constituents that we begin to know their morality (when Athenian democracy excluded slaves from its citizenship, for example, it made a significant statement). India is home to approximately 100 million Muslims, making it one of the largest Muslim communities in the world. Hindu radicals, however, would alter this fact of history either by making the Muslims leave the country or by Hinduizing this vast population. One of the most outspoken exponents of this view is the thirty-year-old *sanyasin* (renunciant) Sadhavi Rithambra, a member of VHP's Marg Darshak Mandal (the central committee). Today she is a household name in India and audiocassettes of her fiery speeches sell by the thousands. She makes her case against the Muslims by using allusions, metaphors, and stories that end up constructing fantasies of Hindu persecution at the hand of the Muslim Other. Only by avenging these imagined historic wrongs can her Hindu audience affirm its religious identity, a line of thought that easily ends up legitimizing all violence against Muslims. Her thinking is exemplified in this quotation from one of her speeches.

My Hindu brothers! Stop shouting that slogan, "Give one more push and break the Babri mosque! The mosque is broken, the mosque is broken!" What mosque are you talking about? We are going to build our temple there, not break anyone's mosque. Our civilization has never been one of destruction. Intellectuals and scholars of the world, wherever you find ruins, wherever you come upon broken monuments, you will find the signature of Islam. Wherever you find creation, you find the signature of the Hindu. We have never believed in breaking but in construction. We have always been ruled by the maxim "The world is one family." We are not pulling down a monument, we are building one. Wherever I go, I say, "Muslims live and prosper among us. Live like milk and sugar. If two kilos of sugar are dissolved in a quintal of milk, the milk becomes sweet. But what can be done if our Muslim brother is not behaving like sugar in the milk? Is it our fault if he seems bent upon being a lemon in the milk? He wants milk to curdle. He is behaving like a lemon in the milk by following people like Shahabuddin and Abdullah Bukhari. I say to him come to your sense. The value of milk increases after it becomes sour. It becomes cheese. But the world knows the fate of the lemon. It is cut, squeezed dry and then thrown on a garbage heap. Now you will have to decide whether you will act like sugar or lemon in the milk. Live amongst us like the son of a human being and we will respectfully call you uncle. But if you want to behave like the son of Babar [the founder of the Mughal dynasty in India] then the Hindu youth will deal with you as Rana Pratap and Chatarpati Shivaji [Hindu cultural heroes who in popular imagination fought against Muslim persecution] dealt with your forefathers." Those who say that we are against the Muslims, lie. We are talking about the birthplace of Ram, not constructing at Mecca or Medina. It is our birthright to build a temple to our Lord at the spot he was born.[37]

In speaking her mind Sadhavi Rithambra clarifies the stance of Hindu fundamentalism on an issue of critical importance for the present discussion: the Muslim citizen can live in the country only by accepting the hegemony of Hinduism, and even when Hindus destroy (for instance, a mosque) they should be seen as engaged in an act of creation. Here the oppressor becomes the liberator; the Muslims are being helped in their cause with a Hindu shrine replacing the mosque, otherwise Muslims will be like squeezed lemons on a garbage heap. It is perhaps not surprising that such rhetoric eventually led not only to the destruction of the over-four-hundred-year-old Babri Masjid in December 1992, but also to some of the bloodiest pogroms against India's Muslims since independence.

These failings of Indic fundamentalism, the terrorism of Sikh militants, and the practice of Hindu radicals baiting their fellow Muslim citizens, do not absolve the "project of modernity" from its sins mentioned earlier, but they do serve as a powerful reminder to all those who see in the rise of Indic fundamentalism the dawn of a new age.

Notes

1. Bruce B. Lawrence, *Defenders of God* (San Francisco: Harper and Row, 1989). See also Martin E. Marty and R. Scott Appleby, *The Glory and the Power* (Boston: Beacon Press, 1992).

2. For background, see Harjot Oberoi, "From Ritual to Counter-ritual: Rethinking the Hindu-Sikh Question, 1884–1915," in Joseph T. O'Connell et al., eds., *Sikh Religion and History in the Twentieth Century* (Toronto: Centre for South Asian Studies, University of Toronto), pp. 136–158; and Kenneth W. Jones, *Arya Dharam Hindu Consciousness in Nineteenth-Century Punjab* (Delhi: Manohar, 1976).

3. See W. H. McLeod, "The Meaning of Sikh Fundamentalism and Its Origins," paper presented at the Fundamentalism Proj-

ect Conference, 1990; Ainslie Embree, "The Function of the Rashtriya Swayamsevak Sangh: To Define the Hindu Nation," in Martin E. Marty and R. Scott Appleby, eds., *Accounting for Fundamentalisms* (Chicago: University of Chicago Press, 1993).

4. Peter van der Veer, "Hindu 'Nationalism' and the Discourse of 'Modernity': The Vishva Hindu Parishad," in Marty and Appleby, *Accounting for Fundamentalisms*.

5. For Bhindranwale's rise to power, see T. N. Madan, "The Double-Edged Sword: Fundamentalism and the Sikh Religious Tradition," in Martin E. Marty and R. Scott Appleby, eds., *Fundamentalisms Observed* (Chicago: University of Chicago Press, 1991), pp. 594–627.

6. For an account of Operation Blue Star,

see Mark Tully and Satish Jacob, *Amritsar: Mrs. Gandhi's Last Battle* (London: Pan Books, 1985).

7. Ganga Singh Dhillon, "Give Us Khalistan and Leave Us in Peace," *Illustrated Weekly of India,* 21 July 1985.

8. In November 1989 Professor Gene Thursby of the University of Florida organized a panel "Belief and Behavior in the Sikh Tradition" at the American Academy of Religion Annual Meeting in Anaheim. For this panel I presented a paper entitled "Sikh Fundamentalism: Ways of Turning Things Over?" in which I argued that the current political struggle of the Sikhs in the Punjab could be understood as an expression of fundamentalism. Although this paper was only a working draft in which I specifically requested that it not be quoted, it received a quick response and continues to be a subject of debate. Kharak Singh, upset with my use of the term *fundamentalism* for the Sikh struggle, writes: "The author's own discussion lends little support to his thesis of Sikh fundamentalism. He is, however, determined to put this tag on the Sikh struggle. . . . In the quest for material to support his unsubstantiable thesis, the author (who is probably an anthropologist) has wandered into area of religion and politics where he does not belong. That is why he has wasted his scholarship on matters which are completely irrelevant to the Sikh struggle. He has missed the real issues" (*World Sikh News,* 24 July 1992, p. 2).

9. For a history of the shrine see Sushil Srivastava, *The Disputed Mosque* (New Delhi: Vistaar Publications, 1991). See also Sarvepalli Gopal, ed., *Anatomy of a Confrontation: The Babri Masjid–Ramjanambhoomi Issue* (New Delhi: Viking Books, 1991); and Asghar Ali Engineer, ed., *Babri Masjid–Ramjanambhoomi Controversy* (New Delhi: Ajanta Publications, 1990). The view that the Babri Masjid was constructed after demolishing a Hindu shrine is argued in the following works: *History versus Casuistry: Evidence of the Ramajanambhoomi Mandir Presented by the Vishva Hindu Parishad to the Government of India in December–January 1990–91* (New Delhi: Voice of India, 1991); Koenraad Elst, *Ram Janambhoomi vs. Babri Masjid* (New Delhi: Voice of India, 1990); and idem., *Ayodhya and After* (New Delhi: Voice of India, 1991).

10. Anonymous, *Angry Hindu! Yes, Why Not?* (Delhi: Surruchi Prakashan, 1988), pp. 3–6.

11. H. V. Seshadri, quoted in Harish Khare, "Advani's Failure Limits of Bluff and Bluster," *Times of India,* 26 October 1990, p. 6.

12. Based on a statement by Kedar Nath Sahni, national general secretary of the BJP, in *Sunday Times of India,* 28 October 1990, p. 5.

13. Jürgen Habermas, "Modernity versus Postmodernity," *New German Critique* 22 (1981): 8.

14. See Benedict Anderson, *Imagined Communities: Reflections on the Origin and Spread of Nationalism* (London: Verso, 1983).

15. My reading of Hegel's reflections on modernity is based on Jürgen Habermas, *The Philosophical Discourse of Modernity: Twelve Lectures,* trans. Fredrick Lawrence (Cambridge: MIT Press, 1990), esp. pp. 1–74.

16. Anthony Giddens, *The Consequences of Modernity* (Stanford: Stanford University Press, 1990), p. 174.

17. G. M. Jagtiani, *Be Proud You Are a Hindu* (Bombay: author, 1982), p. 9.

18. Rajendra Singh, quoted in Yogendra K. Malik and Dhirendra K. Vajpeyi, "The Rise of Hindu Militancy: India's Secular Democracy at Risk," *Asian Survey* 29, no. 3 (1989): 312.

19. The textbook controversy is reported in great detail in Lloyd I. Rudolph and Susanne Hoeber Rudolph, "Rethinking Secularism: Genesis and Implications of the Textbook Controversy," *Pacific Affairs* 56 (1983): 15–37. See also, S. Gopal, "History and Politicians," *Frontline,* 3 January 1992.

20. Note, 28 May 1977, P.M.'s [Prime Minister's] Office U/O No. 40 (277) 77 PMS [Prime Minister's Secretariat]. Quoted in Rudolph and Rudolph, "Rethinking Secularism," p. 16.

21. Purshottam Agarwal, "'Curfew' Tolls the Knell," *Times of India,* 21 April 1991, p. 6.

22. Gurtej Singh exemplifies very well the background and thinking of Sikh intellectuals who are closely associated with the rise of Sikh militancy. For an interesting portrait of Singh, see V. S. Naipaul, *India: A Million Mutinies Now* (New York: Viking, 1991), pp. 427–33, 435–45, 470–77.

23. Gurtej Singh, *Ajit,* 4 October 1992. For an analysis similar to that of Gurtej Singh but a much more elaborate version of the conspiracy theory, see Gurnam Kaur and Kharak Singh, "Blasphemous Attacks," (n.p., 1992), pamphlet.

24. Jasbir Singh Mann, *World Sikh News,* 9 October 1992, p. 15.

25. Sukhminder Singh, *World Sikh News,* 2 October 1992, p. 16.

26. Ernest Gellner, *Postmodernism, Reason, and Religion* (London: Routledge, 1992), p. 81.

27. Abul Barkat's statement is reported in Ram Gopal Pandey, *Sri Ram Janamabhumi Ka Rakt Ranjit Itihas* (Ayodhya: Ram Lakhan Gupta, 1987), quoted and translated by Philip Lutgendorf, "The King, the Baby, and the Bathwater," paper presented at the American Academy of Religion Meeting, Kansas City, Mo., 1991, pp. 13–14.

28. The Sikh scripture, the Adi Granth, states that of itself, that is, apart from the hukam, "the soul does not die and it neither sinks nor crosses over. He who has been active (in creation) is still active. In accordance with the Hukam we are born and we die. Ahead and behind the Hukam pervades all" (W. H. McLeod's translation in *Guru Nanak and the Sikh Religion* [Oxford: Clarendon Press, 1968], p. 201).

29. The following data on Hindu Unity Conferences is primarily based on Neeladri Bhattacharya, "Myth, History, and the Politics of Ramajanamabhumi," in Gopal, *Anatomy of a Confrontation.* Some supplementary information is based on H. V. Seshadri, *Hindu Renaissance under Way* (Bangalore: Jagarana Prakashna, 1984), pp. 139–72.

30. Bhattacharya, "Myth, History," p. 130.

31. Habermas, *Philosophical Discourse of Modernity,* p. 51.

32. Alasdair MacIntyre, *After Virtue: A Study in Moral Theory,* 2d ed. (Notre Dame: University of Notre Dame Press, 1984). See also Christopher Lasch, *The Culture of Narcissism* (New York: Norton, 1979). For a subtle critique of MacIntyre and Lasch, see Charles Taylor, *Sources of the Self: The Making of the Modern Identity* (Cambridge: Harvard University Press, 1989); *The Malaise of Modernity* (Concord: Anasi Press, 1991).

33. MacIntyre, *After Virtue,* p. 113.

34. For one such view, although with Islam as a major focus, see Akbar S. Ahmed, *Postmodernism and Islam* (London: Routledge, 1992). In one part of the book Ahmed observes: "Where nothing is sacred, every belief becomes revisable. Thus fundamentalism is the attempt to resolve how to live in a world of radical doubt" (p. 13).

35. For a report highlighting how Sikh fundamentalist leaders operate, see Kanwar Sandhu, "The Wages of Terrorism," *India Today,* 31 October 1992, pp. 34–36.

36. Taylor, *Sources of the Self,* p. 4.

37. Sadhavi Rithambra, quoted in Sudhir Kakar, "Hindutva Harangue," *Times of India,* 19 July 1992, p. 13.

Fundamentalisms Narrated:
Muslim, Christian, and Mystical

James L. Peacock and Tim Pettyjohn

As academics attempting to describe funda-
mentalists, we might well ask how fundamentalists describe themselves. Perhaps the
central problem of defining fundamentalism lies in bridging the inevitable gap between an abstract set of criteria and a varied empirical phenomenon; "fundamentalism" is never quite able to encompass all the "fundamentalisms."

This is why narrative offers us a useful analytical window into so-called fundamentalist religious traditions. The analysis of narratives leads us to look *at* representation
instead of looking *for* essence. Our materials are stories told by fundamentalists about
themselves, not abstract categories such as "belief" or "faith" (although these certainly find their way into the narratives). The narratives that we examine in this chapter
are positioned strategically between doctrinal precepts and texts on the one hand, and
behavior and practice on the other. A religious leader's life story puts doctrine into
practice, but it also puts life into script. Our interest is in the narrated life, not the
narration *of* the life but the life *as* narrated, not the telling but the told. The literary
form of the narrative and the mode of its telling (style, audience, other contextual
features) are secondary in our analysis to the story told—the "plot" of the life and the
existential world entailed in it, the "narrated self."[1]

The interaction of religion and narrative also calls attention to the process of self-
construction at work whenever an individual represents (literally re-presents) him- or
herself to fellow believers or to outsiders. Theology can form and inform narrative;
that is, it can provide both structure and meaning. Of course, this dichotomy is often
a false one, as will become obvious as we examine our empirical cases.

In our interrogation of the diverse narratives that follow, the basic questions that
we are asked to address in this volume will guide our inquiry. These questions roughly
divide into negative and positive characterizations of the identity of the movement in
question. We ask either what the movement is for or what it is against. Is it reactive or

oppositional, and if so, against what? Is it against modernity, for example, seeking to restore an old order; is it counterhegemonic, seeking to win or reclaim power in some domain that has been lost to the secular? On the positive side, is its identity totalistic, that is, creating a "total way of life?" In doing so, does it appeal to charismatic and authoritarian (especially male) leaders, or to sacred sources of authority characterized as infallible in contrast to the foibles of human rationality? Doing this, must it seek converts, must it be militant, or does it find other ways of relating to outsiders? And do these relations with outsiders render the movement exclusivist, concerned with its own internal purity?

Such issues will be characterized differently according to which aspect of a fundamentalist movement is emphasized—its theology, its organizational structure, its politics. Emphasis on the narratives illuminates yet another side of the questions and raises other questions as well.

The narratives we examine are life stories of four leaders of religious movements among which the senior author has done participant observation. The four can be divided into pairs, each pair representing a polarity within its particular geographic and cultural area. One pair is located in central Java, the Surakarta/Jogjakarta area where a sultanate remains alive, a remnant of the empire of Mataram. Within this area, as scholars have observed,[2] there is a dominant polarity between a purist Islam and a syncretic, mystical stream uniting Hinduist, Buddhist, Sufist, and what might be loosely termed animistic tributaries. The syncretic/mystical pole is represented here by Sumarah, the purist Islamic pole by Muhammadijah. Sumarah, one of numerous Kebatinan (mystical) groups found in central Java, is organized around leaders known as *pamong* who conduct meditation sessions. Muhammadijah, founded in Java but with branches throughout Indonesia, is a large, well-organized Islamic fundamentalist movement that seeks a return to the uncorrupted text of the Qur'an, the word of Allah, and to the pure religion of Muhammad.[3] However, unlike many Islamic fundamentalist groups in the Middle East, Muhammadijah is not a political party, nor is it directly allied to one; this has enabled the organization to survive changes in Indonesia's political climate and grow into the most prominent movement of its type in Southeast Asia. Its members presently number some six million.

The second pair was studied in the upper southern region of the United States but is found around the country in the one case, throughout the world in the other. This pair represent a pervasive polarity within Protestant Christianity; the polarity between the Calvinist and the Arminian (or Wesleyan) soteriologies. The Calvinist professes that God decided before the foundation of the earth who would be saved and who damned, hence one's fate in the next life is predestined. The Arminian holds that the individual has free will to choose whether or not to be saved. Here the Calvinists are represented by Primitive Baptists, who split from other Baptists in the early nineteenth century on the issue of free will (as well as others), while the Arminian/Wesleyans are represented by Pentecostals, who consider not only that the individual can choose to be saved or not, but can also accept or reject gifts of the Spirit, such as healing. The Primitive Baptists affirm the original ("primitive") faith of the early church, and the timeless truth of Scripture; Pentecostals assert the immanent, transformative power of the Holy Spirit.[4] Despite their vast theological differences, both Primitive Baptists and Pentecostals share a tendency toward schism and an absence of hierarchical organization. The approximately 350,000 Primitive Baptists in the United States attend churches that are either loosely federated or independent. Pentecostals, of whom there are over sixty million worldwide, worship in established denominations such as the Assemblies of God, as well as in countless small, independent congregations.

While one would not wish to press these parallels too far, one could see a certain homology between the Primitive Baptists and the Muhammadijans on the one hand, Sumarah members and the Pentecostals on the other. Primitive Baptists and Muhammadijans both seek to return to a scriptural and original faith; in this sense, they conform to the popular conception of "fundamentalist" religion. Equally, both groups hold doctrine to be eternal, an objective verity resting beyond the individual's flawed ability to comprehend it. In contrast, the Sumarah and Pentecostals are more subjectively oriented, even mystical, because their main concern is with spiritual experience, as opposed to the heavily doctrinal focus of Muhammadijans and Primitive Baptists. To the member of the Sumarah meditation group or Pentecostal congregation, experience apprehends what scripture cannot convey, and the ephemeral signals the eternal. Despite the geographical differences, then, certain similarities of logic and patterning justify the choice of these cases for comparison. In any event, there is advantage in that the senior author has enjoyed direct involvement in all.[5]

Dahlan

Dahlan is unique among the cases that we consider in this chapter, in that he is memorialized in a biography. Written by Solichin Salam and published by Muhammadijah in 1962, *K. H. A. Dahlan, Amal dan Perdjoanganja: Riwajat Hidup* (K. H. A. Dahlan, his actions and struggle: Life history) is the official biography of the founder of the Muhammadijah movement.

"Riwajat hidup," or life history, is only one section of the book, the others being devoted to such related matters as the history of Islam and Muhammadijah. The life history is programmatically divided into five sections: "Childhood and Youth," "Education," "As Father and Husband," "Struggle," and "The End of His Life."

The author describes the ancestry of Dahlan, following the Islamic practice of emphasizing the father's lineage over that of the mother, instead of the bilateral balance of the traditional syncretic Javanese. The biographer gives the year of Dahlan's birth (1868 by the Christian calendar, 1285 by the Islamic), but not the day. This again contrasts with the wider Javanese pattern, where often one knows the day of one's birth, but not the year. The Islamic method of reckoning time is concerned with the passing of unrepeatable years—linear time, the Western definition of history—while the syncretist Javanese stress the repeatable day, the cosmic cycle writ small.

Dahlan's siblings are referred to only as a list; he is number four. There are no nostalgic presentations of childhood memories or anecdotes; instead, we are told that the young Dahlan was "diligent, honest, and helpful," and "exceptionally clever with his hands, with which he constructed playthings that made him popular among his playmates." This somewhat Weberian image foreshadows that of the tireless reformer that Dahlan was to become.

His educational experience is also reduced to lists, those of his teachers and the books he studied. This section also relates that he was "ordered" by his father to take the pilgrimage to Mecca. When he returned, his name was changed from Darwisj to Dahlan. This change is simply noted as such; it is not presented as emblematic of any deeply personal religious transformation.

"As Father and Husband" continues Dahlan's story after his return to Jogjakarta. He is described as "replacing his father" by becoming an official of the Great Mosque of the sultan of Jogjakarta. Despite the apparent conflict between his reformist efforts and the conservatism of his post, he occupied this position until his death. He married his mother's brother's daughter, Siti Walidah, then four additional wives, divorcing each after a short time but still retaining his first wife. These wives and his children by each are listed.

"Struggle" (Perdjoangan), a standard category in Indonesian narratives of lives and history, tells how Dahlan came to found Muhammadijah on 18 November 1912, when he was approximately forty-four years old. According to the narrative, as Dahlan was "ordered" to go to Mecca by his father, so was he "urged" to found Muhammadijah by his followers. Perhaps this other-directedness reflects both a prophetic notion of being "called" and a deemphasis of individual initiative and decision in traditional Javanese rhetoric. In either case, there is a remarkable parallel with Primitive Baptist narratives, as we shall see.

In a typically formulaic fashion, the author indicates that Dahlan recognized certain forces as leading to the decline of Islam: syncretic mysticism, Hindu-Buddhism, feudalism, and colonialism. However, Dahlan's (and by extension, Muhammadijah's) struggle against these forces was not couched in the fiery rhetoric of the revolutionary, but rather in an idiom of rational change from within.

One of only two instances of dialogue in Dahlan's biography occurs in the section "The End of His Life." Ill from relentless overwork, Dahlan rejects his wife's plea to rest: "I already feel that my time is almost gone, thus if I work as fast as possible, what remains can be brought to perfection by another." He summoned friends and his brother-in-law to delegate tasks, and died at his home on 23 February 1923.

The author summarizes Dahlan's character as stoical, steadfast, and self-denying, as an active organizer rather than as a meditative intellectual. A similar description of him comes from a Dutch colonial official, who seems to have seen a reflection of his own Calvinist ethic in Dahlan: "[An] energetic, militant, intelligent man some 40 years of age, obviously with some Arab blood and strictly orthodox but with a trace of tolerance. . . . Personally H. Dahlan makes a good impression: one notes a man of character and a will to *do,* which is not seen *everyday* in either the Indies or Europe."[6]

In Dahlan's biography, childhood leads to education, which leads to adulthood and finally death; superficially, this seems to be a straightforward developmental account. But is this really the case? No developmental connections exist to link one phase to the next; in fact, most prominent in each section is a list—of siblings, of books and teach-

ers, of wives and children. There is an absence of a processual narration from "formative years" to "private life," to take two familiar labels from the bourgeois Western
biographical genre. The sections entitled "Struggle" and "The End of His Life" include the only two passages of dialogue, but even these are schematic.

Anecdotal material relegated to the end of the book contains raw material that
could have fleshed out the narrative, but it is not so used. This is because of the manner
in which the conventions and practices surrounding the telling of a "life history"
structure the narrative. Life is portrayed as sequential, as history in the Western sense.
However, this is not to demonstrate how individual experience unfolds psychologically; it is to exemplify by each phase a culturally defined category. Hence the num-
bered lists, ordered not dynamically but thematically.

Dahlan began his struggle after a moratorium, a period of separation from his familiar surroundings. This echoes Erik Erikson's contention that this is a common pattern among reformists and revolutionaries.[7] However, Dahlan's movement from the
female-dominated household to the male-dominated school and mosque is standard
among male children of the *santri* (Islamic) Javanese. Even the solitary (and mascu-
line) undertaking of the pilgrimage was, as Turner notes about traditional pilgrimages,
securely within his social framework, as was his return.[8] Unlike Luther, who entered
the monastery against his father's wishes, Dahlan undertook the pilgrimage at his father's command, returning to "replace" his father in familial, occupational, and religious categories. In contrast to the Christian tradition of celibacy and isolation while
undertaking to change the world (as in the examples of Christ, Paul, or Luther), Dahlan followed Muhammad's example of polygyny and participation in the community
as he instituted his reform. Although he was sometimes perceived as a threat to the
powers that be, his work never destroyed his status in the Jogja hierarchy. Dahlan is
not presented as a visionary, a messenger sent by God to turn the world upside down;
rather, he is a reformer—a fundamentalistic one—who simply went about his vocation
in what Weber would term a "rational-legal" manner.[9] His death is described with
similar understatement; there are no dramatic last words, just arrangements for the
continuation of the organization that he had founded.

Notably absent from this narrative of Dahlan's life is the type of lonely, obsessively
self-questioning spiritual turmoil found in Christian (and, with some differences, Sufi)
life stories. The surface result of Dahlan's reformism is not unlike that of Protestant
figures such as Luther, Calvin, or Zwingli (e.g., the elimination of ritual language and
trappings, reliance on books instead of the sacerdotal power of priests). However,
Luther's theological and ecclesiastical formulations are meaningful only in a culture
where the taint of original sin weighs heavily on the individual *as* an individual. The
reformation of Dahlan was entirely different, an attempt to impose a legalistic Islamic
ethic on a Malayo-Indonesian society. The inspiration was scripture; the method was
systematic application of received creed.

This lack of a dramatic transformative experience was not unique to Muhammadijah's founder. During my fieldwork at a Muhammadijah training camp called Darol
Arqom, I found it to be characteristic of the participants as well. During an exercise
called personal introduction, the trainees (all Javanese men ranging in age from early

twenties to mid-thirties) described how they came to be committed to a faith mani-fested in the Muhammadijah sect. Typical of these public professions was that of a man named Ahmad, who stated that he was reared in a syncretic Javanese family that did not perform the prayers of Islam. But he himself learned to pray, and, praise be to God, he is now a Muhammadijan. Ahmad went on to tell of how he helped to crush a syn-cretic mystical movement that, he said, "threatened the safety of society."

Although these accounts reported conversions and took a form similar to the tes-timonies offered in Christian churches, none of them described Christian-style con-version experiences. In none of the twenty-three accounts that I gathered at Darol Arqom is there a mention of a period of spiritual upheaval or an altered state of con-sciousness. Yet they all describe a shift in belief, membership, and social identity.

The absence of emotional language was especially striking given recent history. This was 1970, only five years after Gestapu, the massacre of some half-million Indo-nesians through a conflict in part between the purist Muslims and the syncretic Com-munists. Members of Muhammadijah, possibly including some of those present at Darol Arqom, had participated in the murder of their own neighbors. Yet this remem-bered violence did not translate into emotional drama even as Muhammadijans nar-rated their conversions from the religion or philosophy of those some of them or their fellows had killed.

I discussed the absence of conversion experiences with one of the instructors at Darol Arqom as we strolled beside a rice paddy during one of our habitual walks. He seemed to recognize the sort of experience I described, but assured me that he had never heard of any Muhammadijan reporting or having one. However, he mentioned that he had heard of such experiences among the Chinese. This is suggestive, and in fact may be the exception that proves the rule: many of the Indonesian Christians (including fundamentalists) are Chinese, highlighting the prominence of the conver-sion experience in Christianity and its virtual absence in Islam.

Evans

The Primitive Baptists of the Blue Ridge Mountains of North Carolina and Virginia offer both parallels and contrasts to the Muhammadijans in their style of narrating lives and events. On the one hand, their strict Calvinistic theology mandates the same deemphasis of individual choice and action that we see in Dahlan's biography, as well as a rationalistic and unsentimental view of earthly existence. In contrast to the Mu-hammadijan and in keeping with the Christian biographical tradition, however, the Primitive Baptist often arrives at this perspective through a tortuous process of self-examination and doubt which, owing to the Calvinist's mistrust of the "dread pre-sumption" that humans may actually know of their soul's fate, can never be brought to closure.

Yet the quest for a sign of God's grace is at the heart of most Primitive Baptist narrative. Primitive Baptists are, as Ruel Tyson and I have termed them, "pilgrims of paradox": while certainty of one's status as one of the Elect, chosen to be spared damnation before the Creation, is elusive, they are ever alert for any sign, and subject their "experimental" (their term for *experiential*) evidence to a rigorous theological/intellectual criticism.

Indeed, this ongoing exercise in biblical hermeneutics is not necessarily a gloomy enterprise for the Primitive Baptists. They often recount with obvious pleasure theological discussions between elders that stretch late into the night and arguments over points of doctrine with the "missionaries" (as they refer, perhaps a bit derisively, to their Arminian neighbors), conducted while on a lunch break at work.

Elder Walter Evans, an eighty-year-old stone mason from the Blue Ridge, exemplifies the Primitive Baptist narrative style in a sermon on pilgrimage: "If you feel today or ever feel, that you're a stranger or pilgrim on the earth, listen to what's said in the following verse: 'they confessed that they were strangers and pilgrims in the earth.' I'm not saying this to make you sad. What I'm dealing with this morning, endeavoring to, has given me perhaps more consolation than any one verse or verses in all the Bible. . . . Because so much of the time . . . I'll not go into that, but I've felt so much of my time in my life, like a stranger."

While Elder Evans hints at feelings of desolate loneliness in these words, he finds comfort in them. How can this be? As he explained later, his feelings of estrangement may suggest that he is one of the Elect, because the Bible depicts the children of God as lonely pilgrims who, like Job, are not taken in by the false comforts and rationalizations offered by the human world.

While Elder Evans may use words such as *felt* to describe his thoughts, his main referent is not psychological, but theological. In narratives of his life and experience, the sensory world is forever checked, in a thoroughgoing manner, against biblical doctrine to determine its validity and interpret its meaning. Inferences, tentative though they may be, can then be drawn—frequently accompanied by a disclaimer heard among Primitive Baptists: "If I am not deceived."

As well as casting grave doubts on all human perception and experience, Calvinist theology eliminates the mediating devices standing between the individual and the Almighty, such as the saints and sacraments. Even the church itself, as a human institution in a hopelessly corrupt world, is compromised; how can it offer sanctuary when it too is suspect? Elder Evans notes his feelings of estrangement as he watches a baptism during a period of spiritual crisis: "As I stood on the bank of the river beholding the scene, I could see no real reason for the action that was underway. It seemed very unnecessary. However, it was performed and the candidate seemed to rejoice in it and those that were looking on. As for me, I got nothing out of it."

This isolation of the individual fundamentally alters the relationship between the faithful and the church. To the Primitive Baptist, Dahlan's smooth ascent in a bureaucratic religious structure would be an empty worldly accomplishment, not a mark of spiritual attainment.

Unlike Dahlan (as biographed) and his fellow Muhammadijans, Elder Evans does not simply state that he came to his convictions in a straightforward manner. While different from the conversion experiences recounted by Pentecostals and other evangelical Christians, Evans nonetheless had a dramatic and transformative experience that brought him to the faith.

> In the latter part of my twentieth year . . . when I cared nothing for God nor his people, satisfied with my big times attending places of worldly pleasure—my father insisted strongly that I attend a meeting being held by people of the Regular Baptist denomination, of which he and mother were members. I finally agreed to go; however, my purpose was to walk home with some of the girls from the meeting.
>
> It was on Tuesday night while standing in the back of the house, a strong power arrested my heart and soul to the extent my body trembled under the weight like a leaf on a tree shaken by a mighty wind. A voice from somewhere, a still voice taut with power said, "You are lost without God or hope in the world."

Walter Evans felt himself a sinner "by nature . . . doomed without God's mercy." He knelt at the altar or "mourner's bench" and "begged God for mercy and pardon for my sins. . . . I was in desperate need of something to give me relief from this awful feeling of condemnation." He left the meeting house and went home. Nothing could bring him relief: "Neither the prayers of Dad and Mother, preachers, nor no one else could reach my case." He prayed fervently, suffering for two days and three nights, until a still voice said, "Your sins are all forgiven." He was raised to his feet "one happy man," and joined the congregation in song. "Before the song was ended, a call or strong impression came to me. . . . O, how I desired to tell what the Lord had done for me. I was in a new world." He was baptized on Sunday, 16 November 1930.

Thus we can see that, unlike Dahlan, Elder Evans relates a specific spiritual crisis as the beginning point of his religious life. But when reading his account of his life, one is also struck by an autobiographical minimalism that is not unlike that of Dahlan. Elder Evans scarcely mentions his family background, working life, marriage, or children. As is the case with Dahlan, his story does not display the didacticism that one might expect from a spiritual autobiography or biography. After the first rather apologetic paragraph (wherein he notes that he wrote down his life story at the behest of others), he does not directly address his audience. He does not imagine himself to be a guide; rather, he is guided, and he works to uncover signs of his predestined fate, as when he notes his grandmother's prediction, made while he was still an infant, that he would grow up to be a preacher. Evans's narrative is one of his pilgrimage, his unceasing effort to understand his life in terms of his theology. To this end he works with the same resigned yet stoical determination as Dahlan did in building his movement, and like Dahlan, his struggle is framed by systematic doctrine grounded in scripture considered to be of ultimate authority: the word of God.

Walter Evans died, at the age of eighty-three, in the winter of 1992. Several hundred Primitive Baptists gathered at Sparta, North Carolina, to hear a sermon and singing before moving to the cold, windy ridge at Salem Church, where Evans was buried beside his father, mother, sister, and son. His friend Lessur Bradley preached the funeral. After nostalgic remembrances, Elder Bradley stated that Elder Evans had requested that his funeral sermon state the doctrine that Evans believed. Bradley then succinctly summarized the doctrinal essence of the Primitive Baptists: predestination, effectual calling, and the hope for grace. He concluded by inviting Evans's descendants to carry on his calling. Evans's life and death were thus framed by systematically explicated doctrine.

Clyde

"I didn't have a very illustrious life coming up, we were just poor folk," says Reverend J. C. Clyde, a traveling Pentecostal preacher from Mississippi. "My dad was just a common laborer, saw mill. My mother was just a housewife. As far as I know she was always a Christian."

At age twelve, he left home, riding a freight train to Memphis. By fifteen he was running a farm for a widow, and by twenty he was a country singer in Nashville. His musical career led him next to Los Angeles, center of the recording industry, as well as the location of the 1906 revival at the Azusa Street Mission, one of the hallmark events in the history of Pentecostalism, the faith that Clyde was soon to join.

The following is the story of Clyde's conversion, quoted from an interview:

I thought I had it made. But it was always just in front of me. It took everything I made for advertising, I never made it then. But my mother never would attend any of our dances, shows or anything, although she lived in Tennessee at this time. I thought why wouldn't she attend those shows, or any of our dances, but she visited me at the radio station one Sunday afternoon. I dedicated her one of the few gospel songs I do, my mother sat and cried audibly there and I was embarrassed. Two months later the call came saying my mother has passed away. I was so glad she never mixed with the world. She lived for God, and I knew where she was. From that hour on I never had a minute's rest, till in Los Angeles, California, about two or three years later. I was sitting in a club there waiting to talk to a man about playing, and God spoke to my heart. I got up, walked out of that club, I don't know how He spoke to me, I just know He did, I walked up and down the street and didn't know which way to turn. I got on the street car and I started home. Right in front of me said a sign, REVIVAL. And I didn't know what kind of church it was. It didn't make any difference, I just knew I wanted to go to church. I went home and told my wife, and she said I'll go with you. And that night I knelt at the altar and gave my heart to God. I turned to my wife before I went to the altar, after the minister got through preaching. She said she would go with me. Our little boy who was just two years old at that time, he didn't know what was with daddy, but when I knelt at the altar he knelt with me there, but he didn't know what it was all about, but today he pastors our church at Los Angeles. I've got a son-in-law that pastors in Atlanta, Georgia, another daughter that is an organist in my son's church and also sings with the Freedom Singers in Southern California. Got another daughter that teaches in the college in Chico, California. God's been so good to me to watch my children grow up to live for God. But I never thought about going into the ministry, I didn't want to go into the ministry.

A woman telephones him, asking "Is this Cowboy Clyde?" "No ma'am, he's dead," replies Clyde. His old self is dead; he is a new creature, born again through his conversion. Muhammadijans may have rejected syncretic religion, Christianity, or atheism to join the movement, and thus may seem as transformed as Clyde, yet they do not so radically separate the old and new phases. However, the Muhammadijans more firmly distinguish the initiation from the postinitiation stage. As noted, Dahlan's initiation (i.e., education) is sharply separated from his vocation (i.e., struggle). When his education is finished, it is not repeated or continued, though the concept derived from it (reformism) is applied. In a sense, Clyde's initiation, his conversion, *is* his vocation; much of his preaching consists of reliving his conversion, in order that others may also undergo the experience. Thus, for the Pentecostal, narrative may serve not only as a bridge connecting believers to each other, but also as a device for carrying out the evangelical mission of saving souls: "More Gospel to be preached, more souls to be reached," sings Clyde in his deep, rough voice.

The narrative and theological contrasts to Primitive Baptist narratives are distinct; while Elder Evans may maintain a cautious hope about his own predetermined fate, his theology discredits any claim that one may save one's own soul, let alone that of another. His story cannot bridge the chasm between fallen humanity and a radically transcendent God, whereas Clyde's conversion narrative seeks to bring God's immanence to bear on the unconverted.

Clyde's conversion did not lead directly or immediately to preaching. He ran an automotive repair shop in Los Angeles while active as a layman in a Pentecostal church, but did not preach "because I didn't have the education, didn't have the words," he says. His call to preach came through his daughter's healing. Clyde maintains that the doctors had given up on the eighteen-month-old girl, who was critically ill with bronchial pneumonia. He prayed, "God heal my baby, I'll preach." While such bargaining with the Almighty would strike the Primitive Baptist as pointless (if not blasphemous), it is a recurrent theme in Pentecostal conversion narratives. God healed Clyde's daughter, and he preached his first revival that Saturday night.

After six years of preaching part-time while he worked at a body shop, commuting 150 miles every night, he contracted pneumonia. Christmas Eve found him in the hospital, broken physically, financially, and spiritually. Then "Jesus walked through that door. . . . God healed me that day." He responded ecstatically: "That was the spell to end all spells. I had the time of my life. From that day to this I have never had to work another job." Clyde has spent the ensuing years as a traveling evangelist, preaching in small Pentecostal churches such as the one in Durham, North Carolina, where I met and interviewed him.

In Pentecostal narratives, the call to preach comes as life reaches a crisis, and linking the pledge to preach and a healing (or the resolution of some other crisis) is common.

To be in a situation when much hinges on your decision, then to "side with the Lord," or "make the choice for Jesus"—this is a pattern prominent in Pentecostal narrative and is not seen in Muhammadijan and not prominent in Primitive Baptist accounts. The decision brings not only comfort and reassurance, but joy and ecstasy; with a revealing cliché, Clyde singles out a unique, revelatory moment: "I had *the* time of my life." No similar peaks appear in Dahlan's story, which portrays time as flat, though progressive: each moment is like the last, except that it is an advance. And in contrast to Elder Evans's epiphany, which is couched in the passive terms of "being lifted up . . . without any effort on my part," and "what the Lord had done for me," Clyde portrays himself as an active agent, choosing, deciding, moving on.

And move on he does; he speaks of the long nights in his van meditating on the Gospel, but he does not mention his days. His work has transformed his routine from that of the farmer or laborer to that of the performer, geared to the draining rhythms of the revival, which in its crises and climaxes plays out the Christian paradigm of the individual drama of salvation.

Whereas Dahlan's bureaucratized struggle is intimately tied to his patrilineal kin as he replaces his father in the local hierarchy, *Brother* Clyde gives himself no ancestry, and his father provides nothing for him to replace, disappearing after the second sentence of his story with even less discussion than Elder Evans grants his family. Clyde's mother moves him toward preaching by embodying Christian virtue, not by establishing a niche in the social structure for him. Perhaps he sees himself as building something of a dynasty, consisting of his children and protégés who carry the Word forward. But, as suggested by the terms *brother* and *sister* by which Pentecostals address each other, the model of the patriarchal hierarchy is not a framework for his church as it is for Dahlan. Anticipating our final narrative, that of Javanese meditation teacher Pak (father or papa) Nyata, we may note that Nyata and Walter Evans are similarly disinclined toward rigid hierarchical structures, the former by his introspective mysticism, the latter by his theological conviction that Election bears no relationship to earthly position. Dahlan's Muhammadijah movement, while originating in a patriarchal and hierarchical setting, is markedly egalitarian in comparison to traditional Indonesian Islam.

In a vision he had while studying Scripture one day, Clyde found himself on the road to Calvary. The guide pointed out a certain spot where Jesus had stumbled under the weight of the cross. Clyde knelt and prayed, waking depressed, feeling that the vision meant that he was seeking an easy path to salvation, instead of suffering as Jesus did when he climbed Calvary. Years later, two days before the beginning of the Six-Day War, Clyde visited Jerusalem and lived his vision; but this time, he climbed Calvary, even though guards tried to stop him.

Clyde lives here in imitation of Christ. No similar imitation of Muhammad is mentioned for Dahlan, reflecting the Muhammadijan emphasis on Shari'a, the law, rather than on the life of Muhammad as a model for imitation (an emphasis found in Sufism, though even there without the mystical/metaphorical link between the believer and the prophet).[10] Dahlan's guide is Muhammad's law, not his life; the linkage is legal, rather than dramatic. Whereas Dahlan built an organization to carry out his mission, Clyde operates independently, outside of the loose organizational boundaries that characterize most Pentecostal churches, with the goal of changing lives with his words.

It is this emphasis on the dramatic and the experiential that distinguishes the Pentecostal narrative from the Islamic or Primitive Baptist. In this respect, Pentecostalism challenges the standard definition of a fundamentalist religion as one that adheres to a strict, legalistic interpretation of doctrine. Marsden explicitly places Pentecostalism outside of the mainstream of American fundamentalism: "The strong concern with the exact meaning of the printed word . . . is one of the principal things that distinguish Fundamentalism from other less intellectual forms of American revivalism or from the more experientially oriented Holiness tradition or—most populist, sectarian, and vocally oriented of all—Pentecostalism."[11]

The goal of the Pentecostal service is the ecstatic union of the believer with the Holy Spirit, as manifested by speaking in tongues or other charismatic signs; it is through these practices that "the Living Word" is made flesh. This subordination of written text to embodied practice is completely at odds with Dahlan's doctrinal and scriptural rationalism, as well as Elder Evans's assertion that the Bible is "a dead letter," inert and unchanging.

Nyata

Sumarah, the type of meditation practiced and taught by Pak Nyata of Java, aims at stilling the inner voices and eliminating the ego-created obstacles that distract the individual from *rasa murni,* the correct perception of reality. Adherents of Sumarah maintain that *alam* (the true, transcendent reality) exists both within and without the individual; meditation is a way of clearing the mind in order to connect the individual's fragment of the totality with its source. In contrast to the Pentecostal service, the Sumarah meditation meeting is not an attempt to bring about an epiphany; rather, it is simply an ephemeral instant in the continuing application of a spiritually liberating discipline. And, our characterization of Sumarah as subjectivist notwithstanding, one of the stated goals of meditation is *tenang* (neutrality or objectivity), a calm state in which one is capable of rasa murni.[12]

Sumarah was founded in Jogjakarta in 1935, spreading out from a small original group of adherents. The following manifesto, signed on 22 April 1940, sets out the goals of Sumarah:

1. The members of Paguyuban Sumarah are certain of the existence of God, Creator of the Cosmos, and acknowledge the Prophets and the Holy Books.
2. They work to be constantly aware of God, by avoiding egoism and arrogance, and by believing in the ultimate truth, through self-surrender to God.
3. They strive toward bodily health, peaceful hearts, and clean spirits, and to refine their character both in words and deeds.

4. They work to strengthen the brotherhood of man through love and compassion.

5. They aim to work toward universal and spiritual harmony, by accepting the responsibilities of daily life, by responding to the needs of society as a whole, and by fulfilling their duty as citizens.

6. They vow to do right, submit to the laws of the country, and respect other human beings; not to defame the beliefs of others, but rather to act on the basis of love, so that all spiritual and religious groups develop toward the same aim.

7. They vow to avoid evil actions, hurting, hating, sinning, and so forth; all speech and actions are to be unpretentious and true, and to be performed perfectly and accurately, without haste or strain.

8. They vow to develop diligently in both spiritual and worldly spheres.

9. They vow not to be fanatical, but to rely on truth, which in the end benefits all people.

While Sumarah has greatly expanded in numbers in the fifty years since its founding, it has not evolved into a tightly orthodox bureaucratic structure. Each local meditation group enjoys a great deal of autonomy, with its particular teachers setting the tone and emphasis for the members.

A thick-limbed, bass-voiced, vigorous man in his mid-forties when I met him in 1979, Pak Nyata teaches in the Sumarah meditation association of Surakarta, Java. His narrative is one of gradual spiritual development, not sudden revelation or rational social planning; neither conversion nor education led him to meditation. He outlines programs of spiritual development, and he refers to his own spiritual progress, noting incidents of psychic disturbance which he has overcome through meditation and careful self-analysis. But this is progress of a kind quite different from the developmental psychology or notion of "personal growth" that the Western observer might expect.

Nyata does not divide his life into clear and discrete phases, as is the case with Dahlan's education followed by struggle or Clyde's conversion, crisis, and preaching. In fact, Nyata emphasizes the continuity of experience; his teaching is still learning. He states, "You find out which of your tools have not yet conformed by giving service, that is by Guiding."

Nyata guides the Sumarah meditation and self-analysis sessions with great power, yet with fluidity and sensitivity. He is capable of shifting from guide to guided, as when he asks someone to "check" (by empathetic meditation) his own spiritual state. He also continues to consult his own guide, Pak H. of Jogjakarta, who advises him on such matters as whether to have more children, how he must psychically release his dead mother-in-law, and how to subdue his attraction to women.

Dahlan is portrayed as completing an education, after which he ceased to learn but spent his life implementing what he had learned. Clyde has a conversion experience at a certain date, then he spends his life replicating it in other people. Nyata's life is represented by him as not so sharply divided into discrete phases, but rather as more fluid, continuous, and dialectical: he continuously enriches his own spiritual state through experiences that deepen his guiding, which in turn is experience.

Nyata is active; he runs a private bank, has a cottage batik industry, and is constantly on his motor scooter traveling to the villages surrounding his home to hold spiritual meetings. The observer may see his life as a bit frantic, but he characterizes his great energy as flowing naturally and effortlessly from his resonance with the widest ground of existence, alam, which is nature but also, he says, God. He describes the apparently draining hours of guiding Sumarah sessions as effortless, for what he says comes not from his consciousness but from a deeper source, alam. He tries to avoid "pulling," that is, striving toward a goal, such as Dahlan's or Clyde's salvation, or Elder Evans's signs thereof. Even a meaningful experience can become an ensnaring goal, he warns (distantly echoing the Primitive Baptist suspicion of appearances), if you try to repeat it, fallaciously valorizing the artifact over the process that creates it. While the language of Western motivational psychology (laden as it is with Weberian Protestant-capitalist overtones) might characterize Nyata as "a productive self-starter," he represents his life as an inevitable expression of energies flowing from the reality with which he resonates.

What of his eschatology? The contrast between his view and that of a salvation religion is illustrated by the following dialogue paraphrased from a Sumarah session at which Nyata was questioned by a young Chinese woman whose Christian affiliation was indicated by the cross on her necklace:

She. What is the source of life? If it goes, can it return?
He. If it's gone, it's not life.

Nyata then drops into a low-toned mumbling conversation with the men about life being tough—this in *ngoko* (low, colloquial dialect) of Javanese language, in a conversational style of *ngomong* and *ngobrol* sometimes termed *ngomel,* an earthy form that debunks the abstract and idealistic. He then shifts into elevated Krama (high) Javanese language, speaking resonantly about meditation being a way of accepting life's sadness, a way to address reality (*nyatane*). Finally, he completes his rhetorical disarming of the girl by turning to us visitors and saying sotto voce in the language she is using, Indonesian: "She doesn't accept my teachings, even though she is silent." She, however, comes back to him: "Pak, what is the source of life?" He replies, "The source of life matters less than life writ small—the daily experience of reality. What is the source?" She points upward, presumably indicating God. He lights a match and watches the smoke, then says, "Life is like that," presumably implying that life has no certain end, path, or source; it just exists and dissipates, returning to alam.

Conclusion

We have sampled a slice of self-definitions: their expression in self-narrations, storied lives by leaders of four movements. What do these narratives tell us about answers to our questions about fundamentalisms?

To a certain degree, the narrated selves are narrations of the theological, ideological, and organizational structures of each movement. This correlation is depicted in table 4.1. Yet this narrative patterning has a distinct logic as well.

TABLE 4.1

STRUCTURE OF LIFE HISTORIES IN RELATION TO STRUCTURE OF RELIGIOUS SYSTEMS

	Life History			
	Dahlan	Clyde	Evans	Nyata
Initiation	education	conversion	uncovering	experience
Vocation	bureaucratic application of education	dramatic replication of conversion	systematic exposition of God's purpose	experience
Termination	continuing application	continuing dramatization	continuing systematic application	experience
Relationship	bureaucratic/causal	dramatic/metaphorical	textual/causal	unity
	Religious System			
	Muhammadijah	Pentecostal	Primitive Baptist	Sumarah
Spirit	transcendent	personal	transcendent	immanent
Form	scriptural/ritual application of spiritual norms	dramatic manifestation of personal spirituality	scriptural exegesis of experience	negated
World	controlled by spirit and form	transformed into spiritual drama	ultimately controlled by spirit	encompassed by larger reality
Relationship	bureaucratic/causal	dramatic/metaphorical	textual/exegetical	unity (as parts seen to fuse into whole)

The oppositional focus is strongest in the "initiation" phase of the narrative for the Pentecostal and the Kebatinan, but in the "vocational" phase of the Muhammadijan and the Primitive Baptist. For Clyde, the struggle is with the Devil and the world prior to conversion. Nyata, although less dramatically, must also combat threatening spirits before he can establish himself as a leader in Sumarah. In neither case do they represent their victories as final; years later, Clyde is haunted by the fear that he is taking the easy way up Calvary, and Nyata endeavors to remain grounded in an all-encompassing reality. For Dahlan, this personal spiritual conflict is absent from the narrative, while the emphasis is on an external battle—the struggle (*perdjoangan*) of Dahlan with various enemies of his movement. The Primitive Baptist is more ambiguous in this respect, for there is an account of Evans's personal struggle prior to conversion and after. However, the devil is not prominent in this account, and oppositional forces come to the fore later, while Elder Evans is a leader and is opposed by physical force (as also happened to Dahlan) from adversaries of his sect.

Such a difference in the patterning of narration is played out in many aspects of the movements. Part of this is what we have termed the subjectivism of the Pentecostals and the Kebatinans versus the objectivism of the Muhammadijans and, to a degree, the Primitive Baptists. The first pair stress inner experience as a crucial marker of identity, whereas the Muhammadijans stress reform and action in the world. The Primitive Baptists are nuanced in their emphasis, skeptical of both inner experience and earthly action, because both are all too human. Yet they affirm the hand of God in both, and this, too, is built into the narrative—note Evans's use of foreshadowing, describing events in such a way as to indicate that God had already discerned and decreed how they would unfold before they do: "In time I would reap what I had sown."

The question of totalism is difficult to address through the narratives alone, for they are only a part of the total experience of the leaders and their movements. Yet the narratives do provide clues, especially given that the question is phrased in terms of intentionality ("does fundamentalism *seek* to provide and direct a 'total way of life'") rather than practice. What do the narratives suggest about totalistic intent?

Dahlan's totalistic commitment to Allah is expressed through the rationalistic application of the Qur'an, which is the signature of the movement he founded, as exemplified by the Muhammadijah women who used ledgers to calculate the percentage of time they wasted each day in sin. This legalistic authoritarianism would not have been out of place in Calvin's Geneva, but this is an area in which the Primitive Baptists depart dramatically from their theological forebears; they are not interested in building a City on the Hill, spurning even the theocratic aspirations of Jerry Falwell's Moral Majority as unscriptural and "missionary" (that is, Arminian). If Primitive Baptists mistrust community, they nonetheless position themselves in a cosmos, a universe, a world. For Elder Evans, God's almighty hand has already written the story of his life, and his narrative describes his effort to apprehend his place in the vast totality that is God's plan. When he receives a sign of God's grace, he speaks of being in "a new world." It is more than mere semantics to note that while Evans enters a new world, Clyde becomes a new man.

This again points to the opposing views of human agency entailed in their theologies. Primitive Baptists hold that human nature is utterly corrupt, incapable of finding (or being worthy of) salvation, redeemable only through the grace of an inscrutable but omnipotent deity. In contrast, harkening back to the teachings of John Wesley, Pentecostalism asserts the possibility of personal holiness, of living a salvation-bound life of closeness to God. As Clyde's narrative demonstrates, electing to undertake such a life is no small decision; the circumstances involve great personal anguish, and the stakes are high. Nonetheless, Clyde made his choice: "I knelt at the altar and gave my heart to God." Yet the contrast between Pentecostal and Primitive Baptist is not strictly self versus other, individual versus cosmos. Paradoxically, the choice to remake the self is a choice to surrender control over it. This is not unlike Nyata's continuing effort to subdue the egoistic distractions from alam; he too must overcome himself in order to gain and maintain resonance with an ultimate reality that permeates all facets of his life. In contrast to the Muhammadijan, the Sumarah member is not interested in legal prescription; since the individual is a microcosm of both the society and the cosmos, balance and harmony begin, and perhaps even end, there. This self = society = cosmos homology is familiar in many Pentecostal churches, which tend to take a dim view of social and political activism, maintaining that "the only social problem is an unsaved soul." Pentecostals, like Sumarah members, bid to transform the outer world by transforming the inner self, both of which embody a deeper reality.[13]

Observing the contrasting logics of the several narratives as they develop the totalistic and sometimes oppositional identity for each movement, other questions posed in this volume are brought into perspective. What is the place of sacred texts, of charismatic and authoritarian (especially male) leaders, for example?

Text works differently in the narratives of the groups that we have termed objectivist than it does in those we call subjectivist. Evans depicts the scripture and its mysteries as a driving force behind his own experience and spiritual development; he confronts a scriptural/doctrinal puzzle, then he is driven to solve it, perhaps in a vision as well as through study and "discourse" (his word). His subjective experiences, then, are narrated as textually motivated. For Clyde, scripture comes into play after an experience, as a way of articulating it. For Nyata, scripture is not an important source of authority; writings of the founders are acknowledged, but authority flows not from them but from meditative contact with alam. For Dahlan, scripture dictates not so much experience as action, and this emphasis shifts focus from scripture as such to what Muhammadijans call ideology (*tjita*), which in their discourse replaces the Qur'an itself as an immediate source of guidance for action.

What about charismatic figures? All four of these leaders are male, possessing a certain charisma and authority. Three of the four draw on an ancestral male, charismatic figure, Christ or Muhammad, for authority. Sumarah, too, was founded by a male, but not of the stature of a savior or messenger of God. This rather gross difference may relate to differences in the place of leadership, which are embodied in the narrations. That is, of the four it is Nyata who most completely embodies the consciousness of his followers. They and he become as one sharing rasa murni (true perception), participating in the ultimate reality encompassing them. Thus, he himself and the concept of self itself are less bounded than is true of the other leaders. In this situation, there is not a bounded narration of Nyata's life in the way that there is for the others. Possibly a factor in this difference is the prominence of a bounded narration of a biography of a founding prophet—Christ or Muhammad—in the traditions of the other three, which is replicated to an extent by their own bounded life stories. Mutatis mutandis, one effect of bounded life stories is to distinguish leader from follower; he has his story, they have theirs. Through varying dialectics—dramatic, bureaucratic, and so forth—linkages are made between the leader's life story and those of followers; conversion is one such linkage. But the flow and fusion embodied by Nyata is precluded for the other three by the tradition of biography/autobiography itself.

God is one, and there is only one God. This is a concept that all four groups confirm, though in different ways. The Muslims unify God but differentiate his opposition; the Christians differentiate God, but unify his opposition; Sumarah transcends both perspectives. Muhammadijans emphasize *tawhid,* the unity of God, but see that oneness opposing a differentiated set of spirits, the evil Setans. The Christians differentiate God into three persons, the Trinity, but unify his opposition as Satan. Sumarah subsumes both God and opposing forces into a unified ground of being, treating all as manifestations of alam; thus, the hood of one Javanese mystic's car is decorated with ornaments representing the Buddha, Siva, the Virgin Mary, and the Javanese clown-god Semar, forming a mobile bricolage of religious symbols.

In a somewhat parallel logic, both Muslims and Christians distinguish between a spiritual realm and the world. The world (*djasmane*) is for the Muslims godless, lacking in morality, and governed by passions (*nafsu*); likewise for the Pentecostals, who speak of living in the spirit versus living in the world or "the natural," or of being *in* the world, but not *of* the world. Sumarah again transcends this distinction, subsuming both world and spirit into a ground of being, an ultimate.

What do the narratives show about such distinctions? What do they not show? The conversionist model of the Christian narratives separate the godless (or actively anti-God, the satanic) and worldly into a preconversion phase, the godly and spiritual into a postconversion phase. While something of this phasing can be discerned in Nyata and Dahlan, it is not pronounced or dramatized. Clyde undergoes a dramatic change, moving from the world, the Saturday nights of juke joints, honky tonks, and country music, to the spirit, the Sunday services of prayer, healing, and gospel music, while Dahlan continued the Friday rituals throughout his life, and Nyata's meditation streams flow gently but firmly throughout his.

Yet the world as well as the spirit continues to be present in the lives of all of these men, even when the narratives downplay it. Sexuality is an example; while all of the groups attempt to, in some form, repress it, they are equally alike in permitting some "return of the repressed." For both Pentecostals and Muhammadijans, the sexuality of women is problematical and suppressed; Pentecostals restrict the use of makeup, while Muhammadijans require that women cover their heads and legs. Yet for both, sensuality emerges in new guises, as in the elaborate coiffures of uncut tresses favored by many Pentecostal women and the skintight dresses of head-covered Javanese Muslim women. Primitive Baptists and Muhammadijans are alike in dealing with sexuality off the record by telling dirty jokes, which are quite similar in content despite the cultural gulf separating them. Nyata contrasts with the adherents of both of these salvation religions by responding to sexuality not by repressing and then uncorking it, but rather by encompassing it; he tells of subduing his desire for a married woman by meditating on her image until it is neutralized by absorption into alam. As a third example, Pentecostals and Muhammadijans are alike in combining desexualization of women in some respects with resexualization of them in others, and enhancing their political and religious power and status in still other spheres. Dahlan's reformism sought to promote the organizational power of women within Muhammadijah; folklorist Elaine Lawless has written with great sensitivity and insight on the ambiguous yet powerful role of women in Pentecostal churches; and Beverly Patterson has shown how even within the patriarchal structure of the Primitive Baptist church, women have a voice (literally) in song.[14] Still, recognition of sensuality occurs only at the edges of the narratives, as for example, in the simple listing of Dahlan's wives.

These examples of style, jokes, song, and female empowerment take us outside of the narratives as such and into their contexts: the *lived* lives of the narrators. That is, of course, another question, for much further discussion. But this also brings us to a point at which we may be able to locate our contribution within other approaches to the comparative study of fundamentalisms. It might be beneficial to refer to a distinction drawn by Bruce Lawrence.[15] He distinguishes between the study of behavior, which he attributes to behavioral science, and the study of text, which he attributes to the humanities. Lawrence views texts as the essential focus of fundamentalism, which leads him to emphasize scripture and doctrinal tracts in his work. Looking at narrated lives, within the context of lived lives, is an approach that strategically bridges the behavioral and the textual; we hope that this chapter proves to be suggestive to others on the topic of this volume.

The relationships that we have discussed between doctrine, experience, and narration are in no sense simple or determinant; doctrine does not straitjacket experience, nor is narrative a simple mirror for doctrine or belief. All interact with, impinge on, and mutually constitute each other. Yet all possess a certain degree of autonomy, an independent dynamic. As we have attempted to demonstrate here, the narrative itself constitutes a world, a world of selves.

And what kind of selves are being constituted? Not primarily psychological selves or ritual selves. Rather, they are cosmological selves. These are stories of the self as part of great cosmic narratives: self as an intersection of opposing forces, God and the Devil, Allah and the spirits, or more abstract negotiations between one's formulation of God's will and one's own life, the ego and the ultimate. Herein lies both the poetry and the power of the fundamentalist's narrated life. We nonfundamentalists may be, in Walker Percy's phrase, "lost in the cosmos." Fundamentalists are trapped in it as well, but they are also empowered by it, struggling within what may seem to us an anachronism, an out-of-date cosmology; yet, so far as their narratives take them, they are victorious.

Notes

1. James L. Peacock and Dorothy C. Holland, "The Narrated Self: Life Stories in Process," *Ethos* Vol. 21, No. 4 (Dec. 1993), pp. 367–383; for the literary and linguistic aspects of conversion stories, see Peter G. Stromberg, *Language and Self-Transformation: A Study of the Christian Conversion Narrative* (Cambridge: Cambridge University Press, 1993).

2. See C. Snouck-Hurgronje, *Brieven van een Wedono Pension* (Leiden: E. J. Brill, 1927); Clifford Geertz , *The Religion of Java* (Glencoe, Ill.: Free Press, 1960); R. M. Koentjaraningrat, *Javanese Culture* (New York: Oxford University Press, 1989).

3. For analysis of Sumarah, see David G. Howe, "Sumarah: A Study in the Art of Living," Ph.D. diss., University of North Carolina, Chapel Hill, 1980. For Muhammadijah, see James L. Peacock, *Muslim Puritans: Reformist Psychology in Southeast Asian Islam* (Berkeley: University of California Press, 1978); and *Purifying the Faith: The Muhammadijah Movement in Indonesian Islam* (Palo Alto, Calif.: Cummings Press, 1978). For Javanese Islam in general, see Mark

Woodward, *Islam in Java: Normative Piety and Mysticism in the Sultanate of Yogyakarta* (Tucson: University of Arizona Press, 1989).

4. For analysis of the Primitive Baptists, see James L. Peacock and Ruel W. Tyson, *Pilgrims of Paradox: Calvinism and Experience among the Primitive Baptists of the Blue Ridge* (Washington, D.C.: Smithsonian Institution Press, 1989), pp. 341–51; for Pentecostalism, see Robert M. Anderson, *Vision of the Disinherited: The Making of American Pentecostalism* (New York: Oxford University Press, 1979) and Grant Wacker, "The Function of Faith in Primitive Pentecostalism," *Harvard Theological Review* 77 (June 1984): 353–75.

5. The four narratives are described in greater detail and with somewhat different interpretation elsewhere; see Peacock, *Purifying the Faith;* idem, "Life History and Religion: An Exploration in Cultural Psychology," in Edward M. Bruner, ed., *Text, Play, and Story* (Prospect Heights, Ill.: Waveland Press, 1988), pp. 94–116; idem, "Belief Beheld," Stewart Lectures in World Religion, Princeton University, 1990; and

Peacock and Tyson, *Pilgrims of Paradox*. "I" in this chapter refers to Peacock, in relation to his fieldwork; the construction and interpretations of this essay are jointly by Peacock and Pettyjohn.

6. Mailrapport, "Reports from Departmen van Kolonien," Ministerie van Binnenlandse, 1914.

7. Erik Erikson, *Young Man Luther* (New York: Norton, 1958).

8. Victor Turner, "The Center out There: Pilgrim's Goal," *History of Religions* 12, no. 3 (1973): 191–230.

9. Max Weber, *Economy and Society* (Berkeley: University of California Press, 1978), p. 218.

10. See Woodward, *Islam in Java*.

11. George Marsden, *Fundamentalism and American Culture* (New York: Oxford University Press, 1980), p. 61.

12. See Howe, "Sumarah."

13. James L. Peacock, "The Creativity of Tradition in Indonesian Islam," *History of Religions* 25 (May 1986): 341–51, argues that mysticism outdid reformism in the transformation of Indonesian culture through a nuanced transition from inner to outer experience.

14. Elaine J. Lawless, *Handmaidens of the Lord* (Philadelphia: University of Pennsylvania Press, 1988); Beverly Patterson, "Sound of the Dove: An Ethnography of Singing in Primitive Baptist Churches," Ph.D. diss., University of North Carolina, Chapel Hill, 1989.

15. Bruce B. Lawrence, *Defenders of God: The Fundamentalist Revolt against the Modern Age* (San Francisco: Harper and Row, 1989).

Religious Fundamentalisms Compared: Palestinian Islamists, Militant Lebanese Shi'ites, and Radical Sikhs

Emile Sahliyeh

With the onset of the processes of modernization and secularization, many theorists of social and political change concluded that the separation of religion from politics is final. The two processes generated widespread expectations that, through the advancement in science and technology and the secular-rational transformation of the traditional values and institutions, individuals— irrespective of their place of residence—would enjoy the benefits of modernization and overcome their economic hardships.

Yet the rise of a militant religious fundamentalism among the Sikhs, the Lebanese Shi'ites, and the Palestinians, among other groups in the 1970s and the 1980s, challenges such assertions. Indeed, fundamentalism among the three groups came in response to the processes of modernization and secularization and highlighted the shortcomings of both, which include crime and "moral corrosion," and the breakdown of the family. In the 1970s and 1980s, members of the three communities increasingly articulated their political and socioeconomic demands in religious terms and explained politics by drawing upon religious historical analogies; in the 1990s, they continue in this fashion, professing to preserve the true belief system, uphold traditional ways of life and religious practices, and observe strict rules of personal and social conduct. This brand of religious fundamentalism is popular among the rural poor, the urban underprivileged, and intellectuals and professionals. Each movement aspires to improve the living conditions of its followers through the formation of a community of believers. For this reason, they have developed authoritarian organizations and established clear boundaries between them and their enemies.

In addition to being a counterresponse to the forces of modernization and secularism, fundamentalism resulted in these three cases from the crisis of national identity, the failure of the local political economy, and class cleavages. Religion, language, race, culture, and ethnonationalism also furnished the bases for religious fundamentalism. A number of external factors accelerated the rise of the fundamentalist phenomenon.

Despite their differences, the three fundamentalist movements share a number of features. This study compares the three religious movements in terms of the explanatory variables that account for their emergence and compares their structures, ideologies, and relationships with the existing power holders. To achieve these objectives, the chapter uses an explanatory framework that consists of crisis theory and resource mobilization models. This conceptual framework helps to point out the common causes and the properties of fundamentalism in the three communities.

Fundamentalism as a Reaction to Crises

The Islamic resistance movement (Hamas) in the Israeli-occupied territories formed in reaction to the increasing secularization of the Muslim Palestinians and their drifting away from their religious beliefs and practices. Hamas's leadership was dismayed by the "erosion of Palestinian morality," which was partly caused by Israel's occupation of Palestine and exposing the Palestinians to an alien culture and values. In a similar fashion, the Sikh fundamentalists were reacting to the growing secularization of their community in postindependence India.

Much of the criticism of the three fundamentalist movements was directed against symbols of secularization and against those coreligionists who drifted away from religious tradition. Certain aspects of modernity were singled out for attack, including television, cinema, secular voluntary associations, ideologies, and political parties. These have been seen as threats corrupting the young and estranging them from their religious beliefs. For instance, Hamas launched a campaign against owners of liquor stores and movie theaters, and those Palestinians who are morally corrupt. In the same vein, Sikh activists, troubled by the increasing secularization of their community, attacked Sikhs perceived as disloyal to their own tradition, including those who shaved or trimmed their beards, or failed to wear a double-edged sword, military shorts, and bracelet-shield.

Fundamentalism in these cases also displayed a strong nationalist overtone. Defining the nation in exclusive religious terms was a common response to externally generated threats to group ethnic identity and political integrity; these threats included rival religions and ethnic groups, and secular elite and political movements. The three communities share a common belief that their cultural, religious, and ethnic identities are endangered by the culture of an alien majority. Such threats compelled them to invoke past traditions so as to preserve their national existence and their cultural purity, and to put forward demands for political independence. The subjugation of the Palestinians and the Lebanese Shi'ites to Israel's military occupation induced both groups to employ religion as a distinctive marker of group identity in order to counter their exposure to Western lifestyles and value systems. The Sikhs, too, felt such threats. The risk to their identity emanated from the Hindu majority, no less than from the secular Indian government seeking to impose its rule on Punjab.[1]

Periodic attacks on the holy shrines of the Sikhs, the Palestinians, and the Lebanese Shi'ites deepened their sense of vulnerability and insecurity and increased the appeal of fundamentalist sentiments. Following the Operation Blue Star military action in early June 1984, in which the Indian army stormed the Golden Temple and killed Jarnail Singh Bhindranwale and some of his followers, many of the Sikhs concluded that their minority status and culture were imperiled by the Hindu majority who controlled the government.[2] Intensification of religious sentiments also occurred among the Palestinians as a result of Jewish extremist attacks on the Islamic holy places in Jerusalem and Hebron. With regard to the Lebanese Shi'ites, throughout the second half of the 1970s and the 1980s, the Shi'ite villages and holy places in southern Lebanon often were subjected to Israeli military attacks. This situation forced the already impoverished Shi'ites to leave their towns and villages in southern Lebanon.

Religious Fundamentalism and Political Economy

The three fundamentalist movements were also affected by the state of the economy, the level of economic development, and unemployment in India, Lebanon, and the occupied territories. Mounting unemployment and the scarcity of social, educational, and health services were linked to the uneven distribution of the benefits of modernization; the resulting religious fundamentalist discourse in each of our three cases accentuated purity (the condition of being free from corruption), equality, and development as the gifts of a return to religious politics.

The deteriorating economic conditions were manifested in the decline of the percentage of peasants working in agriculture. After its occupation of the West Bank and the Gaza Strip in 1967, Israel expropriated 52 percent of the West Bank land and 40 percent of the Gaza Strip, thus reducing the available land for cultivation.[3] By the mid-1980s, the percentage of those Palestinians working in agriculture dropped to 28 percent and 17 percent in the West Bank and Gaza, respectively.[4] Many of these peasants sought employment inside the Jewish state. During the second half of the 1980s and the early 1990s, the economic conditions inside the occupied territories deteriorated further. The massive emigration of Jews from the former Soviet Union and the economic recession in Jordan and the gulf region caused additional unemployment among the Palestinians. It was under these gloomy economic conditions that on 12 December 1988 Hamas joined the political scene of the West Bank and the Gaza Strip.

In India, the uneven economic progress resulting from rapid agricultural development in Punjab polarized Sikh society. Like the Palestinians, the Sikh peasants experienced deteriorating economic conditions and dislocation. The Green Revolution increased social differentiation in Punjab by enriching the already well-to-do farmers and by forcing the poor peasants to leave their land and join the ranks of the unemployed. As a result of the introduction of mechanized farming, 24 percent of the small farmers and 31 percent of the marginal farmers in Punjab lived below the poverty line in 1982.[5] The number of landless peasants increased from approximately 17 percent in 1961 to 38 percent two decades later; the labor force employed in agriculture declined from 38 percent to 11 percent.[6] These deteriorating economic conditions enabled the Sikh radicals to enlist support from among the impoverished peasants, the marginal small farmers, and the poor farmworkers.

The Shiʻite economy experienced a similar trend in the decline of the agricultural labor force. Unemployment among the Shiʻites increased in the 1980s as a result of the movement toward cash crops and farm mechanization. The Shiʻite farmers who continued to use traditional farming techniques were unable to compete in this modern environment. Despite the fact that 68 percent of the agricultural land is controlled by Shiʻite peasants, only 5.1 percent of the national budget was allocated for economic development of these areas.[7]

Religious Fundamentalism, the Secular Elite, and Political Parties

Fundamentalism among the three groups was preceded by the rise of inconclusive secular political movements. Several efforts ranging from extremely conservative to ultraradical ideologies sought to represent the interests of the Sikh community. Among these groups were the Congress Party and the Akali Dal, who alternated ruling Punjab between 1970 and 1985. The Akali Dal, a Sikh party, endorsed a reformist orientation based on an equitable federal form of government. It advocated redistributing power between the central government and the individual states and granting to the latter more autonomy in the areas of economic development and social and religious affairs.[8] It was the belief of the Akali Dal that this federal political system would ensure democracy in India, preserve political rights for all the religious communities, and promote economic development.

The various elite factions and political party rivalries in Punjab, however, encouraged Sikh fundamentalism.[9] Competition existed between the Congress Party and the Akali Dal. The latter party—dominated by rich landowners—failed to bring about a solution to Punjab's economic crisis or to improve the living conditions of the landless peasants.[10] The failures of the Akali Dal paved the road for the emergence of more radical political parties. In 1983, Bhindranwale, the head of the Sikh religious school (Damdami Taksal), formed a new radical political party (Khalsa Dal) as a rival to the Akali Dal party for the control of the Sikh religion. Under the leadership of Bhindranwale, the Khalsa Dal and the Damdami Taksal advocated a militant approach to address Sikh grievances.

Like the Sikhs, Lebanese Shiʻite fundamentalists were subject to modernizing secular movements. Postindependence advancements in Lebanese communications and transportation eliminated the Shiʻites' sense of geographic and social seclusion and exposed the Shiʻites to outside ideologies.[11] As has been widely documented, the needs of the Shiʻites became so intricate and numerous that the traditional leadership could not meet their rising expectations. During the 1960s, they began to participate in a wide range of secular political parties: the Baʻth, the Arab nationalists, the Syrian nationalists, and the Lebanese Communist Party. The failure of these parties to ameliorate the living conditions of the Shiʻites prompted Imam Musa al-Sadr (the religious and political leader of the Shiʻites) in the mid-1970s to form AMAL. The primary aim of this new organization was to promote the political and economic interests of the Shi'ite community and to reform the Lebanese political and economic system.[12] AMAL supported Lebanon's territorial integrity, national sovereignty, and cultural and religious diversity.

Lebanese fundamentalism was also brought about by the failure of the traditional leadership and the new secular parties to address the political and socioeconomic needs of their community. This leadership, which benefited from the existing Lebanese confessional system, ignored the economic and political inequality of their constituents. Similarly, the secular political parties were unable to moderate the rapid urbanization of the Shi'ites or to provide them with equality. Like the secular movements, AMAL failed to reform Lebanon's political system. This situation increased the exasperation of the Shi'ites and created a power vacuum that was eventually filled by Hizbullah.

The Palestinian religious fundamentalists share a comparable experience. Palestinians in the West Bank and Gaza were exposed to secular and traditional politicians in the 1950s and 1960s. These included the Arab nationalists, the Communists, the Ba'th, and the Jordanian government.[13] In the 1970s, they were attracted to Palestinian nationalism and the PLO and its factions. The secular and traditional political parties' elite, however, were unable to bring about solutions to pending problems, because of their political division and rivalries. The insensitivity of the PLO to the political and economic grievances of its followers inside the occupied territories diminished its legitimacy and increased the appeal of Islam among the discontented. The alliance between the PLO mainstream politicians, the middle-class intellectuals and professionals, and some older politicians left unaddressed some salient problems, including the questions of economic development and the place of religion and women in society.[14] The negligence of such developmental issues led to the creation of a psychological gulf between the urban elite and the residents of the rural areas and refugee camps.

This situation contributed to the rise of fundamentalism. To many disillusioned young Palestinians, the stands of the Islamic movement became more attractive. To fill the power vacuum created by the PLO's diplomatic immobilism, the Muslim Brotherhood founded Hamas. The creation of Hamas was intended to give a new image to the conservative nature of the Brotherhood and to underline its commitment to the Palestinian cause.

Organization, Structures, and Resources

The nature of the political system, governmental legitimacy, and the level of popular participation in fundamentalist movements are factors that affect their chances of success. In the three cases, fundamentalism arose in a political climate characterized by a *relative degree of democratization*. In India, Lebanon, and the West Bank and Gaza, trade unions, voluntary associations, and political parties and movements have been part of the local political landscape. This situation enabled the fundamentalists to operate openly, for the most part.

Fundamentalism surfaced also in an environment of religious or sectarian conflict.

Each of the three movements was and is engaged in a power struggle with a rival religious enemy. Hizbullah wishes to establish an Islamic society in Lebanon, a goal that placed the party in direct conflict with the Lebanese Christians; the radical Sikhs aspire to establish Khalistan as a Sikh state free from Hindu domination; the followers of Hamas insist on the formation of an Islamic state in all of Palestine. The cultures of the Sikhs, the Lebanese Shi'ites, and the Palestinians do not distinguish between religion and politics. In Lebanon, religion shapes the cultural milieu and delineates the social and political identity of the individual.[15] To a large extent, the Sikhs and the Palestinians function in a similar cultural setting. In Punjab, for example, the Sikhs encounter the social differentiation and inequality at the heart of the Hindu culture; accordingly, they draw sharp boundaries between themselves and the Hindu majority.

In addition to these contextual factors, the three cases were triggered by major political developments. Hizbullah's emergence was precipitated by the outbreak of the Islamic revolution in Iran in 1979 and by Israel's invasion of Lebanon in 1982. The Green Revolution in India caused economic inequalities in Punjab, a major stimulus to the radicalization of some segments of Sikhism. In turn, Hamas was triggered by the outbreak of the Intifada in 1987 and the leading role that the Islamic Jihad played in the outbreak of the uprising.

Despite the impact of these various forces, however, religious fundamentalism among the Shi'ites, the Sikhs, and the Palestinians could not emerge unless these groups possessed certain distinctive assets and resources that met the needs of adaptation. Charismatic leadership, organizational structures, communication networks, manpower, economic assets, political opportunities, and ideology were the primary resources that facilitated religious militancy.[16]

The Role of Charismatic Leaders and Religious Institutions

Each of the three religious movements was headed by a charismatic leader. These men possessed extraordinary qualities and are distinguished for their mastery of sacred texts. The emergence of such charismatic leadership provided ideological, organizational, and coalition-building skills that proved necessary for the growth of fundamentalism, while the access of those leaders to modern mass media—including television, radio, printed material, communal associations, and places of worship—permitted them to disseminate their ideas among their followers. Access to media also allowed them to increase their recruitment potential and to take their message to the urban poor, the refugee-camp dwellers, and the inhabitants of the rural areas. Unlike the traditional religious leaders who were passive and status quo—oriented, the new appealing leaders were not hesitant to engage in violence and to defy their enemies. The suffering endured by those leaders immortalized them in the eyes of their followers.

The importance of the charismatic leader is clear in the case of Bhindranwale, the leader of the Damdami Taksal, who hastened the rise of Sikh fundamentalism. Bhindranwale sought to contain the growing appeal of secularism and the indifference toward religion by invoking Sikh religious tradition. He believed that the formation of the State of Khalistan would usher in the redemption of the Sikhs.[17] Bhindranwale selected from the Sikh religious traditions of the fifteenth and sixteenth centuries the inseparability of state and religion, and the use of violence to defend Sikh interests. His advocacy of a militant approach not only intensified the Sikhs' fight against the central government, but also made Punjab uncontrollable and weakened the Akali Dal. In 1982, he participated in the "righteous battle" (*har'na yuo'tih*) that was instigated earlier by the Akali Dal against the Indian government. Bhindranwale asserted that in this conflict the cause of his followers would prevail. His death at the hands of the Indian army in June 1984 unleashed a wave of Sikh violence and terrorism.[18]

The case of Shi'ite fundamentalism in Lebanon manifested an analogous pattern. Imam Musa al-Sadr inculcated in his followers the feeling of belonging to Shi'ism and its legacy of revolt and sacrifice.[19] Unlike Bhindranwale, Sadr was not a militant leader. He advocated the reformation of the Lebanese political system and hoped for a better share for the Shi'ites. The vanishing of Imam Musa al-Sadr in Libya in August 1978 provided a rallying point for the Shi'ite community and transmuted AMAL into a major political military force. His disappearance exemplified the missing imam in the Shi'ite tradition and made him a hero among his adherents. The early 1980s witnessed the rise of yet another charismatic religious leader, Sayyid Muhammad Husayn Fadlallah. Fadlallah is the chief ideologue and founder of Hizbullah (the Party of God). His students and colleagues undertook the task of organizing and mobilizing members of the Shi'ite community. These second-tier leaders were usually recruited from among relatively deprived Shi'ite clergymen.

The Palestinian Islamic movement unveiled its own appealing leader, Shaykh Ahmed Yassin, the leader of Hamas.[20] Under his leadership, the Brotherhood changed its passive posture toward Israel and adopted a more militant approach based on military confrontation and the liberation of the entire land of Palestine. Yassin promoted educational and health services in the Gaza Strip and in the development of the Islamic university. He also mediated problems related to marriage, inheritance, divorce, landownership, and family quarrels. In 1983 and 1989, Yassin was arrested on charges of arms possession and anti-Israeli stands. Yassin's imprisonment provided his followers with additional momentum and led them to engage in violence against the Israeli army.

The presence of Imam Musa al-Sadr, Muhammad Husayn Fadlallah, Ahmed Yassin, and Bhindranwale, among others, facilitated the process of religious indoctrination, recruitment, and organization of the discontented. The lifestyles of those leaders contrasted sharply with the luxuries enjoyed by secular politicians. Through teaching, daily contacts with their followers, and the attraction of their message, those religious leaders gave hope to their adherents for a better future where particular grievances would be overcome.

Aside from those charismatic leaders, the crumbling of the old order brought into the political scene a second tier of newly educated religious leaders. Such a change was noticeable in the membership profile of the Shi'ite clerics and the Muslim Brotherhood movement.[21] Unlike the previous generation of leaders, the new clergy had educational training outside the religious institution and have been exposed to contemporary thinking. Some of those leaders have acquired education in medicine, humanities, or engineering.[22]

The holy texts for the three groups serve as additional valuable resources for mass mobilization. The lofty moral precepts embraced in these holy books, such as the commitment to social, economic, and political equity, equip the religious activists with a persuasive moral power over their followers.

The pervasiveness of places of worship is another common resource for the three fundamentalist movements. These sites provide a vehicle for face-to-face communication and offer free or inexpensive social services. In this context, many of the activities of Hamas and the Muslim Brotherhood in the West Bank and Gaza centered on the mosques. A vast network of day-care agencies, religious schools, youth and sports clubs, clinics, nursing homes, and financial assistance programs were established. The creation of the Islamic Center, the Islamic University in Gaza, and several Islamic colleges in the West Bank provided the Muslim Brotherhood with an additional means to advance their political agenda. These institutions served as mechanisms for the recruitment of new members and their indoctrination along Islamic lines. The construction of hundreds of new mosques also promoted fundamentalism among the Lebanese Shi'ites. The growing number of worshipers necessitated hiring more imams, creating new religious organizations, and publishing Islamic books. In the State of Punjab, approximately twenty thousand *gurudwaras* (places of worship and pilgrimage) serve as public accommodation places for the use of the Sikh community.[23] Over the years, some of these sites furnished the radical leadership with a forum for the mobilization and organization of the Sikhs and for educating them on their history and the sacrifices of their predecessors.

In addition to places of worship, the power resources of the religiously active Palestinians, Shi'ites, and Sikhs included organizational structures for the articulation of the demands of the members of the three communities. Such political frameworks took the form of militant political parties, movements, or authoritarian organizations. In the 1980s, the Damdami Taksal, the Sikh religious school, came into existence under the leadership of Bhindranwale.[24] Bhindranwale also formed a radical Sikh separatist party, the Khalsa Dal. The political failures of the more moderate party (the Akali Dal) in the late 1960s and the 1970s, the unsettling social and economic outcomes of the Green Revolution in Punjab, and the rise of Bhindranwale were among the factors that led to the rejuvenation of such political organizations. In addition to being engaged in violence against the Indian government, the Damdami Taksal and the Khalsa Dal convened a number of popular rallies and collectively endorsed resolutions to form a state for the Sikhs (Khalistan) in Punjab.

In Lebanon, the Shi'ites developed several organizations to promote their political and religious programs.[25] AMAL was widely received by the Shi'ites. Following Sadr's disappearance in 1978, a rival organization (Islamic AMAL) was established by Saiyed Hosien Mosawi. The new organization stressed the Islamic identity of the Shi'ites and denied the legitimacy of the Lebanese government. Hizbullah, a third Shi'ite religious movement, was formed to restructure the life of private Lebanese Muslims and to rebuild Lebanon's political-socioeconomic system in accordance with Islamic rules and principles. The party is composed of well-educated and professional Shiʻites.[26] Hizbullah has seven specialized committees: ideological, financial, political, social, judicial, organizational, and military affairs. These committees can be found in areas where Hizbullah operates. The party also keeps a tight organizational structure that allows it to engage in clandestine activities. The demise of the Lebanese central authority enabled the religious activists among the Shiʻites to mobilize their community.

Until the creation of Hamas, the Muslim Brotherhood led the Islamic movement inside the occupied territories. Since Israel's occupation of the West Bank and Gaza, the Muslim Brotherhood operated freely. To avoid any confrontation with the Israeli army, the Brotherhood shied away from immersing itself in the political sphere and confined its activities to the educational and social fields. The restructuring of the goals and the tactics of the Brotherhood in the late 1980s gave a national Islamic coloration to its political rhetoric rather than the previous universal-Islamic tone. This restructuring led to the rise of Hamas.

Though Hamas's support was drawn mainly from the lower and lower-middle classes, it received backing from across the social spectrum of West Bank and Gaza society. Its popular appeal was enhanced by the attacks of its followers on the Israeli soldiers as well as by the decline of job opportunities within and outside the occupied territories. Hamas has a number of paramilitary organizations: the political, intelligence, propaganda, and security departments.[27] Whereas the political and propaganda departments are responsible for the articulation of Hamas's political stands and the promotion of its policies and ideology, intelligence is in charge of collecting information and directing Hamas's secret activities. The military department al-Mujahedoun (the holy warriors) has been responsible for planning and executing attacks on Israeli targets, such as killing and kidnapping soldiers and Jewish settlers and bombing institutions. The security department, al-Majed (glory), interrogates and often executes collaborators. It also gathers information and sometimes "enforces Islamic ethical codes like harassing drug dealers, prostitutes, and those who sell wine and pork."[28]

Religious Fundamentalism as a Function of the Political Space

Political space is another common factor in the rise of the three fundamentalist movements. This political space encompasses the presence of an aggrieved population, the tolerance of the power holders for the activities of this group, and the availability of external support. The flight of the Shiʻites from the poor economic conditions in southern Lebanon in the 1960s and from Israeli military attacks on the PLO's bases in the 1970s and 1980s, and the creation of new slums for the displaced Shiʻites in the outskirts of Beirut aroused their sectarian awareness, made them receptive to radical and revolutionary fundamentalist calls, and rendered them targets for the political induction of religious activists. In a similar vein, high schools, colleges, and refugee camps in the occupied territories provided fertile ground for recruitment of the followers of the Islamic movement. Many of the competent cadres of Hamas and the Islamic movement in general were enlisted from the PLO activists who were in Israeli jails.[29]

After their release, many of those former prisoners assumed a leadership role in their local communities.

Opportunities for political revitalization of religious fundamentalism are not confined to the presence of the aggrieved population and domestic political conditions. The backing of the power holders has also been crucial for the rise of Sikh, Palestinian, and Shi'ite fundamentalism. Governmental permission or denial of political space weighs heavily on the ability of the fundamentalists to operate. The governmental co-optation of these religious groups created an astute atmosphere for the ascension of fundamentalism and allowed it to operate with few political limitations.[30] The Jordanian government's legalization of the Muslim Brotherhood movement in the mid-1950s furnished it with the political space needed to build up mass support in different parts of the country. In the late 1970s and the first half of the 1980s, Israel condoned the activities of the Brotherhood to check the influence of the PLO. It permitted the circulation of Islamic literature, the construction of mosques, and the formation of Islamic political groups. The Islamic movement also benefited from the support of the PLO, which sought to restrain the influence of the Palestinian radical groups by sanctioning the rising Islamic movement in the late 1970s.

Fundamentalism among the Sikhs can also be attributed in part to the political space provided by the local elite. In an effort to widen their popular support and political legitimacy, India's politicians often encouraged the Sikh religious movement. For example, in the late 1970s and early 1980s, Mrs. Gandhi's government supported the activities of the Sikhs. Similarly, after its election loss in the early 1980s, the Akali Dal resorted to agitation in the Sikh community in an attempt to win the next elections.[31]

Outside governmental and private help are crucial in sustaining the fundamentalist movements. Religious groups in the occupied territories, Punjab, and Lebanon gained from the financial, political, and military support of neighboring countries, movements, and individuals. In the 1980s, for instance, the political ascendancy of AMAL and Hizbullah came in response to the external security needs of both Syria and Iran. The ruling elite of Syria (the Alawites) has always regarded the Lebanese Shi'ites as their coreligionists. The taking of Iran by the Islamic revolution in 1978 served as a source of inspiration for many Lebanese Shi'ites. Since that time, Iran has provided them with ideological motivation and financial and military support. By the late 1980s, Iran contributed approximately $30 million per month to promote Hizbullah's political agenda and to support its hospitals, schools, and sanitation services.[32] After 1982, Iran stationed two thousand of its revolutionary guards in the al-Biqa' region, and provided military training and technical support to Hizbullah.

Over the years, the tension between the Indian governments and Pakistan benefited the Sikh fundamentalist groups. The Indo-Pakistani tension prompted the Pakistani government to aid the Sikh separatist insurrection. Following the attack on the Golden Temple in July 1984, the Indian government accused Pakistan of actively supporting the Sikh rebellion.[33] Likewise, the PLO's political standing with the Arab governments controlled the availability of economic resources to the Muslim Brotherhood and Hamas. Periods of intense hostility between the PLO and Jordan and Saudi Arabia increased the financial assistance to the Islamic movement.

Aside from direct governmental support, outside private financial contributions allowed the three movements to render social and charity work, to initiate economic projects, and to build mosques and temples. The sources of such funds are international network groups and transnational kindred or private citizens. The Muslim Brotherhood received financial assistance from Palestinians living in Saudi Arabia and the Arab gulf states as well as from citizens of these countries. Likewise, well-to-do Lebanese Shi'ites in Africa and the gulf region extended generous financial aid to their coreligionists. Similarly, the Sikhs have obtained assistance from fellow Sikhs living in the West.

Ideological and Political Properties and Programs

Aside from the resemblance among the three movements in the areas of explanatory variables and structures and resources, other parallels can be found at the ideological and political levels. Such similarities include the nationalist overtone of the religious movements, the propensity toward violence, the admissibility of modern science and technology, the hostility toward Westernization, the presence of a millenarian vision, and the call for equality.

The Centrality of Ethnonationalism

The fundamentalism of the Sikhs, Shi'ites, and Palestinians has a strong nationalist overtone. Indeed, it is a reaction to outside threats to their individual ethnonational identity. Fundamentalism provides them with a survival technique in the face of Jewish, Christian, and Hindu ethnonational majorities. Profound nationalist concerns are thus central to each of the movements. These concerns are evidenced in the promotion of each group's ethnic identity, cultural purity, and self-preservation. Such basic ingredients of modern nationalism are at the heart of these fundamentalist movements.

Ethnonationalism is expressed in the use of religion by the three communities to advance their political rights and buttress their quest to establish their own independent nation-state. The nationalist component of the Sikh fundamentalist movement is seen in the quest of the followers of Bhindranwale and the Akali Dal to establish a separate nation-state (Khalistan) in Punjab. It is also shown in their animosity toward the Hindu national majority. This ongoing national antagonism has sustained the momentum of the Sikh fundamentalist movement.[34] Analogous nationalist sentiments are found in the fundamentalist movements of the Palestinians and the Lebanese Shi'ites. Their stand on nationalism is strongly anti-Western and anti-Israeli. The nationalist dimension of the Palestinian Islamic groups is explicit in their insistence on the formation of an Islamic state in all of Palestine and their hostility to Israel. From their perspective, Palestine in its entirety is Islamic land, and this fact was not changed by the creation of Israel.[35] Indeed, under the influence of such ideas the Palestinian Muslim Brotherhood assumed a nationalist dimension, which came at the expense of Islamic universalism. To the Lebanese Shi'ite fundamentalists, though their fellow Shi'ites constitute one-third of the Lebanese society, their share in the country's wealth and political power is not commensurate with their numerical size. Indeed, their rivals among the Sunnis and the Maronites have been in control of Lebanon's political and economic fortunes. These inequities prompted the Shi'ites to seek an Islamic state in Lebanon. The complexity of Lebanese society and its sectarian nature, however, compel them to seek the mundane objective of attaining a more equitable place in the Lebanese political and economic system.

The Presence of a Common Enemy

The fixation with an identifiable enemy is another shared ideological property. Each of the three movements points to a specific foe as being the source of its troubles and hardships. Their foes include the former colonialist powers, their present governments, secular nationalists, Communists, modernists, and some coreligionists. Hizbullah and Hamas regard Western imperialism as one of their primary enemies. Hizbullah, for instance, attributes the difficulties and problems of the Muslim world to foreign imperialism and, in particular, to the United States and Zionism.[36] It holds the West accountable for the division and underdevelopment of the Islamic world. For this reason, Hizbullah seeks to fight all forms of imperialism. Like Hizbullah, Hamas singles out the United States and Israel as the principal enemies of the Palestinian people.[37] It does not recognize Israel's existence and is opposed to the Arab-Israeli peace process and the formation of a West Bank–Gaza Palestinian state. In its view, the peace process can neither bring justice to the Palestinians nor restore their rights in Palestine. Such rights can only be attained through the liberation of Palestine and the establishment of an Islamic state. Hamas maintains, therefore, that Palestine's relationship with Israel should be one of relentless hostility and not one of peaceful coexistence. To arrest such a menace, Hamas banned any ties with Israel other than economic contacts; the return to the fundamental tenets of Islam and the waging of a holy war against Israel are the only true alternatives for restoring Palestinian national rights. In the view of the founders of Hamas, the vitality of Islam was proven by its spread to different parts of the world. Though Hamas's adherents in the Gaza Strip and the West Bank regard themselves as the select group who will be the spearhead in the struggle against Israel, such a task can be accomplished only in conjunction with other Muslim people. While the Lebanese state was too weak to constitute a real danger, Hizbullah views Israel as an external imperialist state and its Lebanese Christian allies as the oppressors of the Shi'ite community. Hamas regards the PLO as a secular nationalist movement that is willing to compromise over Palestine.

All three fundamentalist movements view modern secular media—television, cinema, literature—and voluntary associations and political parties as a threat corrupting the young and estranging them from their religious beliefs. Moreover, the three fundamentalist groups distrusted the religious establishment in their individual communities. They regard such traditional clerics as compromising and endangering the survival of the prophetic tradition.

The Propensity toward Violence

Another facet of ethnonationalism is the tendency of the three fundamentalist movements to engage in violence, and the willingness of their followers to die in defense of their cause. The exaltation of personal sacrifice and martyrdom by the Sikh and Shi'ite cultural and religious traditions, and to a lesser extent the Muslim Brothers inside the occupied territories, have furnished powerful ideological motivation to undertake personal political risks that captivated the imagination and admiration of their communities. The recent history of Lebanon, India, and the West Bank and Gaza provides numerous examples of men and women who sacrificed their lives in the name of achieving higher communal goals.

Redemption through martyrdom informs the militancy of the Sikhs and the Lebanese Shi'ites. In both cases, there are numerous historical antecedents for the use of violence against the state and those hostile forces that persecuted them and desecrated their holy shrines. In their prayers and cultural practices, the Shi'ites and the Sikhs recall the history of their heroic ancestors who sacrificed their lives in defense of their religion. While the Sikhs invoked from their religious tradition the teaching of the sixth guru, Hargobind, who warranted the use of the sword, the Shi'ites selected from their religious history the martyrdom of Husayn and Hasan, the sons of the fourth caliph 'Ali, to legitimate their personal sacrifices.

Aside from the religious and historical bases for the propensity toward violence, the experience of the three groups reveals that their engagement in violence is a reaction to governmental actions and policies.[38] The power holders' use of force against the aggrieved Sikhs, Shi'ites, and Palestinians precipitated counterviolence and fundamentalism and often led to the loss of faith in the political process and allegiance to the state. The Indian army's attack on the Golden Temple outraged many Sikhs and compelled them to use violence to achieve their goals. Until that time, many of those Sikhs did not empathize with the politics of fundamentalism.[39] Similarly, Israel's frequent use of force to suppress the Intifada and its aerial attacks on southern Lebanon produced counterviolence among the Palestinians and the Shi'ites.

Selectivity toward Modernization

Another common property of the three movements is the selective attitude toward modernization and the desire to create a pure and virtuous society. Notwithstanding their opposition to aspects of modernization that clash with established moral, social, and religious values, they are not opposed to scientific advancement. In view of the rapid economic change in many parts of the world, Sikh, Shi'ite, and Palestinian fundamentalists do not want to be left behind. This explains the three groups' acceptance of modern science and technology and its application in their particular societies. They widely use modern communication networks and engage in higher education and diverse occupations to advance their goals. While selectively incorporating modern science and technology into their societies, the movements are opposed to the infiltration of Western lifestyles and social values into their social fabric. From their perspective, Western norms and social habits undermine their social traditions and family values, erode morality, and encourage sexuality and social fragmentation. To check such threats, the three fundamentalist groups draw upon their traditions and culture, and spell out certain behavioral rules to govern dress codes, behavior, and reading and viewing material.[40] Social codes ban women from wearing jewelry, cosmetics, and revealing Western-style clothing. Dress codes are meant to draw boundaries between the members of the three fundamentalist movements and the outside communities.

To preserve their traditions and values, each group attempts to build its own community of believers and the harmonious society that is free of social and moral corruption. To achieve this goal, the Sikhs, the Lebanese Shi'ites, and the Islamic Palestinians rely on their sacred books to provide guidance to the individual and the society in all aspects of life. Unlike Islam, however, Sikhism does not have a Shari'a, or jurisprudence, which details the code of behavior for the individual. Instead, the Sikhs have the Rahit-Nama, or the manual of conduct. The Rahit, which consists of oral and scriptural sources, contains a set of axioms specifying distinctive rules for social conduct, dietary habits, and ceremonial practices.[41] As part of its crusade to attain the harmonious community, Hamas heavily stressed the role of education, the distribution of religious literature, lectures and cultural programs, socialization, and the observance of religious holidays. By using these techniques, the Brotherhood seeks to differentiate between themselves and their rivals.[42]

Although the long-term objective of Hamas is to establish an Islamic state in all of Palestine, its immediate goal is to transform the Palestinian society into an Islamic one and undermine the strength of the secular nationalist forces.[43] From its perspective, the persistence of secular nationalism would delay the process of Islamization of the Palestinians. For this reason, the Islamic movement occasionally used violence to contain the influence of the nationalists and to arrest anti-Islamic practices.

Though Sikh fundamentalists consider the entire Sikh community as a single collectivity, the Sikhs have their own chosen community of believers who incorporate a group of chosen soldiers or holy warriors. This is referred to in Sikh mythology as the Khalsa, or the pure. The Sikhs invoked the concept of the Khalsa from the tenth guru, Gobind Singh. To keep away from corruption, lust, and greed, these elect soldiers devote themselves to a righteous life consisting of self-control, continence, and prayer.

Millenarianism and Moral Dualism

Whether it is ending Israel's military occupation, resisting the Indian government's harsh security measures in Punjab, or dealing with unemployment in Lebanon and the occupied territories, members of the three communities have opted to deal with socio-economic and political problems in part by invoking millenarian themes. At the center of this religious tradition is the creation of a harmonious social system free of suffering, corruption, and injustice. The radical Sikhs, the Lebanese Shi'ites, and the Palestinian Islamists maintain that the world is dualistic—divided into good and evil forces—and that ultimately the good will prevail. This sense of moral dualism led the fundamentalists in each group to condemn nonconformists and those who discredit and endanger the community. Though Sikhism is a non-Abrahamic religion and does not share with it a common heritage, millenarianism is an attribute of Sikh fundamentalism's utopian vision of the theocratic State of Khalistan. In contrast to Hizbullah and Hamas, however, the Sikh radicals do not elaborate on their image of how the world should be. The Lebanese Shi'ites are most detailed in their expectations, and alone among the groups exhibit a messianic component; it takes the form of the return of the missing imam, who would intercede on behalf of the faithful.[44]

Equality of the Faithful

Aside from their sense of social and moral superiority, the three fundamentalist movements are politically exclusivist. Each group has its own select members who are presumed to be equal and are distinguishable from the enemy. Moreover, none of these movements makes any special efforts to accommodate its political rivals and allow them to participate in the political process. In this sense, the three groups have antidemocratic and antipluralist orientations. This is manifested in the fact that each of the groups was led by an authoritarian leader.

The advocacy of economic equality is another common aspect among the three religious groups. The focus on equality is rooted in the mounting unemployment among the Sikhs, the Shi'ites, and the Palestinians; the poor health and social services; and the growing class distinction within their societies. Although the three religions highlight the themes of egalitarianism, it is more noticeable in the Sikh movement. The Sikhs' drive toward egalitarianism was caused by the unsettling social and economic consequences of the Green Revolution and by their resentment of the Hindu culture, which emphasizes social differentiation and inequality.[45] The rapid socioeconomic change and the growing class differentiation clashed with the Sikh egalitarian tradition. This situation prompted the Sikhs to champion the formation of a society free from class, racial, economic, and social discrimination.

Conclusion

The preceding analysis yields a number of significant observations that tie the three fundamentalist movements together. First, the causes of religious resurgence are multifarious. The renewed interest in religion has occurred in response to the far-reaching social and economic changes that interrupted the traditional way of life of the Sikhs, the Palestinians, and the Shi'ites. The economic deprivation of these communities, their social exclusion, and political underrepresentation have afforded a suitable environment for the emergence of the phenomenon of religious fundamentalism.

Second, the three religious groups have opted to deal with major social, economic, and personal problems by invoking their prophetic tradition. Issues involving marriage, inheritance, work, and property-related disputes are mediated by religious leaders. Many of these functions have traditionally been performed by the state. In addition, fundamentalism addresses a variety of political questions that are salient to the individual and the society alike. Such concerns have included personal freedoms versus regulated social behavior, ethnonationalism, class cleavages, political autonomy, the place of religion and women in the society, secularism, modernism, and economic development and equality. In a relatively short time, the three groups developed ideas concerning these core issues.

Third, religious fundamentalism gives the individual Shi'ite, Sikh, and Palestinian Muslim a sense of cultural continuity and national existence and furnishes them with a vision for the future. The organizational advantages of the fundamentalists and their access to a sophisticated communication network enables them to include newly emerging classes and social groups in the political process. Indeed, these new groups find religious symbolism—including charismatic leaders and clerics, martyrdom in defense of one's cause, egalitarianism, and divine doctrines—to be valuable assets to buttress their demands for the redistribution of economic resources. Religion also avails these classes of a unifying ideology and institutions to extend social welfare–related services.

Fourth, while providing its followers with numerous benefits, fundamentalism presents a formidable challenge to the forces of secular nationalism. Whether it is in Lebanon, the occupied territories, or Punjab, the fundamentalists seek to redress the status quo. Their long-term objective is to dismantle the existing political and social order and to establish in its place a puritanlike society where religion would guide public and private life.

Finally, although the fundamentalists aspire to establish their exclusivist state, the dictates of political realism would compel them to accept goals short of their ideals. Undoubtedly, the presence of definable enemies will continue to sustain their movements. But the political reality of the existence of Israel and the diverse ethnic and religious composition of both India and Lebanon will compel the fundamentalists to acknowledge such facts. The absorption of such lessons can already be observed. Hamas has occasionally articulated accommodating positions toward Israel, while many Sikhs accept federalism to mediate their grievances against the central government. In their turn, the Lebanese Shi'ites recognize that Lebanon's cultural and religious diversity limits their goal to establish an Islamic republic.

Notes

1. Gurharpal Singh, "Understanding the 'Punjab Problem,'" *Asian Survey* 27 (December 1987): 1277.

2. Mark Tully and Satish Jacob, *Amritsar: Mrs. Gandhi's Last Battle* (London: Jonathan Cape, 1985), pp. 57–58.

3. Cheryl A. Rubenberg, "Twenty Years of Israeli Economic Policies in the West Bank and Gaza: Prologue to the Intifada," *Journal of Arab Affairs* 8 (Spring 1989): 35.

4. Meron Benvenisti, *West Bank Data Report* (Boulder, Colo.: Westview, 1987), p. 19.

5. Harjot Oberoi, "Sikh Fundamentalism: Translating History into Theory," in Martin E. Marty and R. Scott Appleby,

eds., *Fundamentalisms and the State* (Chicago: University of Chicago Press, 1993), pp. 11–13. See also G. S. Bhalla and G. K. Chadha, "Green Revolution and the Small Peasants: A Study of Income Distribution in the Punjab," *Economic and Political Weekly* 17 (May 1982): 826–33, 870–77.

6. Bhalla and Chadha, "Green Revolution and the Small Peasants," p. 870; Arthur W. Helweg, "India's Sikhs: Problems and Prospects," *Journal of Contemporary Asia* 17, no. 2 (1987): 146–51.

7. Many useful tables and figures dealing with the poor economic conditions can be found in Ayla Schbley, "Religious Resurgence and Religious Terrorism: A Study of

the Actions of the Shi'a Sectarian Movements in Lebanon," Ph.D. diss., University of North Texas, Denton, Texas, 1988, pp. 103–9.

8. Oberoi, "Sikh Fundamentalism," p. 32.

9. Joyce Pettigrew, *Robber Noblemen: A Study of the Political System of the Sikh Jats* (London: Routledge and Kegan Paul, 1975), pp. 25–26.

10. Oberoi, "Sikh Fundamentalism," pp. 259–63. On how the Akali Dal favored rich peasants, see Amarjit S. Narang, *Storm over the Sutlej: The Akali Politics* (New Delhi: Gitanjali Publishing House, 1983), pp. 198–99; and Harish K. Puri, "The Akali Agitation: An Analysis of Socioeconomic Bases of Protest," *Economic and Political Weekly* 18 (January 1983): 117.

11. Augustus Richard Norton, "Religious Resurgence and Political Mobilization of the Shi'a in Lebanon," in Emile Sahliyeh, ed., *Religious Resurgence and Politics in the Contemporary World* (Albany: State University of New York Press, 1990), p. 230.

12. For a very useful treatment of AMAL, see Augustus Richard Norton, *Amal and the Shi'a: Struggle for the Soul of Lebanon* (Austin: University of Texas Press, 1987).

13. Emile Sahliyeh, *In Search of Leadership: West Bank Politics since 1967* (Washington, D.C.: Brookings, 1988), chap. 2.

14. Ibid.

15. Michael C. Hudson, *The Precarious Republic: Political Modernization in Lebanon* (New York: Random House, 1968).

16. For a general discussion of the significance of these factors, see Rod Aya, "Theories of Revolution Reconsidered: Contrasting Models of Collective Violence," *Theory and Society* 8 (July 1979): 39–99; Louise A. Tilly and Charles Tilly, eds., *Class Conflict and Collective Action* (Beverly Hills, Calif.: Sage, 1981); Barrington Moore, Jr., *Injustice: The Social Basis of Obedience and Revolt* (White Plains, N.Y.: M. E. Sharpe, 1978); Theda Skocpol, *States and Social Revolutions: A Comparative Study of France, Russia, and China* (Cambridge: Cambridge University Press, 1979), pp. 19–24; and Mancur Olson,

The Logic of Collective Action: Public Goods and the Theory of Groups (Cambridge: Harvard University Press, 1971).

17. Joyce Pettigrew, "In Search of a New Kingdom of Lahore," *Pacific Affairs* 60 (Spring 1987): 1–25; Mark Juergensmeyer, "The Logic of Religious Violence: The Case of the Punjab," *Journal of Strategic Studies* 10 (December 1987): 172–93; T. N. Madan, "The Double-Edged Sword: Fundamentalism and the Sikh Religious Tradition," in Martin E. Marty and R. Scott Appleby, eds., *Fundamentalisms Observed* (Chicago: University of Chicago Press, 1991).

18. Oberoi, "Sikh Fundamentalism," pp. 268–78.

19. Fouad Ajami, *The Vanished Imam: Musa al-Sadr and the Shi'a of Lebanon* (Ithaca, N.Y.: Cornell University Press, 1985).

20. Ahmed Yousef, *The Islamic Resistance Movement: Hamas* (Chicago: United Association for Studies and Research, 1991), pp. 55–60.

21. See, for instance, Ali Jarabawi, *The Intifada and Political Leadership in the West Bank and Gaza Strip* (Beirut: Dar al-Talia, 1989), pp. 111–13.

22. Sayyid Muhammad Husayn Fadlallah, for instance, is a theologian and a scholar. He is the author of many publications, including *Al-Islam wa-muntiq al-quwa* (Islam and the logic of force) and *Al-hiwar fi-al-Qur'an* (Dialogue in the Qur'an).

23. Karandeep Singh, "The Politics of Religious Resurgence and Religious Terrorism: The Case of the Sikhs of India," in Sahliyeh, *Religious Resurgence and Politics*, chap. 17.

24. Oberoi, "Sikh Fundamentalism," pp. 15, 16.

25. Marius Deeb, "Shi'a Movements in Lebanon: Their Formation, Ideology, Social Basis, and Links with Iran and Syria," *Third World Quarterly* 10 (April 1988): 683–98.

26. Ibid., p. 692.

27. Yousef, *The Islamic Resistance Movement*, pp. 22–39.

28. "The Sabra Charter and New Upris-

ing Victims: Suspected Arab Informers," *New York Times,* 2 May 1989, p. A3; Joel Greenberg, "Arabs Decry Non-political Killing," *Christian Science Monitor,* 21 August 1989, p. A3.

29. Ziad Abu-Amr, *The Islamic Movement in the West Bank and Gaza Strip* (Beirut: Al-Quds le-Tibah, 1989), pp. 116–17.

30. Skocpol, *States and Social Revolutions,* pp. 19–24.

31. Karandeep Singh, "The Politics of Religious Resurgence and Religious Terrorism"; Puri, "The Akali Agitation," p. 117.

32. Norton, "Religious Resurgence," p. 238.

33. *Facts on File* (1984), pp. 588–89.

34. Harjot Oberoi, "Mapping Indic Fundamentalism through Nationalism and Modernity," paper presented at the American Academy of Arts and Sciences Conference on Fundamentalisms Compared, Vancouver, B.C., November 1991.

35. For detailed treatment of the political stands of the Palestinian Islamic movement, see Sahliyeh, *In Search of Leadership,* pp. 137–62.

36. Deeb, "Shi'a Movements in Lebanon," p. 693.

37. Yousef, *The Islamic Resistance Movement.*

38. Tilly and Tilly, *Class Conflict and Collective Action,* p. 21.

39. Karandeep Singh, "The Politics of Religious Resurgence and Religious Terrorism."

40. Oberoi, "Sikh Fundamentalism," pp. 22, 23.

41. For more details about the Sikhs, see ibid., pp. 23–25.

42. Mohammed K. Shadid, "The Muslim Brotherhood Movement in the West Bank and Gaza," *Third World Quarterly* 10 (April 1988): 671.

43. Ibid., p. 675.

44. Deeb, "Shi'a Movements in Lebanon," p. 675.

45. Oberoi, "Sikh Fundamentalism," p. 263.

3

Fundamentalisms Compared
within Traditions

Protestants and Catholics in Latin America:
A Family Portrait

Daniel H. Levine

This essay examines the Christian family portrait now emerging in Latin America, and asks how it came to be this way. Particular attention is given to the origins, growth, and character of liberationist Catholicism and fundamentalist Protestantism, and to the relations between them. The central question posed is less to distinguish these trends or to compare one with another than to ask why, since the late 1950s, Latin America should have been the scene of substantial religious innovation of this particular kind: why there, and why at this particular historical moment?

The family portrait of Latin American Christianity has changed in ways that few observers would have anticipated three decades ago. The most striking of these transformations have come in the growth of new churches, in the character of religious organization and practices, and in the nature of religious discourse. A region once confidently assumed to be uniformly Catholic has witnessed innovation and conflict within Catholicism, along with simultaneous Protestant expansion, most notably among churches with Pentecostal messages and connections to North American fundamentalism. There is overt, intense, and widespread competition between churches, and it is now common to encounter large numbers of churches, chapels, and religious meetings where a single Catholic parish once held the field without visible competition. Religious organizations and practices display striking shifts away from the massive public rituals and devotions common to the conventional Catholic culture of the past. Catholics and their Protestant competitors have each developed nets of small, socially homogeneous groups that offer regular and relatively intense religious experiences in familiar settings. In both cases, the norm of religious practice has shifted away from fulfilling minimal sacramental obligations to an informed, literate, and active participation that embraces person, family, and community. A surge of religiously inspired social movements has followed in neighborhoods and communities across the region. Changes in religious discourse hinge above all on the increased centrality of the Bible and devotion to the figure of Christ, as opposed, for example, to saints or particular shrines.

Stressing family resemblances and underscoring shared sources and patterns of change should not obscure substantial differences between the kinds of change represented by liberationist Catholicism and Pentecostal Protestantism in Latin America. Despite the fact that both draw strength from a common pattern of social change, compete for members among similar groups, and have much in common when it comes to discourse and group practices, they remain divided by basic contrasts in the structure of the churches, and in the way each goes about the business of linking faith to family and community life, and to politics. These and related issues are discussed in detail below. To lay a proper foundation for that analysis, let us begin with a look at the origins and pattern of change.

The Family Portrait and How It Got This Way

The simplest place to begin is with the numbers. Most recent discussions underscore the scale and pace of Protestant expansion, and point up the weight of Pentecostal churches and related missionary movements within this pattern.[1] Recent growth differs in character and clientele from earlier Protestant efforts. The new wave of North American missionary effort and church expansion within Latin American countries reaches well beyond the traditional field presented either by foreign communities (e.g., German Lutherans, Scottish Presbyterians) or isolated and mostly nomadic tribal peoples. Further, most of these initiatives are now controlled not by mainline churches but rather by fundamentalist and Pentecostal churches and related parachurch groups.[2]

Although this pattern of growth has been sharpest and fundamentalist preeminence clearest in Central America, Chile, and Brazil, these cases are commonly depicted as just the leading edge of a broad wave of religious change, with major implications for the reconstruction of culture, society, and politics.[3] Observers have been especially preoccupied with the pace of growth, which is commonly described as geometric. In a film I viewed recently (*Onward Christian Soldiers*), a spokesman from the National Association of Religious Broadcasters states that it is no longer a matter of the door being ajar: the hinges are off the door and change is at a flood tide.

It is worth noting that numbers have long been used as weapons in the struggle to legitimize new religious groups and to buttress campaigns for funds, members, and public attention. Current discussions about the pace of Protestant expansion in Latin America recall similar disputes in the early 1980s about the numbers of Christian base communities or CEBs (from the Spanish *comunidades eclesiales de base*) that existed in the region. These groups were widely viewed as the leading edge of religious innovation in Catholicism, tied to the ideas of liberation theology and generative of broad cultural and political change. Subsequent empirical research cast doubt on the validity of the numbers while underscoring variation among CEBs and similar groups. In the process, understanding of the sources, dynamics, and likely impact of change in Catholicism advanced significantly.[4]

Something similar is happening now with the study of Protestant and particularly Pentecostal expansion. A new wave of research has taken a close, critical look at the figures.[5] Estimates of church growth, for example, depend on controversial multipliers (church-supplied membership figures are commonly multiplied by a factor of four). There is evidence of multiple counting, and of failure to address seepage or defections, above all in areas where Protestant expansion has been linked to heavy political and military pressures, as for example in Guatemala.[6] There is also a substantial lack of clarity concerning the social origins of converts to the new churches: class background, gender, and rural or urban setting. These reservations notwithstanding, there is broad agreement in the literature concerning the overall direction and pattern of growth. For present purposes, therefore, I follow Stoll, who takes "evangelical growth as given in order to put certain issues on the table."[7]

Consider, for example, how much recent changes among Latin America's Catholics and Protestants are related to one another. Fear of potential Protestant expansion made initiatives for reform seem particularly urgent to many Catholic leaders in the late 1950s and early 1960s. These early concerns responded less to actual Protestant growth than to two factors that in combination laid the basis for the subsequent emergence of liberationist initiatives. The first was a sense that social changes under way throughout the region would further weaken the church's hold on its mass clienteles. The second was an emerging consensus on the need for reforms of church organizations and practices that would make informed active participation possible.

The conventional wisdom of the matter has long attributed change in Latin American Catholicism to the impact of the Second Vatican Council, adapted and applied to the region in new ways following the landmark 1968 meeting of Catholic bishops at Medellín. Liberation theology crystallized shortly after, along with the now familiar surge of social activism and critical political action by Catholic organizations and activists across the region. This is not the place for extended discussion of these phenomena.[8] My point here is that change did not spring solely from external stimuli (Vatican II). There was much prior innovation throughout the region as Catholic leaders and activists groped for more effective modes of religious organization long before Vatican II crystallized and legitimized the effort.

Innovation in the theory and practice of Latin American Catholicism therefore responded to a double problem that appeared more and more urgent by the mid-1960s. Social, economic, and political transformations were cutting the ground from under long-standing Catholic assumptions about society and politics. In particular, rapid urbanization, the opening up of peasant communities, and growing popular literacy and access to media were making ordinary believers available for new kinds of messages, capable of work with new and more participatory organizations. These changes undermined the effectiveness of existing church structures and methods that relied on static strategies in which clergy took a decisive and directive role. There were not enough clergy to do the job along traditional lines. Population everywhere grew faster

than clergy, and things got worse in the years following Vatican II, which saw considerable shrinkage and aging of clerical personnel. Those priests and sisters remaining
were in any case maldistributed, concentrated in schools and other institutions and
thus not available for work with the general population. At the same time, growing
concern for the promotion of more informed and voluntary participation among
Catholics was energized by translation of texts and liturgies into local languages, by
the new prominence given to the Bible in Catholic practice, and by a host of efforts to
develop new roles for laypeople.

Curious and (for the Catholic hierarchy) mostly unintended consequences followed. Long-standing distinctions marking Catholics off from Protestants faded as
Catholic ritual was simplified and changed to incorporate popular music, local languages, heightened participation, and above all, access to Scripture. Scattered efforts
began across the region to find means of delivering a religious message and encouraging participation even in the absence of clergy.[9] Lay leaders were trained, sisters
given added and more autonomous pastoral responsibilities, and a new model of the
ideal Catholic group appeared in the CEBs mentioned earlier. Limitations of space
preclude detailed discussion of CEBs here.[10] The important point here is to note how
much their logic, structure, and ordinary routine have rested on smallness of size, Bible
study, and active local participation.

These and related changes brought new groups and issues to center stage, and did
much to invigorate Catholic institutions and practices.[11] They also sparked intense and
widespread debate, not only within the Catholic church but also between Catholic
and other institutions. Politics played a central role here. The spread of authoritarian
regimes and an unprecedented surge of intense repression throughout the region
enhanced the resonance of new religious messages about equality and justice. By
shutting off other avenues of social and political expression, repression also drove activists and potential clients to the churches—there was often nowhere else to go. New
religiously inspired groups nurtured a theory and practice of democracy and self-
governance. At the same time, the combination of a more critical discourse about politics and efforts to defend the activities of new church-related groups drew Catholic
leaders into sharp, often violent conflict with civil and military authorities. Throughout the region, church-state conflict reached levels unknown since the mid–nineteenth
century.

All this is well known and has been much documented.[12] Less attention has gone
to the impact that changes in Catholicism had on the growth and character of Protestantism. At the broad level of relations between institutions, it is apparent that authorities in conflict with Catholic leaders (e.g., on issues of social justice or human rights)
often facilitated Protestant activities, in search of legitimation and as a general sign of
their own religious tolerance. Military leaders who saw themselves defending Christian
civilization against godless communism felt betrayed by criticism from their own
church, and condemned Marxist subversion of religion.[13]

At the level of organization and practice, numerous long-standing distinctions between Catholics and Protestants were washed out. Catholicism was "protestantized,"
for example, with heavy stress on discourse over liturgy, on understanding the word

over "mere" acceptance of sacraments, on preaching over praying and ritual, on provision for intense and at least somewhat autonomous community life over submission to hierarchy. To be sure, not everything has changed in the Catholic church, and there has been considerable backlash in recent years, crystallized in Vatican efforts to reaffirm traditional norms of hierarchy, authority, and discipline.[14] But core innovations such as the move to local languages and the encouragement of informed participation remain. In any event, by drawing closer (at least on the surface) to Protestant models of religious organization and practice, innovations in Catholicism opened important doors for Protestant expansion. Protestantism now appeared more legitimate in Catholic circles. Ecumenism was the order of the day, and condemnations were avoided, at least for a while.

A curious and telling dialectic emerges when Catholic and Protestant innovations are set against one another. As Catholics (especially liberationist Catholics) began to emphasize the value of religious experience in small, intense groups, and centered organization and practice on access to the word, at the same time they cut away much of the aesthetic and more mystical sides of religious expression. Of course, prayer and ritual did not disappear, but many conventional and valued aspects of religious practice were clearly underplayed by liberationist groups, whose leaders commonly painted older practices as alienated misunderstandings, obstacles on the way to true liberation.[15] The image of radical priests pressing for action in a congregation wanting to pray is a mainstay of popular folklore. But as liberationists became more "Protestant," the edge of growth among Protestants themselves was increasingly found among churches that—without denying the value of the word or of small groups—placed these in the context of intense spiritual life, with much stress on prayer, healing, personal conversion, and the direct experience of charismatic power.

Catholic innovation opened religious practice to new forms, but may have done so in ways that fatally underestimated the continued appeal of an intense, personal spirituality. I do not mean to suggest that converts to Pentecostal churches necessarily come from those energized and then disillusioned by Catholic innovations. The sheer scale of the numbers suggests that this is unlikely, and in any case, the very logic of liberationist ideas and organizations, and the intensity of participation they demanded, made them more the province of activist minorities than of the rank and file in general.[16] The point is that once doors were opened, liberationist groups were no more than one of several possible options in a religious market. From a consumer's perspective, the issue was no longer going to church or staying away, nor could it be confined to choosing between a conservative church or liberationist CEBs. The religious consumer now faced competition: which church, what kind of organization, which radio preacher, public meeting or crusade. The point holds for rural and urban areas alike. Competition is easier to see in the cities, given the concentration of media and the close proximity of rivals, who often find themselves on opposite corners in the same neighborhood. Competition expanded to the countryside as well, as once-isolated rural communities were opened to new kinds of outside influence all across Latin America. In part this was the result of general economic changes, improved transportation, and growing access to media, especially radio. Declining rural isolation was also spurred by the deliberate efforts of Catholic innovators to engage communities more positively with the outside. Religious innovation of all kinds drew strength from this openness and the legitimacy it gave to the very idea of change. Swanson and Stoll note the ironies for Ecuador, where regions with the strongest and most deeply rooted liberationist Catholic initiatives have also witnessed the broadest and most enduring Protestant expansion.[17]

There has been a tendency lately to assume that in cases of direct competition between liberationist Catholics and fundamentalist Protestants, the former consistently lose.[18] The evidence is unclear, but a few points together suggest why this may be so. Catholicism's lack of institutional flexibility is a basic difficulty.[19] Despite innovations like the CEBs and efforts to create more agile structures (such as vicarates staffed by nuns or pastoral centers in new urban neighborhoods), the Catholic church remains dependent on preexisting networks of parishes and chapels. Protestant churches are newer and much more concentrated in areas of recent urban growth.[20] The home churches and study circles they sponsor are also more vigorous, in no small measure because outreach is a central part of the mission such churches set for themselves.[21]

Structural flexibility is enhanced by the historically fissile character of Protestant growth, and by the extent to which the Protestant scheme of things accommodates and facilitates personal mobility. Protestantism benefits from the availability of choice, building on an image of commitments freely taken and independently pursued. This appeals strongly to populations on the move. In contrast, despite substantial innovations, including those linked to liberation theology, Catholicism's basic ritual patterns and organizational logic remain dependent on a celibate and culturally distant clergy, and on notions of hierarchy. Newly mobile and literate populations find little scope for choice or advancement here.

Despite claims to speak for the people (to be the "voice for the voiceless"), liberationist discourse has often remained alien to its intended clients.[22] Being a voice for the voiceless is not the same as letting the voiceless speak, and even with the best intentions, liberationist activists have had problems shedding directive and paternalistic roles. There are two other reasons the discourse may have remained alien and self-limited. The first concerns the dangers of politics. I noted earlier how much the rise of liberationist Catholicism has been associated with political conflict. Liberationist thinkers and groups saw politics as a necessary field for religious action not because politics was somehow prior to religion, but because in their view a satisfying religious and human life was impossible without a change in the structure of power. This is a political matter, and liberation therefore had to begin with awareness of the causes of oppression, which are taken to be primarily political and structural.[23] But of course politics can be dangerous, and all across the region liberationist groups and activists became prime targets for repression, charged by civil and military authorities with being the "intellectual authors" of subversion. There have been many martyrs.

Politics entails other kinds of risks as well. For example, political activity is culturally perilous for women, who in fact constitute the bulk of CEB members and a majority of converts to the new churches. Carol Drogus suggests that women in the CEBs of São Paulo, Brazil, systematically filter and reconstruct the liberationist message along gender-specific lines: stressing local concerns, moral issues, and conciliation as opposed to conflict and confrontation. They see politics as "men's work"—distant and removed from the core concerns of family, neighborhood, and making a living.[24]

The second reason for the "alien" quality of liberationist discourse concerns its relative deemphasis on issues like prayer, personal morality, or health and healing. Liberationist discourse has stressed collective effort to live well, urging groups to take responsibility for solving their own problems. Ordinary people may see this as blaming the victim for failing to remedy the disease.[25] A deeper problem is that the social emphasis of that discourse undervalues the continuing appeal of moral issues, and of a stress on personal and family responsibility. In the eyes of potential and actual converts, lives can be changed in basic and enduring ways by personal conversion that casts out the devils, and in the process opens individual, family, and community life to the truth of the Bible unmediated by hierarchy, to an upright and self-regulated life, and to health.[26]

One often encounters the argument that fundamentalist stress on personal conversion is a simple and misleading response to complex issues. The "real" solution lies in socially focused collective action.[27] But of course there is nothing "simple" about conversion. The experience is difficult and shattering, and can be enormously empowering. Members of CEBs and converts to Pentecostal churches use similar terms to describe the changes: they speak of going from darkness to light, of gaining self-control and a sense of how to deal with the world, of doors opening to health and to personal and family advancement.[28] Conversion in this sense is best understood not as a wholly otherworldly experience or orientation, but rather as a bridge between worlds, a tapping into charismatic power that then energizes men and women in their life as a whole. As with the Puritans earlier, "Grace imparted by the Spirit regenerates the convert and issues forth in a life of sanctified works. . . . Grace leads ultimately to heaven, but penultimately to a career of holy service suggested by the moral law. Turning does not inhere in a single event; it stretches out through a lifetime of faithful discipline."[29] Karen Fields has also pointed to the tremendous impact of conversion and the sense of personal and social power derived from access to sacred power as central to the links between religious innovation, cultural change, and political resistance in colonial central Africa.[30]

It is impossible to make sense of Pentecostal growth without acknowledging the power and appeal of these experiences. Berryman notes that similar stress on prayer, personal conversion, and openness to charismatic power (including the power to heal) are central to the Catholic charismatic movement, probably the single fastest growing movement in the region.[31] He describes a recent case:

A young woman who was involved in a base community went to a charismatic mass, witnessed speaking in tongues, and responded to the invitation to step forward for healing. She had an ecstatic experience and felt herself healed. Later she told a progressive priest that she had felt at ease and asked whether she had experienced God. He told her he thought it was 90 percent psychological, but admitted to me that the "charismatic movement gets to psychological factors that we in the liberation line don't reach." Among the positive aspects of the charismatic renewal he mentioned were participation, personal renewal, and a festive sense of life. Liberation-oriented pastoral work was deficient in prayer; participants pray in connection with their efforts for change, but such prayer lacks the intensity found in these other church movements.[32]

The differential impact of literacy and access to the Bible warrants separate mention. Every study that I know of affirms the great importance that group members and converts give to the Bible: being able to read it, finding truth in it, learning and being guided by it. Valuation of the Bible appears to be part of a general recognition of the power of the written word, and of education as part of a general process of personal, family, and community improvement. Access to sacred power through access to a text is part of access to power in general. In his careful study of religious change among migrants to Lima, Marzal suggests that access to the Bible has special power because "it comes just at the moment when the migrant is opening up to modern learning, whose symbol is the book. Migrants know that the easiest path for social mobility in our society is education. Getting a good education, at least for the children, is one of the major reasons for migration. In this way, the Bible becomes a symbol of the whole new world that is opening up for migrants."[33]

The scope of access to the Bible is much greater for fundamentalist converts. They also approach the Bible free from the authoritative role of external mediators.[34] Here again, there are important historical parallels. Zaret, for example, stresses the centrality of popular claims to reason, mediated by access to the Bible, in energizing sixteenth-century English Puritans. The distrust of hierarchy and external authority at work in these cases also recalls the surge of popular Christianity in nineteenth-century North America, where barely educated preachers challenged clerical monopolies, disdained formal training, and sparked what Hatch calls a massive "democratization of American Christianity."[35]

The preceding observations clarify several aspects of the Christian family portrait that are often obscured, and point to a few central theoretical issues. Despite conflicts and tensions, the family's different branches clearly have much in common. Religious innovation in Latin America has been centered on a common agenda built around literacy, small and intense groups, flexible organization, and emphasis on personal as well as community responsibility. Protestant and Catholic innovators work in a common context of massive sociocultural and economic changes that make ordinary Latin Americans available for new kinds of messages and more accessible to those promoting them. Both have targeted the same overall population groups: the urban and rural poor and those with some experience of change. Innovations in Catholicism enhanced the legitimacy of Protestantism to former Catholics, and may have unwittingly paved the way for them. But the continuing weight of hierarchy and institutional commitments restrict Catholic ability to act effectively, and limit the potential of Catholic innovations to grow, or even to survive, in their home base.

Liberationist and Protestant churches differ on a number of ideological and structural dimensions. Both reject poverty, for example, but do so for different reasons and with contrasting implications. The analysis crystallized in liberation theology makes poverty hinge on structural exploitation and inequalities. Protestant tradition attributes poverty ultimately to evil, and makes overcoming poverty contingent on conversion and self-mastery.[36] Both positions reflect and reinforce commitments to self-mastery and to work in this world, but liberationist views privilege collective action, while their Protestant counterparts distinguish public from private in ways that delegitimize the effort to form broad transformative political alliances. This does not make the one any more or less "political" than the other. Each affects politics not only through actions explicitly challenging the social and political order, but also as a result of broad efforts to transform cultural expectations, create new social spaces, and build up new forms of community.

Structural differences are not limited to the well-known contrast between churches with multiple transnational connections and those with traditions of local autonomy. There are more transnational linkages among Protestants and greater internal variation among Catholics than this stereotype allows for. The core structural difference is that innovations in Catholicism remain constrained by existing institutional and ideological parameters in ways that do not apply to Protestants, for whom the option of creating a new church has established historical legitimacy. Protestants are therefore freer to innovate but at the same time more subject to the authority of the leader or founder, who is (at least in principle) unconstrained by outside intervention. The curious effect of all this is to affirm the equality of all believers while simultaneously reinforcing the all-encompassing authority of the leader/founder.[37] Contrasting orientations to collective action help make sense out of the conundrum posed by Latin American Protestants' combination of grass-roots equality with stress on acceptance of authority, be it the authority of the father in the family, the pastor in the church, or the military in politics.

The changing family portrait outlined in this section suggests the need for a fresh look at the sources of recruitment to the new churches, and at the reasons for their success in building and holding a mass base. The next section considers alternative explanations.

Explanations

The particular way these changes have developed in Latin America challenges many prevailing theories about religious and cultural transformation. Particular difficulties appear for the comparative discussion of fundamentalism. As Nancy Ammerman has pointed out, Latin American experience does not fit very well with the categories that many scholars have developed to describe and account for the growth of fundamentalism. There is little militant defense of tradition, and scant appeal to the reconstruction of some past golden age. "People whose religious language and lifestyle might look like fundamentalism in North America represent a substantially new religious tradition in areas south of the Rio Grande, and new religious movements have different constituencies and dynamics from movements within traditions."[38]

What then can we say about fundamentalism in the context of religious innovation in Latin America? Is the concept useful at all? A common definition of fundamentalism points to scripturally based movements of religious renovation that strive to rescue core (fundamental) elements within a religious tradition. In these terms, one might argue that liberationist Catholics are the real fundamentalists in this story. Liberation theology clearly emerged as part of an effort to renew an established tradition that appeared in crisis, and to do so in a critical and transformative way.[39] This view is not satisfactory, however, because the organizational dynamics of liberationist Catholicism and the characteristic ways in which its groups work with Scripture do not fit the classic fundamentalist mold. There is no literalism here, and little evidence that texts are used as guides for the authoritative solution of specific problems. Passages are rarely studied in a formal analytical way. Instead, participants jump right in to discuss how what is spoken of in a particular text is happening here and now, to people like themselves.[40] Liberationist Catholic discourse also works with a rationalized and at core optimistic view of the world. It is rationalized because reliance is placed on ethical rules that undergird self-managed efforts at change. Change comes over the long haul, not from unpredictable eruptions of charismatic power. There is no trace of premillennialism here; the vision is fundamentally optimistic, not apocalyptic.[41]

I have argued throughout that the central problem facing analysis is less to fit events in Latin America into general models of fundamentalism as a global phenomenon than to explain why innovation should have taken off with such force in the past thirty years and what accounts for success or failure. I want to proceed by reviewing several explanations that are prominent in the literature: the role of dislocation, anomie, and crisis; the significance of acculturation and cultural loss; and the separation of cultural from political influences and their overall meaning for democratization. I then sketch out an alternative argument, and suggest directions for future research.

Dislocation, Anomie, and Crisis

In an earlier volume of this series, Pablo Deiros attributes the expansion of fundamentalist Protestantism to the dislocation and anomie brought on by urbanization. In this view, the transition out of rural society (presumably integrated and harmonious) to the heterogeneous and unfamiliar world of city and factory life produces a cultural and social collapse that opens migrants to new churches and their message.[42] Deiros also refers to presumed traits of Latin American character ("innate warmth and hospitality, resignation in the face of pervasive natural calamities, a flexibility of spirit producing tolerance, enchantment with charismatic personalities, individualism, and a distinct turn to emotionalism and mysticism") to explain fundamentalism's appeal in the region.[43]

This approach has crippling empirical and theoretical difficulties. Empirically, it is not at all clear that conversions to fundamentalism or growth of fundamentalist churches are disproportionately centered in the cities or drawn from individuals suffering from personal disorientation or anomie. We do know that most new urban churches are physically located in poor neighborhoods and that the bulk of converts and new members are poor people. The poor are leaving Catholic connections and joining Pentecostal groups at a higher rate than other social groups. But the evidence with which I am familiar indicates that new religious recruits in city and countryside alike come from the stable poor. Not the very poorest, not those in abject misery, not the most recent migrants, but rather men and women with some land, relatively steady jobs, and, in the city, an extended experience of urban life.[44]

In theoretical terms, the view that Deiros espouses rests on discredited notions that oppose rural harmony to urban disorganization. The weight of modern research on migration has exploded the notion that moves to the city involve the loss of harmonious integration.[45] Rural communities were never as harmonious as their mythology depicts them, and in any case, we know that migrants are drawn not from the disoriented, but rather from the best qualified and most aspirant of their communities. Individuals rarely arrive in the city without some prior experience of towns and smaller cities, and most come with some contact or connection that gives them a start: the name of a relative, a church, or a regional association. City life is shot through with family and associational connections, and there is a continuing moral discourse in poor communities: anomie is an inappropriate description of the process or its outcome. Research on rural life, migrants, and migration shows that migrants actively work to create a new life for themselves and their families. Religious innovation is just one of many kinds of innovation at issue.

The attribution of religious change to the effects of dislocation and anomie rests on a widely held, but nonetheless distorted, view of crisis. Accelerated social and economic change combined with the kind of political and economic difficulties Latin America has gone through lately is commonly expected to stimulate a turn to religion in search of escape from the pressures of daily life, and solace in dealing with the difficulties it presents. Older social connections are discredited or simply no longer available. Facing a changing and fearful world, individuals bring their new and urgent needs to the encounter with God and with the churches. There has of course been substantial religious innovation throughout Latin America, and in a crude way one might say that innovation and conflict in religion have been most intense where crisis has been sharpest: Central America, Chile, Brazil, or Peru. But Latin American experience presents a few twists that cast doubt on this "crisis-solace" model of conversion and change.

To begin with, the model is too static. It assumes that churches and their clienteles remain unchanged except for the external pressure of crisis. But these are active subjects, and the historical record shows considerable self-moved change at all levels. Churches have been transformed in structure and message, and those coming to religious institutions have changed as well. New work routines, growing literacy and access to media, and migration on a large scale (both within the countryside and from country to city) have altered the rhythms of ordinary life, making popular sectors available for new kinds of messages and innovative organizational forms.

The crisis-solace model also suffers from an unfortunate patronizing tone. The expectation that a turn to religion is sparked above all by the search for solace or escape rests on the same assumptions that for so long dismissed religious belief as epiphenomenal, presumably doomed to privatization and disappearance. Lacking scientific or rational (read Marxist) insight into their problems, ordinary men and women flee crisis by escaping to religion. This view is deeply flawed, and rests on a narrow understanding of what crisis is all about.[46] Undercutting old routines and expectations, crises open horizons, giving institutions and ordinary people a chance to create new bases for action and new criteria of value. Crisis thus presents opportunity along with danger, and regularly finds aspirant social groups reaching out to create and exploit new contacts and connections.

The question that must be asked is not how anomie turns people to religion for escape, but rather why religion (and within religion, specific churches) should appear as a viable and legitimate vehicle for dealing with crisis. The answer is both general to religion and specific to Latin America. In general terms, religions have a unique consolidating power, joining personal to family and community experience, and fusing individual with collective expression through a series of regular, repetitive acts and powerful symbolic expressions. Religions thus work effectively to set proximate acts in ultimate contexts, and do so through structures that are easily accessible and culturally meaningful.

But why Latin America? Why should Latin America have been the scene of such profound and for the most part unanticipated changes? One answer lies in the way crisis has opened doors for religious innovation. Religion has been so closely intertwined for so long with the structure of domination in Latin America that crisis (in the Weberian sense of expanded trade, broadened scale of action, and emerging challenges to legitimacy) made religion a particularly likely focal point for change. Religious themes and metaphors (e.g., Bible stories) are culturally familiar, and thus provide a convenient place from which to begin any effort at cultural reconstruction. Religious innovations of the kind examined here make sense in a setting of "crisis," therefore, not as a response to anomie or personal dislocation, but rather as a consciously chosen and highly prized avenue for change and self-fulfillment.

If we set the expressed consciousness of converts against what we know about their background and overall social condition, it is clear that the process is not one of escape, but rather of self-fulfillment. Marzal's account of the reasons given for conversion to new churches in Lima is suggestive: first is a general sense of change in life, followed (in order) by access to biblical truth, the desire to find Christ, and the experience of healing and health.[47] On reflection, converts to Pentecostal churches have much in common with members of liberationist groups like CEBs. The target group and much of the social process (small intense groups, egalitarian social relations, salience of the Bible) are similar. As Cleary notes for Guatemala, "In effect, pentecostalism and reform Catholicism offer bridges for the socioeconomic and political changes taking place in the country. Both offer symbolic systems by which to live a life adapted to changed conditions."[48] The difference lies in the greater cultural and organizational autonomy the new churches provide.

Acculturation and Cultural Loss

One account that appeals particularly to leaders of both the Catholic church and the Latin American left attributes the force of change to foreign influences. The money, power, and political connections derived from ties with North American churches are painted as the engine of fundamentalist growth. Fundamentalism is depicted as an alien presence, and conversion as an instance of cultural loss and the abandonment of identity.

The external connections of Latin American fundamentalists cannot be denied. There is ample documentation of the relation between fundamentalist growth in North America and its expansion overseas, especially to Latin America. It is also clear that certain sectors of American fundamentalism were closely and explicitly associated with American foreign policy in the region, and with the promotion of right-wing groups and governments, especially but not only in Central America.[49] Having acknowledged this point, however, we must also acknowledge the emergence of a corps of independent churches, leaders, and preachers throughout the region. Some have achieved tremendous growth and broad impact (for example, in Brazil and Chile). As North American evangelism encountered growing difficulties by the late 1980s, these groups have moved to increasing fiscal and ideological independence.

The notion that conversion carries with it loss of culture is popular among the region's Catholic hierarchy, and provides a central theme of preparatory documents for the general conference of Latin American bishops in 1992 in Santo Domingo. The meeting coincided with the 500th anniversary of Columbus's landfall, and the prominence of this theme reflects fear about the "growth of the sects" and a conviction of the need to preserve the core of Latin American culture, inextricably tied to Catholicism from the beginning.

The whole view is deeply flawed. The idea that conversion means loss of culture rests on a static view of culture as something preserved and passed down intact from the past. But exclusive stress on the continuities of some presumed Iberian cultural ethos washes out critical dimensions of conflict and power, ignores variation, and obscures sources of change. Culture is a human artifact, put together by real people in particular historical circumstances. As social, economic, and political configurations change, it stands to reason that cultural formations will also evolve.

The preceding observations suggest that the issue is not well addressed as acculturation or loss of culture, but rather as cultural change. The new element in the equation is the extent to which initiatives of change are being promoted by hitherto marginal and powerless groups. Guy Swanson's account of an encounter between Ecuador's Bishop Proaño and a group of Indian evangelicals is telling. The bishop was a famous advocate of liberation, and served long and well as an ally of Indian groups. He advanced their cause and spoke for them. But he regarded conversion as defection, and accused the converts of abandoning their culture.

A brother said, "Well, Sr. Obispo Proaño, would you like to see us back in the condition our parents were in before us? Their poor feet scarred and a little hat sewed over old ones? Do you want to see us like that? Why don't you want to see us now as transformed people? Or don't we have the right to dress with dignity? So he said, 'Well, yes, but you have changed your culture.' So I said to him, 'We speak Quichua. Here is my wife, she has not lost her language, the dress that we wear, the *bayeta,* the *anauco.*' I explained all this to him. 'We'll talk more about this later,' he said, but we never had another meeting."[50]

Secularization, Politics, and Democratization

In his recent *Tongues of Fire,* David Martin makes the case for fitting religious innovation in Latin America into a general understanding of secularization. He argues that Protestant and particularly Pentecostal expansion in the region represents a break in "the sacred canopy" of culture and power. For the first time, innovation has been spurred "solely at the level of culture".[51] Throughout *Tongues of Fire,* Martin insists on distinguishing politics sharply from culture. Politics operates on a level of "meta-interpretation";[52] locating change at the level of culture means breaking old connections with power, and making possible the assertion of a different, and presumably more autonomous, pattern of group life. The whole argument relies on parallels to Anglo-American experiences with the decay of religious monopolies, and on a view of preexisting Latin American patterns according to which cultural change is impossible without total cracking of the system.[53] According to Martin, the spread of Anglo-American models of religious life in Latin America confronts local traditions that mix religion and politics with imported traditions in which religion operates "on culture alone".[54]

> Once the monopolies begin to crack and lose contact with the core structures of society, evangelical Christianity can emerge to compete within the sphere of culture. There it can stand in for what were once the local territorial units of solidarity, reforming them in an active, mobile, and voluntary format. In this way, it counters chaos and restores moral densities. There is no chance it will become a substitute established church, though it may create a widely shared ethos for some oppressed ethnic group. This dramatic restriction to the cultural sphere is, of course, one aspect of secularization, but whether this means that religion has finally ceased to be socially significant depends . . . on whether culture is regarded as impotent and dependent.[55]

This is not the place for an extended discussion and critique of Martin's provocative and influential work. Despite theoretical ambiguities and problems with the historical parallels and with the evidence, for present purposes it suffices to acknowledge that Martin raises two critical issues. First, if conversion to Pentecostal Protestantism means denial and withdrawal from a historical order of things where culture and power are closely intertwined, can such conversion be understood as the effort to enter a non-political world? Second, how then can we grasp the likely political meaning of the new churches' well-known egalitarianism and stress on personal responsibility, not to mention the impact of the political connections and alliances so often attributed to them?

Because Pentecostal churches, leaders, and converts give so much stress to personal conversion and changing the inner man as opposed to collective organization and structural change, it is easy to take their position as "nonpolitical." But such a conclusion rests on a narrow and excessively conventional view of politics. Politics involves more than states, regimes, or elections. Politics is also a matter of power and legitimacy, and of the way images of self and community are translated into capacities and dispositions to action.

Martin's suggestion that Pentecostals are in some sense "nonpolitical," and in any event notably less political than liberationist Catholic groups, has many echoes in the literature. Many liberationist allies agree, and take the argument further, denying the capacity of Pentecostal churches to promote democracy or democratization. Dodson states that, "unlike Catholic CEBs, Pentecostal churches do not strive to influence the central institutions of power in the society. Because their way of achieving equality and participation does not affect existing structures of power, they cannot alter the causes that make them marginal in the first place."[56] But who is to say that only efforts that begin by targeting "the central institutions of power" can make for change? Why not consider the possibility of change emerging over time as a multiplier of the creation of greater numbers of effective, autonomous groups scattered throughout the social order? Dodson's point that individual members cannot affect their own marginality without directly challenging the structure of power will not stand up to scrutiny. As Stoll puts it, liberation theology

> is the salutary contrast we are supposed to draw because it seems to express the interests of the poor so clearly. Yet there are reasons to be wary, among them the capacity of politicized religion for losing touch with the people it claims to represent. . . . partisans of liberation theology assume that churches can thrive only by fighting for broad social reform. Yet Pentecostal churches have reached mammoth proportions without supporting such causes. Their success in improving the situation of many members suggests that no relation exists between the perspicacity of their social analysis and their survival value to the poor.[57]

The notion that Pentecostals are nonpolitical and hence ineffective rests on the supposition that their visible stress on the otherworldly precludes effective action in this world. The facts suggest otherwise, not only for Latin America, but also for North American cases like the black churches[58] or the fundamentalist rise to activism.[59] As with the Protestants who so occupied Max Weber's attention, the groups before us here are very much in this world, with a spirituality that engages the world in new ways.

If we expand our working notions of politics as suggested above, it is easy to see the profoundly democratizing character of religious innovation in contemporary Latin America. Despite differences in the specifics of their discourse, liberationist Catholics and Pentecostals have a common commitment to demystifying authority by giving the tools of association to everyone. This is accomplished more by opening horizons, energizing person, family, and community, and encouraging a theory and practice of egalitarianism than by making explicitly and narrowly political connections. The self-mastery and mobility nurtured by religious innovation gain political meaning from the outset because they embody new cultural understandings of power and offer paths for the emergence of new strata of leaders working in enduring organizational forms. This is what lays down a foundation for authority or resistance to its claims. It is here that the human solidarities that make any action endure are constructed. From this perspective, explicitly political actions appear as the end of a long chain of events, not the beginning.[60]

Masterless People, Marginality, Crisis, and Culture

How then to account for the surge of religious innovation in Latin America, and to weigh its implications for culture and politics? I suggested earlier that crisis provides a setting in which religious innovation is likely to take on a central role. Acknowledging the salience of religion in moments of crisis and change is important, but by itself this tells us little about the kinds of individuals and groups likely to press for new messages and be open to hearing and acting on them. Drawing on the experience of the Puritan revolution, many observers have pointed to the rise of "masterless men," individuals free of old constraints but not yet bound to definitive new arrangements. The marginal status of displaced peasantries, agroproletarians, new urban migrants, subordinate ethnic groups, or despite the gender-specific formulation, women, are often cited as making them especially critical audiences for and carriers of change.

The marginality in question is not just a matter of being on the "wrong side" of lines of class, wealth, ethnicity, or gender. It is also not a question of social dislocation, anomie, or cultural loss. Marginality also characterizes aspiring classes whose experience of movement leaves them free from the old order but without a secure footing in the new arrangements being put together. Such masterless men and women are a prime source of new leadership and an avid clientele for innovations in religious discourse that underscore equality, identity, and an independent capacity to reason, judge, and act together.

Singly and in combination, these elements are apparent in Latin America. As with other great transformative moments of cultural and political history, contemporary Latin American experience has generated vast enthusiasms along with a sense of movement and openness. In such contexts, the creation of new cultural understandings and social movements through religion is best understood not as a defense against change, but rather as a creative effort to reunderstand the world and reorganize person, family, and community to deal more effectively with it. This is a meaningful and reflexive process, in which human agency plays a central role. Crafting identities that make sense for individuals and groups requires sustained efforts to create resources, to make them accessible and usable, and to open new social spaces where all these can be put to use.[61]

To repeat a metaphor used earlier, crisis takes the hinges off the door to cultural innovation. More is at issue here than the speed by which new ideas are communicated, although that is significant. By pulling and driving experience into new channels, crisis also spurs cultural change, and gives it greater resonance. Neither values nor culture are static, nor can they be understood as superstructure, the epiphenomena of presumably more basic movements of economic or political forces or interests. The interests that individuals and groups pursue do not flow only from their position in the social structure. They are suffused with cultural significance, are value laden from the outset, and hence are as much affected by the dynamics of cultural, as by economic or political change. Experiences change beliefs, and beliefs change behavior at individual and collective levels. Once clientele and message are put together in organizational forms that make sense to those involved, the process of change begins to take on independent force.

Making a Better Portrait

Gustavo Gutiérrez, often described as the father of liberation theology, once noted that, despite pressures for clear definition of the nature and prospects for change in Latin American Catholicism, the process was so new that any judgment was likely to be premature—a prime candidate for being overtaken by events. "At present," he stated, "we are in the position of those trying to decide whom a newborn child resembles. Some will say the father, others the mother; some will even find that the child has this grandfather's nose or that aunt's eyes, whereas still others will be of the opinion that the child does not remind them of any family features known to them. Better to photograph the child and decide later on whom it resembles."[62]

Gutiérrez was searching for the dimensions of the new spirituality being created by the poor in Latin America, but his point has general value. How can we make a better portrait, and be sure that the subject is still part of the same family? How can we avoid having our photograph tainted by the pressure of events, taking incomplete signs as definitive evidence of the shape of things to come? A few considerations follow, in ascending order of complexity.

Future research must avoid the numbers game. As we have seen, the numbers are highly problematic, and in any event obsession with charting curves of growth too often obscures analysis of the social basis and organizational structure of recruitment. Understanding recruitment is more important than charting growth. Analysis of the social basis of the new churches has to be combined with attention to conversion as experienced. This means infusing sociological and political concerns with a phenomenological methodology, one that listens to the language of those involved, and works their own definitions of the process into analysis and explanation.

Cultural stereotypes and easy assumptions about the disorganizing effects of change must also be set aside. They rest on theories that confuse general patterns of change with personal and cultural dislocation and distort the motives and enduring force of conversion. A more fruitful approach will address the relation between messages projected by religious activists and the way these messages are received, understood, and reworked by converts. If twenty years of research on Latin American Catholicism has taught us anything, at the very least it is that popular groups are not infinitely malleable. They bring their own needs and concerns to the encounter with religion, and for this reason if for no other, close attention needs to be paid to the creation and changing content of a new religious consciousness.[63]

There can be no more fatal error than to dismiss the independent role of values and moral discourse. The surge of religious innovation in modern Latin America forcefully reminds us of the energizing and creative power moral argument can have. The point is too often forgotten in the social sciences, whose characteristic view of the world remains steeped in liberal and Marxist assumptions that subordinate values and beliefs to interest narrowly defined. But the drive to construct meaningful vocabularies of moral concern and to build them into community and social life has independent value.[64] Linked with religion, it provides a vital thread of continuity with the past while legitimizing the search for something new. Shared moral discourse is the glue that holds new groups together, a foundation for mutual trust regardless of the group's social or political concerns.

It makes a substantial difference how groups are started, who defines their agenda, and what sort of structures mediate action. Ideas rarely appear in the abstract; they come in specific forms, carried by identifiable kinds of people and with meanings that make sense in context. Competing attempts to shape religion must therefore be specified and each associated with an identifiable organizational and power net. The relative weight of television and campaign strategies as opposed to small group–based organizational diffusion is a case in point. The contrast noted earlier between Catholic and Protestant organizational networks is illustrative. It is harder for Catholics to adapt and change methods. They remain wedded to paternalistic traditions and hierarchical structures, and constrained by preexisting commitments and sunk costs. Pentecostals have more flexibility, in part because of the very newness of their structures, but also because of their greater openness to mobility and influence from below.

The issue of competition warrants separate attention. Competition between Catholics and Protestants is likely to get more intense and explicit over the coming decade. Pentecostal growth has alarmed Catholic leaders, who have responded by making the "invasion of the sects" a central theme in their future plans. The evolution of competition is likely to resurrect older distinctions between Catholics and Protestants, and to provide further opportunity for controlling and restricting liberationist groups. As they prepare to confront the Pentecostals, Catholic leaders are likely to begin by "cleaning house," affirming traditions of hierarchy and ensuring internal discipline. Note that Pope John Paul II began his October 1991 visit in Brazil with a simultaneous attack on liberationist Catholics and fundamentalist Protestants.[65]

The prominence of competition both for institutional strategies and from the point of view of believers has important implications for research. Early work on religious innovation in Latin America (liberationists and Pentecostals alike) was heavily influenced by events in Central America. But Central America is too extreme and polarized to be of much help in charting the overall pattern of change. More representative sites for future research are likely to be found in the big cities of relatively open countries: Venezuela, Peru, and now Chile or Brazil. Here churches of all kinds face surging populations, work with scarce resources, and operate in an environment where competition is the norm. Even the formal presumption of a Catholic monopoly has long passed from these scenes.

The Catholic church's long history of religious hegemony and its close ties with other institutions of power and meaning explain why early work focused so heavily on changes in Catholicism, ignoring (with rare exceptions) the early signs of Protestant growth. We are now into a second or perhaps even a third wave of research on Latin American Catholicism, and it is fair to say that understanding has advanced substantially. Older conventions of legal formalism have been replaced by a wealth of studies on conflict and change in particular countries, on ideological and institutional transformations, on links to politics, social movements, and culture. Empirical work is now less mesmerized by alternatives of reaction or revolution, and much more sensitive to nuance and variation.[66] Research on Protestantism is now poised for a similar evolution. Early work was highly polemical, with much attention going to short-term political connections and to the influence of links with the North American religious right. But recent scholarship and work now "in the pipeline" takes a much more careful and nuanced look at the origins and likely pathways of change.

The next generation of studies can build on these foundations. In the future, research should focus not on one church or another, but rather on religious innovation as a whole. The dialectics of competition between branches of the Christian family, above all in urban settings, will enrich research, with special concern for comparative analysis of recruitment, leadership, and discourse. The scale and direction of change have confounded so many expectations that it is only logical to suppose that future change will continue to do so. Prescriptions that are more specific therefore risk being overtaken by events.

Normal times are not hospitable to dramatic innovation. Movements of religious revitalization find a readier hearing in transformative moments, when crisis sharpens the edge of change and raises the stakes. As new visions emerge and established arrangements are challenged and undermined, the contours of change become clearer. The issues that researchers study are framed by general theoretical interests, and moved in specific directions by the press of events. The interest in fundamentalism that undergirds this and other volumes in this series is a clear case in point. But clearer understanding is not a product only of improved concepts or research tools. Awareness of change is also thrust upon us by those caught up in its midst, whose thoughts and actions, projected time after time on a larger scale, give it life and make it go. The men and women who energize religious change throughout Latin America today resist being confined to the status of subjects for others to study and evaluate. They are active and creative subjects, and it is through their efforts that the familiar is "brought to consciousness as something in need of being ascertained."[67]

Notes

1. See David Stoll, *Is Latin America Turning Protestant?* (Berkeley: University of California Press, 1990); David Martin, *Tongues of Fire: The Explosion of Protestantism in Latin America* (London: Basil Blackwell, 1990); and Edward Cleary and Hannah Stewart-Gambino, eds., *Conflict and Competition: The Latin American Church in the 1990s* (Boulder, Colo.: Lynne Rienner, 1992).

2. See the statistics reported by World Vision in *Time*, 16 February 1987, or in sources such as the *International Review of*

Missionary Research. Examples of parachurch groups that have been active in Latin America include Campus Crusade for Christ, Full Gospel Businessman's International Fellowship, Maranatha Ministries, Youth with a Mission (YWAM), Discipling a Whole Nation (DAWN). For details, see Stoll, *Is Latin America Turning Protestant?*

3. Pablo Deiros, "Protestant Fundamentalism in Latin America," in Martin E. Marty and R. Scott Appleby, *Fundamentalisms Observed* (Chicago: University of Chicago Press, 1991); Martin, *Tongues of Fire;* Stoll, *Is Latin America Turning Protestant?;* Cleary and Stewart-Gambino, *Conflict and Competition.*

4. W. E. Hewitt, *Basic Christian Communities and Social Change in Brazil* (Lincoln: University of Nebraska Press, 1991); Scott Mainwaring, *The Catholic Church and Politics in Brazil, 1916–1985* (Stanford: Stanford University Press, 1986); Daniel H. Levine, *Religion and Political Conflict in Latin America* (Chapel Hill: University of North Carolina Press, 1986).

5. For example, see Timothy Evans, "Percentage of Non-Catholics in a Representative Sample of the Guatemalan Population," paper presented at meetings of the Latin American Studies Association, Washington, D.C., 1991; Bryan Froehle, "The Catholic Church and Politics in Venezuela: Resource Limitation, Religious Competition, and Democracy," in Cleary and Stewart-Gambino, *Conflict and Competition;* Manuel Marzal, *Los caminos religiosos de los inmigrantes a la Gran Lima: El caso de El Agustino* (Lima: Pontifica Universidad Católica del Peru, Fondo Editorial, 1988); Stoll, *Is Latin America Turning Protestant?;* or in a different vein, John Burdick, *Looking for God in Brazil: The Progressive Catholic Church in Urban Brazil's Religious Arena* (Berkeley: University of California Press, 1993).

6. On the numbers, see Evans, "Percentage of Non-Catholics"; Edward Cleary, "Evangelicals and Competition in Guatemala," in Cleary and Stewart-Gambino, *Conflict and Competition;* Froehle, "The Catholic Church and Politics in Venezuela"; Phillip Berryman, *Stubborn Hope: Religion,* *Politics, and Revolution in Central America* (New York and Maryknoll, NY: The New Press and Orbis Books, 1994), esp. chap. 5; and the clear analysis provided throughout by Stoll, *Is Latin America Turning Protestant?*

7. Stoll, *Is Latin America Turning Protestant?* p. 9.

8. See Daniel H. Levine, "Assessing the Impacts of Liberation Theology in Latin America," *Review of Politics* 50, no. 2 (1988): 241–63; Mainwaring, *The Catholic Church and Politics in Brazil;* Christian Smith, *The Emergence of Liberation Theology: Radical Religion and Social Movement Theory* (Chicago: University of Chicago Press, 1991).

9. Phillip Berryman, *Liberation Theology* (New York: Pantheon, 1987); idem, *Religious Roots of Rebellion: Christians in the Central American Revolutions* (Maryknoll, N.Y.: Orbis, 1984); Daniel H. Levine, *Popular Voices in Latin American Catholicism* (Princeton: Princeton University Press, 1992); Mainwaring, *The Catholic Church and Politics in Brazil.*

10. Hewitt, *Basic Christian Communities;* Levine, *Religion and Political Conflict in Latin America;* idem, *Popular Voices in Latin American Catholicism.*

11. Berryman, *Religious Roots of Rebellion;* idem, *Liberation Theology;* Levine, "Assessing the Impacts of Liberation Theology"; Mainwaring, *The Catholic Church and Politics in Brazil.*

12. There have been conflicts over discipline and control within the churches, as new claims to group autonomy and initiative clash with traditional expectations of deference to hierarchy. The edge of conflict has been sharpened by a clear conservative counteroffensive, advanced throughout the last decade by Pope John Paul II. Over the same period, conflicts between church and state have been more intense and widespread than at any other period in the last one hundred years, as church efforts to organize and stand with new social groups have met intense official fear and harsh repression (Berryman, *Religious Roots of Rebellion;* idem, *Liberation Theology;* idem, *Stubborn Hope;* Mainwaring, *The Catholic Church and Politics in Brazil*).

13. This process was not dependent on the presence in high office of a born-again dictator, like Guatemala's General Efraín Ríos Montt. Traditional Catholics like Chile's General Augusto Pinochet also played this role, extending particular public welcomes to visiting North Americans like Pat Robertson and Jimmy Swaggart.

14. Penny Lernoux, *People of God: The Struggle for World Catholicism* (New York: Viking, 1989).

15. The comparison is often made to the Reformation and the Puritan revolution. See Michael Dodson and Laura O'Shaughnessy, *Nicaragua's Other Revolution: Religious Faith and Political Struggle* (Chapel Hill: University of North Carolina Press, 1990). For a general comparative discussion, see Daniel H. Levine, "Religion and Politics in Comparative and Historical Perspective," *Comparative Politics* 19, no. 1 (1986): 95–122; and *Popular Voices in Latin American Catholicism,* chaps. 9 and 10.

16. Hewitt, *Basic Christian Communities;* Levine, "Religion and Politics"; Mainwaring, *The Catholic Church and Politics in Brazil.*

17. Tod Swanson, "Refusing to Drink with the Mountains: Traditional Indian Meanings in Evangelical Testimonies," in Martin E. Marty and R. Scott Appleby, eds., *Accounting for Fundamentalisms* (Chicago: University of Chicago Press, 1993); Stoll, *Is Latin America Turning Protestant?*

18. Burdick, *Looking for God in Brazil;* Martin, *Tongues of Fire;* Stoll, *Is Latin America Turning Protestant?*

19. I consider likely futures in *Popular Voices in Latin American Catholicism.*

20. Froehle, "The Catholic Church and Politics in Venezuela."

21. Berryman, *Stubborn Hope;* Marzal, *Los caminos religiosos;* Stoll, *Is Latin America Turning Protestant?*

22. Burdick, *Looking for God in Brazil;* Deiros, "Protestant Fundamentalism in Latin America"; Carol Ann Drogus, "Religion, Gender, and Political Culture: Attitudes and Participation in Brazilian Basic Christian Communities," Ph.D. diss., University of Wisconsin, 1991; Martin, *Tongues of Fire;* Stoll, *Is Latin America Turning Protestant?*

23. Levine, "Assessing the Impacts of Liberation Theology."

24. Drogus, "Religion, Gender, and Political Culture."

25. Burdick, *Looking for God in Brazil.*

26. Marzal comments on the role of health: "In this way, Pentecostals have mounted a campaign centered on health that draws on elements of collective psychology, such as the faith of people who humbly approach God looking for health in extreme situations, the charismatic force of pastors who in God's name order devils to leave the body of the afflicted, whose illness is charged with ethical meaning, the solidarity of the prayerful community that appeals to heaven on behalf of their sick brother with great emotion at moments when some brothers speak in tongues, which affirms that the community is in the presence of the Holy Spirit. This overall approach to health finds its maximum expression in the spectacular cures that come in the public campaigns of international evangelists such as Jimmy Swaggart or Gigi Avila" (*Los caminos religiosos,* p. 412).

27. Michael Dodson, "Religious Fundamentalism in Central America: General Reflections and a Case Study," paper presented at meetings of the Latin American Studies Association, Washington, D.C., 1991.

28. Levine, *Popular Voices in Latin American Catholicism;* Marzal, *Los caminos religiosos;* Stoll, *Is Latin America Turning Protestant?*

29. Charles Cohen, *God's Caress: The Psychology of Puritan Experience* (New York: Oxford University Press, 1980), p. 6.

30. Karen Fields, *Revival and Rebellion in Colonial Central Africa* (Princeton: Princeton University Press, 1985); see also Jean Comaroff, *Body of Power, Spirit of Resistance* (Chicago: University of Chicago Press, 1985); Jean Comaroff and John Comaroff, *Of Revelation and Revolution: Christianity, Colonialism, and Consciousness in South Africa,* vol. 1 (Chicago: University of Chicago Press, 1986); and for a comparative discussion, Levine, "Religion and Politics."

31. This movement is centered on the idea of recovering charismatic and Pentecostal gifts of the spirit within an overall Catholic framework. From modest beginnings in the Word of God community, founded in Ann Arbor, Michigan, in the 1960s, the notion of a charismatic Catholicism has spread widely, not only in the United States but also in Europe, Latin America, and Africa (Tom Rieke, "The Word of God and Nicaragua," *Ann Arbor Observer,* November 1990, pp. 30–43).

32. Berryman, *Stubborn Hope,* p. 216. Cf. Deiros, who describes speaking in tongues as "the desperate cry of those who cannot make themselves heard in the daily language of society. Visions and eschatological expectations provide a politically acceptable means of expressing the tension of frustration and hope in which the Latin American lower classes must live" ("Protestant Fundamentalism in Latin America," p. 174). This is explaining away the phenomenon, not explaining it.

33. Marzal, *Los caminos religiosos,* p. 414.

34. A similar stance toward the Bible is encountered in CEBs, but such groups face more notable constraints in the Catholic scheme of things. See Levine, *Popular Voices in Latin American Catholicism.*

35. See David Zaret, *The Heavenly Contract: Ideology and Organization in Pre-Revolutionary Puritanism* (Chicago: University of Chicago Press, 1985) and Nathan Hatch, *The Democratization of American Christianity* (New Haven: Yale University Press, 1989). See also Deiros, "Protestant Fundamentalism in Latin America," pp. 168, 180; or Martin, *Tongues of Fire,* p. 164, on the impact that translating the Bible has had in affirming the legitimacy of other cultural and ethnic/linguistic groups. On the general importance of language to the construction of identity, see Benedict Anderson, *Imagined Communities: Reflections on the Origin and Spread of Nationalism* (London: Verso, 1983). The parallel between Anglo-American experience and the innovations of liberationist Catholicism in Latin America has been developed with particular force by Dodson and O'Shaughnessy, *Nicaragua's Other Revolution.*

36. Nicholas Wolterstorff, *Until Justice and Peace Embrace* (Grand Rapids, Mich.: William B. Eerdmans, 1983).

37. James D. Hunter, *American Evangelicalism, Conservative Religion, and the Quandary of Modernity* (New Brunswick: Rutgers University Press, 1983); Susan Rose and Steve Brouwer, "Guatemalan Upper Classes Join the Evangelicals," paper presented at meetings of the American Sociological Association and the Association for the Study of Religion, Atlanta, 1988; Susan Rose and Quentin Schultze, "The Evangelical Awakening in Guatemala: Fundamentalist Impact on Education and the Media," in Martin E. Marty and R. Scott Appleby, *Fundamentalisms and Society* (Chicago: University of Chicago Press, 1993).

38. Nancy Ammerman, "Accounting for Christian Fundamentalisms: Social Dynamics and Rhetorical Strategies," in Marty and Appleby, *Accounting for Fundamentalisms.*

39. See Levine, "Assessing"; Berryman, *Liberation Theology;* and Arthur McGovern, *Liberation Theology and Its Critics* (Maryknoll, N.Y.: Orbis Books, 1989).

40. Berryman, *Liberation Theology;* Levine, *Popular Voices in Latin American Catholicism.*

41. Daniel H. Levine, "Considering Liberation as Utopia," *Review of Politics* 52, no. 4 (1990): 603–22.

42. "For those who migrated, the conditions of anomie produced the possibility of religious change. Uprooted from families and religious traditions, living in slums and at the mercy of criminals and sometimes governmental predators, the urban poor became a fertile seedbed for evangelical proselytism. The weakening of traditional social controls, the sense of confusion and helplessness in the anonymity of city life, the shock of new social values sometimes accompanying the adaptation to industrial work, the absence of familiar community loyalties and of the encompassing paternalism still characteristic of rural employment—all these conditions favored the growth of an acute crisis of personal identity for the migrants. Under such conditions, the exchange of old religious values for new ones was (and remains) likely to

occur" (Deiros, "Protestant Fundamentalism in Latin America," p. 155).

43. Ibid., p. 160; see also p. 174.

44. Evans, "Percentage of Non-Catholics"; Froehle, "The Catholic Church and Politics in Venezuela"; Stoll, *Is Latin America Turning Protestant?*; Burdick, *Looking for God in Brazil*; Martin, *Tongues of Fire*.

45. Janice Perlman, *The Myth of Marginality: Urban Poverty and Politics in Rio de Janeiro* (Berkeley: University of California Press, 1976); Carlos Ivan De Gregori, Cecilia Blondet, and Nicholas Lynch, *Conquistadores de un nuevo mundo: De invasores a ciudadanos en San Martin de Porres* (Lima: Instituto de Estudios Peruanos, 1986).

46. Cf. Karen Fields's comment: "Sociologists of religion did not predict the political resurgence of 'old time religion' here in America, this most secular of modern societies. And we did not foresee that religion would fire a potent revolutionary regime in Iran. Indeed, we have done no better than economists have in predicting major new developments of our times. I do not know what ails economics, but I have become convinced that the problem of rationality, as applied to churches militant, is little more than a translation into scholarly terms of the native folklore about religious belief that is common in secular societies" (*Revival and Rebellion,* p. 22).

47. Marzal, *Los caminos religiosos,* p. 386.

48. Cleary, "Evangelicals and Competition in Guatemala," p. 185.

49. Sara Diamond, *Spiritual Warfare* (Boston: South End Press, 1989); Stoll, *Is Latin America Turning Protestant?*

50. Guy Swanson, "Andean Conversion: Rum and the Circulation of Blessing in the Religious Life of the Puruha People" in M. Marty and R. Scott Appleby, eds., *Accounting for Fundamentalisms: The Dynamic Character of Movements* (Chicago: University of Chicago Press, 1992), p. 94.

51. Martin, *Tongues of Fire,* p. 44.

52. Ibid., pp. 229, 233, 234.

53. Thus, "once we take into account the coiled up resistance of the social mechanisms in Latin American society to any moral initiatives [?] it is not surprising that Pentecostals erect a dualistic wall between the safe enclosure of faith and the dangerous wilderness of the world" (Martin, *Tongues of Fire,* p. 266).

54. Ibid., p. 274.

55. Ibid., pp. 293–94.

56. Dodson, "Religious Fundamentalism in Central America," p. 12.

57. Stoll, *Is Latin America Turning Protestant?* p. 317.

58. Aldon Morris, *The Origins of the Civil Rights Movement* (New York: Oxford University Press, 1984); Albert Raboteau, *Slave Religion* (New York: Oxford University Press, 1978).

59. James D. Hunter, *American Evangelicalism: Conservative Religion and the Quandary of Modernity* (New Brunswick, N.J.: Rutgers University Press, 1983); Robert Wuthnow, "Social Sources of Christian Fundamentalism" in Martin E. Marty and R. Scott Appleby, *Accounting for Fundamentalisms: The Dynamic Character of Movements* (Chicago: University of Chicago Press, 1992). See also Wuthnow, *The Restructuring of American Religion* (Princeton: Princeton University Press, 1988), esp. chaps. 7–9.

60. In all likelihood, our understanding of this issue is clouded by excessive focus on Central America, where matters have been polarized with unusually clear and explicit political ties on all sides, in no small measure because of external pressures and connections. See Deborah L. Huntington, "The Salvation Brokers: Conservative Evangelicals in Central America," *NACLA Report on the Americas* 18 (February 1984): 7–36; and Stoll, *Is Latin America Turning Protestant?* As a practical matter, liberationists have been mostly ineffective at translating group formation and new cultural perspectives into enduring political alliances. Two cases in point are Peru and Brazil, where movements connected with liberation theology, and in the case of Brazil openly backed by the church hierarchy, failed to gain enduring support. Alliances constructed by Pentecostal Protestants, for example in ties to the military in Central America or Chile, or in active support of Alberto Fujimori in the 1990

Peruvian elections, have also been more conjunctural than enduring.

61. Jean Cohen, "Strategy or Identity: New Theoretical Paradigms and Contemporary Social Movements," *Social Research* 52 (Winter 1985): 663–716; Habermas, 1985; Daniel H. Levine, "Constructing Culture and Power," in Daniel H. Levine, ed., *Constructing Culture and Power in Latin America* (Ann Arbor: University of Michigan Press, 1993); Claus Offe, "New Social Movements: Challenging the Boundaries of Institutional Politics," *Social Research* 52 (Winter 1985): 817–68.

62. Jürgen Habermas, "Psychic Thermidor and the Rebirth of Rebellious Subjectivity" in R. Bernstein, ed., *Habermas and Modernity* (Cambridge: MIT Press, 1985), pp. 67–77; Gustavo Gutiérrez, *We Drink from Our Own Wells* (Maryknoll, N.Y.: Orbis, 1985), p. 92.

63. For a detailed discussion, see Levine, *Popular Voices in Latin American Catholicism.*

64. As Habermas states: "We must finally relearn what we forgot during the fascist period . . . that humanitarian and moral arguments are not merely deceitful ideology. Rather, they can and must become central social forces" (citing Marcuse, in "Psychic Thermidor," p. 76).

65. Alan Cowell, "Pope Urges Brazilians to Resist Mirages of Evangelists," *New York Times,* 14 October 1991, p. A3.

66. I review the literature in *Popular Voices in Latin American Catholicism,* chap. 1.

67. Jürgen Habermas, *The Theory of Communicative Action.* Volume 2. *Lifeworld and System: A Critique of Functionalist Reason* (Boston: Beacon Press, 1985), p. 400. Habermas goes on to comment that "sometimes it takes an earthquake to make us aware that we had regarded the ground on which we stand every day as unshakeable."

Unity and Diversity in Islamic Fundamentalism

Said Amir Arjomand

Fundamentalism in the Context of Islamic History

To distinguish fundamentalism from other types of Islamic movements and to compare the contemporary movements within the fundamentalist type, we first must analyze the dynamics of the expansion of Islam as a world religion of salvation.

No sooner were the conquering Arab Muslims transformed into a tribal aristocracy resident in garrison towns, than puritanical Kharijism and millenarian Shi'ism made their appearance in the 680s as rebellious religiopolitical movements. These movements championed Islam as a universalist religion of salvation, and recruited as converts many of the non-Arabs from the client class (*mawali*). Mahdism marks the Shi'ite millenarian rebellion of Mukhtar in Kufa in the 680s; it later passed on to popular Sufism and has generated various Mahdist movements down to the present century. In the same decade, the Kharijites advocated rigorous adherence to Islamic ethics and rejected the established order; they considered nominal Muslims infidels. The Kharijites withdrew from such garrison towns as Basra into areas they termed *dar hijra* (land of withdrawal/migration) on the prophetic model.[1] The puritanical rigorism of the Kharijites and their sectarian rejection of the larger Muslim community find strong echoes through the centuries and among some contemporary militant fundamentalist groups.

But fundamentalism proper appears in Islamic history somewhat later. In historical perspective, fundamentalism can be conceived as the endeavor to purify pristine Islam from subsequent accretions and alien influences by means of a return to its scriptural foundations. It is in this sense that Nagel sees fundamentalism as a reaction to the menacing intrusion of philosophy (in the form of rational theology) and as the mode of thought that rejects the present order as a corruption of the divinely ordained pristine Islamic community depicted in the scriptural sources.[2] The scriptural sources that constitute the fundamentals of Islam are the Qur'an, the standard version of which

179

was established within a generation after Muhammad's death, and the Traditions (*hadith,* singular) of the Prophet, of which several collections, compiled by different schools, were considered authoritative by the end of the ninth/third century. Scriptural fundamentalism has been a powerful instrument of the penetration of Islam into the lower strata of urban society throughout its history, and is thus an integral part of the process of intensive Islamicization. One of the four Sunni schools of law, Hanbalism, whose foundation as a movement against rational theology (*kalam*) went hand in hand with popular mobilization in ninth-century Baghdad, can be considered the medieval archetype of Islamic scriptural fundamentalism according to our conception.[3] Hanbalite fundamentalism was also a reaction to the internal threat of Shiʿism, whose sectarian organization and fusion of theology and jurisprudence it adopted, while counterposing caliphal legitimism to the charismatic Imamate of the Shiʿites.[4] Against sectarian Shiʿism, the Hanbalites advocated the principle of Sunnism—that is, of (prophetic) Tradition (*Sunna*) and the community (*jamaʿa*). Against the rational theology of the Muʿtazila, the Hanbalites maintained that the Qurʾan was the eternal ("uncreated") Word of God, and insisted on unquestioning acceptance of the scriptural propositions. Under the triple threat of the remaining Christian influences of the Crusaders, of the Mongols, and of Shiʿism, Ibn Taymiyya (d. 1328) produced the most forceful statement of medieval Hanbalite fundamentalism.[5]

The Hanbalite tradition produced the Wahhabi fundamentalist movement in Arabia in the latter part of the eighteenth century. Through their dominance in Mecca and Medina, the puritanical monotheistic rigorism of the Wahhabis inspired fundamentalist movements in many parts of the Islamic world, including the neo-Hanbalite "Wahhabism" in India from 1818 onward.[6] The original Wahhabis of Arabia considered contemporary religious practices polytheistic corruptions of the pristine Islam they sought to revive. The current corruption was assimilated to pre-Islamic ignorance (*jahiliyya*), and even Muhammad ibn Saʿud was considered an "ignorant" before embracing the Wahhabi revivalism. The same emphasis on recovery from contemporary corruption by returning to the fundamentals of pristine Islamic monotheism is found in the Wahhabi revival of the beginning of the twentieth century, which produced Saudi Arabia. The Wahhabis of this century, too, conceived of the nominal Muslims as "ignorant," and spoke of their embrace of revivalism as conversion to Islam.[7] The Salafiyya movement, launched by Rashid Rida in the Near East in the first decade of the twentieth century, so named on account of its goal of reviving the pristine Islam of the pious ancestors (*salaf*), was an instance of scriptural fundamentalism. The movement emerged as the successor to the Islamic reform movement of Jamal al-Din Afghani (d. 1897) and Muhammad ʿAbduh (d. 1905), as well as that of the young Ottomans, and was led by a group of marginalized ulama that was partially dispossessed and further threatened by the Ottoman and Egyptian modernizing reforms of the late nineteenth century.[8] In the interwar period, it spread into the French North Africa under the leadership of ʿAbdelhamid Ben Badis. Salafi scriptural fundamentalism bore a strong imprint of neo-Hanbalism: Ibn Hanbal's doctrine that the Qurʾan was the uncreated Word of God, Ibn Taymiyya's opinion that the "pious ancestors" were the soundest authorities on the Traditions, and the Hanbalite limitation of the normative consensus to the Companions of the Prophet were all affirmed.[9]

From the eleventh century on, however, Sufism rather than scriptural fundamentalism was the primary force in the generation of the mass movements that were instrumental in the geographical and social spread of Islam. True, there have been movements for orthodox reform from within popular Sufism since the beginning of the early modern era. These include the "renewal" (*tajdid*) movement in the Naqshbandi order, which has become a very fashionable subject of study and whose exceptionality and importance is anachronistically exaggerated. One could consider these movements a "neo-Sufi"[10] type of fundamentalism. But apart from the objections raised about the historicity of the term,[11] this would obscure the fact that Sufism was historically the rival of fundamentalism. Let me suggest, rather, that Sufism serves our purpose best as a point of contrast. First and foremost, Sufism can be considered the negative counterpart of scriptural fundamentalism on account of the vehement attacks on Sufi spiritual mediationism and popular practices by neo-Hanbalites and Wahhabis. Second, as institutionalized mass movements, the Sufi orders provided a model for those who sought to propagate Salafi fundamentalism in the 1920s and 1930s. Hasan al-Banna was inspired by this model, which he sought to modernize when he founded the Muslim Brotherhood and adopted the Sufi title of *al-murshid al-'amm* (general guide) as its head.[12]

The relation between Mahdism and contemporary fundamentalism is complicated and involves considerable transformation of the notion. Thus Mahdism, too, is best considered a contrasting type of Islamic movement. The absence of millenarian elements in most contemporary fundamentalist movements has been noted by Almond and Sivan.[13] It may be best to make this absence a criterion for distinguishing fundamentalism from other Islamic movements. The containment and transformation of Mahdistic and eschatological expectations played a role in the substitution of clerical for charismatic religious authority in the earliest stages of institutionalization of the ulama.[14] The "renewer [*mujaddid*] of the age" thus appears as a centennial transmutation of the millennial Mahdi, whose initial purpose was the justification of the authority of the jurists of the Shafi'ite school as an extension of the authority of the Prophet.[15] In Sufi revivalism, Mahdism could reappear outright, as it did in the Sudan, or the notion of renewal could revert to its original eschatological meaning, as it did with the Naqshbandi Shaykh Ahmad Sirhindi (d. 1624).[16] Sufi revivalism could easily be harnessed to jihad movements to extend the frontiers of Islam.[17] Such movements have been considered fundamentalist, but this characterization blurs certain important distinctions.[18] What is important is that Mahdist and Sufi revivalist movements have historically been the agency for the unification of tribes and formation of states on the basis of Islam, and that this integrative function devolves upon fundamentalism in the contemporary world.

Shi'ism is our last contrasting movement to scriptural fundamentalism, and was for long its historical negative counterpart. Shi'ism has, for over a millennium, contained Mahdism. In it, the institutional transformation of Mahdistic, charismatic to clerical, traditional authority has proved definitive. The authority of the ulama as the representatives of the Mahdi as the Hidden Imam left no room for that of any "pious ancesters" as the embodiment of pristine Islam. Shi'ite clerical mediationism and popular practices, like the Sufi ones, became targets of Wahhabi attacks, and Shi'ism thus came to constitute a second negative counterpart to its scriptural fundamentalism. Yet under contemporary political conditions, Shi'ism, too, has generated its own fundamentalism. Shi'ite "fundamentalism" in Iran only enhanced traditional clerical authority and eventually extended it to political rule. Thus I have characterized it as "revolutionary traditionalism."[19] For the comparative purpose of this essay, however, it may be termed clericalist fundamentalism.

Contemporary Fundamentalisms: Common Trends and Differentiating Circumstances

Two propositions can be offered to account for unity and diversity in Islamic fundamentalism. First, unity in Islamic fundamentalism stems from what is explicitly affirmed while diversity derives from the negative, and often implicit, counterpart of this affirmation. The affirmation of the scriptural foundations of Islam is fairly uniform across the fundamentalist movements, while what this affirmation is intended to deny and reject varies from case to case, and is the best criterion for differentiating among them.

Some negative counterparts of the formative period of scriptural fundamentalism have left a permanent imprint on the Islamic fundamentalist legacy. The negative counterparts of Ibn Hanbal's traditionalism were rational theology and pragmatic jurisprudence. The denial of these counterparts left a permanent mark on scriptural fundamentalism, on which were superimposed the imprints of neo-Hanbalite rejection of Sufi and Shi'ite mediationism.[20] This fundamentalist heritage was transmitted by the Salafiyya and kindred movements to contemporary Islamic fundamentalists.

The processes of urbanization; the emergence of a public sphere and the development of transport, communication, and the mass media; and the spread of literacy and education—these factors can account for much of the religious revival of the last quarter century throughout the Muslim world.[21] Further, national integration and political mobilization—that is, the integration of the masses into the political society—have politically conditioned this religious revival. The importance of this political conditioning has been generally recognized, and many who consider it the primary feature of the current Islamic revival have given currency to the notion of "political Islam."[22]

My second proposition can be stated in terms of the above-mentioned trends: the first three trends are common to all Muslim countries and have, continuously and everywhere, not only increased a variety of religious activities but also stimulated scriptural fundamentalism. The political conditioning of the Islamic religious revival, on the other hand, has varied considerably from period to period and from country to country, and can account for differences among contemporary variants of Islamic fundamentalism.

The emergence of a political space and the advent of public politics have generally resulted in the superimposition of political elements on scriptural fundamentalism. In the first decade of the twentieth century, the Salafiyya merely superimposed the parliamentary constitutionalism of the modernizers on their call for orthodox reform of

Islam.[23] The same is true of their counterpart in the Ottoman mainland.[24] By contrast, when the superimposed political elements take the novel form of a totalitarian revolutionary Islamic ideology, deviation from scriptural fundamentalism becomes pronounced. Such deviation led one observer to characterize the revolutionary ideology of the Egyptian Sayyid Qutb as "non-scriptural fundamentalism."[25] Deviation from scriptural fundamentalism is pronounced when politicization takes the form of the advocacy of an Islamic state on the basis of the Mandate of the Religious Jurist (*wilayat al-faqih*), as is the case with Shi'ite clerical fundamentalism in Iran and Lebanon. Shi'ite clerical fundamentalism takes the idea of the nation-state for granted, and is conditioned by it.[26] There can thus be considerable tension between some varieties of political Islam and scriptural fundamentalism.

My second proposition implies, on the one hand, that all contemporary Islamic fundamentalisms have some scriptural substratum. On the other hand, it suggests that some fundamentalist movements can successfully resist this political conditioning. This is indeed the case with the Tablighi Jamaat in Indo-Pakistan. The movement belongs to the tradition of Islamic scriptural fundamentalism in India, according to which "the wisest course is to consider the Word of God and the authentic Prophetic Tradition to be the touchstone of the truth or error of the proofs of reason itself, and not the converse."[27] The Tablighis, as other contributors have shown, consider that "true religious faith can be maintained only in freedom from politics" and confirm their cultural critique of an alien society by avoiding all conflict and remaining outside politics.[28] Similarly, scriptural fundamentalism in the Salafi tradition of orthodox reformism (*islah*) sought to combat cultural imperialism and occidentalism in Algeria in the 1920s and 1930s without becoming political. This apolitical fundamentalist tradition was resumed in the 1970s by such organizations as the Association for Moral and Social Reform (*al-Islah al-Akhlaqi wa Ijtima'i*).[29]

As for those fundamentalisms that succumb to their political environments and are conditioned by them, I propose a further analytical distinction between political conditioning by ideological and institutional factors. Institutional factors, most notably the character of political regimes, vary considerably from country to country; ideological factors, in addition to some cross-country variations, are affected by trends in the international political culture, and therefore show considerable variation over time.

The fact that the scientific worldview was an implicit negative counterpart to all scriptural fundamentalism explains many of its apologetic features. Superimposed on these are ideological elements that are oriented toward and conditioned by rival secular political ideologies. Two intellectual watersheds mark the ideological conditioning of contemporary Islamic fundamentalism. The first is Maududi's construction of a distinct Islamic ideology in the 1930s and 1940s, which was emulated in an impressive fashion by the Shi'ite Muhammad Baqir al-Sadr three decades later. The second is the later works of Sayyid Qutb, which became available in the 1960s. The Muslim Brotherhood was already a well-organized movement when Maududi began his ideological endeavor as a journalist. Yet it did not produce anything like the ideological elaboration achieved by Maududi. The reason must be that the Muslim Brotherhood was responding to the concerns of the era of liberal nationalism.[30] Liberal nationalism, the negative counterpart of al-Banna's fundamentalism, did not require a consistent and systematic ideology. Maududi's relative detachment from Indian practical politics, by contrast, oriented him toward communism and fascism in contradistinction to which he put forward a consistent and systematic Islamic ideology.[31] In Maududi, the concern for the Islamic economic, social, and political systems as components of a coherent total ideology replaces the neo-Hanbalite preoccupation with the recovery of pristine Islam, as the salience of the "pious ancestors" is eclipsed by the "pious vanguard" of Maududi's Islamic revolution. As an age of ideology began in the Third World with the decline of imperialism and end of colonialism, Maududi's Islamic ideology was disseminated in translation throughout the Muslim world.[32]

Although Maududi's ideological elaborations included the appropriation of the modern political myth of revolution, this appropriation remained more semantic than substantive. He did not endorse violence as the means for achieving the Islamic revolution.[33] His Iranian imitators in the 1970s would justify revolutionary violence, but in terms of the modern political myth of revolution rather than in genuinely Islamic terms.[34] There was no ideological justification of revolutionary violence in the 1940s. The Egyptian Muslim Brothers and their Iranian imitators, the Feda'iyan-e Islam, did not hesitate to target "corrupt" individuals for assassination, but neither group advocated the overthrow of the established order along Kharijite lines. Their views were in fact similar to Maududi's famous description, in the same period, of the state as a train whose direction could be changed with a change of driver.[35] The Qur'anic justification of revolution had not yet been formulated.

The revolutionary radicalization of the Islamic fundamentalist ideology was conditioned by the monolithic secular state of Nasser's Egypt. In his later writings in Nasser's prison, Sayyid Qutb not only "challenged the ideology of the Nasser regime on almost every key issue"[36] but displayed great intellectual originality in transforming Maududi's ideas into a distinctively Islamic neo-Kharijite sectarian revolutionary ideology.[37] The principle of Qutb's neo-Kharijite sectarianism is this: the profession of faith according to the canonical formula and the belief in the Five Pillars are not the defining mark of a Muslim believer. The believer must in addition reject all man-made laws and governments, which are the foundations of the new paganism. The true believers, the elect, must organize themselves into vanguard groups apart from the new society of ignorance and repeat the original pattern of establishment of Islam through withdrawal/migration, jihad, and conquest of power.[38] This radical modification of scriptural fundamentalism is not intelligible apart from its negative counterpart, namely, the centralized secular state. The claim of the monolithic secular state to legislative power and to authority in areas traditionally considered the preserve of religion now brings condemnation to the nominally Muslim society that sustains it on charges of pagan ignorance and idolatry (*taghut*). To the extent that the imperious presence of the secular state is felt everywhere, the explicit demand for the implementation of the Shari'a (assumed but not conspicuous in Salafi scripturalist fundamentalism) becomes the common denominator of the contemporary political Islamic fundamentalisms.

The utopia of the Islamic state, central to the Qutbist revolutionary ideology, is not intelligible without reference to the anathematized state. This new preoccupation with, and conceptualization of, God's government (*hakimiyya*) on the basis of the Shari'a by Qutb and the Islamic revolutionaries has no counterpart in medieval Hanbalism or in Salafi scriptural fundamentalism, and is entirely a rejectionist reaction to the monolithic secular state.[39] Furthermore, although the neologism *hakimiyya* derives from Maududi, the totalitarian thrust of Qutb's ideology in response to Nasser's monolithic secular state finds no counterpart in Maududi's Islamic constitutionalism. The difference between the two thinkers is brought out strikingly by their respective Qur'an commentaries. The political elements are "astonishingly" inconspicuous in Maududi's commentary on the Qur'an, rendering God's sovereignty devoid of political implications.[40] Qutb's reading of the Qur'an, in sharp contrast, hinges on the very notion of the *hakimiyya* of God.[41] The means for achieving this utopia, however, is none other than the means advocated by the Kharijites of the first century of Islam: withdrawal/migration on the prophetic model, followed by revolutionary warfare to reconquer the lapsed society of ignorance.

Qutb's spirit of revolutionary asceticism spread among the neo-Kharijite[42] sectarian fundamentalists who have formed several *takfir* (excommunication) organizations in the past two decades.[43] These organizations have generally excommunicated the society of ignorance and "emigrated" from it, as had the Kharijites centuries earlier. According to one of the first such organizations in the 1970s, the Society of the Muslims, "after the emigration from the land of Egypt—the land of atheism and abode of war—[true] Muslims would prepare to fight atheistic society and attack the existing political system so as to take over the reins of authority. Thus the movement would follow the same stages of the historical spread of Islam: call, emigration, holy war (*da'wa*, hijra, jihad)."[44]

We have moved a considerable way from the scriptural fundamentalism of the Salafiyya. The replication of the historical pattern of the conquest of pagan Arabia under the leadership of the Prophet has taken the place of the recovery of the pristine Islam as transmitted by the Traditions of the pious ancestors. We have also moved some distance from Maududi's Islamic constitutionalism and his acceptance of political competition under "theodemocracy." According to its founder, Shukri Mustafa, "every Muslim who is reached by the call of the Society of the Muslims and does not join is an infidel."[45] Here, unbeknownst to him, Shukri Mustafa is echoing the equation of the "inactive" Muslim and the infidel by the first-century Azariqa, an extremist branch of Kharijism.[46]

The new Islamic revolutionary asceticism found its most forceful expression in a tract by the engineer M. A. S. Faraj, *The Neglected Duty,* which stated the creed of President Sadat's assassins. In this remarkable justification of tyrannicide, which is apparently influential among young clerics and lay activists alike,[47] Faraj offers a Qutbian view of the contemporary Muslim world as one of ignorance where the believers are constantly forced to submit to earthly idols.[48] "The idols of this world can only be made to disappear through the power of the sword."[49] Faraj argues that the Muslim rulers have suppressed the Islamic law since the abolition of the Caliphate in 1924, replacing it by the laws of the infidels, as the Mongols had done. These secularizing rulers, who are Muslims only in name, have forced the believers to live under the laws of the infidels. They are therefore "apostates" and must be killed, as the punishment for apostasy in Islamic law is death.[50] The absent, neglected duty of contemporary Muslims is to wage jihad against these internal enemies of Islam. Departing from the definition given to the category by Muslim jurists, Faraj thus adapts jihad to justify revolutionary violence. The appropriation of the modern myth of revolution by the Islamic radicals is complete. Our ascetic sectarians thereby become Muslim revolutionary professionals.

In short, ideological, revolutionary, and sectarian variants of fundamentalism have diluted the old scripturalist call "back to the Book!" by deriving answers to new political questions purportedly from the fundamental sources of Islam.[51] What accounts for the novelty of these politicized variants within the Islamic tradition of fundamentalism is (1) the ideological character, which is common to all of them,[52] and (2) the revolutionary asceticism, which is particular to the sectarian radicals.

The Advent of Public Politics and the Political Organization of Islamic Fundamentalism

This brief account of the development, international transmission, and transformation of contemporary Islamic fundamentalisms can now be put in macrosociological context in order to trace different directions of political conditioning of Islamic fundamentalism. In other words, I shall examine the conditions conducive to the recasting of scriptural fundamentalism into a novel ideological framework and, further, into revolutionary sectarianism.

The novelty of contemporary Islamic fundamentalisms and their pronounced ideological character can be understood as a consequence of sudden national and political integration in the absence, or with limited development, of political institutions.[53] In this perspective, politicized Islamic fundamentalism appears as a product of organized but uninstitutionalized mass political participation that results from rapid national integration and enlargement of the political society.

The advent of competitive mass politics in the Muslim world has created certain organizational imperatives. The important contribution of the Muslim Brothers was to carry out these imperatives effectively for the first time in Egypt. They rightly saw their movement as the practical (*'amali*) extension of Salafi scriptural fundamentalism, and their leader, Hasan al-Banna, as the builder (*bani*) of what Afghani had called for.[54] Hasan al-Banna described his mission as that of the Salafiyya; the Society of Muslim Brothers would not deviate from God's Book, the Tradition of the Prophet, and the conduct of the pious ancestors.[55] In the 1930s and 1940s, he built an effective organization that included a secret army and has served as a model for all subsequent Islamic political fundamentalist movements.

Clerical fundamentalism had its origins in the reaction of the ulama to the centralization and modernization of the state in Iran[56] and, as such, belongs to a typical pattern of reactive Islamic activism in modern history.[57] The Shi'ite ulama, however, had to face the organizational imperatives of mass politics as the preservation of its clerical authority required certain organizational adaptations. The Shi'ite hierarchy, like the churches defending their power in modern times, had "no choice but to establish a party organization and to use demagogic means, just like other parties."[58]

Once in firm control of the state in Iran, Khomeini saw no further need for such a tool for mobilization, and the Islamic Republican Party suspended its activity in 1987. The Shi'ite ulama of Lebanon, by contrast, still need to use demagogic means and party organization to take advantage of the political turbulence in that country, and have played a leading role in the Party of God (Hizbullah) since its founding in 1982. Their party, devoted to the eventual implementation of Khomeini's Mandate of the Religious Jurist, has an organized paramilitary wing and has been aptly described as "an Islamic adaptation to the era of Leninist revolutionary organizations." Indeed, the clerical leaders of the Party of God had no compunction in changing the name of its governing body from the Shura Council to Politburo.[59]

The importance of effective organization is clear if we consider the social heterogeneity of the membership in contemporary fundamentalist movements. Like the interwar European nationalist and fascist movements,[60] contemporary Islamic fundamentalism as an integrative movement has tended to recruit its members *both* from the newly mobilized groups and individuals from all strata of society, *and* from social groups and strata dislocated or threatened by industrialization and the modernization of states.[61] This accounts for the social heterogeneity of the Islamic fundamentalist parties. The imitators of the Salafiyya movement, as was pointed out, were partially dispossessed and marginalized ulama of "middling status" whose power and influence had declined under the impact of Ottoman modernization.[62] The oppositional lay intelligentsia played the leading role in the intermediate stages of the Islamic movements from the 1930s to 1970s, and was largely responsible for the creation of the new Islamic fundamentalist ideologies. More recently, the function of popular dissemination of Islamic fundamentalism and mass mobilization has devolved upon clerics and preachers. This social heterogeneity is well illustrated by the dual leadership of the Algerian *Front Islamique du Salut*, with Professor Abbasi Madani representing the socially upwardly mobile intelligentsia, and Shaykh 'Ali Belhadj, prayer leader of a mosque, representing the threatened and disgruntled traditional petite bourgeoisie, and acting as the mobilizer of the lower strata.[63] In Egypt, similarly, we have the bourgeois intellectuals of the Muslim Brotherhood, such as the late 'Umar al-Tilmisani, and the popular shaykhs and prayer leaders of nongovernmental mosques, such as Shaykh Muhammad al-Kahlawi in Alexandria and the famous Shaykh 'Abd al-Hamid Kishk and Shaykh 'Abd al-Rashid Saqr in Cairo.[64] In prerevolutionary Iran, there were the lay intellectuals who tended to follow Bazargan and Bani-Sadr, on the one hand, and the disprivileged clerics, on the other. In all these cases, there has been considerable tension between these two elements.[65]

The dominant role of the intelligentsia, lay and clerical, in Islamic political fundamentalisms can only be understood in light of their life experiences in societies undergoing rapid sociopolitical change. It is not the lower-middle-class background but the *combination* of higher education and social mobility—typically from small towns, and in the more integrated societies such as Egypt from villages, into major cities—that explains their ideological position.[66] The evidence for the urban character of political fundamentalism and the social mobility of its ideologues is overwhelming.[67] The Tunisian fundamentalist Rashid al-Ghannushi typically captures the experience of many: "I am of the generation of Zaytuna [Islamic seminary] students during the early years of independence. I remember we used to feel like strangers in our own country."[68] He became an organizer of the Islamic movement in order to "save human civilization from the domination of Samaritans who worship the golden calf."[69]

Political Regimes and Unification of Fundamentalisms

The relative predominance of the two leading elements can account for some of the differences among the Islamic fundamentalisms. Social recruitment, however, does not take us very far in accounting for diversity among the contemporary fundamentalist movements. The characteristics of political regimes take us considerably farther. The character of the political regimes within which Islamic fundamentalist movements have been organized varies from country to country. This variation is the most important source of diversity in contemporary political fundamentalism. Let me propose a simple model. Our two explanatory factors are the degree of pluralism of the political regime and the extent of integration of the Islamic fundamentalist movements within it. These factors are interrelated and inversely related to (1) ideological radicalism, with constitutional pragmatism and revolutionary sectarianism as the two ends of the spectrum, and to (2) the possibility of an intellectual-clerical alliance. As regards the latter possibility, mutual opposition as a result of full integration (Pakistan) and solid revolutionary alliance as a result of total exclusion (prerevolutionary Iran, Algeria) constitute the two ends of the spectrum.

The British Raj gave Pakistan a pluralistic political system with an independent judiciary, and Maududi and his Jamaat-i-Islami were beneficiaries of this separation of powers more than once, and had coupled their demand for an Islamic constitution with that for the Jamaat's own constitutional right to operate freely.[70] The dominant issue of the formative period for the Jamaat was the creation of the first modern Islamic republic and the formal accommodation of Islam in its constitution. Maududi recast many concepts of constitutional law in Islamic terms, notably substituting the sovereignty of God for national sovereignty, but was in the end prepared to accept as Islamic a constitution that paid only lip service to Islam by the symbolic adaptation of some of his notions.[71] Further ideological elaboration by the Jamaat took place during the campaign against Bhutto's socialism in 1968–70, and again in 1977. The Jamaat remained integrated into the Pakistani political process during the martial law period, when the prominent Jamaat leader Khurshid Ahmad became a confidant of General Zia ul-Haq, who instituted several Islamic measures.[72] This political integration was enhanced when the Jamaat was given four cabinet posts in 1978, and continued, with ups and downs, to May 1992, when it was one of the three partners in the ruling coalition.

After 1954, the Muslim Brotherhood in Egypt was suppressed and totally excluded from the political process. Its leaders were incarcerated, and one of them, Sayyid Qutb, was smuggling his writings out of jail portion by portion. The fundamentalist revolutionary sectarianism was thus born out of total exclusion from the political society. So was clerical fundamentalism in Iran after 1963. The Iranian political regime was monolithic,[73] and the Islamic groups remained excluded from the political process. The result was ideological radicalism of an eclectic and composite kind.[74] Revolution changed total exclusion to full integration, indeed complete control of the state. The fundamentalist revolutionary ideology, developed in total exclusion from the political society under the monarchy, has accordingly given way to clericalist but nevertheless pragmatic and begrudgingly modernized constitution making under the Islamic regime.[75]

A brief comparison of the Jamaat-i-Islami in Pakistan with the Islamic movements in Iran and Algeria can throw light on the relationship between the intellectuals and the other social elements in contemporary Islamic fundamentalism. The Jamaat is socially more homogeneous and far more organized than the Algerian and prerevolutionary Iranian movements. According to Ahmad, its leadership is "almost entirely in the hands of modern educated laymen," and its orientation is modernistic and ideological. The Pakistani counterparts of the Algerian popular shaykhs and prayer leaders do not belong to it and have their own parties. These parties "have in fact challenged the Islamic credentials of the Jamaat more vehemently than the secular parties."[76] The Jamaat has done consistently poorly in Pakistani elections, and its electoral performance has deteriorated further as it has become progressively more incorporated into the political process and government.

This brief comparison suggests that the better organized and the more homogeneously bourgeois and university-based the movement, the further removed is its ideological fundamentalism from the tradition of Islamic scriptural fundamentalism. Furthermore, it suggests that exclusion from the political process is conducive to an oppositional alliance between the Islamic clerics and the lay intellectuals, whereas integration into parliamentary political process is likely to produce a rift among these two elements, whose alliance seems crucial for the success of an Islamic revolution.

The Muslim Brotherhood's suppression and exclusion from the political process ended under Sadat, and the period of its "negative integration" began in 1976, when seven of its members entered the People's Assembly as individuals. This negative integration was enhanced under Mubarak through parliamentary alliances between the Muslim Brotherhood and the New Wafd in 1984, and then, more significantly, with the Liberal and Socialist Labor Parties in 1987, which secured it over thirty seats.[77] As Ramadan shows in meticulous detail, this de facto political integration, at every stage, split the Qutbist vanguard groups from the Brotherhood, whose participation in the elections they vehemently condemned. The Muslim Brotherhood decided to boycott the parliamentary elections of December 1990 while redoubling its very successful effort since the late 1980s to gain control of professional associations. This has so far been condoned by the state in accordance with the policy of negative integration.[78] In exchange, the condemnation of the Qutbist extremists by prominent Muslim Brothers has effectively contributed to the marginalization of the revolutionary sectarians.[79]

The same inverse relationship between integration and ideological radicalism holds in the case of the regular integration of the Muslim Brotherhood into parliamentary politics in Jordan. In 1989, the Muslim Brotherhood won 23 seats in the Lower House of Parliament. Between January and June 1991, the Muslim Brotherhood leaders were among the seven ministers from Islamic groups who entered the cabinet, and controlled the ministries of Education, Religious Affairs, Health, and Social Development. The number of Muslim Brother deputies declined slightly after the 1993 elections when the Brother's political organ, The Islamic Action Front won 16 seats, with a few other deputies who had run independently for the Muslim Brotherhood. There has been no call for the overthrow of constitutional monarchy and the establishment of an Islamic state in Jordan.[80]

The above considerations suggest that partial political integration tends to give rise to practical fundamentalism and splinter ideological radicalism, while political exclusion fosters radical ideological fundamentalism and revolutionary sectarianism.

The case of Algeria is interesting because it seems to suggest that the absence of political pluralism can itself foster radicalization of fundamentalism despite some co-optative integration. Until the constitutional reform of 1989, the monolithic Algerian state propagated a totalitarian political socialist ideology. The followers of Ben Badis were influential in the formation of the *Front de Liberation National* in 1954. After independence, Islam was nationalized,[81] as were land and industry, and was culturally accommodated,[82] with many Islamically (FLN) oriented intellectuals being coopted. The spectacular victory of the Algerian fundamentalists in the elections for the provincial and municipal councils in June 1990 suddenly brought them into the Algerian political process.[83] The violent clashes of June 1991, however, demonstrated that this partial political integration did not result in pragmatism. Furthermore, during the fateful national elections of 26 December 1991, the Front Islamique du Salut stood firm by its official motto of "No constitution and no laws. The only rule is the Koran and the law of God,"[84] and remained uncompromising in its advocacy of an Islamic state. After it was assured of 188 seats (against the ruling Front de Liberation National's 15) in the first round, the Front Islamique du Salut (FIS) did declare its readiness for "cohabitation" with President Chadli Benjedid.[85] But this declaration was never put to the test because President Benjedid declared a state of emergency and stepped down on 11 January 1992, and the government annulled the elections the following day, plunging the country into continuous and deteriorating civil strife. This abrupt ending of incipient democratic pluralism by the military coup makes it impossible to speculate with any confidence on what might have happened. A few observations seem pertinent nevertheless.

The aggressive and intolerant rhetoric of FIS has been correctly underlined by Roberts.[86] His explanation of this intolerance in terms of bungling "manipulation," by President Chadli, of the FIS into "cornering the market in political radicalism,"[87] though interesting, cannot be considered complete. My model offers a complementary explanation of the unabated radicalism of the Algerian fundamentalists throughout 1990 and 1991 in terms of the monolithic structure and ideological totalitarianism of the state under which they have so long lived. The FIS has inherited the antipluralist discourse of national liberation. The model also explains the lay-clerical alliance that doomed the monolithic state's attempt to open up, making Islamic revolution or civil war the only remaining alternatives for Algeria.

Some Recent Changes in the Political Conditioning of Islamic Fundamentalism

The very complex historical conditioning of the Sudanese Islamic fundamentalism by both Sufism and Mahdism, and its more recent political conditioning, require separate treatment and cannot be considered here. The most recent trend in the Sudan, however, is relevant to our concern for classification. Dr. Hasan al-Turabi, the leader first of the Sudanese Muslim Brotherhood, and since 1986, of the National Islamic Front, has certainly been a pragmatic fundamentalist, adept at operating under alternating military and democratic regimes. In 1989, he traded junior partnership in the democratic government of Sadiq al-Mahdi for unencumbered dominance under the Islamicized military regime of General 'Umar al-Bashir. The new partnership initially resembled the relationship between Zia al-Haq and the Jamaat-i Islami in Pakistan until Turabi began the unsavory experiment of turning his organization into the mobilizational arm of Bashir's Islamicized military regime.[88] Turabi had earlier shown concern about the low legitimacy of secular nation-states in the Muslim world, and was groping for a solution in the direction of Islamic internationalism.[89] In the context of a disintegrating nation-state beset by a prolonged civil war, Turabi began to consider a local political regime, Colonel Qaddafi's military-mobilizational *jamahiriyya*, as an alternative to Western democratic political regimes, and one somehow more compatible for the kind of a federal regime with cross-national ties suggested by his idea of Islamic internationalism.

These recent developments in the Sudan indicate the possibility of new factors making for alternative political conditioning and new emergent forms of fundamentalism. I have implied that the disintegration of the nation-state may be one such new factor. This new factor seems to have influenced Turabi's political practice since 1989, but its effect is perhaps more clearly discernible in the political thought of Fadlallah in Lebanon.

Shaykh Muhammad Husayn Fadlallah, a Shi'ite cleric born in Iraq and resident in Lebanon for the past thirty years, and responding at least in part to the disintegration of the state in his adopted and native countries, has departed from his earlier and more typical antithetical focus on the infidel state as the Satanic enemy of Islam. He now considers Islamic government a contingent rather than a necessary goal of the Islamic movement of the disinherited against the powers of oppression. In Fadlallah's recent thought we thus see a relaxation of the revolutionary sectarian obsession with God's government and a move in the direction of what has been described as a theology of liberation.[90]

Conclusion

Unity in Islamic fundamentalism throughout history stems from its affirmation of the central tenets of Islam: belief in monotheism and the conviction of the possession of the final revelation in the Qur'an. This unity rests firmly on familiarity with the Qur'an, partaking of congregational worship, the five daily prayers, and fasting during the month of Ramadan, and is accompanied by the unquestioning acceptance (*bila kayf*) of the literal truth of the holy scripture. It produces a distinct type of God-fearing personality convinced of the possession of the truth of divine revelation and intolerant of alternative truths.

The implicit counterpart of this affirmation, however, varies from time to time and place to place, producing distinct types of Islamic fundamentalism. Philosophy and heterodoxy were the primary cultural counterparts of premodern scriptural fundamentalism. Its political conditioning was complex, but it was largely subsumed by these cultural counterparts, as the main determinants were the political threat of heterodoxy and of the bearers of the philosophical rationalism. Contemporary scriptural fundamentalism, by contrast, is primarily conditioned by the menace of Western culture. In both cases, elements of the rejected cultural counterparts are antithetically absorbed by scriptural fundamentalism. However, the elements thus appropriated—science and technology in the case of contemporary scriptural fundamentalism—become objects of the same attitude of unquestioning acceptance.

Sivan is correct in identifying contemporary Islamic fundamentalism as primarily a cultural phenomenon despite its sharp political edge.[91] Continued reaction to Western culture as their negative counterpart makes a measure of scriptural fundamentalism the common undercurrent of all contemporary fundamentalisms. Culture, however, is intensely politicized throughout the contemporary Muslim world, and the resulting political conditioning has generated a distinct type that deviates considerably from premodern scriptural fundamentalism, and stands in some tension with contemporary scriptural fundamentalism, whose reaction to Western cultural domination it shares. The tension between the new and the old type of twentieth century Islamic fundamentalisms is clearly manifest in the current denunciation of the scriptural fundamentalism of Ben Badis by the Algerian Islamic revolutionaries and the branding of his followers as collaborationists. This new type is political fundamentalism, with four subtypes. The subtypes reflect further conditioning of political fundamentalism by the character of the regime, and by the national and international political culture.

In conclusion, it seems appropriate to offer table 7.1, a typology of Islamic fundamentalism, as a summary of the foregoing considerations. This typological summary does not purport to be exhaustive, and is open to addition of new types by its very logic. In fact, I have alluded to the possibility of the emergence of new types under changing conditions in the previous section. Furthermore, a more general and profound change than the ones mentioned there has been the recent demise of Communism, the more powerful of the totalitarian ideologies that had profoundly influenced Maududi, and through him, the politicized, ideological Islamic fundamentalisms of the subsequent generations. The global demise of totalitarianism and the failure of socialism in the Middle East amount to a radical change in the international political culture that has conditioned Islamic fundamentalism for more than half a century. The current types of Islamic fundamentalism are robust and will persist. At the same time, the new climate in the international political culture can be expected to condition the

TABLE 7.1

TYPOLOGY OF ISLAMIC FUNDAMENTALISM ACCORDING
TO ITS CULTURAL AND POLITICAL CONDITIONING

Type (Example)	Conditioning Factors		
	Cultural Counterpart	Regime	Political Culture
Scriptural			
Premodern (Hanbalism and Wahhabism)	philosophy and heterodoxy		
Contemporary (Salafiyya and Tablighi)	Western culture		
Political			
Pragmatic (Muslim Brotherhood)	Western culture	parliamentary pluralism	liberal democracy (totalitarian ideologies)
Ideological, constitutionalist	Western culture	parliamentary pluralism	totalitarian ideologies (liberal democracy)
Clericalist	Western culture	monolithic state	totalitarian ideologies
Revolutionary sectarian (Qutbism)	Western culture	monolithic state	totalitarian ideologies

emergence of types of Islamic fundamentalism that are less concerned with the creation of an Islamic state and less collectivist—i.e., less hostile to private enterprise and capitalism. These new forms will nevertheless be easily recognizable by what they affirm as the fundamentals; and the affirmative component of their position will unmistakably affiliate them to the fundamentalist tradition within Islam as an Abrahamic monotheistic religion.

Notes

1. Henri Laoust, *Les Schismes en Islam* (Paris: Payot, 1965), pp. 36–48.

2. Tilman Nagel, *Staat und Glaubensgemeinschaft im Islam* (Munich: Artemis, 1981), Vol. 2, chap. 1.

3. Fundamentalism, according to Jeffrey Hadden, can be viewed as "a proclamation of reclaimed authority of a sacred tradition that is to be reinstated as an antidote for a society that has strayed from its cultural mooring. Sociologically speaking, fundamentalism involves (a) a refutation of the radical and the secular that has evolved with modernization and (b) a plan to dedifferentiate this institutional bifurcation and thus bring religion back to center stage as an important factor of interest in public policy decisions."

All we need is to substitute "secularization of government" for "modernization," and Hadden's definition fits medieval Hanbalism perfectly.

4. George Makdisi, *Ibn 'Aqil et la résurgence de l'Islam traditionaliste au XIe siècle* (Damascus: Institut Français de Damas, 1963), pp. 291–97, 326–27.

5. Ibn Taymiyya's first major tract was written in the course of agitation to obtain a verdict against a Christian who had insulted Muhammad. Cf. Donald P. Little, "The Historical and Historiographical Significance of the Detention of Ibn Taymiyya," *International Journal of Middle East Studies*, 4 (1973), p. 312; Henri Laoust, "L'influence d'Ibn-Taymiyya," in Alford T. Welch and

Pierre Cachia, eds., *Islam: Past Influence and Present Challenge* (Edinburgh University Press and State University of New York Press, 1979), p. 15. Much of his effort went to polemics against the Shi'ites who had developed close ties to the Mongol court (H. Laoust, "La critique du Sunnism dans la doctrine al-Hilli," *Revue des Etudes Islamiques,* 34 [1966], pp. 35–60).

6. Marc Gaborieau, "Les Oulémas/soufis dans l'Inde mongole: anthropologie historique de religieux musulmans," *Annales, économies, sociétés, civilisations,* 5 (1989).

7. John S. Habib, *Ibn Sa'ud's Warriors of Islam* (Leiden: Brill, 1978).

8. David D. Commins, *Islamic Reform: Politics and Social Change in Late Ottoman Syria* (New York: Oxford University Press, 1990), pp. 47–48, 142.

9. Ali Merad, *Le Réformisme musulman en Algérie de 1925 à 1940* (Paris: Mouton, 1967), pp. 217–19, 437; Ali Merad, "Islah," in *The Encyclopedia of Islam,* new ed. (Leiden: Brill, 1978), 4:141–63.

10. Fazlur Rahman, *Islam* (Chicago: University of Chicago Press, 1966), chap. 12.

11. R. S. O'Fahey and Bernd Radtke, "Neo-Sufism Reconsidered," *Der Islam* 70, no. 1 (1993), pp. 52–87.

12. Richard P. Mitchell, *The Society of Muslim Brothers* (London: Oxford University Press, 1969), pp. 214–16. Furthermore, when al-Banna founded the battalion system in 1937, he required members in the "formation" stage of their training for loyalty "to carry the burden of jihad, unite on the basis of Sufi 'spirituality' and military 'action' under a strict rule of 'obedience' [*amr wa ta'a*] without hesitation, question, doubt or criticism" (p. 300).

13. See the chapter by Almond and Sivan in this volume.

14. Etan Kohlberg, "Imam and Community in the Pre-Ghayba Period," in Said Amir Arjomand, ed., *Authority and Political Culture in Shi'ism* (Albany: State University of New York Press, 1988); Yohanan Friedmann, *Prophecy Continuous: Aspects of Ahmadi Religious Thought and Its Medieval Background* (Berkeley: University of California Press, 1989).

15. E. Landau-Tasseron, "The 'Cyclical Reform': A Study of the *Mujaddid* Tradition," *Studia Islamica* 70 (1989): 79–117.

16. Friedmann, *Prophecy,* p. 101.

17. For an early example of Naqshbandi jihad in Central Asia in the sixteenth century, see Said Amir Arjomand, *The Shadow of God and the Hidden Imam: Religion, Political Order, and Societal Change in Shi'ite Iran from the Beginning to 1890* (Chicago: University of Chicago Press, 1984), p. 292 n. 70.

18. John O. Voll, "The Sudanese Mahdi: Frontier Fundamentalism," *International Journal of Middle East Studies* 10 (1979): 147–49, for instance, characterizes the Mahdist movement in the Sudan as "frontier fundamentalism."

19. Said Amir Arjomand, "Traditionalism in Twentieth-Century Iran," in Said Amir Arjomand, ed., *From Nationalism to Revolutionary Islam* (London: Macmillan; Albany: State University of New York Press, 1984).

20. It may seem paradoxical that both the Hanbalite Wahhabis and the Salafis emphasize the importance of *ijtihad,* which is also the hallmark of Shi'ism. On closer inspection, however, respective meanings of ijtihad are quite different. The scriptural fundamentalists take the notion to mean individual endeavor to study the Qur'an and the Sunna, whereas in the Shi'ite clericalist and institutionalized interpretation ijtihad assumes the form of competence to engage in authoritative jurisprudence.

21. Said Amir Arjomand, "Social Change and Movements of Revitalization in Contemporary Islam," in James Beckford, ed., *New Religious Movements and Rapid Social Change* (London: Sage, 1986). All these processes contributory to the Islamic resurgence in Algeria have recently been documented by Ahmad Rouadjia, *Les Frères et al mosquée: Enquête sur le mouvement islamist en Algérie* (Paris: Karthala, 1990).

22. Judge Muhammad Sa'id al-'Ashmawy entitled his celebrated critique of Qutbist fundamentalism, published in Cairo in 1987, *al-Islam al-Siyasi* (Political Islam). (French translation, *l'Islamisme contre l'Islam* [Paris: Découverte, 1989].) "Political Islam" has

since appeared in the titles of many recent articles and books, for instance, the special issue of the *Annals of the American Academy of Political and Social Sciences* 524 (1992).

23. Commins, *Islamic Reform*, chap. 10.

24. Şerif Mardin, *Religion and Social Change in Modern Turkey* (Albany: State University of New York Press, 1989), chap. 2.

25. Leonard Binder, *Islamic Liberalism: A Critique of Development Ideologies* (Chicago: University of Chicago Press, 1988), chap. 5.

26. Sami Zubaida, *Islam, the People and the State* (London, 1989), chap. 1. Politicization apart, major doctrinal differences separate Shi'ite clerical fundamentalism from Sunni scriptural fundamentalism. Furthermore, though equally revolutionary, clerical fundamentalism is made distinct from Qutbist revolutionary sectarianism by its clericalism. Qutbist revolutionary sectarians are often anticlerical. For instance, Shukri Mustafa, the leader of the Qutbist Society of Muslims, regarded respect for clerical authority as idolatry. See Gilles Kepel, *Le Prophete et Pharaon: Les mouvements islamistes dans l'Egypte contemporaine* (Paris: La Découverte, 1984), pp. 78–79.

27. M. Q. Nanotawi, "Assessment of Religious Tenets" (1890), in A. Ahmad and Gustav E. von Grunebaum, eds., *Muslim Self-Statement in India and Pakistan, 1857–1968* (Wiesbaden: Harrassowitz, 1970), p. 61.

28. Mumtaz Ahmad, "Islamic Fundamentalism in South Asia: The Jamaat-i-Islami and the Tablighi Jamaat of South Asia," in Martin E. Marty and R. Scott Appleby, eds., *Fundamentalisms Observed* (Chicago: University of Chicago Press, 1991), p. 519; Barbara D. Metcalf, "'Remaking Ourselves': Islamic Self-Fashioning in a Global Movement of Spiritual Renewal," in Martin E. Marty and R. Scott Appleby, eds., *Accounting for Fundamentalisms* (Chicago: University of Chicago Press, 1994), pp. 710–712.

29. Rouadjia, *Les Frères et al mosquée*, pp. 17–25.

30. John O. Voll, "Fundamentalism in the Sunni Arab World: Egypt and the Sudan," in Marty and Appleby, *Fundamentalisms Observed*, pp. 360–366.

31. Charles J. Adams, "The Ideology of Mawlana Mawdudi," in Donald Eugene Smith, ed., *South Asian Politics and Religion* (Princeton: Princeton University Press, 1966).

32. Karl D. Bracher, *Zeit der Ideologien* (Stuttgart: Deutsche Verlagsanstalt, 1982), chap. 6. The demise of the Communist totalitarian ideology in the late 1980s suddenly changed the international political culture. This change will undoubtedly have a profound impact on Islamic fundamentalist ideologies.

33. Ahmad, "Islamic Fundamentalism in South Asia," p. 488.

34. Said Amir Arjomand, "The Emergence of Islamic Political Ideologies," in James A. Beckford and Thomas Luckmann, eds., *The Changing Face of Religion* (London: Sage, 1989), p. 120.

35. Cited in Ahmad, "Islamic Fundamentalism in South Asia," p. 480; see also Abul Ala Maududi, "The Necessity of Divine Government for the Elimination of Oppression and Injustice," in Ahmad and von Grunebaum, *Muslim Self-Statement in India and Pakistan*, pp. 165–66.

36. Voll, "Fundamentalism in the Sunni Arab World," p. 370.

37. Yvonne Haddad, "Sayyid Qutb: Ideologue of Islamic Revival," in John L. Esposito, ed., *Voices of Resurgent Islam* (New York: Oxford University Press, 1983); Kepel, *Le Prophete et Pharaon*, chap. 2; Ibrahim M. Abu-Rabi', *Intellectual Origins of Islamic Resurgence in the Modern Arab World* (Albany: State University of New York Press, 1995), chap. 6.

38. Sayyid Qutb, *Milestones* (Indianapolis: American Trust Publications, 1990); Abdel Aziz Ramadan, "Fundamentalist Influence in Egypt: The Strategies of the Muslim Brotherhood and the Takfir Groups," in Martin E. Marty and R. Scott Appleby, eds., *Fundamentalisms and the State* (Chicago: University of Chicago Press, 1993), p. 156.

39. On the neologisms introduced in this conceptualization, see A. M. Gomaa, "Islamic Fundamentalism in Egypt in the 1930s and 1970s: Some Comparative Notes," in

Gabriel R. Warburg and Uri M. Kupferschmidt, eds., *Islam, Nationalism, and Radicalism in Egypt and the Sudan* (New York: Praeger, 1983); and Arjomand, "The Emergence of Islamic Political Ideologies," pp. 118–19. The moderate eleventh-century Hanbalite thinker, Ibn 'Aqil, maintained that the practice of the Companions of the Prophet proved that there was a political space and politics outside of the Shari'a; one only needed to remember the burning of the variants of the Qur'an in the public interest by the order of the third rightly guided caliph (Makdisi, *Ibn 'Aqil,* p. 527). Even the fiery Ibn Taymiyya insisted that the Qur'an had not decided the form of government in Islam. See Laoust, "L'influence d'Ibn-Taymiyya," p. 22.

40. Charles J. Adams, "Abu'l-A'la Maududi's *Tafhim al-Qur'an,*" in Andrew Rippin, ed., *Approaches to the History of the Interpretation of the Qur'an* (Oxford: Clarendon Press, 1988), p. 322.

41. Abu-Rabi', *Intellectual Origins,* chap. 6.

42. Opponents of the Qutbists among the ulama have compared them to the Kharijites. The revolutionary ascetics themselves, however, seem unaware of the striking similarity between their ideology and Kharijism, and resent the comparison. Faraj, the leading spirit behind Sadat's assassination, is vehement in his condemnation of Kharijism (Johannes J. G. Jansen, *The Neglected Duty, the Creed of Sadat's Assassins, and Islamic Resurgence in the Middle East* [New York: Macmillan, 1986], pp. 179–80).

43. Ramadan, "Fundamentalist Influence in Egypt," pp. 157–64.

44. Ibid., p. 158.

45. Ibid.

46. Laoust, *Schismes,* pp. 44–45.

47. Shabrough Akhavi, "The Clergy's Conception of Rule in Egypt and Iran," *Annals of the American Academy of Political and Social Sciences,* 524 (1992): 95.

48. Ellis Goldberg, "Smashing Idols and the State: The Protestant Ethic and Egyptian Sunni Radicalism," *Comparative Studies in Society and History* 33 (1991): 22.

49. Jansen, *The Neglected Duty,* p. 161.

50. Ibid., appendix.

51. For Ibn 'Abd al-Wahhab, anything not found in the Qur'an was a reprehensible innovation (*bid'a*). Maududi's systems must be making him turn in his grave.

52. This ideological character is attenuated among the Islamic constitutionalists by their implicit recognition of the legitimacy of pluralism in parliamentary representation.

53. Samuel P. Huntington, *Political Order in Changing Societies* (New Haven: Yale University Press, 1968).

54. Gabriel Baer, "Islamic Political Activity in Modern Egyptian History: A Comparative Analysis," in Warburg and Kupferschmidt, *Islam, Nationalism, and Radicalism,* pp. 46, 51.

55. Ramadan, "Fundamentalist Influence in Egypt," p. 152.

56. Said Amir Arjomand, *The Turban for the Crown: The Islamic Revolution in Iran* (New York: Oxford University Press, 1988), chap. 4.

57. Baer, "Islamic Political Activity," p. 49; Commins, *Islamic Reform.*

58. Max Weber in Guenther Roth and Claus Wittich, eds., *Economy and Society* (Berkeley: University of California Press, 1978), p. 1195.

59. As'ad Abu Khalil, "Ideology and Practice of Hizballah in Lebanon: Islamization of Leninist Organizational Principle," *Middle Eastern Studies* 37, no. 3 (1991): 394, 401.

60. It is worth remembering that nationalism, socialism, communism, and fascism were integrative mass movements that arose in Europe, especially in Eastern Europe, in a period of accelerated urbanization, spread of literacy, and higher education, and in the context of an unprecedented process of national integration.

61. Arjomand, *The Turban for the Crown.*

62. Commins, *Islamic Reform,* p. 7. A parallel can be found in the decline of status and influence of the ministers who led Protestant fundamentalism in the United States in the 1910–1928 period. See Martin Riesebrodt, *Pious Passion. The Emergence of Modern Fundamentalism in the United States*

and Iran (Berkeley: University of California Press, 1993), pp. 86–93.

63. François Burgat, L'Islamisme au Maghreb (Paris: Karthala, 1988); Hugh Roberts, "From Radical Mission to Equivocal Ambition: The Expansion and Manipulation of Algerian Islamism, 1979–1992," in Marty and Appleby, eds., Accounting for Fundamentalisms, pp. 448–449.

64. On Kishk, see Jansen, The Neglected Duty, chap. 4; Fedwa Malti-Douglas, "A Literature of Islamic Revival? The Autobiography of Shaykh Kishk," in Şerif Mardin, ed., Cultural Transitions in the Middle East (Leiden and New York: Brill, 1994). On Saqr see Ramadan, "Fundamentalist Influence in Egypt," p. 171.

65. This tension has been well demonstrated by the liquidation of the followers of Bazargan and Bani-Sadr in Iran after the revolution (in 1980–81). In the 1990s, it has generated a heated debate between the leading lay fundamentalist ideologue, 'Abd al-Karim Shorush, and the clerical polemicists.

66. Arjomand, The Turban for the Crown, pp. 199–200.

67. Saad Eddin Ibrahim, "Anatomy of Egypt's Militant Islamic Groups," International Journal of Middle East Studies 12, no. 6 (1980): 423–53; Arjomand, "Social Change"; Uri M. Kupferschmidt, "Reformist and Militant Islam in Urban and Rural Egypt," Middle Eastern Studies 23, no. 4 (1987): 403–18; Mary-Jane Deeb, "Militant Islam and the Politics of Redemption," Annals of the American Academy of Political and Social Sciences 524 (1992): 57–59; Seyyed Vali Reza Nasr, "Students, Islam, and Politics: Islami Jami'at-i Tulaba in Pakistan," Middle East Journal 6, no. 1 (1992): 59–76; idem, The Vanguard of the Islamic Revolution: The Jama'at-i Islami in Pakistan (Berkeley: University of California Press, 1994); Ahmad, "Islamic Fundamentalism in South Asia"; Riesebrodt, Pious Passion, chap. 3.

68. Cited in Norma Salem, "Tunisia," in Shireen T. Hunter, ed., The Politics of Islamic Revivalism (Bloomington: Indiana University Press, 1988), p. 165.

69. Speech made in Tehran in December 1990, cited in Deeb, "Militant Islam," p. 58.

70. Nasr, The Vanguard of the Islamic Revolution, chap. 6. Maududi did not forget that he had been released from detention in 1950 and from imprisonment in 1955 by court orders, and his one substantive criticism of the Constitution of the Islamic Republic of Pakistan was that its clause on "preventive detention" was dictatorial.

71. Leonard Binder, Religion and Politics in Pakistan (Berkeley: University of California Press, 1961), pp. 370–73.

72. Ahmad stresses the dilemmas of cooperation with Zia under martial law. This cooperation does not alter the fact that the Jamaat's demand for the enforcement of the Shari'a was within the rule-of-law tradition and the observance of constitutional procedure.

73. The opening of the Iranian political regime came far too late.

74. The ideology of the movement was a composite of the modern myth of revolution of a disinherited nation against the lackeys of imperialism and Khomeini's idea of theocratic government. It was also eclectic in its selective adaptation of Maududi's and Qutb's notions, especially in slogans. The clerics, who knew Arabic, may also have read Muhammad Baqir al-Sadr.

75. Said Amir Arjomand, "Shi'ite Jurisprudence and Constitution Making in the Islamic Republic of Iran," in Marty and Appleby, eds., Fundamentalisms and the State.

76. Ahmad, "Islamic Fundamentalism in South Asia," p. 509. In this chapter, I am not concerned with the political consequences of integration, which belong to the final theme of fundamentalism and democracy. But it should be noted that the poor performance of the Jamaat-i-Islami in Pakistani elections since 1970 contrasts with the revolutionary victory of the Iranian movement in 1979 and the resounding success of the Algerian movement in 1990. Being tightly organized has increased the social homogeneity of the movement but, given Pakistan's pluralist political system, has thereby greatly reduced its chances of the takeover of the state.

77. Saad Eddin Ibrahim, "Egypt's Islamic

Activism in the 1980s," *Third World Quarterly* 10, no. 2 (1988): 632–57.

78. Gehad Auda, "Egypt's Uneasy Politics," *Journal of Democracy* 2, no. 2 (1991), pp. 70–78; idem, "The 'Normalization' of the Islamic Movement in Egypt from 1970s to the Early 1990s," in Marty and Appleby, eds., *Accounting for Fundamentalisms,* pp. 387–89.

79. Kepel, *Le Prophete et Pharaon,* chaps. 3–4; Goldberg, "Smashing Idols and the State," p. 24; Ramadan, "Fundamentalist Influence in Egypt," p. 173. As Ramadan (p. 172) emphasizes, Sadat's grave mistake in 1981 was to conflate Muslim Brothers (the practical fundamentalists) and the Takfir groups (the revolutionary sectarians). There are indications at the time of this writing (August 1994) that Mubarak is about to repeat the same mistake.

80. Beverley Milton-Edwards, "A Temporary Alliance with the Crown: The Islamic Response in Jordan," in James Piscatori, ed., *Islamic Fundamentalisms and the Gulf Crisis* (Chicago: American Academy of Arts and Sciences, 1991), pp. 100–105. Tim H. Riedel, "The 1993 Parliamentary Elections in Jordan," *Orient,* 35, no. 1 (1994): 58–59.

81. Mohamed Arkoun, "Algeria," in Hunter, *The Politics of Islamic Revivalism,* p. 174. Algerian officials appear reluctant to give up their claim to this nationalized Islam. As late as June 1991, Ghozali would cite a Qur'anic verse (102, 2–3) in his first speech as prime minister.

82. L. Addi, *L'Algérie et la démocratie* (Paris: La Decouverte, 1994), p. 29. The state's attempt at the appropriation of Islam is reflected in the publication of the journal *Al-Asala* (authenticity) since 1971, the conservative family law of 1986, and the appointment of the prominent Egyptian ideologue of the Muslim Brotherhood, Muhammad al-Ghazali, as the rector of the new university of Constantine (Burgat, *L'islamisme au Maghreb,* pp. 151, 168–69).

83. Roberts, "Radical Mission," p. 428.

84. Youssef M. Ibrahim, "Algerian Election Tests Government," *New York Times,* 26 December 1991, p. A3.

85. "Le FIS se dit prêt à 'cohabiter' avec le président Chadli à certaines conditions," *Le Monde,* 31 December 1991, p. 3.

86. Roberts, "Radical Mission."

87. Ibid., p. 469.

88. Judith Miller, "The Islamic Wave," *New York Times Magazine,* 31 May 1992, p. 40.

89. See the statement he made in 1987, as cited in Abdelwahab El-Affendi, *Turabi's Revolution: Islam and Power in Sudan* (London: Grey Seal, 1991), p. 178.

90. Abu-Rabi', *Intellectual Origins,* chap. 7.

91. Emmanuel Sivan, *Radical Islam* (New Haven: Yale University Press, 1985), p. 3.

Muslim Fundamentalists: Psychosocial Profiles

Valerie J. Hoffman

In his book *Islam in Revolution*, R. H. Dek-
mejian devotes a few pages to a psychological profile of the *muta'assib*, the Arab
Muslim "fanatic" or religious extremist. He lists a number of features: alienation, dogmatism, an inferiority complex that resolves itself in an assertion of superiority, activ-
ism/aggressiveness, authoritarianism, intolerance, paranoia, idealism, austerity, obedience, conformity, and conspiratorial tendencies.[1]

Few authors have attempted such a sweeping characterization of the Muslim fundamentalist, even given the restriction to the Arab world. The attempt to draw a
broader social as well as psychological profile of Muslim fundamentalists is a task
fraught with difficulty. For one thing, fundamentalists have seldom allowed themselves
to be investigated by researchers. The few sociological analyses of fundamentalists that
we have are based on very limited samples of particular groups, often only of those
who have been arrested or killed.[2] Furthermore, Islamic groups that might properly
be called fundamentalist pursue a number of different methodologies in their pursuit
of a truly Islamic society: Jamaat-i-Islami, founded by Abul Ala Maududi in India/
Pakistan in 1941, aims at rebuilding Islamic society by reeducating its elite in Islamic
values; the Muslim Brotherhood, founded in Egypt in 1928 by Hasan al-Banna, aimed
to educate the masses in Islam and offered impressive social services to reach out to
them; the "jihad" groups of Egypt and the larger Arab world believe that Arab society
is mainly Islamic in orientation, that the reins of power must be seized from secular
leaders in order to implement Islam from the top; the Takfir wa'l Hijra group of Egypt
led by Shukri Mustafa in the 1970s believed that Egyptian society was in a new stage
of *jahiliyya* (a new "age of ignorance" like that which existed at the time of Muhammad), and they followed Muhammad's pattern of withdrawal from the infidel society
in order to form a Muslim society that would eventually be able to do battle with the
infidels. Today in many countries, Muslim fundamentalists have transformed their

movements into political parties in order to capture the seat of government and bring about the longed-for implementation of Islamic law (*Shari'a*). These different tactics naturally beg the question of whether the different methodologies are reflected in a difference in the composition of these groups. Are we talking about a single "psycho-social profile," or a number of different profiles?

The Fundamentalism Project has published several articles on fundamentalist movements in Pakistan, Iran, and Egypt. Since none of these reflect the experience of the former French colonies, I have added Algeria to the list. Given a paucity of information available on Algeria (with the exception of a spate of recent newspaper articles), due to the amorphous and clandestine nature of the Islamic movement in Algeria until 1989, I have supplemented this with the more plentiful information available on the Islamic movement in neighboring Tunisia, where some of the problems deriving from the French colonial experience (although technically Tunisia was merely a protectorate) are similar.

I also have some personal background in Tunisia. I was a student at the University of Tunis in 1973–74, and was struck by how totally my fellow students in sociology had embraced French intellectual thought. Secularism, even atheism, was the unquestioned ideal for all those who aspired to live a modern and intellectually oriented lifestyle. They assumed that Americans were by definition modern, and were shocked to learn that I had a belief in God. They asked me incredulously why I bothered to study such useless subjects as Arabic and Islamic culture. They all knew French perfectly, indeed the language of instruction at the university was French, and Arabic was deemed inadequate to express modern culture. As for Islamic culture, it had given way before the onslaught of modern French culture (except, however, in the critical domain of family and sexual relations), and was associated only with old or uneducated people.

In late 1979, after the Islamic revolution of Iran had jolted both Muslims and the West to rethink the relevance of Islam to contemporary society, I returned to Tunisia as part of a cultural mission of Arabic-speaking American students. We visited the University of Tunis and talked with a class there. I immediately detected a very different mood in their questions. Instead of the incredulous and somewhat mocking questions concerning the reasons we bothered to study their language and culture, they asked us, "How have you benefited by studying Islamic culture? How has Islam contributed to the West? What do you believe are the greatest strengths of the Arabic language?" A few years later, when the Islamic associations had seized student unions all across North Africa, no one could doubt any longer the strength of the reassertion of cultural pride that accompanied the Islamic resurgence. My experiences in Egypt and Syria in the 1970s also enabled me to see how different the situation was in the Arab east, where there was not such a massive national crisis of identity brought about by cultural hybridism, where great literature continued to be produced in the Arabic language, and where the cultural domination of the West was far less complete than in the Maghreb.

Social Profiles of Islamic Fundamentalism

The Leadership

With the exception of Iran, where clerical leaders played a leading role in the rise of Islamic fundamentalism, the leaders and founders of Islamic fundamentalist movements have had a secular education. Maududi was educated by a personal tutor, because of his father's disdain for the traditional *madrasa* system and his deep suspicion of the British school system. Maududi originally made his career in journalism. Hasan al-Banna was a schoolteacher. Sayyid Qutb was a writer and literary critic. 'Ali Shari'ati, often called the "ideologue of the Iranian Revolution," received a Ph.D. from the Sorbonne.[3] With the exception of Ayatollah Taleqani, the other leaders of the Liberation Movement, a religiopolitical group that played a major role in the Iranian Revolution, were doctors, scientists, and engineers. In addition to the army officers, many of the leaders and founders of Egypt's fundamentalist movements of the 1970s and 1980s were also of these professions. The main leader of the Algerian Front Islamique du Salut (FIS) is Abbasi Madani, a former member of the Front de Liberation National (FLN) and a university professor with a doctorate from the University of London. The leader of the Renaissance Party of Tunisia (formerly the Mouvement de Tendance Islamique [MTI]), Rashid al-Ghannushi, received his early education in the Zaytouna religious school system, and later studied philosophy at the University of Damascus and briefly at the Sorbonne. The Sudanese Islamic leader Hasan Turabi was educated at the Sorbonne and the University of London. The list could go on.

This predominantly secular educational background does not imply, however, complete estrangement from the sources of traditional religious education. Hasan al-Banna's father was a religious teacher who provided his son with a traditional Islamic education in his early years, and Banna at one point was associated with a Sufi order. Sayyid Qutb, who became chief ideologue of the Muslim Brotherhood and was executed in 1966 for inspiring the regrouped Brotherhood in an alleged plot to assassinate Nasser, had memorized the Qur'an by the age of ten, and his early educational formation was traditional, although he went on to study under secular teachers in Cairo in his teens. 'Ali Shari'ati's father is described as a "militant Muslim" who taught Islamic history in local schools, and Shari'ati joined him in the Movement of God-Worshiping Socialists. His father also tutored him in Arabic.[4] Zaynab al-Ghazali, one of the few women who have distinguished themselves in the Islamic movement, was the daughter of an Azhari shaykh and received a traditional religious education at home.[5] Banna, Qutb, Shari'ati, and Ghannushi, among others, were all raised in villages, where traditional values continued to prevail. Most of the leaders of Egypt's jihad movements also have their roots in rural Egypt, often in the religiously volatile south (Upper Egypt), although some were raised primarily in the periphery of Cairo, in densely populated slums inhabited mainly by recent rural migrants.

This combination of traditional cultural roots, often with an early religious education, and later secular education in urban settings where the impact of the West is felt most keenly, has often been cited by scholars seeking an explanation for the birth of fundamentalist movements. It is a point to which we will return later.

First it must be noted that traditional religious scholars are not entirely absent from fundamentalist movements. The most notable case, of course, is Iran, where popular enthusiasm for the fundamentalist revolution focused on Ayatollah Khomeini, who articulated the justification for his own preeminence in the Islamic Republic in his doctrine of "guardianship of the *faqih*." The alliance between the populist clergy, with their roots in the traditional society of madrasa and bazaar, and secular-oriented young intellectuals inspired by Shari'ati, was perhaps based more on a temporary fusion of interests in overthrowing the tyranny of the shah than on a real mutual understanding of the form of Islam that was to be implemented after the revolution. Well before the revolution, Jalal Al-e Ahmad wrote his famous book, *Gharbzadagi* (Westoxication), in which he encourages Iranian intellectuals to renounce their isolation from the masses by forging an alliance with the clerics; a revival of Shi'ite Islam was seen as a "vaccine" against the disease of unreflective embrace of Western ideas and culture.[6] Shari'ati aimed at just such a revival through an activist reinterpretation of Shi'ism. Yet he believed that the clerics had proven themselves unworthy of Islamic leadership, which should be transferred to intellectuals who could transform Islam from scholastic culture to political ideology. Islam, he said, is a revolutionary ideology inspiring people to fight against all forms of oppression, exploitation, and social injustice. His ideas are not really "fundamentalist," in that they are consciously articulated in the tradition of the modernist, Jamal al-Din al-Afghani; like Afghani, Shari'ati advocated a major reformation of Islam, like that which Luther engendered in Christianity.[7] Shari'ati won an instant following of thousands of secondary school and university students and graduates, especially those from devout families who were beneficiaries of the recently expanded educational system. Many clerics denounced Shari'ati for his opposition to their leadership, but Khomeini refused to join in their denunciations. He employed the language of Shari'ati, using phrases like "the wretched," "the rubbish heap of history," and "religion is not the opiate of the masses," thereby encouraging his listeners to see his message and that of Shari'ati as the same. By employing a populist language and remaining vague on specific proposals for the new Islamic society that would be created by the revolution, Khomeini was able to garner the support of the intellectuals who were attracted by Shari'ati, and form a broad alliance that cut across class boundaries. Ervand Abrahamian implies that Khomeini used Shari'ati's popularity and deliberately deceived his following concerning his own position.[8] Shari'ati was more "modernist" than "fundamentalist,"[9] and probably would have been chagrined at many of the developments in Iran since the revolution, had he lived to witness them.

In Algeria, too, the leadership of the main fundamentalist group, FIS, is shared by Professor Abbasi Madani (b. 1931), a middle-aged pragmatist, and the much younger Shaykh 'Ali Belhadj (b. 1954), imam of a mosque in a popular quarter. The two leaders reflect their generational and educational differences in distinctly different leadership styles. While Madani is conciliatory, Belhadj is inflammatory. The difference between the two leaders, however, may represent not an incompatibility of perspectives but "a manageable diversity" within the FIS that enables it to appeal to different audiences.[10] Whereas Khomeini's apparent agreement with Shari'ati may be described as political maneuvering, Madani's apparent *disagreement* with Belhadj may be described in the same terms.

The Jihad group responsible for the assassination of Anwar Sadat also used an Azhari shaykh as *mufti* (a scholar authorized to give verdicts on various issues in light of the Shari'a). Whereas Sayyid Qutb was executed for the role his views had in inciting the Muslim Brotherhood against the state, Shaykh 'Umar Ahmad 'Abd al-Rahman was exonerated by a court for his role in the Jihad's assassination of Sadat, because he did not know in advance how his opinions would be used, and because "the court found his views and activities typical of a man of his background and calling; even his defense of Faraj's book [the manifesto of the Jihad group] was a noncriminal expression of his professional views."[11] Sociologist Chris Eccel believes that the *mujahid,* or fundamentalist, is in fact not far removed from the perspective of the *'alim,* the traditional religious scholar, and that contemporary fundamentalism is a natural outgrowth from the perspectives of earlier reformers like Rashid Rida. "Rida and Faraj are at opposite ends of a long unbroken development. . . . No *'alim* is devoid of sympathy for much of what the *mujahid* fights for."[12]

Members of the ulama have played an important role in recent fundamentalist movements as well. In 1985, for example, Shaykh Hafiz Salama, imam of the al-Nur mosque in Cairo, led a popular movement to implement the Shari'a. The shaykh-centered groups are "intermediate" between the nonviolent mainstream of Egyptian society and the jihad-type militants. The leadership of shaykhs marks an important transition to a higher level of public respectability for fundamentalist activism in Egypt; now even the traditionally sanctioned spokesmen for Islam are increasingly promoting the fundamentalist cause.[13]

In Algeria and Iran, the shaykhs articulated the more conservative, inflammatory, and inflexible Islamic message, in contrast to the more conciliatory or revisionist posture taken by their secular counterparts.

The Rank and File

Who are attracted to the fundamentalist message? Saad Eddin Ibrahim's study of incarcerated members of two Egyptian groups, the Shabab Muhammad, (Military Academy Group) and the Takfir wa'l Hijra group, challenged descriptions of fundamentalists as "acutely alienated."[14] "It is sometimes assumed in social science that joiners of 'radical movements' must be somewhat alienated, marginal, anomic, or possess some other abnormal condition," Ibrahim writes. "Most of the ones we investigated would be normally considered as ideal or model young Egyptians."[15]

However, it would be incorrect to assume that these young men, who in some sense had succeeded according to society's standards, especially in its educational system, were not alienated. How much more acute an alienation from society is there than to declare it all so irretrievably corrupt as to necessitate complete withdrawal from it? The real question to ask, perhaps, is the source of their feelings of alienation.

Let us therefore examine the social characteristics of the thirty-four men interviewed in Ibrahim's project. Both groups recruited followers mainly from among students or recent university graduates, employing kinship, friendship, and mosque attendance as mechanisms. The regional background of the groups differed, the one being centered mainly in Cairo and the Delta, and the other in Cairo and Upper Egypt. The members were all quite young; the median age for one group was twenty-two, and for the other was twenty-four. The leaders of both groups were about fifteen years older than this median age. Two-thirds of those interviewed came from rural or small-town backgrounds and were recent arrivals in the cities when they joined the groups. The sample of the group was entirely male, although eighty women were arrested along with the several hundred men in the breakup of the Takfir wa'l Hijra group. Two-thirds of those interviewed had fathers employed in the middle grades of the civil service, and only seven fathers had a university education; most had an intermediate education. Ibrahim concludes that the class affiliation of most members of these militant Islamic groups is middle and lower middle class. The militants were much better educated than their parents; all but five were university graduates or enrolled in the university at the time of their arrest, and the rest had a secondary school education. A preponderance of the students and graduates were in the academically most competitive fields of science, medicine, and engineering. They were, therefore, "decidedly high on both motivation and achievement." Most militants came from normal, cohesive families that had not experienced any major trauma such as death of a parent or divorce.[16]

Elbaki Hermassi's study of members of the MTI in Tunisia revealed a profile in many ways remarkably similar, although the MTI, a student-based movement modeled on the Muslim Brotherhood, is less extremist in its methods than either of the groups studied by Ibrahim. Over 80 percent of Hermassi's sample were university students, and almost 75 percent of the leadership consisted of either secondary school teachers or university students. The membership included a large number of women. Although the members lived in urban centers at the time of the study, a large percentage were of rural origin. The class membership was somewhat lower than that of Ibrahim's study, as almost half were children of urban or agricultural workers and had illiterate fathers. Fathers who did have education had either only a primary-level education or an education in the traditional Zaytouna religious system. This reflects a broader educational generation gap than the Egyptian study, as well as the longer existence of public education in Egypt. It is also interesting to note that almost one-third (29 percent) of the members of MTI came from families where the father had either died or was an invalid.[17] Although Hermassi does not make this explicit, other studies corroborate the observation made by Ibrahim in Egypt, that the majority of the students in the movement are in the most prestigious and competitive faculties of medicine, science, and engineering.[18]

In Algeria, the Islamic movement is strongly based in the large towns and cities, where the FIS garnered its share of the vote in the June 1990 elections, which enabled it to take control of municipal governments in many parts of Algeria. The FIS drew its recruits from students and university graduates originating mainly from the south and mountainous regions of the country, as well as the urban poor.[19]

The Jamaat-i-Islami of Pakistan has, much more than the MTI, consciously aimed at recruiting its members from the intelligentsia, in the belief that the "good-natured elements" of society would be attracted to them, ultimately bringing about a "revolutionary change" in the "mental makeup" of the people at large. Given this goal of elitist recruitment, it is ironic that the Jamaat-i-Islami is a broader-based movement than either of Ibrahim's groups or the MTI of Tunisia. Its backbone is the lower sections of the new middle class and the traditional petite bourgeoisie. While students have not been the majority of members, the student wing of the Jamaat-i-Islami has been critical in penetrating the mosques and madrasas and mobilizing people for street demonstrations. Although the Jamaat-i-Islami has not been successful in national elections, the student wing has successfully captured the student unions of all major universities. In fact, during the period from 1977 to 1982, they "enjoyed almost complete veto power in most of Pakistan's twenty universities in matters of student's admissions and faculty appointments and promotions."[20]

In view of the prominence of graduates in science, medicine, and engineering in the movements of Tunisia and Egypt, it is interesting to note that Maududi's successors as emir of the Jamaat all attended modern secular schools and obtained graduate degrees in science. The broader leadership of the movement was also drawn from those in modern professions or the business sector, and only 8 percent from the more traditional classes (ulama, landlords, and traditional medical practitioners). Like the Muslim Brotherhood and al-Jama'a al-Islamiyya of Egypt, the Jamaat-i-Islami of Pakistan has succeeded in reorienting much of Islamic thought toward making Islam a political ideology. Unlike the Takfir wa'l Hijra group, the Pakistani Islamic movement does not exist on the fringe—it is very much in the mainstream of Islamic religious thought.[21] In fact, the Takfir wa'l Hijra group is an exception to the larger process of the mainstreaming of the Islamic movement in Egypt.[22] By the late 1980s, much of the vocabulary and thinking of the Muslim Brotherhood had become accepted on a large scale throughout Egyptian society.

In Iran, the fundamentalists ultimately garnered the support of all classes of society in a mass popular revolution against the shah. However, looking at the original supporters and backbone of the movement, one can discern two distinct groups, one the traditional classes of small landowners and merchants led by the clerics, particularly Khomeini, and the other a mass of professionals and university graduates who were primarily inspired by Shari'ati. Shari'ati's political formation was through involvement in the Liberation Movement, a religious and political group founded in the early 1960s by Mehdi Bazargan, a civil engineer who was later to head the provisional government established after the revolution, and Hojjatalislam (later Ayatollah) Mahmud Taleqani, a cleric who studied at the famous Fayzieh madrasa in Qum. Taleqani and Bazargan had two interrelated goals: to show that Islam had answers for modern problems and therefore was relevant to the contemporary world; and "to bridge the deep gulf separating devout believers from secular reformers, traditional bazaaris from modern-educated professionals, conservative antiregime clerics from forward-looking radical intellectuals, and the religious establishment in Qum from the patriotic intelligentsia of the National Front."[23] These goals sound very similar to those espoused by the Egyptian modernist Muhammad 'Abduh in the late nineteenth century, and do not necessarily indicate what we would call fundamentalism, but the Liberation Movement was to play an important role in the Islamic revolution. The other leaders of the movement were all well-educated professionals, mainly in the sciences, medicine, and engineering. Abrahamian attributes the success of the movement partly to the close links it established with Khomeini, and partly to Bazargan's and Taleqani's ability to attract young professionals and radical technocrats, who sought to synthesize Islam and Western science.[24]

The Islamic guerrilla movement, the Mujahedin-e Khalq, drew its members mainly from students in the physical sciences, whereas the Marxist Feda'i guerrillas were drawn from students in the humanities and social sciences. Many Mujahedin came from the traditional (and traditionally religious) middle class, whereas the Feda'is came from the new middle class of secular-minded teachers, civil servants, and professionals. Among the dead guerrillas on whom social data were available, there were three times as many women among the Feda'is as among the Mujahedin.[25]

A consistent pattern emerges, across all these different countries, of fundamentalists drawing heavily from students and university graduates in the physical sciences, usually students with rural or traditionally religious backgrounds. These movements seem to attract the recent beneficiaries of the expanded university systems in all of these countries, people who have, therefore, likely made recent adjustments to a modern urban intellectual and cultural environment after being raised in a fairly traditional milieu.

The smaller, clandestine, and violent groups tend to be heavily male, while the more mainstream groups with large student recruitments often draw considerable numbers of women. The exception is the Takfir wa'l Hijra group, which, despite its extremist nature and its very conservative perspective on the need for women to remain in the home, recruited large numbers of women to serve as the wives of its men. The Takfir wa'l Hijra group is distinguished from the others by its communal nature, necessitating the recruitment of women to foster the formation of a separate society. Since one of the problems the Takfir wa'l Hijra was aiming to solve was the sexual tension caused by the postponement of marriage, typically forced in contemporary urban Egypt by educational and financial constraints, the arrangement of early marriages for its members was one of the pillars of its reconstruction of a new Islamic society. In fact, claims that girls were kidnapped by the group first prompted Egyptian authorities to investigate it.[26]

In none of these countries, with the exception of Iran at the end of its revolution, did the Muslim fundamentalists succeed in drawing the mainstream of traditional society. It is significant that despite the claims of the Renaissance Party of Tunisia (the former MTI) to champion the rights of the oppressed, the infamous bread riots of 1984 took place largely without the participation or instigation of the fundamentalists. The Renaissance Party and the Jamaat-i-Islami have both recognized these deficiencies in their recruitment and have made efforts to actively support the more bread-and-butter interests of the poor, but in fact the backbone of the fundamentalist movements in all countries has been largely the intelligentsia of middle- or lower-middle-class backgrounds.

Sources of Fundamentalist Discontent

Politics

Many authors cite political factors among the main reasons for the rise of fundamentalism. They note, for example, that the intellectual leaders of Islamic movements have made Islam a political movement with a political vocabulary. In Egypt and North Africa, governments deliberately fostered Islamic groups to counteract Marxist influence among students. It is typical of outsiders to dismiss Muslim fundamentalists as politically rather than religiously motivated.[27] Fred Halliday described both Iran's and Tunisia's Islamic movements as "a revolt against the intrusive secular state."[28] Leonard Binder has described the Islamic movements as "in a sense . . . an ideological dimension of the movement to restrict the power of the State."[29] François Burgat describes Islamic fundamentalism as "more language than doctrine . . . a political ideology capable of resisting the great Western ideologies."[30] Some scholars have even gone so far as to describe the fundamentalists as "secular" in their basic orientation and goals, using elements of Islamic tradition like the veil of women as mere political symbols.[31]

The description of Islamic fundamentalism as political certainly has its justification. After all, the goal of many fundamentalists is the Islamization of society by the seizure of government by "righteous" (i.e., fundamentalist) Muslims (whether by coup or by democratic processes). The sense of political impotence prompted the urban middle classes in Pakistan to turn toward Islam. Mumtaz Ahmad describes them as

> psychologically alienated, socially declining, relatively well-off economically, but insecure and politically ineffective. They are reacting against social deprivation at the hands of the upper social classes and government bureaucrats, on the one hand, and against the increasing militancy of the lower classes, on the other. This amalgamation provides the main strength of the urban and small town-based semirevolutionary struggle for an ideal Islamic social order based on justice and equity. The countryside remains almost completely indifferent toward this movement.[32]

It is perhaps not surprising that some have accused the Jamaat-i-Islami of being more interested in power than in religion.[33]

Shari'ati also described the return to one's roots as a political necessity for Third World nations in order to defeat imperialism, overcome social alienation, and eventually borrow Western technology without losing self-esteem. "For us, to return to our roots means . . . a return to our Islamic, especially Shi'i, roots."[34] Shari'ati produced "exactly what the young intelligentsia craved: a radical layman's religion that disassociated itself from the traditional clergy and associated itself with the secular trinity of social revolution, technological innovation, and cultural self-assertion."[35] It is noteworthy that both fundamentalists and modernists—indeed almost all contemporary Muslim intellectuals—are more concerned with making religion relevant to modern social issues than with specifically religious or theological topics.

Uneven Development

Economic reasons are also commonly cited as incentives to join Islamic movements. In Egypt, Sadat's "open door policy," which liberalized the economy by allowing foreign imports, is blamed for widening the gap between the rich and the poor and causing the lower middle classes to slip in the economic scale even as, through education, they seek to attain a higher social status.[36] Many observers speak of the professional frustrations of the educated members of the lower middle class, who often were educated at considerable cost to their families in the hope of upward social mobility. James Rupert describes Muslim fundamentalist students in Tunisia as "would-be professionals—engineers, lawyers, doctors" who "are alarmed at the bleak futures they face in Tunisia, where economic development has stagnated and prospects for climbing into the country's elite classes seem slight."[37] Norma Salem comments, "These are the young upwardly mobile professionals ('yuppies') of the Islamic Third World, caught in a bottleneck."[38] Nazih Ayubi agrees.

> These movements have emerged not really as an expression of moral outrage against a modernisation that was going "too fast," but rather as a reaction to a developmental process that was not going fast enough. . . . The Islamists are not angry because the aeroplane has replaced the camel; they are angry because they could not get on to the aeroplane. There is little doubt in my mind that had Nasserism (and other similar developmental projects) "delivered" in the sixties, we would not be witnessing the same political revival of Islam that we see today.[39]

The proliferation of luxury goods is commonly interpreted as moral degradation,[40] and the austerity embraced by Muslim fundamentalists makes a virtue of what is, for members of this class, almost an economic necessity. Muslim fundamentalists believe they should possess only what is absolutely necessary for living. They avoid all material ostentation, even at their weddings, which normally would be a massive financial undertaking for the average family.[41] In fact, economic factors are largely to blame for the postponement of marriages in modern urban society, which in turn causes moral and social problems as a result of sexual repression. By avoiding the expense of a grand wedding celebration (orchestra, belly dancer, jewels, elaborate gown, etc.), fundamentalists make some progress toward solving an acute social problem.

In all cases, there are problems of uneven development. In every single-country study, major problems that seem to issue in Islamic fundamentalist movements stem from the fact that the development of education, made available at the highest level to all who are qualified, has far outpaced developments on the economic and political levels. In countries where the government promised a job for every university graduate, for years a university education was the key to the high status attached to a civil service job. But as the number of graduates has outpaced the number of jobs to be filled, the overinflated bureaucracies came to reward graduates, often after years of waiting, with unfulfilling jobs that are meaningless, repetitious, and far below their qualifications. Civil service salaries have also remained low and have not made it possible for families to survive on a single income.

In Egypt, for example, it is not unusual for civil servants to double as taxi drivers at night, and in the lower middle class almost all women feel the need to work to enable the family to make ends meet. This engenders contradictions between cultural norms that say a wife should stay at home and the economic requirements of a lower-middle-class family aspiring toward middle-class status. Similar problems may be found in all of the countries under study. All of these countries have a proliferation of higher degrees and insufficient job opportunities for those who have earned them. In Pakistan, the government tries to solve the problem of unemployment by establishing more colleges and liberalizing admissions criteria, thereby generating yet more people with advanced degrees and perpetuating the problem.[42] In Algeria, when Boumédienne came to power in 1965, he inaugurated a vigorous industrializing socialism that generated a high degree of public self-confidence in Algeria's future development. The later disappointment strengthened the growth of Islamic fundamentalism.[43] The Arabization of the educational system, for nationalistic reasons, was not reflected in a corresponding Arabization of public administration and the state sector of the economy, with the result that large numbers of university graduates could not find employment. A high proportion of these *arabisants* came from poor families in the remoter areas of the country, and are the very ones who are most susceptible to fundamentalist appeal in Algeria.[44]

In Iran, one also finds the discrepancy between rapid advances in the availability of education and the unavailability of suitable employment and opportunities for political expression—or any genuine self-expression at all—as fuel for the discontent that led to the revolution. The sudden fivefold increase in oil revenues had also inflated people's expectations beyond what the shah's regime actually achieved. All the great health and educational advances of the White Revolution could not keep pace with the burgeoning population growth and the increase in demand.[45] Actual class affiliation is not as important for the rise of Islamic fundamentalism as "an incongruity between high aspirations and the decrease in economic and political opportunities."[46]

Psychosocial Alienation

Abd al-Salam Yasin, a leader of the Islamic movement in Morocco, rejects these explanations. "To reduce Islamism to economic desperation is simplistic, and does not take into account the subjective factor. People don't come to Islam as an alternative to their social ills. People come to Islam in response to a call, a call which goes very deep into the human spirit."[47] Some scholars also find the reduction of Islamic fundamentalism to political and economic causes unsatisfying. Chris Eccel believes this rationale reduces the fundamentalists to "near automata, angry blisters on the body politic reacting to socioeconomic irritants."[48]

Indeed, we must ask, why should the economic bottleneck and lack of legitimate political expression result in the appeal of Islamic fundamentalism rather than some other form of protest? And why does it appeal particularly to students and graduates in the sciences? Why does it appeal to so many women?

In a perceptive article on the Islamic movement in Tunisia, Susan Waltz analyzes the economic and political arguments for the appeal of Islamic fundamentalism, and finds both these theses unconvincing. She points out that many university supporters of the Islamic movement in Tunisia traced their orientation to experiences at the lycée, and "it hardly seems likely that the class of lycée students destined for the university faculties of science or medicine would have been hardest hit by the frustrations of relative deprivation." Likewise, the most politically discontented students have been those at the Faculty of Letters; "the educational system, and by extension, the economic and political systems, have given the best rewards to students in math and science, not liberal arts. Yet the MTI is built on a class of politically favored young technicians and is all the more threatening to the government because its roots are to be found in the social stratum from which the ruling party itself has drawn its support in the past." Likewise, it is unconvincing to argue that women are involved in the movement because of economic and political frustrations, when the movement itself advocates restricting women from the public sphere, in contrast to the major strides Bourguiba made on behalf of women in that country. Instead, Waltz feels that "an explanation that puts primary emphasis on psycho-social alienation is more compelling."[49]

What is the nature of this psychosocial alienation? One fact stands out in all of the countries under study: Islamic fundamentalism is primarily a revolt of young people who are caught between a traditional past and a higher secular education with all its implications of Western intellectual impact and contact with the materialistically oriented culture of the modern urban environment. The contradiction between the values learned from the past and the realities of the present confront young people with bewildering contradictions and often a multitude of moral choices that create a sense of anxiety, loneliness, and disorientation. Some authors have termed Islamic fundamentalism a "youth revolt," reflecting the particular anxieties created by the necessity to find one's own identity in a world of confusing choices. Issues of identity are most acute in areas where Western cultural impact is strongest: in the cities, in the universities, and perhaps most particularly in the faculties of science, where the embrace of Western learning is most complete. As Waltz puts it, "Liberal arts students studying Western ideas are exposed to the evolution of those ideas and to the weaknesses of Western culture, whereas students in science and technology are more apt to see Western culture as monolithic and properly hegemonic."[50]

The perception espoused by so many Muslim fundamentalists that, to the detriment of all spiritual values, the West is mechanistically and technologically oriented may derive in part from the particular nature of the contact these Muslim students of science have with Western culture. They come to see their lives bifurcated between an Islamic culture that provides moral values, community, and spiritual satisfaction, and a Western culture that provides access to the material improvement of their lives. On the other hand, Mehrzad Boroujerdi sees the absolute dualism of perspective regarding East and West as a type of "Orientalism in reverse," in which the West continues to serve as the standard by which Muslim intellectuals evaluate their own culture. In doing so, they abstract the West in opposition to all Islamic values, just as Orientalism once abstracted Islamic culture as the opposite of all Western values.[51]

Rapid Urbanization

Muslim fundamentalists are only recently urbanized and often come from traditional milieux. Rapid urbanization has been a pervasive phenomenon in all countries under discussion for at least the last thirty years.

Urbanization has contributed to the rise of Islamic fundamentalism in a number of ways: (1) it is partly an expression of disappointment of the hopes engendered by the move to the city; (2) it is partly a result of the increased facility of communications made possible in an urban environment; and (3) it is a result of the perception of moral corruption in the urban environment compared with the more traditional and socially cohesive village environment. For example, one may note the position of the ulama vis-à-vis the rapid urbanization of the 1970s in Iran. The abrupt, uncontrolled migration into the cities created sprawling shanty towns. These, in turn, produced a vast array of new social problems—prostitution, alcoholism, drug addiction, delinquency, suicides, and crime. The ulama saw these social problems not as the result of rapid urbanization and industrialization and uneven development, but as caused by simple moral laxity. The solution, they said, was the strict enforcement of the Shari'a. Unplanned and rapid urbanization in early industrial England inspired John Wesley and his Methodist movement. "In contemporary Iran, the same pressures helped create the Khomeini phenomenon and the Islamic Revolution."[52]

The very personal nature of the struggle of the newly urbanized is captured in Souhayr Belhassen's study of women in the Tunisian Islamic movement. Half the women she interviewed had emigrated to the capital from the interior provinces, and the family was in a state of transformation toward the petite bourgeoisie, thanks to the profession of the woman's older brother, husband, or fiance, who was an engineer, doctor, civil servant, or teacher. In the new phase of the family, the father was losing authority in favor of the person who was the new source of income. The transformation of the family in this way was traumatizing for the daughters, who felt confused as to their own personal identity. Joining an Islamic movement and donning Islamic dress was seen as a solution to an inner struggle.[53]

A Moral Crisis

Whether the discussion concerns politics, economics, or the social dissonance brought about by rapid urbanization, the problems are perceived by the fundamentalists to be ultimately moral in nature. The acquisition of luxury items, particularly in a context of surrounding poverty, is regarded as immoral; we have also seen how rapid urbanization and sudden introduction into this urban environment contribute to perceptions of moral degradation. Concerning the fundamentalists' focus on politics, Nazih Ayubi remarks that "if government is regarded as important, it is not really because of the inherent importance of the 'political' as such (i.e. the representation of interests, the working of institutions, etc.) but because of the crucial role expected from the ruler as a guardian of the moral code, who would oversee the adherence to its stipulations."[54] Because Islamic culture emphasizes external rather than internal moral constraints, it blames the government and the availability of temptations rather than lack of self-restraint for the perceived epidemic of immorality. In Iran as well, many of the previously apolitical clergy turned against the government because they believed it was not doing anything to solve the problems of moral degradation brought about by rapid social change.

Sexuality in Modern Society

Of all potential moral problems, none is so prominent in fundamentalist discourse as those pertaining to sexuality. The centrality of sexuality in the concerns of contemporary Muslim fundamentalists is a function of a number of factors, including but not restricted to the following: (1) the traditional preoccupation in Arab-Muslim society with honor and shame, which translates into an excessive preoccupation with maintaining the chastity and reputation of women, on which so much of the honor of men depends; (2) the profound social changes that have altered the structure of traditional male-female relations, particularly in the urban setting, in a manner that threatens traditional standards of honor and chastity; (3) the introduction of Western films, commercials, and television shows, which entice Muslims with images of a glamorous, materialistic, and sexually liberated lifestyle that goes directly against Islamic cultural norms; and (4) the general unavailability of licit sexual relations to young people in urban areas who postpone marriage for many years in order to complete their education and accumulate the necessary money and furnishings for an apartment and a suitably impressive wedding.

> Frustration at work, or lack of social or educational achievement, accentuated by sexual anxiety and/or repression in the male, may then project itself into a kind of floating aggression, to be released against all female relatives. . . . It has also been argued that the national sense of humiliation suffered by the Arab male as a result of the defeat by Israel, and the social sense of humiliation caused by the prospect of class demotion that may result from the reversal of certain socio-economic policies in a number of Arab countries—these two types of humiliation both leading to a sense of lost dignity—may have contributed to a process that turns women into "an easy target for the 'restoration' of dignity."[55]

Hasan Hanafi, a professor of philosophy who has formed a group he calls the Islamic Left, has written that the fundamentalist is dominated by "a sexual perception of the world."[56] Ayubi notes that both the Moroccan writer Fatima Mernissi and the Syrian writer Bu 'Ali Yasin "corroborate the theory of Wilhelm Reich that sexually frustrated males do not normally externalise their feelings into a rebellion against *all* the manifestations of political, social and economic repression in society, but rather internalise the agony at the level of moral and religious defence." The preoccupation with sexual purity, says Mernissi, derives from the fact that the typical (unmarried) fundamentalist's contact with his own sexuality is in a context deemed impure by his society—sodomy and masturbation. She adds, "It is no wonder that women, who have such tremendous power to maintain or destroy a man's position in society, are going to be the focus of his frustration and aggression."[57]

So despite the fact that Islam has often been called a "sex-positive" religion in contradistinction to Christianity, the youth of contemporary urban Muslim society experience sexuality as a source of anxiety, something tempting (indeed, the enticements are often only too easily available) but socially and religiously forbidden.

The solution? The most obvious solution is to remove women from public view by veiling them and confining them to the home. This not only preserves sexual morality, but also confirms the authority of men over women and their control over their movements. Muslim extremists of the Egyptian Jihad Organization veiled their women and kept them at home, isolating them from neighbors, not allowing visitors, hanging thick curtains on their windows, and not allowing them to put out their laundry. The wife's subordinate position was even emphasized by prohibiting her walking by her husband's side.[58] But these measures alone will not solve the problem of sexual repression. Muslims believe that sexuality is an overwhelming instinct in both men and women, and should be expressed through legitimate means. The only legitimate means of sexual expression is in marriage, so the best solution is to make it possible for people to marry young.

This was in fact the solution effected by the Takfir wa'l Hijra group. The problem of availability of spouses was solved by having the leader arrange marriages for his followers. The problem of availability of housing and saving up the huge sums necessary to place a deposit on an apartment was solved by resorting to furnished apartments, which require no enormous initial deposit. They rent at a higher monthly fee than unfurnished apartments, but they require neither the "key money" to secure the apartment nor money for furnishings, both of which often require years to acquire. Furnished apartments are not usually rented out to Egyptians, but normally go to foreigners and prostitutes. The mere fact that members of Takfir wa'l Hijra rented furnished apartments emphasized their marginality to Egyptian society.[59]

Most groups have not separated from society in as radical a way as Takfir wa'l Hijra and have not pursued such arrangements. Yet belonging to an Islamic group does provide some partial solutions to the problems of getting married. Islamic groups in Tunisia have female matchmakers to facilitate marriages among members, and women enjoy going to meetings in a context where they can meet men without having their personal integrity or reputation threatened. Furthermore, by shunning on moral grounds the expense of a high dowry and an ostentatious wedding, which in Tunisia are the main impediments to early marriage, marriage at a younger age is facilitated.[60]

Women in Islamic Fundamentalist Movements

The foregoing discussion leads naturally to the question of the attraction of the Islamic movement for women. Why would women join a movement that often explicitly seeks to limit their economic and political opportunities and general freedom of movement? François Burgat writes, "Islamist mobilization touches perhaps as many women as men, without seriously or systematically restricting their freedom of action."[61] This indeed appears to be the case with many of the mainline university-based movements like al-Jama'a al-Islamiyya and the MTI of Tunisia. Many of their women, like their men, are single young professionals or students aiming toward a career in medicine or the sciences. The MTI boasts in its literature of the large numbers of women in its ranks, who are Islamic activists in their own right. Rashid al-Ghannushi, the leader of the Tunisian movement, now the Renaissance Party, has even gone so far as to declare that Bourguiba's Personal Status Code is not un-Islamic and need not be repealed, should the Renaissance Party ever come to power. However, his rank and file clearly do not all agree. Many have made the un-Islamic nature of the antipolygamy and divorce provisions of the code a basis for electoral campaigns. Souhayr Belhassen's interviews with women of the movement in 1979 reveal that they believed the Personal Status Code was un-Islamic.[62] And even Ghannushi persuaded his wife to cease her studies at the university when her first child was born, convincing her that her place was in the home.[63]

Women themselves, both within the Islamic movement and outside it, are divided over whether Islam permits women to work outside the home.[64] My own interviews with single young fundamentalist women in Cairo revealed that, although they were studying for some of the most prestigious careers of their society, they intended to cease working once they married or had children.

However, the experience of most women in the middle and lower middle classes of contemporary urban Egypt and, most likely, the other countries under study as well, is that they are unable to give up their employment once they marry or have children. The economic problems discussed earlier force women in this social class in particular to work in order to help provide for their families, especially their children. The double burden of working outside the home and continuing to assume sole responsibility for care of the house and children leaves most women exhausted and resentful, particularly because their jobs are not rewarding or fulfilling.

Arlene MacLeod's fascinating study of women in the lower middle class of Cairo reveals the extent of their frustration. Few of the working women of this class think of pursuing a career, she says, and they view the workplace as relatively unimportant compared to the home. Both women and men say that women do not put themselves as wholeheartedly into their jobs, because their real concerns are elsewhere. Although working outside the home is functional and culturally approved for the single woman, because it enables her to meet a potential spouse, after marriage the husband is often jealous of the wife's contacts with men at work, and once a woman has children, working outside the home is not culturally approved. Women often stress that in Islam the man should provide financially for the household and the woman has no such responsibility, a point often emphasized by the fundamentalists as a major benefit Islam gives to women, and women are resentful that the circumstances of their lives do not allow them to avail themselves of this right. In light of these social realities, is it surprising that many women are far from dismayed when Muslim fundamentalists insist that woman's place is in the home? MacLeod says that the resort to veiling, which in the course of the 1980s came to be embraced by some three-quarters of the women of this class in Cairo, is a way of reconciling the incompatibility of cultural gender norms with the realities of working women. It seldom signals a real change in the religious orientation of the woman, she says, but is a tool particularly of the married woman to assert her respectability and to declare that she is indeed trying to be a good wife and mother, even if she must work outside the home. The veil defuses the conflict working women feel by asserting the primacy of traditional roles. Women, too, feel a loss of dignity and identity in the modern urban world, and "the veil is a symbolic remembering which seeks to recover this lost dignity and place." The veil voices the protest of women over their husbands' failure to appreciate the difficulty of their employed wife's situation. Men grumble over the condition of the house and that dinner is not ready when they come home. But when a woman puts on the veil, her husband must respect her. As one woman said, "It says that I am a good woman, and if they are a good man, they will see that it is right that they treat me with dignity."[65]

Single women also wear Islamic dress in search of dignity, especially because in the cities of the contemporary Muslim world women who walk in the streets or ride public transportation in Western dress are subjected to verbal and physical harassment. In Muslim societies, for women in particular, personal morality is judged mainly by the manner of dress. The woman who wears Islamic dress has freedom of movement that other women do not have. As one young Tunisian woman said, she now had the freedom to stay out till 10 P.M. at the mosque, and no one would bother her or question her integrity. Most of the women in Egypt wearing Islamic dress today are not actually members of an Islamic group, particularly since Islamic dress has become fashionable in the 1980s. MacLeod reports that fundamentalist groups are typically regarded as political organizations rather than genuinely religious, and are best avoided.[66]

Yet in Souhayr Belhassen's interviews with Tunisian fundamentalist women, it was the group itself that was the attraction, offering a network of friends and a common cause. At weekly meetings at the mosque, those with needs are prayed for, and money is collected to help out those among them who are in need. Such rewards of belonging to a group no doubt draw men as well as women, particularly those who are lonely, coming to the city for the first time, often alone, and with few other opportunities to make friends. My own experiences with women at Cairo University and the University of Tunis revealed that women at the university seldom befriend their classmates. Women who are childhood friends often attend the university together and register in the same major in order to remain together, but they regard their classmates, particularly the men, with suspicion. An Islamic group promises a ready-made circle of friends whose moral integrity one can trust.

The Islamic movement often sends a mixed message to women about the roles they should play in society. Although many of their male leaders say that a woman's place is in the home, others emphasize the dynamic nature of Islamic female activism. This contradiction may be observed in Iran, where during the revolution women were encouraged to be inspired by the revolutionary example of the Prophet's granddaughter Zaynab and even of a reinterpreted Fatima, the Prophet's daughter, as an untiring fighter for social justice, but after the revolution the more submissive and domesticated aspects of Fatima's character have been emphasized as a model for women.[67] Zaynab al-Ghazali, the leading woman of the Muslim Brotherhood in Egypt, embodies these contradictions in her own life and writings. In her capacity as editor of the women's section of *Al-Da'wa* magazine in 1981, she wrote that it is contrary to a woman's nature to work outside the home, and that a woman's first duty is to be a wife and mother. "The family comes first. If an urgent need arises, then work in education until you marry; then work stops, except in absolute necessity. . . . Learn, and earn the highest degrees of learning. That is not too precious to be spent in raising a Qur'anic generation of which we are in the greatest need. Return, my dear, to the house. Stay in your home and obey your husband. You will be rewarded for your obedience to your Prophet and to him."[68] However, the models of women she provides for women in this magazine are those of women warriors, including Layla bint Tarif, a member of the extremist Kharijite sect that was largely obliterated in warfare with the larger Muslim community, and the woman who inspired her in her youth, Nusayba bint Ka'b al-Maziniyya, who fought with the Prophet at the battle of Uhud.[69] She also is an unusual model herself. She divorced her first husband because he objected to her Islamic activism and threatened her second husband with the same consequences when he tried to dissuade her from her leading role in the secret regrouping of the Brotherhood in 1964. In her book, *Ayyam min hayati,* she describes her torture and imprisonment during the presidency of Nasser, and depicts herself as the heroic equal of any man. In an interview, she attributed her ability to become actively involved in the Islamic cause to "a great blessing, which would not usually be considered a blessing, that I never had any children." She admitted to me that her case was exceptional, not only because she had no children, but because her husband was a wealthy man, so she had servants to do her housework. He also had other wives, and when he went to visit them, she said, it was like having a vacation from her wifely duties. So she was unusually free to devote herself to the Islamic cause.[70] What is Zaynab al-Ghazali really telling women? That their feminine nature is incompatible with work outside the home, or that women can fight as warriors and resist torture and imprisonment as well as any man? That women should obey their husbands, or that the Islamic cause demands a higher loyalty? That women should concentrate their efforts on raising a "Qur'anic generation" in the home, or that it is more blessed never to have children at all?

The women interviewed by Souhayr Belhassen in Tunisia saw their devotion to the Islamic cause as transcending the boundaries of traditional gender-role definitions. The Islamic woman is a militant for a cause, according to one woman fundamentalist, and she "leaves the usual role of women in our society." Many of the more devoted propagandists felt that they needed to continue to work outside the home in order to devote themselves to spreading the message of Islam, "to propagate Islam, militate, pursue the battle in the field," rather than being removed and isolated from life.[71]

Fundamentalism, Authoritarianism, and Fears of Conspiracy

This keen sense of mission derives from the absolutist nature of the fundamentalist teachings, an absolutism that also lends itself to other features of the fundamentalist personality that are frequently cited: intolerance and aggressive censorship of public morals. From Tehran to Gaza to Asyut to Algeria, wherever fundamentalists have managed to gain ascendancy, whether officially or unofficially, they have not hesitated to function as a kind of morals police. Favorite targets are inadequately covered women, unrelated couples walking together, and mixed beaches. Fundamentalists have not hesitated to punish offenders with violence.[72] The Tunisian leader Ghannushi has publicly disavowed the idea that his party would take responsibility for the moral tutelage of society, saying that after fighting for democracy, they would not become themselves guilty of totalitarianism. "We do not want to assume any guardianship over the people, and Islamists should free themselves from this patronising stance, and believe in the people's ability to make the right choices. . . . We have entered the political arena in Tunisia to fight for freedoms and not to set up an Islamic state."[73]

But the behavior of his followers does not accord with these words. In July 1981, fundamentalist groups tried to enforce the Ramadan fast at schools, universities, and other public places. Their attack on a bar in the Club Mediterranean led to the arrest of seventy-six leading militants of the MTI, including Ghannushi.[74] A bloody attack by militants of the Renaissance Party on the headquarters of the ruling party in February 1991 led to the resignation of the Renaissance Party's second in command, Abdelfattah Morou, along with two other senior members of the movement.[75] The Tunisian movement seems to be suffering from the same split between a moderate middle-aged leadership and its militant young rank and file that has plagued other fundamentalist movements, including the Muslim Brotherhood during the lifetime of Hasan al-Banna.

The attitude of fundamentalists toward society varies. The faith Ghannushi had that the Tunisian people would make the right choice if given the opportunity is not shared by many fundamentalists. Many have embraced the idea created by Maududi and propagated by Sayyid Qutb, that modern Muslim society is in a state of jahiliyya, a new age of ignorance and virtual paganism, even if it theoretically embraces Islam. The need is to create a new Muslim society, and many of the names of these groups—Jamaat-i-Islami, al-Jama'a al-Islamiyya, Jama'at al-Muslimin (the actual name of the Takfir wa'l Hijra group)—convey the sense that they are starting a new society that is truly based on Islam. Only the Takfir wa'l Hijra group opted for total withdrawal from the *jahili* society. The methods of other groups reflect the differences in opinion concerning whether Islamization is best effected by educating the masses or by direct implementation of an Islamic government. The Jihad group that assassinated Sadat apparently expected that the Egyptians would spontaneously rise up in rebellion against the corrupt secular regime once the "Pharaoh" was removed, and they must have been disappointed to see how easily the military and the bureaucracy carried on the machinery of government. Only in their stronghold of Asyut was there a major fundamentalist uprising after the assassination. Yet the way that their leaders in Cairo kept their families isolated from society reflects their low opinion of the moral quality of their neighbors. This is scarcely surprising, since it is the perceived corruption of society that triggers their sense of mission.

Fundamentalists see Muslim society as the victim of a great international plot spearheaded by Zionists and the United States. The West, especially the United States, is perceived as engaged in an unceasing crusade against the Muslims, fostering a new colonialism through its support for the State of Israel, attempting to reduce the Muslim population by supporting family planning, and seeking to undermine Muslim society by striking at the values it holds most dear. Its weapons in this crusade are not only of a military nature, but include the promotion of Christian missionary activities and the proliferation of American media. In Egypt, Coptic Christians, who not only represent an obstacle to the blanket application of the Shari‘a but are frequently more Westernized and educated than Muslims, have been the target of violence by the Jihad group and, more recently, al-Jama‘a al-Islamiyya. Copts are a target because Muslim fundamentalists see them as allies of Western culture, and therefore as an enemy in their midst.[76] American television shows like *Dallas, Knots Landing,* and *Falcon Crest,* which have been widely viewed in many countries, are perceived as truly representative of American life. They depict a society dominated by crass materialism, excessive individualism, and sexual immorality, and are seen as undermining the Muslim family by introducing aspirations toward materialism and sexual liberation.

The equation of Western-style modernity with sexual liberation is pervasive. Before the Islamic movement took hold in Tunisia, in 1973–74, I learned from a Tunisian girl in a secondary school in the provincial town of Jendouba in the northwest that the students of her school had staged a demonstration demanding sexual freedom. The impact of such a demonstration could only be imagined in a town where any association of unrelated men and women was regarded with deep suspicion and would normally result in the summoning of the police. This girl had a naive impression of Europeans, based on her limited acquaintance with French teachers at her school, and believed that, whereas Tunisian men got drunk and beat their wives, European men did not suffer from these vices.

This idealistic depiction of Western society is the opposite of the image promoted by the Muslim fundamentalists. In *Islam and the Orientation of the Contemporary Muslim Woman,* the Egyptian writer Muhammad al-Bahi depicts the West as a society that has fallen prey to a "sexual revolution" of brothels, pornography, and casual intercourse, where normal marital relations are nonexistent and people sell their children in order to buy cars. He warns Muslim women that if they pursue Western-style liberation, Muslim society will likewise soon be plagued with nude nightclubs, nude beaches, pornographic films, and massage parlors where men and women massage members of the opposite sex.[77] According to a tract distributed by al-Jama‘a al-Islamiyya, it is the strategy of international Zionism to bring about the collapse of Muslim society by exposing them to sexual relations via films, "so that they will no longer remain sacred in the eyes of youth. Their greatest concern will be to quench their sexual desires. Then morals will collapse."[78]

The Fear of Social Chaos

In their attacks on women's liberation and other aspects of Western culture, the fundamentalists reveal a basic aspect of their mindset—a great fear of social chaos. Social chaos and moral amorphousness are seen as the greatest evil. Thus many authors argue that Islam improved the status of women over their status in the time of jahiliyya. The historic record does not bear out their claim that women did not have economic or social rights in the jahiliyya. What the jahiliyya lacked was a strict code concerning the proper roles of women. Marriage arrangements, for example, followed a number of different patterns, according to some scholars, including a purely matriarchal arrangement whereby a woman could live on her own and if she became pregnant she would simply name the father, and he would have to accept paternity, regardless of what other lovers she might have had.[79] There is ample evidence from Muhammad's own life that women initiated marriage proposals. What Islam did was guarantee a purely patriarchal form of marriage in which men serve as the guardians for women, women are made economically dependent on men, and only physical paternity is recognized and guaranteed by the seclusion of women. Islam removed the element of flexibility—or chaos—in the social roles of women.

In the contemporary urban setting, Muslims are faced with a new jahiliyya—a new and bewildering set of moral choices. The traditional boundaries set by a cohesive patriarchal society do not exist any more. New bases for status are created through education and the acquisition of nontraditional careers, women assume new roles, and particularly the newly urbanized perceive society as in a state of social and moral chaos. It is extremely revealing that one of the accusations leveled at Boumédienne, the former president of Algeria, was that by destroying the traditional culture and failing to build an adequate new one, he had left the country in a state of chaos (*fitna*).[80] The crisis felt by many is not only alienation from the values of modern society, but a deep insecurity in the face of its complexity and choices.

The craving for security is satisfied through legalistic rigidity and obedience to what is perceived as the absolute authority of the Divine, as represented in his texts and representatives. This craving for legalistic rigidity is evidenced in the great care and concern of those who ask questions on the details of Islamic law in the newspapers and at countless small religious meetings.

The difference between fundamentalists and the merely religious may be highlighted by my observations of two different women's groups in Cairo in 1981. The first was a group attended by mainly young fundamentalist women who were all strictly veiled, often including the face veil, socks, and gloves. They questioned their middle-aged male teachers on details of Islamic law, and by the manner of their questions it was apparent that they inclined toward the strictest interpretations of the law. One woman, for example, asked whether a woman should show her feet, or whether she should wear socks. One of the men chuckled and asked the other, "Who ever said feet had to be covered?" The woman persisted by explaining the potential temptation presented to men by the display of bare feet, and the men finally agreed that it was better that they be covered.

The second group was much more mixed, mainly middle-aged women of the middle or upper middle class, who wore modest dress but not the uniform style enforced by the Islamic associations. In other words, their sleeves were long and their skirts at least to midcalf, but they often wore waisted styles, and their head coverings often did not cover the neck. A young male teacher addressed this group on the importance of wearing proper Islamic dress, and insisted that women should veil even in front of the doorkeeper of their building (who typically runs errands and functions as a sort of servant for inhabitants of the building), and that female medical students should not be allowed to examine male cadavers. The women let out shouts of protest and hoots of amusement at the impracticality of these injunctions. The disparity between the earnest idealism and embrace of legalism by the young fundamentalist women and the rejection of impractical modesty by the middle-aged women was striking. The fact that the more moderate male teachers were middle-aged and the strictly legalistic male teacher was young also lends credence to the idea that fundamentalism is the creed of the young, just as idealism and radical militancy tend to characterize the young more than the middle-aged. In a study conducted by the Egyptian newspaper *Akhbar al-Yawm* in 1981, 87 percent of the young people (ages twenty to thirty-five) surveyed in an open questionnaire said that the problem that most disturbed them was the moral degradation of society, including the "lack of public modesty," and 75 percent believed these problems could best be solved through application of the Shari'a.[81]

The Turn to Fundamentalism: A Conversion Experience?

Fundamentalists have succeeded in bringing an Islamic consciousness to the forefront of cultural identity and political activism, first among educated members of the middle and lower middle classes, and in recent years among the population as a whole in many countries. Striking indeed has been the change in outlook among educated members of Muslim societies in the past two decades, from a secular one to an Islamic one. Such a major reorientation of the educated sectors of Muslim society raises the question of whether Muslim fundamentalists undergo a conversion experience, a major *moral* reorientation. Is conversion, some type of "born-again" experience, a sine qua non for Muslim fundamentalists as it is for Christian fundamentalists?

It does not appear that Muslim fundamentalists have dramatic spiritual experiences that impel them to turn toward fundamentalism. It is not that such types of conversions do not exist among Muslims. They do, indeed, especially among the Sufis. Sufi biographies often begin with the subject's conversion story, which is called the "cause for repentance." Sufi conversions are typically mystical, the process taking place in a short space of time, or even suddenly, accompanied by often exhilarating and awe-inspiring revelation of spiritual realities, resulting in a profound moral change and an entirely new perspective on life.[82] Muslim fundamentalists do not speak of their experiences in this way at all. Few of them tell tales of leading irreligious lives before their embrace of fundamentalism. Rather, most of them say they come from religious families, and their stories do not usually indicate that they slipped from that moral milieu into hedonism or criminal behavior, or even the neglect of their religious obligations. On the contrary, for many of the fundamentalist leaders of this century, the greatest spiritual influence on their lives was their father. My interviews with fundamentalist women in Egypt in 1980–81 also revealed that the strongest influence on many of them was their father.

In the early 1980s, the donning of Islamic dress in Egypt was a reliable indicator of fundamentalist tendencies. This is no longer the case, as in Egypt some form of Islamic dress has become the fashion and the mark of a respectable, not necessarily a religious, woman. In the early 1980s, some of the Egyptian women I interviewed pondered wearing the hijab (Islamic dress for women) for a long time before undertaking the commitment to wear it. "I want to wear the hijab, but I'm not ready yet," one woman remarked to a group of *muhajjabat* (women who wear the hijab) at a Qur'an lesson outside the Mustafa Mahmud mosque in Cairo, and the women all nodded in understanding.

Wearing the hijab appears to mark the culmination of a process of "turning to Islam" after having been deluded into taking cultural cues from the West. But many women who wore it said they were not more religious after wearing the hijab than they had been before wearing it. They had simply become better educated, and therefore more aware of the need for modest dress, through reading and attending lectures, or being persuaded by teachers, classmates, colleagues, friends, or relatives. Many of the women denied that people are actually more religious today, but said that people were simply better educated. The increase in Islamic publications, one woman explained, is not evidence of a resurgence of Islam, but an indication that there is more freedom to write and publish on religious themes. People were just as religious when Nasser was president, but they simply did not have the freedom to express their Islam openly in Nasser's day as they do today.[83]

Sayyid Qutb declared that he "was born in 1951" when he returned that year to Egypt from the United States and joined the Muslim Brotherhood.[84] His sense of new birth came from his wholehearted embrace of an entirely Islamic identity, after his deep disillusionment with American culture. This does not mean that he had ever rejected Islam or become irreligious, but his encounter with the perceived evils of Western society led to a reaffirmation of his Islamic identity. The transformation was not a moral one, but rather a discovery that *all* of life must be based on Islam, that even the areas of so-called Western superiority must be governed by Islam. His later experience of government repression intensified and radicalized that commitment, as it did for many Muslim Brothers in the 1950s and 1960s.

Muslims who turn to fundamentalism in the United States speak of being "born again" into fundamentalism. This appears to imply not an adoption of a phrase familiar in Christian fundamentalism, but their sense of a truly new orientation toward Islam after their wholehearted embrace of Western culture. For them, the embrace of fundamentalism is a radical change in response to the shock of rejection by the Western culture they had hoped to join. This contrasts sharply with the experience of Muslim fundamentalists who do not leave their home countries, who generally say they simply become more observant (*multazim*) when they turn to fundamentalism.[85]

This does not mean, however, that all fundamentalists see their families of origin as truly Muslim. Fundamentalist women in Tunisia consistently claimed to come from families that were secular. Members of extremist groups in Egypt likewise typically saw their families as not truly Muslim. But the "secular" environment of the homes of the Tunisian fundamentalists likely reflects not a rejection of Islam, but an ignorance of the manner in which daily life should be forced to conform to Islamic standards; Belhassen says that in these "secular" home situations, *Muslim* was a nationality and

Islam an inheritance, but the family was ignorant of the true meaning of religion.[86] A middle-aged woman I interviewed in Cairo had donned Islamic dress under the influence of her daughter, a medical student at Cairo University. She described the difference between today's religious environment and the one in which she was raised: "Islam was something we inherited as a tradition. But by going to lectures we learned to be Muslims by conviction, not by inheritance."

The shift appears to be away from a communal religious identity, toward greater individual responsibility to lead a religious life. Previously religion was a part of culture that was accepted without question; today it must be studied, acquired, and consciously embraced. Islam has become not just a part of Muslim culture, it can also be culture-challenging. The sources of religious teaching have become numerous and sometimes mutually contradictory. Muslims, more than in the past, have to make choices about what they are going to believe.

The writer Safi Naz Kazim, who has been described as a blue-jeaned Marxist who suddenly converted to Islam in 1972 and donned the hijab, likewise denies that she was ever anything but a believing Muslim.

> I was never a Marxist or Communist a single day of my life. . . . I was an enthusiastic nationalist and partisan of Arab nationalism and Arab socialism as a form of salvation for our masses. I thought the foundation of all that thought was Islam. But I repented to God after it became clear that Nasser, Saddam Husayn and others of their type exploited Islam to their own advantage, and given the opportunity they slaughtered only the Muslims. . . . I look critically at my whole life before I donned the *hijab* after I performed the hajj in January 1972. I find that although I was a Muslim in faith and belief every moment of my life, I was robbed of my Islam: it was a belief unconnected to my behavior. I suffered on a personal level from a schizophrenia between belief and behavior, and it is the same schizophrenia suffered by our society as a whole. Our society is not an unbelieving society . . . our society is robbed of its Islam, and it seeks it and will certainly find it, God willing.[87]

Safi Naz Kazim is describing not a change in religious belief, but a change in her perception of the degree to which society in fact conformed to the standards of Islam, and consequently a shift in her attitude toward the course society and politics should take.

This is not to say that no Muslims have entertained genuine doubts about the truth of Islam or even the existence of God. On the contrary, Muslim students in the urban centers most thoroughly imbued with Western ideas in the 1950s and 1960s did sometimes entertain serious doubts about the compatibility of religion with the intellectually oriented life they came to esteem so highly. In his book on his conversion from atheism to a Hindu-like belief in the essential unity of all being to an Islamic concept of God, the Egyptian writer and physician Mustafa Mahmud blames his doubts about God on the time in which he lived, a time when the progress of human civilization led many to have supreme confidence in the human intellect, and gifted individuals like himself became so bedazzled by their own brilliance that they failed, in his words, to respond to the knowledge of God's existence that is instinctive in human nature. "The

West was progress. The East was backwardness, weakness, humiliation, being crushed under the feet of imperialism. It was natural for us to imagine that everything that came from the West was light and truth and the way to strength and salvation. . . . From a scientific point of view, whatever cannot be perceived with the senses does not exist." He defines the Antichrist as materialistic progress, power, and luxury, for they are the idols of this age.[88]

But whether Islamic fundamentalism consists mainly of individuals who experienced firsthand an actual conversion from atheism to Islam is questionable. What the fundamentalist students seem to be discovering is that an Islam they never really doubted can be affirmed in the context of modern civilization, that their cultural identity is Muslim regardless of how far they advance in the study of Western sciences. None of the fundamentalist leaders, including those in French North Africa, appears ever to have entertained doubts about the essentials of Islamic faith; their radicalization was engendered by observing the cultural impact of the marginalization of Islam in social life and politics. Fundamentalists are not people raised in heavily Westernized environments, but those who are introduced to Western ideas and lifestyles during adolescence, in disharmony with their Islamically oriented upbringing. This disjunction produces a crisis that is resolved only through the wholehearted embrace of Islam as the governing principle of all aspects of life.

Sufi conversions are recognizably *religious* experiences, often accompanied by visions, illumination, ecstasy, and moral reorientation. Fundamentalists do not speak of visions, miracles, or other supernatural events precipitating their embrace of Islamic ·fundamentalism (although they may experience such things in times of trial),[89] nor is there evidence of an abrupt moral change, but rather a slow awareness of the social meaning of Islam, an acceptance of its consequences, and a conscious grounding of personal identity on allegiance to Islam.

Although Paul's "Damascus road" experience and the Western Christian revivalist conversions have often been paradigmatic in studies of religious conversion, scholars define conversion much more broadly, so as to encompass a wide variety of experiences, and these include the experiences of the fundamentalists.[90] In 1970, Richard Travisano defined conversion as "a radical reorganization of identity, meaning, life."[91] In 1977, Max Heirich defined it as "the process of changing a sense of root reality" or "a conscious shift in one's sense of grounding."[92] William James defined conversion as "the process, gradual or sudden, by which a self hitherto divided, and consciously wrong, inferior and unhappy, becomes unified and consciously right, superior and happy, in consequence of its firmer hold upon religious realities." Certainly this definition encompasses the Islamist experience. James goes on to explain, "To say that a man is 'converted' means that religious ideas, previously peripheral in his consciousness, now take a central place, and that religious aims form the habitual centre of his energy."[93]

James draws on the ideas of Edwin Starbuck, who noted that "the 'conversion' of young people in evangelical circles closely parallels that growth into a larger spiritual life which is a normal phase of adolescence."[94] The process of conversion resembles the process by which an adolescent's insecurity is resolved in a new sense of mature identity that results in self-confidence, but conversion compresses the process so that it reaches a crisis and resolution in a shorter space of time than normal adolescence. Fundamentalist conversions most closely resemble this type of resolution or break-through from a bifurcated into a more integrated personality.

Through their conversions to a new intensification of Islamic identity, fundamentalists discover their own selves, their cultural and spiritual identities. The transformation is not so much an alteration in belief or moral orientation, but the integration of all aspects of life after the dissatisfaction of feeling divided. By grounding themselves in culturally accepted—"authentic," to use the popular term—models of identity, fundamentalists affirm continuity with the culture of their parents and the relevance of Islam in contemporary society.

It may not be far-fetched to suggest that the fundamentalist conversion experience is becoming characteristic of the Muslim world as a whole, for, more and more, fundamentalist ideology is becoming the common property of large portions of Muslim society. Safi Naz Kazim in fact does abstract her experience to that of Egypt as a whole which, like her, was Muslim but "robbed" of its Islam, and, having finally seen the failure of Nasserism, has turned toward Islam. She happily observed in 1983 that at the popular beach of Ra's al-Barr, near Alexandria, no girl over twelve wore a bathing suit, and the mothers all wore Islamic dress. To her, this indicated a triumph of Islamic consciousness and a rejection of Western cultural hegemony and of the definition of "progress" as imitation of the West. She expressed her jealousy of the young people of today who do not have to go through the struggles of her generation, which had to experience the failure of Western cultural models before turning to Islam.[95]

Egypt's rejection of secular ideologies and the general trend to favor an Islamic orientation in all aspects of public life may be seen as a type of national conversion and reorientation precipitated by its defeat in the June 1967 war, a conversion that was mirrored in countless lives. At this level, some of the supernatural phenomena associated with Sufi conversions come into play: the apparition of the Virgin Mary at the church in Zeitoun from 1968 to 1970 was perceived by millions of Egyptians, both Muslims and Christians, as an indication that Egypt should return to God and would be granted victory if it did.[96] The "victory" of October 1973, which secured Egypt's new Islamic identity and orientation, was likewise accompanied by visions of angels and the Prophet himself in the sky over the soldiers' heads, leading the Egyptians to victory.[97] These are *national* religious experiences marking the conversion of an entire nation.

For the new generation of students, the orientation toward Islam is a given, and provides a ready standard against which society is judged. For this new generation, an individual conversion may not be required, for the collective memory of national identity crisis suffices.

Conclusion

The message of Islamic fundamentalism is capable of attracting a broad spectrum of society because it links the core beliefs of Islam, shared by the vast majority of the population, with the solution of such basic problems as identity, morality, and economics in a rapidly changing society. In an age when secular solutions have been discredited by the failures and repressions of earlier governments, when rapid modernization meant the introduction of new social problems perceived as moral, the promise of a comprehensive "Islamic" solution is appealing, even if doubts concerning details are expressed by many. Many Muslims see religion as the major moral force in society, without which human beings become animals. The perception of Islam as a comprehensive code for all aspects of life, and its intimate connection with both personal and national identity, grant the Islamic solution an authenticity no other ideology could have.

Given the acuteness of the anxiety evoked by the problems of modern urban society, as long as Muslim fundamentalists are not allowed to test their solutions by actual application, it is unlikely these movements will die out. Government repression has not succeeded in eliminating Islamic fundamentalism, partly because of its ideological legitimacy, and partly because religious gatherings cannot be outlawed (though they may be strictly controlled), and mosques offer a ready forum for the expression of religiously legitimate views that may prove politically volatile. Algeria's decision not to allow a fundamentalist victory at the polls and the incarceration and execution of the leaders of the FIS has not extinguished fundamentalism from that country.[98] Like Egypt's crackdowns on Muslim fundamentalists since the 1950s, which in 1992 escalated into daily battles in Upper Egypt and the cordoning of an entire section of Cairo, suppression appears to lead only to the further radicalization of those advocating an Islamic form of government, and leads to widespread sympathy among those who would not otherwise be drawn to fundamentalism.

Although the dilemmas of identity and alienation are more keenly felt by the young, and as fundamentalists move into middle age they may abandon some of their earlier dogmatism, there is a ready pool of new recruits to take their place. Implementing economic policies that reduce the gap between the rich and the poor may help defuse a potentially volatile situation, but they will not, by themselves, remove the incentives for seeking societal solutions in Islam. The fundamentalist movements have had varied political success, but their success at reorienting Islamic discourse toward political and social issues has been considerable, and the impact of the movements is evident in the broader resurgence of Islam that can be witnessed all over the Muslim world today. Although the violent fringes are often discounted as "crazy," the words of the fundamentalists often make a good deal of sense to many people. It is unlikely that for some time to come people will easily dismiss Islam as irrelevant to social and political life.

Notes

1. R. Hrair Dekmejian, *Islam in Revolution: Fundamentalism in the Arab World* (Syracuse: Syracuse University Press, 1985), pp. 32–36.

2. The most famous such study was conducted by Saad Eddin Ibrahim with members of two groups, Shabab Muhammad, which launched an abortive coup in 1974, and Jama'at al-Muslimin, better know as the Takfir wa'l Hijra group, which assassinated a

former minister of religious affairs in 1977. Ibrahim's study was conducted with members who were still alive and in prison. His results have been published in "Anatomy of Egypt's Militant Groups," *International Journal of Middle East Studies* 12 (1980): 423–53, and in "Islamic Militancy as a Social Movement: The Case of Two Groups in Egypt," in Ali E. Millal Dessouki, ed., *Islamic Resurgence in the Arab World* (New York: Praeger, 1982), pp. 117–37. The only other sociological study done with the cooperation of fundamentalists is Elbaki Hermassi, "La société tunisienne au miroir islamiste," *Maghreb-Machrek* 103 (January–March 1984), in which he interviews members of the Mouvement de Tendance Islamique (MTI) in Tunis. Ervand Abrahamian was able to interview members and former members of the Iranian Mujahidin for his book, *The Iranian Mojahedin* (New Haven: Yale University Press, 1989). In *Iran between Two Revolutions,* Abrahamian utilizes data concerning dead guerrillas for his analysis of the composition of guerrilla movements ([Princeton: Princeton University Press, 1982], pp. 480–81). Much of the data about the much-discussed Jihad group responsible for the assassination of Sadat in Egypt was obtained from court records and newspaper articles rather than from direct interviews with members of the group.

3. It is generally said that Shari'ati was a sociologist, because he often called himself such, but Mehrzad Boroujerdi says that in fact his Ph.D. was in Persian philology (1965) ("Orientalism in Reverse: Iranian Intellectuals and the West, 1960–1990," Ph.D. diss., Washington, D.C.: American University, 1990, p. 249).

4. Abrahamian, *Iran between Two Revolutions,* pp. 464–65.

5. Interview with Zaynab al-Ghazali, June 1981, recorded in Valerie J. Hoffman, "An Islamic Activist: Zaynab al-Ghazali," in Elizabeth W. Fernea, ed., *Women and the Family in the Middle East: New Voices of Change* (Austin: University of Texas Press, 1985), pp. 233–54.

6. Boroujerdi, "Orientalism in Reverse," pp. 145–64.

7. Ibid., pp. 258–60; Abrahamian, *Iran between Two Revolutions,* pp. 464–71.

8. Abrahamian, *Iran between Two Revolutions,* p. 479.

9. The differences between Islamic modernism and fundamentalism may not be as great as we sometimes assume, since both share in a great deal of conservatism. See W. Montgomery Watt, *Islamic Fundamentalism and Modernity* (London: Routledge, 1988), pp. 51–53, regarding the very traditional outlook of the famous modernist Muhammad 'Abduh of Egypt.

10. Hugh Roberts, "A Trial of Strength: Algerian Islamism," in James Piscatori, ed., *Islamic Fundamentalisms and the Gulf Crisis* (Chicago: American Academy of Arts and Sciences, 1991), p. 136.

11. A. Chris Eccel, "'Alim and Mujahid in Egypt: Orthodoxy versus Subculture, or Division of Labor?" *Muslim World* 78 (1988): 203. Shaykh 'Abd al-Rahman was later the subject of much media attention in the United States as a result of the 26 February 1993 bombing of the World Trade Center in New York by a worshiper at Shaykh 'Abd al-Rahman's mosque in Jersey City. Shaykh 'Abd al-Rahman came to the United States in 1990 on a tourist visa and secured a green card despite his presence on the State Department's "watch list." He has denied complicity in the bombing and has condemned the media for implying that Islam endorses terrorism. Nonetheless, he condoned the assassination of Sadat and said that the current president of Egypt, Hosni Mubarak, "deserves the same thing" (*New York Times,* 19 March 1993, p. A7).

12. Eccel, pp. 203, 204.

13. John O. Voll, "Fundamentalism in the Sunni Arab World: Egypt and the Sudan," in Martin E. Marty and R. Scott Appleby, eds., *Fundamentalisms Observed* (Chicago: University of Chicago Press, 1991), p. 388.

14. Dekmejian, *Islam in Revolution,* p. 33.

15. Saad Eddin Ibrahim, "Anatomy of Egypt's Militant Groups," p. 440.

16. Saad Eddin Ibrahim, "Islamic Militancy as a Social Movement," pp. 128–31.

17. Hermassi, "La société tunisienne au miroir islamiste," pp. 31–33.

18. Susan Waltz, "Islamist Appeal in Tunisia," *Middle East Journal* 40 (1986): 651–70.

19. John Entelis, "Islamism and the State in the Maghreb: From Conciliation (Algeria) to Containment (Morocco) to Crackdown (Tunisia)," paper presented at Workshop on Muslim Fundamentalism in the Maghreb, Council on Foreign Relations, New York City, 5 June 1991.

20. Mumtaz Ahmad, "Islamic Fundamentalism in South Asia: The Jamaat-i-Islami and the Tablighi Jamaat of South Asia," in Marty and Appleby, *Fundamentalisms Observed*, p. 483.

21. Ibid., p. 501.

22. Voll, "Fundamentalism in the Sunni Arab World," pp. 376–90; Andrea B. Rugh, "Reshaping Personal Relations: Islamic Resurgence in Egypt," in Martin E. Marty and R. Scott Appleby, eds., *Fundamentalisms and Society* (Chicago: University of Chicago Press, 1993), pp. 151–80.

23. Abrahamian, *Iran between Two Revolutions*, p. 459.

24. Ibid., p. 462.

25. Ibid., p. 491. Abrahamian had information on the social background only of guerrillas who had been killed.

26. Gilles Kepel, *Muslim Extremism in Egypt: The Prophet and Pharaoh*, trans. Jon Rothschild (Berkeley: University of California Press, 1985), pp. 86–88.

27. A recent and altogether typical assessment of the fundamentalist movement in Gaza is given by Ziad Abu Amer, a political science professor at Bir Zeit University: "The Islamic revival in Gaza is principally motivated by politics. This is a counterbalance to Judaism, Zionism and Israel" (Sabra Chartrand, "The Veiled Look: It's Enforced with a Vengeance," *New York Times*, 22 August 1991, p. A4).

28. Fred Halliday, "Tunisia's Uncertain Future," reprinted in *The Renaissance Party in Tunisia: The Quest for Freedom and Democracy*, a compilation of articles and documents put together by the Renaissance Party, Washington, D.C., 26 July 1991, pp. 91–93.

29. Leonard Binder, *Islamic Liberalism: A Critique of Development Ideologies* (Chicago: University of Chicago Press, 1988), pp. 16–17.

30. François Burgat, *L'islamisme au Maghreb: La voix du sud* (Paris: Karthala, 1988), p. 70.

31. Mohamed Arkoun, "Algeria," in Shireen T. Hunter, ed., *The Politics of Islamic Revivalism* (Bloomington: Indiana University Press, 1988), p. 184; Jean-François Clement, quoted in Burgat, *L'islamisme au Maghreb*, p. 71.

32. Ahmad, "Islamic Fundamentalism in South Asia," p. 67.

33. Emma Duncan, *Breaking the Curfew: A Political Journey through Pakistan* (London: Michael Joseph, 1989), p. 225.

34. Abrahamian, *Iran between Two Revolutions*, pp. 469–70.

35. Ibid., p. 473.

36. Saad Eddin Ibrahim, "Contemporary Islamic Fundamentalism: A Quest for Understanding," unpublished paper, quoted in Nemat Guenena, *The "Jihad": An "Islamic Alternative" in Egypt*, Cairo Papers in Social Science, vol. 9, monograph 2 (Cairo: American University in Cairo, 1986), pp. 77–78. Fadwa El Guindi also associates the rise of the Islamic movement with Sadat's *infitah* (opening) of the economy ("Veiling *Infitah* with Muslim Ethic: Egypt's Contemporary Islamic Movement," *Social Problems* 28 [1981]: 465–83).

37. James Rupert, "Tunisia: Testing America's Third World Diplomacy," *World Policy Journal* 4 (Winter 1986–87): 24.

38. Norma Salem, "Tunisia," in Hunter, *The Politics of Islamic Revivalism*, p. 160.

39. Nazih Ayubi, *Political Islam: Religion and Politics in the Arab World* (London: Routledge, 1991), pp. 176–77.

40. See Rivka Yadlin, "Militant Islam in Egypt: Some Sociocultural Aspects," in Gabriel R. Warburg and Uri M. Kupferschmidt, eds., *Islam, Nationalism, and Radicalism in Egypt and the Sudan* (New York: Praeger, 1983), p. 171.

41. See Souhayr Belhassen, "Femmes tunisiennes islamistes," in *Annuaire de l'Afrique du Nord, 1979* (Paris: Editions du Centre National de la Recherche Scientifique, 1980), pp. 90–91.

42. Ahmad, "Islamic Fundamentalism in South Asia," p. 70.

43. Arkoun, "Algeria," p. 177.

44. Hugh Roberts, "Radical Islamism and the Dilemma of Algerian Nationalism," *Third World Quarterly* 10 (1988): 566–67.

45. Abrahamian, *Iran between Two Revolutions*, pp. 427, 443–46.

46. Salem, "Tunisia," p. 160.

47. Burgat, *L'islamisme au Maghreb*, p. 72.

48. Eccel, "'Alim and Mujahid in Egypt," p. 195.

49. Waltz, "Islamist Appeal in Tunisia," pp. 662–65.

50. Ibid., p. 666.

51. Boroujerdi, "Orientalism in Reverse."

52. Abrahamian, *Iran between Two Revolutions*, pp. 473–74.

53. Belhassen, "Femmes tunisiennes islamistes," pp. 78–79.

54. Ayubi, *Political Islam*, p. 35.

55. Ibid., citing the perspective of Hani Shukrallah (p. 40). The article is by Hani Shukrallah, "Political Crisis/Conflict in Post-1967 Egypt," in C. Tripp and R. Owen, eds., *Egypt under Mubarak* (London: Routledge, 1989).

56. Hasan Hanafi, *Al-turath wa'l-tajdid* (Heritage and renewal) (Cairo: Al-Markaz al-'Arabi, 1980), p. 42; quoted in Ayubi, *Political Islam*, p. 45.

57. Fatima Mernissi, *Beyond the Veil: Male-Female Dynamics in Muslim Society*, rev. ed. (London: Al-Saqi Books, 1985), pp. 160–64; Bu 'Ali Yasin, *Al-thaluth al-muharram* (The forbidden trinity: A study on religion, sex, and class struggle) (Beirut: Dar al-Tali'a, 1985), pp. 66–70; Ayubi, *Political Islam*, pp. 40–41.

58. Yadlin, "Militant Islam in Egypt," p. 169.

59. Kepel, *Muslim Extremism in Egypt*, p. 89.

60. Ibid.

61. Burgat, *L'islamisme au Maghreb*, p. 116.

62. Belhassen, "Femmes tunisiennes islamistes," p. 90.

63. Waltz, "Islamist Appeal in Tunisia," pp. 662–63.

64. Belhassen, "Femmes tunisiennes islamistes," pp. 88–89; Arlene Elowe MacLeod, *Accommodating Protest: Working Women, the New Veiling, and Change in Cairo* (New York: Columbia University Press, 1991), p. 93.

65. MacLeod, *Accommodating Protest*, esp. pp. 121, 133, 136.

66. Ibid., pp. 40–41.

67. Shahla Haeri, "Obedience vs. Autonomy: Women and Fundamentalism in Iran and Pakistan," in Marty and Appleby, *Fundamentalisms and Society;* MacLeod, *Accommodating Protest*, p. 78.

68. Zaynab al-Ghazali, "Al-mar'a 'l-muslima," *Al-Da'wa*, January 1981, p. 34.

69. Ibid., and "Sayyidāt muslimāt: Layla bint Tarīf," *Al-Da'wa*, January 1981, p. 35.

70. In "An Islamic Activist," I translate portions of my first interview with Zaynab al-Ghazali, on 17 June 1981, as well as a chapter of her book. I met her a second time on 13 September 1988.

71. Belhassen, "Femmes tunisiennes islamistes," pp. 87–89.

72. John Entelis reports that these "negative" tactics have been less used in Algeria away from the coastline in the more Arabized, religious interior ("Islamism and the State in the Maghreb," p. 164). On Gaza, see Chartrand, "The Veiled Look." On Asyut, see Michael Youssef, *Revolt against Modernity: Muslim Zealots and the West* (Leiden: Brill, 1985), p. 93. On Iran, see Farah Azari, "The Post-revolutionary Women's Movement in Iran," in Farah Azari, ed., *Women of Iran: The Conflict with Fundamentalist Islam* (London: Ithaca Press, 1983), pp. 190–225.

73. Abdelwahab Effendi, "The Long March Forward," *Inquiry* (October 1987), reprinted in *The Renaissance Party in Tunisia*, p. 105.

74. Salem, "Tunisia," p. 162.

75. Entelis, "Islamism and the State in the Maghreb," p. 173.

76. On the murders of Christians by Jihad before Sadat's assassination in 1981, see Kepel, *Muslim Extremism in Egypt*, pp. 204–9. On the more recent and potentially more serious attacks on Christians in Upper Egypt, see Youssef M. Ibrahim, "Muslims' Fury Is Falling on Egypt's Christians," *New York Times*, 15 March 1993, pp. A1, A4.

77. Muhammad al-Bahi, *Al-Islam wa ittijah al-mar'a 'l-muslima 'l-mu'asara* (Cairo: Dar al-I'tisam, 1979), pp. 26–27, 35–36, 14.

78. *Risalat al-mar'a 'l-muslima* (Cairo, n.d.), pp. 12–13. Other writers have also commented on the widespread suspicions of Western and Zionist conspiracy against Islam among members of the new Islamic movement: Saad Eddin Ibrahim, "Anatomy of Egypt's Militant Groups," p. 430; Yvonne Y. Haddad, *Contemporary Islam and the Challenge of History* (Albany: State University of New York Press, 1982), pp. 33–45.

79. See Mernissi, *Beyond the Veil*, pp. 65–85.

80. Arkoun, "Algeria," p. 183; Roberts, "Radical Islamism," p. 585.

81. *Akhbar al-Yawm*, 3 July 1981, cited in Yadlin, "Militant Islam in Egypt," pp. 166–67.

82. On Sufi religious experiences in contemporary Egypt, see Valerie J. Hoffman, *Sufism, Mystics, and Saints in Modern Egypt* (Columbia: University of South Carolina Press, 1995).

83. Valerie J. Hoffman-Ladd, "The Religious Life of Muslim Women in Contemporary Egypt," Ph.D. diss., University of Chicago, 1986.

84. Gilles Kepel, *Le Prophète et Pharaon: Les mouvements islamistes dans l'Egypte contemporaine* (Paris: La Découverte, 1984), p. 43.

85. These points were raised by Yvonne Haddad, from her studies of Muslims in America, and Marcia Hermansen, from her research in Pakistan, during a discussion following the presentation of my paper "Transformation and Continuity in the Religious Experience of Islamists and Sufis" at the American Academy of Religion annual meeting in San Francisco, 23 November 1992.

86. Belhassen, "Femmes tunisiennes islamistes," p. 79.

87. Safi Naz Kazim, *'An al-sijn wa 'l-hurriyya* (Cairo: Al-Zahrā' li 'l-I'lam al-'Arabi, 1986), pp. 30–31, 33.

88. Mustafa Mahmud, *Rihlati min al-shakk ila 'l-iman*, 2d ed. (Cairo: Dar al-Ma'arif, 1980), pp. 8, 10, 11, 96–97.

89. Zaynab al-Ghazali and the mother of Khalid al-Islambuli, Anwar Sadat's assassin, both speak of visions they received in times of acute trial and stress (Zaynab al-Ghazali al-Jabili, *Ayyam min hayati* [Beirut: Dar al-Shuruq, 1977], p. 52; Khalid al-Islambuli's mother's vision is related in Kazim, *'An al-sijn wa 'l-hurriyya*, p. 232).

90. For a typology of conversion experiences, see John Lofland and Norman Skonovd, "Conversion Motifs," *Journal for the Scientific Study of Religion* 20 (1981): 373–85.

91. Richard Travisano, "Alternation and Conversion as Qualitatively Different Transformations," in G. P. Stone and H. Farberman, eds., *Social Psychology through Symbolic Interaction* (Waltham, Mass.: Ginn-Blaisdell, 1970), p. 594.

92. Max Heirich, "Change of Heart: A Test of Some Widely Held Theories about Religious Conversion," *American Sociological Review* 83 (1977): 674.

93. William James, *The Varieties of Religious Experience* (1902; London: Macmillan, 1961), pp. 160, 165.

94. Edwin Starbuck, *The Psychology of Religion* (New York: Scribners, 1911), pp. 224, 262, cited in James, *The Varieties of Religious Experience*, pp. 167–68.

95. Kazim, *'An al-sijn wa 'l-hurriyya*, pp. 49–52.

96. Otto F. A. Meinardus, *Christian Egypt: Faith and Life* (Cairo: American University in Cairo Press, 1970), pp. 264–69; Cynthia Nelson, "Stress Religious Experience and Mental Health," *Catalyst* 6 (1972): 48–57.

97. Haddad, *Contemporary Islam and the Challenge of History*, p. 43; Hasan Hanafi,

"The Relevance of the Islamic Alternative in Egypt," *Arab Studies Quarterly* 4 (1982): 54–74, esp. p. 62; Emmanuel Sivan, *Radical Islam: Medieval Theology and Modern Politics,* enlarged ed. (New Haven: Yale University Press, 1990), esp. pp. 120–21, 134.

98. See Chris Hedges, "Denied Election, Algeria's Muslims Counterattack," *New York Times,* 12 May 1993, p. A3.

Buddhism, Nationhood, and Cultural Identity: A Question of Fundamentals

Gananath Obeyesekere

In the well-known *Encyclopedia of Religion* edited under the aegis of Mircea Eliade, published in 1987, there is no listing under *fundamentalism* per se; rather it is subsumed under the heading "Evangelical Christianity and Fundamentalism." The earlier Hastings *Encyclopaedia* of 1921 has no reference to this phenomenon at all. This is not surprising, since the term was invented in the United States in the 1920s to designate conservative offshoots of evangelical Christianity, dogmatic and uncompromising in their literal interpretation of the Bible and their exhortations to return to the biblical, spiritual, and moral injunctions and conceptions of an ideal society and world order—all based on the idea that the world has fallen into a state of spiritual decay. With the rise of Islamic historical and political self-consciousness, especially in Iran after the overthrow of the shah in 1979, the term *fundamentalism* developed a new reference; it was effectively displaced from evangelism and transferred in toto to Islamic movements. This shift occurred in both the popular and scholarly media, the one reinforcing the other, such that the term became more or less restricted to Islam and to movements elsewhere that exhibited "family resemblances" to Islamic fundamentalism. With the displacement of the term *fundamentalism* to Islam and then to other religions, Christian evangelism ceased to be fundamentalist and instead was reclassified descriptively in such terminological labels as *televangelism* or the *religious right,* or in terms of specifiable *cults.* Concomitantly *fundamentalism,* like the term *nationalism* itself, gradually became in the American popular imagination a pejorative and often demonizing label for religious and political movements elsewhere, most particularly in Islamic nations.

The virtual demise of the self-referential term *fundamentalism* in the United States is due to the dawning recognition that it hides much more than it reveals, a recognition based on the knowledge that there are a variety of movements in the Christian evangelical tradition, and that the term *fundamentalism* does not adequately discriminate among them. I suspect this to be one of the underlying reasons why every religion, including Christian evangelical sects, resists using this term for self-characterization. Besides, it has now become a pejorative label to be avoided. There are a multiplicity of fundamentalisms in any larger movement that calls for a return to an authentic scriptural tradition; moreover, some of these fundamentalisms are passive and quiescent movements whose members simply go on minding their own business of personal salvation.

The scholarly resurrection of this term as an analytic tool poses a problem endemic to the human sciences, namely, the transfer of a loaded term in popular usage to a different level of intellectual discourse. This particular discourse seeks to define and explain the rise of religious movements that reify the past scriptural tradition, or even invent one, mostly as a reaction to a variety of historical conditions, especially colonialism and those complex forces subsumed under the term *modernity*. I am not denying the usefulness of this enterprise in bringing a disturbing modern trend into the forefront of academic and popular consciousness and subjecting it to a critical understanding. My goal is different: following the spirit of the Fundamentalism Project I attempt to reformulate fundamentalism, or at least one broad form of the larger genus, in another intellectual idiom that brings to the fore issues pertaining to a critical feature of our times, namely, the preoccupation with issues of personal and cultural identity and the reconstitution of the past to create a sense of modern nationhood. Buddhism, I think, is a good case for exploring this issue because it problematizes the nature of fundamentalism at different levels.

The Idea of Buddhist History

I begin with Buddhist history rather than with its doctrines because it is Buddhist history that is associated with cultural identity, violence, and intolerance of others. This history, like many other histories of both literate and preliterate peoples, begins with a founder, the Buddha himself, who, as the tradition defines it, is a historical personage. The Archimedean point of Buddhist history is the death or *parinirvāṇa* of the founder. This date may vary in different traditions, but everywhere it is the key chronological event to which past and present are related. Unlike the founding myths of many preliterate peoples, the life and death of the founder are never ritually enacted, though sometimes conceived as a myth of an eternal return. A chronological imperative dates the reigns of kings and other important events from the death of the founder. Chronological specificity is important in Buddhist history, quite unlike the situation in the Hindu traditions. Further, Buddhist societies are self-conscious about their past and exhibit what one might call a "historical self-consciousness." It is interesting to compare Buddhism with the great monotheisms—Judaism, Islam, and Christianity—in this regard. In the powerful self-conceptions of these contending monotheisms, history is the operation of the divine will. Along with this is a conception of a moral and social order the believer must live by. Modern fundamentalistic movements in these monotheisms are an attempt to reconstitute society and the world in terms of these divinely ordained postulates of an ideal sociocultural order.[1] Insofar as this order expresses the will of God, it brooks little compromise. Consequently it contains the seeds of radical intolerance.

The situation is quite different in the Buddhist *doctrinal* tradition. Here, there is little evidence of intolerance, no justification for violence, no conception even of "just wars" or "holy wars" that are important for systems of jurisprudence based on monotheistic values. Moreover, very crucially, unlike the god of the monotheisms, the Buddha is no longer active and can therefore have no say over the unfolding of history. The legend of the Buddha and the stories of his past lives are in the past; they contain virtually no map of the future. In fact the religion is thoroughly negative even in regard to its own future: an ancient and popular tradition states that the monk order will last only five hundred years! Further, the Buddhist doctrinal tradition cannot produce the passions that characterize the prophetic traditions of the great monotheisms. Doctrines such as the four noble truths, no soul, dependent origination, the fleeting nature of the five constituent elements of the body, and the theory of impermanence might be intellectually satisfying; it is doubtful whether one can go to war over such things. The person of the Buddha, though no longer alive, is internalized in the Buddhist conscience—but as a totally benevolent being. He is radically different from God, the Father; if at all he is closer to the Son. It is impossible for the Buddha to say "vengeance is mine" without a radical distortion of Buddhist eschatological principles. The question I now pose is this: Where then lies the fury and passion that one sees in Buddhist societies such as Sri Lanka today? Where, if at all, are their antecedents in the Buddhist past?

Admittedly, the specific nature of violence that occurs in a particular historical period must be seen in relation to the socioeconomic and historical conditions of that period. Thus, looking at the political and economic conditions of the colonial and postcolonial period—in turn embedded in the geopolitics of larger regional and even global networks of our own times—is necessary to assess the specific kind of violence and its frightening intensity that one sees today in Sri Lanka. But in as much as one can make an assertion that Buddhist doctrine is *impossible* to reconcile logically with an ideology of violence and intolerance, and *difficult* to reconcile with the practice of violence, can we make a parallel case that shows endemic violence in Buddhist societies right through its history? Let me give a recent example. A few months ago the *New York Times* had a picture of a Yugoslav soldier with a gun in hand praying in a church. Even in the most violent periods of Buddhist history it would be hard, though not impossible, for a monk or layman to pray at a Buddhist shrine for success in war and impossible for a person to do so with a gun in hand, even now when considerable redefinition of Buddhist values is taking place. I am suggesting that while the soteriological traditions—not just the Pāli canon but the worship of the Buddha by ordinary Buddhists—do not justify violence and war, the reverse is true of Buddhist history. In other words, while violence is rarely reconcilable in ideology or practice with Buddhist soteriology (except in our own times), this is not true of Buddhist history. Violence is endemic there and is highly variegated in character. This distinction and the resultant tension between history and soteriology is not so clear-cut in the great monotheisms and in most types of Hinduism.

When we look at the histories that were written in the Theravāda societies, one is struck by the fact that they are self-consciously Buddhist histories, but of a special sort whose nature we must try to understand. These histories express the operation of Buddhism in the unfolding of history although the Buddha himself has no active intercessory role in it. Buddhist history then is a *construction,* of a special sort, based on a coalition of monks and kings, that begins with the death of the Buddha and exists for most purposes outside of the fundamental tenets of the doctrine. It is about kings who are, or should be, the guardians of the *sāsana* (the Buddhist order) and the people of Sri Lanka (often inextricably intertwined). The stories of these kings constitute Buddhist history. If Buddhist doctrine is fundamentally soteriological, Buddhist history is practical and world-oriented as is any history that must deal with problems of political order and disorder, violence pertaining to succession and access to political power, the ambitions of rulers, and endemic warfare. Buddhist history describes political events that occurred, with a few exceptions, after the death of the Buddha and exists almost entirely outside the Pāli canon. If Buddhist doctrine and ethics are universal, Buddhist history is particularistic and concerned exclusively with the political events in the various Theravāda nations. The Buddhist monks who wrote these histories had to face a moral dilemma, namely, to justify the acts of Buddhist kings who were, on the one hand, guardians of the doctrine and, on the other, secular rulers greedy for power and given to violence and war, murder, parricide, and sexual misconduct. If one picks up the great *Mahāvaṃsa*, the prototype Buddhist history written in the fifth century and the model for all Theravāda histories, one is struck by the enormity of the violence recorded therein. Even Asoka, the ideal Buddhist king who reigned in accordance with the ethical postulates of the religion, began his career in an orgy of violence: in order to ascend the throne he killed ninety-nine of his hundred brothers, sparing only his full brother. The enormity of Asoka's crimes is only redeemed by his later repentance, his renunciation of violence, and the initiation of a specifically Buddhist welfare polity.[2] These acts of violence pertain to political power, especially succession; and in most cases the violence is by Sinhalas against Sinhalas in internecine warfare. Violent kings in turn assuage their guilt and their fears of a bad rebirth by enormous acts of public piety, especially the construction of religious edifices, whose positive karmic effects might, they hope, cancel the bad karma acquired through violence—a position difficult to justify in terms of doctrinal Buddhism. Nevertheless, because these acts of Buddhist piety enhance the glory of the religion and the material well-being of monks, the compilers of Buddhist history must provide some kind of legitimation for kings who violate the basic tenets of their faith. Unlike in the Bhagavad Gita, Buddhist soteriology cannot provide a dharma of duty for kingly violence, yet in fact there is a similar notion implicit in Buddhist history that I will now explore.

The paradigmatic story that deals with this issue in the *Mahāvaṃsa* and in the Sinhala imagination is that of King Duṭṭhagāmaṇi Abhaya, popularly known as Duṭugämuṇu. This story is also a myth charter for Sinhalas who want to define their nation as Sinhala-Buddhist. Because this story is well known, I shall present only its briefest outline.[3] The *Mahāvaṃsa* devotes almost one-third of its text to Duṭugā-muṇu, who wrested the northern seat of the Sinhala kings from Elara, the Tamil, portrayed as a righteous king but also as a usurper and an unbeliever. Duṭugāmuṇu is saddened by the large number of Tamils killed in battle, and he cannot sleep as a result of his guilty conscience. But the monks console him and tell him that this will be no hindrance to heaven because the enemies he has killed were "not more to be esteemed than beasts. . . . But as for thee, thou wilt bring glory to the doctrine of the Buddha in manifold ways; therefore cast away care from thy heart, O ruler of men!"[4] This statement is a terribly important development in Buddhist history because it produces a theory, or at least a rationale, for killing one's enemy that contradicts the Buddhist doctrines and the Buddhist faith, and overthrows the primary Buddhist ethical postulates of compassion and nonviolence. It is close to the dharma of duty enunciated by Arjuna to Kṛṣṇa on the field of battle: Kṛṣṇa ought not to be troubled by his conscience because he is acting selflessly and without personal motivation, thereby fulfilling the dharma of royal duty. The *Mahāvaṃsa* retranslates this ethic in terms of its own view of Buddhist history: it is justifiable to kill one's enemy for the glory of the Buddhist "church" or sāsana. Duṭugāmuṇu's action is exempt from bad karma, as in the Gita, because the king is doing his royal duty and not acting out of greed for kingship.

Here then is a partial answer to the question of how Buddhism, a religion of radical nonviolence, has produced in our own times an intensity of political violence that has overwhelmed the physical and psychic space of Sri Lanka. Buddhist history is either the instigator or legitimator of violence, and insofar as this is associated with war, political power, ethnic identity, and the succession to rulership, it has also the capacity to overwhelm the humane philosophy and ethics of its soteriology.

Imagining a Buddhist "Whatever"

I have deliberately refrained from employing terms like *nation, nation-state,* or even *state* to describe the situation in precolonial Sri Lanka. For the moment I want to bracket these words from the Western lexicon and substitute *whatever* instead, till I have presented the empirical material. The idea of sovereignty was clearly recognized, however. It was an ideological construct, a fiction, though a very significant one.

Sovereignty was claimed for all of Sri Lanka, even by kings who had effective control over only a minuscule area (such as the Tamil kings of Jaffna after the fifteenth century). In reality the provinces were practically independent though they paid ideological homage to the "seat" of sovereignty. For most of ancient and medieval history the province of Ruhuṇa in the south was a virtually independent kingdom, an ideological replica of the seat of sovereignty in Anurādhapura (and later in Polonnaruva) in the *rajaraṭa* (the royal province), so named because the seat of sovereignty was located here. In the Kandyan period—after the fifteenth century—Buddhist kingdoms became what Tambiah has called "galactic polities," where the provinces were emulating and moving toward a center though effectively independent of it.[5] Hence the characteristic of all these Buddhist polities: structurally disparate, yet ideologically imagined as a unified Buddhist "whatever." For the most part the center was politically unstable, yet the ideology of a Buddhist whatever was constant.

How then is this Buddhist ideological unity conceived and expressed in the popular imagination?

According to the *Mahāvaṃsa* the Buddha, flying through the air by virtue of his supernormal powers, landed in Sri Lanka three times, chasing demons to a distant isle known as *giri dīpa* (rocky isle) and settling a dispute among contending *nāga* (snake being) kings living in the north and converting them. He visits places that later became sacred sites: Kälaṇiya near Colombo and Mahiyaṅgaṇa in the northeast, where his collarbone relic was later enshrined. In his third visit he placed his foot on the top of the spectacular peak known as Sumanakūṭa, named after the guardian of the peak, Sumana or Saman, later to become one of the guardian deities of Buddhist Sri Lanka. The myth of the Buddha's visits is uncontested. Their significance is equally clear: the island was rid of malevolent demons while the benevolent nāgas were converted to the true religion. Major religious centers have been sanctified by his presence, and his foot is indelibly inscribed on the peak at the very center of the land, later to become the most important pilgrimage site for Buddhists. It is as if the land is consecrated as a place where Buddhism will flourish, as virtually all historical texts recognize.[6] This land is made ready for the coming of the founding ancestor of the Sinhalas, Vijaya.

Vijaya (victory) was the son of Sinhabāhu, a parricidal king who killed his father, a lion, and then married his own sister and lived in Sinhapura (lion city) in northern India. Owing to Vijaya's violent and unlawful behavior, Sinhabāhu banished his son by putting him in a boat with seven hundred of his followers. Vijaya landed in Sri Lanka on the very day the Buddha passed into final nirvana; thus Vijaya the victor is the secular counterpart of the other victor, or *jina,* the Buddha himself. The Buddha entrusted Sakra (Indra) to protect Vijaya, and Sakra delegated this task to Viṣṇu, who blessed Vijaya when he landed by tying a Buddhist protective charm on his person. Viṣṇu (Upulvan), like Saman before him, became one of the guardian deities of the land and a future bodhisattva. Vijaya married a demoness whom he subsequently betrayed; from this union sprang the Väddas, the aboriginal hunters of Sri Lanka (who to this day claim Vijaya as their ancestor). Subsequently, in a formal ceremonial, he married a princess from South Madurāpura (in the Tamil country, distinguished from North Madurāpura, the land of Kṛṣṇa). There were no heirs from this marriage, and Vijaya's brother's son was brought from Sinhapura to take over the kingship.[7]

This foundational myth for Sri Lankan history is an inescapable part of the historical consciousness of the Sinhalas. Modern scholars have scarcely noted the fact that it is a myth of ethnic separation and integration. The land is consecrated and cleansed of evil spirits by the Buddha for Vijaya to land; the aborigines are descended from Vijaya but by an inferior union, and hence outside the pale of legitimate kingship and Buddhist history and civilization. The Tamils are affines; they do not inherit the dynasty; it goes back to Paṇḍu Vāsudeva, whose name resonates with that of the protagonists of the Mahābhārata. Yet unlike the Väddas the Tamils are both kinsfolk and cofounders of the nation. This aspect of the myth has been almost completely forgotten or ignored in recent times. The rest of the Vijaya myth appears everywhere and is so powerful that even modern scholars treat it as an empirically, or at least symbolically, correct beginning of Sri Lankan history.

Village rituals, whether for gods or demons, virtually everywhere start with a standard phrase: *Sasiri bara, me siri laka* (Heavy with prosperity, this blessed Sri Lanka). Take the implication of this phrase: it does not express a geographic conception at all, but an imagination of a place. This imagined place has an internal geography recorded in *kaḍaimpot* (boundary books) and paralleling the cosmic geography of Buddhist texts. Though for insiders the place is always known as Sri Lanka, it is often called Sinhaladīpa (the island of the Sinhalas) by outsiders. The divergent terminology indicated that the people living in this place were sensitive to internal ethnic differentiations, whereas outsiders adopted a more simplistic naming procedure after the dominant ethnic group.

Following the preliminary incantation quoted above, the Buddhist hierarchy is recounted in virtually every ritual text: the Buddha, the dhamma (doctrines), and the sangha (the monk order). Then the great guardian gods are named, followed by a list of minor local deities who exhibit considerable regional variation. Thus, though the rituals might vary in content and form from region to region, there is a recognition of a pan-island hierarchy of named deities, specifically the Buddha and the guardian gods who act as protectors of Buddhism and of the place, Sri Lanka. When one moves from these village rituals for gods and demons into Buddhist temples, there is a strong standardization of rituals and prayers for the Buddha, in spite of different types of monk orders and fraternities. The Buddha figure is also internalized in the conscience of believers as a benevolent figure, an almost maternal one, although he is formally recognized as a male. This standardization is made possible because Buddhist temples and monks (and other kinds of Buddhist religious virtuosi) are everywhere present and accessible to all.

All these cultural expressions permit the plurality of Sinhalas to imagine themselves as Buddhists. Yet is imagining a community all that is necessary to create a sense of belonging to a community that transcends local boundaries and allegiances? Contrary to Anderson I think there are no "concrete communities": all communities are imagined, but imagined in different ways.[8] The ethnographic or historical task is to describe the manner in which communities are imagined. But this is not sufficient: the imagined community, even that of a modern nation, must be "concretized" in a variety of ways—in parades, national events, collective gatherings ranging from football to political meetings, and so forth. Unlike Durkheim's Australian aboriginal corroboree,[9] these concretized gatherings of modern nations permit mass vicarious participation through their refractions in the media; and these media presentations in turn bring into question the very distinction between imagined and concrete. These diverse representations are intrinsic to the imagining of modern nationhood, and they nourish it. The question I pose with respect to Buddhism is, How was this sense of belonging concretized in the Buddhist case in precolonial times prior to the development of mass communications? I suggest that this concretization happens through the crucial mechanism of the "obligatory pilgrimage."

Such a pilgrimage takes place in Rambadeniya, an isolated village in the northeast-
ern hills of Sri Lanka where Stanley Tambiah and I did fieldwork in 1958–60.[10] After
each harvest the villagers of Rambadeniya gather in a collective thanksgiving ritual for
the gods known as the *aḍukku*. During this festival the priest of the *dēva,* or deity cults
(never the Buddhist monk), pays formal homage to the Buddha and the great guardian
deities and then actively propitiates the local gods, especially their main deity known
as Baṇḍāra Deviyo (*baṇḍāra* means "chief" rather than "king," which is the term
reserved for the guardian gods). These rituals help define the village as a "moral community" under the benevolent care of Baṇḍāra Deviyo. Once every year, however,
some of the villagers go to the great pilgrimage center of Mahiyaṅgana, about thirty-
five miles away, which the Buddha himself consecrated by his presence and which now
contains his collarbone relic enshrined in an imposing stupa. As they proceed through
the forest, they hang branches or twigs on trees sacred to local deities, implicitly acknowledging that they are no longer under the care of the local deity but under the
aegis of another whose *sīma* (boundary) they are now crossing. In a matter of a few
hours other villagers taking different pilgrim routes join them, and there is a literal and
dramatic expansion of the moral community, which ultimately becomes a vast sea of
heads at Mahiyaṅgana. Right along the pilgrims sing religious songs mostly in praise
of the Buddha, since this is the shared idiom that makes sense in the context of an
expanded community. At the pilgrimage site they bathe in the river and purify themselves and pray to the two guardian gods represented there—Saman and Skanda—and
then worship the Buddha and perform exclusively Buddhist rituals. An important shift
in allegiances has occurred: villagers have temporarily renounced their parochial local
deities and are united under the common worship of the Buddha and the guardian
gods. The once separate and discrete moral communities now lose their identities in
the larger moral community of Sinhala Buddhists.

A powerful act of concretization has occurred, fostering the imagination in a special
way, reinforcing and nourishing ideas of being Sinhala and Buddhist that a person has
learned by simply living in a village community and participating in its round of activities. Concretization is a physical, psychic, and imaginative experience, as Durkheim
rightly noted.[11] The trip to Mahiyaṅgana is but one station in an ideal pilgrimage
round of sixteen, a number that comes from at least the eighteenth century. Rambadeniya folk rarely made it beyond Mahiyaṅgana, but all did make it to Mahiyaṅgana
some of the time.

Let us for the moment go beyond this particular case to consider transnational
pilgrimage centers that are out of reach for most members of a moral community. Even
in this situation the community is not imaginatively isolated from the experience.
Those who go on distant pilgrimages communicate their experiences to others and
nourish stories and other cultural scenarios that exist in the village. Consider the elaborate ritual practices undertaken by the pilgrim going to Mecca. For a whole year the
prospective pilgrim is beset with a powerful *shawq* (longing), and this emotion is communicated to friends and relatives who also identify with his longing. Prior to leaving,
the pilgrim bids ceremonial farewell to his fellows, who weep for him and give him
vicarious authority to pray on their behalf. The return of the pilgrim, now known as

the hajji, is also thoroughly ritualized. The members of the community have pitched their tents for two or three days, and they welcome him joyously with festivities involving the slaughter of many sheep.[12] In this process the hajji himself becomes a symbol of aspirations waiting to be fulfilled. The imagination at work here relates to narrativization and other ways of representing the missed experience as against its immediate representation and visualization as in modern television. Different ways of imagining the community are involved in the two cases.

The obligatory pilgrimage also has an important political function in fostering a sense of a larger consciousness in Buddhist societies, as it did in Chaucer's England.

> And specially, from every shires ende
> Of Engelond, to Caunterbury they wende,
> The holy blisful martir for to seke,
> That hem hath holpen, whan that they were seke.

It is very likely that these obligatory pilgrimages set the stage for the later development of a more powerful sense of nationhood in Elizabethan England.

The obligatory pilgrimage makes it possible for us to identify the whatever that eluded us thus far: it is sāsana, the term that I previously translated as the Buddhist "church." By contrast *nation* is an alien word that has no parallel in the Sinhala lexicon. Sāsana takes its place. In the doctrinal tradition sāsana refers to the universal Buddhist community or church that transcends ethnic and other boundaries. This meaning coexists with another meaning that is found in postcanonical historical texts: sāsana is the Buddhist "church" that is particularized in the physical bounds of the land consecrated by the Buddha—in the present instance, Sri Lanka. Here is the word we were looking for: it is the sāsana of Sri Lanka or, for most purposes, simply the sāsana. Sāsana in a particularistic sense is locked into Buddhist history; sāsana in a universalistic sense is locked into Buddhist soteriology. This tension between the two meanings of sāsana is intrinsic to Buddhism. Thus Duṭugāmuṇu is fighting the Tamils not for the glory of sovereignty but for the glory of the sāsana—in its entirely particularistic sense. Sinhalas had no term that could be translated as *nation;* they had a term that perhaps belonged to the same polythetic class as *nation,* namely *sāsana.*

Representing the Tamils

In today's ethnic conflict the Tamils are the hated Other for most Sinhalas; the feeling is mutual as far as the Tamils are concerned, except that for the latter there also exists the hated Muslims in their own midst. It is a mistake to think that this is a primordial conflict rooted in the nation's history. The fact that history imagines a Buddhist sāsana in the island of Sri Lanka does not mean that the Tamils were exclusively depicted as enemies. One also must not be deluded by European language use by defining Other as a radically exclusive conception, because one can be an Other in respect of some specific defining category or attribute but not in respect of another feature. Many scholars, retrojecting the past from the present, have read the *Mahāvaṃsa* simply as a text that represents the Tamils as enemies who should be destroyed. This is of course extrapolated from a contemporary reading of the Duṭugāmuṇu story. But in the *Mahāvaṃsa*, and more generally in the Sinhala-Buddhist imagination, the Tamils (i.e., South Indians) were represented in a variety of ways that I shall briefly demonstrate below.

Take the foundational myth–charter itself. Vijaya marries a queen from South Madurāpura, which is in the Tamil country, and his seven hundred followers find wives from the same place. Thus the charter myth says that Tamils are affines, and given the myth's proclamation that these unions produced the Sinhalas, it is clear that Sinhalas have Tamil blood, since "blood" is bilaterally inherited. If there is any doubt that South Madurāpura is not in the Tamil country (but the south of the Madurāpura in North India), this is easily dispelled in popular texts that say that Vijaya married the Pandya (Tamil) king's daughter. This charter represents a political reality in Sri Lankan history, where right down to the nineteenth-century kings contracted alliances with South Indian royalty.

Tamils are enemies to be vanquished, as the Duṭugāmuṇu myth exemplifies. Sometimes Tamils are distinguished from other South Indians, sometimes not. Owing to the presence of internecine wars, however, the Sinhalas themselves are as often enemies to be vanquished. Thus Duṭugāmuṇu fought with his own brother and killed thousands of his own countrymen. It is important to recognize, however, that the disparaging references to one's enemies are to Tamils and other invaders—Javanese, Kālingas, Portuguese, and other Westerners.

Tamils are allies. Many kings sought Tamil support in their wars and took sides with one Tamil king against another. Some kings sought refuge in the Tamil country in order to escape from their Sinhala enemies. And Tamil mercenaries were a standard feature of ancient and medieval society.

Tamils can be kings, though subsequently Sinhalized and Buddhicized. Some of the greatest Sinhala kings had South Indian origins, such as Kirti Sri Rājasinha (1741–80), and Bhūveneka Bāhu VI (1469–77), who, as Sapumal Kumāraya, was one of the great heroes of the Sinhalas and, ironically, the conqueror of the Tamil kingdom of Jaffna.[13] Tamil queens are of course much more common, owing to the logic of affinity. An interesting feature of both the written texts and the popular tradition is that the Tamil queens are often mothers of illegitimate offspring, so that the illegitimate son is from a Tamil woman rather than the chief queen (*mahesi*). Thus the parricide king, Kaśyapa I (473–91), was not of the right status, according to the *Mahāvaṃsa*, and, according to popular tradition, was born of a Tamil woman. Another great king, Rājasinha I, was the son of a dancing woman, but "dancing woman" is a code name for Tamil.[14] These Tamil dancing women are in their own way idealized in the Sinhala popular imagination in such texts as *Kamacci sinduva* (The song of the erotic lady), and *Mādevi kātava* (The story of the dancing girl, Mādevi).[15] They parallel the *veśya* (courtesan) of the classic texts.

Tamils are sorcerers and powerful ritual specialists. This has been a historically consistent theme that I have discussed elsewhere. A few examples from the contemporary scene will illustrate what I mean. In spite of the enormous hostility to Tamils, some of the most popular shrines for Buddhists are the Kali temples at Munneswaram, thirty-five miles north of Colombo, and in the city of Colombo itself, both controlled by Tamil priests. In Colombo there are Tamil priests who have recently set up an institution for reading *nāḍi vākyams,* astrological sheets written in Tamil, supposed to have been compiled by *rishis* (saints) thousands of years ago and to contain the horoscopes of most human beings of the past, present, and future. These are enormously popular with Buddhist middle classes, and even Buddhist monks patronize these priests for horoscopic readings. It is also well known that past presidents and prime ministers have consulted astrologers from South India for the timing of most state events and the solution of personal crises and anxieties. Former President Premadasa imported magicians and astrologers from Kerala and housed them in Colombo as spiritual consultants.[16]

I am not suggesting that these images of Tamils were consistently operative, but some were operative all the time in the precolonial period. Some images, such as Tamils as enemies to be vanquished, must have surfaced during invasions from South India, while at other times affinal connections must surely have been important. One also cannot assume that these diverse images did not imply that Tamils were not seen as Others, because their language and customs were in fact not Sinhala-Buddhist. Otherness was not a total exclusion but rather a series of identity boundaries that tended to be fuzzier in some periods of history than in others. Because the whole problem of identity is crucial to understanding "fundamentalism," it is now time to examine this issue at some length. I shall do so in a preliminary way by introducing an important type of ritual drama that occurs in many collective ritual performances and folk dramas among Sinhala Buddhists.

The basic scenario common to all these ritual dramas is as follows: In the ritual arena two performers take the role of the Buddhist guardian deities of the island. They hold a stick that acts as a barrier and also as a *kaḍavata,* literally an entrance to a city gate, but at another level of symbolic remove the entrance to Sri Lanka itself. An alien deity or magician or merchant (or groups of them) try to break thorough the barrier and enter Sri Lanka, but the gods prevent them. These aliens speak a funny kind of Sinhala with a strong Tamil accent, and they constantly utter malapropisms, unintended puns, and spoonerisms. They inadvertently make insulting remarks about the gods at the barrier; they are ignorant of Sinhala and Buddhist customs, and the audience has a lot of fun at their expense. Gradually the alien visitors recognize their errors of speech and custom; they learn to speak properly; they begin to properly worship the deities and acknowledge the superiority of the Buddha. Then the gods open the barrier, and these aliens enter Sri Lanka. I think these rituals give symbolic expression to a important historical process: the foreign visitors are "naturalized" as Sri Lankan Buddhists, and only then can they be legitimized as "citizens." These ritual performances parallel what I have previously described and dubbed as colonization myths—myths that describe the arrival and incorporation of South Indian people into Sri Lanka and their subsequent Sinhalization and Buddhicization (or better still their sāsanization).[17] In my work on the goddess Pattini I have shown how the ritual texts of these migrants were soon translated into Sinhala.[18]

The Creation of Axiomatic Identities

"Axiomatic identity" refers to those statuses and social positions that one takes for granted and that simultaneously carry an important though varying emotional investment, the root of which is birth. Thus *son* is a status in the conventional sociological sense of a bundle of rights and duties; as an identity, however, it is associated with birth, together with emotional investments of various kinds, as for example, feelings of filial piety as well as all sorts of ambivalences. As a status it is taken for granted; but this taken-for-grantedness can get a jolt, for example, if I begin to question whether my father deserves my love or whether fatherhood is not a bourgeois institution that ought to be abolished, and so forth. The questioning of axiomatic identities, precisely because of their taken-for-granted quality, can be profoundly troubling and agonizing. Axiomatic identities are woven into one's sense of worth, wholeness (Erikson's "ego identity"), and well-being. When one talks of an axiomatic identity, one can also examine the processes whereby an identity is created, reproduced, broken, changed, and reconstituted. Thus the Freudian Oedipal crisis is, among other things, a process whereby an identity crisis pertaining to the axiomatic identity of sonship takes place. The processes or mechanisms that help create identity formation can also be depicted, such as the "introjection" of paternal values and an "identification" with the father.

I do not want to make a sharp distinction between individual and group identities, for, following Freud, the individual does not stand alone but is related as brother, sister, father, spouse, and so forth to a larger entity, the family, and, I might add, to even larger structures like lineages and clans.[19] While recognizing the fuzziness of these boundaries, let me nevertheless, for heuristic purposes, refer to group identities that also have an axiomatic quality, for example, caste identities in India; or lineage identities; or ranks such as aristocracies; or, in the largest sense, modern nations; or even the emerging forms of transnational identities such as a universalizing Islamic cultural consciousness; or that recent formation struggling to emerge, namely, Europeanness. In all of these cases axiomatic identity is an end product. Yet this end product did not emerge from the blue; there had to be a lot of work to create it. Even if the axiomatic identity is already in place, it must be reproduced or recreated or refashioned according to changing sociohistorical circumstances. Axiomatic identities need not necessarily produce intolerance, though that possibility always exists. To say one is French is certainly to say one is not Dutch or English; it need not be a statement about enmity. However, in times of crises such as wars or football games, the axiomatic identity gets an infusion of passion and commitment; and it gets sharpened in opposition to an equally simplistically defined and opposed Other. Thus strengthening-weakening is a dialectical process inextricably associated with axiomatic identities. Naturally these processes depend on historical circumstances that must be contextualized for each case.

I noted that the critical feature of axiomatic identity is birth: it is the one incontestable feature of any kin relation or membership of a lineage, caste, nation, and so forth. Thus the popular word for caste in many South Asian languages is *jāti*, which means "birth." The modern word for race is *jāti;* when Sinhalas think of themselves as a nation they also use the term *jāti*. The origin of the European word *nation* is also birth. What modern nationhood has effected, as Eugen Weber shows for France, is to refigure the idea of birth associated with axiomatic identities by transfusing it into a larger domain, namely, nation—an enormously difficult and complicated task.[20] Being born into a group identity is in fact the critical mechanism that renders an identity axiomatic. In European thought an identity associated with birth is "natural," a cultural idea that has resonances in other traditions, for example, in the ritual dramas discussed earlier where the alien is assimilated through forms of cultural learning, or in other cases through marriage. In Europe the person who adopts an axiomatic identity has therefore to be "naturalized." Parallel with this is another notion in modern nationhood: birth is not in any place but in a particular "land." In the precolonial Sri Lankan case one notices similar metaphors: this blessed isle, this Sri Lanka—blessed by the Buddha himself as a place where the sāsana will flourish. In modern times even more powerful familial metaphors are invoked in both nationalistic and ethnic discourses everywhere: patria, fatherland, motherland. In the latter instance the violation of the land is associated with sexual violation and rape of the mother. *Patria* is associated with juridical rights that have to be defended in the name of the father, often associated with duty. Both can lead to an extraordinary level of violence.

Neither birth nor land is sufficient to create the content and substance of the complex identities associated with such things as nationhood, ethnicity, or being Buddhist. Let me come back to my previous discussion of the obligatory pilgrimage. This can now be seen as another mechanism for creating and recreating an axiomatic identity. So is it with the great historical text, the *Mahāvaṃsa*. The *Mahāvaṃsa* is not only a text that provides information on historical matters, including information on "ethnic identity"; it is also a text that in fact helps construct such an (axiomatic) identity. In his important book *Forms of Nationhood*, Richard Helgerson shows the deliberate manner in which six major Elizabethan writers attempted to construct an idea of an English nation through their literary works.[21] The *Mahāvaṃsa* performs a similar task; I am sure it is easy to find examples in any literate tradition. So is it with the ritual dramas and colonization myths discussed earlier.

The kind of axiomatic identity created in Buddhist Sri Lanka is now clear: to be Sinhala is ipso facto to be Buddhist: they are twin facets of the same identity. As far as Buddhists are concerned, the tension between the two meanings of sāsana resurfaces in the historically constructed and essentialized axiomatic identity. Buddhist soteriology denies any enduring reality to the body or the self: the doctrine emphasizes the fluctuating and senseless nature of all structures of existence. Therefore an axiomatic identity in Buddhist soteriological terms is a kind of false consciousness. Nevertheless, such an identity is the self-perceived true consciousness of Buddhist history and lived existence. Thus in Buddhist history there is expectably a continual Buddhicization (i.e., a sāsanization) of South Indian groups, including their gods, magical practices, language, and texts, which if translated into the European language is a form of life that is called naturalization. Viewed in long-term historical perspective, Sinhalas have been for the most part South Indian migrants who have been sāsanized. It is interesting to note that sāsanization embraced virtually all the castes in the Sinhala system. Sāsanization has been facilitated by the relative absence of contestation by immigrant groups in areas dominated by Sinhala speech communities. A parallel process perhaps took place in the northern peninsula, which after the fifteenth century at least was controlled by Kerala and Tamil peoples who in their own way assimilated previous Sinhala speakers.

Given our discussion of axiomatic identities and modes of representing the Tamils, it is difficult to accept the positions taken by several leading scholars regarding the attitude to Tamils in Sri Lankan texts. Thus Tambiah, following an important paper by Guṇāwardana, thinks that the relations between Sinhalas and Tamils were traditionally harmonious until the changes brought about by colonialism and the imperial conquest. By contrast Dharmadasa looks at another set of historical sources to prove the very contrary.[22] Thus in typical social science fashion each protagonist brings forward historical evidence to advance one hypothesis against another. My position is that "evidence" of this sort is indicative of debates that were going on in the society at large, and these debates could easily have coexisted in any particular time span. Stated in another way, people could have had both views of Tamils at any particular time; or in some periods of history one set of views may have dominated over the other. The debates between these scholars provide evidence of debates in the society at large; they cannot be used as "facts" to vindicate one scholarly hypothesis over another. Even today in spite of the virulence of the ethnic conflict, there are a variety of views about Tamils, though the predominant view is that of the hostile Other.

Colonialism and Buddhist "Fundamentalism"

A critical feature of fundamentalism as it was defined in the United States pertains to the literal interpretation of the Bible. This meaning of fundamentalism is not particularly modern because it is a part of the faith of all evangelical movements. What makes fundamentalism a modern phenomenon is the idea that in our own times the world has moved away from the simple, profound, and ethically meaningful world order propounded in the doctrinal texts of the great monotheisms. These monotheisms have within them conceptions of an ideal order the true devotee must live by; the intention of the new fundamentalisms is to implement that order in the present degenerate age where atheism and antireligiousness have taken root. Any form of "demythologization" is anathema to modern fundamentalism.

Buddhism, as far as I know, never had to confront similar issues until modern times. No one for a moment thought that the word of the Buddha was anything but literally true. Powerful commentarial traditions dealt with doctrinal interpretation and exegesis, but rarely with symbolic interpretation and demythologization. Buddhism did not possess a conception of a world order that the believer must live by, and, unlike the Hindu Dharmaśāstras, it did not even possess a social theory of any significance. Thus the aspect of fundamentalism that called for a reconstitution of the world simply could not arise in Buddhism. Moreover, there were no radically opposed worldviews, like that of modern science, to question the exclusive world picture of Buddhism. The various Hindu faiths provided an arena for continuous argument, but this historical dialectic only helped to reinforce the truth value of Buddhism. Thus as far as the meaning of fundamentalism as doctrinal literalism is concerned, Buddhism has always been "fundamentalist." It was a nonproblematic issue.

The matter is rendered much more complicated, however, by the fact that the Buddhist texts were the exclusive preserve of the monks, and there was no single easily available text like the Protestant Bible or the Qur'an for authoritative consultation or elucidation. The voluminous Buddhist texts were enshrined in what scholars have called the Pāli canon, consisting of the Suttas (doctrinal discourses), the Vinaya (rules of monk discipline), and the Abhidhamma (philosophical commentaries). Steven Collins has shown that a formalized "canon" was invented in the first century B.C.E. when the Buddhist texts were put into writing and that even then there might well have been contending versions.[23] The word *canon* is a European rendering of the more open term *tripitaka* (three baskets). The texts were in Pāli, and hence a more or less exclusive preserve of the literati, in effect monks. Even great kings like Asoka were probably unfamiliar with the doctrinal corpus. A good part of the canon—the Vinaya—dealt exclusively with the regulation of monastic life; and the commentarial and psychological texts were for the most part irrelevant for ordinary laypersons. But, unlike the Latin Vulgate, the monkish exclusiveness had a soteriological point: this is the distinction recognized very early in Buddhism, that the doctrine was "against the current" and meant for those who have renounced "home," in effect monks. Laypersons were involved in the home, and home involvement is an impediment for salvation (nirvana). Thus the laity is expected to lead good moral lives that will ensure a happy rebirth, the very thing the virtuoso tries to abolish. However the layperson who lives a good life according to the moral precepts can also achieve nirvana—but only in some future (and perhaps remote) rebirth.

Thus the "canon," however defined, possessed contents that were for the most part alien to the layperson. It was fetishized as a body of sacred texts and on occasion paid homage to or worshiped (though never to the degree that the Bible and Qur'an were fetishized). However, a significant portion of the canon known as the Khuddaka Nikāya (minor collection) intersects with lay lives. "It is the mass and the home of many minor branches of the True Idea (Dhamma)," says one of its texts.[24] It is doubtful whether monks even thought of it as containing information that was false or only symbolically or parabolically true or "noncanonical." These texts of the minor collection were strongly influenced by the popular religion and in turn influenced that tradition. Perhaps the most important part of this corpus is the Buddha legend and the collection of the lives of the Buddha known as the *jātaka* tales.

A characteristic feature of the minor collection is that it exists in both Pāli and

Sinhala, in the canon and outside of it. The minor collection then influenced an important development—a huge body of vernacular literature that I have labeled "intermediate texts," neither belonging to the canon nor to the oral tradition of folk literature.[25] These intermediate texts are crucial to the Buddhism of the laity. When you enter any Buddhist temple, you will see frescoes that deal with the stories from these intermediate texts with brief captions in Sinhala to give the viewer's memory a jolt to help recollect the full story. They were widely read or diffused orally through a variety of sources, including monks' sermons. Monks used these stories to illustrate in concrete form the abstract doctrinal ethical ideas important to Buddhism, such as the Four Noble Truths; concepts like karma, *anicca* (impermanence), *anatta* (no soul), and *saṃsāra* (existence); and ethical ideas such as nonviolence, compassion, nonretaliation, and so forth. The ethics and doctrines, selectively filtered, entered the popular consciousness through these intermediate texts in the form of stories. The main body of the canon was never translated into vernacular languages until very recent times.

If raising the scriptural tradition for fundamentalist reflection was a complex non-issue, this was not so with the advent of colonialism, particularly with the coming of the British, who subjugated the last Buddhist kingdom in Kandy in 1815. Prior to this, during the period of Dutch rule in the "low country," Buddhist missions were sent to Thailand to revive the lapsed ordination in Kandy. In the low country areas controlled by the Dutch, monks from disprivileged castes instituted new Buddhist fraternities that derived their ordination from Burma. These fraternities were active in the Dutch occupied territories; some were committed to a more doctrinally orthodox and austere lifestyle than were the monks of Kandy who had received their ordination from Thailand. From the early period of British rule in Sri Lanka, monks, particularly from the new fraternities, began a process of revivifying Buddhism and attempting, not very successfully, to challenge the intrusion of the missions. The great Buddhist monk (and later king) Mongkut of Thailand, who introduced some radical reforms in the organization and constitution of the Thai order, was perhaps influenced by these early Sinhala movements.[26]

After the middle of the nineteenth century Buddhist monks of all the fraternities started to confront the missionary presence in a more active manner. Here they had an unexpected resource: the emerging work of European Indologists, some of whom saw the teachings of the Buddha embodied in the major doctrinal texts as a more rational religion than the Christian monotheism. This work not only gave a fillip to the flagging self-esteem of Buddhists whose religion was disestablished with the conquest, but it also gave them powerful ammunition for counterattack. It should be remembered that these Western Indologists redefined the Buddhist "three baskets" as the Pāli canon. From the rationalist Indological perspective, the Pāli canon of Theravāda contained the pristine teachings of Buddhism, compounded occasionally with popular superstition. From their perspective these superstitions were later accretions; especially dubious and virtually noncanonical was the minor collection. Thus the very portion of the canon that linked the lay tradition with the monastic was defined as not quite Buddhist. Monks at this time did not share this view, but they could use the European defense of Buddhism to good effect against the missions. For Buddhists, Indologists became, quite unintentionally, benevolent traitors to their own European religious traditions.

Buddhist monks were the literati of society, and they took the initial leadership against the missions. They began to emulate missionary tactics by starting their own printing presses and tracts as a response to the missionary ones, most important from an organization begun in 1862 known as the Society for the Propagation of Buddhism. This was one of the very first attempts by the Buddhists to take over organizational styles from Christianity—in this case an imitation of the Society for the Propagation of the Gospel. A second thrust consisted of public debates between Buddhists and Christians, the most famous held in Panadura, a village south of Colombo, in which, by Buddhist accounts, they trounced the Christian representatives. These confrontations brought to the fore a powerful orator, Miguṭṭuvattē Guṇānanda, who gave up the sedate style of Buddhist sermonizing and adopted instead the active, polemical, vituperative stance of the missions. After these momentous events the Buddhists effectively used the European views of Buddhism and atheistic critiques of Christianity in their attacks on the missions. Reginald Copleston, the bishop of Colombo, noted in 1789 that the secretary of "an obscure society" was corresponding with monks, "hailing them as brothers in the march of the intellect" and praising them for their spirited antimissionary and anti-Christian challenges. "This nonsense had a good deal of effect, I think, on the common people, while the more educated, having really become free thinkers, welcome the extravagant encomiums passed on the true, original Buddhism by European writers."[27] The "obscure society" that Bishop Copleston referred to was the Theosophical Society, and its secretary was an American colonel, Henry Steele Olcott. Olcott wanted to consolidate these early communications with Buddhists, and on 17 May 1880, he, Madame Blavatsky, and several other theosophists arrived in Sri Lanka for this purpose. Soon after his arrival Olcott founded a local branch of the Theosophical Society, but soon he became aware of the larger role that Sri Lankan Buddhists expected of him. Olcott enthusiastically accepted his role as a Western champion of Buddhism against the Christian missions. As a Westerner and an anti-imperialist American who had fought in the Civil War, Olcott possessed enormous charisma, reinforced no doubt by his discovery of his own capacity to heal the lame and the paralyzed.

I refer the reader to my earlier account of Olcott's contribution to the "Buddhist revival": here I shall focus on his almost single-handed construction of a fundamentalist Buddhism.[28] Note that by this time there was a powerful and hostile religion with its missionary adversaries. There was also another important force that any modern religion had to contend with, namely, science. The intellectual and political climate was right for pitting Buddhism against Christianity and justifying its tenets in terms of science. What kind of Buddhism, though? It was clear to Olcott that it had to be the "pure" Buddhism of the textual tradition as defined, or rather redefined, by Western Indologists. This rational Buddhism was also perfectly consonant with his own theosophy.[29] Consequently, he formally declared himself a Buddhist by taking the five precepts of Buddhism administered by a monk. He wrote in his diary:

Speaking for her [Blavatsky] as well as for myself, I can say that if Buddhism contained a single dogma that we were compelled to accept, we would not have taken the *pansil* [precepts] nor remained Buddhists ten minutes. Our Buddhism was that of the Master-Adept Gautama Buddha, which was identically the Wisdom Religion of the Aryan Upanishads, and the soul of ancient world-faiths. Our Buddhism was, in a word, a philosophy and not a creed.[30]

A key event in the foundation of modern Buddhism is the publication in 1881 of Olcott's *Buddhist Catechism,* which he compiled after reading ten thousand pages of Buddhist books from English and French sources.[31] The monks to whom he showed the draft threw out overt or hidden elements of theosophy, but they agreed to the final version.

The *Catechism* contains almost everything that is found in modern Buddhism, though it also excludes much. Insofar as Olcott used French and English translations of texts and expositions of Buddhist doctrine, it was inevitable that the *Catechism* should be oriented to a Western intellectual view of Buddhism. Olcott noted that the missions "taught that Buddhism was a dark superstition" and that the few government schools that existed did not teach the religion at all (p. 31).[32] Consequently, he made the not unusual outsider's inference that "our Buddhist children had but small chance of coming to know anything at all of the real merits of their ancestral faith" (p. 36).[33] Olcott was ignorant of the fact that Sinhala children were traditionally educated in Buddhism in a variety of ways. Like many intellectuals of our own time, he implicitly accepted the Orientalist critique of Buddhism. Olcott speaks of *dēvales* (shrines) for Hindu-derived gods (*dēvas*), located adjacent to Buddhist temples, as an "excrescence on pure Buddhism, left by the Tamil sovereigns of former days" (p. 42).[34] This condemnation of popular religion is carried over into the *Catechism* and spelled out in detail there.

Q: What was the Buddha's estimate of ceremonialism?

A: From the beginning, he condemned the observance of ceremonies and other external practices, which only tend to increase our spiritual blindness and our clinging to mere lifeless forms. . . .

Q: Are charms, incantations, the observance of lucky hours and devil dancing a part of Buddhism?

A: They are positively repugnant to its fundamental principles. They are surviving relics of fetishism and pantheism and other foreign religions. In the Brahmajāla Sutta the Buddha has categorically described these and other superstitions as Pagan, mean and spurious.

Q: What striking contrasts are there between Buddhism and what may be properly called "religions"?

A: Among others, these: It teaches the highest goodness without a creating God; a continuity of line without adhering to the superstitious and selfish doctrine of an eternal, metaphysical soul-substance that goes out of the body; a happiness without an objective heaven; a method of salvation without a vicarious Savior; redemption by oneself as the Redeemer, and without rites, prayers, penances, priest or intercessory saints; and a *summum bonum,* that is, Nirvāṇa, attainable in this life and in this world by leading a pure, unselfish life of wisdom and of compassion to all beings (pp. 41–42).[35]

Olcott was the son of a Protestant minister, and it should not surprise us that he introduced a Protestant and "purified" form of Buddhism. He also used the words of the missionary lexicon—*idolator, pagan,* and so forth—a vocabulary further developed later by his disciple Dharmapāla to castigate the Christians themselves. Olcott did not concern himself overly with public morality, but he roundly condemned polyandry and polygyny and extolled monogamy as the proper kind of marriage—all in the name of the Buddha (who we know was simply not interested in such mundane matters). The British had already legislated monogamy as the only legal marriage, and Olcott's vindication of it soon found a sympathetic audience among the newly emerging indigenous bourgeoisie.

The most systematic modernist aspect of the *Catechism* is a justification that the doctrine is not only perfectly compatible with "science" but also vindicated by modern science. Early in the *Catechism* Olcott poses the question whether the karma theory is consistent with modern science and replies, "Perfectly consistent: there can be no doubt about it" (p. 29).[36] He then develops this theme in a whole section entitled "Buddhism and Science" (pp. 76–87).[37] Here he justifies Buddhism as a "scientific religion" and notes its support of education and science. But perhaps the most interesting part is where he justifies the supernormal powers of the Buddha and the saints (*arahants*) in terms of contemporary scientific experiments on "auras." Like his own capacity for healing, which he argued was based on "animal magnetism" and hypnosis, the powers of Buddhist saints were simply products of mental cultivation and meditation. Here then is a striking feature of modern Buddhism in contrast with evangelical fundamentalism: it was perceived as perfectly congruent with science.

The foregoing discussion suggests that, by its redefinition of doctrinal Buddhism, Indology created the beginnings of Buddhist "fundamentalism," in the sense of a return to a pristine Buddhism suited to the modern world. The reification and transfer of this fundamentalism into Sri Lanka and elsewhere was the work of Olcott, whose *Catechism* was translated into twenty-two languages and went into at least forty editions in his own lifetime. The Sinhala translation was employed in Buddhist schools, and a variety of similar works in both English and Sinhala appeared soon afterward. The modern Buddhist curriculum in practically all schools has been influenced, directly or indirectly, by the *Catechism.* However, the transfer of the *Catechism* into Buddhist nations cannot explain its acceptance by the Buddhist populace of laypersons and monks. The minimum requirement for the acceptance of Buddhist fundamentalism contained in the *Catechism* depended on the emergence of educated laypersons in the very schools created by Olcott and his successors in Sri Lanka. With this emergence the leadership of Buddhism ceased to be the exclusive preserve of monks.[38] Perhaps Olcott anticipated what would eventually have happened anyway as Buddhist nations moved toward modernity.

Olcott's selective reification of pure Buddhism shares a feature of the Buddhist doctrinal tradition as a whole: it is in fact quite benign! It cannot produce the sound and fury that one normally associates with fundamentalism. It is true that in the popular imagination this form of Buddhism has been reified and even fetishized; but it is difficult to produce from this body of doctrine a law of the Father for whom one can go to war, or to associate it with a violated motherland. I have shown elsewhere that this form of Buddhist modernism led to the decline of the tradition of stories that concretized the abstract doctrine and ethics. These stories went to constitute the Buddhist conscience; consequently this may have had the effect of weakening that conscience and indirectly loosening the moral bulwark against violence.[39] Nevertheless I think it is the case that neither the Pāli canon nor its selective reification in the *Catechism* can arouse the passions or provide justifications for the violence that one associates with contemporary monotheistic fundamentalisms. Yet it is undeniable that a powerful passion is associated with the ethnic conflict in Sri Lanka by all parties involved. As far as the Sinhala Buddhists are concerned, the answer is relatively clear: it does not come from Buddhist soteriology; it comes from Buddhist history.

The Resurrection of Buddhist History

The attempt to bring together Buddhist history and a catechistic or doctrinal fundamentalism was not the work of Olcott but of his disciple, the great religious reformer Anagārika Dharmapāla, whose life and career are now well known.[40] Dharmapāla was Olcott's protégé and secretary of the Buddhist Theosophical Society that Olcott founded. Like Olcott, Dharmapāla was interested in Buddhist fundamentalism and ecumenism, but unlike him Dharmapāla was centrally interested in Buddhist history. Olcott moved mostly with Buddhist intellectuals, whereas Dharmapāla was influenced by the powerful orator monk Guṇānanda, who, as noted earlier, led public debates against Christian missions. The antagonism against the missions masked a deeper antagonism against British rule. It was Guṇānanda's adoption of the missionary style of discourse that soon began to take the place of the more sedate (even somnolent) style of monkish sermons. I do not want to go into the details of that history here; suffice it to say that Dharmapāla, in addition to his other roles, soon became a founder of an anti-imperialist and antimissionary movement. Olcott had little understanding of Dharmapāla's populism and little sympathy for it. Ultimately Olcott and Dharmapāla fell out, ostensibly over an argument regarding the sacred tooth relic, which Olcott claimed was an animal bone. For Dharmapāla, who knew Buddhist history, this relic was intrinsically associated with the sovereignty of Sinhala-Buddhist kings. To treat it disparagingly was to disparage Buddhist history. Dharmapāla was a fundamentalist of Olcott's type: he reified the Orientalist canon, downplayed the jātaka tales and the Buddha legend, and was almost totally ignorant of what I have called intermediate texts. His knowledge of Buddhism came primarily from Orientalist sources. But as a patriotic anti-imperialist he also wanted to mobilize Sinhalas against the British regime. To do this it was necessary to reify Buddhist history. Let me quote a few extracts from his voluminous writings.

You should assault the lawless British wherever you see them. In front of every house make a scarecrow of the white man with banana trunks, deck the scarecrow with a pair of trousers, and beat it in front of your children. Then when your children grow up they will assault the alien British.[41]

The sweet gentle Aryan children of an ancient historic race are sacrificed at the altar of whiskey-drinking, beefeating belly god of heathenism [i.e., Christianity]. How long, oh! how long will unrighteousness last in Lanka.[42]

Arise, awake, unite and join the army of Holiness and Peace and defeat the hosts of evil.[43]

My message to the young men of Ceylon is . . . Believe not the alien who is giving you arrack, whisky, toddy, sausages, who makes you buy his goods at clearance sales. . . . *Enter into the realms of our King Duṭugämuṇu in spirit and try to identify with the thoughts of that great king who rescued Buddhism and our nationalism from oblivion.*[44]

Dharmapāla upheld the Sinhala past as an ideal worth resurrecting. "There exists no race on earth today that has had a more triumphant record of victory than the Sinhalese."[45] The present degradation is due to evil Western influence—both missionary and colonial. The country, as he perceives it, is Sinhala-Buddhist, and there is hardly a place for "filthy Tamils" and Muslims who are viewed as exploiters. Christians are condemned as meat eaters of "low caste." "The country of the Sinhalese should be governed by the Sinhalese."[46] The old themes about the land and its peoples have been resurrected once again.

This Buddhist history, redefined and elaborated in a variety of ways, exists in confrontation with the very recently invented yet equally polemical Tamil-Hindu history. These are the discourses that scorn compromise. Here reigns passion, physical and polemical violence, the quest for boundaries, the isolation and the demeaning of the Other. Buddhist history can coexist with the benign fundamentalism derived from the doctrines, but the two can hardly be reconciled. In my exhaustive reading of Dharmapāla's work, in both Sinhala and English, it is impossible to come across passages that bring the doctrinal tradition into harmony with the historical. This was also the dilemma of King Duṭugämuṇu. His Buddhist conscience, like Asoka's, was tormented by the killing of his enemies; ironically the monks console him by saying that the killing of the enemy is justified. The discourse of these monks is impossible to reconcile in terms of fundamentalist ethics; they were articulating a vision of Buddhism that was not doctrinal, but invented and activated during a period of internal turmoil and waiting to be revived at appropriate historical moments. Even today in the context of the interethnic struggle, one can hear plenty of talk about Buddhist (and Tamil) history, but very little of a fundamentalist justification for it.

What then is the fate in Buddhism of the other critical feature of monotheistic fundamentalism, namely, its attempt to reconstitute the present in terms of a scriptural ideal of a righteous social order? Because there has been no such ideal in the Buddhist scriptural tradition, it can only be invented. Buddhist intellectuals have attempted to invent an economic ethics and schemata for living in the Theravāda societies of Asia, the most famous being the Sarvōdaya movement of Sri Lanka.[47] But here is the irony: the moment one invents an economic ethics or a blueprint for a new social order on the basis of the doctrinal tradition, it tends to be quite benign, as the doctrines themselves are! There is no passion, no violence in them: all one could say of them is that they are unrealistic, naive, or downright fatuous. What then about the histories? Do they contain such ideals? The histories provide charters for ethnic violence, but they do not provide models for a new revitalizing social order. It is therefore no accident that Dharmapāla himself idealized capitalism in its Japanese and American forms, and modern political leaders are quite content with some form of Western socialism or capitalism. Thus, however one looks at modern Buddhism, it hardly fits the label *fundamentalism*. To resolve this issue one must go back to the problem sketched at the beginning of this essay, namely the idea of nation and nationalism, for it is this idea rather than fundamentalism that has family resemblances to the past of Sri Lankan Buddhism, particularly in its conception of the sāsana institutionalized in the physical space of that entity, Sri Lanka.

Conclusion: Fundamental Implications of Buddhist Fundamentalism

It seems to me that what Buddhists are attempting to do is to construct a new cultural identity that will ipso facto be a national identity in the modern sense of belonging to a nation and a state, if not a nation-state. Quite unlike their ancestors the idea of a nation or nation-state is thoroughly familiar to Sri Lankans, owing to a powerful, yet little discussed, legacy of colonialism—that it provided a ground for socializing colonies and training colonial bureaucrats and politicians on the virtues of the modern state. Many of the founders of the independent movements in the colonies studied in the imperial capitals, and, even if they were Marxist, they were imbued with the idea of the modern state as centrally organized and manifesting an overall political unity. It is doubtful whether their experiences in England, France, or Germany provided them with models for political or cultural pluralism. Such pluralism was, however, a fact of their home situation. To construct an axiomatic identity that paralleled the idea of British or French or German nationhood was a well-nigh impossible task. Much easier and more appealing is the already available resource—that of ethnicity, however defined—for in it are contained the crucial features necessary to both ethnicity and nationhood, the taken-for-granted or axiomatic nature of that identity. But this form of creating nationhood can even minimally work in the modern world only if there is a relative degree of cultural homogeneity. If there is a significant minority like the Tamils, then there is going to be a strong resisting force. In the dialogical contestations that govern ethnic conflict the two contending parties begin to mirror each other's aspirations, both attempting to construct some political position that is based on a common or shared ideological stance ("ethnicity") in which the fundamental idea is that of birth in a land, an idea that in turn is enveloped in myths and metaphors that tap a huge emotional reservoir. In relation to the Sri Lankan ethnic conflict one must not forget that Buddhism is not the only issue; Catholic Sinhala speakers have had to invent their own ideological stance based on other metaphors, but minimally involving the idea of language, birthright, and land. And what about the Sri Lankan Tamil Catholics? Neither type seems to exist in the scholarly literature on the Sri Lankan "ethnic conflict," since their presence confounds the notion of both ethnicity and fundamentalism.

The question worth posing in light of the Buddhist example is, How much of the preceding discussion throws light on the monotheistic fundamentalisms? It is hard to deny that the moving force in these religions is also a sense of history, and a resurrection or an invention of a past that offers a vision for the present and the future. But more than this: it is also an attempt to create a larger entity out of this ideological vision—something that resembles "nation." This is what the "Islamic fundamentalism" of the Iranian Revolution achieved and what the several monotheistic fundamentalisms are attempting to achieve. They all have a similar vision: the fact that they have not achieved this vision is irrelevant, because all fundamentalisms must begin with a vision and most of them will in all likelihood end up with nothing more than the vision. But the failure of a group of people or a "sect" to transform the vision into a larger sociopolitical conception that could be realistically implemented must not lead us to underrate the power of this vision. For this vision is locked into issues of personal identity as well as that of the cultural identity of the group or sect. In some places, like the United States, there is little likelihood of creating a "nation united under God" on the basis of a fundamentalist vision; but it would be naive of us to believe that some fundamentalist groups cannot create other unifying transsectarian entities that might even challenge the order of the secular nation-state. Others will simply continue to believe in their faith privately, like "fundamentalists" everywhere, without much political or public fuss.

What is happening in the erroneously labeled Hindu fundamentalism is not altogether different, except that one can actually see the invention of a transforming axiomatic ideology and identity, namely, that of "Hinduness." Since "Hindu" is a modern invention, it is tautological to talk of a traditional Hindu fundamentalism. There was no canon that could constitute a rationale for fundamentalism and no unifying history and accompanying institutional arrangements that could form the basis for uniting the various communities and kingdoms on the subcontinent. The unifying entity "India" was created by colonialism and, as in Sri Lanka, accepted by its politicians and peoples. One can argue that a secular, democratic ideology is necessary for India's survival as a viable political entity, but it is doubtful that it can serve as a transforming ideology for a plurality of people. What then from the past, from history, can create such a transforming ideological vision? Not the Vedas: they are not a canon in the narrow monotheistic sense, or in the broad Buddhist sense of something contained in baskets. They are sacred texts, not a depository of doctrine. Moreover there are hundreds of thousands of texts and doctrinal corpuses, mostly "revealed." Revelation was everywhere, from medical texts to village myths. Given this situation, one can understand why the attempts by the Arya Samaj to search for a canon and to locate it in the Vedas was futile.[48] For even if people were to acknowledge the Vedas as authoritative, they cannot provide a unifying vision for a new sense of Hinduness. Many traditional texts have conceptions of an ideal social order, but such conceptions are for the most part locked into caste ideology. Social thinkers from Dayananda to Ananda Coomaraswamy were compelled to make naively idealistic interpretations of caste. Modern religious reformers reacting against a secular and pluralistic polity also feel the need to reconstitute their history, an enormously difficult task in a landmass that has many histories, but no single unifying history. Hence the contemporary relevance of the epics: the Rāmāyaṇa and Mahābhārata are the only master narratives that straddle the subcontinent. Though located in a specific part of India, they can be delocalized and relocalized in their continual narrative retellings. For example, the *karaiyar* castes of Tamil Nadu and Sri Lanka could, until recently, imagine themselves as descendents of the *kauravas* of the Mahābhārata. The new localization of Rāma's birth place by the Hindu nationalists is an attempt to reconstitute a foundational myth for the new Hinduism, which is simultaneously a new nationalism. Conjoined with a set of cultural practices, this myth can produce a kind of unifying communal consciousness that must inevitably, and in devastating fashion, produce a violent confrontation with those groups who must with equal inevitability challenge its hegemonic and totalizing vision.

"A unifying communal consciousness": in Buddhism this is an old game! Therefore let me end at the beginning. The *Mahāvaṃsa* that defined the idea of Buddhist history and particularized its conception of sāsana was written in the fifth century. Every single Buddhist history since that time takes it as axiomatic that the country is Buddhist. The land is sacred soil blessed by the Buddha; the tree under which the Buddha achieved enlightenment is no longer in India but here in Sri Lanka, in the sapling planted by Mahinda, Asoka's own son according to the texts. The saplings of that sapling as well as the relics of the Buddha are enshrined in sacred spots at different points throughout the length and breadth of the island; kings are Buddhist sovereigns and guardians of the religion. These ideas receive concrete manifestation in the obligatory pilgrimage. The problem is that nowadays people are trying to translate these ideas of being Buddhist into modern political conditions that do not permit them to succeed and instead provide violent confrontations. Ironically, in the context of the present Fundamentalism Project, a glimmer of hope for the future might well lie in a Buddhist fundamentalism that could perhaps mitigate the dark underside of the political religion that I have called Buddhist history. But what about the Tamil Hindus? What benign fundamentalism do they have to fall back into? What hope . . . ?

Notes

This article is part of a larger project on the national and international dimensions of the current "ethnic" conflict in Sri Lanka between the Sinhalas, the Tamils, and the Muslims; and of the crucial internecine conflict between the government and the radical youth among the Sinhalas themselves. The project was supported by a grant from the John D. and Catherine T. MacArthur Foundation.

1. For a discussion of the differences between Buddhist and monotheistic religions, see Gananath Obeyesekere, "The Rebirth Eschatology and Its Transformations: A

Contribution to the Sociology of Early Buddhism," in Wendy Doniger O'Flaherty, ed., *Karma and Rebirth in Classical Indian Traditions* (Berkeley: University of California Press, 1980), pp. 137–64 ; and S. N. Eisenstadt, "Fundamentalism, Phenomenology, and Comparative Dimensions," chap. 11 in this volume.

2. See *The Mahāvaṃsa, or The Great Chronicle of Ceylon,* trans. and ed. Wilhelm Geiger (London: Pali Text Society, 1980), p. 29.

3. Ibid., pp. 146–227.

4. Ibid., p. 178.

5. Stanley J. Tambiah, *World Renouncer and World Conqueror* (Cambridge: Cambridge University Press, 1976).

6. *Mahāvaṃsa,* pp. 1–13.

7. Ibid., pp. 51–61.

8. Benedict Anderson, *Imagined Communities: Reflections on the Origin and Spread of Nationalism* (London: Verso, 1983), p. 74.

9. Emile Durkheim, *Elementary Forms of the Religious Life,* trans. Joseph Ward Swain (London: George Allen and Unwin, 1954), pp. 205–34.

10. I draw heavily upon my article "The Buddhist Pantheon in Ceylon and Its Extensions," in Manning Nash, ed., *Anthropological Studies of Theravāda Buddhism,* Cultural Report Series no. 13 (Detroit: Cellar Bookshop, 1966), pp. 1–26. In using the term *obligatory pilgrimage* I was influenced by Gustave E. von Grunebaum's *Muhammedan Festivals* (New York: Schuman, 1951), pp. 15–51.

11. Durkheim, *Elementary Forms of the Religious Life,* pp. 209–19.

12. I am indebted to my colleague Abdellah Hammoudi for information on the return of the hajji.

13. The Kandyan rulers from the time of Sri Vijaya Rājasinha till the reign of the last king, Sri Vikrama Rājasinha (1798–1815), were South Indian Nayakkars. See C. S. Dewaraja, *The Kandyan Kingdom, 1707–1760* (Colombo: Lake House Press, 1972).

14. For a discussion of the king's women, see Gananath Obeyesekere, *The Work of Culture: Symbolic Transformation in Psychoanalysis and Anthropology* (Chicago: University of Chicago Press, 1982), pp. 201–14.

15. These texts were until recently freely available as broadsheets sold in public places. For details on *Mādevi katāva,* see Gananath Obeyesekere, *The Cult of the Goddess Pattini* (Chicago: University of Chicago Press, 1984), pp. 238–39, 572–74.

16. Premadasa was assassinated in 1993.

17. For details, see Obeyesekere, *The Cult of the Goddess Pattini,* pp. 306–12.

18. Ibid., pp. 521–28.

19. See Sigmund Freud, *Group Psychology and the Analysis of the Ego,* standard ed., vol. 18 (London: Hogarth Press, 1981), p. 69.

20. Eugen Weber, *Peasants into Frenchmen: The Modernization of Rural France, 1870–1914* (Stanford: Stanford University Press, 1976).

21. Richard Helgerson, *Forms of Nationhood: The Elizabethan Writing of England* (Chicago: University of Chicago Press, 1992).

22. For details of this controversy, see Stanley J. Tambiah, *Buddhism Betrayed* (Chicago: University of Chicago Press, 1992); R. A. L. H. Guṇṇāwardana, "The People of the Lion: The Sinhala Identity and Ideology in History and Historiography," in Jonathan Spencer, ed., *Sri Lanka: History and the Roots of Conflict* (London: Routledge, 1990), pp. 45–85; and K. N. O. Dharmadasa, "'People of the Lion': Ethnic Identity, Ideology, and Historical Revisionism in Contemporary Sri Lanka," *Ethnic Studies Report* 10, no. 1 (Colombo: International Centre for Ethnic Studies, 1992), pp. 27–59.

23. Steven Collins, "On the Very Idea of the Pali Canon," *Journal of the Pali Text Society* 15 (1990): 89–126.

24. *The Minor Readings: The First Book of the Minor Collection,* trans. Bhikkhu Nanamoli (London: Pali Text Society, 1978), p. 3.

25. For further information on intermediate texts, see Ranjini Obeyesekere and Gananath Obeyesekere, "The Story of the Demoness Kali: A Discourse on Evil," *History of Religions* 29, no. 4 (1990): 318–34.

26. See Kitsiri Malalgoda, *Buddhism in Sinhalese Society: A Study of Religious Revival and Change* (Berkeley: University of California Press, 1976).

27. Cited in ibid., p. 230.

28. Gananath Obeyesekere, "Buddhism and Conscience: An Exploratory Essay," *Daedalus* (Summer 1991): 219–39.

29. I have since qualified my views on Olcott in a paper delivered in Sri Lanka, "The Two Faces of Colonel Olcott: Buddhism and Eurorationality in Nineteenth-Century Sri Lanka." In this paper I deal with some of the irrational elements in Olcott's theosophy and show that the Buddhist monks in Sri Lanka were instrumental in Olcott's conversion to Theravāda Buddhism.

30. S. Karunaratne, *Olcott's Contribution to the Buddhist Renaissance* (abridged version of Olcott's diary, *Old Diary Leaves*) (Colombo: Ministry of Cultural Affairs, n.d.), p. 58; Henry Steel Olcott, *The Buddhist Catechism* (Colombo: Ministry of Cultural Affairs, n.d.), p. 4.

31. Olcott, *Buddhist Catechism*, p. 4. Hereafter, pages are given in text.

32. Ibid., p. 31.

33. Ibid., p. 36.

34. Ibid., p. 42.

35. Ibid., pp. 41–42.

36. Ibid., p. 29.

37. Ibid., p. 76–87.

38. For details, see Malalgoda, *Buddhism in Sinhalese Society;* and Richard F. Gombrich and Gananath Obeyesekere, *Buddhism Transformed: Religious Change in Sri Lanka* (Princeton: Princeton University Press, 1988).

39. Obeyesekere, "Buddhism and Conscience"; Gananath Obeyesekere "Duṭṭhagāmaṇi and the Buddhist Conscience," in Douglas Allen, ed., *Religion and Political Conflict in South Asia* (Westport, Conn.: Greenwood Press, 1992), pp. 135–60.

40. See Gananath Obeyesekere, "Sinhalese-Buddhist Identity in Ceylon," in George de Vos and Lola Romanucci-Ross, eds., *Ethnic Identity: Cultural Continuities and Change* (Palo Alto, Calif.: Mayfield Publishing Co., 1975); Gombrich and Obeyesekere, *Buddhism Transformed*, pp. 202–24; Sarath Amunugama, "Anagārika Dharmapāla (1864–1933) and the Transformation of Sinhala Buddhist Organization in a Colonial Setting," *Social Science Information* 24, no. 4 (1985): 697–730.

41. Cited in David Karunaratne, *Anagārika Dharmapāla* (in Sinhala) (Colombo: M. D. Gunasena and Co., 1965), p. 103, my translation.

42. Anagārika Dharmapāla, *Return to Righteousness: A Collection of Speeches, Essays, and Letters of the Anagārika Dharmapāla,* ed. Ananda Guruge (Colombo: Government Press, 1965), p. 484.

43. Ibid., p. 660.

44. Ibid., p. 510, my italics.

45. Ibid., p. 735.

46. Cited in Ananda Guruge, Introduction to Dharmapāla, *Return to Righteousness,* p. lvii.

47. See Gombrich and Obeyesekere, *Buddhism Transformed,* pp. 243–55.

48. For details, see Daniel Gold, "Organized Hinduisms: From Vedic Truth to Hindu Nation," in Martin E. Marty and R. Scott Appleby, eds., *Fundamentalisms Observed* (Chicago: University of Chicago Press, 1991).

4

New Disciplinary Approaches
and Interpretations

Fundamentalism, Phenomenology, and Comparative Dimensions

S. N. Eisenstadt

Fundamentalism is often seen as an antimodern phenomenon, as a sort of eruption of strong traditional forces that were repressed, as it were, by modern regimes, by modernity, by modern cultural programs—just as contemporary ethnic movements have sometimes been described as such an outbreak of natural primordial forces suppressed by the ideology of Enlightenment and of the modern nation-states. Yet this is not the case with respect to either the ethnic or the fundamentalist movements. Fundamentalism is not an eruption of long-suppressed natural forces, nor is it a manifestation of resentment by traditional circles against the existing ways of the religious establishment, about the depravity of contemporary mores or some vague millenarian dream about good old days, or about the original good state of mankind. In fact, fundamentalism is a thoroughly modern phenomenon. It is not only that chronologically movements have been called fundamentalist that have emerged only in the nineteenth century, originally among Protestant groups in the United States. Later this term was applied also to other movements—first of all in Islam, later in Judaism, then, albeit in different modes, in other civilizations, especially Hinduism and Buddhism. These latter movements—beyond the original Protestant ones—did not call themselves fundamentalists; they were rather so dubbed by Western scholarly and more general discourse.

Nor is it the close relation between fundamentalist movements and organizational and communication technologies that is of crucial importance here.

Beyond these—no doubt very important—aspects of the relations of fundamentalist movements to modernity is the fact that these movements are characterized by a highly elaborate ideological and political construction that is part and parcel of the modern political agenda—even if their basic ideological orientations and symbols are antimodern.

Axial Civilizations—Bridging the Transcendental and Mundane Orders

Truly enough, modern fundamentalist movements share many characteristics with what may be called protofundamentalist ones, with movements of religious reconstructions that developed above all in those religions or civilizations that have a broad space for reinterpretation and reconstruction of the basic religious visions and premises and of their major institutional applications—that is, especially the so-called axial civilizations.[1]

By Axial Age civilizations (to use Karl Jaspers's nomenclature), I refer to those civilizations that crystallized during the thousand years from 500 B.C.E. to the first century C.E., within which new types of ontological visions, of conceptions of a basic tension between the transcendental and mundane orders, emerged and were institutionalized in many parts of the world—in ancient Israel, later in Second Commonwealth Judaism and Christianity, ancient Greece, Zoroastrian Iran, early imperial China, Hinduism and Buddhism, and, beyond the Axial Age proper, Islam.

The crystallization of these civilizations can be seen as a series of some of the greatest revolutionary breakthroughs in the history of mankind, which changed the course of human history. The central aspect of these revolutions was the emergence and institutionalization of new basic ontological conceptions of a chasm between the transcendental and mundane orders referred to above. These conceptions, which first developed among small groups of autonomous, relatively unattached "intellectuals"—such as prophets or visionaries (a new social element at the time)—particularly among the carriers of models of cultural and social order, were ultimately transformed into the basic "hegemonic" premises of their respective civilizations; that is, they have become institutionalized. That is, they became the predominant orientations of the ruling and many secondary elites, fully embodied in their respective centers or subcenters—as was the case for instance in the institutionalization of the monotheistic vision attributed to Moses in ancient Israel, or of Confucianism, or of Christianity.

The development and institutionalization of such conceptions of a basic tension, a chasm between the transcendental and mundane orders, gave rise in all these civilizations to attempts to reconstruct the mundane world–human personality and the sociopolitical and economic order according to the appropriate transcendental vision, to the principles of the higher ontological or ethical order. The given, mundane, order was perceived in these civilizations as incomplete, inferior, often as bad or polluted—at least in some of its parts—and as in need of being reconstructed by bridging over the chasm between the transcendental and the mundane orders, according to the precepts of the higher ethical or metaphysical order—that is, in Weberian terms, "salvation"—basically a Christian term, some equivalents of which are to be found in all the axial civilizations. All these civilizations developed a very strong urge to implement the transcendental vision or visions prevalent in them.

The political order as the central locus, or one of the central loci, of the mundane order was usually conceived as lower than the transcendental order and so had to be restructured according to the precepts of the latter—above all according to the perception of the proper mode of overcoming the tension between the transcendental and the mundane order, of "salvation" or of the implementation of the appropriate transcendental vision. It was the rulers who were usually held to be responsible for organizing the political order according to such precepts.[2]

Alternative Visions and Heterodoxies in Axial Civilizations

These new modes of reconstruction of the social and civilizational orders and of social and cultural change gave rise to continuous tensions in the very premises of these civilizations and, above all, in their institutionalization. The root of such tensions lies in the fact that the institutionalization of the perception of the tension between the transcendental and the mundane order and of the quest to overcome this tension, generates an awareness of a great range of possibilities or visions of the very definition of such tensions and of the proper mode of their resolution, as well as an awareness of the partiality or incompleteness of any given problem of institutionalization of such vision. Moreover such institutionalization was never a simple peaceful process. It has usually been connected with a continuous struggle and competition between many groups and between their respective visions.

This very multiplicity of alternative visions gave rise in all these civilizations to an awareness of the greater range in the possible definitions of such tension and, above all, of alternative modes of overcoming this tension, of alternative ways of salvation and of the possibility of constructing alternative social and cultural orders. No single definition or resolution could be taken any longer simply as given.

This very multiplicity of alternative visions led to an awareness in all civilizations, of the potential uncertainty of different roads to salvation, of the existence of alternative conceptions of social and cultural order, and of the seeming arbitrariness of any single solution. The consciousness of such alternatives became a constituent element of the structuring of self-awareness in these civilizations, especially among the carriers of their great traditions. It was closely related to the development of a high degree of "second-order" thinking, of reflexivity that was inspired by the awareness of alternative means of bridging the chasm between the transcendental and mundane orders.[3]

From the point of view of their contents or orientations, such alternative visions tended to develop in several directions and combinations. One such direction was to reformulate the nature of the tension between the transcendental and mundane orders—for example, the Buddhist reformulation of the premises of Hinduism or the Christian reformulation of the premises of Judaism.

Another direction was to deny (either in highly ideological terms with strong transcendental orientations or in more simple terms of little tradition) the emphasis on the tension between transcendental and mundane orders. This could lead to a "return," usually among small groups of intellectuals, to a highly sophisticated conception of parallelism between the transcendental and mundane orders (as for instance among some Gnostic circles) and to concomitant attempts to go back to a pretranscendental, "preaxial" state, and in the periphery, to a deaxialization of the predominant orientations.[4]

A third direction was to elaborate a great variety of religious and intellectual orientations—above all the mystical and esoteric ones—which go beyond any given, established, routinized, and orthodox version of the resolution of the transcendental tension. Such elaborations may be related to the development of strongly antinomian tendencies negating ideologically the tendencies to rationalization inherent in most such official resolutions of the conception of the chasm between the transcendental and mundane orders.

A fourth direction was—as can be seen among many Christian monastic groups or among the Indian renouncers—to uphold the prevalent conceptions and ideals in their pristine form, as against their necessarily compromised concretization in any institutional setting.

All these alternative visions were usually combined with the perennial themes of social protest—themes such as the emphasis on equality and solidarity, on the suspension of social division of labor, and the like.

Utopian Visions in Axial Civilizations

Out of the combination of the conception of possible alternative roads to salvation, of alternative cultural and social orders, and the structuring of the time dimensions, there emerged utopian visions of an alternative cultural and social order beyond any given place or time.[5] Such visions contained many of the millenarian and revivalist elements that can be found in pre–Axial Age or nonaxial civilizations such as Japan as well; but they go beyond them by combining them with the search for an alternative "better" order beyond the given one, a new social and cultural order that will be constructed according to the precepts of the higher transcendental order and which will negate and transcend the given one.

These alternative visions usually contained a high potential for reconstruction of the basic conceptions of ontological reality, of the conception of the transcendental order as well as and of their relations to the basic institutional conceptions and of the relations between them, which were institutionalized in these civilizations. Some such visions often denied the validity of the very definitions of ontological reality upheld in the respective civilizations. Most of them, however, were oriented above all against the specific concrete relationship between such definitions and institutional premises (the ground rules that regulated the different arenas of social life), that is, against the concrete institutionalization of such definitions of their institutional spheres. These visions were usually articulated by special actors who presented themselves as the bearer of the pristine religious and/or civilizational visions of these civilizations. Illustrations of such carriers are the holy men of antiquity, the Indian or Buddhist renouncers, Christian monks, and the like—in other words, religious virtuosi, who often stood in some dialectic relationship to the existing ways of institutionalizing the transcendental visions, often acting from within liminal situations. These actors often attempted to combine such visions with wider movements of protest.[6]

Protofundamentalist and Fundamentalist Utopias

Protofundamentalist and the later modern fundamentalist movements—which in some cases built on the tradition of the earlier protofundamentalist ones—constitute one type of such utopian movements.

Protofundamentalist movements constitute one of the utopian heterodoxies that develop in these civilizations, although the contents of their utopias differ, of course, from what has usually been conceived by the term *utopian*. They usually developed together, side by side with many other types of religious movements—especially different types of reformist ones, as well as different types of popular religiosity. The basic characteristics of protofundamentalist—and fundamentalist—movements and ideologies crystallize through their confrontation with such other movements, as well as with the existing religious establishments and ways of life of their respective societies.

Like other sectarian utopian movements, protofundamentalist (and fundamentalist) movements also promulgate visions of an alternative cultural and social order beyond any given place or time, certainly beyond the given place and time. Such visions emphasize the necessity to construct the mundane order according to the precepts of the higher transcendental one, with the search for an alternative "better" order beyond the existing one.

In common with other utopian programs, protofundamentalist (and fundamentalist) movements entail an eschatological vision that combines the reconstruction of the mundane world according to a sharply articulated transcendental vision. In contrast, however, to the so-called progressive utopias of the modern era, many of which were grounded in older Christian eschatological visions which promulgated visions of the unfolding of a semieschatological progress entailing the continuous expansion of reason, the fundamentalist movements tend to envisage the reconstruction of the world according to a past-oriented vision.

Fundamentalist utopias are also aiming at a future reconstructed according to their vision. But their vision aims at the reconstruction of the existing order, according to what is promulgated as the pristine "original" vision of the given religion—a vision most fully realized in the past—and they are oriented against the existing situation into which religion has degenerated. Similarly, in contrast to so-called progressive utopias, modern fundamentalist movements do not emphasize social or individual emancipation and reconstruction.

As do other utopian sectarian groups, protofundamentalist and fundamentalist movements emphasize very strongly the construction of sharp symbolic and institutional boundaries; they stress the distinction between purity and pollution—the purity of the internal fundamentalist community as against the pollution of the outside world.[7] They are highly totalistic-ideological, attempting to construct a self-enclosed universe that demarcates and organizes clearly all arenas of life. The strong tendency to rituals and ritualization that developed in these groups was closely related to such attempts.

Modern Fundamentalist Movements

All these characteristics became more fully developed in the modern fundamentalist movements.

The fullest crystallization of the fundamentalist movements and ideologies took place indeed in modern times, and the encounter with modernity has shaped many of the most distinctive features of these movements. While the modern fundamentalist movements share many of these characteristics—especially the utopian orientation—with the protofundamentalist ones, they tend to construct their visions in specifically modern ways.

The close relations of fundamentalist movements to modernity are manifest, first of all, as I have alluded to above, in many of their organizational characteristics, such as the very tight partylike discipline, and in the use of modern communication technologies and modern propaganda techniques. The composition of these movements, as we shall see in greater detail later on, has also differed greatly from that of the protofundamentalist movements of earlier periods, very much in line with the composition of some of the more militant modern movements.

But it is above all with respect to some of their ideological features, to the mode of construction of their ideologies, that the relations between the fundamentalist movements and the modern world, modernity, are most conspicuous. Here we encounter yet another rather paradoxical situation. The basic ideology of fundamentalism is antimodern: the negation of some of the basic tenets of modernity—of the autonomy of the individual, of the hegemony of reason, of the ideology of progress, and the like—and of modernity as a civilization, although not necessarily of its technological or organizational aspects.

Yet at the same time most fundamentalist ideologies—the different ideologies of the various fundamentalist movements in their common orientations—exhibit some very distinct modern characteristics.

The most important of these characteristics is their strong predisposition to develop not only a totalistic worldview and patterns of organization, which is characteristic of many "traditional" sectarian movements, including the protofundamentalist one, but also overarching totalitarian all encompassing ideologies, which emphasize a total reconstitution of the social and political order, and which espouse a strong universalistic, missionary zeal. These characteristics of the modern fundamentalist movements are reminiscent of the great revolutions.[8] Just as the great revolutions had their roots in the heterodoxies of the axial civilizations within which they developed, so did the fundamentalist movements, especially those that developed in the monotheistic civilizations; and just like the great revolutions, they have transformed these heterodox tendencies into potentially full-fledged political programs and missionary visions.

Many of the fundamentalist movements share also with the great modern revolutions the belief in the primacy of politics—albeit in their case of religious politics or of politics guided by a totalistic religious vision to construct society, or sectors thereof.[9]

As with many revolutions, the fundamentalist movements tend also to minimize the importance of primordial components of collective identity—as against the universalistic religious ones—for instance, the Islamic against the Iranian ones.

The emphasis on primordial components becomes strong only in special cases—first of all in cases, like in Judaism, in which the primordial orientations constitute a basic component of the universal religion, in which nationalist fundamentalist orientations are predominant.

Second, such emphasis on primordial elements may become, paradoxically enough, strong in especially otherworldly civilizations, like Hinduism or Buddhism, the religious premises of which are not—as we shall see in greater detail later on—very conducive to the development of pure pristine fundamentalist orientations.

In other words, these movements bear within themselves the seeds of very intensive and virulent Jacobinism, seeds that can, under appropriate circumstances, come to full-blown fruition. The fundamentalist movements are among the bearers and promulgators of modern Jacobin components and orientations, and they impose such Jacobin orientations on the more traditional ways of life—making the ideological formulation of a pristine tradition into the overarching basic organizing principle.[10]

This strong totalitarian, Jacobinlike component or orientation is visible first in the attempts to effect the reconstruction of the centers of their respective societies in which they develop, in the almost total conflation of center and periphery, negating the existence of intermediary institutions and association—of what can sometimes be called civil society.

Second, this potential Jacobin element can be found in the strong tendency to sanctification of the reconstruction of the center as a continuous liminal arena, and third, in the closely related tendency to missionary expansionism.

Because of this Jacobin tendency or predisposition, these movements face a continuous tension—a tension that is inherent in most sectarian movements, but that is exacerbated in the modern fundamentalist ones, between the strong participatory orientations—rooted very much in the modern conceptions of center-periphery relations—which develop within them, and the authoritarian ones inherent in their basic ideologies.

The strong modern components of many of the fundamentalist movements—even of the most extreme ones—can also be seen in some aspects of their institutionalization. When the Islamic revolution triumphed in Iran, it did not abolish the most modern of institutions—basically without any roots in Islam—such as the parliament and election to it. Both the Majlis and the mode of election to it were reconstructed—with some very strong Jacobin elements, clothed in an Islamic garb. Interestingly enough, one of these garbs—the institutionalization of a special Islamic court to supervise "secular" legislation—was not so far removed from the special place of judicial institution that is characteristic of modern constitutional regimes, even from the principle of judicial revision.[11]

Reconstruction of Tradition—Tradition as Ideology

Thus, the antimodern attitude that develops within the fundamentalist vision is not just a reaction of traditional groups to the encroachment of new ways of life, but a militant ideology which is basically couched in a highly modern idiom.

While in many ways the fundamentalist movements are reactive, this general designation can also be applied to other, for instance reformist, movements; hence, it does not delineate the specific characteristics of the fundamentalist movements.

The way in which fundamentalist movements and groups reconstruct tradition and select different themes from the reservoir of theories available to them differs greatly from that of the various reformist movements.

The most important such selection is the very emphasis on some original pristine vision or symbol of a tradition—especially on some book or some pristine canon, or for instance on the sanctity of the Land of Israel in the ideology of Gush Emunim—as the main, even the single, focus of the tradition.

It is not, however, just the selection of a certain theme or symbol of tradition as against others that is characteristic of the various fundamentalist movements. It is rather the attempt at the totalization of this vision that is crucial here—the subordination of different aspects and layers of tradition under the presumed implications of this single principle and their concomitant hierarchization.

The same is, of course, true of the emphasis on some basic pristine premise embodied in some text—whether in the form of a book, or a message, or even a set of symbols.

The central characteristic of the movements' "reaction" to modernity is their totalistic construction of a closed utopian-sectarian vision and its legitimation in terms of ideologized tradition.

Such constructions of the fundamentalist utopian universe are accordingly characterized by several paradoxes.

Although seemingly traditional, in fact these movements are in some paradoxical way antitraditional. They are antitraditional in the sense that they negate the living tradition, with its complexity and heterogeneity, and instead they uphold a highly ideological conception of tradition as an overarching principle of cognitive and social organization.

Thus, fundamentalist traditionalism is not to be confused with a "simple" or "natural" upkeep of a given tradition. Rather, it denotes an ideological mode and stance oriented against new developments; it promulgates certain themes of the tradition as the only legitimate symbols of the traditional order and upholds them against the existing situation.

The fundamentalist groups espouse a principled denial of interpretation, which does, of course, in itself constitute a distinct, new and innovative mode of interpretation.

The fundamentalists are oriented in principle against any innovation or lenience within the existing traditions—even if such innovation has been a continuous component in such tradition. The Hatam Sofer's—a major figure in modern Eastern European fundamentalist Jewish Orthodoxy in the first half of the nineteenth century—famous injunction that "anything new is forbidden from Torah" went against the great and continuous tradition of interpretation and innovation that characterized the classical (medieval and early modern) Jewish tradition. Such injunctions and attitudes were in fact themselves innovations—but innovations presented as representations of simple, pristine, "old" tradition.[12]

Fundamentalist movements are accordingly characterized by a *principled*—though not easily observed in practice—differentiation between different layers of "tradition" in terms of their relation to the pristine vision, and especially by the ideological symbolization of many customs, such as pattern of dress, calendrical observance, and the like, which can be used as markers of collective identity, to demarcate the boundaries between the internally pure space and the externally polluted one.

As many other such sectarian-ideological movements, the fundamentalist ones also exhibit a very low threshold of tolerance of ambiguity on both personal and collective levels.

In practice they may often waver between, on the one hand, sharp segregation between "traditional" (ritual, religious) and nontraditional spheres of life, without developing any strong connective symbolic and organizational bonds between the two, and, on the other hand, a strong predisposition or demand for some clear unifying principles that would connect and unify both arenas.

As a result, a tendency can develop toward "ritualization" of the symbols of traditional life, on the personal and collective levels alike. Increasing attempts to impose traditional symbols on the new secular world in relatively rigid, militant ways may then alternate with the total isolation of these traditional symbols from the impurities of that world.

The Heterodox Nature of Fundamentalist Movements

In close relation to this attitude to tradition, fundamentalist movements are characterized by yet another paradox. Although these movements present themselves as the pure orthodoxy of their respective religion, in fact, in any given situation they are heterodoxies, in sharp conflict with the existing religious establishment and ways of life. Indeed, in many cases the leaders of the fundamentalist movements were intellectuals with strongly antinomian tendencies, their antinomianism being above all oriented against the prevalent modes of interpretation of tradition.

The basically heterodox nature of the fundamentalist movements is evident also in the fact that within any single religion there may develop, at any single point, not one but several fundamentalist movements.

Such variety may be due to different sociopolitical circumstances or to changing constellations of the relation between the various fundamentalist groups with the political rulers and of the possible incorporation of some of the fundamentalist themes or symbols by the rulers.

However, such variety is also inherent in the very nature of the religious sectarian dynamics of these religions, and of the fundamentalist movements themselves. Although each such movement claims to be the only representative of the original pristine vision of its religion, in fact they all are new constructions, and they may differ with respect to which aspect or symbol of their religion they portray as the essence of the original pristine vision.

One of the clearest illustrations of the almost coterminous development of different fundamentalist movements in the fold of the same religion can be found in contemporary Israel, where both the anti-Zionist haredim and the ultranational Gush Emunim claim to present the pristine vision of Judaism.[13]

Yet another illustration of such variety of fundamentalist or protofundamentalist movements can be found in the quite numerous revivalist Islamic movements in the eighteenth century.[14]

Differing Directions of Fundamentalist Visions and Movements

There are, of course, far-reaching differences in the intensity and direction of different fundamentalist and protofundamentalist movements, in the extent to which they are totalistic, and to which they attempt to shape all arenas of life, as well as in their rigidity, especially the differentiation between internal and external, pure and polluted forces. Such differences were already fully visible in the protofundamentalist movements of different axial civilizations.[15]

These differences were shaped first of all by those very conditions that generated them. First, these differences were influenced by the concrete definitions of the chasm or tension between the transcendental and mundane orders, especially whether the basic chasm between them was couched in relatively secular terms (as in Confucianism and classical Chinese belief systems and, in a somewhat different way, in the Greek and Roman worlds) or the tension was conceived in terms of a religious hiatus (as in the great monotheistic religions, and in Hinduism and Buddhism). Within the latter cases, an important distinction is the one between the monotheistic religions, in which there was a concept of God standing outside the universe and potentially guiding it, and those systems, like Hinduism and Buddhism, in which the transcendental cosmic system was conceived in impersonal, almost metaphysical terms, in a state of continuous existential tension with the mundane system.

Second, such differences were influenced by the conception of salvation, of the soteriological bridge prevalent in the respective civilizations, of the nature of the transcendental vision or visions, as having to be implemented in the respective civilization. Here, following Weber, the primary distinction is between purely this-worldly, purely otherworldly, and mixed this- and otherworldly conceptions of salvation. It is probably no accident that the "secular" conception of this tension was connected, as in China, Greece, and Rome, with an almost wholly this-worldly conception of salvation, or that the metaphysical nondeistic conception of this tension, as in Hinduism and Buddhism, tended toward an otherworldly conception of salvation. The great monotheistic religions, by contrast, tended to stress combinations of this- and otherworldly conceptions of salvation. The ontological conceptions also influence what constitutes the embodiment of this pristine vision in the fundamentalist movements of these civilizations seen as such embodiments by different fundamentalist groups.

The fundamentalism, which developed within the fold of American Protestantism, focused on a book—on the Bible—as the embodiment of the original as the guide for the reconstruction of the world. This was probably to a large extent also the case in Islam. In both these cases one book was seen as the direct source of ultimate authority—not mediated by any institution such as church or pope and hence accessible to all believers. But not all the axial civilizations saw a book as such an embodiment.

While the New Testament did of course play a very important role in Catholic (as well as eastern) Christianity, it did not attain the same position as the Old Testament in Protestantism or the Qur'an in Islam. This might have been due to two interconnected facts: the very strong emphasis on mediation through the pope and church in Catholic Christianity and of the church in eastern Christianity, and the fact that, unlike the Old Testament and Qur'an, the prescriptive legal dimension is not very strong in the New Testament.

In Judaism, the situation was more complex; the Jewish Bible—the "Old Testament"—did not enjoy in the Jewish tradition such authority as the Qur'an or the Bible in Protestantism. It was, at least in rabbinical Judaism, open to many interpretations. Indeed, the Karaite movement, which denied the validity of the oral law and harked back only to the Old Testament, constituted probably the first fundamentalist movement to develop within the fold of rabbinical Judaism—or rather, to be more accurate, in conjunction with the full institutionalism of this Judaism. Later on different aspects of the oral law, sometimes in combination with the Bible, could serve as the foci of the different fundamentalist visions.[16]

In other axial civilizations such original, pristine vision may be embodied not necessarily in a book or in its interpretation, but in other arenas or in other exemplary religious experiences.

Distinctions between Orthodoxy and Heterodoxy

These various ontological conceptions and the conceptions of what constitutes the locus of the pristine transcendental visions have also greatly influenced, among others, the mode of distinction and confrontation between orthodoxy and heterodoxy or sectarianism that developed in these civilizations, and hence also some of the most important characteristics of the protofundamentalist and fundamentalist movements that developed in these civilizations.[17]

From the point of view of such distinction, the most crucial difference is between those civilizations to which it is legitimate to apply the term *heterodoxy* and those in which it is more appropriate to talk "only" about sects and sectarianism.

The term *heterodoxy* is applicable only to cases when one can talk about orthodoxy, and this term is in its turn a certain type of both organizational and cognitive doctrinal structure.

Organizationally the crucial aspect is, of course, the existence of some type of organized church that attempts to monopolize at least the religious arena and usually also the relations to the political powers. But of no lesser importance is the doctrinal aspect—the organization of doctrine, that is, the very stress on the structuring of clear, cognitive, and symbolic boundaries of doctrine.

With respect to both the organizational and the doctrinal aspects, the major difference among the Axial Age civilizations is between the monotheistic civilizations in general and Christianity in particular on the one hand, and, on the other, Hinduism and Buddhism, with Confucian China constituting a sort of in-between type.

It is within Christianity that these organizational and doctrinal aspects of orthodoxy developed in the fullest way. Thus it was in Christianity that there developed full-fledged churches that constituted potentially active and autonomous partners of the ruling coalitions. In Judaism and Islam these developments were weaker. There developed rather powerful, but not always as fully organized and autonomous, organizations of clerics.

But of no lesser importance is the fact that in Christianity and to a smaller, yet not insignificant, degree also in Judaism and Islam, there developed strong tendencies to the structuring of relatively clear cognitive doctrinal boundaries.[18]

First, this tendency was rooted in the prevalence, within the monotheistic civilizations in general and within Christianity with its stronger connections to the Greek philosophical heritage, of strong orientations to the cognitive elaboration of the relations among God, man, and the world. Second, this tendency was rooted in the fact that, in all these monotheistic religions, with their strong otherworldly orientation, the mundane world was seen—even if in different degrees—as at least one focus of otherworldly salvation, and hence the proper designation of such activity became a focus of central concern and of contention between the ruling orthodoxies and the numerous heterodoxies that developed within them.

The importance for the struggle between orthodoxies and heterodoxies, of the structuring of such cognitive boundaries, of the elaboration of visions, of the reconstruction of the mundane world according to transcendental otherworldly vision, is best seen, in a seemingly negative way, in the cases of Hinduism and Buddhism.[19]

In both these cases we find, despite a very strong transcendental and otherworldly orientation, that the structuring of cognitive doctrines (as distinct from ritual) and above all of their bearing on mundane matters, did not constitute a central aspect or premise of these religions or civilizations. Hence even when, as in Buddhism, it is not impossible to talk about something akin to church—albeit a much more loosely organized one—it is very difficult to talk about heterodoxy. At the same time sectarianism abounds, Buddhism itself being in a sense a sect developing out of Hinduism.

Hence the various Hindu sects, Buddhism itself, did indeed have far-reaching impact on the structuring of the mundane arenas of their respective civilizations. First, they extended the scope of the different national and political communities and imbued them with new symbolic dimensions. Second, they could also change some of the bases and criteria of participation in the civilizational communities, as was the case in Jainism, in the Bhakti movement, and, of course, above all in Buddhism, when an entirely new civilizational framework was constructed.

Buddhism introduced new elements also into the political scene—above all that special way in which Sangha—the Buddhist "clergy," usually politically a very compliant group, could in some cases, as Paul Mus has shown, become a sort of moral conscience of the community, calling the rulers to some accountability.

But this impact was of a different nature from that of the struggles between the reigning orthodoxies and the numerous heterodoxies that developed within the monotheistic civilizations. Of crucial importance has been the fact that in these latter cases a central aspect of such struggles was the attempt to reconstruct the political and cultural centers of their respective societies and that, because of this, these struggles became a central part of the central political processes in these civilizations—processes that often lead to or were connected with wars of religion.

Here indeed the comparison between Protestantism and Catholicism is of great interest. It is not accidental that it was within Protestantism, especially sectarian Protestantism, that fundamentalism developed in some of its most crystallized ways, while such developments were always much weaker in Catholic Christianity—their fullest crystallization being always confronted by the mediating functions of the pope and the church.[20]

The fullest development of the various characteristics of protofundamentalist movements and ideologies analyzed above takes place, first, in those religions and civilizations in which the mundane world constitutes a major arena for the implementation of the transcendental vision with strong otherworldly components. In other words, such tendency is stronger in those civilizations in which transcendental vision, the basic conception of salvation, does include a very strong this-worldly orientation but which is not exclusively this-worldly, or, in other words, in which there is a strong emphasis on the reconstruction of the mundane world on the basis of a transcendental otherworldly vision. It is in such religions or civilizations that the political dimensions of fundamentalism become strongest.

Second, such tendency is stronger in those civilizations in which there is relatively heavy emphasis on doctrine and on logocentric exposition thereof, and in which it is relatively easy to identify a clear version.

Third, such tendency to the development of fundamentalist ideologies and movements is stronger in those axial civilizations in which no institution or group monopolizes the access to the interpretation thereof, thus increasing the range of possible interpretation and above all facilitating the possibility of any group's presenting itself not just as opposing the existing religious authorities and their interpretation of religion, but as embodying the true vision of their religion.

But under some probably rather exceptional circumstances, even within these civilizations, there may develop sects or groups with very strong fundamentalist movements. The Sikh case—albeit a case of a monotheistic sect—is one such exception.[21] In Theravāda Buddhist countries, in which already in medieval times there developed a strong tendency to conflate Buddhism with specific countries (as can perhaps be least seen in medieval Ceylon or Sri Lanka), fundamentalist seeds were planted—to flourish in modern times.[22]

However, even in those axial civilizations, in which there is a strong emphasis on mediation and a strong otherworldly orientation, protofundamentalist tendencies may indeed develop, but they are usually weak or the contents of their utopian vision will be less fully articulated or structured—and their internal organization is looser and their orientation to the political arena weaker.

Extent of Development of Fundamentalist Movements

Such differences in the ontological conceptions prevalent in different civilizations—especially the relative centrality of the political arenas in their soteriological conceptions—also greatly influence the extent of development of fundamentalist movements in modern times. They influence the extent to which the Jacobin tendencies crystallize fully in different movements according to the basic premises of the respective religions within which they develop and according to changing historical conditions.

Such Jacobin tendencies are strongest, most fully manifest, in the more politically oriented fundamentalist movements, but the seeds thereof are to be found in all of them. Given, however, the centrality of the political dimension in the expansion of modernity—even in otherworldly civilizations, such as Buddhism and Hinduism—there may develop fundamentalistlike religious movements with strong political orientations, and many political movements tend to clothe themselves in religious, often fundamentalist garb. Thus, as Gold has shown, there developed in India several trends of Hindu fundamentalism.[23] But these fundamentalist movements had to use Western colonial structures and to invent doctrinal moral contents or canons—in ways contrary to whatever was seen as the center of "classical" Hinduism. Such inventions entailed attempts at a soteriological revaluation of the political arena, far beyond what existed in the historical tradition of these civilizations.

The same is true—even if to a smaller extent, given the stronger political orientations of Theravāda Buddhism—of Buddhist countries, especially of Sri Lanka, even if there may in these circumstances develop other apolitical fundamentalist orientations, groups, or movements.[24]

In all these societies and civilizations fundamentalist ideologies constitute only one mode of response to processes of change, and their importance varies greatly in different situations and settings.

Timing of Fundamentalist Development

Fundamentalist movements tend to arise in periods of rapid social and cultural change, especially in situations in which there develop— as a result of either internal economic and technological developments, of the internal expansion of the religions, of impingement of other civilizations or cultures, or of some combination of all these factors—growing differentiation, growing diversity of ways and styles of life.

Such diversification, the crystallization of many new heterogeneous modes of life, usually weakens the hold of existing traditions on many arenas of life, tends to differentiate between different layers of tradition, and gives rise to many arenas that are, as it were, "tradition-neutral."

While the impingements of external forces, especially those of technology and of other civilizations, may make some groups see many such developments as polluted, it is above all in situations when all these are seen by some groups as a threat to the basic premises of their civilization that fundamentalist—and earlier on protofundamentalist—movements tend to arise. The most central focus of such a threat is not just the feeling among some groups that many sectors of the society, and above all the religious establishment, deviate from the traditional life and give in to the temptation of power, an easy life, and the like. It is rather when such developments are seen by some groups as being closely interconnected with the potential undermining of the basic premises of their religion by emphasis on what seem extrareligious criteria, above all by "reason" or the like. The tension between reason and some ultimate religious premise or commandment—above all, as in the monotheistic constructions, revelation—has been part of the internal tensions of most axial civilizations. In those situations in which the impact of internal change and internal impingement may be seen as undermining, in the name of autonomous reason—however defined—the ultimate religious premises and their hegemony, the tendency to development of fundamentalist movements becomes strongest.

The most central focus of the attack of fundamentalist movements is that many sectors of the society, and above all the religious establishment, deviate from the traditional life and give in to the temptation of power and wealth.

Fundamentalist movements develop among those groups that perceive their civilizations—the basic religious premises of their civilization—as threatened by others, especially by the component of reason; in modern times by modern (Western) civilization. But they gathered momentum in situations and periods when there occurred certain political and ideological weakening of Western civilizations—or of the nonfundamentalist, often reformist regimes in different non-Western societies—and when the perception of such weakening became relatively strong among active religious groups, as was the case after the October War and the oil shortage in the West.

In such situations, the encounter with fundamentalism became part of the internal Western discourse. This was also true of many of the encounters between fundamentalists and the predominant liberal groups in the United States. Indeed, it was in this discourse that these movements were dubbed fundamentalist, and the confrontations between them and the predominant rebel secular or religious groups have sometimes been portrayed in terms of an internal "Western" cultural discourse, and have often been perceived as internal cultural critique.

Who Participates?

The social groups or categories that promulgate the various fundamentalist visions and those that are responsive to such promulgation vary greatly in different civilizations, but they seem to share several common characteristics. Probably their most common shared characteristic is dislocation from the more central (not only in economic, but also in cultural) sectors of the economy and from sociopolitical centers.

It is not just "simple" economic deterioration or dispossession that is of importance here, although these processes may greatly help in generating fundamentalist predispositions. Rather, the crucial fact is the dispossession from (old and new) cultural and political centers. The promulgators of fundamentalist vision tend to come mostly from older and new intellectual groups that are dispossessed, or feel that they are dispossessed, or banned from access to the center.

One most vivid illustration of such processes of dislocation can be found in Iran under the Shah.[25] It is not only the dislocation of the Shi'ite clergy from strong positions in the cultural center or close to it that is of importance here. Of no smaller importance has been that the worldly, mobile occupational and professional groups, which developed to no small extent as part of the processes of modernization, controlled by the Shah, were barred from any autonomous access to the new political center or participation in it—very much against the premises inherent in these processes.

The broader sectors that tend to be responsive to such messages are not necessarily the lowest economic echelons. They are probably the middle or lower echelons of more traditional economic and broader groups, who either experience some downward social and occupational mobility or feel that their occupations and ways of life have lost their traditional standing as being worthwhile or as epitomizing virtues that are highly valued in terms of the central vision of the religion and society. Needless to say, the extent and exact location of such groups in various societies should constitute one of the most important topics of research.

It is with respect to the composition of the fundamentalist groups—the leaders and the followers—that some important differences between premodern (proto)fundamentalist and modern fundamentalist movements can be indicated. In contrast to the premodern situations, in which the major bearers of the fundamentalist vision were usually some sectors of the traditional religious leaders and communities, in modern fundamentalist movements a much more central part was played by various "modern" educated groups—professionals, graduates of modern universities, and the like—who find themselves dispossessed from access to the centers of their respective societies.

The scope of the fundamentalist movements, their impact on their respective societies, depends greatly first on the extent to which the feeling of dispossession from the respective centers of their societies and of threat to their respective civilizations is widespread among the different sectors of these societies. Second, such scope and impact are dependent on the placement of the more active fundamentalist leaders in their respective society and on the resonance of broader, potentially or actually dispossessed groups to the messages of these leaders.

The basic characteristics of fundamentalist movements, of their leaders and followers, also greatly influence the processes of their institutionalization. But the analysis of these processes is beyond the scope of this paper.

Notes

1. Shmuel N. Eisenstadt, "Cultural Traditions and Political Dynamics," *British Journal of Sociology,* no. 2 (1981); "The Axial Age: The Emergence of Transcendental Visions and Rise of Clerics," *European Journal of Sociology* 23, no. 2 (1982): 294–314.

2. Shmuel N. Eisenstadt, ed., *The Origins and Diversity of Axial Age Civilizations* (New York: State University of New York Press, 1986); *Kulturen der Achsenzeit,* 3 vols. (Frankfurt: Suhrkamp Verlag, 1992).

3. See Shmuel N. Eisenstadt and Ilana Friedrich Silber, eds., *Knowledge and Society: Studies in the Sociology of Culture: Past and Present,* vol. 7 (London: JAI Press, 1988), particularly S. N. Eisenstadt, "Explorations in the Sociology of Knowledge: The Soteriological Axis in the Construction of Domains of Knowledge," pp. 1–72.

4. For some instances of deaxialization, see Erik Cohen, "Christianity and Buddhism in Thailand: The 'Battle of the Axes' and

the 'Contest of Power,'" *Social Compass* 38, no. 2 (1991): 115–40.

5. Adam B. Seligman, "The Comparative Studies of Utopias," "Christian Utopias and Christian Salvation: A General Introduction," and "The Eucharist Sacrifice and the Changing Utopian Moment in Post-Reformation Christianity," in A. Seligman, ed., *Order and Transcendence* (Leiden: E. J. Brill, 1989), pp. 144; Shmuel N. Eisenstadt, "Comparative Liminality: Liminality and Dynamics of Civilization," *Religion* 15 (1985): 315–38.

6. Ilana Friedrich Silber, "Opting Out in Theravada Buddhism and Medieval Christianity: A Comparative Study of Monasticism as Alternative Structure," *Religion* 15 (1985): 251–78.

7. Mary Douglas, *Purity and Danger* (London: Routledge and Kegan Paul, 1966).

8. On the dynamics of the great revolutions and their roots in the axial civilizations, see Shmuel N. Eisenstadt, "Frameworks of the Great Revolutions: Culture, Social Structure, History, and Human Agency," *International Social Science Journal* 133 (August 1992): 385–401.

9. On the primacy of politics in the great revolutions, see Claude Leforte, *Democracy and Political Theory* (Minneapolis: University of Minnesota Press, 1988), pp. 57–163; John Dunn, "Totalitarian Democracy and the Legacy of Modern Revolutions—Totalitarian Democracy and After," International Colloquium in Memory of Jacob L. Talmon, Jerusalem, 21–24 June 1982 (Jerusalem: Hebrew University, 1984), pp. 37–56; François Furet, *French Revolution* (New York: Macmillan, 1970); idem., *Interpreting the French Revolution* (Cambridge: Cambridge University Press, 1981). On the primacy of politics in many contemporary Islamic fundamentalist movements, see Bassam Tibi, *The Crisis of Modern Islam* (Salt Lake City: University of Utah Press, 1988).

10. On the Jacobin components of modern political discourse, see Albert Cochin, *La crise de l'histoire révolutionnaire* (Paris: H. Champion, 1969); *La révolution et la libre pensée* (Paris: Plon-Nourrit, 1924); *Les sociétés des pensées et la démocratie: Études de l'his-*toire révolutionnaire (Paris: Plon-Nourrit, 1921); and *L'esprit du jacobinism* (Paris: Presses Universitaires de France, 1979).

11. See, for instance, Said Amir Arjomand, "Constitutions and the Struggle for Political Order: A Study in the Modernization of Political Traditions," *European Journal of Sociology* 33 (1992): 39–82.

12. Michael K. Silber, "The Emergence of Ultra-Orthodoxy: The Invention of a Tradition," in J. Wertheimer, ed., *The Uses of Tradition* (Cambridge: Harvard University Press, 1992).

13. Samuel C. Heilman and Menachem Friedman, "Religious Fundamentalism and Religious Jews: The Case of the Haredim," and Gideon Aran, "Jewish Zionist Fundamentalism: The Bloc of the Faithful in Israel (Gush Emunim)," in Martin E. Marty and R. Scott Appleby, eds., *Fundamentalisms Observed* (Chicago: University of Chicago Press, 1991), pp. 197–264, 265–344.

14. John O. Voll, "Fundamentalism in the Sunni Arab World: Egypt and the Sudan," and Abdulaziz Sachedina, "Activist Shi'ism in Iran, Iraq, and Lebanon," in Marty and Appleby, *Fundamentalisms Observed*, pp. 345–402, 403–56; Tibi, *The Crisis of Modern Islam*.

15. Many of the implications of these differences were explicated in Eisenstadt, *The Origins and Diversity of Axial Age Civilizations* and *Kulturen der Achsenzeit*.

16. On the Karaites, see Salo W. Baron, *A Social and Religious History of the Jews*, vol. 6 (New York: Columbia University Press, 1958); Z. Cohen, "The Halakha of the Karaites," unpublished thesis, New York, 1936; "Karaites," in *Encyclopaedia Judaica* (Jerusalem: Keter, 1971), 10:775–85; Zvi Ankori, *Karaites in Byzantium* (New York: Columbia University Press, 1959); Leon Nemoy, ed., *Karaite Anthology: Excerpts from the Early Literature* (New Haven: Yale University Press, 1952).

On rabbinical Judaism, see Haim Hillel Ben-Sasson, *History of the Jewish People*, part 5 (Cambridge: Harvard University Press, 1970); Isadore Twersky, *Rashi* (in Hebrew) (Merhavia: Ha-Po'alim Press, 1946); Ephraim E. Urbach, *The Sages: Their Con-*

cepts and Beliefs (Jerusalem: Magnes Press, Hebrew University, 1975); Joseph Dan and Frank Talmage, eds., *Studies in Jewish Mysticism* (Cambridge, Mass.: Association for Jewish Studies, 1982); Joseph Dan, *Jewish Mysticism and Jewish Ethics* (Seattle: University of Washington Press, 1985); Jacob Katz, *Tradition and Crisis* (New York: Free Press of Glencoe, 1961); idem., *Exclusiveness and Tolerance* (London: Oxford University Press, 1961); Yosef H. Yerushalmi, *Zakhor* (Seattle: University of Washington Press, 1975); Gershom Scholem, *The Messianic Idea in Judaism* (New York: Schocken Books, 1971); idem., *Major Trends in Jewish Mysticism* (New York: Schocken Books, 1961); Raphael J. Z. Werblowsky, *Joseph Karo: Mystic and Lawyer* (London: Oxford University Press, 1962); Haim Hillel Ben-Sasson, *Rezef u-temurah* (Continuity and variety) (Tel Aviv: 'Am 'Oved, 1984).

17. On the distinction between orthodoxy and heterodoxy in general, see Shmuel N. Eisenstadt, "Heterodoxies, Sectarianism, and Dynamics of Civilizations," *Diogene* 120 (1982): 5–26; and *Kulturen der Achsenzeit.*

18. See the various papers in Eisenstadt and Silver, *Knowledge and Society.*

19. On sects in Hinduism and Buddhism, see Friedhelm Hardy, *Virama Bhakti: Early Development of Krsna Devotion in South India* (Oxford University Press, 1981); J. Lele, ed., *Tradition and Modernity in Bhakti Movements* (Leiden: E. J. Brill, 1981); K. Schormer and W. H. McLeod, eds., *The*

Saints: Studies in a Devotional Tradition of India (Berkeley and Delhi: 1985; John B. Carman and Frederique A. Margolin, eds., *Purity and Auspiciousness in Indian Society* (Leiden: E. J. Brill, 1985); S. C. Malik, ed., *Dissent Protest and Reform in Indian Civilization* (Simla: Indian Institute for Advanced Study, 1973).

20. See J. Coleman, "Catholic Integralism as a Fundamentalism," in C. Kaplan, ed., *Fundamentalism in Comparative Perspective* (Amherst: University of Massachusetts Press, 1992), pp. 74–95.

21. T. N. Madan, "The Double-Edged Sword: Fundamentalism and the Sikh Religious Tradition," in Martin E. Marty and R. Scott Appleby, eds., *Fundamentalisms Observed,* pp. 594–627.

22. Donald K. Swearer, "Fundamentalistic Movements in Theravāda Buddhism," in Marty and Appleby, *Fundamentalisms Observed,* pp. 628–90.

23. D. Gold, "Organized Hinduisms: From Vedic Truth to Hindu Nation," in Marty and Appleby, *Fundamentalisms Observed,* pp. 531–93; Swearer, "Fundamentalistic Movements in Theravada Buddhism."

24. See Gananath Obeyesekere, chap. 9 in this volume.

25. See, for instance, Farrokh Moshiri, "From Westernization," in Jack A. Goldstone, Ted R. Gurr, and F. Moshiri, eds., *Revolution of the Later Twentieth Century* (Boulder, Colo.: Westview Press, 1991).

Fundamentalism as a Comprehensive System: Soviet Marxism and Islamic Fundamentalism Compared

Ernest Gellner

Refuting the Secularization Thesis

If one were asked some twenty years ago to sum up the conventional wisdom about the role of religion in human society in our age, it would run roughly as follows, in three propositions.

1. By and large, the secularization thesis is correct. Religion used to be important, is less so now, and is getting even less so. The most naive and common theory would be an intellectualist one: the evidence has gone against the propositional content of religion, and this has undermined belief in it. People more sophisticated sociologically would adopt instead some kind of variant of either the Durkheimian or the Weberian theory of why religion is declining. According to Durkheim, religion is the expression of social organization, and in an anomic, fluid society, the weakness of the social organization is reflected in the weakness of its ritual expression. That is why secularization is taking place.[1] The Weberian view holds that, among religions, the most powerful in the end turned out to be a form of religious life that cut its own throat, through rationalizing its own beliefs; in the end, it rationalized itself out of existence.[2]

In these and other versions of the secularization thesis, it is assumed that religion has lost much of its social and political clout.

2. Nevertheless, religion is dreadfully tenacious among the educationally less privileged strata of society. This is a kind of Enlightenment sadness of the enlighteners: while preaching Enlightenment among sensible people like ourselves, the philosophers looked at the masses and despaired—how is one ever going to eradicate all those dreadful superstitions? Religion, although declining, is nevertheless strangely tenacious.

3. One of the by-products of secularization was the emergence of secular religions, functionally similar to religion, but which in their doctrinal content were careful to

stay within the limits of this world, and try to share in the prestige of science. Among these kinds of secular religions the one which had by far the greatest social impact, and which in effect became a major world religion and the official doctrine of a number of important states and of some unimportant ones, was Marxism. Secular religion was expected to resemble the literal religions in terms of its tenacity.

This was the conventional wisdom. Yet the conventional wisdom has been refuted twice over by two major events of our age. If the conventional wisdom was indeed what I say it was, then it is incorrect for a number of reasons. First, secularization simply has not taken place within Islam.[3] The hold of Islam over both the masses and the elite in Muslim countries is as strong now as it was a hundred years ago, and in some ways it is stronger. Thus, whatever merit there is in the logic of the secularization argument, it does not seem to apply in at least one of the four major culture zones of the Old World, even if it holds in various ways in the other three. An interesting question is, why not? The failure of the secularization thesis to hold in one large and important zone constitutes a part of its refutation.

On the whole, the West has only noticed this in connection with the Iranian revolution, and since the recent emergence of militant fundamentalist movements in various parts of the Middle East and North Africa. The phenomenon is in fact much older—approximately a hundred years old—but Westerners failed to observe it. The contentious aspect of this claim is: there is a continuity between the reformation that has been taking place in Islam over the past hundred years, and the politically more obvious movements which have emerged recently. These recent movements, in other words, are merely the more visible—the noticeable—part of the iceberg.

The conventional wisdom has also been refuted by the dramatic events since 1985 and particularly of 1989, which demonstrated that, although Marxism clearly resembles world religions in other ways, it does not seem to have the same tenacity. Its failure—its lack of hold over the psyches of the populations who had been subjected to it—is really quite astonishing. Here there really is something about which one can ask, where are the snows of yesteryear? The faith has gone to an astonishing degree, and the interesting question is, why so? Given that this belief system did in *other* ways resemble religion, and given that early on it had a very, very powerful hold over many people, why did it fail to sustain this hold?

To get into the factual basis of my question, it seems to me obvious that the Marxist world and the Soviet Union, up to approximately the age of Khrushchev, was a zone of faith. I read with care, for instance, Sakharov's memoirs.[4] Sakharov was a supremely intelligent man, who, moreover, in his professional interests was concerned with questions which overlapped with Marxist themes and theses. Wherever they overlapped on concrete points, he had a complete and total contempt for Marxism, for its specific propositions. He despised its Lamarckism, the poor quality of its mathematics, and its scholasticism. Nevertheless, he accepted it as a totality, as a kind of general vision. He acknowledged that a very dramatic and profound social transformation, a transformation of the human condition, was taking place as a result of and under the inspiration of the October Revolution. Although he had a deep contempt for Marxist epistemology and all the specific theses with which it was connected, he accepted the vision as a whole and in outline. In that respect and others he was not at all untypical. And then, of course, something happened during the period of stagnation, in the period between Khrushchev and Gorbachev, which thoroughly and, it seems, definitively undermined that faith.

So we have two phenomena which contradict the conventional wisdom: the powerful hold of Islam, and the weak hold of Marxism. This essay is an attempt to highlight this interesting contrast.[5]

Stages of History

The two areas are mirror images of each other from the viewpoint of Westerners committed to liberal values. We have the curious contrast of the Marxist world, totally devoid of its faith, but possessed of a strong longing for Civil Society. A rather interesting phenomenon is the reemergence of that phrase, its migration from the dullish area of history of ideas into a living political slogan—and, by contrast, the Muslim world, where the craving for Civil Society, though not wholly absent, is sadly weak, but where the literal Faith is astonishingly strong. How are these phenomena—these two rather neatly paired phenomena—to be explained?

To begin with, allow me to offer a slightly megalomaniac brief summary of world history—of the intellectual history of mankind. Mankind has passed through four stages, and here I must acknowledge Fustel de Coulanges, Emile Durkheim, Karl Jaspers, and Shmuel Eisenstadt. The first stage, the Durkheim–Fustel de Coulanges stage, was one in which the religious life of mankind was essentially centered on ritual, and religion was basically the choreography of social life. I accept the Fustelian-Durkheimian thesis.[6]

Stage two, the Axial Age as proposed by Jaspers and as reintroduced by Eisenstadt, is based on the idea that there was at a certain stage a crucial shift of gravity from ritual to doctrine.[7] This, of course, had enormous social implications, because it meant that religion became detached from any particular social-political-ethnic group, and became a kind of platonic entity, which can and does sit in judgment on the societies which adhere to it.

The subsequent stage three is fairly short (things always get foreshortened because we take our own period more seriously), and could also be called stage 2b, in that doctrine continues to be central. This third stage is anticipated in the Reformation but really begins with the Enlightenment and runs to 1989. The period remains axial—you still have doctrine that claims to be independent of any one society, and to sit in judgment on the entire social order—but this time the doctrine is this-worldly. The basic view of the Enlightenment was that mankind had been subject to priests and kings, to false doctrine and oppression, tyranny, hierarchy—to illegitimate hierarchy—but a newly emerging true doctrine will also engender a just social order. The Enlightenment's central correlation was false doctrine with oppression, and true doctrine with liberation. When the French monarchy collapsed through financial bankruptcy and other reasons, this doctrine failed to work. As thinkers considered this failure and attempted to find the answer, Marxism emerged as the most famous, the best orchestrated, and the most influential of the solutions.

Marxism held that the Enlightenment was right in the end in proclaiming the possibility of a just social order based on truth, just as previously there had been an unjust order accompanied by illusion. According to Marx, it is not quite as simple as that, however, because we must combine the Enlightenment insight with the functionalism of the reactionaries (who claimed, in defense of the old order, that the injustices are socially functional). In other words, Marxism sought to understand the functionality of the social injustices and determine how they can be removed. The reactionary functionalists were 98 percent right, so much the Marxists admitted, but it's the 2 percent which counts: the functional systems are not completely functional, and they will eventually come unstuck. And, at the end of time, there will still be a just order, based on truth. This view, of course, persuaded a lot of people, and found its implementation from 1917 onward. But by 1989 it was abandoned for various reasons, which are part of my problem.

At that point, we come to the fourth stage of human history, which I shall, without prejudice but with malice, call the "Californian" stage. It is characterized by the abandonment of the Enlightenment supposition that the society based on science and powerful technology will have a social order rooted in the true understanding of nature. In its place there is a firm detachment of social belief from economically and technologically operational belief. This is, technologically, a most sophisticated society, in which, however, as the phrase has it, "anything goes," and a kind of total permissiveness in belief prevails. The social order partly relies on effective knowledge, and partly tolerates any old belief in the spiritual life of its members.

This is my background schema. Fundamentalism, as we have been studying it, is a phenomenon largely connected with the emergence of stage four. This leads to a point about the strategy of defining fundamentalism.

Defining Fundamentalism

I am tactically in disagreement with a discussion which includes "reactiveness" in the very definition of fundamentalism. I prefer not to actually include this trait in the definition, but just say that, *in fact,* fundamentalisms are reactive. The reason for such a procedure is, if we refrain from including it in the definition, we can perceive more clearly the connection between fundamentalism and the earlier phenomena to which the fundamentalism is reacting.

It is important to note that among belief systems, or ritual-doctrinal-moral complexes, some are more fundamentalism-prone than others. The proposition with which I was inclined to toy, though it has now been refuted, was that whereas the doctrinal and theological religions are fundamentalism-prone, it is inconceivable that there should be Hindu fundamentalism. Well, the inconceivable *has* happened, and so one must make some adjustments to the theory, and I would now be tempted to say something like this: when a religion which has its center of gravity outside doctrine, being rather a system of praxis, nevertheless goes fundamentalist, it can only do so by, as it were, platonizing itself a bit, by coming in some measure to resemble the more doctrinal and theological religions. This is an ad hoc hypothesis, but it may well be correct.

When approaching fundamentalism, one should first exclude the reactiveness from the definition so as to be able to note the continuity between contemporary fundamentalism and certain earlier phenomena—namely, what I might call the Reformation-prone religion systems, those "axial" systems which are relatively detached from social organization and which are soteriological, and *generically* soteriological. They are not, like the systems of support offered by the Fustelian-Durkheimian kind of religion, caste- or segment-specific, and they are not ailment-specific. They offer a kind of generic salvation *for all comers,* a kind of total remedy for the human condition; and it is these generic, to-whom-it-may-concern, socially disembodied religions that were historically engaged in a struggle with the persistent tendencies of the social order to return to a more Durkheimian variant of faith. This struggle is quite characteristic of Islam, and it seems inherent in the Abrahamic religions in general. Neither is it absent from Buddhism.

The striking thing about the traditional order is that these reformations are in the end unsuccessful, but when one Reformation was for once successful, it thereby engendered the modern world. The continuity between reformations, whose enemies were the folk incarnation of the sacred, and modern fundamentalisms, which are basically a reaction to a kind of relativist-ecumenical spirit, in which religion is emptied of its literalness and seriousness, must not be exaggerated, so as to make the two seem identical. The enemy is different, above all. Yet there is also a marked similarity between them. This is something which the system of definitions I am proposing would highlight. To make all this concrete: Wahhabism was a reform movement within Islam, reacting to internal backsliding; it first arose prior to the impact of the modern world. Contemporary Muslim fundamentalism is *both* a continuation of internal self-purification, *and* a reaction to the ecumenical-relativist diminution of religion by the modern world.

The Necessity of the Sacred and the Profane

Why did Muslim Fundamentalism succeed so strikingly, and Marxism fail so remarkably? The clue, in both cases, is perhaps the notion of routinization. My basic claim is: it is very often said, especially by some pro-religious propagandists, that the human soul, or human society, cannot do without the sacred. One could add, however, that it also cannot do without the profane—profanity, or the routinization of life, must be present, if faith is to work. The existence of a profane zone of life is a precondition of the effective functioning of faith.

Let us start with the failure first, the failure of Marxism to maintain itself as a faith. Various obvious theories claim to explain this. One is that Marxism is soteriological but also uncompromisingly collectivist: it offers salvation to mankind as a whole, but not to the individual sufferer. It has nothing to say to the individual, the person who suffers tragedy, other than "Devote your life to the liberation of mankind." Well, some may take that way out, but not everybody can. A second explanation points to the poverty of the Marxist life-cycle and crisis rituals. The Soviets, of course, tried to remedy this in various ways, and there are various studies of the Soviet attempts at ritualization of life; but these were not terribly successful. Then there is the obvious fact that it might be a disadvantage for a religion to be—and claim to be—entirely of this world, and therefore find itself open to factual refutation. I am not persuaded by this argument, however, because the sharp separation between the transcendent and the this-worldly is not present in people's minds, and there really is not much difference in practice. Furthermore, other faiths, even if transcendent, nevertheless say quite a lot about this world which often is not true, yet on the day in which prophecy fails, the religion itself does not fail but, on the contrary, is frequently fortified. It is not very clear why Marxism should have collapsed on the day on which it became obvious that one of its crucial claims—namely, that it constituted a shortcut to prosperity—was emphatically refuted.

The failure of Marxism is connected with the impossibility of routinization within it. Marxism claimed to overcome the alienation or estrangement of man. This is an obscure, muddled notion. The texts concerning this claim in the Marxist-Hegelian tradition are untidy, and you can never get anything very clear out of them. Nevertheless certain ideas seem to emerge. Marx's repudiation of civil society had something to do with the separation of the economic and the political. In the political sphere, man was a member of a community, but in the economic sphere he was a ruthless individualist, and this alienation of the two parts—the alienation of the economic and the political activities—was to be rejected. Marxism tried to overcome this estrangement and the separation of the spheres. Its tragedy was that it succeeded. The main feature of the social order actually implemented under the banner of Marxism was precisely the catastrophic unification of the three aspects of life—the fusion of the political, the ideological, and the economic hierarchies in one single nomenclatura—and this had a number of consequences. One of them is that it is desperately inefficient, as had become only too visible, because in a single hierarchy, people simply are compelled by the logic of their work situation to direct all their attention to their intrigues within that hierarchy, rather than on technical efficiency—a phenomenon not unknown outside of the Soviet world but, of course, catastrophic and decisive within it, because the unification of bureaucracies was nearly total.

But what was economically disastrous seems to be also disastrous from the viewpoint of the belief system. The age of terror was still also the age of faith, and not only because people were frightened to express any doubts. The terror was a kind of vindication of the faith. There was a heightening of conviction during the times when an enormous and random and drastic terror was going on, and people at the same time still *believed*. Clearly, this was a kind of human sacrifice on an enormous scale, which underwrote the transformation of the social order. It would have been absurd if the total transformation of the human condition were not accompanied by some kind of bloodletting, and this kind of reasoning operated even in the minds of people like Sakharov: that *was* an age of faith. When the Marxist hierarchy stopped shooting each other and started bribing each other, however, faith evaporated. The faith quietly evaporated in the Brezhnev era. Now, why should it?

I think the answer is precisely because Marxism was a sort of grandchild of Spinoza. The line of Spinoza-Hegel-Marx presents a kind of continuity. There is a kind of logic in Spinozan pantheism: if anything is sacred, then everything is. You must not discriminate. But, from the viewpoint of actual social life, it does not work, and the total sacralization of everything, notably of the economy, could not survive the squalor, the squalid mediocrity and corruption, of those years of stagnation. What ultimately killed Marxism was this absence of religious slack into which people could retire when faith was at a temporary low ebb.

Perhaps no one really knows why this total evaporation of belief took place, why that loss of faith which became so obvious the moment Gorbachev took the lid off the system and enabled people to recognize and say to each other that they did not believe. That is my guess: here was a society which had become squalid, opportunist, at a low ebb—but nothing very dramatic was happening. People were no longer shot arbitrarily—the political prisoners who remained had, in fact, done a little bit against the system. They were counted in hundreds, or at most in thousands, but no longer in millions. It was, on the whole, a much more acceptable society than the one which had preceded it, but it no longer believed in itself, and it did not believe because it was expected to believe too much, and had no escape into routinization. That is the hypothesis I offer you. The pantheistic sacralization of the whole social order, including—and particularly stressing—the economy, was as disastrous for faith as the unification of hierarchies was for the economy.

Now, by contrast, why is Islam so astonishingly secularization-resistant, and so successful in the modern world? Again, the hypothesis runs as follows: Islam is, indeed, by some sociological criteria, the most developed of the Abrahamic monotheisms. (It was an embarrassment to Hegel that it came last and consequently should be the highest; he had to correct the historical timetable and make Christianity the highest, by some peculiar reasoning. That Islam should be the highest form of faith was of course unacceptable to him, but the idea has merit.) When Islam settled into a fairly stable form, it became permanently polarized into a high variant and a low variant, where the high variant was very "Protestant," that is, rule-oriented, individualistic, scripturalist, puritan, and entirely suitable for the tastes of urban scholars and urban bourgeoisie, but not at all suitable for the requirements of rural populations, still enclosed in largely Durkheimian units.[8]

Moreover, I accept the Martin Hinds–Patricia Crone thesis that Islam was not Sunni at the very beginning, but that Sunnism was projected back onto it. There was originally a folk Islam with a de facto clergy, a de facto sacramental personnel; it was ritualized, with an ethos of loyalty rather than an ethos of rule-abiding. There emerged a puritanical, egalitarian, scripturalist High version. These two wings, of course, did not openly separate themselves. It was during the early generations of Islam when the polarization between scripturalism on the one hand, and the cult of personality on the other, led to the initial Sunni-Shi'ite-Kharijite split. But later on, when things settled down, Muslims learned how to play within the rules and avoid a further split.

There emerged an unacknowledged tension, but also frequently a happy symbiosis; very regularly, of course, the tension bursts out into an internal jihad, in which the High version tries to convert the Low version, and a Reformation is attempted. For social reasons, however, this was never successful in the past. Come the modern world, however, come the impact of the industrial world on the Muslim world, this changed: the colonial and postcolonial state was in the arid zone strong enough, for the first time, to conquer and administer and erode those rural, self-administering units (generally known as tribes) which had been the social basis for the Fustelian version of Islam—and so the Reformation succeeds at last. The political and economic atomization and, at the same time, the centralization of society also favor a centralized variant of Faith; and so, in the last hundred years, the central variant of Islam for the first time in history actually carried out a *successful* Reformation. But it was only noticed by the West, on the whole, in connection with the somewhat untypical case of Iranian Shi'ism, where it very effectively erupted on the political scene.

Said Arjomand pointed out, in response to an earlier draft of this essay, that when the nineteenth-century renewal movements, advocating reform from within Sufism, became an important social force, there was always a *mixture* of the Fustelian-Durkheimian and reformationist elements. He contends further that the Fustelian-Durkheimian element is there, certainly in Iran and even in the Sunni contemporary movements. The emphasis on community certainly is very important. So could it be that routinization may be still more important? The fact that Islam can still harness the Fustelian-Durkheimian force of religion, albeit in a minor key, may be, according to Arjomand, more important for its success than its Protestant feature.

Iran may not be that much of an exception to the overall pattern I have described, however, given Khomeini's Sunnification of Shi'ism. From the viewpoint of revolutionary potential, Shi'ism was ideal because in the course of preparing for the revolution the martyrdom theme, and its cult of personality, made it much more accessible to the masses. Masses are not interested in jurisprudence and legal theory; but they do find inspiration in martyrdom. Thus a Shi'ite scholar, who is an expert on the biography of the martyr as well as an expert on law, may well be able more readily to communicate with the masses. This is a part of the astonishing success of the Iranian Revolution, which, like perestroika, contradicts all the conventional wisdom about revolutions following a defeat in war and financial bankruptcy. Iran before the revolution was a rich state with an undefeated army—the only thing that fits the conventional requirements of a revolution was the alienation of the intellectuals. Once Khomeini succeeded, he in effect pensioned off the Hidden Imam by denying his political relevance. In the final analysis Khomeini's revolution is about the law: Islam is the application of the law, whether the Hidden Imam returns or whether we, the scholars, serve in his place for the time being. The cult-of-personality element in Shi'ism is thus deemphasized in the shift to the authority of scholars. The modern world thus provides a framework for Khomeini's Republic of the Scholars; had he operated his revolution in some earlier age, the scholar would have had to compromise with some tribal leader to help him to get to the power, thus leading to another monarchy.

Islam survived its identification with the Ottoman Empire and the collapse of that empire. Many people's lives were largely unaffected by it; the Anatolian peasants went on living their same lives. (By contrast the collapse of the Soviet empire has penetrated the whole of society.) The interesting fact about the new reformation—the hundred-year-old reformation of Islam—is that it has been stronger and more effective in the areas like Egypt or Algeria, where the link between religion and the state was weaker, where the ulama were not compromised by their association with the state. Islam survived its association with a collapsing empire, but its association with that empire did, at the old center, lead to the Kemalist attempt at a secularized state. By contrast, it is clear that Marxism has not survived its association with a collapsed Bolshevik empire. Thus I agree with the generalization that religions generally live longer than states do.

The consequence of this successful reformation is that the Muslims escape the dilemma—the generic dilemma—of underdevelopment, that is, the dilemma of a society whose own traditional values are threatened by the economic superiority of the industrial world, and which is therefore caught in the option between either westernizing or populism. Normally, the argument is that the ancient regime clearly has failed us; so we can either imitate the Westerners in order to become as powerful and as rich as they are, or if we do not like spitting, as it were, on our own values, we can idealize the folk variant of our society, because the rulers have failed us. This typical dilemma of backwardness is escaped by some, of course—the Prussians and the Japanese evaded it by modernization from above—but on the whole, this is the characteristic dilemma, which Islam escapes for a different and very simple reason: there is a genuine local tradition, perhaps wrongly identified with the first generation of Islam, but rightly claiming to be genuinely local—namely, the High variant, which is endowed with many virtues which make it compatible with the modern world: low loading of magic, a kind of symmetry of believers, and all those "Protestant" characteristics of orderliness and a rule ethic—features which make it compatible with the drive toward industrialization, and an advance to an industrial society. So the drive toward self-discipline and self-reform can be imposed, not in the name of emulating the alien or in the name of a less than fully convincing idealization of the local folk culture, but in the name of a genuine indigenous tradition, which at the same time has a kind of dignity and acceptability by the criteria of the modern world.

This seems to me the main plot of Muslim history of the last hundred years, and explains how Muslims escaped what might be called the Russian nineteenth-century dilemma between populism and westernizing, *and* it explains why Islam now has this astonishing force. Islam fulfills some of the very function which nationalism performs elsewhere—the transition to a modern society where, for the first time in history, high culture has become the general culture of the total society. This phenomenon, which elsewhere expresses itself as nationalism, expresses itself in the Muslim world as religious revivalism, as fundamentalism, which takes religion seriously. It enables rustics, migrating to the shanty towns, or finding themselves under the shadow of the towns, to express their rejection of their own past ignorance. It also allows them, of course, to criticize their own new technological Mamluks and to sit in judgment on them—and also, of course, to define themselves against the foreigners.

So it has these multiple effects, and at the same time it *permits routinization*. On the one hand, it provides guidance in daily life, by surrounding it, reinforcing it, with rules of guidance and general orientation, suitable for the fourth stage of humanity, thus providing a corrective to disorientation, where there are no longer the cozy Gemeinschaften of the first stage. On the one hand, it is supportive, yet, unlike Marxism, it is not excessive in its demands. It does not really sacralize economic life. It may surround it by rules. They do not even sacralize marriage too much. Life is surrounded by rules, but the rules make it fairly prosaic.

Thus routinization *is* possible, and it makes possible that curious compromise of the Muslim world, which is so paradoxical to outsiders: the combination of moralism and political cynicism—which to Westerners wrongly often seems hypocritical, but is not such really—and the strong expectation that government should enforce, or at any rate not contradict, the Law. On the other hand, there are no great political expectations. Politics is simply a matter of conflict of clientelist groups, which is accepted as being in the nature of things, and does not seem to outrage the population: this leads to the acceptance of opportunist mafia politics, but also to a high moralism in the implementation of the formal religious rules. All this seems to me beautifully adapted to current needs: the possibility of the routinization, the giving of the slack, enables it to both provide guidance, yet not to be overdemanding, and thereby to provoke rejection. By contrast, Marxism turned out to be the other way around. It was precisely its proud attempt to overcome "alienation," to reunify the various aspects of human life, and to sacralize it all, which was its undoing. When life was squalid and the supposedly sacred economy ineffective, this undermined the faith.

Conclusion: Comparing Fundamentalisms

In the Fundamentalism Project discussions, Ninian Smart raised a question about the interpretive scheme I am proposing, namely, the implications of this scheme for other religious traditions which also offer generic soteriology: Buddhism, for example, and the Hindu tradition in its modern form, have made adjustments which have been in certain ways very successful—in fact, he maintains, in certain ways they have been more successful than Islam. Smart takes as an example the Indian ideology of Vivekananda: if all religions point to the same truth, Hinduism is superior to other religions only in the sense that it has known it all along. This kind of ideology has been a remarkably successful basis for the pluralism of the Indian constitution, which has, until very recently, allowed India to avoid some of the clashes which follow upon the application of the Shari'a. Smart then suggests that the notion of the Shari'a is, in the modern world, a weakness for Islam. On the other hand, what is obvious in the Islamic case is the importance of ritual: the very fact that Islam has a ritual discipline makes it immediately personally meaningful to individuals and is an enormous strength; this contrasts with the weakness of the rituals of Marxism.

This line of comparison is worth pursuing. There are striking parallels between the Buddhist reform movement and the Islamic one. Buddhists have not had the same level of success, as far as I can see, for purely demographic reasons: the classical Buddhist countries are relatively low in population, and the Mongolians and the Tibetans simply could not assert themselves against the big empires, against the Chinese and the Russians and the British. Had they only been as populous, we might have seen a Buddhist Algeria, that is, a purified, revivalist Buddhism in Mongolia.

Hinduism might well be an embarrassment for my theory. However, modern Hinduism seems to have developed in two rather different directions. One is a kind of high intellectual theory—the truth has many forms and so on—in which form it appeals to intellectuals but is not an adequate base for a popular mobilization movement. Once, after a lecture I gave in Rajasthan, the Hindu audience was absolutely furious. Their basic line was, "You're really telling us that these fanatical, ignorant, rigid, intolerant Muslims are more compatible in the modern world than us Hindus! We are practically the Enlightenment; we are the Enlightenment in Eastern form . . ."

While this kind of version of Hinduism appeals to intellectuals, it is not a mobilizing force for the masses. A second form of Hinduism, based on the social realities of Hinduism, may fit generally within my analysis. Yet I am quite puzzled about how this can become a mobilizing force, how something which is so centered on *caste* can become a mobilizing force in the modern world. Wendy Doniger reminds us of the statement made by a member of the Rashtriya Svayamsevak Sangh, the Hindu fundamentalist group, about the Muslims. The argument is that Hindus are the most tolerant people in the world and therefore they should own India, and the Muslims, who are less tolerant, should be disenfranchised in India.[9] By such reasonings modern fundamentalists legitimatize their programs, not only in Islam but in other religious traditions as well.

Notes

1. Emile Durkheim, *The Elementary Forms of the Religious Life* (1914; New York: Free Press, 1965).

2. Max Weber, *The Protestant Ethic and the Spirit of Capitalism*, trans. Talcott Parsons (New York: Scribners, 1976).

3. See the argument in Ernest Gellner, *Muslim Society* (Cambridge: Cambridge University Press, 1991).

4. Andrei Sakharov, *Memoirs*, trans. Richard Lourie (New York: Alfred A. Knopf, 1990).

5. It so happened—I didn't plan it that way—that the two areas in which I did research are these two contrasting areas.

6. Numa-Denis Fustel de Coulanges, *The Ancient City: A Study on Religion, Laws, and Institutions of Greece and Rome,* trans. Willard Small (Boston: Lothrop, Lee, and Shepard, 1920).

7. Karl Jaspers, *Vom Ursprung und Ziel der Geschichte* (München: Piper Verlag, 1949); S. N. Eisenstadt, "The Axial Age: The Emergence of Transcendental Visions and the Rise of Clerics," *European Journal of Sociology* 23, no. 2 (1982): 294–314.

8. Patricia Crone and Martin Hinds, *God's Caliph: Religious Authority in the First Centuries of Islam* (New York: Cambridge University Press, 1986).

9. Transcripts of Fundamentalisms Compared, a conference of the American Academy of Arts and Sciences, Chicago, 14 November, 1991.

From Orthodoxy to Fundamentalism:
A Thousand Years of Islam in South Asia

T. N. Madan

This day, O true believers, I have perfected your religion for you,
and brought my mercy upon you to its completion. I have chosen
for you Islam to be your religion.
The Qur'an (V, 3)

Islam desires, above all, that people should commit themselves entirely to
God's Truth and that they should serve and worship only God. Similarly,
it desires that the law of God should become the law by which people lead
their lives. . . . Only when power in society is in the hands of the Believers
and the righteous, can the objectives of Islam be realized.
Sayyid Abul Ala Maududi, The Islamic Movement *(1984)*

Santayana's famous dictum that one compares only when one is unable to
get to the heart of the matter seems to me . . . the precise reverse of the
truth. It is through comparison, and of comparables, that whatever
heart we can actually get to is to be reached.
Clifford Geertz, Local Knowledge *(1983)*

Introduction

A major conclusion of current studies of re-
ligious fundamentalist movements is that we should speak of fundamentalisms in the
plural rather than the singular, for such movements and their underlying ideologies
are everywhere characterized by significant cultural and historical specificities.[1] We
must not, however, altogether abandon a general notion of fundamentalism, for it
reminds us of the indispensability of comparison in our studies and paves the way for
it. The understanding of each time-, space-, and culture-bound fundamentalist movement is facilitated, and indeed deepened, by the exploration of similarities as well as
differences among such movements. All fundamentalist movements may not be exactly
similar, but they are said to share certain "family resemblances."[2]

Thus, it has been asserted that fundamentalism is essentially a modern phenomenon. Everywhere it has been shaped in confrontation with the processes of moderniza-

tion and its shibboleths, notably secularism and nationalism, which have, however, been proven inadequate in respect of their soteriological promises. The excesses or failures of modernization, both entailing enormous cultural costs, are regarded by many intellectuals as a condition for, if not a cause of, the emergence of religious fundamentalism. In other words, a return to religion, which lies at the core of the fundamentalist quest, makes no sense unless the people concerned first experience or witness a departure from it.

In this sense religious fundamentalism is "inseparable from the specter of its dreaded enemy: the 'Enlightenment,'" which is at once its "precursor" and "foil."[3] The ideals of the Enlightenment were diffused outside the West through colonial education and administration and the process of Westernization that these generated. The disaffection with these ideals and processes is, however, a twentieth-century phenomenon, though the first stirrings are in some parts of the world more than a hundred years old.[4] As a particular form of antimodernism, fundamentalism in the West is no older than the early years of the present century; elsewhere it is considered a post–World War II phenomenon.

The exponents of the foregoing view acknowledge that fundamentalism, though antimodernist, is by no means a fanciful retreat into the past. Actually it is serious business, and it is modern, not merely in the sense of being novel or contemporary, but also in the significant sense of being based on a recognition of the instrumental value of modern technologies and modern methods of organization (of work), management (of resources), and communication (of information) in the reordering of social life. Some scholars have felt persuaded to regard fundamentalist movements as secular, though dressed up in religious garb,[5] but that seems going too far. As Bruce Lawrence has pointed out, "the core contest is between two incommensurate ways of viewing the world, one which locates values in timeless scriptures, inviolate laws, and unchanging mores, the other which sees in the expansion of scientific knowledge a technological transformation of society that pluralizes options both for learning and for living."[6] Viewed thus, religious fundamentalism is, in the words of an Islamicist, "a sort of holding operation against modernity. And though it has no doubt a sharp political edge, it is primarily a cultural phenomenon."[7]

There are two problems with this way of looking at fundamentalist movements. First, models of modernity other than the Western are excluded. Second, the perspective has a shallow depth in time. When confronted with individual preachings or collective movements from earlier times, which are concerned with culture, scripture, and power, one excludes them by definition from the rubric of fundamentalism: "Fundamentalism has historical antecedents but no ideological precursors."[8]

If one were to bracket (not abandon) the criterion of a narrowly defined antimodernism, but retain that of a concern with cultural critique and recovery, with scriptural inerrancy and authority, and with power, one could then compare, not only synchronically across religious traditions, but also diachronically across different periods of a particular religious tradition over a fairly long period of time. Such an exercise would liberate us from the stranglehold of the peculiar concerns of the present, such as *gharbzadagi,* that is, being smitten or plagued by the West.[9] This malady afflicts not only non-Western societies, spawning fundamentalist movements in reaction, but also to some extent our studies of the latter. It is well to remember the sane advice of Karl Marx that an age is not judged best by relying upon its self-consciousness alone. The introduction of the historical perspective, going beyond the present century, not only would be welcome, but also seems imperative in certain cases.[10] And this is what I will briefly attempt to do in this essay, with reference to Islam in South Asia.

Islam in South Asia has had an eventful and richly documented history of about thirteen hundred years, and is therefore well suited to the kind of longitudinal inquiry I have suggested above. A large body of high-quality literature in English, written from a variety of perspectives, is available as a secondary source for this purpose. I will occasionally refer to the primary sources and also draw upon interpretations and analytical insights of a number of distinguished historians and Islamicists.

There are more Muslims in South Asia today, numbering more than 300 million, than in any other region of the world; and, although divided into a number of regional communities (such as the Malabar, Bengal, or Kashmiri Muslims), Islam and the "Indian environment" have played critical roles in the making of their diverse histories. Maulana Muhammad 'Ali, the Indian political leader who was one of the key figures in the Khilafat movement (for the restoration of the spiritual and temporal authority of the Ottoman sultan as the caliph of Islam) in the early 1920s,[11] thought of "India" and "the Muslim world" as "two circles of equal size but which are not concentric." Maulana Abul Kalam Azad, who served twice as the president of the Indian National Congress, declared in 1940: "I am a Muslim and profoundly conscious of the fact that I have inherited Islam's glorious traditions of the last thirteen-hundred years. I am not prepared to lose even a small part of that legacy . . . I am equally proud of the fact that I am an Indian, an essential part of the indivisible unity of Indian nationhood, a vital factor in its total make-up without which this noble edifice will remain incomplete. I can never give up this sincere claim."[12]

Yet there is a crucial element of ambiguity or tension in the relationship of the Muslims of South Asia and their cultural and political environments. It is a relationship that has, right from the very beginning, carried within itself the potential for the emergence of fundamentalism. As Yohanan Friedman puts it:

> There was, on the one hand, the feeling that the Indian Muslims were constantly in danger of being overwhelmed by an environment which could only be described as an anathema to their ideal of monotheism. The apprehension created an intense desire to preserve Islam in its pristine purity and to protect it assiduously from any encroachment of Indian customs and beliefs. . . . Diametrically opposed to it was the attempt to find a common denominator for the two civilizations. . . . This conciliatory trend was always weaker than the orthodox one.[13]

This essay is not concerned with "communalism" (i.e., Hindu-Muslim conflict) in modern India, nor is it offered as a contribution to the history of Islam in India. It is rather an attempt to construct an argument, on the basis of selected materials, about the character of Muslim fundamentalism in South Asia in our time. Briefly, the argument runs as follows: while a concern with *orthodoxy* and *orthopraxis* is only to be expected among the carriers of a religious tradition when they enter an alien sociocultural environment and make converts, their anxiety about the loss of the pristine purity of belief and practice at a later stage of consolidation expresses itself in the form of efforts at *reform* and *revival*. If and when the reformist-revivalist stage develops into a situation of crisis, so perceived, because of the loss of political power (or, maybe, its acquisition), one is faced with the phenomenon of fundamentalism bringing together the elements of scriptural dogmatism, cultural critique, and the quest for power. The encounter with colonialism and the resultant cultural impact of the West is a particular expression of this crisis, not its only true form.

The Arrival of Islam in India: Opportunities and Dilemmas

The western seaboard of India was known to seafaring Arab traders long before the advent of Islam. The Malabar coast derives its name from the Arabic word *mabar*, "crossing"; the Muslims living there, the Moplahs, trace their name from *mappilla*, meaning bridegroom or child, and pointing to intermarriage between Arab men and local women belonging to the matrilineal Nair community.[14] The impact of Islam must have been felt by the Indo-Arab communities during the time of the Prophet. Islam cast its missionary-cum-military eyes on India during the caliphate of Umar bin al-Khattab, and finally arrived in A.D. 712,[15] when Sind was conquered by Muhammad bin Qasim on behalf of Hajjaj bin Yusuf, governor of the eastern provinces of the Umayyad caliphate. Muhammad conquered the kingdom of Dahir, a Hindu raja, and stayed to establish Islam as a political force in Sind. Although Hajjaj sent the military expedition because Dahir refused to provide to Arab trading vessels protection from pirates in the Arabian Sea,[16] the eastward push was likely part of a larger plan of a political nature.[17]

It was one thing to conquer an alien land but quite another to establish a stable Muslim state among a people whom Muhammad was obliged by his faith to judge as idolatrous infidels. Objectively judged, however, these infidels were legatees of Brahmanical and Buddhist cultures with varied achievements to their credit. As Peter Hardy puts it, "The century following the Arab conquest of Sind was therefore one in which Hindu culture could encounter the Arabs in the hope of giving more than it was forced to receive."[18]

Immediately, Muhammad's task was to set up an administrative structure and to receive the obedience of the people whose ruler had been defeated. These objectives would be impossible to achieve without the support of the existing administrative functionaries, who happened to be high-caste Hindus. While some conversions to Islam were effected, the conqueror had to call upon non-Muslims to hold office under him, and this posed a dilemma. Muhammad would have to either abandon his political mandate and refrain from seeking the cooperation of infidels, or abandon orthodoxy and seize the opportunity of consolidating the extended dominion of dar al-Islam. As it turned out, political expediency won over orthodoxy.

Muhammad persuaded his religious advisers to allow him to extend the status and rights of "the protected class" (*zimmi*) to the Hindus of Sind, although they were not, strictly speaking, "People of the Book" (*ahl-i-kitab*), that is, followers of God-given but superseded religions.[19] The Umayyad state adapted the doctrine regarding non-Muslims for purely secular purposes, and the Hanafi school of law, which became preponderant in India, endorsed the view. "This conciliatory policy was not only desirable but necessary. The Hindus accepted [Muslim] rule on the guarantee that the state would not interfere with the practice of their religion."[20]

The Hindus who did not embrace Islam were treated as noncitizens of the caliphate, in it but not of it. They were required under Islamic law (Shari'a) to pay poll tax (*jizya*) on a graduated basis, the propertied classes paying four times as much as the poor. In return, their lives were spared and their properties were exempted from confiscation; they were excused from rendering military service and paying surplus property tax (*zakat*), both essential obligations for Muslims. What is more, Muhammad felt obliged to confirm the privileges of upper-caste Hindus, particularly the Brahmans, who traditionally received tribute from lower castes. In conformity with the practice of the Umayyad caliphate, he did not discard the existing administrative structure,[21] and ruled through Hindu village headmen (*rais*), chieftains (*dihqans*), and prefects whose work was overseen by Muslim governors. This gave rise, in due course, to the administrative category of *amils* in Sind who looked after revenue administration. "The management of all the affairs of the state, and its administration, I leave in your able hands," Muhammad proclaimed, on a hereditary basis.[22]

Simultaneously, the high ecclesiastical office of *sadru-I-Islam al affal* was created and the secular governors subordinated to it. This gave the appearance of an Islamic state. The opportunity for making converts to the new faith was also seized, apparently without great success. Although some chieftains and common people embraced Islam at the invitation of Muhammad, most of them were Buddhists, or Buddhists recently reabsorbed into the Hindu fold. Sind became a Muslim majority province only very gradually.[23] In this respect the social dynamics in Sind were no different than in any other area newly conquered on behalf of Islam. It took centuries for even a country like Egypt to have a Muslim majority among its people.

What lay at the core of the new setup was compromise on the part of both antagonistic communities between religious orthodoxy and political expediency. The Hindus saved their religious faith by submitting to Muslim political power, without acknowledging its legitimacy or authority,[24] and consequently agreed to work for the alien rulers. The nature and extent of the Muslim compromise is indicated by the decree of Hajjaj bin Yusuf.

> [T]he chief inhabitants of Brahmanabad had petitioned to be allowed to repair the temple . . . and pursue their own religion. As they made submission, and have agreed to pay taxes to the Khalifa, nothing more can be properly required from them. They have been taken under our protection, and we must not in

any way stretch out our hands upon their lives or property. Permission is given to them to worship their gods. Nobody must be forbidden or prevented from following his own religion. They must live in their houses in whatever manner they like..[25]

Since the Buddhists and Hindus were grouped together as zimmis, their legal status presumably provided them some protection against conversion. In any case, the early Arabs were not enthusiastic proselytizers.

Whatever the sadru-I-Islam thought of this, the subordination of religious authority to the power of the state at the highest level had been asserted. The compact was between two groups of elites—the native and the alien—and the guardians of religious orthodoxy on either side, namely the Brahmans and the ulama[26] (the latter were not yet quite a well-defined category or as influential as they became later), apparently kept aloof.[27] Muslim religious authority in India was to be alternately asserted and challenged by Muslim royal power, during the next one thousand years. The tension was internal to the Indian Muslim communities, but the Hindu environment was a significant factor in its ebb and flow.

Simultaneously, the relations between Muslim rulers and the non-Muslim ruled also were to see many ups and downs. The relations of the Indo-Muslim rulers "to the indigenous heritage were always a live issue."[28] On the cultural front, "[t]he history of medieval and modern India is to a very considerable extent a history of Hindu-Muslim religio-cultural tensions, interspersed with movements or individual efforts at understanding, harmony and even composite development. The divisive forces have proved much more dynamic than the cohesive ones."[29] Smooth-working arrangements were nonetheless worked out at the local level.[30] The prevalence of tensions at the macrolevel may not be denied, however, nor indeed the ideological divide.

It would be apposite to point out here that the assimilative character of the Hindu cultural environment was, in the eyes of the Muslim elites (most of them of foreign origin—Arabs, Turks, Iranians, Afghans, etc.), a serious threat to the Muslim way of life as well as to Muslim secular power, and called for "constant vigilance and effort."[31] Indian Muslims "were a people living, as it were, in two worlds; one of their immediate surroundings and the other was the world of the sources of inspiration which sustained their spiritual experience,"[32] and there was discord between them. Muslim fundamentalism in India has its roots deep in the twin predicaments of the Indo-Muslim community, namely the perceived threat of the Hindu cultural environment (which became in course of time a breeding ground for various kinds of Sufi deviations) and of Muslim secular power, or in modern times, of political expediency.

Religious Authority versus Secular Power in Medieval India

When Muhammad bin Qasim was recalled by the new caliph, three years after he had annexed Sind in 712, he had already designed the basic structure of administration in Sind; pushed northeast to conquer Multan, bringing half of what is Pakistan today under Muslim rule; and, above all, worked out a modus vivendi with the Hindu elites. His experiments in administrative and social engineering became the basis for more elaborate and refined arrangements in the following millennium.

The next happening of equal significance for Islam in India, in its threefold aspects of religion, culture, and power, was the appearance of Mahmud, king of Ghazni, in 1000 at Lamghan in the northwest (not far from present-day Peshawar). During the next quarter of a century he invaded India seventeen times. He overran the Muslim settlement in Multan, which had been taken over by the Isma'ili sect, slaughtered many Isma'ilis, and destroyed their mosques. He pushed eastward toward the Gangetic plain and southward to Gujarat, and ruthlessly pillaged Hindu temples and killed large numbers of Hindus.

In an astute move, Mahmud submitted himself to the authority of the Abbasid caliphate. "In his mind the two processes, submission to a 'universal' khilafat and the invasion and occupation of 'infidel' Indian territory were clearly inter-connected."[33] His vow to cleanse "pagan" India of its "ignorance" and false religions had been the occasion for the first investiture at the hands of the caliph al-Qadir; his sack of the rich Hindu temple of Somnath resulted in the honor of a second investiture. Mahmud thus appeared in India as the champion of Sunni orthodoxy, defending it against the heretic and the infidel. In his concern for orthodoxy he may have appeared to be on the side of the ulama rather than secular power, but he did not let down the state: he had Hindus in his multiracial army.[34] Mahmud's successors ruled over northwest India for well over a century and a half, making Lahore a kingly city.

The signal for heightened tension between the spokesmen for orthodoxy and the authority of the ulama, on the one hand, and the power of the king, on the other, came later during the period known as the Delhi Sultanate (the thirteenth to the early sixteenth century). Formally, the sultanate was part of the eastern caliphate and the fiction of caliphal authority was kept alive beyond the sack of Baghdad in 1258 by the Mongols. Gradually the Delhi sultans began to call themselves by a title formerly reserved for the caliph, namely *zillillah* (the shadow of God). Sultan Ghiyas ud-din Balban (ruled 1265–87) apparently realized the potential utility of this concept in the furtherance of the scope and legitimacy of royal power.[35]

The Turkish-Afghan connection, which began with the invasions of Mahmud Ghazni, and was extended by the Ghurids, ended with the death of Muhammad Ghuri in 1206, when his general, Qutb ud-din Aibak, took over the Indian possessions of the sultan and declared himself the new king. The significance of this development was that the sultanate was no longer subject to the original Ghurid base but an Indian state, which was nominally part of dar al-Islam. However, these sultans, with the sole exception of Firuz Tughluq (ruled 1351–88), did not insist on the promulgation of the Shari'a, though they could not have disregarded the consensus (*ijma*) of the ulama on doctrinal issues. The distinction between spiritual authority and temporal power is of crucial importance; which has the upper hand in a particular situation depends on the prevailing circumstances.

The great empire builder Ala ud-din Khalji (ruled 1296–1316) challenged the authority of the ulama, who had come to prominence all over the Muslim world after the decline of the Abbasid caliphate in the tenth century. He decreed whatever seemed to him to be for "the good of the state" and also "opportune under the circumstances," without worrying whether it was in conformity with the Islamic law, which he did not claim to know well.[36] Naturally, the ulama did not approve. He was roundly condemned for his disregard of Shari'a by the supporters of clericalism, most notably Zia ud-din Barani, an outstanding historian of medieval India (ca. 1280–1360); but the approvers were not absent, and the very distinguished scholar-historian-Sufi, Amir Khusrau, addressed him as khalifa.

Muhammad Habib writes that the empire of Delhi during the fourteenth century "was not a theocratic state in any sense of the word. Its basis was not shariat of Islam but the *zawabit* or the state laws made by the king. . . . their foundation was . . . nonreligious and secular. . . . Barani leaves us in no doubt that in cases of conflict the state-laws overrode the shariat."[37] Habib's judgment on the issue of religious orthodoxy versus political expediency is noteworthy: "It is true that Muslim kings, mostly of foreign extraction, sat on Indian thrones for some six or seven centuries. But they could only do so because their enthronement was not the enthronement of Muslim rule; had it been otherwise, they could not have lasted for a single generation, for India could not have been properly governed without help from the sons of the soil."[38]

The two tensions—between Islam and its Hindu environment, and between religious authority and secular power—which emerged when Muhammad bin Qasim established a Muslim (not Islamic) state in Sind early in the eighth century, persisted in full force in the medieval period. They were exacerbated by the expanding demands of administration and divisions among the ulama. Hindu administrative skills, business acumen, and even military prowess, had become a strong pillar of the Muslim kingdoms: "the relatively small numbers of Muslim invaders and the vastness of the areas to be controlled, inhibited the Muslim conquerors from seeking to fulfill their true intentions which were to Islamize the whole country, if necessary by force." Otherwise, the attitude toward Hindus was "wholly offensive" and "virulently hostile."[39] The bending was mutual, but that was no consolation to the upholders of orthodoxy.

The guardians of correct belief and action were corrupted by proximity to power. A class of ulama—*ulama-i-su*—emerged, who specialized in jurisprudence (*fiqh*), and became functionaries of the Muslim state. They were not above time-serving interpretations of the tradition, and even of the Qur'an, so long as they were cosharers of power.[40] The ulama who devoted themselves to religious pursuits, however, upheld the supremacy of Shari'a and kept aloof from the corridors of power. The Sufi were similarly divided between those who were close to the masses and abhorred both kings and the ulama, and those who hobnobbed enthusiastically with kings and courtiers and assumed a variety of roles far removed from those of the saint and the ascetic. The 'alim-Sufi distinction was not meaningless, though never as deep and clear-cut as the Sunni-Shi'ite divide.

In the midst of these differences a courtier of aristocratic birth, whose intellectual passion was historiography, raised his voice in defense of religious orthodoxy as he perceived it. Zia ud-din Barani, a Sunni, lived and wrote in the overwhelming presence of Hindus, whom he rejected. He even hated Hindus who embraced Islam, for religion was for him a matter of birth, though this was contrary to the fundamental teachings of Islam. Some historians attribute this hostility to the fear that the privileges of the Muslim nobility (Barani's class) were threatened by the Hindu rural aristocracy, "with whom the Sultans had been inevitably led to strike a compromise."[41]

Barani made his livelihood in an economic system dominated by the Hindu groups.[42] He advised the Muslim kings to deal with Hindus by offering them the choice between Islam and death. Since he did not believe that conversion could redeem any non-Muslim, or improve the character of the lowborn (it was lower-caste Hindus who embraced Islam), there was no real choice available. Barani wrote that the Muslim king would not be able to establish the supremacy of Islam unless he strove with all his courage to overthrow infidelity and eliminate its leaders (*imams*), who in India were Brahmans. Further, if the kings, despite their royal power and prestige, were content to preserve infidelity in return for the tribute and the poll tax, how could they give effect to the tradition of the Prophet, which says, "I have been ordered to fight all people until they affirm 'there is no God but Allah'"? "The religious perfection of the Muslim kings lies in this—they should risk themselves as well as their power and authority and strive day and night to establish truth at the centre."[43]

Barani's concern was to confront the threats to religious orthodoxy from the Hindu environment and from the runaway royal (secular) power. Although he was not a theologian, he attempted to bring the royal function and power under the hierarchical control of religious authority. The two functions (or domains) were autonomous but needed to be made complementary. While "prophethood is the perfection of religion," "kingship is the perfection of worldly good fortune." Further, "these two perfections are opposed and contradictory to each other, and their combination is not within the bounds of possibility."[44] Muslim kings, Barani believed, had to follow the policy of pre-Islamic Iranian emperors, "which breaks the headstrong" and "subdues the rebels" in order to establish the supremacy of the state. The rulers of Islam, too, "have adopted the policy of unbelievers in God (the Iranian emperors) for establishing their own power so that they may utilize their authority and strength for the protection and promotion of the Faith, for ensuring the greatness of the True Word by constant holy wars (jihad) intended to overthrow idolatry and polytheism [both deemed as typical Hindu sins] and for raising the prestige of Islam by killing and slaughtering the enemies of the Faith."[45] The kingly function was thus derived from the religious function. Barani's exemplary king is a properly instructed, pious sultan, who is "twin brother" of the prophet[46] and who has virtuous ulama for his advisers.[47] He uses his secular power to eradicate false beliefs.

Barani's grievance was that real-life Muslim kings of India, from Sultan Balban to Ghiyath al-din Tughluq (1266–1325), had fallen far short of this ideal, and therefore orthodoxy was in peril. Royal power had not yet reached the heights it was to attain in the Mughal Empire, and departures from orthodoxy, too, had not yet become so alarming as to make the ulama give the call for a return to the fundamentals of the faith. For this to happen, India had to witness the rise of Jala ud-din Akbar as emperor.

Religious Syncretism and Revivalism

The five centuries between the last of Mahmud Ghazni's invasions (1026) and Babur's conquest (1526) saw the spread of Islam far and wide in India and the rise and fall of Muslim kingdoms and dynasties on the subcontinent. But it did not see India, though nominally dar al-Islam, become so de facto. Those who professed Islam as their religion (*din*), whether immigrants or converts, remained a minority. Those who, through their association with Muslim aristocracy and administration, came to imbibe Muslim high culture (*adab*) also remained a minority. In the heartland of north India where many battles for orthodoxy, and not only for political supremacy, were waged, and from where the twentieth-century demand for a separate Muslim homeland derived its strongest support, Muslims constituted only 14 percent of the total population at the time of partition (the figure for India as a whole was about 25 percent).

Not that efforts to convert non-Muslims were not made—both persuasion and force were employed—but success was limited. Muhammad Habib concedes that by medieval times, "the Muslim Faith had made no progress in the rural areas of the provinces that now constitute the Indian Union," but he refers to "a landslide in favor of the new faith in urban areas."[48] Sayid Athar Abbas Rizvi, however, questions this: "[T]he Hindu architects and masons, who constructed the mosques and minarets of the thirteenth century were not necessarily willing workers. Many worked under duress, although subsequently some of them embraced Islam. The same was the case with the Hindu artisans." All rulers, beginning with Muhammad bin Qasim himself, forcibly secured converts, until Akbar forbade the practice, in keeping with the Qur'anic injunction that there should be no compulsion in the matter of faith.[49] For Akbar, "true Islam meant tolerance and understanding and an extension of the human rights and privileges reserved in earlier Indo-Muslim political philosophy for Muslims alone, to non-Muslims, including the rights of conversion and reconversion, . . . freedom of worship and construction of the houses of worship."[50]

In Akbar's time a certain loosening of the structures of orthodoxy had occurred as a result of the emergence of different versions of it. The ulama included the puritans, who stayed away from the kings and disowned political concerns, as well as the courtiers. The ulama tended toward "fanaticism" and the lack of "character" and "spiritual sensitivity."[51] The Sufi, generally of ascetic disposition and closer to the populace, were also divided between a strict adherence to a disciplined way of life and a tendency to sycophancy and pantheistic drift. Not surprisingly, heresies came to be associated with the Sufi more than with the ulama. Indeed, "the popularity and success of the Chishti saints in India was due to their understanding of the Indian conditions and the religious attitudes and aspirations of the Indian people,"[52] which often meant a willingness to adopt Hindu customs and ceremonies.

The nature and extent of Indian contributions to Sufism are a matter for debate. What is not disputed is the fact that the Sufis, who derived their immanentist ideas primarily from Ibn al-Arabi, generally found the Indian cultural environment congenial, and their attraction to certain aspects of Hinduism (notably "devotionalism," or *bhakti*) resulted in deviations from Islamic orthodoxy, which emphasizes the "otherness" and the "awesome majesty" (jalal) of God. This provoked negative reactions from stricter Sufis and of course the ulama.

The edge to these struggles between Sunni orthodoxy and different kinds of heterodoxy (Shi'ism, "erroneous" Sufism, secularism, etc.) was provided by the tendency of Muslim kings to give first preference to their personal or dynastic interests and the interests of the state (usually the former) and to disregard the claims of orthodoxy. Second, it was provided by the character of the Muslim masses, who were mostly converts and who never completely forsook their original faiths and ways of life. Conversions had a multiplicity of causes and were not generally the result of strong religious conviction alone. Coercion, opportunism, and economic and ecological pressures, and so forth, were also influential in different degrees in various places and times.

The converted, particularly those in rural areas, did not cut off all social and economic relations with their former coreligionists. Hindu values and practices survived conversion and resulted in a poverty of Muslim mass culture that was the source of much dismay to both the ulama and the bearers of elite culture (adab). Akbar's personal religious beliefs and his respect for religious faiths other than his own "are . . . important because they represent the culmination of trends which had been active in the life of the community for some time." [53]

The court of Jala ud-din Akbar (ruled 1556–1605) was certainly not lacking in opinionated advisers, including the ulama, who were represented "by corrupt and degenerate men." [54] Nevertheless, Akbar was in the early years deferential toward these purveyors of traditional orthodoxy. [55] He did not please them by taking an interest, even at that young age, in the teachings and practices of Sufis and Hindu yogis. Akbar encouraged religious controversy at the court and wanted even the Qur'an discussed and interpreted. For this purpose he established the House of Worship in 1575, a debating hall where rationalist inquiry received the emperor's approval. The discussions were at first confined to Sunni Islam, but later other Muslim and non-Muslim religious leaders also were invited to participate. [56] Akbar came to acknowledge the revealed and valuable truths of faiths other than his own, and came to adopt a syncretistic position on religious matters.

Akbar was obviously interested in more than exposing arrogance and charlatanry among the ulama; he was also concerned about the legitimation of the imperial state, the majority of the subjects of which were non-Muslims. The problem had become much more complex. Islam had come of age in India and developed its own internal complexity, complete with divines and mystics and their theological disputations; the caliphate's foothold on the subcontinent, overseen by a governor, had also grown into an empire. While the expanding central authority was grounded in "explicitly Islamic principles," a pluralist legitimation must have seemed appropriate to Akbar. [57] This would not have been readily possible without the tension between the emperor and the ulama being resolved in his favor. He had to be the principal 'alim himself.

Such a resolution was achieved through a declaration, drawn up by Shaykh Mubarak, a maverick of considerable learning who had earned the wrath of the ulama for his unconventional experimental attitude toward religious beliefs, [58] and signed by high-ranking ulama, including the chief *qazi*. Issued in 1579, it held the "just ruler" (*sultan-i-adil*) to be superior in the eyes of God than any eminent authoritative divine (*mujtahid*), and asserted the emperor's right to settle in favor of a particular interpretation or opinion, when there was conflict among the appointed divines (*mujtahidun*) on a particular issue.[59]

While this decree did not deprive the divines of their normal function or invest the emperor with arbitrary powers in religious matters,[60] it did combine the two functions that Barani had argued were irreconcilable contraries: the king would no longer be a mere "twin brother" of the prophet but more than his equal; the kingly function thus became preeminent. Moreover, the 1579 manifesto defined the principles that would guide the king, and these were secular principles, namely the "benefit of the people" and "the betterment of the administration of the country,"[61] subject, of course, to conformity with Qur'anic injunctions as interpreted by Akbar. (These principles had been cited by Ala ud-din Khalji as the guiding principles of his policy.)

Two years after the declaration, Akbar went one step further and announced the doctrine of "divine unity" (*tawhid-i ilahi*) as the basis for the oneness of humankind. He sought to make reason the basis of the approach to religion. Not only were all Muslims to be united—his mosque at Fatehpur Sikri is home to a Chishti shrine—he also affirmed moral principles derived from other religious traditions, "including the Jain dislike of killing that which possesses life and the Catholic virtue of celibacy."[62] He showed, however, "surprising indifference to Hinduism."[63] The underlying motive was "to create a high inter-confessional moral and even religious level through the example of the court itself and even in some measure through legislation" decreed by the emperor.[64] Muhammad Mujeeb highlights another objective, namely the "emotional integration of the Indian people."[65] In this regard the Sufi ideal of universal or total peace (*sulh-i kul*), advocated with great passion by Abul Fazl, Akbar's spiritual counsellor and admiring chronicler, appealed enormously to him.[66]

The importance of this experiment in religious syncretism must not be exaggerated: the new faith was not intended to displace Islam.[67] Akbar obviously did not attach too much importance to it, and its tenets were not stated in any detail. Akbar's critics were, however, alarmed by the promulgation of what appeared to be a new faith. They particularly denounced the efforts of enthusiasts like Abul Fazl to bestow on the emperor the mantle of prophethood, and even to suggest a quasi-divine status for him.[68] According to them, Akbar had already given evidence of wayward tendencies and been guilty of un-Islamic actions. These included abolition of the poll tax on Hindus, appearing in the manner of Hindu kings before his subjects to be seen by them, recognition of prostration (*sijda*) as a form of showing reverence for the emperor, wearing of Hindu dress, a visit to the third Sikh guru, Armar Das, and observance of non-Muslim festivals. In the critics' eyes, Akbar had ceased to be a Muslim— a judgment rejected by all serious historians except a few obviously prejudiced ones.[69] In any case, *din-i ilahi* had in Akbar a reluctant proselytizer, and it never acquired more than a very limited following. It died with the emperor, but not before it had aroused hostility among the ulama who considered Islam to be in danger. The time had come to call halt to dangerous innovations (*bid'a*) and reassert the purity of the faith. The concern was not merely with orthodoxy but with the imperative of reviving the faith and restoring its purity.

Akbar's innovations are framed by the earlier messianism of Sayyid Muhammad of Jaunpur, and the later revivalism of Shaykh Ahmad Sirhindi.

In the early years of Akbar's efforts to contain the influence of the ulama, he had found excellent interlocutors on his behalf in Abul Fazl and Abdul Qadir Badauni, two very able pupils of Shaykh Mubarak. The shaykh himself had been deeply influenced by the Mahdawi movement of the first half of the sixteenth century, particularly by the role played in its development by Sayyid Muhammad, who introduced messianism in Indian Islam—a radical innovation—and claimed that he was the messiah (*mahdi*) promised to Muslims for the rejuvenation of the faith and the redemption of the faithful. Claiming the authority of Qur'anic revelation, he called for a reassertion of the supremacy of Shari'a, elimination of the ulama and the aristocracy, and the reordering of Muslim society in India on a moral basis.[70] Inevitably he came into conflict with the ulama. More importantly, he—and perhaps even more, the idea of a "savior"—had a profound impact on Akbar and inspired some of his actions in the cause of religious reform mentioned above.[71]

Akbar's religious reforms were attacked by Shaykh Ahmad Sirhindi (1564–1624). He was a brilliant Sufi thinker of the Naqshbandi order and claimed descent from 'Umar, the second caliph of Islam. He affirmed having mystical experiences suggestive of prophethood and inevitably earned the hostility of the ulama, of the worldly among whom he himself was sharply critical. He also claimed divine inspiration for his self-proclaimed mission of restoring Sunni orthodoxy to its pristine glory. His followers bestowed on him the title of *mujaddid-i alfe-e sani* (the renovator of the second thousand years).[72]

The shaykh acquired a reputation for scholarship early in life, during the last years of Akbar's rule, but resisted efforts to be drawn into the emperor's circle. On the latter's death, he denounced the compromises with Hinduism that he thought Akbar had made to the detriment of Islam.[73] Characterizing the news of the death of Akbar as "good tidings," he called upon all God-fearing people to put pressure on "the king of Islam," namely Jahangir (Akbar's successor), to mend the harm done by his father, enforce the holy law (Shari'a), and strengthen the community of true believers. He invoked the traditional authority of "the consensus of the community" for pronouncing judgment on all "innovations" as had indeed been the practice "in the very early days of Islam,"[74] thereby repudiating the authority that Akbar had claimed for himself as the just king. Shaykh Ahmad emphasized that the "example of the Prophet" alone could be the ultimate guide to righteous behavior. In relation to non-Muslims, he called for the reimposition of the poll tax on infidels, the resumption of cow slaughter (a practice deeply repugnant to Hindus), and the denial of high secular office to Shi'ites as well as to Hindus.[75] He maintained that the power of the state was essential for the maintenance of the holy ways of Islam.[76]

The significance of Shaykh Ahmad's call for restoration of orthodoxy is threefold. First, it represented not merely a deep concern with orthodoxy but also the contention that remedial action in the form of revival was called for. A retreat from orthodoxy had occurred, in the shaykh's judgment, owing to the baneful influence of the worldly ulama, the ignorant Sufis and the heterodox Shiʻites, and the un-Islamic actions of kings, particularly their tolerance of infidels. The enemies of Islam were not only outsiders but also, and more injuriously, insiders. The situation could only be remedied by reviving the original purity and missionary spirit of Islam. Second, Shaykh Ahmad stressed the imperative of strengthening the Muslim community by sharply defining its boundaries with reference to infidels and reviving the principle of consensus. Lastly, he underscored the importance of the state as a necessary instrument of renewal. This coordinated program involving the faith, the community, and the state was not merely a restatement of the holistic conception of Islam—as revelation, as a way of life, and as worldly power—but also an anticipation of the fundamentalist turn that was to be witnessed later, from around the middle of the eighteenth century onward.

While Akbar's immediate successors, Jahangir and his son Shahjahan, backed away from the radical religious syncretism that he had set in motion, they did not entirely abandon his attitude of tolerance.

Aurangzeb (ruled 1658–1707) was a learned and devout Sunni Muslim. His goal was to govern "by the precepts of Shariʻa for the benefit of the Indian Muslim community." Conversion of the "infidel" population was to be encouraged, and, "failing that, [he] would rule fairly but sternly over the majority population. Increasingly, the political culture of the empire would be defined in exclusively Muslim terms."[77] Gradually, he abolished laws and conventions, or prohibited practices, that offended against orthodoxy as defined by the ulama. A major landmark was the reimposition of the poll tax in 1679, with a view to "curb the infidels and distinguish the land of the faithful from the infidels."[78] The poll tax "was often a heavy tax, and was exacted in a humiliating manner."[79] By 1669, Aurangzeb had ordered "destruction of Hindu temples on various pretexts."[80] Many historians believe that the most significant development that influenced the emperor's religious policy was the emergence, in western India, of the Maratha challenge to Muslim hegemony. This of course does not mean that the Marathas were concerned exclusively about religion any more than the Mughals were. Power was the key element of historic confrontation. Eventually it became "a vicious circle"[81] with discriminatory measures against non-Muslims acting as both cause and effect of Maratha, Jat, and Sikh rebellions. Aurangzeb "may have felt that the answer to such threats was greater discipline within the Muslim camp, which for him would include tighter religious discipline."[82] Thus we see the role of external *and* internal threats to the religious life of a community in the emergence of alarmist responses, including an insistence on orthodoxy.

Although Aurangzeb was still the emperor of Hindustan, and the country was at least nominally part of dar al-Islam, apprehensions that all was not well were widespread. "Aurangzeb's pluralism had a positive and negative side. Its positivism was directed towards a reformulation of the Muslim society in India. Its negative aspect was the denial to his non-Muslim subjects of social and spiritual rights conceded earlier by Akbar."[83] Aurangzeb not only failed to prevent the disintegration of the empire, but also failed in what he had perceived as his "first task," namely "the preservation or establishment of Shariʻah-minded Sunni rule."[84]

Loss of Power: Dar al-Islam to Dar al-Harb

Aurangzeb died in 1707. His heirs were small men, and within a dozen years the Mughal Empire was beginning to break up into regional kingdoms. The mantle of the moral leadership of the Muslim community of north India (Hindustan) was donned by a farseeing intellectual of high caliber, Shah Wali-Ullah (1703–62).[85] At the age of sixteen this precocious scholar became head of the Delhi branch of the Naqshbandi order of Sufis, and applied himself single-mindedly to the task of saving Indian Muslims. The foundations of his scheme were, first, "purification" of the prevailing Muslim way of life, corrupted by survivals from pre-Islamic Arab religions, borrowing from Hinduism, and general laxity and, second, the revival of Muslim political power.[86] In his judgment, the fundamental cause of both the moral and the political decline of Indian Muslims was their ignorance of the Qur'an and the Prophetic tradition. He was not, however, intolerant toward other religions as such.[87]

Wali-Ullah considered Sunni-Shi'ite differences and the scholasticism and mutual exclusiveness of the four schools of Islamic law largely injurious. His advice to his coreligionists was to overcome dissensions of all kinds, including the theological differences among the three Sufi orders. He exhorted them to put their trust in a rational and broad-minded interpretation of the fundamentals of Islamic belief, thought, and practice and, in its light, to try to evolve a new legal system. To promote such an endeavor, he took a revolutionary step: he translated the Qur'an into Persian (in 1737–38) and followed this up with a formulation of the elements of Qur'anic hermeneutics, emphasizing the exercise of independent judgment on an individual basis (*ijtihad*). As for the larger Indian society, he adhered to the pluralist model, classifying the citizenry into three mutually exclusive classes, namely, unquestioning acceptors of Islam, obeyers of Islamic laws with mental reservations, and infidels/zimmis, and advocated the realization of the poll tax from the third category. In other words, while divisions within Muslim society were to be cemented, the boundaries separating Muslims from non-Muslims were to be given sharper definition.

To overcome both kinds of foes of the faith, internal as well as external, possession of political power was, in his judgment, essential, but Wali-Ullah looked in vain toward Delhi, Hyderabad, and elsewhere for the revival of the Islamic state. Ultimately he invited Ahmad Shah Abdali (of Afghanistan) to invade north India, which had by then come under the rule of non-Muslims, notably the Marathas, who had pushed as far as Lahore in the northwest, beyond Delhi. The Marathas were defeated at Panipat in 1761 by the combined forces of Ahmad Shah Abdali and two Indian Muslim chiefs, and the Mughal emperor Shah Alam was reinstated in Delhi. The political fortunes of Islam in north India however, continued to decline. Abdali, whose "sole interest in India was to get his tribute punctually year after year"[88] to help him consolidate his empire in his homeland, failed to fill the political vacuum,[89] although he tried to bring together different Muslim chieftains of the area. The fate of Islam in the subcontinent could hardly be said to have been his main concern. In fact, Abdali's invasions "proved hardly a contribution to the glory of Islam."[90] A year after the battle at Panipat, Wali-Ullah died.

The significance of Wali-Ullah's contributions to Islamic renewal for the present discussion lies in their form—the combination of several strategies. Unlike Barani and Sirhindi, who believed that the true Islamic way of life had not been supported adequately by the sultan or the padishah, the shah was faced with the collapse of the state. This was an unprecedented crisis and called for a many-sided response. His concern was not only with the revival of the faith in its pristine purity, but also with the reestablishment of the state. The new situation included all three elements—namely reassertion of scriptural authority, revival of the true way of life, and reestablishment of the religious state—that distinguish fundamentalism from revivalism and orthodoxy. The key variable here is the quest for power.

Wali-Ullah's eldest son, Shah Abdul Aziz (1746–1823), carried forward his father's attempted work of Islamic revival with the help of his brothers, one of whom, Abdul Qadir, translated the Qur'an into Urdu in the hope of reaching out to the Muslim masses. Abdul Aziz pronounced on the character of non-Muslim rule, which included in his time British and not only Hindu and Sikh rule. Unlike the Marathas, who had displaced the Mughals in the eighteenth century as the imperial power, but continued to apply the laws made by the Muslims, the British followed an interventionist policy, replacing Shari'a by new laws, particularly in the area of crimes. The very year in which the British established their control over Delhi, without doing away with the powerless Mughal "emperor," that is in 1803, Abdul Aziz declared that the areas under non-Muslim rule had become *dar al-harb*, "the land of war."

Sind had been included in dar al-Islam early in the eighth century, and Muhammad bin Tughluq had six hundred years later regarded his empire as part of it. More than a thousand years of dar al-Islam in India were ending. As Aziz put it in his *fatwa* (judicial opinion), "Islamic law did not prevail in Delhi and the law of the Christian overlords was current without any hindrance."[91] He did not, however, call for migration (*hijrat*) or holy war (jihad), which were the only legitimate options available, according to his father's teaching, in such an imperfect state. Actually, Abdul Aziz softened his attitude toward the British after the initial denunciation.[92] These options were, however, availed by Abdul Aziz's disciple Sayyid Ahmad Barelwi (1786–1831), known by the honorifics of *mujaddid* (renewer) and *shahid* (martyr) among his followers. As a pupil he proved himself more strictly orthodox and less gradualist than his mentor. Continuing the earlier efforts to unify the Muslims and to purify their way of life of its Hindu elements and superstitions, he gave a call to follow the example of the Prophet of Islam (*tariqa-i-Muhammadiya*).[93] Not content with his religious studies, he obtained military training by joining the army of a Muslim chieftain of Rajasthan. Deeply concerned about the moral and political decline of the Muslims, he set two goals for himself, namely, the purification of the lifestyles of all strata of Indian Muslims and the realization of the ideal state (*madinat al-tamma*).

While he and his followers tried to reach out to the masses, through the written and spoken word, the establishment of an important Muslim state had by far the highest priority: only in such a state could true Islam, freed from semipagan practices, be practiced. This necessitated the supreme act of sacrifice, jihad, or a religious war.[94] Preparation for jihad included pilgrimage to Mecca and Medina in 1822, where he stayed for a year and a half, and even dared challenge the orthodoxy of the Wahhabis, provoking their hostility. Sayyid Ahmad and his companions returned home in 1824.

Two years later, he set out on jihad. Traveling westward through Gwalior and Rajasthan, then heading northwest through Sind and Baluchistan, the "warriors," or *mujahidin* (as they were called), reached Kabul in Afghanistan at the end of the year. Turning back into India, having gained a foothold on Muslim soil, from where alone jihad could be launched, and having enlarged the size of his "army" threefold (from 500 to 1,500), Sayyid Ahmad sent an ultimatum to Ranjit Singh, ruler of the Sikh kingdom of Punjab, and almost immediately thereafter attacked a Sikh camp. An early victory here enabled him to establish a theocratic dispensation among the Pathan tribesmen whom he set out to make better Muslims. This was not easily done, for the Pathans were unwilling to give up such elements of their traditional culture as were considered violative of the fundamentals of Islam by Indian judges.[95] Beset with many problems of reform and reorganization, Sayyid Ahmad tried to expand his territorial base, and the social space available for his experiments, by wresting Kashmir from the Sikhs. An attack was launched from the west in 1831, but it failed and Sayyid Ahmad was killed in the hostilities. The mujahidin movement survived for many decades, but it changed the focus of its interest and became increasingly involved in the situation in Afghanistan. It was finally crushed by the British in 1858 when the "warriors" allied themselves with the Indian "mutineers." They had failed to establish the ideal Muslim state in India, though they maintained their presence on the frontier well into the twentieth century.

Contemporary with the north Indian developments but independent of them, militant reformist movements, with similar political agendas, arose among the Muslims of Bengal. The most prominent of these was initiated by Shariat-Ullah (1781–1840) after his return to east Bengal in 1820 from Hijaz, where he had spent twenty years, during which he would have been exposed to the fundamentalist scripturalist movement of 'Abd al-Wahhab. Shariat-Ullah's movement was called Faraizi because of the insistence on *farz,* the fundamental obligations of a Muslim derived from the Qur'an and the Sunna (orthodox tradition). Its leaders rejected Shi'ism, were more wary about Sufism than the north Indian reformists, and prohibited customary practices suspected to be of Hindu derivation. Their attitude to Hindus was deeply colored by the economic situation resulting from the land settlement policies of the British, which had led to the expropriation of Muslim landlords and the impoverishment of Muslim peasantry. In view of the resentment against both the Hindus and the British, Shariat-Ullah unhesitatingly declared Bengal to be dar al-harb, and even prohibited the Friday community prayers and the celebration of the Id festivals. But he did not advocate migration or jihad.[96] The anti-British attitude was softened later on, when the movement was led by Shariat-Ullah's son. West Bengal too witnessed a reformist movement during 1827–31. More militant and openly anti-Hindu, its leaders were the disciples of Sayyid Ahmad Barelwi.[97]

These nineteenth-century Bengali movements did not achieve their objective of cultural renewal ("Islamization") in the desired measure, partly because of the composite character of Bengali society. The great majority of the Muslims of Bengal were descended from Hindus converted to Islam. It has been argued that Islam flourished in Bengal only when certain Muslim cultural mediators of the medieval period interpreted it to the masses in a locally familiar and originally Hindu idiom.[98] The nineteenth-century reformers' concept of Islam was West Asian. These reformers also did not succeed in their political objective of recapturing power. They did, however, generate a social and political awakening among the masses, which bore rich fruit a hundred years later when Bengali Muslims chose to cast their lot with the Pakistan movement. The nineteenth-century movements were narrow in scope, being "essentially the response of the ulema to the loss of their world [of privilege] which they sought to regain by a return to the primitive society of Islam."[99] Yet a new India was taking shape in which new power equations were to be negotiated and new strategies for cultural survival were to be shaped.

The Revivalist Hope: Redemption by Education

With the collapse of the so-called Mutiny of 1857, and the banishment of the nominal Mughal "emperor," who had served as its figurehead, Muslim rule in India on a subcontinental scale finally ended. It was replaced by British supremacy—direct rule in the conquered territories and "paramountcy" in the surviving "native" states, which included some Muslim principalities. The new ground realities also highlighted in Indian Muslim consciousness the overwhelming numerical preponderance of Hindus. How were the Muslims to hold their own alongside of or against the Hindus under British rule? In other words, how could the Islamic way of life be safeguarded in a non-Muslim environment and in the absence of political power?

Sayyid Ahmad Khan (1817–98) of Delhi shaped and spearheaded the modernist response. He attached greater importance to Western rationalism, science, education, and pedagogy (use of English as the medium of instruction was a basic tenet of his faith in modern education) than to traditional Islamic knowledge. He did not, however, reject the latter altogether. Moreover, he was second to none in demanding a return to Islam in its pristine purity. Sayyid Ahmad also attached greater importance to cooperation with the British than confrontation with them over who should rule and how, that is, the issues of legitimacy and character of the state. He was anxious that Muslims should not lag behind Hindus in seizing the new opportunities that were opening in public life for educated Indians. He saw the future of the Muslim community in India to lie in the pursuit of these religious and secular goals. The alternatives of unquestioning retreat into tradition and opposition to British imperium would, he argued, mean spiritual and material ruin.

Actually, Sayyid Ahmad Khan initially sought to further the reformist ("purificationist") program of Shah Wali-Ullah in the direction of "limitless rationalist speculation" in order to build a bridge between Islam and post-Enlightenment Western thought. In a bold move, he called for the rejection of all the "sayings" attributed to the Prophet, that is, the classical Hadith, that were repugnant to human reason. He even introduced a distinction between Muhammad's personal opinions, which he did not consider binding, and the revelations made by God to him. He went on to trace the roots of modern thought in the revelation itself. A key idea on which he built his thought was "that the Work of God and the Word of God can never be antagonistic to each other." [100] Therefore, the Word could be interpreted by the Work. This made the study of nature by the methods of inductive and experimental sciences imperative and earned for Khan the sobriquet of *nechari*, (the naturalist) from the shocked ulama and other critics. Moreover, he said that the adaptation of the modern world demanded the liberalization of Islamic law.

Sayyid Ahmad Khan attached the greatest importance to modern education, alongside of which traditional studies could be pursued critically. He declared, "The Muslims have nothing to fear from the adoption of the new education if they simultaneously hold steadfast to their faith, because Islam is not an irrational superstition; it is a rational religion which can march hand in hand with the growth of human knowledge." [101] Ideas such as these became the basis for the establishment of a Scientific Society and a modern school for Muslims in 1864 and the Anglo-Muhammadan Oriental College at Aligarh in 1874. The college was modeled on Cambridge, and grew in due course to become the celebrated Aligarh Muslim University.[102] "There is evidence that towards the end of his life Sayyid Ahmad was himself disappointed in the first crops that grew at Aligarh. These were gentlemen who . . . prided themselves on a smattering of modern ideas but were either a-religious or anti-religious." [103] A synthesis of tradition and modernity was more problematic than Sayyid Ahmad Khan had anticipated.

Meanwhile, the revivalist hope continued to generate scripturalist responses in north India, along sectarian lines, well into the late nineteenth century. They all attributed the decline of political and social fortunes of the Muslims to the failure of the community to live within the bounds of Shari'a. They mainly depended upon interpretations of Islamic law in their efforts for renewal (*tajdid*) and reform (*islah*), and vacillated between contextualized traditionalism (yielding to local customs such as saint worship) and scripturalist universalism. A similar vacillation also marked various educational experiments that preceded and followed Sayyid Ahmad Khan's efforts, but remained opposed to them.

The most notable of the traditionalist educational programs of this kind, though not the oldest, was a seminary founded by a group of ulama, led by Muhammad Qasim Nanotawi, in 1867 at Deoband, not far from Delhi. The institutions at Aligarh and Deoband both derived inspiration from the theological teachings of Wali-Ullah. While the Aligarh college developed the element of religious speculation, the Deoband Dar ul-Ulum stressed orthodoxy. The Deoband theological seminary was to attain "great distinction, unrivalled, except for al-Azhar." [104] Its goal was to synthesize "the two main streams of Islamic tradition, that of intellectual learning and that of spiritual experience" [105]—that is, the traditions of the ulama and the Sufis. The strategy adopted was to "return to the tradition of the 'tongue and the pen' and train ulama 'dedicated to reformed Islam.'" They were expected to preach in mosques, issue fatawa on specific theological and social questions, and provide spiritual guidance to those fit to receive it. In a radical departure from past practice, they were to serve the community rather than the state.

Accordingly, a fairly wide-ranging but fixed curriculum stressed the study of juris-prudence (fiqh) and the Prophetic tradition (Hadith), but also asserted that the Shari'a could not be subjected to rational inquiry. The Deoband ulama were actually against the teaching of the rational sciences of logic, philosophy, and jurisprudence. "No single concern was more central to them than the quest for correct belief and practice in the light of the classical texts."[106] They adhered to the Hanafi school of law, disap-proved of interscholastic eclecticism of the kind advocated by Wali-Ullah, and pre-scribed strict conformity. They also limited severely the scope of individual interpre-tation (ijtihad) to such injunctions as were characterized by a revealed inner meaning but a flexible outer form.

In short, the Deoband ulama were intellectual isolationists who "denied the need and value of further knowledge."[107] New ideas were suspect, and innovation was con-sidered a bad thing. The fatawa they issued expressed their puritanical zeal.[108] Thus, they were critical of Ahl-i Hadis (another reformist group) for not being orthodox enough, warned against Shi'ite influences, disapproved of Sufi excesses (such as the belief in the power of intercession claimed for the saints), discouraged social relations and religious disputations with Hindus, and denounced the Ahmadiyya notion of sec-ondary prophets after Muhammad. Some of them went to the extent of opposing the celebration of the Prophet's birthday on the ground that it reflected Hindu influence and encouraged false beliefs.[109] On the whole, the Deoband ulama steered clear of controversies: thus, they did not attack the Aligarh experiment although they did not approve of it. They kept a low political profile, which does not mean that they did not appreciate the uses of political power. Actually they were deeply concerned with the shaping of ways of being Muslim under colonial rule. This amounted to pulling away from the state until such time as the ulama may rule again. The retreat from an active program of reestablishing the Muslim state was more tactics than the enunciation of a new principle. The Deobandis' conception of the Dar al-Ulum was of an institution "from where jihad for observance of the shari'ah could be carried on."[110] The expec-tation referred to not only the "greater" jihad of self-purification but also to the "lesser" one against nonbelievers. The seminary discretely maintained contact with the caliph-sultan of Turkey and entertained a pan-Islamist view of the future. They even visualized the possibility of active collaboration in the event of hostilities breaking out between Britain and Turkey.[111] At home, they were suspected to have supported the largely Sikh *ghadir* rebellion of 1915[112] and, ultimately, "formed the spearhead of the nationalists among the Muslims."[113]

In 1919, after the end of the First World War, the ulama of Deoband joined hands with those of Farangi Mahal and Nadwat ul-Ulama, both of Lucknow, to establish a political organization that they called the Jamiyyat-ul-Ulama-i-Hind, the party of the ulama of India. It aligned itself with the Indian National Congress and supported the Khilafat movement, which protested the imposition of the treaty of Sèvres on Turkey.[114] Ironically, the modernist Aligarh Muslim University was the cradle of the leaders of the Muslim separatist movement. In fact, one of the reasons the Jamiyyat was founded was that the leadership of the All-India Muslim League (founded in 1906) was too modernist for the liking of the ulama. While the league leadership was expected to strive for a modern (presumably secular) state, the Indian National Congress was known for its pluralist orientation, under which one could hope to make room for Muslims to live according to their own lights. In short, the Deobandis' twin quest for a scriptural religion combined with, eventually, the rule of the ulama marks them as moderate fundamentalists.

The Muslim League worked for the founding of Pakistan and restored political power to the hands of Muslims, though not on an all-India basis.[115] Moreover, a homeland for Muslims did not automatically resuscitate dar al-Islam. In fact, some concerned Muslims looked upon the demand for Pakistan as un-Islamic because of its emphasis on the Western notion of "nation" and "nationalism." Such critics emerged as the Muslim fundamentalists of twentieth-century South Asia, widely influential but until now (the 1990s) not wholly successful.

Islamic Fundamentalism in South Asia in the Twentieth Century

Muhammad Iqbal (1876–1938) and Abul Kalam Azad (1888–1958) shared the Deobandis' distrust of the modernists. The youthful Azad, educated in the Arab lands (he studied for a while at al-Azhar also), sought answers to all significant questions about the universe and the place of humanity in it in the Qur'an, and called for a return to it in the pages of his widely circulated magazine *Al-Hilal.* The older Iqbal, who studied philosophy in Cambridge and Munich, called for "the reconstruction of religious thought in Islam" (in his poetical works generally and specifically in a set of lectures published in 1934). He cautioned his listeners and readers that such reconstruction was a more "serious" enterprise than "mere adjustment to the modern conditions of life." The task of interpreting the Islamic tradition involved, according to Iqbal, the full realization of the Prophetic message and example. The ultimate principles were unchanging, but their significance in a changing world were open to exploration through reasoned judgments (ijtihad). He regarded Islam as a "cultural movement" and considered ijtihad "the principle of movement."

Both Azad and Iqbal were revivalists and advocates of pan-Islamism, but otherwise were intellectually dissimilar. Azad modified his pan-Islamism by adopting a pluralist view of nationalism[116] and a comparativist position in the field of religion.[117] Iqbal overcame an early romantic view of the love of the land of one's birth to proclaim Islamic universalism and argue for a cultural space for Indian Muslims, which in other hands became the demand for Pakistan.[118]

While agreeing with the Deobandis' antimodernist stance, Azad and Iqbal disapproved of the tendency of the ulama, from the earliest times, to place their own opinions and interpretations above the original text. As Azad put it, "[W]hen the commentators found that they could not rise to the heights of the Quranic thought, they strove to bring it down to the level of their own mind."[119] A third critic who joined in the criticism of the ulama was the gifted editor of the official organ of the Jamiyyat-ul-Ulama-i-Hind, Abul Ala Maududi (1903–79).

Maududi's principal grievance against the Deoband ulama, and the others who together with them composed the Jamiyyat, was their support of the movement for independence under the auspices of the Indian National Congress. In his judgment, no well-educated and honest Muslim could subscribe to the Western ideology of nationalism, for his worldview would be religious. The very notion of the nation was, according to Maudidi, a Western and false concept. While the political attitudes of the so-called nationalist Muslims were bad enough, the situation became quite alarming in his eyes when the All-India Muslim League, building upon the ideas of Iqbal and others, adopted a separate Muslim homeland on the subcontinent as its political goal. Such a state, Maudidi declared, would "safeguard merely the material interests of Indian Muslims" and neglect their spiritual life, as none of the leaders, including Muhammad Ali Jinnah, had "an Islamic mentality or Islamic habits of thought." [120]

From 1933 Maudidi's journal *Tarjuman ul-Qur'an* has been the principal vehicle of his ideas. In 1941 he founded an organization, sociocultural and religious rather than directly political in character, and called it Jamaat-i-Islami (literally, the Islamic Association). Arguing that there could be no Islamic state without an Islamic revolution, he concentrated on expounding the fundamentals of Islam and announced that he was opposed to the demand for Pakistan. When Pakistan was established in 1947, he migrated there and started a campaign for the establishment of an Islamic state. "Indeed," he wrote, "if a secular and Godless, instead of Islamic, constitution was to be introduced and if the Criminal Procedure Code had to be enforced instead of the Islamic Shari'a what was the sense in all this struggle for a separate Muslim homeland?" [121] He pronounced Western secular democracy to be the very antithesis of Islam. [122]

Maudidi was in and out of prison in Pakistan from 1948 onward. In 1953, when he assumed the leadership of the anti-Ahmadiyya movement and counted Pakistan ulama among his followers, the government held him responsible for street violence in Lahore, and a military court sentenced him to death. The sentence, which had been imposed on flimsy grounds, was commuted soon afterward. [123] In India, his followers were denounced by the ulama of Deoband, who issued a fatwa in 1951 asking Indian Muslims to "shun the Jamaat-i-Islami and treat it as deadly poison"; supporters of the organization were pronounced sinners. [124]

Maudidi's importance as a twentieth-century exegete of the fundamentals of Islam, who has been influential not only among the Muslims of South Asia but also in the heartlands of Islam in West Asia, lies not so much in any profundity of thought as in the compelling simplicity of his message and its clarity of argument. He wrote in Urdu, and his writings were translated into Arabic and English, contributing to his wide-ranging influence. Among the creative scholars influenced by him the most notable, perhaps, was Sayyid Qutb of the Muslim Brotherhood (al-Ikhwan al-Muslimun) of Egypt. [125] The core of Maudidi's message is a call "for a return to the real and original fountains of the Islamic ideal," dispensing with "all the excess intellectual and religious baggage accumulated by the community in its journey through the centuries." [126] He writes, "The objective of the Islamic movement, in this world, is . . . [that] a leadership that has rebelled against God and His guidance is responsible for the suffering of mankind has to be replaced by a leadership that is God—conscious, righteous and committed to following Divine guidance." [127] His teaching represents "a triumph of scripturalist doctrine."[128] To elaborate, the Qur'an and the exemplary life of the Prophet are, according to Maududi, the foundation of the Islamic way of life. The law that God gave is comprehensive and perfect. In Maududi's words, "The *shari'ah* is a complete scheme of life and an all-embracing social order—nothing superfluous and nothing lacking."[129] Whatever seems not to be clearly given may be derived from the original sources through personal legal deduction (*taffaquh*). The exercise of personal reason (ijtihad) is legitimate, for true reason is Islamic. This is a point of fundamental importance: it goes beyond the rationalist formulation that Islam conforms to reason.

No individual is, however, an island unto himself: the existence of the social group, of society, is imperative for the Islamic way of life to be pursued. No Muslim society would survive as such if power were not in the hands of reasonable Muslims. Maududi observes that "in human affairs the most important thing is, 'who holds the bridle reins?' If these are in the hands of righteous people, worshippers of God, then it is inevitable that the whole of social life be God-worshipping. . . . None of the purposes of religion can be accomplished so long as control of affairs is in the hands of *kaffirs*."[130] This being so, the Islamic state must be "totalitarian," resembling formally even the Fascist and Communist states, but unlike such ungodly regimes, it is, of course, based on submission to divine law: that is what Islam means, total submission.[131]

Power lies at the very center of Maududi's concept of true Islamic society, and all varieties of legitimate power are for him only expressions of God's sovereignty (*hakimiyya*). He writes, "[T]he everlasting truth which the Quran expresses . . . is that kingship in the heavens and the earth [alike] is kingship of a single essence only."[132] Human beings, like all that God has created, whether it is animate or inanimate, obey his law by their very nature. Choice is granted to them alone in the sphere peculiar to their state, namely the moral domain. Those who would be saved must submit to God's command here also; only then would they be true "submitters," that is, Muslims. Maududi interprets the first part of the Muslim confession of faith, "There is no god other than the God" (*la ilaha illa Allah*), to mean that "There is none other to be obeyed but God."[133] Those who argue for traditional personal monarchy as an idea sui generis, or those who advocate modern secular democracy investing sovereignty in the people, defy God's law, give evidence of their ignorance, and produce total chaos. Ignorance (*jahiliyya*) was the state of society in Arabia prior to the bestowal of the mantle of prophecy on Muhammad. Islam in modern times has, according to Maududi, reverted to the pre-Islamic state of ignorance. Hence the central importance of "holy war for the spread of Islam" (jihad).

In his 1929 essay on jihad he first stated his fundamentalist position and attracted widespread attention.[134] Jihad is "but another name for the attempt to establish the Divine order; the Quran therefore declares it to be a touchstone of belief."[135] In other words, it is total struggle, offensive or defensive as the need may be, against the usurpation of God's sovereignty, whether by pseudoreligious monarchists or Westernized secular democrats. What is more, its aim is to embrace all of humankind. Just before leaving India for Pakistan in 1947, Maududi appealed to Hindus to resist modernization and search for "detailed guidance" in their own religious tradition: "if you do not find [it] it does not mean that God has never given it to you. It means you have lost all or part of it. . . . We are presenting to you the same guidance sent by the same God. Don't hesitate to accept it." [136]

The significance of the rhetoric of Abul Ala Maudidi was above all that, it uttered in general terms the fundamentalist concerns of Indian Islam and sought to overcome the specificity of the predicament of South Asian Muslims. I have tried to show in this essay that the major preoccupation of the traditional guardians of Islamic orthodoxy in India, mainly the ulama, has been the threat posed by internal divisions—of sects, schools of law, and Sufi orders—and the external Hindu religiocultural tradition and social organization. Its enormity was accentuated by the large numbers of imperfectly Islamized converts who swelled the ranks of the Muslims during the heyday of Muslim political power. As long as Muslims enjoyed such power, the guardians were concerned to see that the values of religion would not be sacrificed for the sake of the interests of the state, that kings and emperors did not accommodate heretics and their Hindu subjects in a compromising manner. Such compromises did occur, however, throughout the thousand years of Muslim suzerainty in India.

The Muslim state in India had long been defunct when Maudidi began his career as reformer in the 1930s. The not-so-new imperial power on the subcontinent was Great Britain, and a national liberation movement, dominated by Hindus, had taken shape over the previous half century. The Muslim response to this development had been, as stated earlier, a divided one. The ulama sided with the nationalists against the British, and the modernists with the British against the nationalists. The radicals among the former (the modernists) later spawned the separatists, who won a separate Muslim homeland. Maudidi redefined the terms of the choice in religiocultural rather than political terms, more sharply than Iqbal had done, and rejected all three options. He envisaged a future for Indian, and later Pakistani, Muslims in which they would be cosharers of Islamic destiny on a global scale: in his own words, "a rational nationality of believers" constituting "a world community of Islam." [137] As soon as power appeared to be not only within reach but also definable in nonsecular, Islamic terms, he lost no time in stressing its importance. He emerged as a fundamentalist par excellence.

Not all of Maudidi's South Asian contemporaries thought highly of his incessant efforts for the promotion of Islamic society and government. The extreme hostility of the Deoband ulama and of successive governments in Pakistan (up to the time of President Zia ul-Haq, who was an admirer of Maudidi's fundamentalist ideas, notably the notion that sovereignty "belongs" exclusively to Allah) has been noted above. Muhammad Mujeeb accuses him of equating "assertion" with "proof" and of the "disregard of thirteen hundred years of Muslim history." [138] Fazlur Rahman, who regarded Maudidi as "a journalist rather than a serious scholar" and as a superficial writer, observes, "Maudidi displays nowhere the larger and more profound vision of Islam's role in the world." [139]

Such criticism notwithstanding, Maudidi's influence has survived his own lifework, and the Jamaat-i-Islami is an active organization in Pakistan, Bangladesh, and (to a lesser extent) India. [140] Within India, there is a separate Jamaat-i-Islami in the state

of Jammu and Kashmir, which is a major force behind the armed secessionist movement there and has given the call for Islamic society and government: "As Kashmiris
it is our duty to struggle for . . . independence . . . and to establish that social order in
the state which we would like to see triumphant in the whole world."[141]

Concluding Remarks: Lessons of Comparison

This essay was written with a limited objective in mind: namely, to review the concern
with Islamic orthodoxy in north and northwest India, over the long duration and at
the macrolevel, with a view to looking for the lessons that such an exercise must have
for understanding the contemporary worldwide phenomenon called fundamentalism.
Regrettably, this approach has resulted in the neglect, first, of significant regional variations,[142] and, second, of the sociologically interesting accommodations at the micro-
level that have been gradually worked out by the people in the course of their everyday
life in both the intrareligious (within Islam) and interreligious (between Muslims and
Hindus) contexts. The assumption with which I began the exercise was that all religious traditions are concerned—more in some situations than in others—with safe-
guarding "correct beliefs" and "correct practices." It was further assumed that, while
the guardians of tradition are usually an identifiable category, attempts to arrogate this
role may be made by others—individuals or groups—particularly in times of crisis.
Thus, the Iranian Revolution of 1979 bestowed a novel interpretation on the role of
the Islamic jurists as the guardians of the state and the society (*wilayat al-faqih*), although this was only a minor strand in Shi'ite political thought (constitutionalism was
the dominant one). Similarly, the emergence of militant fundamentalism within the
Sikh religious tradition during the 1980s saw new categories of functionaries don the
mantle of the guardians of orthodoxy.[143]

Islam, it is often asserted, has been particularly prone to giving rise to fundamentalist movements concerned with restoring the pristine purity of belief and practice.
The reasons for this tendency are said to be manifold. Thus, as a way of life believed to
be ordained by God, revealed in the pages of a single book, reinforced and extended
by the exemplary traditions associated with Muhammad (regarded as the last true
prophet) and the first four "rightly guided" khalifas, Islam has certain well-defined
fundamentals. Belief in the unity of God in his angels, prophets, and the revealed book
and submission to his final judgment form the core of orthodoxy, supplemented by
daily prayers, the month of fasting, charity, and if possible the pilgrimage to Mecca.

The clarity of the basic tenets is, however, offset by sectarian divisions, such as the
one between Sunnis and Shi'ites, which are as old as Islam, by the almost equally ancient differences between the ulama and the Sufis, by the mutual exclusiveness of the
schools of Islamic law, and by the rather ambiguous status of the king, or a substitute
secular authority, and the laws that they make. The dangers of heterodoxy are further
heightened by the absence of the church.

The above characteristics are true of Muslim communities everywhere. Further, the
very fact that Islam is a world religion means that it is subject to the pressures of diverse

environments. I have tried to show in this essay that, when Islam traveled eastward to India from its locus classicus in West Asia, it confronted a highly developed civilization, the religious traditions of which were radically different. The immigrants—whether Arabs, Turks, Mughals, or Pathans—were everywhere on the subcontinent a privileged and self-conscious minority, and depended heavily on proselytization to constitute local Muslim communities. Islam in India, therefore, often generated anxieties and movements for the protection of the purity of the faith.

The tensions that thus simmered at the very core of the Muslim presence in India never settled down to a stable equilibrium of coexistence. As Francis Robinson puts it, "there [has been] continual, if sometimes slow and barely perceptible, movements between visions of perfect Muslim life and those which ordinary Muslims lead."[144] The last two, or two and one-half, centuries in particular have been, Robinson says, "a period of considerable vitality in which versions of high Islamic tradition have come to make noticeable inroads into the custom-centered tradition."[145] Employing the terminology used in this essay, one may say that the eighteenth century witnessed the replacement of an abiding concern with orthodoxy by deeper and more organized revivalist or fundamentalist movements. How, then, may the difference between orthodoxy, revivalism, and fundamentalism be characterized?

From the evidence presented here, it seems that, despite the differences in the perceptions of the Muslim kings and the guardians of Islam in the medieval period, the state was seen by all concerned as ideally the protector of the true Islamic way of life (Shari'a), even though it did not always discharge its role well. The principle of the legitimacy of kingship was given precedence over actual practice. In Akbar's time, however, it would have appeared to the guardians of orthodoxy that the principle itself was being redefined. When the deviation from orthodoxy involves either large numbers of a community or its most significant individuals, for example the king, the situation calls for a sterner response than the routine expression of concern about orthodoxy. Such a response came for Shaykh Ahmad Sirhindi, who gave the call for the renewal of the original impulse of Islam.

While Sirhindi's concern at the beginning of the seventeenth century arose from the alleged misuse of royal power, Shah Wali-Ullah's angst in the middle of the eighteenth was owing to the loss of political power and the general decline of the moral character of the community. The protective shield of the Islamic way of life had fallen, and without it the community was adrift. Political power, then, emerges as the key variable in the transition from orthodoxy to fundamentalism. Fundamentalist movements are Janus-faced: they are as much concerned with regaining power as they are with recovering the purity of the way of life and renewing its impulses. One endeavor is seen as inseparable from the other. In other words, cultural sociology and secular history must be reintegrated. As Wilfred Cantwell Smith puts it, "[t]he fundamental malaise of modern Islam is a sense that something has gone wrong with Islamic history. The fundamental problem of modern Muslims is how to rehabilitate that history . . . so that Islamic society may once again flourish as a divinely guided society should and must."[146]

If power is of critical importance, how do we evaluate Maududi's lack of interest in the political independence of India in the pre-1947 days? It is not at all obscure that for him power, or the quest for it, was not unimportant but had to be subordinated to the right purpose. Since neither the independence of India nor the demand for Pakistan was intended as the means for the establishment of a true Islamic society, he wrote about the Islamic state only in general terms and concentrated on religiocultural reform. As soon as the establishment of Pakistan opened the way for the establishment of an Islamic state, Maududi lost no time in entering the political arena.

The linkage of culture and power inevitably results in the totalitarian ambition of world domination. Fundamentalist movements lay claim to exclusive possession of "the truth," brook no dissent, and proceed to show "the right path" to everybody who is not an "insider." Such an attitude comes naturally to Muslim fundamentalists, because Islam does not in principle attach any importance to race, language, or nationality. In practice all primordial bonds that separate one Muslim from another are to be submerged in the universal brotherhood of Muslims (*umma*). This, at any rate, is the ideal goal.

To carry home the message of umma to various peoples, in different places and at different times, calls for adjustment and innovation. Without these nothing can be done. Paradoxical though it may seem, fundamentalists, who are self-proclaimed renewers, must necessarily be innovators. From Shah Wali-Ullah to Abul Ala Maududi all South Asian Muslim fundamentalists have been innovators. The former's translation of the Qur'an into Persian, his plea for eclecticism in the field of Islamic law, and many other exhortations were innovations. Maududi, it has been pointed out, has more in common with the modernist Sayyid Ahmad Khan than with the ulama, though he disagrees with him as well as them.

Maududi has been considered the archconservationist, a scripturalist, claiming Shari'a as an unchangeable, complete, and valid way of life for our times, but it would be an error to consider his polemics timeless. He is as much situated in the twentieth century as the modernists he criticizes, and like them he reformulates Islam in the process of protecting it against the spirit of the modern age, which in his opinion is summed up in the notion of rationality. This conviction led Maududi to one of his startling and innovative formulations: it will not do to say that Islam accords with reason; one must assert that true reason accords well with Islam.

This formulation is obviously a response to the challenge of the West, for had not no less a Muslim intellectual luminary than al-Ghazali inveighed against reason? Similarly, Maududi's concern with Islamic governance reflects not an original emphasis on the Shari'a, which is mainly concerned with the regulation of personal matters rather than affairs of the state, but a modern preoccupation. As Charles Adams puts it, "it is difficult to avoid the conclusion that Mawdudi . . . [was] profoundly determined by historical circumstances."[147] So indeed was Ayatollah Khomeini.[148] It follows, then, that the confrontation with past-Enlightenment modernity, which I bracketed at the beginning of this essay to enable me to look back a thousand years for the roots of Islamic fundamentalism in South Asia, can now be reintroduced as a characteristic feature of twentieth-century fundamentalist movements.

The rearrangement of emphasis in the received tradition, in the manner indicated above, is tantamount to a selective retrieval of tradition. Fundamentalist movements appear to be characterized by a tendency first to redefine tradition in the light of perceived contemporary challenges and only then to give the call for a return to the fundamentals of the faith. This is as true of the Sikh and Hindu fundamentalist movements as of the Muslim.[149]

An attempt to understand developments in the history of Islam in South Asia in the narrative mode yields certain insights into the making of fundamentalism (which is by no means all there is to this history). These insights include an appreciation of the critical role of, notably, exclusive claims to the possession of scriptural truth, cultural critique, political power, ambitions of domination, and the willingness to innovate and redefine the received tradition. All these, however, will remain inchoate elements in the absence of determined if not charismatic leadership and a formally organized movement. The foregoing commonalities notwithstanding, there will always be critical differences, too, and there will be diverse fundamentalisms, even diverse Islamic fundamentalisms. Their "family resemblance," implied in their being called so, points to "a oneness residing not in any supposed essential features of 'Islamic' . . . but in the logic of relations between the meanings given to prescription and those given to circumstances."[150]

Notes

I am grateful to Semma Alavi, R. Scott Appleby, Raymond Jamous, Barbara Metcalf, Harbans Mukhia, Francis Robinson, and W. R. Roff for their valuable criticisms of the first draft of this paper.

1. See Martin E. Marty and R. Scott Appleby, eds., *Fundamentalisms Observed* (Chicago: University of Chicago Press, 1991).

2. Martin E. Marty, "Fundamentalism as a Social Phenomenon," *Bulletin of the American Academy of Arts and Sciences* 42 (November 1988): 15–29.

3. Bruce Lawrence, *Defenders of God: The Fundamentalist Revolt against the Modern Age* (San Francisco: Harper and Row, 1989), p. 8.

4. See Ashis Nandy, *The Intimate Enemy: Loss and Recovery of Self under Colonial Rule* (Delhi: Oxford University Press, 1983).

5. See, e.g., Mohamed Arkoun, *Rethinking Islam Today,* Centre for Contemporary Arab Studies Occasional Papers (Washington, D.C.: Georgetown University, 1987).

6. Lawrence, *Defenders of God,* p. 232.

7. Emmanuel Sivan, *Radical Islam: Medieval Theology and Modern Politics* (New Haven: Yale University Press, 1990), p. 3.

8. Lawrence, *Defenders of God,* p. 100.

9. The theme of gharbzadagi was elaborated by Jalal Al-e Ahmad, an Iranian author, in a book bearing that title and published in 1961. It received more scholarly treatment at the hand of 'Ali Shari'ati (see Kenneth Cragg, *The Pen and the Faith: Eight Modern Muslim Writers and the Quran* [London: George Allen and Unwin, 1985], pp. 72–90). Fazlur Rahman has noted several Indian writers, notably Abul Kalam Azad, Zafar Ali Khan, and Abul Ala Maududi, used the term *maghrib zadah,* "West-stricken," in their work to describe "modern-educated and westernized classes." See Fazlur Rahman, *Islam and Modernity: Transformation of an Intellectual Tradition* (Chicago: University of Chicago Press, 1982), p. 72.

10. See T. N. Madan, "The Double-Edged Sword: Fundamentalism and the Sikh Religious Tradition," in Marty and Appleby, *Fundamentalisms Observed.*

11. See Gail Minault, *The Khilafat Move-*

ment: *Religious Symbolism and Political Mobilization in India* (Delhi: Oxford University Press, 1982).

12. See Syeda Saiyidain Hameed, ed., *India's Maulana, Abul Kalam Azad: Centenary Volume II: Selected Speeches and Writings* (Delhi: Vikas Publishing House, 1990), p. 161.

13. Yohanan Friedman, "Islamic Thought in Relation to the Indian Context," in Marc Gaborieau, ed., *Islam and Society in South Asia (Purusartha 9)* (Paris: Editions de l'Ecole des Hautes Etudes en Sciences Sociales, 1986), p. 79.

14. See Ishtiaq Husain Qureshi, *The Muslim Community of the Indo-Pakistan Subcontinent, 610–1947* (The Hague: Mouton and Co., 1962), pp. 12–14.

15. All dates in this essay are according to the Christian era.

16. See Qureshi, *The Muslim Community*, p. 35.

17. See Sayid Athar Abbas Rizvi, *The Wonder That Was India: A Survey of the History and Culture of the Subcontinent from the Coming of the Muslims to the British Conquest, 1200–1700* (London: Sidgwick and Jackson, 1987), 2:9.

18. Peter Hardy, "The Foundations of Medieval Islam," in William Theodore de Bary, gen. ed., *Sources of Indian Tradition*, vol. 1, compiled by A. L. Basham et al. (New York: Columbia University Press, 1970), p. 371.

19. See Yohanan Friedman, "The Temple of Multan: A Note on Early Muslim Attitudes to Idolatry," *Israel Oriental Studies* 2 (1972): 180–82.

20. Hafeez Malik, *Moslem Nationalism in India and Pakistan* (Washington, D.C.: Public Affairs Press, 1963), p. 5.

21. See Aziz Ahmad, *Studies in Islamic Culture in the Indian Environment* (Oxford: Clarendon Press, 1964), p. 101.

22. See Khaliq Ahmad Nizami, *Akbar and Religion* (Delhi: Idarah-i-Adabiyat-i-Delli, 1989), p. 96.

23. See Qureshi, *The Muslim Community*, pp. 42, 53–54.

24. See Peter Hardy on this theme, though for a later period ("The Growth of Authority over a Conquered Political Elite: The Early Delhi Sultanate as a Possible Case Study," in J. F. Richards, ed., *Kingship and Authority in South Asia,* South Asia Studies, no. 3, 2d ed. [Madison: University of Wisconsin, 1981]).

25. Malik, *Moslem Nationalism in India and Pakistan*, p. 4.

26. *Ulama* is the plural of the Arabic noun *'alim,* which literally means "one who knows," "a learned person." It is specifically used to refer to a person who is a formally educated authority on religious and legal matters. The ulama as a body are an essential element of Islamic governance. Their judicial opinions (*fatawa,* sing. *fatwa*) help in the regulation of the domestic and public life of a Muslim community.

27. See Romila Thapar, *A History of India* (Harmondsworth: Penguin Books, 1966), 1:302.

28. Marshall G. S. Hodgson, *The Venture of Islam: Conscience and History in a World Civilization,* vol. 3, *The Gunpowder Empires and Modern Times* (Chicago: University of Chicago Press, 1974), p. 59.

29. Aziz Ahmad, *Studies in Islamic Culture,* p. 73.

30. See, e.g., Susan Bayly, *Saints, Goddesses, and Kings: Muslims and Christians in South Indian Society, 1700–1900* (Cambridge: Cambridge University Press, 1992); and T. N. Madan, "Religious Ideology in a Plural Society: The Muslims and Hindus of Kashmir," *Contributions to Indian Sociology,* n.s., 6 (1972): 106–41.

31. Qureshi, *The Muslim Community,* p. 103.

32. Ibid. See also Aziz Ahmad, *Studies in Islamic Culture,* p. 77 et passim.

33. Aziz Ahmad, *Studies in Islamic Culture,* p. 5.

34. See Rizvi, *The Wonder That Was India,* pp. 12–18.

35. See Malik, *Moslem Nationalism in India and Pakistan,* p. 18.

36. See Muhammad Mujeeb, *The Indian*

Muslims (London: George Allen and Unwin, 1967), pp. 73–74.

37. Muhammad Habib and Afsar Umar Salim Khan, *The Political Theory of the Delhi Sultanate* (including a translation of Zia ud-din Barani's *Fatwa-i Jahandari*, ca. 1358–59) (Allahabad: Kitab Mahal, n.d.), p. vi.

38. Muhammad Habib, "Politics and Society during the Early Medieval Period," in Khaliq Ahmad Nizami, ed., *Collected Works of Professor Muhammad Habib* (New Delhi: People's Publishing House, 1981), p. 356.

39. Hardy, "The Growth of Authority," pp. 192, 204.

40. Thapar, *A History of India,* p. 290.

41. Harbans Mukhia, *Historians and Historiography during the Reign of Akbar* (New Delhi: Vikas Publishing House, 1976), p. 39.

42. Habib, "Politics and Society during the Early Medieval Period," p. 424.

43. See Habib and Khan, *The Political Theory of the Delhi Sultanate,* pp. 46–47.

44. Ibid., p. 39.

45. Ibid., pp. 39–40.

46. See Barani's formulation in Hardy, "The Foundations of Medieval Islam," pp. 459–60.

47. See Peter Hardy, *Historians of Modern India: Studies in Indo-Muslim Historical Writing* (London: Luzac and Co., 1966); and "Unity and Variety in Indo-Islamic and Perso-Islamic Civilization: Some Ethical and Political Ideas of Diya al-Din Barani of Delhi, of al-Ghazali, and of Nasir al-Din Tusi Compared," *Iran* 16 (1978): 27–35.

48. See Sayid Athar Abbas Rizvi, "Islamic Proselytisation (Seventh to Sixteenth Centuries)," in G. A. Oddie, ed., *Religion in South Asia* (New Delhi: Manohar, 1977), p. 21.

49. Ibid., pp. 22, 31.

50. Aziz Ahmad, *Studies in Islamic Culture,* p. 175.

51. Ibid., p. 83.

52. Khaliq Ahmad Nizami, *Some Aspects of Religion and Politics in India during the Thirteenth Century* (Aligarh: Muslim University, 1961), p. 178.

53. Qureshi, *The Muslim Community,* p. 137.

54. Aziz Ahmad, *Studies in Islamic Culture,* p. 168.

55. See Hodgson, *The Gunpowder Empires,* p. 66; and Nizami, *Akbar and Religion,* pp. 100–163.

56. Aziz Ahmad, *Studies in Islamic Culture,* p. 168.

57. See Hodgson, *The Gunpowder Empires,* p. 66.

58. See Rizvi, *The Wonder That Was India,* p. 107; and Mukhia, *Historians and Historiography,* p. 48.

59. See Qureshi, *The Muslim Community,* pp. 140–41; and Nizami, *Akbar and Religion,* pp. 127–31.

60. This is a controversial issue. Ishtiaq Husain Qureshi, who can hardly be called an apologist on behalf of Akbar, writes, "The decree . . . has been wrongly termed a decree of infallibility, which it certainly was not" (*The Muslim Community,* p. 141).

61. See Sri Ram Sharma, *The Religious Policy of the Mughal Emperors* (Bombay: Asia Publishing House, 1962), pp. 31–32.

62. Aziz Ahmad, *Studies in Islamic Culture,* p. 171.

63. It may be noted here that the fundamentalist Abul Ala Maududi asserted the contrary view: "The new religion . . . in reality, was intended to favor all religions to the complete exclusion of Islam. . . . The most favored creed, however, was Hinduism" (*A Short History of Revivalist Movement in Islam* [Delhi: Markazi Maktaba Islami, 1981], p. 65).

64. Hodgson, *The Gunpowder Empires,* p. 67.

65. Mujeeb, *The India Muslims,* p. 258.

66. See Mukhia, *Historians and Historiography,* p. 77; and Azra Alavi, *Socio-religious Outlook of Abul Fazl* (Delhi: Idarah-i-Adabiyat-i-Delli, 1983), p. 49.

67. See Qureshi, *The Muslim Community,* pp. 145–47; Aziz Ahmad, *Studies in Islamic Culture,* pp. 171–73; Mujeeb, *The Indian Muslims,* pp. 263–64; Hodgson, *The Gunpowder Empires,* p. 84.

68. See Mukhia, *Historians and Historiography,* p. 80.

69. See, e.g., Malik, *Moslem Nationalism in India and Pakistan,* p. 39.

70. See Hodgson, *The Gunpowder Empires,* p. 70; and Rizvi, *The Wonder That Was India,* pp. 258–61.

71. See Aziz Ahmad, *Studies in Islamic Culture,* p. 168.

72. See Hodgson, *The Gunpowder Empires,* pp. 84–85.

73. See Qureshi, *The Muslim Community,* pp. 149–58; Mujeeb, *The Indian Muslims,* pp. 244–47; Nizami, *Akbar and Religion,* pp. 261–68.

74. See de Bary, *Sources of Indian Tradition,* 1:447.

75. See Rizvi, *The Wonder That Was India,* pp. 162, 269–70.

76. See Mujeeb, *The Indian Muslims,* p. 247.

77. John F. Richards, "The Mughal Empire," in *The New Cambridge History of India* (Cambridge: Cambridge University Press, 1993), 1:172.

78. See Malik, *Moslem Nationalism in India and Pakistan,* p. 67.

79. Hodgson, *The Gunpowder Empires,* p. 95.

80. Two contributors to *The New Cambridge History of India* take somewhat different positions on this thorny subject. While John Richards ("The Mughal Empire") endorses the view adopted here, Catherine Asher suggests that "when Aurangzeb did destroy temples, he did so not out of bigotry but as a political response when his authority was challenged" "Architecture of Mughal India," in *The New Cambridge History of India* [Cambridge: Cambridge University Press, 1992], 1:254.

Romila Thapar writes, "To the Muslims the Hindu temple was not only a symbol of a pagan religion and its false gods, but [also] a constant reminder that despite their political power there were spheres of life in the country over which they ruled to which they were strictly denied access" (*A History of India,* 1:279).

81. Aziz Ahmad, *Studies in Islamic Culture,* pp. 198–99.

82. Hodgson, *The Gunpowder Empires,* p. 93.

83. Aziz Ahmad, *Studies in Islamic Culture,* p. 197.

84. Hodgson, *The Gunpowder Empires,* p. 98.

85. Mujeeb, *The Indian Muslims,* p. 277.

86. See Sayid Athar Abbas Rizvi, *Shah Wali-Allah and His Times* (Canberra: Marifat Publishing House, 1980).

87. See Aziz Ahmad, *Studies in Islamic Culture,* p. 209.

88. See Malik, *Moslem Nationalism in India and Pakistan,* p. 121.

89. See Sayid Athar Abbas Rizvi, *Shah Abdal-Aziz, Puritanism, Sectarian Polemics, and Jihad* (Canberra: Marifat Publishing House, 1982), p. 15.

90. Wilfred Cantwell Smith, *Modern Islam in India: A Social Analysis* (London: Victor Gollancz, 1946), p. 46.

91. See Mujeeb, *The Indian Muslims,* pp. 390–91.

92. See Rizvi, p. 236.

93. See Aziz Ahmad, *Studies in Islamic Culture,* pp. 210–12.

94. Ibid., p. 214.

95. See Rizvi, *Shah Abdal-Aziz,* pp. 484–93.

96. See Rafiuddin Ahmed, *The Bengal Muslims, 1871–1906: A Quest for Identity* (Delhi: Oxford University Press, 1981), pp. 39–71; and Muin-ud-Din Ahmad Khan, *History of the Faraidi Movement in Bengal, 1818–1906* (Karachi: Pakistan Historical Society, 1965).

97. See Aziz Ahmad, *Studies in Islamic Culture,* pp. 216–17.

98. See Ashim Roy, *The Islamic Syncretistic Tradition in Bengal* (Princeton: Princeton University Press, 1983).

99. See Ahmed, *The Bengal Muslims,* p. 41.

100. See William Theodore de Bary, *Sources of Indian Tradition,* vol. 2, compiled by Stephen Hay and Ishtiaq Husain Qureshi

(New York: Columbia University Press, 1969), p. 192.

101. Ibid, pp. 193–94.

102. See David Lelyveld, *Aligarh's First Generation: Muslim Solidarity in British India* (Princeton: Princeton University Press, 1978).

103. Fazlur Rahman, "Muslim Modernism in the Indi-Pakistan Subcontinent," *Bulletin of the School of Oriental and African Studies* 21 (1958): 84.

104. Ibid., p. 105.

105. Barbara Daly Metcalf, *Islamic Revival in British India: Deoband, 1860–1900* (Princeton: Princeton University Press, 1982), pp. 139, 87, 100.

106. Ibid., p. 140.

107. Mujeeb, *The Indian Muslims,* pp. 522–23.

108. In the first hundred years of its existence the Dar ul-Ulum claimed to have issued 269,215 fatawa, many of which went into the minutest details of everyday life. See Metcalf, *Islamic Revival in British India,* p. 146. They were too many, and only too often banal, to be described as the enunciation of the fundamentals of Islam.

109. See ibid., p. 150.

110. Mujeeb, *The Indian Muslims,* p. 522.

111. See Malik, *Moslem Nationalism in India and Pakistan,* p. 192.

112. See Wilfred Cantwell Smith, *Modern Islam in India,* p. 295.

113. Mujeeb, *The Indian Muslims,* p. 558.

114. See Minault, *The Khilafat Movement.*

115. See Farzana Shaikh, *Community and Consensus in Islam: Muslim Representation in Colonial India, 1860–1947* (Cambridge: Cambridge University Press, 1989).

116. See Abul Kalam Azad, *India Wins Freedom* (Delhi: Oxford University Press, 1959); and Syeda Saiyidain Syeda Hameed, ed., "India's Maulana: Abul Salam Azad," in *Selected Speeches and Writings,* vol. 2 (New Delhi: Vikas Publishing House, 1990).

117. See Abul Kalam Azad, *The Tar-juman al-Quran,* vol. 1, ed. and trans. Syed Abdul Latif (Bombay: Asia Publishing House, 1962).

118. See Hafeez Malik, ed., *Iqbal: Poet-Philosopher of Pakistan* (New York: Columbia University Press, 1971).

119. See Aziz Ahmad, *Studies in Islamic Culture,* p. 176.

120. Aziz Ahmad, *Islamic Modernism in India and Pakistan* (Berkeley: University of California Press, 1961), p. 214.

121. See de Bary, *Sources of Indian Tradition,* 2:303.

122. See Abul Ala Maududi, *The Political Theory of Islam* (1965; Delhi: Markazi Maktaba Islami, 1989).

123. See Charles J. Adams, "The Ideology of Mawlana Mawdudi," in Donald Eugene Smith, ed., *South Asian Politics and Religion* (Princeton: Princeton University Press, 1966), pp. 37–38; and Leonard Binder, *Religion and Politics in Pakistan* (Berkeley: University of California Press, 1961), p. 302 et passim.

124. See M. S. Agwani, *Islamic Fundamentalism in India* (Chandigarh: Twenty-first Century India Society, 1986), pp. 86–87.

125. See Leonard Binder, *Islamic Liberalism: A Critique of Development Ideologies* (Chicago: University of Chicago Press, 1988), pp. 170–205; and Sivan, *Radical Islam,* pp. 22–23 et passim.

126. Adams, "The Ideology of Mawlana Mawdudi," p. 85.

127. Abul Ala Maududi, *The Islamic Movement: Dynamics of Values, Power, and Change,* ed. Khurram Murad (London: Islamic Foundation, 1984), p. 71.

128. Binder, *Islamic Liberalism,* p. 171.

129. See Adams, "The Ideology of Mawlana Mawdudi," p. 388.

130. Ibid., p. 389.

131. See Maududi, *The Political Theory of Islam,* pp. 27–34.

132. See Binder, *Islamic Liberalism,* p. 176.

133. See Adams, "The Ideology of Mawlana Mawdudi," p. 381.

134. See Maududi, *The Political Theory of Islam.*

135. See Maududi, *The Islamic Movement,* p. 79.

136. Cragg, *The Pen and the Faith,* p. 10.

137. Malik, *Moslem Nationalism in India and Pakistan,* p. 278.

138. Mujeeb, *The Indian Muslims,* p. 402.

139. Rahman, *Islam and Modernity,* pp. 116–17.

140. See Mumtaz Ahmad, "Islamic Fundamentalism in South Asia: The Jamaat-i-Islami and the Tablighi Jamaat of South Asia," in Marty and Appleby, *Fundamentalisms Observed,* pp. 457–530; and Rafiuddin Ahmed, "Redefining Muslim Identity in South Asia: The Transformation of the Jama'at-i-Islami," in Martin E. Marty and R. Scott Appleby, eds., *Accounting for Fundamentalisms* (Chicago: University of Chicago Press, 1994).

141. Agwani, *Islamic Fundamentalism in India,* p. 76.

142. Such as are insightfully discussed in Ahmed, *The Bengal Muslims;* Roy, *The Islamic Syncretistic Tradition in Bengal;* Richard Eaton, *The Sufis of Bijapur, 1300–1700: Social Roles of Sufism in the Medieval India* (Princeton: Princeton University Press, 1978); Bayly, *Saints, Goddesses, and Kings.*

143. See Madan, "The Double-Edged Sword."

144. Francis Robinson, "Islam and Muslim Society in South Asia," *Contributions to Indian Sociology,* n.s., 17 (1983): 2010.

145. Francis Robinson, "Islam and Muslim Society in South Asia: A Reply," *Contributions to Indian Sociology,* n.s., 20 (1986): 97–98.

146. Wilfred Cantwell Smith, *Modern Islam in India,* p. 41.

147. Adams, "The Ideology of Mawlana Mawdudi," p. 395.

148. One of Ayatollah Khomeini's closest and most learned colleagues, Ayatollah Mutahhari, in his critique of secularism from the vantage point of Shi'ite Islam, shows a remarkable awareness of the implications of Western science for Islamic thought, and his exposition of the fundamentals of Islam is deeply influenced by this awareness. See Ayatollah Murtaza Mutahhari, *Fundamentals of Islamic Thought,* trans. R. Campbell (Berkeley: Mizan Press, 1985). See particularly his discussion of evolution, which he accepts and rejects, pp. 205–16.

149. See Madan, "The Double-Edged Sword."

150. See also William R. Roff, "Islamic Movements: One or Many," in William R. Roff, ed., *Islam and the Political Economy of Meaning* (Berkeley: University of California Press, 1987), p. 47.

What's So Funny About Fundamentalism?

Gideon Aran

Mephistopheles:
Since you, O Lord, once more approach and ask
If business down with us be light or heavy—
And in the past you've usually welcomed me—
That's why you see me also at your levee.
Excuse me, I can't manage lofty words—
Not though your whole court jeer and find me low;
My pathos certainly would make you laugh
Had you not cast off laughing long ago.
Goethe, "Prologue in Heaven," Faust

Zealotry and Humor: A Radical Embrace

Fundamentalists with a sense of humor are the heroes of this essay. While common wisdom holds that fundamentalists are completely humorless—indeed, a lack of humor is often used to characterize the very nature of fundamentalism—I have met many fundamentalists who do have a sense of humor, including some who have made fundamentalism itself the butt of their wit. In the course of extensive fieldwork, I have become intimately acquainted with fundamentalist Muslims, Christians, and Jews—leaders as well as rank and file—who are aware that, whatever its precise meaning, the term *fundamentalism* applies generally to them, and they are intrigued by it. Of these, many know how to joke, and their humor provides an excellent introduction to contemporary zealotry in general, and to fundamentalism in particular. The true believer with a sense of humor can guide us in an exploration of contemporary radical religion.[1]

Listening to the jokes that fundamentalists tell enables us to study fundamentalism from a previously unexplored angle. And this humor reveals important aspects about the nature of fundamentalism—that it can be wise, sensitive, and self-conscious. Humor, for example, requires the ability to see both sides of the coin, to perceive nuances, to tolerate ambiguity, and to be attracted to paradoxes. It presupposes the ability to see the world from a certain distance and to maintain one's detachment—if only for a moment—from what is familiar and dear, including one's group, one's values, and oneself. Hence humor assumes subtlety and perspective, while zealotry is conventionally understood as the very antithesis of subtlety and lacking in all perspective. Zealots are usually characterized as one-dimensional, closed, and categorical, as seeing the world solely from their point of view. Yet there are zealots who also possess subtlety and perspective, who can laugh out loud, like the Palestinian Sunni fundamentalist who boasted to me that he has "a Jewish sense of humor."[2]

While not negligible, humor is certainly not dominant among fundamentalists. Let us not, however, lose a sense of proportion. As some true believers have remarked to me, humor is also scarce among opponents of fundamentalism from the secular-liberal camp. (They gently note that among observers of fundamentalism in the media and academia, humor has completely disappeared, making room for dryness and pomp.) EE, a major figure in Gush Emunim, a Jewish fundamentalist movement known for its aggressive opposition to Israel's withdrawal from territories conquered in the 1967 war, derives moral authority both from her marriage to a rabbi who heads a yeshiva defiantly located in an area densely populated by Palestinians hostile to Israel, and from her own pious style of life. She penned a satiric "Lexicon of Important Religious and Political Values," intended for internal use only, excerpts of which were published in the Gush Emunim periodical. Item 3 in the lexicon reads, "*Jewish Fundamentalism*— Capricious obstinacy in calling our country the Land of Israel and spitefully holding on to it merely because, according to archaic superstition, it was promised to the Patriarchs."

Puncturing pretensions is a practice turned inward as well. The senior pastor of a group of messianic Christians in Jerusalem working covertly to missionize, addressed his congregation as if revealing a hidden truth. He noted the pragmatic principle behind conversion to his relatively small group: "When you seek a new God, you don't have to wait in line." This is an appealing metaphor in a bureaucracy-ridden society. Similarly, when a Jewish messianic group took the risk of publicly announcing the imminent arrival of the Messiah, disappointment and public embarrassment followed the failure of the Messiah to appear at the announced time. Members of the group explained, "No problem; we'll have another Messiah tomorrow." This reaction confirmed their understanding of the ABCs of messianic dynamics!

Humor glories in the ability to laugh at absolute values; thus, from the point of view of true believers, humor is sheer heresy. Like the sciences, humor is skeptical regarding absolutes. In jokes on religion, as in the sociology of religion, true believers see iconoclasm. And yet the true believer manages to live with the dissonance, and even to capitalize on it. Both the true believer and the sociologist deal with the same sensitive material: the world as a changing, fragile, unclear, ambiguous, and sometimes ugly reality. Both humor and sociology probe what has become conventional, arbitrary, imposed by terror, and sanctified. Like the trained sociologist, the supple fundamentalists with a sense of humor are aware of themselves and their surroundings.

Western secular culture criticizes what it regards as the tendency of religious radicals to impose their will on others, even though this coercion stems from a sincere desire to save them. Thus the beneficiaries of religious radicalism are under assault by it, and those saved by it are in consequence its victims. I heard acknowledgment of this irony several times from Moslem and Jewish fundamentalists who attribute this propensity to each other. In their words, "A true believer is someone who will kill you for your own good."

The Somber Visage

It is difficult to find something amusing in zealotry that has proven that it is capable of bloodshed. Fundamentalism is tested by stern discipline, total commitment, and absolute standards; it is not supposed to seek relief from tension or to recognize alternatives or to compromise. Those able to sacrifice themselves and their contemporaries on the altar of an ideal surely take themselves seriously. And we had better take them seriously, too. We had better, then, relate to their humor, and with seriousness.

There are many who draw a straight line of humorlessness from the Puritan revolutionaries of England to the Jacobin revolutionaries of France to the Bolshevik revolutionaries of Russia; those who sought the millennium toward the end of the Middle Ages in central Europe to the founders of the Thousand Year Reich in the same locale only two generations ago; and all these to the fundamentalists in America, Asia, and Africa today. It is assumed that the pathos, the solemnity, and the portentous sense of destiny that typifies different kinds of holy emissaries preclude any possibility of humor. This supposition holds true for all types of radicalism and true belief; it holds for parties that claim absolute truth, movements with a new gospel, alternative world communities and sects of world reformers; it holds for revolutionaries, prophets, and messiahs in the past, and for religious zealots in modern times.[3]

This is the image fundamentalism wants to project to the world. The somber visage of Khomeini has become a symbol of the entire phenomenon: thick eyebrows, clenched lips, scraggly beard, gaunt frame, wrinkles, black turban, and the eyes, especially the eyes. Khomeini has been photographed only with a dour, angry expression, or else the censor has prevented the distribution of any other kind of picture. I have dozens of photos of fundamentalists. Although they represent different places and cultures, they are much alike, so that one can talk about a common denominator. Not only do the beards and headgear appear time and again, but also the message transmitted in body language, facial expressions, and the code of dress: the leader of the zealots with a piercing look of castigation, the mass of zealots with clenched fists lifted in threat.

This, no doubt, says something about fundamentalism. But perhaps it also says something about those of us who are looking at fundamentalism, who study the phenomenon, and who are the consumers of these reports. While I did not find the shadow of a smile in these photos, through my years of fieldwork I often encountered situations of humor if not outright laughter among radical groups. Indeed, the very seriousness of fundamentalism is suggested by the fact that it also knows how to laugh. And this humor serves a number of important functions, which we shall now examine.

Against this pessimistic background, humor may take root and help grapple with draconian norms and a stark atmosphere. Thus, the somber hue of radical religion is speckled with elements of amiability, sentimentality, lust, satisfaction, childishness, naughtiness. I have witnessed moments of letting-go among fundamentalists that bear orgiastic features: radical religious leaders who are studying holy scripture or discussing political issues late at night suddenly breaking the tension by jokes and playfulness. This can also occur on long journeys, or when idle under police arrest. These moments when fundamentalists are free of outside supervision and internal restraint can be viewed as moments of truth: situations in which the true believers are unveiled, presumably as their genuine selves. In clowning, the fundamentalist can either identify with true belief or express hidden ambitions—not generally acknowledged even to oneself. Time out can be taken from the onus of fulfilling expectations to the point of criticizing dogma, something that religious radicalism does not normally allow within its ranks. There are moments of freedom that disclose a special, authentic existence which brings to mind the effects revealed in extreme situations of collective behavior.

In the midst of a Palestinian Islamic wave of terrorism that swept Israel in the spring of 1993, I had a long conversation with AZ, a forty-year-old member of Hamas, the Sunni resistance movement in the territories notorious for its murderous attacks on Israelis. AZ had been imprisoned because of his active membership in this group, and he was trying to convince me and his son-in-law who was present of the greatness of Islam. He grew more and more excited as he spoke, and I became increasingly uneasy, with the three of us alone in a field. "Don't worry," said AZ, noticing my apprehension, "I won't kill you, but not out of fear of the army." From didactic and doctrinaire, he erupted into raucous laughter. "Killing you is small change, and probably wouldn't secure my place in the world to come or turn me into a martyr!"

Moments of hilarity can occur at the height of success, following escape from crisis, or even when despair and anxiety prevail. In the first instance, the humor is crude and self-congratulatory, while in the second, it may be subtle, bitter, and even ironic. In the mid-1970s, the conflict between the government of Israel and Gush Emunim, the radical national religious movement, reached a peak with direct, sometimes physical, confrontations. Fear of a civil war was voiced, and the leaders of Gush Emunim were called to an urgent meeting with the prime minister. At one point, they asked to meet by themselves and were given use of an adjoining room normally used for meetings of the cabinet. During their discussion the true believers were swept into a kind of role playing. It began as a joke. Each person imagined himself to be the minister on whose chair he was sitting. Rabbis and young yeshiva students became, for a few moments, the rulers of Israel and did what they wanted without constraint or inhibition. The fundamentalist minister of defense announced the expulsion of the Arabs across the Jordan River. The fundamentalist minister of the interior ordered all citizens to fast in order to end the drought then prevailing in the land. The minister of finance imposed a new tax to fund the rebuilding of the ancient Temple in Jerusalem. The room was filled with hilarity. Afterward they told no one what had happened. Some years later, a number of these members of Gush Emunim formed a group that became known as the Jewish underground, which carried out clandestine terrorist actions in which a number of Palestinians were killed and injured. They were apprehended just as they were about to plant bombs in buses loaded with Palestinians. As expected, they used their trial to proclaim their credo and were subsequently incarcerated. One day in the prison yard, they suddenly began parodying their courtroom speeches. Exaggerating the intonation and flowery language, they moved from overidentification to mockery of their ideological stand. In these instances, laughter evolved spontaneously; when the game went too far, it was abruptly halted. An effort was then made to disengage from the clowning, to define it as an aberration in the radical religious routine.

On some occasions, attempts will be made to show that the humor is not surrealism but hyperrealism, emphasizing continuity between the game and the sphere of serious fundamentalism. Among the leaders of Gush Emunim is a radical group of professionally mobile settlers. They determine the front line of Jewish presence in the territories by establishing a settlement, handing it over to second-level cadres, and moving on to establish a new one. They preach about the Promised Land as encompassing areas far afield of the borders of modern Israel. Once a simulation game spontaneously evolved: establishment of a new settlement near Iraq. Smiling, they bent over maps, divided responsibilities, and were swept into phases of operational planning. One person took on the problem of lack of water in that arid area. Another brought a group of young people to the site and guided them on a tour. They carried on raucously, but when the game was over, they decided that it was not meant to be funny. Their intention was serious and so was the hope of realizing it. They compared their parody to an army contingency plan, in which what appears farfetched one day can become reality the next.

Institutionalizing the Outburst

To ensure intense commitment and enthusiasm over a long period of time, the radical religious community is subject to strict control, which gives it the characteristics of a "total institution."[4] Monitoring encroaches on privacy in all aspects of life. As a result, fundamentalists need release from the unbearably heavy burden of commandments and restrictions. Outbursts allow them to let off steam. Sometimes these outbursts are regulated. Controlled enclaves of abandonment and hilarity are created—"institutional respites"[5]—that contribute to the efficient performance of the system. These are structured ritually and become part of the group culture. Such respites are well known in anthropology. They allow one to act out alienation and protest, and at the same time to absorb and channel these feelings. They allow the formation of alternative worlds and an antistructure in a contained and sublimated mode.

Take, for example, the Jewish festival of Purim, which commemorates the deliverance of the Jewish community in Persia (fifth century B.C.) from a plot to annihilate it. Besides the prayers, Purim is celebrated by masquerading, drinking to intoxication, performance of humorous plays, and carousing. During Purim there is license not only for raucousness, but for challenging that which is sanctified. Jewish fundamentalists take Purim seriously, including the injunction to joy. They observe Purim by wild costumes and pranks, sometimes drinking to unconsciousness, but they also recognize the dangers of running wild. Radical religion that encourages joy knows that it is playing with fire. Thus, a typical ambivalence develops, characteristic of contemporary radical religion, which is both aware of humor and of itself. The zealot's Purim has the dialectical logic of fundamentalists who are swept away yet pull back. While the true believers exalt the festival, they also convert the joy into gravity. Hence Purim foolery is subject to strict supervision. Limits are set on costume and repertoire. With some ultra-Orthodox, for example, it is forbidden for a man to masquerade as a woman.

Some yeshivot have censored certain subjects for parody. The phenomenon of students mimicking their rabbis at the pulpit is condemned. Edicts have been published that forbid Purim mockery of ludicrous halakhic decisions.

The Purim festivities of the hard core of Gush Emunim settlers in Hebron are especially raucous. This group is known for its right-wing extremism: aggressive against liberal Israelis and violent against Arabs. During Purim, inebriated activists have been known to roam the alleys of the Casbah in Hebron, throwing stones at Arab homes, smashing windows, and shooting at water tanks on the roofs. N., one of their leaders, came to synagogue on Purim wearing jeans, John Lennon glasses, and a T-shirt emblazoned with the symbol of Peace Now, the left-wing group diametrically opposed to Jewish fundamentalism. True to his masquerade, N. appeared for prayers without a skullcap on his head. After the initial shock at his daring, it turned out that he was wearing a wig, so that he could appear to be bare-headed and yet be head-covered at the same time. Purim provided him with an excellent opportunity for tasting the forbidden fruit of the enemy.

Heirs to the Court Jester

A society institutionalizes humor not only by fixing a special time, bound in advance and ritually structured, but by creating the role of humorist for one or more individuals. The humorist is heir to the court jester with the privilege of mocking things that others dare not laugh at, including the king himself. The function of a quasi-official humorist is especially necessary for groups with an authoritarian regime. Some radical religious groups handle humor by concentrating it in a particular person or small group. Fundamentalist Christians have "messianic clowns" whom they invite to gatherings of fundamentalist congregations for their amusement. Their permanent repertoire includes jokes about "televangelists."[6] Among ultra-Orthodox Jews, this role is filled by the rhymer. This figure often appears at weddings at the end of the ceremony, when only family and close friends remain for a ritual dance. The rhymer calls on each dancer, offering praise and slipping in jibes. After working over the newlyweds and the family, the rhymer will often introduce more general material. He begins with a safe routine, jokes against rabbis and Hasidim who belong to other sects. By settling accounts with rivals, he wins over the crowd. Then he becomes more daring and slips in some digs at the group itself. The roaring laughter of those present is then replaced by nervous giggles as they glance around to make sure everyone present belongs to the intimate circle of true believers.

Among the fundamentalist Jews of Gush Emunim, the court jester has a functional substitute in the satire column of the internal settler newsletter. The column is popular with the settlers, although it may snipe at them too, though this is rare. An analysis of the contents of twelve issues of the publication shows that over 95 percent of the column is aimed at others—Arabs, secular Jews, ultra-Orthodox, politicians, and the Israeli establishment. But there are exceptions. As the columnist himself confesses, "One day the satirical writer sat alone, his door locked, and took out a sheet of paper to note down all the doubts and certainties" pertaining to his radical religious identity. The following is a sample, a self-conscious testament to the dilemma of a fundamentalist humorist:

> Why I should stop wearing a skullcap, once and for all: (1) so they won't think I'm one of those fanatics; (2) if I—who am religious—write as I do, imagine what the seculars will say about religion; (3) to show them I'm the same as anyone (also getting bald). Now why I should not stop wearing a skullcap, once and for all: (1) perhaps it's better if they don't see I'm getting bald; (2) I've gotten used to wearing it; (3) the seculars will respect me more—they'll see that religion has other types, not just Gush Emunim and ultra-Orthodox fanatics; (4) my dealings with religious people are more effective when I wear a skullcap. It proves I'm brave and know them from the inside.

According to the columnists and their readers, the items sniping at Gush Emunim and its members elicit a much greater response than do those sniping at their adversaries. Articles of self-satire become the talk of the town. The following clipping, for example, was widely circulated in Gush Emunim circles, including their yeshivot, which turned it into the subject of educational discussion. It was titled "Openness."

> She grew-up in Kiryat Arba, Elkana, perhaps in Kedumim or in Ofra; and passed her childhood years in the local school; she also studied, of course, in the Girls' Yeshiva in Kiryat Arba, Elkana, perhaps in Kedumim or in Ofra; she then did her national service in Kiryat Arba, Elkana, perhaps in Kedumim or in Ofra; there she met a likeable chap who was born in Kiryat Arba, Elkana, perhaps in Kedumim or in Ofra; and they decided to set up home, of course in Kiryat Arba, Elkana, perhaps in Kedumim or in Ofra; and they will have (with God's help) eight children (may they be healthy) who will live in Kiryat Arba, Elkana, perhaps in Kedumim or in Ofra. And what does she really detest? Those leftists who shut themselves up in their kibbutzim; and those ultra-Orthodox who never leave the ghetto of Bnei Brak.

Modern Strands of Ancient Humor

The question of humor in contemporary radical religion touches on the question of humor in religion in general and of humor in particular religious traditions.[7] A common perception is that Jewish fundamentalists engage in more humor than do Christian fundamentalists. Protestantism is assumed to be relatively earnest, and Puritanism is a byword for seriousness. There are those who say that Islam is even more bereft of festivity, that it is as arid as the desert in which it grew.[8] Muslim fundamentalists have said to me, "Hilarity is not Islamic; one must suppress it." But when they soften up a bit, they disclose that the holy Hadith carries the words—explicitly and more than once—"The prophet laughed until you saw his back teeth."[9]

I have observed Islamic Palestinian fundamentalists in detention camp in which

hundreds of suspects and convicted perpetrators of terrorism against the Israeli occupation were incarcerated. The radical Sunnis, known as Hamas, were crowded together in their own separate enclosure, over which hovered an air of seriousness. In
contrast with the secular PLO prisoners, remarkably few signs of merriment emanated
from the Moslem true believers. Although one could hear occasional bursts of laughter, these were always directed inward toward themselves, with their backs to the fence.
When my eyes would meet those of a smiling PLO prisoner, he seemed to exaggerate
his smile, as if to express autonomy and assertiveness. On the other hand, Hamas prisoners caught in the act of smiling immediately wiped it off their faces, as if guilty for
having heard a joke. Indeed, those who did tell jokes covered their faces with their
hands while doing so. Fundamentalists' jokes are a secret.

It is difficult to determine to what extent fundamentalist jokes maintain traditional
humor or invent it anew. Some strands may be hundreds of years old, alongside contemporary influences. Modern Jewish fundamentalist humor clearly differs from traditional Jewish humor and even from that produced 50 to 150 years ago at its initial
encounter with the secular Western world. One finds reflections on the problems of
religion in modern secular surroundings, as well as assimilation of some aspects of
these surroundings.

Fundamentalism tries to deny and eradicate old humor, but at the same time it
benefits from and sanctions it. All shades of radical Jews continue to enjoy, sometimes
surreptitiously, humor drawn from Jewish Orthodoxy in general, and from the medieval Diaspora religious tradition in particular. Both the ultra-Orthodox and Gush
Emunim repeatedly use old jokes in response to stimuli and needs that have not altered. Naturally there are changes, such as shifting the butt of the jokes from European
Christians to Arabs and Muslims. But there continue to be universal problems whose
sting has not subsided, and humor is one way to deal with them.

Sex is one example of an old problem. Though fundamentalists claim that sex is
conspicuously absent from their humor, this is not so. In fundamentalism, and in the
world of the yeshivot in particular, there is a variety of dirty jokes, and a vain struggle
to uproot them. These are sexual jokes told in a religious style, with imagery and expressions from the Scriptures. Some of the jokes are quite daring not only sexually but
religiously, such as the pun from a chapter in the Bible, known to every Torah student,
implying that God (Heaven forbid) masturbates.[10]

Many modern Jewish fundamentalists are immersed in the heritage of the Mussar (morality) movement, which was an awakening of moralistic religious fervor in
nineteenth-century eastern Europe. In daily mussar lessons—a type of preaching for
sincerity in faith and for enthusiastically fulfilling the commandments—the rabbis emphasize the ban on laughter and merriment. On the other hand, Jewish fundamentalists cannot ignore Hasidism, the nineteenth-century religious revival movement related to the mystic-ecstatic tradition, which excels in the spirit of joy. Ultra-Orthodox
of the Hasidic school exhibit more joy than ultra-Orthodox of Lithuanian background,
who find fault with this joy. But the difference between the two movements is not one
of pure joy versus pure solemnity. With Hasidim, joy is not spontaneous; it is primarily
organized—singing, dancing, professional clowns—and theologically mandated. The
duty to serve God with joy is one of the main tenets of Hasidic doctrine, and it is

rigorously adhered to. As for Lithuanian Jews, under cover of the seriousness that has become their trademark—and against the background of their conflict with the Hasidim—they have developed a humor that outshines that of the Hasidim in sophistication, realism, and directness. Indeed, a major part of serious Lithuanian humor is aimed at the Hasid. In particular, Lithuanians mock Hasidim for deifying their rabbis. When one Hasidic group brought its messianic fervor to unprecedented heights, intimating that its rabbi—a sick, aged man on his deathbed—was the Messiah, and calling on Jews everywhere to prepare for the imminent messianic advent, the Lithuanians reacted by distributing caricatures titled "Here he comes . . ." But this Messiah was not riding a white donkey, as tradition prescribes; depicted instead was a pair of exhausted white arms stretched out, leaning with difficulty on a walker. This barb, it should be noted, concealed their own embarrassment and anxiety, as the revered Lithuanian rabbi is himself well advanced in age.

Zeroing in on Taboos and Tension

There are fundamentalists who are aware of the lack of fundamentalist humor and comment—seriously—on it. One member of Gush Emunim turned to his friends with a severe rebuke in his sermon.

> If only we possessed a little humor, we would have realized our goals long ago. Comrades, without humor, you aren't serious. You stern-faced believing settlers, smile! A little bit of grace, God help us, won't do any harm, nor would a trace of irony . . . Why the constant grimacing, hard-set countenances in the holy, liberated territories? Why walk on hot coals all the time? I know people who behave properly and who know how to laugh, but they are embarrassed to do so. They're afraid of being considered frivolous, for "redemption is acquired through suffering." . . . I'm not saying (God forbid, God forbid) that one should laugh all day and night, though no one has ever died of it. But this severity, this ascetic, diligent, pious teeth-gnashing is one reason so many people distance themselves from us. One constantly hears our hysterical shouting and apocalyptic threats, or sees the admonishing finger and the contentiousness. If we want to sway the masses, we simply have to be a little more pleasant.

One may regard humor as exceptional in fundamentalism, yet attribute to it the same importance as to social deviance, from which we may learn about the norms of a society. It is possible that humor in fundamentalism is abnormal, yet humor is necessary to soften the ramified system of rules and to define gradations of freedom within it. If mechanical rigidity is comical and laughter is its punishment,[11] then humor certainly fits fundamentalism. Beyond a normative system, true believers must have common understandings about who they are and what the world is like. This shared understanding of themselves and the world can be implied by gestures, of which jokes are one. In fact, joking is one way for fundamentalists to maintain their "conversation of gestures" about reality that supports their lives as true believers.[12]

Humor is not only an effective tool for marking the rules of the game, it is also a subtle instrument for negotiating them. In a radical religious context in which there are limitations on the negotiation of rules, humor can be helpful in bypassing them. In every society, humor aids in dealing with taboos. In fundamentalist enclaves, which are loaded with taboos and whose surroundings challenge these taboos, humor is especially important. Listening to jokes can provide us with something that analysis of radical religious sermons cannot: hints of a latent structure that is sometimes inconsistent with manifest standards, and hints of covert dynamics that touch on sensitive and "illegal" issues.

Through humor, heretical thoughts slip in. Such are the jokes that characterize radical religion when it is seized by anxiety. There is a standard set of jokes, used repeatedly when the fundamentalist Jewish community encounters a crisis in religious stability, or some cracks in their faith. In the midst of the Gulf War (1991), which aroused fears of mass destruction, a humorous story appeared among the ultra-Orthodox. This story had roots in the 1967 war, in which there was anxiety about collective existence, and again in the 1973 war, which carried a sense of impending doom. The story: The leader of the ultra-Orthodox group that takes a moderate position regarding the Zionist state meets on the street the leader of the most militant anti-Zionist group. Against the background of the possibility of a military catastrophe, the more moderate rabbi says to the other: "It seems that you were right: the godless State of Israel has no future. Behold, the kingdom of wickedness will soon fall as a punishment from heaven." His anti-Zionist compatriot replies: "Don't worry. The word is that they have an excellent air force." All those listening—who had heard it again and again— burst out laughing. A number of ultra-Orthodox rabbis whom I asked for an explanation of this laughter stood on their heads to convince me that this is actually a case of laughing at the secular state which relies on its own physical strength. But they could not deny that this is also the nervous laughter of true believers who, lacking any other viable option, place their reliance on the state.

Humor zeroes in on forbidden matters; it is drawn to subjects that cause controversy, embarrassment, and anxiety. Humor thrives on internal tension within the collective. While the jokes single out problematic social subjects, they also point to a way of confronting these problems. For example, the very profusion of jokes about the redoubtable old age of their leaders is an indication that this phenomenon, prevalent in many fundamentalist groups, does indeed trouble true believers and is viewed as a potential crisis. These jokes suggest attempts to partially respond to this distress. The venerable Rabbi Schach, for example, ninety-six years old in 1994, is the undisputed leader of the Lithuanian school of Jewish fundamentalism. Among his followers, many stories circulate about the dissonance between Rabbi Schach's age and his prowess. In one well-known statement, for example, it is said of Rabbi Schach, "He will soon grow teeth." [13] Clearly there is an element of mockery here, but the ultra-Orthodox claim that they compare their aged leader to an infant in admiration for his vitality. Over time, the Lithuanian establishment adopted and disseminated this joke to express love for its leader.

Another source of tension for internal jokes in the radical religious world is the female true believer. There are many jokes about women, singling them out as a threat to the male true believer. Allegedly female traits—materialism, practicality, compromise, a desire for comfort and security, and others—supposedly constitute an antithesis to the complete realization of religiosity. In religious folklore, woman represents the seductive force vis-à-vis the male religious hero, enticing him to stray from the path of zealotry.[14] However, current radical religion has nurtured on a mass scale what was once a rare phenomenon: the woman zealot. Today, women are on the front line of fundamentalist movements, where they take a position formerly reserved for men. These women are at times more radical than men, and the reaction of men is quite ambivalent. While they may praise the radical women, they do so in a patronizing manner and minimize their worth. Humor serves this purpose well. The husbands "explain" the fervor of their wives and daughters as stemming from the fact that they have not deeply studied the sources, and thus their understanding is limited, which accounts for their extremism. Fundamentalist humor thus turns superreligiosity into inferior religiosity.

True believers may try to impress outsiders with the humor behind fundamentalism. A number of fundamentalist groups in Jerusalem—Muslim, Christian, and Jewish—told me in confidence that their leader actually had hidden features that are contrary to what was generally thought about him: humane, smiling features. True believers keep recycling curiosities from the lives of their leaders, treading the thin line between admiration and mockery, while attempting to render these anecdotes sympathetic if not instructive. In one case, I was present at a Torah lesson given by Rabbi Kook, the spiritual leader of Gush Emunim, to his closest pupils. About twenty of us sat crowded together in a small room of his home. Suddenly the skullcap slipped off the aged rabbi's head. The lesson halted. A tense silence prevailed, and pupils jumped as if bitten by a snake to pick up the skullcap from the floor. Rabbi Kook reacted with a calm smile and said casually, "Look here, my God-fearingness is wallowing in the dust of the earth." A burst of laughter was heard over this unexpected heretical remark. During the years since then, I have heard this episode recounted in many versions, some with little resemblance to the original. The story was turned into a bedrock of fundamentalist Jewish lore and was repeated as a joke with a double message. First, we learn about the character of the fundamentalist leader: wise, modest, endearing, and capable of irony. At the same time, there is a message of the superiority of intent and devotion over carrying out commandments by rote.

Jewish fundamentalism is full of examples of spontaneous humor slipping into canonical humor. In many cases, jokes such as the one above have taken on the characteristics of "Hasidic Tales."[15] The joke serves as a pedagogic tool and a theological statement, a kind of guide to matters of faith and religion and, in itself, a religious tenet. In a sense, repeating the story—or joke—becomes an act of worship.

Ambivalence and Informers

Among fundamentalists there is ambivalence to humor; radical religion is itself confused about whether humor is an expression of strength or weakness. The Jewish fundamentalist group called the Temple Mount Faithful is dedicated to rebuilding the

ancient Temple in Jerusalem. Its journal contains articles about which priestly garments should be worn in the rebuilt Temple and how to conduct animal sacrifices
there, intermingled with reports of political-legal struggles. Needless to say, the tone
is serious. At some point, after considerable discussion and postponements, the group
introduced a satirical column to the journal in response to a need to relieve frustration;
implicit was an admission of a certain helplessness and despair. The appearance of the
column was accompanied by remarks from the editors and movement leaders about
the real and hypothetical opposition to having humor in the movement journal. They
addressed the criticism that jokes and caricatures are incompatible with the holiness of
the Temple, promising that only material that furthered the aims of the movement
would be employed. They resorted to a defense that could be considered the essence
of the rationale of Jewish humor, "As we have no strength to cry anymore, there is
nothing left to do but laugh," adding, "Who knows, perhaps our redemption will
come precisely thanks to laughter." The column appeared, delivering trenchant barbs
against Muslim believers and the State of Israel and its police, reserving the most bitter
words for the Orthodox establishment and mainstream Orthodox Jews. And yet after
only three issues, explaining that it was not respectable enough and might harm the
struggle, the Temple Mount Faithful put an end to the daring venture.

Fundamentalist apologists for humor often emphasize that jokes on religious subjects don't reflect alienation from religion, but are a luxury that the totally committed
can afford. Messianists, for example, assert that they would never laugh at the Messiah
if they were not seriously awaiting him. They claim that jokes about true belief are not
a product of faithlessness, but rather prove the steadfastness of that faith. This is why
such jokes should be told only to those whose loyalty to the faith is beyond question.

Fundamentalists are aware that their own jokes can be used against them by opponents, and Jewish fundamentalists illustrate this as follows. A satirical piece entitled
"She Goes Modestly" appeared in an internal newsletter of Gush Emunim settlers.
The piece poked fun at the tendency among radical religious women to become ever
more extreme in their attire. This self-satire caught the attention of secular Jews, and
appeared in a major newspaper where opponents used it to support their claim that
radical Judaism and Khomeinism are identical. True believers who had initially laughed
at the piece were now offended, and the author was forced to declare that he would
never have published it, had he known how it would be misused.

Muslim fundamentalists describe the act of making their humor available to those
around them as "arming those who besiege us in the midst of a battle for life or
death." Humor is censored by fundamentalists to prevent it from reaching the ears of
a hostile environment, or to prevent it from raising awareness to and prominence of
things they don't wish to admit. Telling jokes about fundamentalism to nonbelievers
is comparable to disclosing confidential information or incriminating evidence. Radical religious individuals who divulge inside jokes to outsiders are subject to severe
sanctions, to the point of banning and excommunication. Lithuanian ultra-Orthodox
compare true believers who leak jokes to outsiders with those who convey information
to the police or gossip to the press: they are all *mosrim* (informers), a stigma that
evokes deep wells of associations with treason against Jewry. Under a heading that

quotes the "blessing over apostates" which decrees death for informers, the fundamentalist Yeshiva Council published a document denouncing followers who collaborate with the Zionist enemy. It includes a description of those who poke fun at the
beliefs and customs of radical religion, its leaders, and its institutions. These jokers are
described as "loosing all bonds"; indeed, "a glint of idolatry" can be detected in their
eyes. At the end of the document they are likened to "a priest who places an unclean
carcass in the cellar of a rabbi's house."

Fundamentalist Humor as Social Control

Through humor, one can trace the parameters of conformity and deviance within radical religious groups. True believer jokes are a valid test of the values and norms of such
groups. A joke can confirm and support what is officially expressed in sacred canons
and codices; it can also adapt them and mark the standards actually practiced. Through
laughter one can simultaneously sketch two sets of coordinates, the ideal and the real.
Those who hear the joke—researchers as well as believers—learn what is desired and
what is actual, and the gap between the two.

Fundamentalist humor reflects a clear hierarchy of radical religious leadership.
While the top echelon of leadership is rarely a butt of humor, the second and third
levels are not spared. At times it seems as if the top echelon has given license to laugh
at those below, as if to make sure they know their place in the hierarchy. Commonly
among fundamentalists, there is a division of labor in the leadership between those
who specialize in "pure" spiritual matters and those who specialize in organizational
work, regulating conflicts, mobilizing and allocating resources, and relations with the
surroundings; the former are spared the scoffing whereas the latter are its favored victims. In various radical religious groups, it is more difficult to find jokes at the expense
of religious authority proper, whereas there are numerous jokes about the religiopolitical authority. The latter, however, react to instigation against them with jokes
about the "spirituality" of the others. While there is respect for the heads of yeshivot,
for example, one finds a jocular attitude toward representatives of the ultra-Orthodox
and Gush Emunim in the Knesset. The jokes mock their addiction to the good life and
the rewards of office, their cozying up to the political establishment, and their willingness to compromise. The jokes reflect a value statement, but they also articulate jealousy and the frustration of political dependence; and they express a practical dread.
Fundamentalist movements are fearful that their politicians will be swept away from
religion to politics, and that others will be swept away with them. Humor is enlisted
to counter this, too. Through humor, fundamentalism reins in those forces within it
which, while vital to the functioning of the movement, threaten its purity and are liable
to damage the sources of its authority. It is not only those who fill important political,
financial, and social tasks—on whom there is much dependence as well as contempt—
who are victims of fundamentalist humor.

A similar attitude is expressed in jokes toward individuals whose position places
them on the fringes of the radical religious group and who are mandated to cross the

boundaries on occasion. These are the intermediaries between the fundamentalist community and the modern secular world. For the sake of the radical religious cause, these cultural brokers must take on some attributes of the surrounding culture, considered negative and threatening. The jokes at their expense serve as a constant reminder to them of where they come from and to where they must return.

The observation that jokes set social boundaries has long been regarded as trivial, especially in a social setting of cultural cleavages, intergroup tension, minority-majority relations, and horizontal and vertical mobility. Radical religious humor, like ethnic or national humor, aids the threatened collective to demarcate who belongs and who does not. Jokes against the Other—whether the liberal elite or the religious establishment—produce a sharply defined profile of the rival camp. The radical religious are thus able to unite on the basis of their confrontation with the outside world. But beyond the jokes themselves, one must look at their creators and consumers. Only individuals considered by the authorities and their associates to be—beyond any doubt—complete true believers are permitted such humor. A covenant with an underground flavor develops among those initiated into this exclusive humor. The joke contributes to solidarity, esprit de corps, and the rejection of those not deemed worthy.[16]

The discreet and esoteric nature of the fundamentalist joke is jealously guarded. True believers explain this by saying that strangers lack the knowledge and associations to appreciate their jokes. As evidence, they cite jokes that only those fluent in the sacred writings could understand. For example, the settlers in Hebron, the most militant of Gush Emunim members, say of their leader, "Rabbi Levinger has the title, *Yoreh Yoreh.*" The Hebrew word *yoreh* has two meanings. One is a teacher of religious faith and laws; the other is one who fires a gun, referring here to shooting at Arabs. True believers sometimes deliberately tell such jokes in situations where those present could not possibly understand, thereby emphasizing their superiority and cohesiveness, and distancing others. In similar fashion, the ultra-Orthodox sometimes seek to insult Israeli outsiders by telling a joke with a punch line in Yiddish. Such jokes can create solidarity among rival fundamentalist groups, in the same front line against secular surroundings.

Raising the Volume on Opposition Jokes

From the function of social control in humor, we now look at its converse—opposition. This relates to what is generally called "political humor," a phenomenon that may flourish in liberal democracies, but which takes on particular significance in totalitarian regimes, including fundamentalist ones. Humor often represents the debunking of authority and convention. As with political jokes, fundamentalist jokes also stick a pin into an inflated balloon—whether king or priest, the constitution or Scriptures. Fundamentalist jokes about radical religion can be an expression of frustration and protest, even of cautious and well-disguised rebelliousness. Humor focused on internal weaknesses points out these flaws and hence also hints at potential sources of crisis and change. Humor, however, has the capacity to sublimate frustration, thus rendering harmless the cumulative aggression against irksome norms and values. This liberating effect enables the system to continue to function. This is why fundamentalist movements, like Bolshevik or Fascist states, tend to show a measure of tolerance toward self-humor and even to encourage it, as long as it is contained. It is better to institutionalize jokes against oneself than to have people stop paying membership dues, demonstrate in the streets, or plant bombs. As with heads of state, so mullahs, pastors, and rabbis sometimes manage to co-opt jokes and then recirculate them.

Fundamentalist jokes walk a tightrope between reconciliation and rebellion, security and insecurity, loyalty and estrangement. Fundamentalist humor at the expense of its leaders is an example of this. To wit, the jokes about Rabbi Kook (the son), the charismatic spiritual leader of Gush Emunim, who suffered from a number of physical handicaps, including a lisp so severe that it was almost impossible to understand his speech. According to his disciples, "His mouth uttered pearls of wisdom which welled up in such profusion that when they reached the narrow opening, they pressed together, bumping each other." This began as an ironic comment by a few jokers among Gush Emunim, but it was quickly adopted by circles close to the rabbi. There are many examples of such a "career" for a fundamentalist joke. Initially the joke pokes fun at the cleric, gradually it takes on an apologetic character that seeks to conceal the believers' embarrassment at deficiencies of their leader, and eventually the joke becomes a kind of ode to the leader's greatness. Rabbi Kook also suffered from a severe disability in his legs, similar to that of Shaykh Ahmed Yassin, spiritual leader of the Hamas movement, who is paralyzed from the waist down. In both cases, true believers have chosen similar forms of humor to cope with the incongruity inherent in the fact that healthy young people defer to physically weak, paralyzed figures. Wheelchairs become royal chariots and walking sticks, lethal weapons.

In radical religion, as in politics, a genre of humor takes aim at figures of authority. Beside the motif of old age and physical limitations, a frequent subject is their lack of orientation in the here and now. While many leaders of Protestant fundamentalism enjoy a fresh, alert, and active image, as reflected in their appearance and behavior, and are viewed as professionals in the realms of organization, economics, and politics, the leaders of Islamic and Jewish fundamentalism—with a few exceptions, such as the Imam Musa al-Sadr[17]—are rather eccentric characters. Although not weak or sickly, their familiarity with modern life is limited. For example, they seem to be incapable of basic commercial transactions or of using technology that has long since become an integral part of urban life. This phenomenon is sometimes so pronounced that the leaders appear strange, out of sync, which could cast doubt on their ability to master the world and to guide the true believer within it. This is a popular subject for internal fundamentalist jokes, which offer caricatures of leaders who cannot distinguish between different values of currency, can't drive a car, don't read newspapers, and have never seen a movie. Yet even the most mocking jokes can turn these flaws into merits. Humor helps present this impractical nature as proof of utter spirituality. The more ridiculous the figure seems, the more sublime the religious qualities that afford a better perspective on reality.

Fundamentalist humor is subversive in three respects. The jokes are a transparent medium for opposition to the modern secular world, a more subtle vehicle for intra-fundamentalist opposition, and an even more cautious tool for self-criticism. Coop-tation of jokes can never completely neutralize their sting. Even when the laughter appears to be open, it always carries a hidden thought, something approaching a con-spiracy. In fundamentalist humor against radical religion itself, undercurrents can be sensed which both compete and merge with the dominant currents. Many of these jokes are a counterpoint and eventually become an integral part of a complex music. Here we raise the volume of the voice of opposition over the first voice, which is rela-tively known and usually appears in solo. But if we listen to both voices, we can see fundamentalism as a highly tense, essentially dialectic phenomenon.

Jokes can sometimes force people to face a cruel and unpleasant truth; yet people continue to listen to jokes at their own expense just as they continue to look in the mirror. It is a way—almost the only way—for the fundamentalists to examine who they are. For all their apparent conviction, religious zealots are astonishingly anxious to engage in self-examination, and thus eager to hear jokes about themselves. Like the rest of us, true believers pay close attention to the legendary fool who exploits his liberty to say what is forbidden to others, and they enjoy what he says even when it is harsh.[18] The thirst of fundamentalists to learn more about themselves surpasses their fear of criticism. This is reflected in the obsessive interest of zealots to hear what the secular world thinks of them, and what doubting fundamentalists think about funda-mentalism. So they listen to jokes.

Self-examination through humor enables fundamentalists to make sensitive sub-jects negotiable and to explore daring new ideas. All jokes, perhaps particularly radical religious ones, contain an element of heresy rooted in the reflexivity which is the foun-dation of the fundamentalist joke. The truth reflected in a fundamentalist joke is tol-erated so long as it is limited to a situation clearly defined as humorous. Jokes push matters to the very edge, just as contemporary radical religion does. Indeed, humorists and zealots share a common trait: both go to the brink, challenging their limits and the limits of their culture. Joke tellers and fundamentalists balance precariously be-tween order and chaos, the forbidden and the permitted, old and new, true and imagi-nary, possible and impossible. Behind humor lies the painful awareness of human con-straints, fragility, and finitude. In this respect, humor is always tragic, and contains an essentially religious nucleus. In its laughter, radical religion recognizes how pathetic and ridiculous it is. Fundamentalist jokes are a commentary on its own insignificance and humanity, a reminder to themselves and to the world that they are an inseparable part of it.

Demonizing the Other

The most elementary function of humor is to confront the Other. Through humor it is possible to unify the ranks, to solidify ideals, and especially to hurt those in the opposing camp by depicting them as preposterous and despicable. The use of humor for internal indoctrination and external propaganda has been known to various groups in history and certainly to dictatorial regimes in recent generations. What the Soviets, the Nazis, or for that matter the English and the French did to each other by means of jokes, the fundamentalists do just as well. To the extent that radical religion is associated with laughter, it is in terms of this "external humor"[19] (which some claim is not genuine humor). Modern religious radicals, like all radicals, also use humor to settle accounts with opposing factions of fundamentalism.[20]

Fundamentalists who take themselves seriously and therefore suppress joking at themselves also take their opponents seriously, which is why they make fun of them. Hence, jokes directed against adversaries to radical religion can be particularly vicious, designed to humiliate and oppress their opponents. This humor idealizes radical religion and demonizes the outside world. The jokes release aggression that seeks to delegitimize and even dehumanize secular moderns as well as the religious establishment.

In the world of the yeshivot—the stronghold of both Zionist and anti-Zionist Jewish fundamentalism—humor is at once condemned and exploited. It appears in lessons and sermons as a didactic device and in attempts to foil the external threat to religion. When humor is used in the service of a holy war, fundamentalism relaxes its restrictions. "All jesting is forbidden, except for jesting about idolatry" says the Talmudic tract (Sanhedrin 63). Among the ultra-Orthodox, for example, books of jokes are popular, though these are intended for common folk and children rather than yeshiva students. The books have a clear moral—the superiority of the Jew over the Gentile, of the Torah scholar over the ignoramus, of the believer over the heretic, and of the observer of religious commandments over those who do not observe. In recent years, a popular book in ultra-Orthodox circles was a four-volume collection of Jewish humor,[21] which legitimated itself as "a guard against the despair of exile," referring to the exile of the ultra-Orthodox in the secular state of Israel. In each anecdote of conflict, the adversary is overcome.[22]

While modern rabbinic texts scarcely bear a trace of humor, the audiocassettes, which have become an important means of communication in the Jewish radical religious world, are replete with humor. In these recorded sermons, jokes intended to humiliate sinners and heretics are skillfully woven into the rhetorical flow. After listening to a number of such cassettes, one notices that a scorn of the secular has been casually introduced. The word *secular* (in Hebrew, *hilonim*) is subtly transformed into the word *sick* (*holanim*)—a minor change in pronunciation and spelling. Most of the jokes are vulgar parodies on the materialism, vacuity, and corruption of modern Israeli life. Others settle accounts not only with seculars, but also with various types of religious Jews, including opposing ultra-Orthodox camps. Some of these jokes exhibit self-irony. A preacher who belongs to the most extreme group—Neturei Karta—describes "the impending funeral of the evil instinct," stating that this will be "the greatest funeral in the world, attended by ultra-Orthodox Zionist collaborators, by religious Zionists, and by secular Jews from the communist left to the fascist right . . . as well as by Neturei Karta. After all, they all seem to have known the deceased."

Exposure to humiliating jokes against them prompted true believers to consider giving the opposition a taste of its own medicine. Although many still oppose this technique, Jewish and Muslim fundamentalists of various types have decided to use humor to fight the enemy, and caricature is a natural medium. Modern religious zeal-ots, like their predecessors, have found that a vulgarized portrait of the forces of dark-ness at battle with the forces of light can be a potent medium for spreading the gos-pel. These ultimate struggles can be found among the Hamas, which depict scenes of resistance to the demonic Israeli army, and among the ultra-Orthodox in scenes of resistance to the demonic Israeli police. Caricatures appear in the semiofficial press, underground leaflets, huge street posters, wall paintings, and graffiti.

Within this wealth of caricatures one can distinguish a striking thematic and graphic similarity. First, the stereotypes of the forces of evil are constant. Thus, more or less the same figure of the demonic Jew appears in the caricatures of the Palestinian Hamas, the Lebanese Hizbullah, and the Egyptian Jihad (and this is the same old Jew who was depicted in German and Russian propaganda until not long ago). Also, modern West-ern civilization is the common enemy of both Moslem and Jewish fundamentalists, and frequently appears in their caricatures as a combination of a greedy American and a licentious whore.

More surprisingly, when the caricatures of fundamentalist movements relate to op-posing fundamentalist movements, they often borrow images from each other. Thus, the Jewish zealot in Moslem fundamentalist caricatures is remarkably similar to the Moslem zealot in Jewish fundamentalist caricatures—the same hooked nose and evil black eyes. Meanwhile, the secular media borrow and lend their own version of the fundamentalist image, and this cultural Ping-Pong results in a stereotype of the arche-typal fundamentalist. The Western press, for example, uses the dervish to represent the Moslem fanatic; this figure is then applied to fanatic Jews, and rabbis are depicted as dervishes wearing robes and bearing an insane gaze. In one case, the zealot holds a dagger in his mouth; in another, an Uzi submachine gun dangles from his shoulder. A zealot looking at a caricature of a zealot could be forgiven for being confused. Is this a sympathetic depiction of himself or of a rival believer?

Fundamentalists are eager to see caricatures of themselves drawn by both seculars and rival believers. Both sources provide information to understanding themselves and their surroundings. This phenomenon reaches its height when true believers adopt the caricatures drawn by others as a way to describe themselves, possibly with the same measure of humor. External humor thus becomes self-humor. Gush Emunim, for ex-ample, has been confronted with its public image in Israel through caricatures in which its members appear over and over again with the same features: the prominent skull-cap, dangling fringes of the prayer shawl, thick eyeglasses, army jackets, and, of course, a weapon. The wife of the settler has her own stereotype: the same military jacket, a long denim skirt, and always pregnant. It will not be long before members of Gush Emunim begin to depict themselves the same way. At this point, the gap between mocking the other and self-irony is closed, and "they" becomes confused with "we." A variation of the "identification with the aggressor" syndrome appears. Some mem-bers of the movement are aware of this and have criticized it in closed forums, likening it to Diaspora Jews who take on the properties that anti-Semites attribute to them.

Fundamentalists learn serious things about themselves from humor directed against them, and they might also learn to laugh at themselves. Following a recurring pattern of violence committed by radical Jews after they scornfully ignored laws, government orders, and court rulings, a caricature appeared in the Israeli press showing three identical structures—same size and shape, all at ground level. The first is labeled "the legislature," the second "the executive," and the third "the judiciary." High above, a cloud drifts past on which sits a bearded, skullcapped man with the features of a well-known radical religious leader, a broad smile on his face. True believers understood the message well and happily adopted the caricature, proudly displaying and distributing it.

What makes a caricature effective is a stripping away of camouflage and an accurate reading of reality. Even a hostile, vicious caricature must reveal an interest and sensitivity toward the subject. If the caricatures of rival fundamentalists are to strike home, they must reflect some measure of empathy with the zealot rival. Laughter at the expense of one's rival does not preclude laughter at one's own expense. Indeed, humor unites the two in a common alliance transcending recognized boundaries.

Jewish Humor—Old and New

A distinction can be drawn between "normal" humor that aims to glorify the in-group and belittle the out-group, and what is known as "Jewish" humor, whose hero is both the creator of the joke and its victim. This is a sarcastic form of humor that seeks to debunk the whole world, particularly the strong, but it can also lead to the deconstruction, depreciation, and desacralization of the ideals of the weak—the Jews themselves. It is an ironic type of humor that deals obsessively with the flaws and limitations of the narrator. A prime example was the satire that appeared in Gush Emunim's internal newsletter under the title "O Us!" This was a tongue-in-cheek critique of Gush Emunim's tendency to exalt themselves and belittle others, in which a member of the movement ridicules his comrades who see themselves as an unblemished elite. This attack has become a milestone in the life of the movement, and the expression "O Us!" a reminder that often appears in their discourse.

Jewish jokes settle scores with religious institutions and their officials, with Torah and faith, and even with God. This is the humor of pious blasphemy, a humor which can be a sign of heretical thoughts masking great faith or of great faith masking heretical thoughts. Jewish humor appears to show that, in the context of complete trust in God, His omniscience and His omnipotence can be tried. Doubt can be cast on divine justice only in the context of a complete lack of skepticism concerning His reality and greatness. While the believer loves God, he can also be angry with Him, negotiate with Him, and make loyalty to Him conditional on the fulfillment of certain expectations. In the past, when religion was natural and a given and religiosity was spontaneous, evident and a matter of routine, and there was not even a hypothetical alternative to Divine Providence, humor could emerge which could risk humanizing or even debasing God. This provocative humor seems to have disappeared with modernization, in which religion is no longer taken for granted. Modernity has impaired the familiarity between the believer and God.

While Jewish humor presupposes religious naiveté, fundamentalism is anything but naive. Fundamentalism watches itself like a hawk, and shields itself by a well-processed rationalism. It does not flirt uncontrolled or joke with the sacred. Fundamentalism is at war, and—à la guerre comme à la guerre—must maintain seriousness. In this war, all true believers are on the front line, therefore discipline must prevail at all levels. Except that here and there one finds deviations of humor, of the type that is simultaneously innocent and daring. This, however, no longer causes spontaneous laughter and relaxation, but rather embarrassment and tension.

With the modernization of Judaism that began during the eras of emancipation and enlightenment in the nineteenth century, and the transformation of religion into free choice from among a range of attractive options, a new type of Jewish humor emerged. It is similar to its predecessor in terms of its skepticism and self-criticism, but completely different in its sources and context. This is a sophisticated Jewish humor that revolves around the dilemma of collective identity, previously a much less acute problem, and is a function of balancing an existence between two worlds in conflict. Paradoxically, this type of Jewish humor, which is identified with enlightened Judaism and assimilated Jews, is the same as that found in radical religious Judaism.

Humor characterized by a keen awareness of the surrounding world and by self-awareness is typical of two opposing forces: those who have left religion, and those who are trying to restore its glory. In both cases, religion is no longer an organic part of the background but a problematic element in the foreground of consciousness. A similar type of humor is shared by both adversaries for whom religion is a battleground. Old Jewish humor with its total religious security has been replaced by Jewish humor rooted in the absence of religious security. This is also characteristic of the Jewish fundamentalist whose humor reflects the true believers' need to constantly check themselves against their surroundings, to test the limits of their faith. Take, for example, the competition announced by Gush Emunim humorists for new designs for skullcaps. Hundreds of suggestions poured in, from Adidas and BMW trademarks to the cynical use of holy verses. One suggestion showed a labyrinth underneath which appeared a Talmudic verse used in the Jewish burial ritual: "Know whence you came and where you are going."

The phenomenon of laughing at oneself is not, of course, confined to the Jews; it typifies all threatened or persecuted groups. This is the humor of the underdog, and it is arguable whether it reflects inferiority or arrogance, whether it is (self) pitying or brutal, whether it accepts or protests reality, whether it is optimistic, realistic, pessimistic, or cynical. This is the humor of groups who are attentive to their surroundings in an effort to understand themselves. Some see this humor as "neurotic" since it involves acute self-awareness and radical self-questioning. Humor of this type, which appeared with the modernization of religion, has now reappeared in the form of fundamentalist humor.

An ironic element of fundamentalism, by nature self-critical, is its tendency to appropriate humor aimed at it from the secular world without. This includes jokes, parodies, caricatures, rhymes, slogans, and epithets that modern Western culture uses to ridicule and vilify fundamentalists. Some of these jokes are vulgar and malicious to true believers, yet this does not prevent the latter from adopting them, recycling them, and indeed preening themselves with them. In secular Israel, the following street song can be heard: "Trample on every black coat / Degrade every ultra-Orthodox / Curse the worshiper / Piss on the believer." In Hebrew, the song rhymes and is catchy; it is obscene and amusing. And there is hardly a single young ultra-Orthodox Jew who doesn't know these lines by heart and derive pleasure from repeating them to friends and secular Israelis alike. This allows the fundamentalists to identify with those mocking them and their point of view, while at the same time scorning and rejecting them.

Similarly, fundamentalists are often aware of the epithets by which seculars refer to them, and the natural tendency is to ignore them out of shame and contempt. Sometimes, however, true believers take pride in these labels. Thus the term *fundies* is how fundamentalist Protestants in Jerusalem, with a knowing wink, refer to themselves. They do not hide their pleasure in repeating names intended to hurt them, in an expression of their sense of superiority and invulnerability. In the 1950s, the nickname *doss* came into use; it means "religious" in Yiddish, and is used as a scornful anti-Orthodox term. In recent years, various ultra-Orthodox groups have adopted the word and given it prominence in their humor as an amusing term of self-reference employed to rail against both themselves and their environment. I have also heard Jewish, Christian, and even Sunni fundamentalists refer to themselves publicly as "Khomeinists." "Yes, we are Khomeinists," they may say, meaning, we know what you think of us; we know what Khomeinism is; but we are not what you think.

What could better express the fundamentalists' mastery of the nuances of modern secularity than their fluent rehashing of jokes about fundamentalists? Thus the use of secular humor enables religious fundamentalists to clarify to the seculars that their faith is not based on ignorance of the alternatives. This buttresses the claim of true believers: "We are familiar with your way of life, but we prefer the way of God . . . which proves that it must be better."

Many fundamentalists regularly collect and share every scrap of humor they can find about fundamentalism, and some specialists document these jokes and present them in public. For years, the bulletin of Gush Emunim included a column that quoted verbatim the comments of adversaries. Indeed, the more brutal the laughter, the more the Gush Emunim readers seemed to enjoy it. True believers themselves have suggested that there may be some masochism in this, and there have indeed been instances when fundamentalists' enjoyment of jokes about fundamentalism appears to be a form of self-degradation for purposes of purification and elevation. The editors of the column, however, assert that its purpose is educational: to show the members of the movement how biased their opponents are, and how spurious their claims. For this purpose, caricatures or items of demonization are most effective, since they are patently absurd. Radical religious leaders, fearful that followers might be demoralized by humor against them, resort to a preemptive policy by bringing in these jokes and exposing followers to them, accompanied by corrective commentaries.

Importing jokes also sometimes gives the opportunity to give them a positive twist. For example, when messianic tension reached a peak in one group, it placed enormous billboards across Israel declaring "Prepare for the Coming of the Messiah!" When the Messiah showed no signs of appearing, however, the adversaries of this messianic group—particularly the secular Zionists—distributed stickers that mimicked the posters but bore a different message: "I came but you were out." The laughter that this produced in Israel caused great pain to the messianists, but instead of ignoring the paraphrase, some publicized it, transforming the joke into a reproof: the Messiah had indeed come, but since you were not worthy of receiving him, he left until you mend your ways.

Fundamentalist groups collect digs against them and disseminate them within the community, which copes with them as a group. Repeating jokes is a test of the community and a tool for building it. The declared aim of fundamentalism in presenting collections of jokes against itself is to relate to the indecent creators of these jokes and not to their objects. In turn, opponents of fundamentalism view these collections as the expression of a sanctimonious and arrogant attitude on the part of the believers. Moreover, these collections are another indication of the obsession of true believers with what the modern world thinks of them, in an attempt to find out who they themselves are. Through secular satire of them, fundamentalists satisfy their curiosity and a desire for self-analysis.

While there is an endless flow of jokes into the radical religious group, attempts are made to sabotage their export. The qualified legitimacy given to the import of jokes serves as authorization for home-grown jokes. Limitations placed on self-humor by the fundamentalist authorities are overcome by passing it off as external humor. Some of the most brutal jokes about fundamentalism have been told by fundamentalists, but presented as "This is what seculars say about us." This is a form of fundamentalist reconnaissance in search of itself.

Miracles, Messianists, and More Catholic than the Pope

We turn now to a sample of three motifs that are unique to radical religious humor. Not surprisingly, these motifs relate to unresolved core issues for radical religion, issues that are the subjects of interest and tension. The jokes, accordingly, suggest the fascination and disquiet with which fundamentalists regard these subjects, and their ambivalence toward them.

The first motif relates to an eternal religious question that has been given renewed prominence by radical religion: miracles. Contemporary radical religion has benefited from increased religiosity among broad sections of society that had been immersed in processes of modernization and secularization, and radical religion has promoted this trend. However, there are elements in this popular religiosity that radical religion finds vulgar and primitive. Prominent among these is a mechanistic view of miracles. Although fundamentalism has been associated with a certain rehabilitation of the status of miracles, fundamentalism is engaged in a war against the subculture of miracles.[23]

Miracles of both Jewish and Moslem origin prospered during the Gulf War. Over a period of several weeks, about forty SCUD missiles landed in population centers in central Israel. The missiles caused considerable damage—hundreds of houses were destroyed and there were injuries—yet extraordinarily there were no fatalities. This is ideal ground for the revival of faith in miracles. The promoters of the miracle boom were the spokespeople of radical Judaism, above all ultra-Orthodox preachers. Yet the critics of those who promoted miracles as explanations for strange occurrences included both pro- and anti-Zionist ultra-Orthodox Jews, who joked: "Saddam Hussein is bombarding Israel—with miracles"; "Were it not for the American, British, and French air forces, there would be far more miracles"; "The hospitals have classified patients according to the degree of miracle—light, moderate, and severe miracles"; and so on.

Another area fertile for anecdotes about miracles during this war relates to the air-raid sirens in Israel, which gave civilians four minutes to seek shelter. The siren was broadcast over the radio, which created a problem for Orthodox Jews, as they are prohibited from listening to a radio on the Sabbath. On the other hand, there is also a religious commandment that sanctions the transgression of religious laws if necessary to save life. The rabbis were required to rule on the dilemma between these two injunctions. Their decision was an invitation to parody: the radio was to be covered by a blanket and placed in a closet so that music and words could not be heard during the Sabbath—but the siren would still be audible. Even Jewish fundamentalists could not help but react with humor. Ultra-Orthodox satire told of "a miracle that occurred when a missile destroyed a house, but the radio remained safe and sound in the ruins since it was well padded. As for the residents, they were also saved, having already left the house, afraid they would be considered sinners for listening to the radio . . ."

A second motif is that of the Messiah. As with miracles, the Messiah raises classic religious problems, hence it is only natural that it be handled by religious humor. Gush Emunim is a radical religious movement that proudly declares its messianism. Whenever messianic tension peaked in the Gush, there was an expectation that true believers would abandon their full-time study of Talmud and devote themselves entirely to settlement activity in the territories. Students of the Merkaz Harav yeshiva declared that immediate settlement was "the key to accelerating and completing the process of redemption," and therefore they called on people to "close the books of Torah and realize the Torah in concrete terms." In response, an ironic complaint was heard among both rabbis and students in the yeshiva: "For two thousand years, Jews prayed daily for their return to Nablus, Hebron, Bethel, and Jericho, but in vain. Now that it's actually happening, for Heaven's sake, does it have to happen to us?" Instead of happiness, we see reservations and complaints. True believers are somewhat reluctant to accept what they so badly wanted. The opportunity to realize the messianic dream is threatening. Thus while religious jokes in the past were based on the belief that the Messiah's arrival was not immediate, contemporary fundamentalist jokes express the insecurity resulting from the Messiah being imminent. Not only would the coming of the Messiah force religion to submit to a test that could end with the obvious failure of its prophecy, vindication would also be dangerous since it would present Torah and faith as no longer relevant—after all, conventional and radical religion are intended primarily for an unredeemed world.

The 1993–94 revivalist campaign of the Lubavitch (Habad) Jews focused expectations on the coming days or weeks, and pointed to the Lubavitcher rebbe as the concrete incarnation of redemption. Yet this personification of messianism fell ill—so ill that he was paralyzed, unable to speak or think clearly, and on the verge of death. Given the anxiety of the believers, this only intensified the messianic fervor. Needless to say, this was a great opportunity for adversaries of messianism. Not only secular but also religious Jews, particularly the radical religious, exploited the moment to knock the Lubavitch camp, and what better way than through jokes, particularly those combining themes of the Messiah and redemption with illness and death? "Hospital corridors are filled with sick people desperate to die quickly so they will be on time for the resurrection of the dead." Jokes of this kind circulated among Israelis, including the rival Lithuanian ultra-Orthodox, as well as other ultra-Orthodox and even the Gush Emunim, who are themselves messianists. Happiness at the misfortune of the Lubavitch masked confusion, fear, and subsequent relief. True believers of various kinds dreaded the prospect of success of Lubavitch messianism since fulfillment of the dream would have demanded profound religious changes from them. Elements within the Lubavitch camp itself were equally alarmed at such a possibility. Attempts were made to find an escape clause from their investment in redemption. The repetition of secular jokes about the Messiah by Lubavitch Hasidim themselves was an expression of reservation and role distance which would enable them to find a way out of the maze. Jokes adopted by messianists revealed both their sophistication and nervousness. Consider, for example, the following satire, phrased in the style of traditional Talmudic reasoning. (The passage should be chanted in the sing-song learning style of the yeshiva.) "If the Messiah dies before the Messiah comes, then there's no problem—he will awake in the resurrection of the dead when the Messiah comes. But if the Messiah tarries and dies only after the Messiah has come, then who will wake him?"

At an advanced stage, when messianic tension was unbearable, a jocular mood seized the Lubavitch camp. Laughing at oneself gained legitimacy and could soothe the shame at the eventual denouement. A joke that criticized the fragmentation of the ultra-Orthodox world was seized by the frustrated Lubavitch. It was claimed that the Messiah had in fact arrived, but had turned around and fled since believers began to bombard him with questions—which synagogue did he pray in? following whose tradition and tune? (and did he believe that the Lubavitcher rebbe was the Messiah?).

Right up to the end, messianic true believers continued to cling to the life preservers offered by the holy texts, particularly the position that any setback on the road to redemption guarantees redemption. This is an example of the logic that "the worse things are, the better they are." As explained by the principle of cognitive dissonance, the fact that the man destined to be the Messiah is dying leads not to an abandonment of faith, but rather to the eruption of an additional pulse of messianic enthusiasm. However, as the rebbe's illness became more severe, even true believers could not avoid admitting the absurd level the messianic tension had reached. This acknowledgment and distress were reflected in their laughter. Illuminating in particular was the laughter of the children of these messianists. During the last days before the declared coming of the Messiah, many children in the streets of religious neighborhoods, including throngs of Lubavitch followers, threw off all restraints. They openly transgressed prohibitions that none would normally have disobeyed—retorting to their parents, mocking their teachers, and teasing their rabbis. When asked to explain their insolent behavior, they answered, affecting innocence—indeed in a subtle reproach—that according to the Talmud, sinful behavior will reach its peak on the eve of the Messiah's coming. The mischievous children forced their fundamentalist parents to confront the ironic dimension of their faith, revealing the extent of its absurdity. That is chutzpa; this is redemption.

The next motif of fundamentalist humor, ultraextremism, draws us even closer to an understanding of the true believer. In traditional religion, religious authorities could not impose extreme religious norms for fear that many would be unable or unwilling to bear the demands. Present-day radical religion, however, appeals to a homogeneous and self-selected group for whom extreme religious norms are a distinguishing factor. In traditional religious society, believers who took their religious zeal to extremes posed a threat to the community and to its leaders, so institutionalized ways were found to deal with them. Sometimes they were removed from the community, and an institutional framework, such as monastic orders, was created for them.[24] But modern fundamentalism expects the entire community to live up to high standards of religious virtuosity. Within fundamentalist groups, as within the monastery, dealing with the danger posed by extremists is more complex. Jokes are one way of handling it.

Conventional religious jokes concerned those who were negligent in performing the commandments or who performed them out of a sense of duty with no feeling. The ideal objects of these jokes are those who neglect the required blessings when they imagine they are not being observed. Radical religious jokes, on the other hand, concern those who obey every detail of the commandments according to the strictest interpretations and who appear overly enthusiastic. The butt of these jokes is the individual who insists on blessing God even in minor matters when there is no requirement to do so. Jewish true believers, like their Muslim counterparts, laugh both at those who take shortcuts in their prayers and at those who lengthen them unreasonably; at least the former, they say, are not burdened by hypocrisy. One can also find traditional Jewish humor among the ultra-Orthodox. When faced with a plague of chattering in a fundamentalist synagogue, cards were distributed with the inscription, "The authorities note that it is forbidden to pray while chatting."[25] Social control of extremists also uses traditional methods such as accusing the extremists of putting on airs or mocking the histrionic nature of their worship.

A new type of humor shows awareness of the latent rules of the radical religious game. Take, for example, a one-liner which fundamentalist Jews tell about themselves. Two ultra-Orthodox meet on a Sabbath morning. One turns to the other and asks eagerly, "Have you got a new *khumra* for me?" The word means stricture and refers to a rabbinical ruling which is particularly difficult to observe. In other words, true believers are competing with each other in ultra-piety and conspicuous devotion. Yet the fear of aberration is no less acute concerning excessive religiosity as sacrilegious behavior.

Fundamentalists whose zealotry threatens fellow believers and the fundamentalist establishment are curbed through humor. From Jewish fundamentalists studying in a yeshiva renowned for its strictness, I heard a parody of a rabbinical argument that mocks extremism: "Why is it forbidden to urinate on the Sabbath? Because if one does so in a bathroom, one is guilty of the transgression of 'making a musical sound,' and if one does so in the yard, one is guilty of the transgression of 'watering the grass seeds.'"

A good number of fundamentalist jokes emanate from the tension between strict observance of the commandments and laziness or greed. Jewish and Muslim fundamentalists tell of a radical religious Jew who found coins on his way to the synagogue on the Sabbath—when it is forbidden to handle money—so he lay down on top of them until the end of the holy day. Among Sunni radicals in Israel, a repertoire of jokes has developed around the veiling of fundamentalist women. Many jokes relate to the endless attempts by husbands to force their wives to cover their bodies and remain hidden away in the home. These jokes tacitly admit that the effort is useless since "it runs counter to the nature of women." Among Palestinian true believers, one finds several versions of a story in which chairs are chained inside the homes so that wives and daughters who want to be out on the balcony will have nothing to sit on, so they will stay indoors. More interesting are the jokes that imply the absurdities on the path to true religion. For example, one source of self-satire is the dilemma of the Muslim true believer who must choose between his desire for his wife to pray in the al-Aqsa mosque on Fridays during the holy month of Ramadan and his desire for her not to leave home. One path of religious excellence negates another. Furthermore, jokes on this subject are sensitive to the fact that growing fundamentalism can push women into a protofeminism. Radical religion encourages female true believers to cover their limbs and faces and to blur their figures with long wide clothes, yet, at the same time, it leads them to expose themselves in street demonstrations or as spokespeople on TV.

Fundamentalists can also laugh at themselves in matters of modesty and abstention—qualities on which they pride themselves. This is true concerning modes of dress and entertainment, but above all concerning relations between the sexes. Certain ultra-Orthodox groups and Gush Emunim yeshivot are so strict about the separation of men and women that even married couples are not supposed to appear together in public. When they go out on the street, the wife walks a few paces behind her husband. Fundamentalists relate that once they met a rabbi walking in town. After walking a few paces, they met the rabbi's wife and told her, "We saw your husband a few minutes ago." "Yes," she replied, "we went out for a stroll together." Other religious fundamentalists say that in a particular neighborhood, a well-known rabbi was seen walking side-by-side with his wife. When passers-by asked in amazement how he dared do this, he answered that she was not *his* wife, but the wife of another rabbi who could be seen walking ahead in the distance.

Among Jewish and Muslim fundamentalists who are viewed as behaving "more Catholic than the pope," born-again converts are prominent. Veteran true believers have noticed this and ask, "When can we be sure that they are really part of us?" The answer: "When they start to chat during prayers." The extremism of those who have newly joined radical religion threatens those who have long been part of the community, and the latter scornfully attempt to discredit the newcomers. Fundamentalist jokes suggest that showy ritualism can mask ignorance, as in the following example from Jewish fundamentalism: There is a religious injunction to wash one's hands before eating, and all rings must be removed before this ritual. Radical religious women often hold their rings between their lips while washing. The story is told of a born-again woman who was standing in a long line of women waiting to wash their hands. When her turn came, she asked her neighbor to lend her a ring so that she could hold it between her lips while washing.[26]

The Secret Diary of a Fundamentalist

In an internal newsletter circulated among some Gush Emunim settlements, a column appeared entitled "Just between Us," whose declared aim was "to unveil the inner world of the [Jewish settlers], relating their hardest moments and toughest struggles against those who seek to destroy them, Arabs and Jews—especially Jews, and including extensive details of some of their own idiocies." The column was unsigned, but it eventually became known that the author was HS, who had been a member of the Jewish underground in the territories. The author had been convicted and imprisoned for his participation in setting bombs that had seriously injured Palestinian mayors of towns close to his settlement.

This column of humorous soul-searching is offered as a model of radical religious satire. Although much of it parodies secular Israelis and rival religious streams, it also interjects an ironic view of the true believers themselves. HS's satire spills over from mocking criticism of the outside world to mocking self-criticism and back again. Even passages that reveal the faults of the radical religious movement show a kind of license taken by those who believe themselves faultless. On the other hand, enumeration of all the weaknesses of the movement and a glimpse at its ridiculous side—even if there is an element of preening—demands a courageous measure of introspection and is insightful. Take, for example, the adjectives that are applied to radical religion. Gush Emunim satire about Gush Emunim is replete with labels such as Khomeinists, fanatics, obscurantists, inquisitors, medieval, primitive, and so forth. Humor permits the rejection of these labels while in a way it accepts them. The droll adoption of these images undoubtedly reflects a flaunting superiority on the part of true believers toward their critics, yet, however tentative, this adoption also has its effect.

Caricatures of fundamentalism in this document run the gamut of fear, contempt, hatred, and criticism of radical religion. Some episodes concern the true believer "who rolls his eyes up to heaven while he clings to his assault rifle," and his wife who is, needless to say, pregnant and "who recites concoctions of terrifying biblical verses while leaping in front of the menfolks crying out for Jihad in the name of the rabbis." One episode presents the viewpoint of a Muslim Palestinian regarding the Jewish settlers. The passage sharpens the conflict between the two; it also hints at their similarity and mutual dependence, and the contempt toward the enemy couches within it a tone of understanding and sympathy. The author, who had once described violent missions against Palestinian leaders as "axing the limbs of those who postpone redemption," presents his fellow fundamentalists with a monologue by an Arab laborer, father of eleven children of whom "only six are at home since the others are being held in an Israeli army detention camp after being caught throwing stones at Jewish cars." The evident identification with the Palestinian enables Gush Emunim to be examined at point-blank range, in a mirror image.

Throughout the monologue, this Muslim is torn between his fearful hatred of the settlers (he believes that their "shaykh," Rabbi Levinger, is planning to kill all the Arabs) and his feelings of security in the face of their naiveté, respect for their fairness, and gratitude for their humanity (the wife of a rabbi makes sure that he has food for his children and unthinkingly changes his name from the Arabic Yusuf to Yossl, an affectionate Yiddish variation). At the end of the passage, he fantasizes slaughtering all the settlers—"may God have mercy on them"—in the name of Allah, but by now he has already had the chance to confront the settlers with some uncomfortable truths about themselves. In particular, he explains to them that "without us [the Moslems of the area surrounding the radical Jews], there is no Gush Emunim, there are no settlements, no rabbis—nothing." He claims that "realization of the goal of transfer [expulsion of the Palestinian population] would be tantamount to suicide on their part."

A number of heroes reappear throughout the satiric series. They are a gallery of true believers, representatives of different shades of Gush Emunim, from Rabbi Tahori (Rabbi Pure), the man of spirituality; through down-to-earth types who bring redemption by daily life in the settlements, such as Artzieli (Mr. Land of Israel); to the radical religious woman settler who runs an ideal home, is involved in charity, and shows expertise in *makhshav* and *makhshava* (computers and mystic nationalist thought). It was not difficult to identify the real-life figures of Gush Emunim behind the fiction. Oroti (Lights), for example, who, as his name implies, is a Kookist (i.e., a follower of the Rabbis Kook, father and son, all of whose books include the word *lights* in the titles). The Oroti character is drawn from idiosyncratic vocabulary to relationships within his family to style of driving, surrounded by considerable affection, yet revealed in all his absurdity. In him, readers in the yeshivot and settlements laughed at themselves. YH, one of the founders of Gush Emunim and a prominent activist for many years, had no problem recognizing himself as this figure, but he enjoyed the piece and told the author that on the whole he was willing to accept the description. Another character in the satire whom there was no point in even trying to camouflage, appears by the name of "Rabbi Moyshe," the reference being to Rabbi Levinger leader of the most zealous wing of the Gush. The author describes himself as "just an anonymous guy with a knit skullcap and a word processor."

When the thirst of the true believers for satire became evident, the author collected some of the episodes into a booklet entitled *Imaginary Settlement.* This opens with a *haskoma,* a device common in the yeshiva world, in which the first page of religious books is an endorsement letter signed by an important rabbi to indicate that the publication is politically correct and to promote its sale. This satirical haskoma holds a double-edged sting. First, it mocks the absurdity of this ultra-Orthodox mechanism that combines censorship and sales promotion; and, second, it mocks members of Gush Emunim who condemn the ultra-Orthodox for their "Diasporalike" customs, which they themselves are increasingly inclined to adopt. The author adds an apology to the endorsement, asking forgiveness from the victims of his critique in language that parodies the flowery and archaic quotes of spiritual leaders.

Such an introduction helps smooth the way for readers who could be offended by an exhaustive list of their faults, until an absurd mirror image is created. Thus, a fundamentalist Jew with a sense of humor provides a fascinating insider's look at fundamentalism, particularly its hidden and quite illegitimate aspects. From satire to satire, we see the enjoyment true believers derive from secretly reading the heretical press, which they prefer to the boring, indoctrinating, internal press. We learn about the true believers' efforts to place themselves in the center of the world: their desire to be the focus of attention of political leaders and the masses, their fondness for filling headlines and the TV screen. The true believer tendency for histrionics and their attraction to the scandalous are other recurrent themes, as is their awareness of the gulf between the power and success attributed to them and their actual limitations and situation. Other passages lampoon the discrepancy between their pretension to know better than anyone else what is good for the nation and their inability to manage well the affairs of their own small group. The merciless list of the true believer's faults continues: the admission of their boredom with the lengthy sermons and long prayers; the fear of what their neighbors might say, which leads them to initiate charities that no one needs and to force these charities on people who become needy against their will; and their bitter struggle against the devil who tempts them to drop the holier-than-thou competition and to relax in their attempt to make their daily lives meet the principle that "redemption is won through suffering."

The fundamentalist satire shows scenes of radical religious leaders who are manipulated like puppets by their wives, or rank and file who excel in terrorism against their enemies and maneuvering with state leaders, but who are helpless before their own children, who are apathetic to the cause and interested only in American movies, clothes, and food. Another scene depicts the bitter disputes and the endless schisms among radical religious Jews . . . with each substream dubbing itself the "Unity of Israel." Still another scene depicts the mouthing of holy verses in response to any question, even those that deal with prosaic matters such as sewage and parking problems in the settlements—after all, "There is no matter, however small, that is not related to redemption or to the sanctification of the Lord." But in really important matters, the true believers adopt a "fearless and unequivocal" stance: "Ask the rabbis." The author, after exhausting his repertoire of negative images, admits, "Sometimes I don't have time to run to the mirror to check if we're still nice."

Particularly blunt passages separate radical religion from its own rhetoric. While mocking academic studies of fundamentalism that cannot crack the code of the movement and attribute far more to them than is really the case, the author suggests that true believers themselves might examine the relationship between their pretentious language and what they really mean. Thus "the average liberal dove and leftist doesn't realize that when a fanatic fundamentalist settler answers a difficult question with the comment 'If God so wills,' he actually means 'maybe.'"

One of the most revealing passages discusses the desperate need of the radical religious to be loved by the surrounding world, which they condemn and against which they struggle. They long for the approval of those whom they negate; this preoccupation with their own popularity harms their drive to realize their ideals. While they declare that no importance should be attached to what other people think of them, they obsessively read opinion polls about themselves and survey every taxi driver and housewife, hoping to win their hearts. They are even willing to give credit to a university professor who is among their opponents if his statistics show an increase in popular support for radical religion. In one episode, a Gush Emunim activist invents "a sophisticated machine for assessing the precise distance at any given moment between Rabbi Moyshe [Levinger] and the rest of the Jewish people."

In some episodes, the fundamentalists talk about the Messiah, and again we infer that the redemption for which they pray is actually embarrassing: "One fine day early in the summer of 1975, I heard a voice telling me to gather together all my chattel and to prepare my wife mentally for what was to come." The longed-for great moment arrives and whatever happens, happens. The passage ends with a fantasy. "Sometimes I plan a terrible revenge. Early one morning I will telephone Rabbi Moishe, Rabbi Tahori, and Rabbi Oroti [the heads of Gush Emunim] and announce in a choked voice that the Messiah arrived about two hours ago in the nearby settlement Beth El, and has just left on his way to our settlement [Ofra]. When they respond tensely, saying, "Yes, but, why are you only telling us now? . . . Our white shirts are in the laundry!" then I'll torture them happily, "Oh ye of little faith—you had almost six thousand years to get ready!"

One poignant passage may serve as a conclusion to this essay. The true believer pauses to reflect on the growing radicalism of his cofundamentalists, and wonders where it is all leading. In "The Diary of a Sane Religious Man," the hero moans that an hour and a half of Jewish studies have been added to his children's curriculum so that they no longer study ancient Japanese or the history of southeast Australian tribes; the curls of the women in the settlement no longer peek out from behind their head coverings; and the skullcaps of the men have become larger and their beards longer. In response, he sighs, "It feels sometimes as if the Heavens have fallen in on us," and wearily adds, "They seem to be closer to us now than they ever were."

Notes

My thanks to Scott Appleby for his editorial assistance on this essay.

1. For an analysis of classical thought about humor from Plato through Kant to Freud and Bergson, see J. Morreal, ed., *The Philosophy of Laughter and Humor* (Albany: State University of New York, 1987). See C. Powell and G. Paton, eds., *Humor in Society* (London: Macmillan, 1988), for an updated and comprehensive anthology of different aspects of humor. For a review essay on the sociology of humor, including an annotated bibliography, see A. Zijderreld, "Trend Report: The Sociology of Humor," *Current Sociology* 31 (Winter 1983), special issue. See also M. Mulkay, *On Humor,* Basil Blackwell, 1988, and, M. Koller, *Humor and Society,* Cap and Gown Press, 1988. (With special chapters on the social functions of humor and religious humor—Jewish and Christian).

2. One of the definitions of Jewish humor is "Self-awareness pushed to self-analysis, turned to self-criticism" (Leo Rosten, *Joys of Yiddish* [New York: McGraw Hill, 1968]).

On Jewish humor, see also: W. Novak and M. Waldoks, *The Big Book of Jewish Humor* (New York: Harper and Row, 1981) and Henry Spalding, ed., *Encyclopedia of Jewish Humor* (New York: Jonathan David, 1969).

3. E. Methvin, *Rise of Radicalism: The Social Psychology of Messianic Extremism* (N.Y.: Arlington House, 1973) and A. Haynal et al., *Fanaticism* (N.Y.: Schocken Books, 1983).

4. E. Goffman, *Asylums* (Garden City, N.Y.: Anchor Books, 1961).

5. B. Schwartz, "Notes on the Sociology of Sleep," *Sociological Quarterly* 11 (1970): 485–99; Gideon Aran, "Parachuting," *American Journal of Sociology*, 80, no. 11 (1984): 124–52.

6. I learned about this phenomenon from Protestant fundamentalists in Jerusalem, with reference to their communities in Canada.

7. Material on humor in religion is on the whole sparse. Interesting and rare exceptions are: J. Alston and L. Platt "Religious Humor," *Sociological Analysis* 30, no. 4 (1969); on humor in the bible, Edwin Marshall Good, *Irony in the Old Testament* (Philadelphia: Westminster Press, 1950); and on making fun of the sacred in Middle Ages' Catholicism, V. Kolve, "Religious Laughter," in *The Play Called Corpus Christi* (Stanford: Stanford University Press, 1966). In a provocative thesis on religion, humor is presented as signifying a transcendental dimension of human existence (P. Berger, *A Rumor of Angels* [Middlesex, Eng.: Penguin, 1971], p. 90). A recent insightful publication "Religion, Laughter, and the Ludicrous" argues provocatively that traditional religion is pregnant with humor. It also suggests the affinity between humor and religion (I. Gilhus, *Religion* 21 [1991]). For more on humor and religion: C. Hayers, ed., *Holy Laughter* (New York: Seabury Press, 1969); N. Voss, *For God's Sake, Laugh* (Richmond, Va.: John Knox Press, 1967); G. Webster, *Laughter in the Bible* (St. Louis: Bethany Press, 1960); and H. Cormier, *The Humor of Jesus* (New York: Alba House, 1977).

8. Concerning the bleak outlook of Islam, see M. Cook, *Muhammad* (New York: Oxford University Press, 1983).

9. See F. Rosenthal, *Humor in Early Islam* (Leiden: Brill, 1956).

10. In his daily evening prayer, a Jew says, "Hamake be'evrato b'chorei mitzraim." In the Ashkenazi accent prevalent in the yeshivot, this sounds like God is striking his sex organ.

11. Henri Bergson, *On Laughter* (New York: Macmillan, 1911), p. 18.

12. George Herbert Mead, *Mind, Self, Society* (Chicago: University of Chicago Press, 1934); P. Berger and T. Luckmann, *The Social Construction of Reality* (New York: Doubleday, 1966).

13. This joke was brought to my attention by M. Horowitz, a former yeshiva student and an intimate of Rabbi Schach; he later left Orthodoxy and became active in a liberal secular Zionist party. A similar version appeared in his book, *Shemafteyach b'yado* (Jerusalem: Keter Pub., 1989).

14. According to a kabbalistic tradition dealing somewhat jocularly with the very essence of zealotry, the band of Rabbi Lurie the Holy from Safed (fifteenth century) was offered an opportunity to welcome the Messiah. Had they reacted as true zealots should, that is, left everything and proceeded to Jerusalem right away, the Temple would have descended on them from Heaven. But the students felt they had to go tell their wives about their plans to leave for Jerusalem, and so the messianic moment was lost. Once again the failure to pass the test of zealotry was blamed on women.

15. A collection of hasidic tales. See M. Buber, *Or ha-ganuz* (Jerusalem: Schocken, 1957). On the function of tale telling as a form of worship, see H. Rabinowicz, *Hasidism* (Northvale, N.J.: 1988).

16. This phenomenon has an interesting parallel on the language level. Even if an outsider knows the true believer's idiom, the latter will usually talk to him in the outsider's own language. Thus, when addressed by secular Israelis in Yiddish, the ultra-Orthodox will switch to Hebrew, keeping their Yiddish unsullied for communication among insiders only.

17. F. Ajami, *The Vanished Imam* (Ithaca: Cornell University Press, 1986).

18. See, e.g., M. Douglas, "Jokes," in *Implicit Meanings* (London: Routledge and Kegan Paul, 1975).

19. See W. Cameron, "The Sociology of Humor," in *Informal Sociology* (New York: Random House, 1963).

20. Polemics on matters of principle, conflicts of interests and prestige, and simple quarrels among different sectors of the ultra-Orthodox world as well as between the ultra-Orthodox and the secular Israeli world are often conducted by billboards, one of the major communications media for radical Jews. True believer posters are sometimes couched in violent language, though they don't lack a touch of irony. They are called *pashquil,* meaning a sharp satire, a lampoon.

21. M. Z. Porush, *Had V'Halak* (Tel Aviv: Hamol, 1987). (In Hebrew.)

22. I have heard similar jokes from radical Moslems. In the classical encounter between a shaykh, a rabbi, and a priest, the shaykh is the winner, and the other two are disgraced as fools and crooks.

23. See the case of the Virgin Mary vision at Zeitoun. Many researchers point to this miracle as an important event in the history of Sunni fundamentalism in Egypt.

24. See M. Hill, *The Religious Order* (London: Heinemann Educational Books, 1973).

25. This is a variant of an old Hasidic joke: when simple Jews used to chatter during prayer in the synagogue, the rabbi addressed God in a loud voice: "O Lord, look how god-fearing members of my community are. They take care to mention thy name even while talking about important matters."

26. An observation by my colleague Tamar El Or.

Antifundamentalism

Mark Juergensmeyer

In many parts of the world, not only "fundamentalism" but the fear of it has become a problem; in some cases this fear has led to a violation of human rights. A resident of Punjab told me that the Indian government's brutal campaign that effectively quelled the Sikh rebellion in 1992 was often indiscriminate in its targets: "anyone could be killed," he explained, if he or she was "accused of being a fundamentalist."[1] The Punjabi compared the government's recent attitude to that of thirty years ago when it quashed an incipient revolt by militant Marxist Naxalites through similarly brutal measures. Then, he explained, to be labeled a Naxalite also was tantamount to receiving a death threat.

In Tajikistan, former Communist leaders used the accusation of fundamentalism as a reason for attacking and destroying the country's democratically elected Islamic government, leading to what one Tajik journalist described as a "genocide" of Islamic opponents in 1993.[2] One of the Communist leaders, in justifying his party's actions, explained that "Islamic fundamentalism is a plague that spreads easily."[3] In Bosnia in the early 1990s, one of the major reasons given by Serbian nationalists for their policy of "ethnic cleansing"—decimating whole populations of Muslim villages—was their alleged fear that the Bosnian Muslims would establish "a fundamentalist Islamic state." They claimed that "fundamentalists" would use Bosnia as a base for Islamic expansion across Europe.[4]

In many cases, the fear of fundamentalism is grounded in legitimate concerns. Often the animosities against militant, antimodern religious movements have been brought on by the movements themselves, when they have employed what are often strident slogans, violent tactics, and dictatorial leadership styles. In these instances, they have provoked a hostility so deep and pervasive that it has begun to rival the old Cold War in its intensity, its ideological posturing, and its global scope.[5] It is a conflict that pits neighbors against neighbors within nations as well as between nations: religiously oriented countries have become aligned against their common foe, the secular West.

As in the old Cold War, moreover, the creation of stereotypes about the opposition leads to additional problems. When the Other is portrayed as an intractable enemy who possesses predictable and virtually demonic characteristics, someone accused of being a partisan of that camp can become a target for all the hostility felt toward the stereotype. During the Cold War, Communists were branded as satanic foes of the "free world" of the West. The McCarthy era in the United States is a familiar example of the abuses of anticommunism during that period; in Spain and other countries, the anticommunist animosity was even more severe. In the incipient new Cold War between secular and religious nationalism, stereotypes also abound. Religious activists have characterized secular government as "the forces of evil" and as "agents of satan."[6] Secular writers, for their part, have referred to religious nationalists as "fundamentalists" and worse; they have been labeled "hatemongers" and "neo-Nazis."[7] Much has been written about the religious fear of secularism, but relatively little about this latter fear: the sometimes irrational hatred that some secularists harbor against the potency of religion.

This hostility in its extreme forms might be called "fundaphobia"—the irrational fear of fundamentalism. Let us assume, however, that in most cases this hatred is not pathological but is an attitude that is provoked by specific situations, and will change if the situation improves. I prefer, then, to call this attitude "antifundamentalism." It contains the word *fundamentalism* within it, not because I find that term useful in itself, but because those who are most virulently opposed to modern religious activists inevitably refer to them as "fundamentalists." When they use the term it is pejorative, but it should be noted that it is possible to use the word nonjudgmentally: increasingly, for instance, *fundamentalism* is employed in scholarly discourse as the accepted way of labeling the cross-cultural phenomenon of antimodernist religious activism. In the academic context, presumably, there is no moral judgment attached to the use of the term: there can be good fundamentalists as well as bad fundamentalists. Still, I find the pejorative resonance in the term troubling, and the use of the term in non-Western contexts restrictive.[8]

Moreover, in the charged atmosphere of political competition between secular and religious nationalists, to be accused of being a fundamentalist is a serious matter. In addition to the alleged atrocities committed in the name of countering "fundamentalism" in such places as Bosnia, Tajikistan, and Punjab, there are other instances where the reaction has not been as extreme but the attitude is the same: there, secular governments have taken abnormal liberties with the democratic process as a way of countering what they perceive to be a fundamentalist threat.

In this chapter, I will look at three recent cases where the accusation of fundamentalism has led to unusual and possibly undemocratic procedures: the annulment of elections won by Islamic nationalists in Algeria, the eviction of Islamic activists in Israel, and the banning of Hindu nationalist organizations in India. Each of these cases has created a crisis of conscience for democratically minded citizens within these countries and around the world, and they raise critical issues regarding how one deals with the threat of religious activism within the context of democratic institutions.

The Algerian Elections

The Islamic movement has been a thorn in the side of Algerian nationalists ever since they won independence from the French in 1962. In 1990, after the Front Islamique de Salut (FIS) won 55 percent of the vote in local elections, the army attempted to arrest and intimidate members of the party, and in the summer of 1991, four thousand of them lost their jobs as a result of going on strike against the government. When the first stage of the national elections was held on 27 December 1991, the FIS garnered an impressive 40 percent of the parliamentary seats: it was expected that after the run-off elections were completed on 16 January 1992, the party would gain 60 percent of the seats and control the government. Leaders of the FIS jubilantly proclaimed that a new stage in the independence movement had begun, and that the country had formed "a firm beginning for building an Islamic state."[9]

This was not, however, the vision of an independent Algeria that many of its old-guard leaders had in mind. In January 1992 the army annulled the elections and established a secular military junta, accomplishing, as the leader of a local mosque put it, "a coup d'etat against the [Algerian] Islamic state before it was created."[10] Leaders of the FIS were jailed, and a ban was imposed on meetings at mosques, which had become venues of protest and organization for the Islamic opposition. The leader of the FIS, Abdelkadir Hachani, urged his followers to respond nonviolently to the military and to confine their protests to attendance at mosques, which swelled significantly after Hachani was jailed on 22 January 1992.

On 5 March the FIS was outlawed, and for the rest of 1992 and 1993 the country was locked virtually in civil war. Hundreds of supporters of the FIS were killed, and on 29 June 1992 Mohammed Boudiaf, the civilian head of the military-supported Council of State, was assassinated in a complicated attack involving bombs and automatic-weapons fire as he was giving a speech in the Mediterranean port city of Annaba. Boudiaf, a hero of Algeria's war of independence against the French, had defended the ban on the FIS and openly opposed the concept of an Islamic state.[11]

The termination of the democratic process in Algeria and the institution of a military dictatorship was met with nervous silence by most Western powers. Although most officials were relieved that an Islamic government was not allowed to take the reins of power and create what many expected to be another Khomeini-style revolution, they were also uncomfortable at having Algeria's most thoroughly democratic elections so summarily abandoned.

In the United States, the official silence was punctuated by vague and confusing statements. Soon after the elections were suspended, the State Department made something of an international faux pas by declaring—incorrectly—that the assumption of power by the Algerian military was in conformity with the Algerian constitution. The next day, 14 January 1992, the State Department "modified" its statement, asserting that the United States had no desire to intervene in an internal constitutional debate. Washington's official response was one of "concern."[12]

Richard W. Murphy, the State Department's Middle East expert in the Reagan administration, explained that a government based on Islamic fundamentalism would apply religious law in a way that would be inherently undemocratic and would "end the chance for multi-party democracy" in Algeria. Margaret Tutwiler, the Bush administration's State Department spokesperson, cautioned that one should not generalize about the matter: "The term 'Islamic fundamentalism' is used in different ways by different people," she explained, indicating that it is "not a single coordinated international movement." But although the United States had had "excellent relations" with Islamic governments and parties in the past, she said, it would continue to promote "democracy and human rights" throughout the world, and "resist the efforts of extremists of whatever stripe to undermine those principles."[13]

The State Department position was widely interpreted as tacitly condoning the Algerian government's actions. Most American newspapers editorially condemned the seizure of power, including the *Wall Street Journal*, which argued that democracy should be allowed to "run its course."[14] The *Washington Post* and *New York Times* took similar stands. Some writers accused the State Department of being complicit in the Algerian government's actions. George Black, a contributing editor to the *Nation*, quoted I. F. Stone: "[F]ree elections are stopped without protest from us, if not with our connivance, where we fear the results." Black went on to observe that in Stone's day "the excuse was communism; now the reasons lie elsewhere—in the fear of Islam."[15]

The French government's position was even more confused than the State Department's, veering first one direction, then another. The immediate response to the cancelled elections was to take a wait-and-see attitude. The Foreign Ministry said that it was not up to France to "judge these events," and that it would view the situation "with great attention."[16] The French newspapers took more extreme positions: *Le Figaro* cheered the Algerian army's decision to derail the elections, saying that the former colony was not yet ready for democracy. *Le Monde,* on the other hand, was critical of both Algerian and French governments, condemning the French government for its relative silence and accusing it of tacitly supporting the Algerian army's actions.[17] On 16 January, however, Mitterand issued an official statement on Algeria, urging the Algerian leaders to "re-tie the threads of democratic life."[18] The Algerian government, angered by what they described as the "condescending and unacceptable" tone of Mitterand's remarks, withdrew their ambassador to France. Later in 1992, the Algerian regime accused Paris of providing support for the Islamic revolutionaries who assassinated Boudiaf.

In 1993, however, a new government was in power in France, one that adopted quite a different stand, promising financial aid to Algeria. In a June 1993 meeting of the French minister of foreign affairs and his visiting Algerian counterpart, the minister pledged "the will of the French government to aid Algeria in the fight against extremism and fundamentalism."[19] Apparently the French had capitulated to the Algerian position, that the threat of fundamentalism is sufficient justification for suspending the democratic process.

The Israeli Eviction of Hamas Supporters

In Israel in 1992, the fear of fundamentalism also precipitated radical, undemocratic measures by the government. The fundamentalist group that evoked these fears was Hamas, a potent new Islamic resistance force that had emerged within the Palestinian liberation movement in the late 1980s during the Intifada.[20] Hamas opposed both Israel and the secular PLO. In a remarkable way, however, its rhetoric paralleled that of Jewish nationalists like Meir Kahane and the leaders of the Gush Emunim, who also were opposed to the secular Israeli government. In this four-sided war, it was understandable that two of the adversaries—the secular leaders of Israel and the PLO—would reconcile their differences in the face of both Jewish and Islamic religious extremism. The threat was especially real in Gaza and parts of the West Bank where Hamas had replaced the PLO as vanguard of the Palestinian resistance.

During the months preceding the peace accords in 1993, Israeli authorities made every effort to control the Islamic wing of the Palestinian movement, and indirectly to support their partners in the peace talks, the secular PLO. In October 1991, Israeli courts convicted the leader of the Hamas movement, Shaykh Ahmed Yassin, of ordering the deaths of four suspected Palestinian collaborators. The cleric, who was virtually paralyzed from a childhood accident and suffered from lung and eye ailments, was sentenced to life imprisonment. During the same month that the shaykh was jailed, the Israeli-Palestinian peace talks began. From the beginning, Hamas was skeptical of the outcome, and the PLO made every effort to exclude them from it.

Over a year later, the peace talks continued to be held in Washington—albeit at a sluggish pace—and Shaykh Yassin was still in jail. At the same time that representatives of the Israeli government and the PLO were entering into secret negotiations in Norway, leaders of Hamas were accelerating their own campaign to free Shaykh Yassin. On 13 December 1992, following a series of encounters with Israeli troops in Gaza and the West Bank, a militant Hamas cadre kidnapped an Israeli police officer and threatened to kill him if the shaykh were not released. In response, the Israeli government rounded up over 1,300 Hamas activists and detained them, although Prime Minister Yitzhak Rabin assured the captors that he would negotiate with them if they could prove that the police officer were still alive. The Israelis broadcast a tape-recorded plea from the imprisoned Shaykh, urging his colleagues to spare the officer's life, at least until the authorities had time to respond.

Two days later, the officer was killed. In Lebanon, a military leader of Hamas said that the action was taken because Israel had been slow to respond, and because it had detained the Palestinians. He hinted that his group might conduct even more kidnappings in the future. Rabin, who had previously been criticized for his willingness to negotiate with the kidnappers, felt compelled to take a hard line: he vowed to wage a "merciless" campaign against Hamas. He claimed that it was the intention of Hamas to kill not only Jews but also the peace process itself.[21]

On 17 December, Israeli military commanders issued orders to deport over four hundred of the detained Palestinian activists to Lebanon for a period of up to two years. After an unsuccessful effort to block the deportation by legal action through the Israeli courts, the Islamic activists were taken by bus to the Lebanese border. There each was given food, a blanket, and US $50, and sent walking across the no-man's-land toward the Lebanese border. When the Lebanese border guards refused to let them in, they turned back; the Israeli border guards then shot rifles over their heads to discourage them from returning. So the ragtag crowd settled down on the barren, frozen land for what would become for many of them an almost year-long hiatus, in which they would be kept alive with bread and cheese from Muslim Druze living in the area and with international contributions from the Red Cross.

Few of the detainees were charged or convicted of any crime; their only mistake was to have been associated in some way with one of the Muslim groups aligned with Hamas. Some members of the Israeli cabinet who supported the deportations did so as a direct response to the killing of the kidnapped Israeli soldier, in an effort to impose a kind of "collective punishment" on the Palestinians. Others, however, emphasized the importance of the peace negotiations and the threat that Hamas posed to a long-range solution in the region. For them, the kidnapping incident was simply the last straw in a series of Hamas activities that needed to be curbed.

The specter of four hundred cold and pious Muslims shivering on the rocky fields of southern Lebanon brought virtually worldwide condemnation against the Israeli government. In Israel itself, the human rights group B'tselen made a last-minute appeal to Rabin on 16 December to reconsider his plans. The international response was just as swift. The day after the deportations began, on 18 December, the United Nations Security Council agreed to condemn Israel and send the secretary general to Jerusalem to discuss what the council described as "this serious situation."[22]

The United States supported the Security Council's actions and voted in favor of condemning Israel. In one of his first statements on the Middle East following the November 1992 elections, President-elect Bill Clinton voiced his approval of the Bush administration's position, saying that he feared that the deportations would imperil the peace talks. The *New York Times* echoed Clinton's comments, censuring Israel and stating that the Hamas kidnapping and killings were "clearly meant to provoke the Israelis into reprisals," and that Israel had fallen into the trap. Its actions, the *Times* claimed, would "only inflame the confrontation."[23]

It is interesting to note that Rabin used exactly the same reason to justify the deportation of the Islamic activists as Clinton and the *New York Times* used in denouncing it: keeping alive the peace talks between Israel and the PLO. According to several Israeli officials, the deportation was intended to undercut the credibility of Hamas and strengthen support for the PLO. "You have to bear in mind," Rabin explained, "that we are fighting Islamic fundamentalist groups that are trying to kill Palestinians, Israelis, and the peace."[24]

If this was the real intention—to undercut support for Islamic fundamentalism— then the Israeli actions were a failure, at least in the short run. The immediate effect of the deportations was to make martyrs out of the four hundred Muslim deportees, and some observers claimed that Palestinian support for Hamas rose as a direct result of the Israeli actions.[25] Moreover, Yassir Arafat's Fateh branch of the PLO felt compelled to side with Hamas in openly condemning the deportations. Later in 1993, the secret negotiations between Israel and the PLO did indeed lead to the historic peace accord signed in the Rose Garden in Washington, D.C., but it is unlikely that the deportations significantly aided the process. Moreover, Hamas continued to be a serious and dangerous foe of both PLO and the fragile peace. The Israeli efforts to isolate and weaken the Islamic activists by extreme and undemocratic means may have seriously misfired.

The Ban on Hindu Organizations

Recent events in India provide another case where attempts to crush "fundamentalists" may actually have strengthened their cause. On 6 December 1992, in the north Indian town of Ayodhya, following a Supreme Court ruling that forbade the state government from completing the construction of a Hindu temple that would eventually replace a Muslim mosque, an angry mob of 200,000 Hindu *kar sevaks* (action servants) and lower-class Hindus from nearby towns descended on the ancient Moghul edifice with iron bars taken from an adjacent fence and hacked the mosque to rubble. The nation was shocked, and within days the central government invoked its emergency powers. In the weeks that followed, some three thousand people were killed in riots involving Hindus, Muslims, and the police. Leaders of the Hindu nationalist party, the Bharatiya Janata Party (BJP), appeared to be surprised by the destruction of the mosque. The day following the attack, L. K. Advani, founding president of the BJP, publicly took responsibility for the debacle and resigned as leader of the opposition in parliament; the BJP chief minister in Uttar Pradesh resigned as well.[26] Advani, who is said to have personally assured Prime Minister P. V. Narasimha Rao that the BJP would uphold the decision of the Supreme Court, appeared "visibly shaken," and India's most popular Hindu politician, A. B. Vajpayee, said that the Ayodhya incident was the BJP's "worst miscalculation."[27]

For the first few days, the Ayodhya tragedy could be seen as a setback for the BJP. By the middle of January 1993, however, the harsh measures of the ruling Congress Party against the Hindu party had backfired against the Congress, and made martyrs out of the BJP leaders. In a series of measures that one journalist described as "too much, too late," the government suspended the four state governments controlled by the BJP, arrested Advani and hundreds of other BJP leaders, and banned five organizations, including three Hindu nationalist movements: the Rashtriya Svayamsevak Sangh (RSS), the Vishwa Hindu Parishad, and the Bajranj Dal.[28] The ban would have entailed sealing the organizations' offices, freezing their bank accounts, and detaining key members of the associations. In the case of the RSS, this would have involved 35,000 branch organizations and over two million members. The ban was never effectively implemented, and soon was lifted. Most of the leaders were also soon released from jail. Prime Minister Rao had been forced to react harshly not only because of pressures within his own party, but also because of strident public demands, led by the middle-class English-language press. The leading newsmagazine in India, *India Today,* published scathing anti-BJP editorials and ran news reports that questioned the veracity of the BJP leaders it quoted. When Advani and other leaders expressed unhappiness over what had happened at Ayodhya, for instance, the reporter added that these words "ring hollow and expose them as the grandmasters of calumny."[29]

To some extent, the journalists were responding to the way that they had been treated by Hindu activists. The Hindus, perhaps accurately, had identified the English-language media as foes. During the Ayodhya incident, reporters and photographers were subject to both verbal and physical abuse. International correspondents suffered as well. The *New York Times* correspondent was pushed to the ground, the *Los Angeles Times* correspondent was beaten with a bamboo staff and hit with a brick, an American freelance photographer was chased by a man brandishing a sword, a Swiss photographer fought off an angry sadhu who tried to strangle him, and a TV cameraman was pushed off a rooftop into a tar pit. According to Bob Drogin of the *Los Angeles Times,* the cameras, recording equipment, and other gear of journalists were smashed or stolen.[30] Many were pushed or jostled. Most critically injured was Peter Heimlein, the New Delhi correspondent for *Voice of America,* who was hit on the back of the head with an iron rod: he was carried, bleeding, to a nearby temple and then to a hospital. It was not surprising, therefore, that the tone of the journalists' reports was decidedly negative, describing what the *New York Times* correspondent called the "savage intolerance" of Hindu "fundamentalism."[31] The foreign ministries of most Western countries were silent over Ayodhya and the Congress Party's attempts to throttle the Hindu nationalists by repressive means. Rather than censuring Prime Minister Rao for his actions, the *New York Times* and other representatives of the international press chided him for not having acted sooner.[32] A *Washington Post* editorial explained that Rao had to move "vigorously" in order to "take the immediate situation in hand," and that "secularism" had to be restored in order "to build a democracy."[33] The *Wall Street Journal* described the country as being divided between voices of reason and "a howling mob," and regarded Rao and the Congress Party as the last defenders of reason.[34] Only the occasional op-ed piece asserted that the leaders of the BJP were not necessarily wild-eyed fanatics but could be "moderate and tolerant" politicians who represented a "broad social movement."[35] Later in 1993, when the Congress Party went so far as to ban the BJP's peaceful demonstrations in Delhi, the *New York Times* proclaimed that it had gone too far, and that in its handling of Hindu nationalism it may have "lost its bearings, lurching between ineffectiveness and authoritarian posturing."[36]

Increasingly large numbers of the Indian public had already come to that conclusion, having seen the Congress Party's attempt at repressing Hindu nationalism as a sign of weakness rather than strength. According to a poll in the 15 January 1993 edition of *India Today,* the majority of the public disapproved of the Congress government's attempts to repress the Hindu nationalist movement in general and the BJP in particular. Moreover, the poll indicated that if new parliamentary elections were held at that time, the BJP would gain over 50 seats (from 119 to 170), and the Congress Party would lose 12 (from 245 to 233; other BJP gains would come from losses in other parties).[37] The rise of BJP popularity in the wake of the destruction of the mosque made many observers wonder whether the party might not have orchestrated the destruction after all.

The zealousness of the Congress Party's response had given Advani and the BJP a great gift of martyrdom, which they were quick to exploit for political purposes. Perhaps more important, the actions of the Congress leaders caused them to lose the moral high ground. By abrogating democratic processes and dictatorially silencing the opposition, they seemed hostile to the very rights and freedoms they were pledged to protect, and which they claimed the religious nationalists were undermining.

The Antifundamentalist Threat to Human Rights

Running through each of these cases—the banning of Hindu organizations after Ayodhya, the deportation of Hamas supporters to the Israeli-Lebanon border, and the cancellation of elections in Algeria—is a common theme. In each case, the fear of fundamentalism propelled a democratic regime to take extraordinary, possibly undemocratic, measures to prevent groups it regarded as fundamentalist from accruing greater political power. In each case, the action provoked a great deal of controversy within democratic circles, and in each case, the efforts to crush fundamentalism may actually have made the religious resistance stronger.

It may be true that in each case there were real and particular dangers that justified some sort of action on the part of the government. But it is also true that the general pattern of these cases betrays a common logic, one that involves some questionable assumptions about what fundamentalism is and how it affects society. The antifundamentalism syllogism goes as follows:

Assumption 1. There is a known syndrome of human behavior called fundamentalism, which is dogmatic, intolerant, and hostile to human rights. It is dangerous and infectious.

Assumption 2. Adherents of fundamentalism, known as fundamentalists, desire power in order to spread fundamentalism and destroy human rights.

Assumption 3. It is therefore excusable to use whatever means necessary, including the violation of human rights, to prevent fundamentalism from spreading and to prevent fundamentalists from achieving positions of power.

Each of these assumptions is problematic. The third—that any means are justified against fundamentalism—raises basic questions about proportionality in response to a political threat, and it poses the possibility of a Vietnam type of response: destroying human rights in order to save them. It also opens the doors to witch hunts—as in Bosnia, Tajikistan, and Punjab—where old grudges are settled by those who accuse the other side of being fundamentalist in order to justify attempts to eliminate it.

The second assumption—that religious activists will cruelly enforce their prejudices when they gain power—is also questionable: religious regimes sometimes soften their rhetoric when they gain positions of leadership. The Iranian government has mellowed considerably since the harsh years after the revolution when the Muslim clerics had considerable influence. After the death of Ayatollah Khomeini, the new president of Iran, Ali-Akbar Hashemi Rafsanjani, has followed a line of foreign policy aimed at making Iran a more acceptable member of the international community.

When the leaders of the BJP came into power in 1991 in several Indian states, they also seemed eager to demonstrate that they could be good citizens and responsible officials. The party attempted to present a more moderate face to the Indian electorate. Early in 1992, at the party's annual caucus, the BJP adopted Gandhi as its ideal in an overt attempt to employ on its behalf the Mahatma's reputation for moderate Hindu politics. In fall 1992, the Indian press spoke of a "honeymoon" between Congress and BJP leaders, in which they came to an agreement over how to deal with the sensitive Ayodhya matter: the BJP pledged to uphold the constitution and the rulings of the Supreme Court. In a meeting with a group of American academics in Berkeley in October 1992, Advani spoke of the virtues of Hindu tolerance, and claimed that his party's policies would fit easily into the mainstream. In fact, he asserted that the electoral success of his party would help to foster harmony among competing religious groups precisely because it was sensitive to religious concerns. In the months following the destruction of the mosque at Ayodhya, however, radical members of the BJP chided their leaders, claiming that this kind of moderate talk invited repression, and that it showed that there was no need for the party to sell its soul to secular political interests. In this case, then, the assumption that Hindu fundamentalists were fanatics may have helped to move the BJP further in that direction.

The most troubling assumption of those who are stridently opposed to fundamentalism, however, is the first one, the notion that there is such a thing as "fundamentalism": a known, predictable entity that is by definition opposed to human rights. It obscures the fact that religious politics comes in many shapes and forms, especially in the modern world. In Egypt, Tajikistan, and many other countries, religious activists have attempted to develop notions of religious law that will be tolerant to minorities and protect the abuse and exploitation of individuals. And although Iran is still a very harsh and authoritarian society, the constitution of the Islamic Republic of Iran is a remarkably tolerant document: it lists the rights of minority religious communities, the rights of women, and the economic rights of the oppressed among the many rights of its citizenry.[38]

In the cases of Palestine, Algeria, and India, the antipathy against fundamentalism is a volatile matter in large part because religious politics are so common, and a great variety of people can, at one time or another, be labeled "fundamentalist." Those who have been attracted to religious ideologies are unpredictable: some are poor and ignorant, and some are middle-class. In Algeria, many of the supporters of the Islamic movement have been educated in Western universities and pursue professional urban careers. In India, the urban middle-class supporters of the BJP have been branded as scuppies, "saffron-clad yuppies." They see in Hindu political parties a stabilizing influence on the country and not a narrow dogmatism.[39] Allied with these urban scuppies, however, are Hindu shopkeepers, lower-middle-class workers from India's towns, and the often ragtag band of religious mendicants who help get out the vote. Their notions of what aspects of a religious state they might support are quite diverse.

Although there are many kinds of religious politics in the world, what unites the modern religious activists of various hues is their resistance to the secular ideology of the modern state. They are also united by their common label of being called fundamentalist. For that reason those opposed to them help to define them, and must share responsibility for the emerging cold war between secular and religious forces. As in the old Cold War, each side is fond of demonizing its opponents—the Iranians character-ized America as "the Great Satan," for instance. But according to Hasan Abdullah Turabi, the leading Islamic strategist in Sudan, the post–Cold War West also needs a new "empire of evil to mobilize against," and for this reason has made fundamentalism into a demonic global foe.[40]

This new cold war rhetoric was employed by Israeli leaders in justifying their de-portation of four hundred followers of Hamas to the Israeli-Lebanese border. In ex-plaining why such extreme measures were called for, Yitzhak Rabin placed his actions in the wider context of a worldwide struggle against fundamentalism. "We call on all nations, all peoples," he said, "to devote their attention to the great danger inherent in Islamic fundamentalism," which he claimed "threatens world peace." Just as Israel was one of the first countries to face Iraq's nuclear threat, he said, Israel stands "on the line of fire against the danger of fundamentalist Islam," and explained that "the world in general will pay if the cancer of radical-fundamentalist Islam is not halted."[41] Foreign Minister Shimon Peres painted an equally grim picture of what he called the spread of "Khomeinism," which he compared to the threat of communism: "Khom-einism has many of the characteristics of communism. It is fanatic, it is ideological, it is religious [*sic*] and it claims, like communism, that the goal justifies the means. . . . Most of all, it has the same inclination to export its ideas."[42]

In India, where communism has never been as greatly feared as it has been in Israel or America, the rise of Hindu "fundamentalism" has been compared to Nazism rather than to communism. In the 15 January 1993 edition of *India Today,* the editors claimed that "the parallels between the rise of Nazism and the tactics of [Hindu na-tionalists] are difficult to ignore."[43] Accompanying the editorial was a drawing that portrayed a swastika emerging in the shadow of the BJP's political symbol, the lotus flower.

The bombing of the World Trade Center in New York City on 26 February 1993 led to a new outburst of fundaphobia. In the United States, newspapers throughout the country speculated on the global rise of fundamentalist terror, and the *Los Angeles Times* editorially condemned what it described as "the new enemy" of a new cold war.[44] In Egypt, the World Trade Center bombing and a series of bombings in Egypt allegedly plotted by Islamic extremists—including bombs thrown at coffeehouses and tourist boats on the Nile, and a plan to attack the pyramids—provided the pretext for a new crackdown on religious activists. Some observers in Egypt described it as the Egyptian government's "most sweeping series of executions for political crimes in more than four decades." Human rights officials, however, complained that the con-victions were made at quick military trials without witnesses, and that they were send-ing a "wave of victims to the gallows without even rudimentary guarantees of fair trial."[45]

In the midst of the hostility toward fundamentalism evoked by the World Trade Center bombing came moderate voices from two surprising sources: Moorhead Ken-nedy, one of the hostages held by Iranians in the American embassy, and Salman Rush-die, the novelist who was given a death sentence by Ayatollah Khomeini. Kennedy, in a *Los Angeles Times* op-ed piece entitled "Why Fear Fundamentalism?" explained that much of the attraction to Islamic politics stemmed from an attempt to expel the excesses of Western culture that have taken root "deep within themselves and their societies."[46] Rushdie, in a *New York Times* article, attempted to make distinctions between good religious nationalists and bad ones, insisting that it would simply exacerbate tensions to tar all religious activists with the same fundamentalist brush.[47]

London's *Daily Telegraph* also cautioned that "the greatest danger for the West" in the present age is "to demonise Islam as monolithically bad."[48] A number of American scholars of Islam warned about the possible backlash that might come from the repression of Islam in Egypt and other countries. John Esposito of Georgetown University expressed concern about "a growing number of governments" that are "cracking down on Islamic movements, both extremist and moderate," and warned that the repression would be "contributing to radicalization." He added that, since America often defended these governments in its repression, "their actions reinforce an anti-Americanism or anti-Westernism."[49]

Under the Clinton administration, however, the U.S. State Department has reaffirmed the stand taken by Assistant Secretary of State Edward P. Djerejian in a little-noticed speech at Washington's Meridian House conference center in June 1992. On that occasion Djerejian said that "the U.S. government does not view Islam as the next 'ism' confronting the West or threatening world peace," and stated that U.S. policy would judge each situation on its own merits.[50] Still, many observers have noted the absence of strong State Department objections to the actions of the Egyptian government, the Israeli deportations, the Algerian suspension of elections, the Indian ban on Hindu organizations, and the repression of religious nationalists in Tajikistan and Punjab. This silence has allowed the State Department's policies to be characterized as antifundamentalist.

American leaders have been perplexed by their own ascription to the virtues of tolerance. On the one hand, a tolerance for ideological diversity in the world should allow the United States to be open to at least moderate forms of religious nationalism. On the other hand, the same virtues make it difficult for America to support a regime that it judges to be intolerant. The critical issue is whether some form of religious politics is inevitable: if it is, then it is futile to oppose it. The challenge is to find the most moderate and acceptable forms to support.

It is increasingly difficult to ignore the significance of what George Weigel calls the "unsecularization of the world," and which he goes on to describe as "one of the dominant social facts of life in the late 20th century."[51] Samuel P. Huntington, in a provocative article in *Foreign Affairs* entitled "The Clash of Civilizations?" claims that what he calls "the growth of civilization consciousness" is enhanced by "a return-to-the-roots phenomenon" that he sees occurring "among non-Western civilizations—the 'Asianization' in Japan, the end of the Nehru legacy and the 'Hinduization' of India, the failure of Western ideas of socialism and nationalism and, hence, the 're-Islamization' of the Middle East, and now a debate over Westernization versus Russianization in Boris Yeltsin's country."[52]

Such a momentous historical change on a virtually global scale is more significant and complicated than the trivializing appellation *fundamentalism* would imply. Yet it is a change to be taken seriously: neither lightly accepted nor easily rejected. Secular leaders would be well advised to avoid the excesses of antifundamentalism in their language and actions, and learn to live in a world where religious nationalism is increasingly a fact of life.

Notes

1. Interviews in Amritsar, India, 5 June 1993.

2. Timur Klychev, Tajik journalist in exile in Moscow, quoted in Cary Goldberg, "A Grim Prophecy Fulfilled," *Los Angeles Times,* 30 January 1993, p. A1.

3. Tahir Akhmedov, a Tajikistan Foreign Ministry official, quoted in ibid.

4. Quoted in John F. Burns, "Serbs Would Deny Muslims a State," *New York Times,* international ed., 18 July 1993, p. 7.

5. I expand on this point in my book, *The New Cold War? Religious Nationalism Confronts the Secular State* (Berkeley: University of California Press, 1993), pp. 1–2.

6. Ibid., p. 22.

7. *India Today,* 5 January 1991, p. 9.

8. Regarding my reservations about using the term *fundamentalism* as a category for cross-cultural analysis, see "Why Religious Nationalists Are Not Fundamentalists," *Religion* 23 (Spring 1993): 85–92.

9. Abdelkadir Hachani, quoted in Kim Murphy, "Algerian Election to Test Strength of Radical Islam," *Los Angeles Times,* 26 December 1991, p. A18.

10. Robin Wright, "Muslims under the Gun," *Los Angeles Times,* 28 January 1992, p. B1.

11. Jonathan C. Randall, "Algeria Leader Assassinated during Speech," *Los Angeles Times,* 30 June 1992, p. A1.

12. For background on Algeria, see John P. Entelis, *Algeria: The Revolution Institutionalized* (Boulder, Colo.: Westview Press, 1986); and Hugh Roberts, "Radical Islamism and the Dilemma of Algerian Nationalism: The Embattled Arians of Algiers," *Third World Quarterly* 10, no. 2 (1988): 567–75.

13. Statement by State Department spokesperson Margaret Tutwiler, 13 January 1992, quoted in Norman Kempster, "U.S. Delivers a Mild Rebuke to Algeria for Canceling Vote," *Los Angeles Times,* 14 January 1992, p. A10.

14. "Going Wrong in Algiers," editorial, *Wall Street Journal,* 14 January 1992, p. A14.

15. George Black, "Our Love for Democracy Is Selective," *Los Angeles Times,* 19 January 1992, p. M5.

16. Quoted in Alan Riding, "France Voices Concern on Algerian Situation," *New York Times,* 14 January 1992, p. A7.

17. *Le Monde,* 15 January 1992, p. 4. I appreciate the research assistance of Darrin McMahon in preparing summary English translations of French newspaper articles and government statements on the Algerian case.

18. François Mitterand statement cited in *Le Monde,* 16 January 1992, p. 2, trans. McMahon.

19. Quoted in *Le Monde,* 21 June 1993, p. 18, trans. McMahon.

20. Juergensmeyer, *The New Cold War?* pp. 69–77.

21. Yitzhak Rabin, quoted in Michael Parks, "Body of Kidnapped Israeli Border Officer Found," *Los Angeles Times,* 16 December 1992, p. A5.

22. United Nations Security Council, quoted in Paul Lewis, "Security Council Moves to Condemn Israeli Expulsions," *New York Times,* 19 December 1992, p. 1.

23. "Don't Orphan the Peace Process," editorial, *New York Times,* 18 December 1992, p. A38.

24. Yitzhak Rabin, quoted in Clyde Haberman, "400 Arabs Ousted by Israel Are Mired in a Chilly Limbo," *New York Times,* 18 December 1992, p. 5.

25. See Joel Greenberg, "Oustings by Israel Raise Arab Militants' Esteem," *New York Times*, 20 December 1992, p. A14.

26. Yubaraj Ghimire and Rahul Pathak, "Too Much, Too Late," *India Today*, 31 December 1992, p. 50.

27. Inderjit Badhwar with Yabaraj Ghimire, "Masters of Deception," *India Today*, 31 December 1992, p. 35. The reporter expressed skepticism over the genuineness of Advani's and Vajpayee's comments.

28. The other banned organizations, the Islamic Sevak Sangh and the Jamait-i-Islami Hind, were Muslim opponents of the Hindu nationalists who might have become caught up in the communal warfare.

29. Badhwar, "Masters of Deception," p. 35.

30. Bob Drogin, "Hindu Militants Raze Mosque, Stir India Crisis," *Los Angeles Times*, 7 December 1992, p. A1. Drogin wrote in detail about the attack on himself and other journalists in the following issue of the paper, "Scrambling for Safety amid a Merciless Mob," *Los Angeles Times*, 8 December 1992, p. H3.

31. Edward A. Gargan, "Savage Intolerance: Fundamentalism in South Asia Isn't All Islam," *New York Times*, 13 December 1992, sec. 4, p. 1.

32. "Pulling Down India's Temple," editorial, *New York Times*, 8 December 1992, p. A24.

33. "Explosion at Ayodhya," editorial, *Washington Post*, 11 December 1992, p. A26.

34. "India's Difficult Progress," editorial, *Wall Street Journal*, 29 December 1992, p. 10.

35. James C. Clad, "Subcontinent Ultranationalists May Rule," *Los Angeles Times*, 11 January 1993, p. B7. Clad is a senior associate of the Carnegie Endowment for International Peace.

36. "India at the Edge," editorial, *New York Times*, 24 February 1993, p. A18.

37. *India Today*, 15 January 1993, p. 14.

38. *Constitution of the Islamic Republic of Iran*, trans. Hamid Algar (Berkeley: Mizan Press, 1980).

39. Madhu Jain, "BJP Supporters: Invasion of the Scuppies," *India Today*, 15 May 1991, pp. 18–19.

40. Hassan Abdullah Turabi, quoted in Kim Murphy, "Islamic Militants Build Power Base in Sudan," *Los Angeles Times*, 6 April 1992, p. A9.

41. Yitzhak Rabin, quoted in Michael Parks, "Israel Sees Self Defending West against Militants," *Los Angeles Times*, 2 January 1993, p. A22.

42. Shimon Peres, quoted in ibid.

43. "Fight the Menace Politically," editorial, *India Today*, 15 January 1993, p. 9. The term the editors used for Hindu nationalism was the *Sangh*, by which they meant the RSS, the leading Hindu nationalist organization behind the BJP.

44. "Beyond the Cold War: The New Enemy," editorial, *Los Angeles Times*, 3 March 1993, p. B6.

45. Kim Murphy, "Egypt Curbing Muslim Militants—and Civil Rights, Critics Say," *Los Angeles Times*, 6 August 1993, p. A5.

46. Moorhead Kennedy, "Why Fear Fundamentalism?" *Los Angeles Times*, 15 March 1993, p. B7.

47. Salman Rushdie, "The Struggle for the Soul of Islam," *New York Times*, 11 July 1993, p. E19.

48. "Danger of Demonising Islam," *Daily Telegraph*, 3 April 1993, p. 1.

49. John L. Esposito, quoted in Robin Wright, "Security Fears, Political Ties Cloud U.S. View of Islam's Rise," *Los Angeles Times*, 9 March 1993, p. A1.

50. Edward P. Djerejian, quoted in ibid.

51. George Weigel, quoted in Samuel P. Huntington, "The Coming Clash of Civilizations; Or, the West against the Rest," *New York Times*, 6 June 1993.

52. Samuel P. Huntington, "The Clash of Civilizations?" *Foreign Affairs*, Spring 1993.

The Rhetoric of Fundamentalist Conversion Narratives

Wayne C. Booth

Introduction: A Fundamentalist Confesses

I was raised as a Mormon fundamentalist. Though back in the twenties and thirties I never heard the term, my 100% "Latter-day Saint" family clearly emphasized the restoration of fundamentals. Until my middle teens I was an unquestioning, often zealous believer in Joseph Smith's stories about how God the Father and Jesus Christ and the Angel Moroni had finally restored, after nearly two millennia of Christian backsliding, the only true Gospel: the fundamentals of Christian—and indeed of Judaic—faith.

Only a very small number in my generation were fundamentalists of the kind now attacking the Salt Lake City leaders for betraying the fundamentals that Joseph Smith restored, especially the most fundamental practice of all, plural marriage, polygamy. Though my parents and grandparents did not practice polygamy, they still believed that it was a fundamental: it would someday be restored as the most important marital custom. And so did I for a while. In one story that I heard again and again, my great-grandfather Eli Brazee Hawkins, born when his convert parents were crossing the plains to Utah, had gone to jail for refusing to give up his second living wife. I can remember a portrait of him in striped prison garb, displayed proudly on the piano in the parlor. He had gone to prison as what was called a cohab rather than give up polygamy. But by the time I came along, "Aunt Hattie Pepper" had simply disappeared from our lives, leaving behind only our belief that the marriage had been itself righteous.

The stories I heard did not dwell only on cheerful affirmation about the glories of restoration. Like recent fundamentalist narratives, ours were enriched with a fine collection of enemies—not just those who had murdered our prophet but those who were still persecuting our missionaries. The last days were upon us, and there was a lot of talk, some of it quite violent, about how we could share in destroying the wicked. Some of my Sunday school teachers believed that all other churches were essentially wicked; Roman Catholicism, for example, was that "great whore and abomination" described in the New Testament. More of them taught that *some* other churches had *some* truth and that many, maybe even all, of their members would finally embrace Mormonism. We often sang in a hymn, as current Mormons no longer do, words I remember as "Long may his [Smith's] blood / Which was shed by as-sas-sins, / Stain Il-li-nois . . ."

As I think back on our daily discourse about our claims to world-shattering uniqueness, I find the low ratio of argument to story striking. Endlessly repeated stories about how our ancestors had been converted were the very substance of our lives, the daily confirmation that who we were made ultimate sense.

In our monthly testimony meetings, when someone wanted to express why the Church was the only true Church, the testimony was almost never in the form of doctrinal argument; it was always a story: "I believe that the Lord Jesus Christ and God the Father appeared to Joseph Smith in the Sacred Grove and gave unto him the power to translate the gold plates that are the Book of Mormon, which I know to be the true word of God." Or: "I thank our Father in Heaven for the miracle I experienced on January 30, 1910, when I was dying of a mysterious illness. The elders came and laid their hands upon my head and they gave unto me a blessing, and the illness was instantaneously lifted from me. At that moment I knew with a certainty I had never known before that . . ." Or: "Just before my fifteenth birthday, thirty years ago, in this very meeting house, Sister Ashby was taken with the spirit and spoke in tongues, and Sister Anderson was given the power to translate what the spirit had spoken."

I came along a bit too late to witness any actual talking in tongues; I never even saw anyone dramatically cured by the laying on of hands with the holy oil. But such experiences were real for me, often realer than my memory of what had happened the day before. I lived the truth of them not only in official testimony meetings but also in family prayer sessions morning and evening. And always in our stories was our claim to possess a unique and truly grand story, the story of early America as told in *The Book of Mormon,* a story to rival in importance and literal truth the Bible itself.[1] And that story conveyed another story that was grander still: the account of what really happened in the three days after Christ was crucified (he visited America!) and of what that visit meant in the history of all creation.

This relative dominance of stories over doctrinal propositions persisted as I began, in my teens, to question the stories' literal truth. My questions usually boiled down to the one literal question, "Did Joseph Smith tell a *true* story?" Having been taught by literalists, I always defined the truth I sought in the most literal terms possible: Did the prophet have gold plates or didn't he? That literal question naturally led to a polarization of possible answers. As the protagonist of the grand story, Smith was either—we would say—the greatest prophet who ever lived or the greatest fraud who ever lived. There was simply no middle ground.

Accepting the literalist's notions of what constituted truth, I inevitably encountered a crisis when I finally decided that, no, sadly enough, the plot of Joseph Smith's epic had to be revised; he had not had any actual gold plates, whether he thought he had or not. No literal Father and Son appeared to him as flesh and blood figures, as he claimed, in the best known of his various versions of his first vision. Christ must not have really visited America during the three days before the resurrection. And so on, into further doubt, anxiety, and frequent misery.

My problem for decades, then, became that of finding some new story, not just about Joseph Smith and the Mormons, but about the world, about my own path through life. I could hardly expect that path to be as meaningful as it had seemed when I had been promised that *if* I kept my nose clean and followed every Church requirement, I could someday, eons onward, become the god of another planet of my very own. What a comedown, to lose the hope of a world all my own! How could I hope to find a story equal in power to the glorious tales I had now discarded?

Narrative as Fundamental to Fundamentalisms

Because of this early experience with the way in which story dominated our discourse, experience that has now been echoed by my recent forays into other fundamentalist territory, I am convinced that fundamentalisms cannot be compared adequately without direct confrontation with how their diverse stories *work as stories*. They can of course be mined for comparison of explicit doctrines or recommended practices, but what happens when narratives are treated as distinctive "truth practices" in their own right?

My claim, by no means mine alone on the current critical scene, is that stories, even the simplest of stories, teach us more than we usually acknowledge and often more than the storytellers consciously intend. They may teach us for good or for ill, but they teach us. Indeed they do more than teach, in the usual sense of that verb. They affect us not so much in their open propositions or moral summaries, though of course they do that, as in their very way of embedding us in transforming experience. Stories transform listeners (a term that will here cover readers as well) because they unite tellers and listeners in an embrace of a shared "world," a world that is always intended as "higher" than the one we live in day by day. That world—which could of course be called by other equally ambiguous names like "total values" or "universe of norms" or "pattern of concerns"—determines the listener's view of the significance of every detail. Every character, every choice, every event in even the simplest of stories makes sense only as seen within a "world" that only rarely if ever seems identical with the "world" that the listener lives in before the story begins.

The two worlds must of course overlap in essential ways or the story will not work at all. But when it works, it seduces travellers into a kind of emigration from the listener's native land into what can sometimes be strange or incredible or even frightening alien territory. Fundamentalist narratives, and particularly fundamentalist conversion narratives, are accounts of such emigration journeys that have become permanent; the protagonist, like Bunyan's Pilgrim, has traveled far from what I shall call Badland and has found a true home, which I shall call Homeland. And the Pilgrims, or their biographers, use their stories as open invitations to listeners to join them: Come, ye misguided ones! Immigrate into the only country of light, the City of the one true God. Come home! Come home! Ye who are weary, come home!

The claim that the living experience of the journey is a better clue to a religion's "truthfulness" than are doctrinal tests runs counter in some ways to the still widespread view, especially among social scientists who were trained in earlier decades, that knowledge about a subject like ours can best or perhaps only be expressed in demonstrable propositions about doctrine and behavior: "Do you believe in God?" or "Do you believe in life after death?" or "Do you believe in miraculous healing?" In a world dominated by studies based on such questions, the stories believers tell are at most icing to the cake, with no genuine truth content as story.

The alternative view that I pursue here, and that James Peacock and Tim Pettyjohn suggest in chapter 4 as well, is increasingly popular today in many academic fields, though by no means yet dominant.[2] In it the literal content—Were there or were there not any gold plates buried in the hill Cumorah? Did Jesus physically rise from the dead? Is the Qur'an in fact a direct dictation from Allah or even a text that preceded creation?—becomes relatively unimportant. What matters more is whether the structure embodies, as a metaphorical tracing, a spiritual path that is true to . . . but it is not easy to finish that sentence. True to what? The truth about the one and only strait and narrow spiritual way? The truth about how we should live in the world? The truth about what kinds of belonging to what kinds of groups make for the best life? The truth about what it is to be a creature in a universe like this one? The psychological truth about what can provide a structure for a productive life? The truth about who the true enemy is? In trying to complete the sentence we have risen from the literal world into the metaphorical or allegorical or symbolic.[3] And the tests for truth enter a different world from the literalist's at the moment we ask, Is this narrative structure one that in itself, as story, has religious value?

Most scholars, even today, will attempt to explain fundamentalisms by a propositional analysis—or even by the construction of a tenfold grid of propositions (see tables 17.2 and 17.3 in this volume, for example). But that grid will seem to most fundamentalists at best peripheral. Ask fundamentalists to explain their belief, and they'll almost always tell you a story of a conversion experience, either their own or someone else's, or a story of the founding of the world or the establishment of the one true church—a story with a beginning, middle, and end. "I was living a life of sin, and I was visited by saint X"; or "I visited shrine Y, and suddenly a light flashed"; or "a voice spoke"; or "an image was remembered . . ." And when you ask what precisely they believe in, having experienced that story, they tell you other stories: stories of how the world came to be, or of how their own place in it came to be. Just like those we do not call fundamentalists, they feel compelled to explain their beliefs by telling a story that they find makes sense not just of their personal lives but of the entire scheme of things in which those lives are led. The stories enfold the believer as in a total nurturing medium; they become the true account of nature itself.

This means that—though few if any fundamentalists would ever put it this way—the borderline for them between what makes a *good* story and what makes a *true* one is extremely vague, if not non-existent. The true story is the one that is persuasive, *as story,* the one that makes narrative sense, the one that resonates with its plain rightness. But even without investigation one can predict that what makes narrative sense—what in fact moves listeners to enter a narrative world fully—will vary radically from fundamentalism to fundamentalism. That's why literalists claim that story has, in itself, no testable truth value.

In exploring what is to me new territory in a different sense—not just fundamentalist stories but the effort to understand the variety of such sacred travel brochures—I have found myself raising more questions than I can answer. But beyond the many puzzles in what follows, I hope that my main point will remain clear: attending closely to how narrated fundamentalist worlds either work for us or, if we remain cold, how they might work for receptive listeners, is the best road to understanding not simply any one fundamentalism but the intricate relations between any two of them. What will not become as clear as one might wish are the various borderlines this study uncovers: between the scholar's reading and the believer's reading; between truth and narrative effectiveness; between good secular stories and good fundamentalist stories. In opening what I see as neglected questions, I am asking us all to emigrate, as it were, into territory that at first is likely to feel alien.

Seven Variables That Affect Narrative Quality

What marks distinguish good from bad fundamentalist stories? Some of these clearly distinguish good stories for all tellers and listeners; some will seem more specific to fundamentalist stories. The ambiguities inherent to this difference will become troublesome.

One could predict that I would ultimately resemble the fundamentalists in finding it hard to distinguish sharply the good and bad of narrative technique and structure from what I see as the good and bad of ethical or religious doctrine. We are all caught in this problem: the very narrative stroke that will seem brilliant when it appears in a story whose world we embrace can appear cheaply manipulative in a story whose world we abhor. The relation of ideological agreement about worlds to what we call aesthetic judgment will always be complicated and controversial. Thus it will be best to begin with a simple version of the question: What makes a good conversion story as experienced *by any believer*? The ambiguities in the word *good* will quickly become evident, as will my own biases. But we have to begin somewhere. What are the marks, in any conversion narrative, that are likely—at least for the listener who shares the major doctrinal premises of the storyteller—to carry cognitive and emotional force?

The Degree of Overt or Implied Fictionality

Does the story claim to be true or is it a novel or fantasy or allegory? The most striking impression as I began to look around for representative narratives was the dearth of openly fictional works by and for fundamentalists. A great majority of conversion narratives claim to be true stories, strictly literal accounts of what happened either to the author or to someone the author knows or has studied. I have not, for example, been able to find any full-length fundamentalist Islamic fictions; to a non-Muslim reader the biographies I have found seem heavily fictionalized, but they explicitly claim to be literally true. It is easy to see why: if a religious experience actually happened, its portrayal provides a stronger argument for belief than if it is simply made up. My two main examples below discard this advantage, though they both implicitly rely on the literal truth of the New Testament narratives.

Distance between Badland and Homeland

Does the protagonist (whether the story is first or third person) experience a lengthy and perilous journey or only a change of address from one street to the next? Many a fundamentalist story is not a conversion story at all, the distance between beginning and end is so slight. A saint is born in Homeland and exhibits the necessary stages of growth as citizen of that land, the City of God. Such stories are faith-promoting for the genuine Citizens, whether by birth or naturalization. But they tend to be far less inviting to Foreigners than are those that, like the conversions of Paul, Augustine, St. Francis, Charles Colson, Malcolm X, and Eldridge Cleaver, claim that Badland and Homeland are at opposite ends of the universe (traditionally one end is "far up there," the other "far below"). Creation in these stories is best explained as a place of dramatic distances to be traversed only by narratable event. And the stories of individual experiences are almost always closely parallel in structure to the story of humanity as a whole: the heroes were born clean in Homeland, lost their way into Badland, and are now restored. The truth about life, the truth about *this* life, is thus something that can only be expressed in a chronology, leading from Homeland to Badland to Homeland: from error to truth, from sin to forgiveness, from misery to bliss, from a world wicked, damned, or meaningless, to a world redeemed.

The distance traveled by the protagonist clearly makes a great difference in the dramatic impact. But our study is complicated by the fact that what is an immense distance for one reader, intellectually, psychologically, culturally, or temporally, may seem to another like just moving next door. "I was a Methodist and one day I saw the light and became a Baptist": to any Muslim reader that must seem like at most a change of neighborhoods—not a very interesting story. But to the Native Citizen of Methodism, it may feel huge. "I was a Roman Catholic and I became a Muslim": that will seem to most of us a broad and perhaps even an inexplicable leap—the very quality that may well heighten the drama when viewed by Citizens of Islam; but to a passionate atheist, the trip may look like no more than a change of superstitions. "I was a sinner so vicious that nobody would ever have dreamed that I might be saved": that is the distance traveled by Malcolm X, in the story he tells Alex Haley; it is the distance dwelt on by Eldridge Cleaver in his various accounts of his life. Yet can we not imagine readers for whom such transformations will seem trivial?

The distance variable is complicated further because some leaps that appear intellectually broad are psychologically—and perhaps even religiously—narrow: a fanatic can slide quickly, like Paul at Damascus, from one fanaticism to another that appears to be its opposite. The move from being an ardent Communist to being an ardent follower of Jerry Falwell may look like a great leap, but to someone whose life is determined by the effort to obtain a totally encompassing worldview, or to a perceptive psychoanalyst, it may seem to cover less ground.

It remains true that no conversion narrative will work well, as story, unless something is done to dramatize—or even exaggerate—the distance traveled.

Clarity of Dramatic Irony

The best conversion narratives, like the best transformation narratives in general, emphasize not mere suspense but dramatic irony: just what Homeland consists of is made emphatically clear from the outset, so that listeners can experience the thrills of watching protagonists stumble, in their ignorance, first away from it and then toward it. Tellers and listeners in a sense dwell in Homeland looking down upon the wandering characters, hoping that they will finally make it Home, but also enjoying the spectacle of their mistakes and sins. In this perspective, one can often distinguish not just my original two "worlds" but three. The wandering characters in the story are often shown sinning in a world considerably worse than the one listeners think of themselves as inhabiting before and after the story is told. Yet the world those characters enter at the end is always considerably *better* than the listeners inhabit day by day. Thus the ironic distances multiply.

Instrument of Conversion and Resulting Pace

There is a great difference between conversions that spring from some shattering change in external circumstances and changes that spring from internal meditation or gradual growth or surprising mystical experience or hard thought. The first kind will for most readers prove most effective *as story*.

Here are two summaries of personal conversions. Are the authors talking about an experience that is in any sense the same? The first convert, Debora Kaufman, "saw the rabbi," and "I knew this was a Divine messenger—I was intoxicated. It was an immediate and complete conversion for me."[4] The second, Douglas Hyde, gives a long account of hard thinking, spread over several years, about principles and about the behavior of adherents to communism and Catholicism, and concludes: "That I was a Communist and am now a Catholic has . . . little to do with either the supposed appeal of discipline imposed from above or the attraction of monolithic organizations. It had much more to do with the conviction, which I had for long held, that a man should have a philosophy which is capable of forming a basis for all his judgements, values and activities."[5]

The first of these is described as if it were just the miracle of encountered truth embodied in a particular human being. The second shows a transformation that occurred gradually as Hyde discerned logical contradictions in the Communist position and in his own way of adhering to it. The turning point for Hyde came when he was asked to debate with Catholics and realized that in order to do well in the debate he must read carefully the best Catholic literature he could obtain. "That was my undoing as a Communist," he reports. "As I prepared my defence, the weaknesses in my own position were gradually revealed." Kaufman does not even mention doctrinal coherence; Hyde's story is about little else.

Which one of these two makes for the "best" conversion narrative? To me, heavily laden with my academic prejudices, Hyde's is much the more persuasive. Yet the one Kaufman reports seems more dramatic according to most narrative criteria. The most dramatic fundamentalist stories are bound to be those with the most dramatic, most tangible, most easily imagined agents, producing the most rapid-fire changes in the protagonist. As sheer story, they will work best—except of course for those listeners like me who respond more fully to a quite different kind of story, one that includes much more meditation or argument.

It is of course tempting to consider as the defining mark of fundamentalist conversion an instantaneous, emotion-charged moment of radical change, while accounts of prolonged, detailed thinking about "fundamental ideas" would have to be called something else. Here we touch once again on a definitional problem that has run through all of the volumes of the Fundamentalism Project. If seekers are converted to their fundamentals through hard thought, does that automatically wipe the *-ist* from their label as Fundamentalists?

The nature of the agent of change is so closely tied to the pace of change that they can hardly be distinguished. One kind of God will prefer, we might say, that we come to embrace Her truths in a sudden flash, while the God of Thomas Aquinas, say, will prefer that we spend a lifetime thinking about every implication of our emotional commitments. The fact remains that even the most "instantaneous" of conversions will never make a good story if actually told in a sentence. All accounts will profit from some form of what rhetoricians call amplification: listeners savor a pace that to some degree stretches out even the changes that occurred in a flash. This taste in turn dictates more complete dramatization of the instrument of change.

Consequences of the Transformation

Some conversions, especially those to religions that stress faith, not works, exhibit no practical consequences except in the words with which the converted describe their feelings, as if to say, "My life was transformed—but don't expect to see the transformation in an increase in my almsgiving." The more dramatic accounts, however—judged, that is, by usual standards of compelling narrative—exhibit amazing changes of behavior.

Most authors of these stories emphasize strongly the contrast between "How I—and other people—behaved in Badland" and "How I—and other converts—behave in Homeland." Or the consequences can be how the heavens treat me: before I was cursed and now I am blessed, whether with health, or gold, or just comfort of the spirit in my enduring-but-now-unimportant poverty. For those readers who themselves dwell in a superstitious Homeland, the best stories lead to or are based on miraculous cures, as in Christ's healing of the blind. If a hero lacks a physical ill to be cured, the narrator can always give him one: no matter what was Paul's visual acuity at Damascus, a skillful narrator would have turned him blind so that he could, after conversion, be made to see again.

Of course the ultimate proof of grand consequences is the willingness to sacrifice life itself in the new cause: to die willingly is the final proof that the believer was sincere. Most impressive are the great martyrs, like Christ and the many later Christian saints and saints from other religions killed by Christians. Clearly the more nearly voluntary the death the more powerful the example. To be killed by a mob, like Joseph Smith, is a great step forward. But his biographers usually heighten the story, often in contradictory ways, by showing that he knew in advance what was coming and embraced it, or by heightening his choices along the path to the shooting. At this point we often find a confluence of conversion narratives and biographies of saints: the saint's miracle in a sense enacts the conversion that the reader is intended to experience.

Short of chosen death, the most impressive accounts of consequences are quite explicit about the change of values and behavior: not just "My life was transformed," or "God blessed me," but "I am now willing to sacrifice such-and-such values, values that in Badland are important and even might be still considered as real though subordinate values by us in Homeland." The greater the surrendered value, in the eyes of the listener, the more impressive the surrender—up to the point at which the lost value will seem something more precious than any possible gain. It is not surprising that most accounts stress the discarding of values that listeners are already inclined to discard or to hold lightly: hardly ever "I joyfully gave up my family" (though Christ at one point seems to urge that), or "I no longer felt the need to be kind." Rather: "I gave up drinking . . ." or drugs . . . or fornication.

Sometimes the claims of dramatic sacrifice are indeed a bit comic because to the Foreigner they look too easy, as when a thirty-year-old woman says of her recent return to Orthodox Judaism: "I knew I had committed myself to orthodoxy when I finally gave away my Bob Dylan records" (quoted by Kaufman). Yet when a value runs deep, its surrender can require or justify a good deal of narrative amplification, and the greater the ostensible value of the surrendered good, the more impressive the presumed effect. When Maryam Jameelah (now a Muslim, formerly Margaret Marcus, daughter of liberal Jews) recounts her conversion from Judaism, it is all about "the impact on my life" of "the holy Prophet." In a relatively short autobiography prefacing her lengthy "Refutation of the Modern Way of Life,"[6] she moves quickly to how her "quest for absolute values" was satisfied, partly by giving up the destructive values of the West. She then tells her own favorite story about surrender, to emphasize how much she had been happy to give up. The story concerns Fatima, the "most loved daughter of [the] Prophet." Fatima did the housework, and she worked so hard at it that she wore calluses on her hands and scars on her breast (from carrying water). A friend suggested that she obtain from Muhammad one of his slaves to help her do the work. She was too shy to ask, but the friend attempted to intercede with him. The prophet replied: "Fatima! Fear Allah! Acquire *Taqwa* (piety) and when you go to bed, recite, *Subhanallah* 33 times, *Alhamdulillah* 33 times and *Allahu Akbar* 34 times. This you will find more helpful than a servant." Fatima said: "I am content with Allah and His Prophet" (p. 7). Maryam Jameelah is fully aware that any non-Islamic reader will wonder how she, raised in a non-observant Jewish home in America, could succumb to the world of this story, with its supreme sacrifice of women's freedom. "This will not appeal to the advocates of the so-called 'Women's Liberation.' The immediate reaction of the modern-minded woman to this is dismay. She will certainly ask me how I as a twentieth-century woman, born and reared in modern America could possibly endorse such an apparently poor and limited life? The answer is that to the Holy Prophet, depth of experience was more important than breadth" (p. 6). There follows a paragraph describing the miserable life of "modern American women" whose purpose in life is only enjoyment, contrasted with the genuine happiness of the Muslim woman whose purpose in life is "achievement": "one's emotional satisfaction in one's duties being conscientiously performed for the pleasure of God to gain salvation in the life to come."

In accounts of consequences, what is gained is thus often more important than anything given up. Every conversion narrative suggests that what has been gained is simply everything: total bliss in this life—or at least in the next. For many Jewish returnees the gain seems to be what it was for the Orthodox woman interviewed by Kaufman: like the convert to Islam, she has found bliss in this world: "Every moment of my waking life is so full of the sense of my holiness as a woman." For others it is escape from a world with no community, a world with confusing or non-existent "moral discourse," a world that has felt "impossible" because it provides no "moral absolutism." For some, though, the gain is intellectual clarity. "The Torah has answers for all the key questions of life," a newly orthodox Jew tells Kaufman.[7]

Consider how Christopher Isherwood puts the reward of surrendering to Vedanta.

> Every moment of my conscious existence had contained within itself this riddle—"What is life for?"—and its answer: "To learn what life means." Every event, every encounter, every person and object I had met, had restated question and answer in some new way. Only I hadn't been ready to listen. Now, as I came to learn something about practical mysticism, I was greatly astonished to find how closely the recorded experiences of Hindu and Christian (not to mention Buddhist and Taoist, Sufi, and Jewish) mystics are interrelated. And thus another group of my anti-Christian prejudices was liquidated, along with my ignorance. "What is the meaning of life?" Now [that I have found Vedanta] I have it.[8]

Maryam Jameelah says, "Thus the Holy Prophet has revealed to me personally and to all mankind for all times in all places the purpose of human life and what is important and what is not." I could fill these pages with similar statements by converts to Mormonism, or to Jehovah's Witnesses, or—for that matter—to mainline Catholicism or Episcopalianism.

I'll return later to another major gain, that of falling into the bosom of a loving community of brothers and sisters. A complementary gain is a new and clear-cut enemy or group, a group that may include former friends who must now be sacrificed. Every fundamentalism I've looked at provides jumbo jets loaded with enemies. Perhaps enemies are essential to all religion, since any ideal implies a search for explanations of why the ideal is never reached. As Kenneth Burke often quipped, "Yeah, I know you are a Christian, but who are you a Christian *against*?"

The enemy can range from a specific person, as Salman Rushdie has become a target for many Muslims, to a whole culture that seems overwhelmingly threatening. Islamic biographers never tire of excoriating the evils of the industrial, nominally

Christian but essentially wicked West. For fundamentalist Christians various idolatries will serve: the Catholic Church, Islam, and dishonest and greedy clergymen of any alien denomination.

Nature and Quality of Intended (Implied) Listeners [9]

The degree of pre-established credulity of the audience will partially determine, for narrators who consciously think about listeners, the speed of the account. If the audience is thought to be already believers or half believers, if they thus already share the language of Homeland, the moments of conversion can be covered briefly yet still seem credible. If the listeners are made up of Foreigners whose primary vocabulary, from the perspective of the teller, is that of Badland, the account may require, like that of Maryam Jameelah, a whole book or series of books. And of course the choice of which details to explain and which to take for granted will always vary according to audience.

Evidence for this variable can be found in thinking of the differences between conversion narratives in Christian communities before and after the decline of widespread orthodoxy. In the nineteenth century, if someone wanted to write plausibly about conversion to belief in the Christian God, the account could be as brief as "It was at the age of twenty that I finally saw the light." But if someone wanted to write plausibly about deconversion, whole books of self-explanation and justification would emerge: Olive Schreiner's *Story of an African Farm* or Butler's *Way of All Flesh*. A few decades later intellectuals writing their autobiographies could dismiss God in a sentence or two. But if they wanted to explain their return to him, they knew that their audience would require lengthy explanation: C. S. Lewis's *Surprised by Joy,* Thomas Merton's *Seven Storey Mountain,* G. K. Chesterton's dozens of books and hundreds of articles explaining his conversion first to the Church of England and then, when he was almost fifty, to Roman Catholicism. Anthony Burgess, reared as a Roman Catholic but soon tempted into various forms of doubt, feels no strong need, in his *Confessions,* to argue for the doubts; he knows that most readers take them for granted.[10] It is quite understandable that he saw no need in a time like ours to dwell on the reasons for doubt, while Chesterton, living in a similar time of triumphant skepticism, believing that his conversion was primarily a matter of thinking things through, felt the need to go on and on arguing about it through book after book.

Coherence of Stated Values with Implied Values of the Story

The final variable—and in my judgment of the full religious worth of the story, the most important one—is the degree to which the values *implied* by the story told, with its distances, its losses and gains, its saved and loving community and hated enemies, harmonizes intellectually and emotionally with the *stated* values of Homeland. Every Foreigner will feel justified in asking, "Does the story itself, *in its narrative nature, in the world it asks us to inhabit,* embody the supreme values that its protagonists in effect preach?"[11] Does the author implied by the very existence of the tale, embracing as he or she must the tale's rewards and punishments, harmonize with the values that the "saved" characters, including the narrator, urge upon us? Or has the author allowed the requirements for making a really good story (or perhaps his or her deepest but tacit convictions) to undermine those values in any way? We will come to obvious instances of disharmony on this variable in my two main examples below.

This criterion is tricky, because—as current literary critics urge upon us—every literary world will betray *some* disharmonies if pressed hard enough. Like the world we live in, the worlds created by our brothers and sisters can be deconstructed to show how even the wisest creator, even God himself, creates some "incommensurables." But there are disharmonies and disharmonies. Some conflicts most readers will easily accept. But if a story "preaches" love and "practices" hate, if a story "preaches" Christ and "practices" a revenge ethic, any reader who notices the clash is sure to draw back.

Summarizing these variables, we can see why the most famous conversion narrative in the Christian tradition is that of a brief moment in the life of Paul, when he traveled the greatest possible distance—from active hostility to total commitment—in the shortest possible time, produced by the most striking of agents, the Lord of the universe, with miraculous consequences, including a new "family" and new enemies—all in the service of an even more striking sacrificial act, that of Christ himself. This story is most often read by readers who know the outcome in advance and can thus savor the dramatic irony to the full. Now that makes a story that *is* a story, one clearly qualified to inspire the tens of thousands of amplifications it has received. (Whether that story is self-harmonious is a debatable question; Jewish critics have generally thought not.)

There are no doubt further variables that we might explore: the duration of the conversion portrayed—the longer it lasts and the more appalling the temptations against it, the more convincing; or the degree of self-evident "surface" artifice—the more the narrative manipulation is visible, the weaker the persuasive effect for listeners hoping to hear the direct and undoctored word of God. The stories that claim truth tend to deny all artifice: "this is exactly how it happened." The resistance in many traditions to all fictions, and the late arrival of novels in traditions like Christian fundamentalism, can be partially explained as caused by a sense that only true stories can carry the truth. The Bible, the Qur'an—these are legitimate stories to listen to, for believers. But save us from the liars.

Examples of Fundamentalist Fictions Crammed with Conversion Narrative

The two novels we approach now are both apocalyptic fantasies highly successful with American Christian fundamentalists. It is hard to tell whether Roger Elwood, author of *Wise One,* and Frank E. Peretti, author of *This Present Darkness,* have consciously thought through the variables I have described, but they both write as if they were deliberately exploiting at least some of them.

Wise One, published by the Moody Bible Institute in 1991, was recently on display in multiple copies in their Chicago Avenue bookstore. It is a blatantly polemical work, announcing its theses aggressively in its preface. The novel is designed, Elwood says, to help cast out the money changers from the temple. It deals with "the selling not of lambs . . . but of the Lamb Himself, the commercialization of salvation, including one of the most alarming deviations of all: the virulent cult of personality" now flooding the TV and radio channels. The novel was written with a battle in mind, a battle against the multiple "cancers" that threaten the true church today—not just those televangelists who commercialize Christ but more dramatically "the intentions of the Islamic fundamentalist movement." The preface concludes with an appeal not to worry about "being too hard on the Muslims" but rather about "being too *easy* on them in this age of lack of convictions often masquerading as humanistic tolerance both within and outside the Body of Christ."

The story that follows is, when judged by me as Foreigner, implausible in every respect: the plot moves relentlessly toward the last-minute conversion and salvation of a small number of characters and the damnation of those who resist conversion, all combined with the destruction of as many Muslims as can be heaped up as corpses. The characters are all made sympathetic or antipathetic less by what they do than by what they claim to believe. Like many in this tradition, this story is not about being saved through good works: being born again is all.

The cast includes (1) assorted Western money-obsessed villains so wicked as to be beyond salvation and obviously slated from page 1 to die damned; (2) one prophet/ angel, the Wise One, who warns everybody to repent or die; (3) one Christian convert from Islam who tries ineffectually to warn the backsliding villagers that they should listen to the Wise One; (4) a village full of nominal Christians who, because they have discovered oil in their backyard, have lapsed from their faith and must either repent or die; (5) innumerable devout Muslims who have been driven from the village by the Christians and are determined to kill every Christian they can get their hands on; (6) two well-meaning but misguided Westerners who hope to be saved for their good works, in itself a serious mistake, but who get converted to the true faith, are crucified by the Muslims, and are then, along with other genuine converts, divinely transported out of the holocaust that concludes the book; (7) a fanatical Muslim woman who leads the Muslims in their massacre of the Christians, who stabs her own son to death because he betrayed Allah by converting to Christ, and who at the end, because her son forgives her, in the name of Christ, as he dies, cries out as *she* perishes, "Praise the Holy Name of Jesus" (presumably she then goes to Heaven even though she led the Islamic battle against the Christians and has killed her own son); and (8) the one main character who is left alive and kicking at the end, the most vicious of all the Westerners, a grasping evangelist who turns every Christian matter into material profit and who expects to sell off souvenirs memorializing the holocaust we have just witnessed. He is obviously damned, yet he is left alive for reasons that the book does not make explicit but that are clear enough: we need him as a continuing threat to the reader, who must repent or be damned, and who must be prepared to fight to the death the two grand and powerful enemies, materialist evangelists like him and the Muslims.

The twists of the plot are all designed to provide either a bloody thrill—the physical nastiness throughout is striking—or an occasion for a sermon about what is wrong with the modern world and about what true belief entails. This book is especially revealing as an effort to pack into one volume as many appeals as possible from the extremist end of each of the narrative variables.

The success of *Wise One* with Citizens (as a best-seller) clearly comes from its exploitation of most of the dramatic possibilities I have described above. Yet it makes no effort to claim *literal narrative truth*. It is a barefaced fantasy that purports only to provide an up-to-date, pop-adventure analogy for Armageddon. Most of its actual battles are fought on the literal location of the original Garden of Eden, somewhere in the Middle East; the spot has become a kind of antique collection of physical remnants both of Eden and of Golgotha. (At one point the skeleton of the original serpent comes alive and bites one of the villains; *the* crown of thorns is prominently displayed.) Such obvious fantasy might conceivably weaken the argument even for Citizens; to compensate, Elwood fills the book with specific references to everyday modern reality, including details of the Gulf War.

Wise One does require most of its dramatized converts to travel the *greatest possible psychological and cultural and doctrinal distance*. None of the characters was born and raised as a Citizen, fully in the truth. One was converted as a young man from Islam to Christianity. One had Christian training as a child, but gave it up. But no character has been raised steadily in the true faith. They are all thus either unsaved dogmatists of Badland, doomed to die, or uneasy inhabitants who are about to escape into Homeland. The plot unfailingly abides by—but of course never states—the principle I have described: the greater the distance between Badland and Homeland the better the story, especially for listeners who know in advance exactly where Homeland is and can thus savor the dramatic irony. Some rebirths in this fictional world are far more important than others: the Muslim who stabs her Christian son for betraying Islam, and who is converted by her son's forgiveness, is by the very distance of her instantaneous journey a greater triumph for the Lord than is Derek Sparrowhawk, the doomed televangelist, a relatively sympathetic character who is not shown as having ever done anything positively evil. The distance between now and then is also maximized: much of the action takes place literally in the Garden, with the suggestion that we are seeing both the remains and at one moment the coming back to blooming life of the Garden that died about six thousand years ago.

We always know just *who our enemies are* and where we are required to stand, as we watch the follies and sins of all those in the fallen world. No one even half-naturalized into this Homeland could fail to have fun watching the stupidities of all those wicked folks "down there." At the same time "we up here" can take a warm pleasure in observing the half-good folks stumbling toward our platform. Wise One, the ancient powerful prophet, controls much of the action, appearing and disappearing irregularly and mysteriously. But of course the *true agent* is Christ—and, by implication, God himself. Through these two agents, *Wise One* is made as dramatic as possible, with a good deal of magical folderol, including the incredible physical strength and divine foresight of Wise One. The agency is often some character's Christlike act of unconditional forgiveness. A great deal is made of how demonstrations of unconditional love by believers produce conversion in others, a message that is violated by the hate-ridden structure of the story itself. The chief actor, however, is always the Lord and Master of the universe—from the Citizen's perspective the most dramatic of all agents.

Turning to the final narrative variable, the *consequences of conversion:* these frequently *clash with the values* implied in the story, though they are presented as logically following from them. The consequences for individuals are a surrender of all that one has in order to follow the Lord and Savior. Country, parents, friends count for nothing in the light of the new birth and a claim to have found an all-embracing love. Some of the key characters seem able even to cast off hatred and actually to love their enemies. But that is something that the story itself cannot manage; in its implied code, its world, it seems to me vicious to the core. It cheerfully tortures and kills off thousands of people, many of them innocent of any sin except being in the vicinity when the holocaust strikes, and many others guilty only of not being Elwood's kind of Christian. The implied consequences of conversion are that one must buy into this mass destruction as a good thing—thus raising, in acute form, the nasty problem that the original Christian story also raises by making the massacre of the innocents an essential part of the divine plan. Here is where the structure of the story, as story, determines its fundamental teaching; all the surface preaching of love cannot counteract what the pattern of pleasures provided by the story implies. Citizen-readers have lived along a hate-filled path; when they leave the book, they leave it pleased to be rid of many enemies, but facing more enemies than when they began.

What is gained? Here we find similar disharmonies. Part of the bliss offered is total clarity about who the enemies are. As we saw in the quotation from the preface, Elwood fears that many readers will not believe that Islam is as hateful and criminal as he claims, so he spends a lot of time quoting from the Qur'an passages that sound as vengeful as the most vengeful (but mostly *not* quoted) passages in the Hebrew Bible. Thus every last problem about secular life for those who surrender to Christ is solved, including the problem of wrestling with one's own temptation to hate and destroy: it is blessed to hate the followers of Satan and, as the story requires, to revel in their destruction.

In short, any reader who succumbs to *Wise One* will leave the book with thoroughly polarized views of the world and its possibilities. The world is simply an immense battleground, with a tiny remnant of good guys who preach love confronting hordes of bad guys who must be hated and killed. The last days are upon us, and he who is not with us is against us—and deserves to die. What the work implies is that—as in all other kinds of warfare—just about any means are justified: it's kill or be killed. The commercial evangelists and the Muslims are after us. Though by the end the battle has been won in that small area of the Middle East, the rest of the world is desperately threatened by the unsaved. To arms, to arms.

Who, then, is the implied listener to this story that as Foreigner I cannot really listen to? This is a difficult question. One criterion is easy: readers are expected to be Islam haters. But what about the attack on televangelists? Surely most of the expected readers will be adherents of one or another of those disciples of Mammon. Since we are given no examples of evil television preaching, readers are presumed to know that the preachers are simply out for money. To drive all those folks into outer darkness, as the book does, should surely reduce the number of possible believing readers drastically. And to convert those readers into believers who detest all televangelists would take more narrative effort than the novel expends.

Though the book seems from one angle simply an effort to exploit a given pre-sold audience, in this one respect it seems to be sacrificing audience for a sincere assault on Mammon. Indeed, the kind of preacher the novel attacks has usually promised that conversion will yield financial success—and as Mark Twain once said about the attractiveness of Christian Science to the American temper, the "appeal of such a message ["all illness is an illusion"] is as universal as is the appeal of Christianity itself. . . . Its clientage is the Human Race. Will it march? I think so" (*Christian Science* (1907), chapter 6). With so many televangelists equating salvation with "get rich," and with their message "marching" so grandly with their gullible audiences, does not Elwood's attack on greed present a core of integrity that should modify my reservations?

Though set not in the Middle East but in the Middle West, Frank E. Peretti's holy-war thriller takes us into roughly the same home territory. Published by Crossway Books in 1986, it was into its twenty-ninth printing by 1991 when my copy was purchased. I assume that the readers of this book overlap with the readers of *Wise One:* the ultimate salvation of the heroes in the two books seems identical. The enemies who must be destroyed, however, are in many ways quite different.

As in *Wise One,* we can see from the beginning that we are entering upon an allegorical battle of worlds. On one side are the forces of good—God and his representatives, some of them angelic (all male) and some of them flesh-and-blood. On the other are the forces of evil: Satan and his representatives, some of them demonic (all male) and some of them earthly creatures. The double forces on each side, supernatural and natural, battle in parallel actions for possession of a small town. The seemingly innocent setting is presented, like the disputed territory in *Wise One,* as a crucial testing ground for the apocalyptic battles to come. In both novels the two domains are ambiguously related—that is, though the angelic and demonic forces can and do affect material events directly, their power is curiously and inconsistently limited. Usually but not always, their ability to enter human affairs depends on direct invitations from human characters: the angels respond to the prayers of the tiny remnant of the born-again; the demons answer calls from the wicked characters, in the form of evil incantation or "spiritual" meditation.

Once again we find that the author has tried his best to exploit each of my variables. Though the two main conversion stories in the novel are to some degree subordinated to the warfare of the gods, they are clearly designed to work best on a Citizen reader—and perhaps nearly as well, though with less effective dramatic irony, on the reader who is already tempted to apply for naturalization papers.

We open and close with the vividly portrayed warfare—at first only threatening but quickly moving to violence—between two vast armies of angels and devils. First the angels—not called such—enter the town that they know to be besieged by the devils. "[T]all, at least seven feet, strongly built, perfectly proportioned" (p. 9), they are determined to save the town—and they do save it, with the help of the absolutely pure minister of one small church and his righteous friends. At the end of the novel the angels leave for Brazil, where, though "the revival is going well," "the enemy is concocting some plan against it" (p. 376). Thus the reader is again asked to see the local triumph as only one episode in the great continuing war. And again the true Citizen is sure to think the world threatened by more enemies than had seemed true before reading.

Within this large scheme, there are of course lesser triumphs and disasters. Many people, and even more demons, are killed. A psychologist/witch who preaches the virtues of meditation in order to seduce college students into devil worship is exposed as leagued with the devils and finally killed. A clever angel "general" and his minions succeed in annihilating the demonic forces in a final battle described in apocalyptic physical detail: "Rip! Rafar's sword took off a corner of Tal's wing. Tal kept darting and flitting, dodging and swinging, and he clipped Rafar's shoulder and thigh. The air was filled with the stench of sulfur; the evil darkness was thick like smoke" (p. 370). The human beings who are shown as vicious, including one up-to-date capitalist from the big city who has been buying up the town to turn it over to the forces of evil, are similarly destroyed.

Meanwhile, what about the conversions? Some minor characters are converted through having their devils exorcised by the saintly pastor. Others are converted by witnessing incontrovertible evidence of the supernatural. Two central characters are a bright, cynical, but courageous and honest woman and a bright, unbelieving, but equally courageous and honest male, both journalists. Both are by different routes led to acknowledge the literal reality of the various supernatural events, and once they do so they have no choice but to invite Jesus into their lives.

The enemy here is considerably more diverse than in *Wise One:* "humanist religion" (p. 65); liberal or broad beliefs (pp. 69, 74); mere respectability (p. 72); adultery; video games; Buddhism (p. 217); meditation; and the wicked belief that "God is within you." When a minor character is purged of devils, they come out one by one personified as Fortune-telling, Confusion, Madness, Hatred, Witchcraft, Rape, and Cruel Violence (pp. 151–54); in short, "whatever description or definition fits, whatever shape, whatever form it takes to win a person's confidence and appeal to his vanity, that's the form they [the devils] take. . . . Eastern meditation, witchcraft, divination, Science of Mind, psychic healing, holistic education" (p. 314).

Since almost every Foreigner will have committed—or may even be committed *to*—one or another of the sins listed, one might think that Peretti has narrowed his potential converts down almost to zero. But to think that way is to forget that recognition of being sinful is a prerequisite for entering this Homeland. Readers sufficiently interested to enter Peretti's book are sure to find their special sinfulness addressed here.

The list of explicit marks of virtue is similarly diverse: honesty, courage, reliance on the Bible, being blond rather than dark, the practice of prayer, blind credulity concerning supernatural events. Of course none of these ranks as high as the embrace of Jesus. Next to that, or even in some sense identical to it, is the humble acknowledgment that the demons are real and thus that evil is literally besieging the village.

So much for the explicit values and their dramatic heightening. But what about our last variable—the harmony between such explicit values and the experience of the story as story? First, as in *Wise One,* there are really no important gradations of good and evil. Either you are saved or you are not. It's true that there is a middle, double category: those who are destined to be saved and those who are destined to be damned. But all are viewed, as they would be viewed in an Islamic narrative, strictly according to whether they will be among those who are accorded eternal bliss. Though the characters seem to choose freely, they are in fact foreordained.

Second, there is in fact a world war on, a war between good and evil. There can be no compromise. As in *Wise One,* to compromise, to tolerate, to excuse is to play into the devil's hands. A member of the good pastor's flock commits adultery. He is promptly excommunicated, with no sign whatever of the pastor's engaging in confession or counseling, as would occur in a Catholic narrative; he is driven out "for his own good"—and of course it turns out that indeed the punishment cures him and he gets saved.

Third, everything is clear, painted in plain black and white, for those who have eyes to see and ears to hear. Simple acknowledgment of the supernatural events is the only mental activity needed—except of course a prayerful reading of the Bible and a trusting of those who trust it. At the end the forces of evil are still out there, as they were at the end of *Wise One;* they can still achieve local victories—perhaps even in you. Therefore, beware: you are surrounded by sinister, invisible forces (we might here call them "other fundamentalisms"). In fact, the devil is actively at work, here and now, and whatever bad things happen in the visible world can be attributed to a living evil presence. Be especially suspicious of anyone who tries to help you, spiritually or temporally, unless he or she is offering Christ through the Bible. Professors are among the worst—especially if they are psychologists recommending meditation or claiming that "God is within you." Colleges are dangerous—it is through the town's college that the greatest wickedness has been promulgated.

To a Foreigner like me the novel is not just weak; it is—I am tempted to borrow the Homeland vocabulary—wicked. Of course some extremely naive and inexperienced Foreign readers might be unharmed by it—reading it perhaps just like a piece of science fiction. But it is hard to imagine that such readers would actually read through to the end. To read to the end you must be either a dutiful critic, like me, or a full Citizen or good prospect for Citizenship. So here I am, once again finding myself totally outside a community that seems to be growing rapidly—those special Christians who have made the book a best-seller in their special City.

I find it hard to understand why such a book becomes a best-seller even among the most devout Citizens. Most of them will know that the particular demons and angels are simply made-up names, that the battles are not real. Will they not see that the whole thing is radically unlike anything that happens in life? Will they not spot the absurd inconsistencies? But who am I to say what is their picture of "what happens in life"? If one has actually witnessed the exorcism of devils, what is so strange about showing one in a novel? Similarly, though from the perspective of my own world the conversions in the story seem to travel quite short distances and are thus undramatic and boring, for the born-again Christian the "distance" from liberal "complacency" to the prayer of contrition is as great as any conversion distance could be.

A Subtler Transport

So far I have treated these stories as if their effects were all blatantly didactic: their authors hope to win converts, or to strengthen the faith and allegiance of those who already claim to be believers, or to sharpen the dividing line between true believers and false prophets and followers. Most of the tellers I have tried to listen to—invariably with only limited success—talk as if their motives must fall somewhere among these three. Almost none of them says anything openly about a subtler effect, in both tellers and listeners, that is always present—at least for the Citizen who enters *any* story fully: the reward of being lifted temporarily—or should one say "temporally"?—out of the fallen world into a "world" that one would prefer to live in. It is an effect we all experience when we become fully engrossed in reading (or viewing) any powerful fiction, as we rise into the fictional world and enjoy the dramatic irony entailed in observing characters who fail—and only sometimes finally succeed in joining us who are "up here." It is an effect made explicit in the best Christian allegories—*The Divine Comedy* say, or C. S. Lewis's Perelandra stories: we long, as Lewis constantly reminds us, for a return to the world before the fall.

The implied author of all tales offers an invitation that is accepted by every surrendering reader: "Come live with me for a while in this other world, a world inhabited by at least one 'saved' human being, namely me. Join me and you will at least temporarily escape the world you know is just not good enough, not interesting enough, not virtuous enough, not vital enough—not the one you'd prefer to live in, given a choice. In telling you this tale I, the implied author, have risen, for the time being, into a world of light, and I invite you to join me here." This similarity between the invitations offered by all fictions and the promised offerings of all religions has to my knowledge never been adequately pursued. (The word "all" in any claim should make any scholar uneasy; for obvious reasons I feel more confidence in using it about all fictions than about all religions. I hope that by pushing my universalist claims further here I can challenge others to go deeper than most programs in "religion and literature" have been willing to go.)

Without space sufficient to argue my claim about the structural similarity, I must simply assert it one more time. The one belief common to all religions, fundamentalist or not, is an awareness that the world as we find it is just not as good as a world ought to be; there simply must be another better world somewhere—in the past, in the future, or perhaps even right here and now. And it is not just that the world "ought" to be better; *we* must somehow become better than we manage to be in our quotidian world. Facing this universal longing, every religion I know anything about offers the possibility of transport from the fallen or falling or cursed world into another, whether in the future or in some mystical experience. Similarly, the one experience common to all fully-engaged reading of fictions is a departure from an inferior world into one that is not just more interesting but more desirable (if it were not, we would not be reading). Thus every fiction, secular or religious, implicitly offers a transport, however trivial, that resembles in structure what religions claim to achieve: not simply a future possibility of "salvation" but an actual experience: we become better persons living in a superior world as we read. (I deal with the ambiguities in the word "better" throughout *The Company We Keep*—see footnote 11).

Christian fundamentalist fictions unite religious and fictional transports, reinforcing the implicit invitation "upward" with an explicit set of doctrines. They offer the transport both in the future—heavenly reward—and now: the bliss of feeling saved, of living among the saved and looking down on the damned. Explicitly they offer a set of religious convictions; implicitly they offer, just by being fictions, a piece of redeemed—"transported"—time during the hours of reading. (On another occasion I would extend this claim about "reading time" to "listening time": music at its best turns us into "better persons" living in "better worlds" for the duration of the listening.)

In other words, telling the story of the hero's spiritual journey, whether that journey is turbulent and accompanied with metaphorical wars or serene (as in most Islamic and Buddhist and many Catholic accounts I have seen), is not just showing listeners how to be saved, with the consequences of the listening postponed until afterward; it is giving them the experience of salvation here and now, in the act of dwelling in story. Citizen listeners experience a transcending of this world, "for the time being"—from the first moment when they "buy into" the world of the story. The teller—not a dramatized narrator but the author implied by every choice he or she has made—is experienced as already a companion, a friend, a saved one, dwelling in a consecrated world. The listener is lifted into that world in the act of listening or reading. We know nothing about Elwood or Peretti, as real men. But we experience Elwood and Peretti as dwelling "up there," and if our pre-reading values are close enough to theirs, the secular world is redeemed for us during the non-time of reading.

Every reader knows that to dwell fully in any story is to leave the ordinary world with its mundane time scheme and conflicting values and to escape into an entirely different world with a different time scheme and ordering of values: in a sense a "timeless" time scheme, since the values and their ordering never change in the course of a given reading. The word *escape* may be a dangerous one: most critics feel some contempt for mere "escape fiction." But the contempt conceals a sublime fact: to enter the world of even the cheapest fiction is to transcend everyday time.[12]

Once we take seriously this fact, it becomes clear that something very profound is going on in this worldwide flood of conversion narrative, something far more important than the usual view of stories as a form of mere evangelical persuasion. The difference between falling into the clutches of "non-religious" tales—a gripping murder mystery, say, or *Kidnapped*—and listening to fundamentalist narratives is that for the latter the experience of transcending the world of time is "thematized," as current critical jargon puts it: not only do I, the listener, enter another world, as I do in reading *Kidnapped,* but I am told explicitly that it is a world infinitely truer, realer, than the one I will fall back into after listening. The best stories, in whatever tradition, *incarnate* not just their heroes but the gods their heroes worship and the experience of living—for the duration of the listening—in the world created and inhabited not only by a holy implied author but by those gods. The incarnation is not indeed physical, in the usual sense. One cannot ask to touch the body of story, like some doubting Thomas. But it enters "tangibly" through the senses of hearing or sight as the listener lives, for the time of the telling, lives in the divine world with the hero or heroes—and more subtly with the person who tells the story, whether that person claims to be the hero or not. Obviously the temptation to live increasingly in that divine world becomes greater as the secular world becomes less tolerable.

Sometimes listeners do not discover explicitly that they have been living in that special world until late in the tale, when conversion is portrayed; sometimes the listener is told from the beginning that the world of the book is not the everyday visible world, thus producing less ordinary suspense but more opportunities for dramatic irony. But always that special world is implicitly inhabited throughout the listening, just as Augustine, for example, dwells in that world from the beginning of his *Confessions,* even though the younger self he tells about was living elsewhere.[13] The "saintly" implied author leads us to dwell "up there" and to choose to dwell there "forever." The better world—far more than just the explicit characteristics of Homeland that I described earlier—is thus implicitly and totally circumambient, transforming the nature of every detail, from "the beginning." In the beginning of every tale, in short, is the "word" that validates that tale *as story,* that makes it work as an intelligible tale: every word exhibits an incarnation of that story's "world." For the believing listener, the true Citizen of that world, every word is heard resonating with the contrast between the world incarnated in the story and the world from which the listener has come and to which he or she must return.

In short, this effect does not unfold as the story unfolds; it enters from "the beginning." The spiritual battle does not take place "out there," witnessed at a distance; it is an incarnated moment in the eternal war, with "me" from the beginning on the side of the holy forces, a knowing yet unsure reader, passionately hoping that my side will win. Meanwhile, for the reader who finds that these novels do not "work" as story, the leap upward fails to occur—except, in my case, as a wish that it *could* work for me; the young fundamentalist part of me would still love to live in such salvational certainties.

"True Stories" and the Tourist

To describe the difference between Foreigners and Citizens in this way sharpens the question of how a critic might deal with the search for critical criteria. We cannot escape the difference between experiencing an incarnation and watching others *think* that they are experiencing it. What, indeed, are we studying, if we cannot even claim to have encountered fully the thing studied?

One answer would be that of many traditional anthropologists when encountering divergent cultures with divergent norms: develop a total relativism of fundamentalisms and do our best to adopt, for the nonce, the total world of the story, all judgments postponed. Acknowledge that you can never enter an alien world fully; stop trying and abandon all judgments.

But I think we can no longer take that comfortable path, not only because of the general collapse by now of the anthropologists' cultural relativism but because of what we know about our own responses: no listener can surrender to all narrative worlds with equal abandon. We can of course dodge the problem by refusing really to engage with *any* story, retreating to linguistic analysis or various theoretical abstractions. But insofar as we really try to listen, we find that even if we attempt to postpone judgment, pursuing fairness and objectivity, our basic commitments judge for us.

Milestones

To dramatize the problem of judging rival fictional worlds fairly it is helpful to turn from stories that announce themselves as fictions to those that claim to be historically, literally true. Consider the difficulties non-Muslims face when trying to listen to any of the several biographies of Sayyid Qutb, the most famous of the Muslim fundamentalist martyrs under Nasser. One of these is by S. Badrul Hasan, Qutb's translator, in a preface to Qutb's *Milestones*.[14] Reading it, I cannot escape the fact that I come to it as a distant Foreigner. As a white Western Mormon-raised secularized miracle-doubter, I have not been prepared, as Hasan clearly expects his readers to be, to be thrilled by examples of total Islamic faith. Qutb is portrayed as living in that faith, as if from the day he was born. Though I can work to earn the title of Friendly Investigator—or at least open-minded Tourist—the title would rightly raise some skepticism in any alert Muslim.

Hasan's version, unlike some others, shows Qutb as absolutely serene in the faith from his earliest years: "he worshipped the Holy Qur'an in his childhood in keeping with the heartiest desire of his revered mother," and there is no hint of his ever questioning a single line of the holy book. Unlike most Christian biographies and autobiographies, this one reveals no effort to portray the hero as ever having lived anywhere but "up there"—there is no falling away and there is little if any spiritual distance traveled from birth to death. Sayyid was born into a family in which "verily every member . . . appears a unique pearl," a family that was "all sun" (p. 1). His mother "had very [*sic*] keen attachment with the Holy Qur'an" (p. 2). His father was "a very religious and derwish-like [*sic*] person" (p. 3). So Sayyid Qutb was guided by Providence (and in the same paragraph, to my no doubt blasphemous amusement, by "good luck"!) throughout a life that never faltered in total sanctity (p. 4).

Hasan's version of the hero's two years attending American colleges is crucial in its picture of absolutely unfaltering devotion (pp. 4–5). In interesting spiritual biographies the education years are usually presented as the years of temptation, even years of great sin: Augustine as gratuitous pear thief and fornicator; Gandhi relishing beef and fancy clothes as a young man in London. In another version of Qutb's life by Yuonne Haddad, he had a period of "enchantment" with the values of the West; he became an "intellectual" who at an early age fell under the misguided "influence of Abbas al-Aqqad and his Westernizing tendencies."[15] He was for a time "enamored of the West" and then had to undergo "a transformation in the late 1940's." That to me is a much more interesting Qutb than the one portrayed by Hasan: "[T]he sojourn in America for a short period proved of imme[n]se value and blessing for him. He witnessed the devastation brought about by the materialistic life with his own eyes. Thus he felt more satisfied with the truth and veracity of Islam, and he returned with the reinforced conviction that the real well-being of humanity lay only in Islam" (p. 5).

Because this Qutb has had no struggle, and because spiritual struggle is for me as Foreigner one test of genuine religious depth (one of my fundamentals), I am not prepared properly, when Qutb's trials inevitably come, to respond as I should. He was persistently persecuted by the Egyptian government for having become active in the movement known as al-Ikhwan al-Muslimun. One of his students describes what happened: "Syed Qutb was subjected to mountainous persecutions. He was branded. Police dogs dragged him between their jaws. Water, sometimes cold, at others hot, was continuously poured on his head. He was belabored with fists and kicks. He was insulted with painful words and gestures but all these things added to his faith and conviction and he became more steadfast on the path of rectitude" (p. 8). This wording of course might be taken as implying that he was not perfectly steadfast on that path before the torture, just as words like *reinforced*, in the account of the American experience, might imply moments of weakened conviction or satisfaction of the kind described by Haddad. But surely that is not what the student means here. He must mean that Sayyid Qutb, always invulnerable, happy and secure in Homeland, could never be dragged down into our world. It is a faith made up of elements only some of which I can embrace, probably the very ones that Sayyid Qutb himself would see as minor. If I probe to deep metaphorical levels, I can find among my strongest convictions some that are *like* some of Sayyid Qutb's—most notably a longing to dwell in a Homeland—but the very effort to locate them distracts me and produces further distancing.

In other words, whatever joining I manage is not emotionally intense enough to allow the story of his further persecution and execution to achieve even a faint echo of the kind of engagement that I have been calling an incarnation. I observe with sympathy for him as Sayyid Qutb is arrested, released, arrested again, and executed, and I come to admire his courage. I am impressed by his refusal to compromise. I am absolutely convinced that Nasser's persecution was as unjust as the persecution of the various Christian saints whose lives I have read, or the assassinations of Joseph Smith or Malcolm X or Martin Luther King. But at no point do I enter Sayyid Qutb's world fully. Though I abhor his torture, the feeling is shamefully lukewarm as compared with what it might have been if he had not been portrayed as a saint so far above ordinary mortal condition that nothing could really faze him. I suspect that other biographers, no matter how skillful in "Western" narrative techniques, would fail to move me into that world, so long as they insisted on adhering to the convention of a hero born in the truth, never once doubting the truth, never once tempted by other truths, and dying along with other unquestioning heroes—heroes whom I find it hard not to label with pejorative terms like *fanatic* or *fundamentalist*. (I have heard non-Christians make the same claim about trying to respond emotionally to the story of Christ's persecutions: "He's not really hurting; he's not one of us.")

One more example of the obstacles to full listening: In a study of conversions to

Christianity, James Craig Holte finds contrasting patterns between the typical Protestant conversions—dramatic, sudden, shattering, moving from depravity to a sudden inflowing of Grace—and the dominant Catholic conversions, stressing "lengthy preparation" and a "search for God" that includes, as in Thomas Merton, deep and prolonged intellectual questioning of a multiplicity of tenets and their potential coherence.[16] Similarly, Christine M. Bochen has compared conversions to Roman Catholicism in the nineteenth century with what she and others take to be typical "revival" conversions to Protestantism. She finds that the Roman conversions tend to result not from suddenly overwhelming illumination but from a "patient searching of the heart done with calm deliberation."[17]

No reader of this non-dramatic essay will be surprised to learn that I find it easier to enter the world of the second kind than the first. Reading C. S. Lewis's *Surprised by Joy* and G. K. Chesterton's *Autobiography* and dwelling with them as they struggle through decades of hard thought, I find when I come to their final transport—Chesterton almost fifty and Lewis just over thirty (though he "feels" much older to me)— I am "with" them even though my description of Homeland would be far different from theirs. Part of Lewis's narrative triumph is that he brings into the crucial moment the very intellectual problems that might otherwise distance me from his experience.

> You must picture me alone in that room at Magdalen, night after night, feeling, whenever my mind lifted even for a second from my work, the steady, unrelenting approach of Him whom I so earnestly desired not to meet. That which I greatly feared had at last come upon me. In the Trinity Term of 1929 I gave in, and admitted that God was God, and knelt and prayed: perhaps, that night, the most dejected and reluctant convert in all England. I did not then see what is now the most shining and obvious thing; the Divine humility which will accept a convert even on such terms. The Prodigal Son at least walked home on his own feet. But who can duly adore that Love which will open the high gates to a prodigal who is brought in kicking, struggling, resentful, and darting his eyes in every direction for a chance of escape? . . . The hardness of God is kinder than the softness of men, and His compulsion is our liberation.[18]

Such an account is most likely to capture a reader who knows how it feels to struggle resistingly, seeking in every direction an escape route. Though I cannot take Lewis's or Chesterton's final steps with them, their stories make me want to. My fundamentals are close enough to those they discover, after long, thoughtful inquiry, to place me into the class of Honest Investigators, and thus I am narratively seducible. I can mime that "temporary suspension of disbelief" that critics have too often claimed should be the aspiration of all readers of all fiction.

Note that to achieve this effect on me the stories have to be quite long. They are immeasurably longer than accounts of the lives of Muslim saints, or of conversions of liberal Jews to radically fundamentalist Judaism or of mainline Mormons to polygamist groups, or of Catholics to this or that Protestant fundamentalism.

Consider the account by Maryam Jameelah of her conversion from secularized Jew to passionately committed Muslim. She writes more skillfully than the other fundamentalists I've quoted. She is educated in scholarly practices, and surprisingly devoted to citing and refuting, in detail, all that can be said by various enemies against Islam. As she tells it, she was determined from the beginning to find "the absolute Truth which alone gives human life its meaning, direction and purpose" (p. 1). The consequence is that she does not tell a story, or rather, that the story she tells is so curt and lacking in persuasive detail that one finds little but a conceptualized account of the world one is being invited to enter. It is as if the fundamentalism itself prevents her even considering the kind of "telling" that would be persuasive to an outsider.

> As soon as I was able to think and comprehend at all, I was repelled by the dominant values of my society, the purpose of which is happiness, pleasure and enjoyment while I longed above all else to achieve something eternally worthwhile. . . . My quest was always for absolutes. . . . Neither Judaism nor Christianity could satisfy me. I was repelled by the narrow, parochial-mindedness of the synagogue and horrified by the atrocities of Zionism against the indigenous Arabs of Palestine. . . .
>
> In Islam, my quest for absolute values was satisfied. In Islam I found all that was true, good and beautiful and which gives meaning and direction to human life (and death) while in other religions, the Truth is deformed, distorted, restricted and fragmentary. If anyone chooses to ask me how I came to know this, *I can only reply that my personal life experience was sufficient to convince me* [my emphasis, W.B.]. . . . Since I have, I believe, always been a Muslim at heart and by temperament, even before I even knew there was such a thing as Islam, my conversion was mainly a formality, involving no radical change in my heart at all but rather only making official what I had been thinking and yearning for [for] many years.[19]

She seems to imply that it would be impossible or repugnant to provide any vivid rendition of what kind of "personal life experience" could have given such clear evidence for the truth of Islam. It is precisely here that we meet the most interesting question about the rhetoric of conversion narratives—but it is one that "we," by definition, cannot answer: Does her brief, unembellished narrative provide, for the Citizen of Islam, anything even remotely resembling the "incarnation" experience that a fully developed, dramatically heightened, and technically enriched account would?

It will not do to say only that of course her account, and that of many another hagiographer, could be improved by thinking harder about the rhetorical variables I have described—and thus writing a narrative "better" not just by my standards but by theirs as well. For all we know such elaboration might repel the believer. At the same time it is obvious that the sheer process of editorial selection and publishing narratives entails passing judgments on better and worse. Though full Citizens may resist any kind of deliberate, overt criticism of any story that celebrates Homeland, in practice they must make judgments all the time, rescuing from heaps of poorly told saint's tales and conversion allegories those few that really *incarnate*—as Bunyan's allegory was rescued, in spite of elite critics' denigration, by the incarnational experience of generations of non-elite listeners, many of them literally listening because they could not read.

A Foreigner Struggles for a Conclusion about Stories by Natives

The questions raised by an inquiry of this kind multiply rapidly, and most of one's tentative answers turn out to be relevant only to *some* of the stories that might be called fundamentalist. No doubt I am not the first author in the ambitious Fundamentalism Project who has discovered that struggling to understand contrasting movements can produce a conversion experience of its own kind: a shattering of scholarly pride, and a strengthening of the humility that every serious religion urges upon us as a major, if not the supreme, virtue. I can thus only offer here at the end, instead of the confident conclusions one might have hoped for, a feeble echo of that ancient and exasperating convention employed by social scientists: "I hope I have raised some possibilities for further study." We need a body of serious studies of the special problems that fundamentalist narratives raise for us—and for the world's future: by philosophers, especially those who wrestle with the problem of universals; by literary critics, perhaps especially those who have engaged with post-modernist movements; by social historians; by students of secular fundamentalisms like Stalinism and free-marketism; by politicians concerned with the rise of violence; by students of popular rhetoric; by theologians pursuing ecumenical formulations; by social reformers searching for ways to build community. To me the most important of all our questions is the one raised by the entire Fundamentalism Project: What common ground can we hope to find among so many movements that declare that there can be no common ground?

We face an obvious paradox: those fundamentalists whose words I've reported might deplore my project, or even hate me for it, rejecting out of hand any hope for common ground. I have questioned their hatred of some things and some people and beliefs that I cherish. I have given in some detail accounts of two novels that "we here" can deplore, because they seek to convert us all to a fundamentalism that teaches hatred. And I have discussed a few shorter narratives that we can look down on from our platform as superior students of fundamentalisms. Is it not sheer paradox to seek real bridges between ourselves and all those "others"—Elwood and Peretti and Maryam Jameelah and Sayyid Qutb and his hagiographers, not to mention others?[20] Can any similarities we might trace between their accounts and Lewis's, Chesterton's, Merton's, my daughter's account of her embrace of (one version of) Judaism, the accounts of my ancestors converting to Mormonism—suggest that we are all brothers and sisters under the skin of our contrasting fundamentalisms?

It is painfully clear that most of those we meet will tell us to give up the absurd quest: "Come join the one true way." Are they not right in insisting that our fundamentals clash fundamentally with theirs? After all, many on "our side" are deeply committed to seeing a huge difference of value between those stories that imply a final brotherhood and sisterhood of all (that is, conversion is available to all and will finally come to all—or at least to most fellow human beings) and those that imply or state that salvation is inherently confined to a tiny remnant. In some versions of Calvinism and some versions of Islam, the list of the to-be-saved is already written in Heaven, and therefore no written story can make any difference in who gets saved and who damned. Does this mean that those fundamentalists who have opposed the very idea of storytelling (except for the sacred scriptures, fixed for all time) are absolutely justi-

fied in their opposition? Is there not indeed a "war in heaven" between some fundamentals and all human storytellers, and between some fundamentalists and all students
of storytelling?

We cannot hope—I repeat my main point—even for limited success with such
questions if we confine ourselves to the explicitly formulated doctrines of the various
faiths. Whatever "deep" commonalities and genuine differences are to be discovered
will be found in the way the various narratives *work*. They will be discovered in patterns
of ultimate desire that the questers reveal.

Thought about those deepest patterns may uncover one slight hope for a meeting
ground: my storytellers share with me two convictions. On the one hand, you do not
search for or find the truth alone: you find it by discovering other pilgrims who have
made some progress in the quest. Second, among those others there is a supreme
Other, or Otherness, that/who has created (or as in Buddhism at least now sustains)
us and our fellow questers. God and his Church, Christ and his Saints, Allah, Buddha,
Kṛṣṇa—these provide, along with the loving community of the orthodox, what many
have been calling the "we feeling" that is perhaps the chief validator of all fundamentalisms—and, in my view, all church memberships and indeed most secular communities too. Some fundamentalisms seem at times to reduce the size of this in-group to
two—the convert and God. Yet the central structural points are the same in all: "I am
no longer alone" and "I hereby surrender to a Center infinitely more wonderful and
powerful than *we* are." In this perspective, the "fundamental" drive even of narrators
as "foreign" to me as those who write bigoted, hate-filled best-sellers is not so different from that of the rest of us as they (and perhaps we) would like to think.

Can we not say that we all tell one another conversion narratives, stories of belief
changes that, though much less dramatic than those we have met here, seem to us as
revolutionary, and as important? Do we not always imply, like Peretti and Elwood and
Sayyid Qutb and Maryam Jameela, that we have always lived embedded in the truth,
even though ignoring it and even though it takes so long to find it that many never
arrive? The truth-of-things, how-things-really-are, the full-reality-of-Creation was always there surrounding us, but we could not see it? Isn't it obvious that even the most
negative of nihilists, explaining how they have discovered that there is no truth, are
claiming that they, like all the rest of humankind, have been dwelling in *that* truth,
even though ignoring it and even though it takes so long to find it that many never
arrive? Was not the truth-of-things, how-things-really-are, the full-reality-of-Creation
always there, surrounding us, but we could not see it?

Such tentative explorations of "fundamental" similarities may only heighten the
apparent paradox facing anyone studying comparative fundamentalisms. All serious
conversion narratives tell us that if we pursue the new life they offer we will have a
reason for knowing that all other people, those who have not seen the light, are wrong,
or damned, or benighted, or ignorant. That claim almost always seems to me con-
temptibly vulgar. But how can I say *that* without implying that I dwell in a light these
believers do not share? Thus I exhibit one of their vices: arrogance. But do they not
also share one quality that even on my most humble days I think of as a virtue: my
sense that the life I am living, the life we are living, *requires redemption?*

On the one hand the life we actually live, "down here," has provided us, blessedly, with clues about what would be an ideal life. On the other it has deprived us, in innumerable ways, of the actuality to match our ideals. All the fundamentalist conversion stories begin with a recognition that something is wrong here and the hope that something will be or can be made right "up there." Does the fact that to my taste they all show much too much confidence that the "up there" has been found imply that I know more about it than they do? And would not that claim already betray the essential humility that to me ought to unite all who probe into the great Mystery?

Notes

1. Thus my fundamentalism had what most fundamentalisms still lack, a full-length sacred book to rival, in its miraculous claims, the Bible and the Qu'ran. In his book *Sacred Writings: A Guide to the Literature of Religions* (London: William Collins and Sons, 1961; original, *Heilige Schriften,* 1956), Gunter Lanczkowski includes *The Book of Mormon* as one of eighteen "unquestionably Sacred Books," books that have claimed and gained the status, among their followers, of the Talmud or the New Testament. My experience with fellow Mormons confirms his choice.

2. See Wendy Doniger, "Preface to the English Edition of the Complete Work," in *Mythologies,* compiled by Yves Bonnefoy (Chicago: University of Chicago Press, 1991).

3. For a careful argument about terminology in such matters, see Lynn Poland, "The Bible and the Rhetorical Sublime," in Martin Warner, ed., *The Bible as Rhetoric: Studies in Biblical Persuasion and Credibility* (London: Routledge, 1990). Poland argues persuasively that *allegorical* should be preferred to *symbolic* for what we have in mind.

4. Debora R. Kaufman, *Rachel's Daughters: New Orthodox Jewish Women* (New Brunswick: Rutgers University Press, 1991), p. 31.

5. Douglas Hyde, in Bernard Dixon, *Journeys in Belief* (London: Allen and Unwin, 1968), pp. 139–40. A fuller and more complex account of his conversion is given in Hyde's *I Believed: The Autobiography of a Former Communist* (London: William Heinemann, 1951).

6. Maryam Jameelah, *Islam and Western Society* (Lahore: Mohammad Yusuf Khan, 1976).

7. Kaufman, *Rachel's Daughters,* pp. 27–28, 44–45, 155.

8. Isherwood, p. 132.

9. For extensive treatment of how narratives postulate or imply or create "readers," whether reading or listening, see my *Rhetoric of Fiction,* 2d ed. (Chicago: University of Chicago Press, 1983); and Wolfgang Iser, *The Implied Reader: Patterns of Communication in Prose Fiction from Bunyan to Beckett* (Baltimore: Johns Hopkins University Press, 1974).

10. Anthony Burgess, *Little Wilson and Big God* (New York: Weidenfeld and Nicolson, 1986).

11. See my *The Company We Keep: An Ethics of Fiction* (Berkeley: University of California Press, 1988), for detailed analyses of how one might do ethical criticism not by judging expressed codes but by exploring the kind of "harmony" I touch on briefly here.

12. (Each of the following "bests" is preceded with "to my limited knowledge.") The best fictional account of just what this can mean to the fully engaged listener is Proust's, as Marcel describes, early in *Du côté de chez Swann,* his total immersion in the tales he read as a young boy. The fullest and best scholarly explorations of how the chronological, "horizontal" dimension entails the eternal, the "vertical," is Paul Ricoeur's in *Time and Narrative,* 2 vols. (Chicago: University of Chicago Press, 1984; original, *Temps et récit,* 1983). His analysis of how Augustine struggles to explain the rela-

tion of time and eternity should be studied by everyone who cares about how narrative relates to religion. For the way in which all language, including narrative, implies hierarchies leading to God terms, see Kenneth Burke's *Rhetoric of Religion: Studies in Logology* (Boston: Beacon Press, 1961). The best short treatment is the one I have cited earlier by Lynn Poland.

13. Again Poland's essay is essential here.

14. Sayyid Qutb, *Milestones* (Karachi: International Islamic Publishers, 1982), introduction and translation by S. Badrul Hasan.

15. Yvonne Y. Haddad, "Sayyid Qutb: Ideologue of Islamic Revival," in John L. Esposito, ed., *Voices of Resurgent Islam* (New York: Oxford University Press, 1983), pp. 67–69).

16. James Craig Holte, *The Conversion Experience in America: A Sourcebook on Religious Conversion Autobiography* (New York: Greenwood Press, 1992).

17. Walter Elliott, quoted in Christine M. Bochen, *The Journey to Rome: Conversion Literature by Nineteenth-Century American Catholics* (New York: Garland, 1988), p. 68.

18. C. S. Lewis, *Surprised by Joy: The Shape of My Early Life* (London: Geoffrey Bles, 1955; reprint, Fontana Books, 1969), pp. 182–83.

19. Jameelah, *Islam and Western Society,* pp. 1–4, my italics.

20. See also A. C. Bhaktivedanta Swami Prabhupada, "His Divine Grace," founder of the International Society for Krishna Consciousness, *Kṛṣṇa: The Reservoir of Pleasure* (Borehamwood, England: Bhaktivedanta Book Trust, 1990).

5

Fundamentalisms Comprehended

Fundamentalism: Genus and Species

Gabriel A. Almond, Emmanuel Sivan, and R. Scott Appleby

Introduction: Methodological Considerations

To explain is to make "plain" in the physical sense of leveling out unevenness. We use other physical metaphors such as "seeing" or "grasping" in defining *explanation*. We see something that was previously obscure; we grasp something that has eluded us. We try to make sense of an anomaly brought to us by our senses. All of the many papers and chapters contributed to the American Academy of Arts and Sciences' study of fundamentalism—even those consisting mostly of description—are concerned with explaining the movements in this larger sense of "making plain" or "making sense of" fundamentalism. When we describe a fundamentalist movement, specify its properties, observe where and how it originated, how it grows and develops, what it does, how other groups react to it, we are explaining it, grasping its meaning, making sense of it.

Ernest Nagel writes of four varieties of explanatory logic—the deductive, the statistical, the functional, and the genetic.[1] In deductive logic, often presented as the "genuine" form of explanation toward which all science should aspire, a conclusion follows invariantly from a set of premises: if A occurs, B must occur. Given the laws of the conservation of energy, for example, there is an invariant relationship between atmospheric pressure and the boiling point of water.

The probabilistic or statistical logic of explanation, meanwhile, establishes recurrent relationships among variables that fall short of invariance. We are speaking of a tendency, a probability: if A occurs, B usually occurs, but not invariably. Meteorologists advise us that, given a particular set of atmospheric conditions, the probability of rain is 70 percent in the next twenty-four hours.

The third explanatory logic, functional explanation, takes the form of a set of interacting variables that, at given states, explain each other as well as the condition of the larger system of which they constitute parts. Thus if the overall condition of a biological organism A is of a given order and quality, there is a high probability that B, C, and D are occurring. If one's cat, for example, is thriving, then the cat's digestive, cardiopulmonary, and neurological systems are interacting within certain ranges.

Finally, there is genetic explanation, favored by historians, in which a given set of preceding conditions are used to explain a set of subsequent conditions. Tocqueville's *Ancien Régime et la Révolution française* is a classic example of this explanatory logic; it describes the structure of French institutions and the character and mood of the French aristocracy, bourgeoisie, and peasantry on the eve of the revolution, showing how and why these history-shaping events unfolded as they did.

These logics of explanation are not mutually exclusive. Functional and genetic explanations involve probabilistic explanatory components. And some of the devotees of hard science espouse a program that would reduce the other varieties to the nomological, deductive one. In the empirical and analytical studies of this series one finds many examples of probabilistic, functional, and genetic explanation, but none of the deductive variety. The relations between the Green Revolution in Punjab and Sikh fundamentalism; between the emigration from Eastern Europe and the rise of ultra-Orthodox Jewish fundamentalism; between the Six-Day War and the Yom Kippur War on one hand and the rise of religious Zionist fundamentalism, Gush Emunim style, on the other; and between the development of the audiocassette and the spread of Iranian fundamentalism—these are among the examples of probabilistic explanations.[2] Functional explanations appear in the discussions of the interdependence and interaction of fundamentalist ideology, programs, and organization.[3] The various accounts of the histories of fundamentalist movements contain numerous examples of genetic explanation: the contemporary settlement and clothing patterns of ultra-Orthodox Jewish movements are explained, for example, in terms of earlier normative "shtetl" culture; radical Sikh garb is explained by a warrior past; and so on.[4]

Philosophers of science and of social science disagree, however, on the place of the nomothetic or deductive model in the explanation of human affairs. Nagel, Braithwaite, and Hempel, among others,[5] tend to insist on the essential unity of science, and the amenability of social as well as physical reality to deductive explanation. Popper, Kaplan, and others defend a more complex ontological model,[6] arguing that, in the social sciences, learning and creativity limit the confidence with which we can establish social patterns and regularities. These relations are at best probabilistic, and they tend to erode over time as a result of human learning.

Recent experience with theory building in the social sciences raises questions about earlier confident beliefs in a methodological hierarchy with deductive and statistical approaches at the top, and case studies at the bottom. Increasing rigor and systematization in case study research, comparative historical analysis, and the adaptation of statistical analysis to small numbers suggest that the choice of methodologies should be governed by the kind of problem under study, and that they are best employed in combination.

In seeking to explain fundamentalism we are in the quandary of trying to generalize about causation from a relatively small number of very complex cases. Arend Lijphart and David Collier would characterize this situation as the "many variable, small *n* dilemma," a situation in which it is difficult to establish relationships with high confidence.[7] More than twenty years ago Lijphart examined various methodologies from the point of view of their appropriateness in dealing with social movements and other political phenomena. He points out that the two more scientific methodologies—experimental and statistical—are not readily applicable to the study of political movements. We cannot place such movements in laboratories, and subject them to controls. And given the possible relations among their many variables, there are not enough cases to enable us to establish statistical significance with confidence. At the same time, with rare exceptions, individual case studies at best produce hypotheses, not rigorous explanations. Collier, summarizing progress that has been made in comparative studies, points to improvements in the case study approach associated with the work of Harry Eckstein through the selection of "crucial," theoretically powerful cases, and that of Alexander George through focused comparison and rigorous "process tracing."[8] He also points to the development of quasi-experimental techniques through the comparative study of the impact of the same public policy on areas having different characteristics.

Collier refers to two alternative ways of comparing a small number of cases—the "most similar systems" and the "most different systems" designs. The most-similar-systems approach seeks rigor and control through matching cases on as many dimensions as possible, other than the presumed "cause and effect variables." While it is difficult to find in nature or in history what can be made to occur through deliberate control in the laboratory, this kind of controlled small n comparison does produce theory, or at least very persuasive hypotheses. Let us take two Sunni Islamic countries, Egypt and Algeria. While ranking closely in the Physical Quality of Life Index, which combines life expectancy, infant mortality, and literacy, the two nations manifested differing degrees of fundamentalist mobilization in the late 1980s and early 1990s (prior to the military crackdown in Algeria). In this particular comparison the explanatory difference seems to be in the political dimension, with Algeria having established a more open political system prior to the crackdown, and having a more mobilized population (with borders more open to penetration by Islamic extremists). Egypt, on the other hand, had a more authoritarian system and generally succeeded in suppressing the fundamentalists. One result was that the 1991 Algerian election produced a fundamentalist plurality. (The result was reversed in an authoritarian coup.)

In the preceding chapters of this volume, the contributors employ controlled comparison as a way of generating explanatory hypotheses. Thus Said Arjomand's chapter, "Unity and Diversity in Islamic Fundamentalism," and T. N. Madan's, "From Orthodoxy to Fundamentalism: A Thousand Years of Islam in South Asia," hold religious tradition constant, and examine how other aspects of society, culture, and economy interact with fundamentalism. On the other hand, Daniel Levine's "Protestants and Catholics in Latin America: A Family Portrait" and Harjot Oberoi's "Mapping Indic Fundamentalisms through Nationalism and Modernity" hold the socioeconomic context constant, and vary the religious-doctrinal dimension. Both approaches have the virtue of introducing analytic controls—the same religion in differing sociocultural contexts, or different religions in the same context.

Adam Przeworski's approach to comparison—the most-different-systems design—requires a set of cases as diverse as possible, but all containing a dose of the same phenomenon. The value of this approach is that it forces us "to distill out of that diversity a set of common elements with great explanatory power."[9] Such a design also has the virtue that it enables us to sort out the varieties of the phenomenon, to establish the common properties, as well as the properties of the subspecies.

In the present essay we approach the explanation of fundamentalism in two steps. First, we classify these movements according to their characteristics, thereby establishing the properties of the "genus" called fundamentalism as well as its varieties. In other words, we first identify what it is that we are trying to explain. Second, we examine the historical and contextual variables in each case, in a search for the causes of fundamentalism in its various manifestations.[10]

The Properties of Fundamentalism

We see fundamentalism neither as a "new religious movement" (in the technical sense of that term) nor as simply a "traditional," "conservative," or "orthodox" expression of ancient or premodern religious faith and practice. Rather, fundamentalism is a hybrid of both kinds of religious modes, and it belongs in a category by itself. While fundamentalists claim to be upholding orthodoxy (right belief) or orthopraxis (right behavior), and to be defending and conserving religious traditions and traditional ways of life from erosion, they do so by crafting new methods, formulating new ideologies, and adopting the latest processes and organizational structures. Some of these new methods, structures, ideologies, and processes seem to be in direct violation of the actual historical beliefs, interpretive practices, and moral behaviors of earlier generations—or to be, at the least, a significant departure from these precedents, as well as from the praxis of contemporary conservative or orthodox believers. Indeed, fundamentalists often find fault with fellow believers who want to conserve the tradition but are not willing to craft innovative ways of fighting back against the forces of erosion. In other words, fundamentalists argue that to be "merely" a conservative or a traditionalist in these threatening times is not enough.

At the same time, fundamentalists would reject the suggestion that they are doing something radically new; a crucial element of their rhetoric and self-understanding is the assertion that their innovative programs are based on the authority of the sacred past, whether that past be represented in a privileged text or tradition, or in the teaching of a charismatic or official leader. While fundamentalists are neither restorationists nor primitivists—that is, they do not wish to return society to the conditions "wherein the greatest excellence and happiness existed at the fount of time," nor are they marked by a special or distinctive longing for "a simpler, less complex world"[11]—they are nonetheless careful to demonstrate the continuity between their programs and teachings and the received wisdom of their religious heritage. A pronounced rootedness in scripture and/or "purified" tradition, coupled with a reluctance to embrace New Age philosophies or Spirit-inspired new revelations, characterizes fundamentalism as a religious mode. Thus Christian fundamentalists, strictly speaking, do not belong to Pentecostal churches or movements, which rely heavily on the immediate leading of the Holy Spirit; similarly, one would not expect Sufi orders to produce Muslim fundamentalists, given the former's emphasis on mystical experience as opposed to religiolegal revelation.

Nonetheless, the twentieth century is characterized by religious syncretism, and that blending of influences affects even conservative movements known for their boundary maintenance. Thus we see new expressions of fundamentalism—which we call synthetic fundamentalism to distinguish these expressions from "pure fundamentalism"—in which Christian Pentecostals and Bible-believing fundamentalists make common cause for political purposes; or in which members of Sufi orders may in fact swell the ranks of fundamentalist movements; or in which Hindu nationalists borrow religious structures and concepts from the Abrahamic religions.

The concept of fundamentalism as used in this study refers to specific religious phenomena that have emerged in the twentieth century, particularly in the last several decades, in the wake of the success of modernization and secularization. For much of the nineteenth century and for the first half of the twentieth, the Western world was in the grip of a "culture of progress," the spreading confident belief that humanity, through the power of reason, the triumphant discoveries of science, the magnificent inventions of technology, and the secular-rational transformation of traditional institutions, was on a clear course toward the mastery of the evils of the human situation. In much of the contemporary world, religious communities and elites had been put on the defensive, retreating into cultural ghettos, or adapting to and compromising with the spreading secular world. Fundamentalist movements are the historical counterattacks mounted from these threatened religious traditions, seeking to hold ground against this spreading secular "contamination," and even to regain ground by taking advantage of the weaknesses of modernization. These weaknesses include costly and threatening "side effects" such as crime and "moral decay," the breakdown of the family and the community, environmental pollution, and the like.

The properties of fundamentalism as specified in this study have been derived and abstracted from recent and contemporary manifestations of the phenomenon in various parts of the world. The term was first used by Protestant ministers and scholars in the early decades of the twentieth century to refer to their commitment to adhere to the fundamental beliefs of Christianity in the face of the threats of modern science and the secular world, and their will to resist the modernizing, adaptive trends in their denominational establishments. The growth of militant ultra-Orthodox movements in Jewish and Israeli public life in the decades following World War II and the explosive Islamic resurgence in Iran, and elsewhere in the Islamic world, produced a version of the concept that traveled across religious traditions. Were these non-Christian movements the same, or even similar, kinds of movements? In recent years there has been a tendency for every expression of religious militance and extremism reported in the media, whatever the religious context, and wherever it may occur, to be called fundamentalism.

Since religious movements are shaped by the ideological and organizational properties of the religious traditions from which they emerge, and are constrained in other ways by cultural, economic, and political conditions and influences, it goes without saying that the blanket use of the concept of fundamentalism to encompass these phenomena all over the world creates problems. Not all religious traditions make clear separations between the sacred and the secular, have the same kinds of religious establishments, posit an "end of days" deliverance by a savior or a messiah, or have clearly formulated doctrines and codes imputed to divine origin. Nor have all religious traditions been confronted in the same way and degree by modernity and secularism. Secular modernity may have been introduced endogenously as in Europe and North America, through the industrial, technological, and scientific revolutions; or it may have been introduced by ethnoreligiously alien, imperialistic, and exploitative forces as in the Middle East, Asia, Africa, and Latin America. The program and organization of fundamentalist movements will have been affected by the auspices and structure of the secular threat to their survival on the one hand, and the structure and composition of their religious tradition on the other. Thus the fundamentalisms of Protestant or Roman Catholic Christianity, Sunni and Shi'ite Islam, and Judaism will differ in important respects in view of their very different histories, and they will be alike in certain other respects by virtue of their sharing in the Abrahamic tradition of monotheism, messianism, and sacred, codified doctrine and law. It is easier to establish a fundamentalist movement when religious fundamentals are spelled out explicitly in sacred texts and codes.

What is called fundamentalism in South Asia will bear the marks of Hindu, Sikh, and Buddhist religiosity, as well as the history of the various parts of the area—the movement of peoples and religions, their sub- and superordination, warfare, conquest, and changing boundaries. It should not surprise us that the concept is "culture bound," and that family resemblances become strained the farther one strays from the religious epicenter, from the point at which the movement was named and acquired its identity.

Religion is not the only matrix out of which fundamentalismlike movements emerge. Race, language, and culture may also serve as the bases of revivalism and militance. It is not unusual for ethnicity and religion to combine, as in Hinduism. We shall observe that Hindu fundamentalism is ethnonationalist as well as religious. The two spheres are not separated. This may also occur in Christian contexts such as Northern Ireland, where militant Protestantism is as much ethnonationalist as religious, in its opposition to the Catholic Irish.

On the question of the proper use of the term *fundamentalism,* a case can be made for limiting its use to its original manifestation in North American Protestantism at the turn of the present century, and its later development in the American cultural context. Or if its reference is expanded, then a case might be made to limit its applicability to the religions of the Abrahamic tradition because of their common origins and content. Finally, a case can be made for the inclusion of all instances of militant religiocultural movements that have come to be called fundamentalist, regardless of their heterogeneity. The justification for this third strategy is that simply through tapping this larger universe of militant, revivalist cultural movements, without procrustean anxieties, it becomes possible to spell out more precisely the essence of the genus fundamentalism, to determine the dimensions and degree of variation among species in the larger genus, and to uncover varieties erroneously assigned to the genus because of superficial resemblances. This "what's in a name" strategy, though seeming to be imprecise, actually is more likely to generate interesting hypotheses, through the introduction of more cultural and structural contrasts, than would be the case if the purist Protestant Christian strategy or the Abrahamic strategy were to be followed.

As the properties of fundamentalism have been specified in the course of this project, some nine characteristics—five ideological and four organizational—have recurred. They are described below.

Ideological Characteristics of Fundamentalism
Reactivity to the Marginalization of Religion

Fundamentalism is reactive to and defensive toward the processes and consequences of secularization and modernization, as they have penetrated the larger religious community itself. Protestants, Catholics, Muslims, Jews, Hindus, and Sikhs are losing their members to the secular world outright, or to relativism (the assumption any given religion is culture bound and thus relatively true or false) which leads, fundamentalists believe, to the same end: the erosion and displacement of true religion. Fundamentalism is a militant effort to counteract this trend.

What is being reacted against may include other consequences of secularization and relativism; some movements may be reacting to heightened ethnic or religious pluralism, for example, or to competing ideologies of nation. *But to qualify as genuine fundamentalism in our understanding, a movement must be concerned first with the erosion of religion and its proper role in society.* It must, therefore, be protecting some religious content, some set of traditional cosmological beliefs and associated norms of conduct.

A movement may seek to gain control of the state in order to resacralize or desecularize that powerful instrumentality. The movement may be ethnoreligiously preemptive—that is, it may seek to limit, suppress, or expel from the national community other ethnoreligious groupings (e.g., the Hindus versus the Muslims in India, or the Sinhala Buddhists versus the Hindu Tamils in Sri Lanka). Or the movement may be ethnonationally defensive—that is, it may seek to survive in the face of majority preemptive ethnoreligious movements (e.g., the Christians of south India versus the Hindus, or the Palestinian Muslims versus the occupying Israelis). In short, the threat to the religious tradition may come from the general processes of modernization and secularization, from other religions and/or ethnic groups, from a secular state (imperial or indigenous) seeking to secularize and delimit the domain of the sacred, or from various combinations of these.

This reactivity has a dual aspect. Fundamentalist movements also seize upon opportunities provided by the processes of secular modernization. That is, these movements react to secularization both by opposing it *and* by exploiting it for their own purposes. Here we note the fundamentalist adoption and mastery of modern means of communication and recruitment, the fundamentalist readiness to compete in an open marketplace of ideas and a society of fragmented loyalties, and the fundamentalist imitation of the late modern tendency to appropriate history and tradition selectively.

Selectivity

Fundamentalism is selective in three general modes. First, it is not merely defensive of the tradition, but selects and reshapes particular aspects of the tradition, especially those that clearly distinguish the fundamentalists from the mainstream. For this purpose Protestant fundamentalists of the United States select the apocalyptic prophesies to be found in the Books of Daniel and Revelation; the Italian Catholic movement Comunione e Liberazione selects Barthian theology, among other ideas; the Shi'ite movements of Iran, Iraq, and Lebanon select beliefs in the responsibility of learned jurists in political affairs in times of crisis.

Second, fundamentalisms select some aspects of modernity to affirm and embrace. Much of modern science may be accepted, for example, and modern technology such as radio, television, VCRs, telephone banks, and modern mailing techniques are effectively employed. In reacting to threats and in selecting the parts of the religiocultural tradition to be especially defended, fundamentalismlike movements such as the Hindu variant may create a kind of synthetic fundamentalism by imitating the theological and organizational structures of threatening religions and cultures. In other words, the fundamentalismlike movements, primarily those of the non-Abrahamic traditions, are creative and imitative in a special way, selecting elements from the enemy they oppose as well as from the religious tradition they seek to uphold.

Third, fundamentalisms select certain consequences or processes of modernity and single these out for special attention, usually in the form of focused opposition (as in the cases of the tourist trade in Egypt, abortion on demand in the United States, and "land for peace" in Israel). As with the other two types of selectivity, the precise content of what is selected may change with time. Just as different texts or traditions are selected, just as different positive features of modernity are embraced at different times, so, too, will different particular issues be contested at different times.

More important, these three modes of selectivity are interrelated, so that the retrieved texts match the significant issues, the modern methods chosen convey or support the fundamentalist opposition, and so on. Thus a different text and tactic will be selected if the issue is abortion rather than, say, evolution.

Moral Manicheanism

A dualistic or Manichean worldview is one in which reality is considered to be uncompromisingly divided into light, which is identified with the world of the spirit and of the good, and darkness, which is identified with matter and evil. Ultimately, light will triumph over darkness. For fundamentalist movements the world outside is contaminated, sinful, doomed; the world inside is a pure and redeemed "remnant." If the movement does not guarantee perfect purity to its members, it does provide certitude and a minimum standard by which members may be assured at least of protection from contamination. The sinful world outside may be graded in degrees of contamination. For the independent Baptists of Protestant Christianity, the world of evil would first include the mainstream denominational authorities who have compromised with the secular world, and then the secular world itself. For the Shi'ite Muslims the sinful world would include first the secularized Shi'ite Muslims, then the Sunni Muslims, and then the various infidel Satans great and small.

Absolutism and Inerrancy

The Torah, the Talmud, the halakha, the Qu'ran, the Shari'a, the Bible, and the Granth Sahib are of divine (inspired) origin, and true and accurate in all particulars. Here, of course, the degree to which there can be a belief in "inerrancy" or its analogues (e.g., papal infallibility, a privileged school of Islamic jurisprudence, etc.) depends on whether there is a sacred code, set of codes, or canon in the religious tradition. This is true of the Abrahamic religions which have a divinely transmitted law and canonical interpretations generally acknowledged within the entire religious community. In Eastern religions, gurus, monks, or priests may have a freer hand in retrieving sacred texts. In Hinduism, for example, texts are cited, but their normative character is more ambiguous and in the nature of the case less authoritative. Nevertheless, in these movements as well there is an affirmation of the absolute validity of the "fundamentals" of the tradition.

Fundamentalists, then, share a recognizable approach to religious sources. First, they steadfastly oppose hermeneutical methods developed by secularized philosophers or critics; these are not appropriately applied to sacred texts and traditions. This is not to say that fundamentalist interpretation itself is monolithic, only that it does not submit to the canons of critical rationality. Instead of following philological or historical methods, fundamentalists employ their own distinctive strategies of interpretation, including "hardened" and "updated" traditional approaches, designed in part to reify and preserve the absolutist character of the sacred text or tradition.

Millennialism and Messianism

History has a miraculous culmination. The good will triumph over evil, immortality over mortality; the reign of eternal justice will terminate history. The end of days, preceded by trials and tribulations, will be ushered in by the Messiah, the Savior; the Hidden Imam will come out of hiding. Messianism and millennialism promise victory to the believer, millennialism by promising an end to suffering and waiting, messianism by promising an all-powerful mediator. Abrahamic cosmology offers both; the non-Abrahamic traditions lack such fully elaborated assurances. The promised outcome for the Hindu movements and the Sinhala Buddhists are nations safeguarded from threatening alien penetrations, though the Kingdom of Ram, Khalistan, and the purely Buddhist "kingdom" of Sri Lanka have millennial overtones.

Organizational Characteristics of Fundamentalism

Elect, Chosen Membership

Fundamentalist movements tend to have an "elect," a chosen, divinely called membership, described variously as "the faithful," "the remnant," the "last outpost," the "Covenant keepers," those who "bear witness," who "walk with the Lord," and the like. Some movements divide their adherents into an elect—a fully committed inner group—and a periphery of sympathizers.

Sharp Boundaries

The theme of separation, of boundaries between the saved and the sinful, is general among these movements. The notion of a dividing wall and other spatial metaphors are characteristic markers. This wall may be physical in the sense in which the ultra-Orthodox haredi Jews require their members to live within easy walking distance of the synagogue, and who require that in each town, or community, extradomestic life be organized around the sanctified precincts of the *talmud Torah* (the school), the synagogue, the kosher slaughterhouse, and the *mikva* (the ritual bath). Separation may be implemented through audiovisual boundaries, through a distinctive vocabulary, and through control over access to the media.

Authoritarian Organization

Membership in fundamentalist movements is voluntary, and orthodox insiders are presumed to be equal. This imparts a certain weakness to the decision-making process. Bureaucracy in the sense of rational-legal division of power and competence has no place in this type of community, and its appearance is usually associated with a decline in mobilization and militance.

The typical form of fundamentalist organization is charismatic, a leader-follower relationship in which the follower imputes extraordinary qualities, heavenly grace, special access to the deity, deep and complete understanding of sacred texts to the great rav, the rebbe, the imam, the virtuous jurist, the minister. One man is set apart from all others. He may have trusted associates who implement his decisions, but they are not "officials" with clear divisions of competence and tenure. The distance between charismatic leaders and followers is illustrated in body language and rituals such as kissing the hand of the emir, or touching the prayer garment of the rebbe. This tension between voluntarism and equality and charismatic authority makes these movements somewhat fragile. Since there can be no loyal opposition, there is a tendency toward fragmentation.

Behavioral Requirements

Broadly speaking the member's time, space, and activity are a group resource, not an individual one. Elaborate behavioral requirements create a powerful affective dimension, an imitative, conforming dimension. There is distinctive music, hymnals, Hasidic chants, Qur'anic psalmodies. There are rules for dress—the Muslim white galabia and headdress, the haredi black coat and hat; long beards for the haredim, trimmed beards for the Muslims; shorts and *lathis* (staves) for members of the Hindu *shakhas* (small troops), turbans, uncut hair, and knee-length shorts for the Sikhs. Sinful behavior is proscribed in detail—rules about drinking, sexuality, appropriate speech, and the discipline of children abound. Likewise, there is censorship of reading material, and close supervision of listening and viewing practices. Dating, mate selection, and the like are strictly regulated.

Relations among Properties: Functional Explanations

In the discussion that follows we argue that these nine properties are not just a checklist, but that they are interrelated in important ways, that they constitute a functional system of interacting properties. Thus, reactivity is the basic impulse behind the other eight properties. Indeed, it constitutes the very essence of fundamentalist movements. They are by definition militant, mobilized, defensive reactions to modernity. Millennialism and messianism, on the other hand, may or may not be present. But when they are present they serve as powerful catalysts.

The seven remaining properties coalesce in three overlapping clusters—selectivity, boundaries, and election. Selectivity revolves around the need to pare down the tradition to its essentials, because of the danger that it faces. Boundaries relate to the challenge of keeping the group's identity in an open and often tempting society, a task rendered all the more arduous as the group cannot adequately reward its members in material or in "normal" status terms. Election is an answer to the challenge of how to maintain efficient decision making in a group that stresses equality among its members; this very equality is in turn an answer to the inadequate material and status resources possessed by the group. Each of these three draws into its cluster other properties that help sustain it.

Reactivity

By reactivity we refer to religious reactivity—a movement mobilizes against secularizing forces in the modern world. The traditional religion is attenuating, adherents are slipping away. Or the community that the fundamentalist movement seeks to defend is threatened with absorption into a pluralistic, areligious milieu. Reactivity draws other properties with it: selectivity, moral dualism, and inerrancy accompany the defense against threat. There are mixed cases in which reactivity is of an ethnonationalist-cultural sort, either of a majority preemptive variety like the Hindu Rashtriya Svayamsevak Sangh (RSS), the Sinhala Buddhists, and the Kach movement of the late Rabbi Kahane, or of the minority defensive sort like the Christians in south India or the Muslims in Soviet Asia. In these cases it is difficult to separate the religious from the cultural and ethnonationalist components. The movements themselves may differentiate the religious component, rework the pantheon a bit, rearrange the sacred texts in order to be more effectively deployed on the cultural battlefield. In such cases it is inaccurate to dismiss the religious motivations or aspects of the movement altogether, but it is important, on the other hand, to note that these religion-cum-ethnonationalist movements behave differently as a category than do movements inspired more exclusively by strictly religious considerations.

Table 16.1 shows how these groups in the Christian, Jewish, Islamic, and South Asian religious traditions perceive and react to the threats in their environments—threats against which they mobilize. The table shows that in almost all cases these movements perceive their own adaptive, compromising religious establishments as endangering the survival of true religion; they see the interventionist secular state as intrusive in the religious sphere, or as failing to provide support to it; and, finally,

TABLE 16.1

THE PERCEIVED ENEMIES OF FUNDAMENTALISM

Religious Movement	Religious Establishment	Secular State	Civil Society	Religious Competition	Ethno-national Competition	Imperialism and Neo-colonialism
Christian						
U.S. Protestant I	XX	X	X	X		
U.S. Protestant II	X	X	XX			
Guatemalan Pentecostal			X	XX		
U.S. Catholic traditionalist	XX					
Italian Comunione e Liberazione	X	X	XX			
South Indian		X	X		X	
Islamic						
Egyptian jama'at	X	XX	X	X		X
Algerian FIS	X	XX	X			X
Hamas	X		X		X	XX
Iranian Khomeini	X	XX	X	X		X
Iraqi Shi'ite	X	XX	X	X		
Lebanese Hizbullah			X	X	X	XX
Pakistani Jamaat-i-Islami	X	X	XX	X	X	X
Indian Tablighi Jamaat	X		X	X		
Jewish						
Haredi first wave	XX	X	X	X		
Haredi second wave	X	X	XX	X		
Habad	X	X	X	X	XX	
Gush Emunim		X	X		X	
Kach		XX	X		XX	
South Asian						
Hindu RSS		X	X	XX	XX	X
Sikh radical	X	XX	X	XX	X	
Sinhala Buddhist	X			X	XX	

they judge the civil society to be corrupting and corroding of religious belief and practice.

The exceptions to a pattern of seeing the religious establishment as the enemy are the Guatemalan Pentecostals, the South Asian Christians, the Hizbullah in Lebanon, the Israeli Gush Emunim and Kach, and the Hindu RSS. In each case special conditions explain why the religious establishment is not viewed as the enemy. Guatemalan Pentecostals have recently converted to Protestantism from their Catholic or pagan backgrounds; their former religion thus appears as a competing religion. The South Asian Christians are very loosely organized, lacking in much of an establishment to hate. The Shi'ite clergy in Lebanon are not sufficiently coherent to threaten the Hizbullah. The concerns of the Gush Emunim and Kach in Israel are nationalist and ethnic, as well as religious, and some rabbis of the "religious establishment" have lent support to their causes; in any case, the religious establishment is not the primary enemy. In the case of the Hindu RSS there is no religious establishment as such. Otherwise, regardless of religious tradition, fundamentalist movements are pitted against their mainstream establishments in a struggle to halt the trend toward secularism.

The second most commonly perceived enemy of fundamentalist movements is the secularizing state, with its rationalized bureaucracy, which has penetrated all spheres of life by introducing secular education and/or prohibiting religion and religious practices in the schools, and by permitting or encouraging sinful practices such as divorce, extramarital sex, homosexuality, abortion, and the like. Fundamentalists direct their antagonistic efforts toward the state as frequently as they oppose the religious establishment. Again the exceptions are easily explained. The Guatemalan regime (particularly under Ríos Montt) was supportive of the Pentecostals as an alternative to the left-inclined Catholic liberationists. In the case of the Hamas movement in the occupied territories, the Israeli state is viewed as an external imperialist state. In Lebanon there was no powerful state for the Hizbullah to fear or oppose.

Similarly, the civil society is viewed as a threat by the fundamentalists of all of these religious traditions. Among the forces working to alienate the faithful and particularly the young from their religious beliefs and affiliations, fundamentalists blame the corrupting media, including television, cinema, and secular literature; secular voluntary associations and political parties; and the world of secular education.

Fundamentalists, then, can be said to share this family resemblance: across the board they identify three antagonists—the tepid or corrupt religious establishment, the secular state, and secularized civil society—as objects of sustained opposition by true believers.

The last two columns of table 16.1 show how these movements differ in their goals and antagonisms. Thus the Christian movements—with the notable exception of the South Asian groups and the Ulster Protestants—are not involved in ethnonational competition, nor are they engaged in anti-imperialist, neocolonialist antagonisms. The South Asian Christians are defensive against the preemptive pressures of Hindu extremism. All of the Islamic movements are strongly anti-imperialist (Israel being the representative of "imperialism"); and the Lebanese Hizbullah, the Jamaat-i-Islami in Pakistan, and Hamas in the occupied territories are also in competition with ethnoreligious opponents. In the Lebanese case the conflict is with the Lebanese Christians; in the Pakistani case the conflict is with the Hindus, Christians, and Ahmadis; in the case of Hamas, conflict occurs with radical Jewish settlers. The Jewish fundamentalist movements (with the exception of some haredi movements) are in ethnonationalist conflict with the surrounding Arab peoples. The Hindus of India and the Sinhala Buddhists of Sri Lanka are involved in efforts to "purify" their societies religiously and ethnically, of Muslims and Christians in the case of the Hindus, and of the Hindu Tamils in the case of the Sri Lankans. The Sikhs are concerned with establishing a Sikh nation, cleared of Hindu domination.

Selectivity: Inerrancy, Boundaries, Behavior

Selectivity results from the particular state of siege in which the religious tradition finds itself. In such a state of siege, it is possible to defend only so much; one has to highlight the fundamentals. This is more likely to occur in a well-defined religious tradition where principles are explicit—the more codified and explicit the better. Jews can select from the Shulkhan 'Arukh, where one can emphasize certain rules; Muslims from the Shari'a, where one can pick one of the four schools, such as Hanbalism; Roman Catholics from certain papal encyclicals, or conciliar doctrines; Protestants from Christian eschatology, where one can pick either pre- or posttribulationism. But selectivity is possible even among the Sikhs, whose codified doctrine is rather limited. It is even possible among the Hindu and Buddhist "fundamentalists" who, in their efforts to compete with Western fundamentalists by imitation, may create a canon.

The companion to selectivity is inerrancy. In a doubting and cynical world one needs a reliable and sure proof. The doctrines are not only clear-cut, they are of divine origin or inspiration, and they are true beyond doubt. Inerrancy promotes unambiguous behavioral rules, enabling a movement to draw clear boundaries between the saved and the sinful, in behavior as well as doctrine. Selectivity may have the strategic purpose of setting the movement clearly apart from its enemies. Often "shocking" (to outsiders) themes are selected—as papal infallibility, the completely inerrant Bible, the Hidden Imam, the "sacred spark" in Hasidism and among the Jewish radicals of Gush Emunim.

Boundaries: Behavior, Election, Manicheanism

Having sharp boundaries enables a group to maintain the cohesion of a more or less egalitarian elite of the virtuous. This is crucial because the core group, being beleaguered, cannot reward adherents materially or with power, but only with status. If group demands on time and conduct are too heavy, gradations may be created—elect, auxiliary, periphery—as among the haredim, Comunione e Liberazione, the Jama'at. The absence of a core may weaken the group, as in the case of the Tablighi Jamaat of Pakistan, in contrast to missionary-type groups such as the Habad and Comunione, which have a strong core and a broad periphery. The sense of being both elect and beleaguered is amplified by moral dualism. However, moral dualism or Manichaeanism is by no means a distinguishing mark of fundamentalism. All of our cases manifest dualism, simply as a consequence of being militant. What distinguishes fundamentalist dualism is that it is directed more strongly against drifters from one's own tradition (e.g., sinful Muslims) than against competing religions, atheists, and agnostics. Thus Hamas in Gaza fights "Westoxicated," morally corrupted Muslims first, and infidel Israelis second.

Election: Authority, Charisma, Selectivity

To operate effectively, selectivity requires authority. If one is to keep the core of the elect happy while the group is lacking in remunerative and coercive power, however, the membership should be as egalitarian as possible, equal and sharing in virtue. The solution to this dilemma is to have as few leaders as possible, that is, a "small hierarchy" (in Mary Douglas's terms), at the apex of which there is leadership of even higher and undisputed virtue, that is charisma, touched with divine or supernatural grace. One thinks here of the Hasidic rabbi, or the emir of the Muslim jama'a. The development of a bureaucratic hierarchy may signal the transformation and possible decline of a movement, as in the case of the Jewish movement Aguda haredim. The movement loses much of its "enclave" solidarity and militance, its cohesiveness, once it becomes bureaucratized.

This process of bureaucratization has affected several fundamentalist groups, especially those of longer duration and multiple generations. The Muslim Brotherhood in Egypt is one of several examples; bureaucratization set in after the assassination of Hasan al-Banna in 1948; and today the original, noncompromising fervor of the mainstream Brotherhood has waned as it has participated in "mainstream" politics (even while spawning radical offshoots, which reject the bureaucratizing, compromising tendencies of the main body).

Nevertheless, some groups retain their fundamentalist character over generations. Fundamentalist Baptists in the United States, for example, succeeded in combining the decentralized authority of the local community governed by a charismatic pastor with a measure of control of the denominational bureaucracy in a number of key areas (teaching materials, nomination of pastors from an approved pool of candidates, etc.).

The charismatic leader may be a "cleric"—a minister, priest, rabbi, guru, and so forth—and there has been a decline in the role of the laity in clerically led groups such as the haredim and some Protestant and Catholic movements. But clerical leadership is not an absolute necessity; among Sunnis, for example, the ulama in general were discredited earlier in this century by collaboration with the powers that be, and self-taught charismatic leaders emerged from among the laity.

Charismatic leadership is not always a source of strength, nor is it the only source of strength. Splits may occur when two charismatic leaders clash. Or when the charismatic leader disappears, leaving no real heir, the internal egalitarian core may be weakened, and with it the movement as a whole. This has been the case with Rabbi Kahane and the Kach movement, with Rabbi Kook the Younger and Gush Emunim, and with the Ayatollah Khomeini in Iran. It will also likely be the case with Habad, now that its nonagenarian leader, Rabbi Isaac Schneerson, has passed from the scene (May 1994). The demise of a charismatic leader could even endanger Agudat Yisrael with the death of its leader, Rabbi Schach.

Millennialism and Messianism

Messianism and millennialism are not always present in fundamentalist movements. Movements can flourish when messianism is in a minor key (e.g., Comunione e Liberazione, the Sunnis, the haredim, the radical Sikhs) or even absent. Yet it certainly contributes to morale when millennial beliefs are strong (Habad, Gush Emunim, Protestant Christians). The expectation of the end of normal history, when the rules of the game will be changed, endows a beleaguered movement with the expectation of ultimate victory. Hence risks and costs are bearable. And as this miraculous outcome is to be preceded, more often than not, by an apocalypse, it also confirms, in the short term, the validity of the group's pessimistic vision of historic reality. Yet even groups where messianism is in a minor key tend toward an apocalyptic interpretation of reality in moments of crisis. Thus weakly millennialist groups in Islam and in Judaism developed apocalyptic visions during the 1991 Gulf War, comparable in power to those of their Protestant counterparts who are strongly millennialist.

Examining the Cases

The first task is to sort out the twenty-two movements of table 16.1, according to the ideological and organizational traits presented above. For the purposes of tables 16.2 and 16.3 we have grouped the various Sunni jama'at of the Middle East and North Africa together, and the Shi'ite movements of Iran, Lebanon, and Iraq together, giving us eighteen clusters of movements. This enables us to begin creating a fundamentalist typology. The scheme has three values—high, low, and absent.

If we run our eyes over tables 16.2 and 16.3, ten of the eighteen clusters of movements appear to have the defining characteristics of fundamentalism. Among the

TABLE 16.2

IDEOLOGICAL RATINGS OF FUNDAMENTALIST MOVEMENTS

Religious Tradition	Reactivity	Selectivity	Dualism	Inerrancy	Millennialism
Christian					
U.S. Protestant	High	High	High	High	High
Catholic traditionalist	High	High	High	High	Low
Comunione e Liberazione	High	High	High	High	Low
Guatemalan Protestant	Absent	Low	High	High	Low
Ulster Protestant	High	High	High	Low	Low
South Indian	High	High	High	High	Low
Islamic					
Sunni jama'at	High	High	High	High	Low
Shi'ite	High	High	High	High	High
Jamaat-i-Islami	High	High	High	High	Low
Tablighi Jamaat	Low	Low	Low	Low	Low
Hamas	High	High	High	Low	Low
Jewish					
Haredi	High	High	High	High	Low
Habad	High	High	High	High	High
Gush Emunim	Low	High	High	High	High
Kach	Low	High	High	Absent	Low
South Asian					
Hindu RSS	Low	Low	High	Absent	Low
Sikh radical	High	High	High	High	Low
Sinhala Buddhist	Low	Low	High	Absent	Low

TABLE 16.3

ORGANIZATIONAL RATINGS OF RELIGIOUS MOVEMENTS

Religious Tradition	Elect-Chosen	Boundaries	Charismatic Leadership	Authority/ Behavior
Christian				
U.S. Protestant	High	High	Low	High
Catholic traditionalist	Low	Low	Low	Low
Comunione e Liberazione	High	High	High	Low
Guatemalan Protestant	Low	High	High	Low
Ulster Protestant	Low	Low	High	Low
South Indian	Low	Low	High	Low
Islamic				
Sunni jama'at	High	High	High	High
Shi'ite	High	High	High	High
Jamaat-i-Islami	Low	High	Low	High
Tablighi Jamaat	Low	Low	Absent	Low
Hamas	High	High	High	High
Jewish				
Haredi	High	High	High	High
Habad	High	High	High	High
Gush Emunim	High	Low	High	High
Kach	Low	Low	Low	Low
South Asian				
Hindu RSS	Low	Low	High	High
Sikh radical	Low	Low	High	High
Sinhala Buddhist	Absent	Low	Absent	Low

Christian cases the U.S. Protestants have high ratings in all particulars except charismatic leadership, which, although low, is still present. Similarly, the Italian Catholic movement, Comunione e Liberazione, has all the specified properties and has more highs than lows. Among the Islamic movements the Middle East/North African Sunni jama'at and Shi'ite cases, Hamas, and the Jamaat-i-Islami of South Asia come out high on these defining characteristics. Among the Jewish cases the haredim, Habad, and Gush Emunim fall in this same category. There is only one case with high ratings among the South Asian religions—the Sikhs. This reflects the fact that our definition of the properties of fundamentalism has been derived from a focus on Christian, Islamic, and Jewish cases, all of which have sacred texts and codified religious laws and share in a millennial-messianic cosmology. Inerrancy is more likely to be asserted where there are well-established sacred texts and codes. Millennialism and messianism are more likely to be present in fundamentalist movements coming out of religious traditions that share an end-of-days cosmology, a viewpoint not present in the South Asian religions. Both millennialism and messianism are present in the Abrahamic movements. Messianism is not present in the South Asian cases, and millennialism only on a limited scale. It is of interest that one South Asian movement, the Sikhs, has a sacred text—the Granth Sahib—and in most other respects that movement fits the category.

Abrahamic Fundamentalism

Thus similarities in religious tradition attributable to a common heritage explain the association of fundamentalism, as we have defined it, with Christianity, Islam, and Judaism. We speak of movements sharing in these characteristics, in these religious traditions, as Abrahamic fundamentalisms. Fundamentalism was defined from an examination of Abrahamic cases, since it was first observed and studied in these traditions. Militant, restorative-revivalist religious movements in other religious traditions, which do not share important features of Abrahamic theology and practice, or where some features have been introduced imitatively, may perhaps be called fundamentalist-like movements. Though not an Abrahamic religion, the Sikh case shares almost all of these specified characteristics. If we include the Sikhs in this category, we can account for ten of the eighteen movements listed in tables 16.2 and 16.3.

As we have suggested, the defining properties of fundamentalism are connected in complicated ways, with one precipitating or requiring the others. And when the movement is in decline, as one property attenuates, so do others. While we have been examining these properties here in synchronic terms, as dialectically interdependent, we can also examine these movements with a diachronic or genetic logic as they emerged and acquired these characteristics, each creating its own "package." We offer a brief sketch of these ten movements to make this point.

Among the Christian groups the *U.S. Protestant fundamentalists* emerged in the first decades of the present century in reaction to rapid urbanization and industrialization, the spread of education and science, the decline of belief in sacred texts and religious tradition, and attenuating religious discipline. The fundamentalist reaction took the form of affirmation by conservative Protestant clerics and scholars of the inerrancy of the Bible, with emphasis on the biblical account of the Creation, and the promise of the return of the Savior. Millennial or apocalyptic passages of the Old and New Testaments, promising salvation after an end-of-days tribulation, were selected. Fundamentalist discourse constituted an elect—a saved "remnant" separated from lapsed Christians and the secular world by sharp boundaries, Manichaean beliefs, and the elect's pious behavior. Bible-believing Christians were governed in individual, autonomous congregations by authoritative ministers, often known for their charismatic preaching, who supervised the community's interpretations of sacred sources and divine purpose.

Comunione e Liberazione emerged in Milan in a time of rapid social change and explosive political division. Although in time it responded directly to these challenges, the movement developed as a reaction against secularization. Father Luigi Giussani became well known in the 1950s and 1960s for his classes and study groups in which modern authors from Dostoyevsky to Camus were sympathetically read and subjected to a Christian critique. The movement grew in the 1960s and 1970s primarily among university students, attracting many who were disillusioned with revolutionary radicalism and the moral corruption of Italian society. The intellectual attack on secularization was thus joined to a political problem and an organizational solution. Revolutionary protest was bound to fail because there was no one to protest against, but the alienation of modern life could be overcome by the creation of communities based on common belief and shared activities. These communities in turn could conquer and transform society, and Comunione e Liberazione developed programs and publications devoted to a wide range of issues as well as extensive missionary activities.

At the center of all this is Father Giussani's charismatic authority; the *scuole* or communities of Comunione e Liberazione are modeled on the first ones in Milan and privilege a selection of Catholic teachings, largely interpreted by Giussani's writings, which in turn emphasize the role of the laity in renewing "Christendom" through communal living and the personal experience of Jesus Christ. Boundaries are maintained by personal ties (new members adopt a big brother from those who already belong), daily contacts, frequent devotions, and study groups within the community and by mutual support and elaborate personal networks within secular society, from professors to Christian Democrats.

The Islamic *Sunni jama'at* movements of Egypt, Syria, and Tunisia represent reactions to Arab secular nationalism fostered in the nation-building movements of the immediate post–World War II decades, and resulting from the mass exodus to urban centers during this same period. Since the state was the prime instigator of this social revolution, the clergy and Islamic laity selected the part of the Shari'a most suspicious of state authority, the Islamic legal school (Hanbalism), as inerrant doctrine. The primary question raised by the movement, whether the state is Muslim, was answered in the negative. Faith in Islam among the people is said to be undermined by the secular state. The first order of the day for the movement's leadership was to organize the "remnant" against an all-penetrating state, and against contamination by lax nominal Muslims. Hence the movement's concern with boundary maintenance and the enforcement of behavioral requirements. Authority is in the hands of the founders, usually charismatic figures (Sayyid Qutb in Egypt, Marwan Hadid in Syria, Rashid al-Ghannushi in Tunisia). Millennialism is a minor element, but dualism is strong against fellow Muslims, especially Westernized elites.

The *Jamaat-i-Islami* of Pakistan was founded by an authoritarian leader, Maulana Maududi, who was not charismatic but who provided a religiopolitical idiom for Islamic fundamentalism. His ideology was dualistic, drawing sharp boundaries between Muslims and infidels. In developing an Islamic politics, he selected Islamic concepts that would be amenable to political constructions.

The *Shi'ite* fundamentalist movement of Iran also represents a reaction to state-instigated secularization under Reza Shah Pahlavi, coupled with industrial development and urbanization. The movement had a strong charismatic figure from the outset in the Ayatollah Khomeini, who enjoyed integral authority over a small hierarchy of leading ulama. Khomeini selected the doctrine of the Guardianship of the Jurist and the hitherto minor activist strand in the Shi'ite tradition. Dualism is very strong, with the elites (political and otherwise) and, secondarily, the lapsed coming in for condemnation; outside Islam are the various greater and lesser Satans. The behavioral requirements of the movements are heavy and centered on political action. The strategy was to build strong boundaries around an elect, the saved remnant, and then to employ these reliable forces in political action and missionary activity in the society at large.

Messianism is present in the form of the expectation of the ultimate return of the Hidden Imam, and in the sense that Khomeini was viewed as the "just jurist" and the "vicar" of the Hidden Imam.

The founder of *Hamas,* Shaykh Yassin, was reacting to laxity in belief and practice among fellow Palestinian Muslims; he and his followers were alarmed by the erosion of an outside boundary, through Israeli domination of Palestine. Both infidel and modern, the way of life under Israeli occupation contaminates the Muslim community. Hence two sets of stringent behavioral rules emerged, prohibiting "innovations" and any contact other than economic with the Israelis. Hamas selects an activist approach out of the neo-Hanbali tradition, which would lead its members to holy war. The Hanbali text becomes inerrant. Hence a very strong dualism. The charismatic authority of the founder, Shaykh Yassin, legitimizes this selection and the rules that follow therefrom. Around the Shaykh an elite of the elect is formed with sharp, sometimes clandestine boundaries, dedicated to imposing this rule.

The emergence of *haredi* Jewish fundamentalism can be dated to the formation of the Agudat Yisrael in 1912. The Agudat brought together the yeshivot, surviving local Jewish communities, and Hasidic courts of Eastern Europe in reaction to the depopulation of the shtetl at the turn of the century. In the more liberal atmosphere of those decades Jews assimilated in substantial numbers to secular culture and migrated to Eastern European cities, or emigrated to other European countries and in very large numbers to the United States. Secular nationalist aspirations were fostered by Zionism, and atheistic socialist views by the Bund. The leading figure in this reaction to secularization was the Hafetz Haim, who sought to bring together the "remnant of Israel" as an elect, guided and protected by the Shulkhan 'Arukh as an inerrant text, selected and adapted for vulnerable Jewish life in anonymous urban centers, in the czarist army, and in the United States. Fear and hostility were directed against lapsed Jews rather than against Gentiles. *Frumkeit* (pious behavior) was required—wearing the ritual undergarment, use of phylacteries in morning prayer, strict observance of the Sabbath, and the like. The maintenance of boundaries was urged; in cities one should settle in the immediate neighborhood of the synagogue in order to avoid violation of the Sabbath and the temptations of mixed neighborhoods. One should not socialize with Gentiles after 5:00 P.M., since there might be temptations of various kinds. Messianism was present in a minor key, but as a remote prospect about which one could do nothing. It was kept in check by recalling the catastrophe of the false messiah, Shabtai Zvi, in the seventeenth century. Rabbinical authority in the yeshivot was based on learning. The greatest and most inspired scholars such as the Hafetz Haim were endowed with charisma.

Under its first four rebbes *Habad* (the Lubavitcher Hasidim) was a very traditional movement. In the late nineteenth century, under the fifth rebbe, the movement became mobilized and militant in reaction to the depopulation of the shtetl because of assimilation and emigration. Charismatic authority was present from the very beginning because of the Hasidic mystical tradition. The movement was missionary toward the larger Jewish community, with an elect surrounding the rebbe and implementing his programs. Thus the boundaries of Habad established an enclave and a periphery. The halakha and the Tanya (the sayings of the first Lubavitcher rebbe) were selectively plumbed. Charismatic authority was very strong, as was messianism. Behavioral regulations for the enclave were very strict, with dress fixed in the style of the eighteenth century, and with ritual garments and the use of phylacteries in morning prayer required.

The first nuclei out of which *Gush Emunim* formed took shape after the 1967 war when what seemed to be the miraculous victories of the Israeli forces were viewed as ushering in the messianic era. The Yom Kippur War in 1973 made these prospects seem problematic, but it was interpreted by Rabbi Kook the Younger as meaning that Jews must play an active role in assuring the triumph of the messianic era. Charisma and messianism thus were built into Gush Emunim from its very formation. The members were an elect, chosen for this last holy role. The one mitzvah (commandment) selected by the Gush as the most important in the age of Redemption was the reestablishment of the Jews in the entire land of biblical Israel. The stringent behavioral requirement was to establish settlements on the West Bank and the Gaza Strip. The boundaries of the Gush were not sharp; members were ready to collaborate with lapsed Jews just as long as they shared their goals. Dualism was expressed in the attitude toward Arabs.

Though not in the Abrahamic tradition the *Sikh radicals* share in these fundamentalist qualities in almost all respects. The Sikh radicals originated out of groups reacting to the growing secularization of their community in postindependence India as well as to the encroachment by the dominant Hindu community upon the Sikhs. They selected the Granth Sahib as a salient and inerrant text out of the tradition, a text governing behavior (dress, diet, conduct). They declare the whole community to be the elect, there being no sharp internal boundaries. From the very beginning dualism vis-à-vis the Hindus was high. Authority by tradition is in charismatic hands, that is, gurus and sants.

The remaining eight cases either belong in a fundamentalistlike category or are not fundamentalist movements at all.

Fundamentalistlike Movements

The fundamentalistlike movements tend to be those in which ethnocultural features combine with religion. These movements are inspired less by strictly religious considerations than the actual fundamentalisms profiled above. Whereas fundamentalist movements are most at home in a religiocultural enclave, but find themselves drawn into politics as a result of their religious beliefs, fundamentalistlike movements tend to reverse the process. That is, they reach for religious justifications, tactics, and organizational patterns in order to mount the most effective opposition possible, based on ethnicity, community, and religion. These movements include the Ulster Protestants, South Indian Christians, Hindu RSS, Sinhala Buddhists, and Kach movement in Israel. The militance and reactivity of these movements is not primarily toward modernization and secularization but tends to be an affirmation of ethnonational—identity in the face of threatening ethnonational minorities, or preemptive ethnonational majorities.

The *Ulster Protestants* are ethnonationalist, anti–Catholic. On one hand they exhibit strong fundamentalist characteristics. The founder of the Free Presbyterian Church and the Democratic Unionist Party, the Reverend Ian Paisley, is a strong charismatic leader whose personal authority has almost single-handedly forged the movement; a "small hierarchy" of supporting ministers echo his teachings. Likewise, Paisley's rhetoric is reactive and defensive; he traces his movement to the seventeenth century, when the cycle of "oppression" began (at Catholic as well as British hands). Properties of fundamentalism such as inerrancy, millennialism, and so forth, are present. On the other hand, Paisleyism is clearly an ethnonationalist movement: followers rally around the political rather than the strictly religious cause; the religious rhetoric and mobilizing capacity is generally understood to be at the service of ethnonationalist politics. In the absence of the ethnonationalist component, in other words, it is doubtful that this kind of religious "fundamentalism" would have emerged.

The *Christian movements of South India* similarly are threatened by Hinduizing and syncretic propensities in their own communities, and the preemptive ethnonationalism of the Hindu majority. These movements are secondarily threatened by modernization and secularization, primarily through the activities of the Indian state. In their active competition they have developed fundamentalist traits such as inerrancy, millennialism, and charismatism. In their efforts to compete with the Hindu pantheon with its aggressive and bloodthirsty deities, the Christian movements have turned Jesus and the saints into militant and avenging forces.

The *Guatemalan neo-Pentecostals* are unlike fundamentalists in that they are not retrieving or defending their age-old religious tradition; to the contrary, they have rejected Roman Catholicism for something relatively new, the evangelicalism imported by missionaries over a century ago, but given a new profile by the Ríos Montt regime. Yet this new profile includes a fundamentalistlike emphasis on biblical inerrancy, strong moral requirements, millennialism, and support of a political order that seems to favor their growth.

The *Hindu RSS* is a preemptive ethnonationalist-cultural movement mobilized against the dilution of Hindu identity by the penetration of the secular, pluralist Indian state, and against the inroads of Islam and Christianity. In reaction to these threats it has created a kind of synthetic fundamentalism, extracting a religious component out of Hindu culture, according priority to the god Rāma, and privileging certain ancient texts.

Sinhala Buddhist extremism is not a religious mobilization against modernization and secularization, but rather a movement among the Sinhala-Buddhist majority against the threat of the Hindu Tamils emigrating from South India. It is much more of a political movement than a religious one, concerned with domination of the Sinhala state and the Sri Lankan territory. The Sinhala Buddhists are seeking to repossess the northern parts of Sri Lanka from the Hindu Tamils. Their readiness to resort to violence on a large scale separates them from their own Buddhist heritage.

The *Kach movement* of Rabbi Kahane is to be understood as a quasi-Fascist movement, drawing on strong antiestablishment sentiment—directed at both the Right and

Left in Israeli politics—and ready to engage in street hooliganism, terrorism, and generally extrasystem, extraparliamentary, and extralegal action. It laid claim to the Maccabean and Zealot tradition in Jewish history, advocating the expulsion of the Arabs from biblical Israel, attacking the ruling parties as having become Hellenized and "Gentilized." Though Rabbi Kahane favored the elimination of all forms of Judaism other than Orthodoxy, specific religious interests and activities played a small role in the movement.

These fundamentalistlike movements are primarily ethnonationalist movements, mobilized as preemptive majorities against the threat of minorities; or as minority ethnoreligious movements defending themselves against a majority nativist threat. In these cases religion is not separated from other cultural practices (e.g., Hindu India) or where it is, as in Northern Ireland, it may be instrumental to ethnonationalist goals. The affirmation of religious tradition against secularization is a secondary theme.

Nonfundamentalist Movements

Some cases may have superficial resemblances to fundamentalism, but properly do not belong in the category. If the Tablighi Jamaat of South Asia had been included among the paradigmatic cases, it would strain the definition of the category. In tables 17.2 and 17.3 it was evaluated as low in all nine characteristics. It was formed near Delhi in the 1920s by an Islamic religious scholar, Maulana Ilyas, who wished to correct the lax and Hinduizing practices of the Islamic population in northern India. The local population had been converted to Islam, but only partially: most of their rituals were based on Hindu culture. They could not recite their prayers correctly; there were no religious schools; they had few contacts with the centers of Islamic culture in India. The new movement sought to deal with these problems by missionary activity, carried on by volunteers. The missionary activity involves the teaching of prayers, rituals, and elementary knowledge of Islam, by small mobile units of volunteers sent out to the villages. Organization of the Tablighi Jamaat is informal. There are no full-time workers. There is no clear-cut separatism or boundaries. The leadership of Maulana Ilyas was expressed in saintliness and dedication, a low-key charisma. The aims of the movement were to make better Muslims out of the half-Hindu peasantry of northern India and, as time went on, to protect them from the secular influences in the area. The extent of organization is minimal and communitarian, involving intense personal relationships among the leaders and the rank and file. Membership takes the form of participation in missionary activity. Moral suasion rather than exercise of authority is the mode of decision making. A single small volume is distributed to villagers, containing the "Tablighi curriculum," with appropriate material from the Qur'an and the Shari'a. Each member is asked to contribute forty days of missionary work each year, traveling to neighboring areas, delivering simple sermons, and exemplifying proper Islamic behavior. The movement is not activist or political in its aspirations. Its program is limited to the improvement and intensification of Islamic religious practice. Millennialism is relatively low-key, but nevertheless present. The movement is very successful. A recent international conference, held near Lahore, attracted more than a million Muslims from all over the world.

The *U.S. Catholic traditionalist* case is an example of a strong fundamentalist ideology in search of an organizational structure, resources, and personnel—in short, an ideology in search of a movement. (Contrast the rankings in tables 16.2 and 16.3). Neither the host religion nor the American religious culture proved useful to the mounting of a fundamentalist movement; these macrostructural elements *inhibited* traditionalists from exploiting fully the confusion and discontent felt by conservative Catholics in the years immediately following the Second Vatican Council (1962–65). Resources were abundant in American Catholicism of the twentieth century, but they did not become available to the postconciliar traditionalist movement, for a number of reasons. Catholicism had experienced a revival leading to a newfound prominence and respectability on the American scene in the 1940s and 1950s. The revival was conducted under the ideological canopy of Vatican-sponsored neo-Thomism. Thus, for all of their technical innovation and lay involvement, the new Catholic Action groups actually perpetuated and deepened a cosmology centered on the triumphant true Church of Christ, identical with the Roman church under the headship of the magisterium (the bishops in full communion with the pope). In short, the "cadres" trained in these revival movements were inclined to take their cues from clerical leadership and, ultimately, from Rome; this did not change after the Council. Meanwhile, the GI Bill made higher education accessible to a generation of Catholics, who moved to the suburbs in great numbers and adapted to middle-class American culture and lifestyle.

To the future members of the traditionalist movement, Vatican II seemed to lift up the more revolutionary elements of the revival, emphasizing an apostolic rather than a medieval paradigm of the church and all but abandoning the traditional emphasis on absolute, exclusivist truth claims. Ideological boundaries between members of "the One True Church" and "heretics" were erased almost overnight. The worst suspicions of the traditionalists were confirmed by the "triggering event" of Catholic traditionalism, the implementation of the Novus Ordo Mass. But the movement never really took off, in large part because of organizational problems.

Among cases considered elsewhere in the Fundamentalism Project series, the *Ecuadoran Puruha* do not exhibit selective reaffirmations of tradition in response to the threats of modernization and secularization. Rather than reacting against modernity, affiliation with the new movements is a step toward the modern world in the sense of the adoption of orderly family life and sober work habits.

Islamic movements in the Soviet Union since glasnost and in the early post-Soviet era have been marked by the revival of religious practice and belief, and ethnonationalist fragmentation, with control being decentralized to the different Islamic regions—Kazakhstan, the North Caucasus, Azerbaijan, and the like. There is a tendency for individual mosques to be taken over by different ethnic groups. Ideologically the revival of Islam under glasnost rejects the adaptive strategy followed by the Muslim clergy under the old Soviet Union; the new ideological trends in this period were revivalist and traditionalist rather than fundamentalist. In some cases such movements are anti-Russian in the ethnic sense, but they are not organized, focused reactive movements possessed of a charismatic leadership, clear lines of authority, and a mythologized or aggrandized enemy against whom they preserve purity and erect boundaries. Thus they are not, at this writing, even fundamentalistlike.

Conclusion

In this chapter we have examined the characteristics of oppositional movements in Christian, Islamic, Jewish, and South Asian religious traditions. We have established that the first three types of oppositional movements, descended from the Abrahamic tradition, share close ideological and organizational family resemblances. We also suggest that these common ideological and organizational characteristics tend to cohere, to require one another, in a functional logic. Among South Asian cases, the Sikhs come closest to fundamentalism.

We describe a second category of movements exhibiting these characteristics as fundamentalistlike. In most of these cases, ethnonational considerations dominate religious elements. These cases include Hindu and Buddhist nationalist movements, as well as Ulster Protestants. Interestingly, many Islamic cases tend to be borderline between these two categories in the sense that they combine strong religious fundamentalist commitments with strong nationalist, anti-imperialist tendencies. The Sikhs are an interesting deviant case arising at the point of historical contact and synergism between Hindu and Islamic culture. The religious "host" of Sikh radicalism thus had acquired Abrahamic qualities through culture contact and conflict. Like its Islamic counterparts, it also combines religion with nationalism.

Other movements assigned to the fundamentalistlike category, including Guatemalan and South Indian Pentecostals, are activist, but they are religiously closer to evangelical and Pentecostal strains of their respective host religions.

As we shall see in chapter 17 and 18, however, fundamentalist and fundamentalistlike movements share four identifiable patterns of activism in relation to the "world" outside the movement. Before turning to these patterns, however, we must attempt to account for fundamentalist and fundamentalistlike movements by examining the conditions and circumstances under which they originate and grow into powerful forces in the contemporary world.

Notes

1. Ernest Nagel, *The Structure of Science: Problems in the Logic of Scientific Explanation,* 2d ed. (Indianapolis: Hackett Publishing Co., 1979), pp. 20 ff.

2. See, for example, Gideon Aran, "Jewish Zionist Fundamentalism: The Bloc of the Faithful in Israel (Gush Emunim)," in Martin E. Marty and R. Scott Appleby, eds., *Fun-*

damentalisms Observed (Chicago: University of Chicago Press, 1991), pp. 272 ff.; and T. N. Madan, "The Double-Edged Sword: Fundamentalism and the Sikh Religious Tradition," in the same volume, pp. 612 ff.

3. Functional explanations are to be found especially in volume 4, Martin E. Marty and R. Scott Appleby, eds., *Accounting for Fundamentalisms* (Chicago: University of Chicago Press, 1994), especially Robert Frykenberg, "Accounting for Fundamentalism in South Asia: Ideology and Institutions in Historical Perspective," pp. 591–616; Samuel Heilman, "Quiescent and Active Fundamentalism: The Jewish Cases," pp. 173–96; and Nancy Ammerman, "Accounting for Christian Fundamentalism: Social Dynamics and Rhetorical Strategies," pp. 149–70.

4. See Emmanuel Sivan, chapter 1 of this volume, for elaboration of these points.

5. Ernest Nagel, "Methodological Problems in the Social Sciences," in Nagel, *Structure of Science;* R. B. Braithwaite, *Scientific Explanation* (Cambridge: University of Cambridge Press, 1953); Carl Hempel, *Aspects of Scientific Explanation* (New York: Free Press, 1965).

6. Karl Popper, *Objective Knowledge: An Evolutionary Approach* (Oxford: Clarendon Press, 1972), pp. 210 ff.; Abraham Kaplan, *The Conduct of Inquiry* (San Francisco: Chandler, 1964).

7. Arend Lijphart, "Comparative Politics and the Comparative Method," *American Political Science Review* 65 (September 1971): 3; David Collier, "The Comparative Method," in Ada Finifter, ed., *Political Science: The State of the Discipline* (Washington, D.C.: American Political Science Association, 1993), p. 112.

8. Alexander George and Timothy McKeown, "Case Studies and Theories of Organizational Decision-Making" in *Advances in Information Processes in Organizations,* 2: 21–58. See also Harry Eckstein, "Case Study and Theory in Political Science," in *Regarding Politics* (Berkeley: University of California Press, 1992).

9. David Collier quotes these observations from a personal communication from Adam Przeworski ("The Comparative Method," p. 112.)

10. Cf. Gary King, Robert Keohane, and Sitney Verba, *Scientific Inference in Qualitative Research* (Cambridge: Cambridge University Press, 1994), pp. 167 ff. Their concluding chapter, "Causal Inference with Few Cases," summarizes and evaluates the literature cited in the present introduction, and provides a set of standards that may be used in judging the validity of the arguments we advance in this chapter.

11. Richard T. Hughes, "Introduction: On Recovering the Theme of Recovery," in Richard T. Hughes, ed., *The American Quest for the Primitive Church* (Urbana: University of Illinois Press, 1988), p. 3.

Explaining Fundamentalisms

Gabriel A. Almond, Emmanuel Sivan, and R. Scott Appleby

In chapter 16 we identified in abstract terms the characteristic traits of "fundamentalism." When we observe these traits in action—when we look at fundamentalism in its particular historical manifestations—we see that fundamentalist *movements* are quite complex phenomena. They are founded and organized, they develop programs and devise tactics which are more or less successful in acquiring members and resources and achieving their goals. Whatever one may posit of generic "fundamentalism," actual fundamentalist and "fundamentalist-like" movements come in a confounding variety of shapes, sizes, and types; they are found in different settings. Yet these disparate movements share not only a set of identifiable traits, but a certain "logic" in their unfolding. They follow certain patterns of relating to the world. Furthermore, the pattern followed by a given movement at a given time is determined by a set of factors which we classify under the rubrics of structure, chance, and choice. In this chapter we will describe the patterns themselves; and we will explain the ways that structure, chance, and choice combine to determine the patterns. In the next chapter we will illustrate this "logic" of fundamentalism by reference to specific cases.

Patterns of Relating to the World

All fundamentalists, by our definition, intentionally *interact* with the outside world in some way. Different fundamentalist movements—or the same movement at different times in its life—relate to the world according to various patterns or modes of behavior. Some spread throughout the society gradually; others attempt to overthrow their enemies in a dramatic, concerted campaign; still others may withdraw to the periphery, or decline, or even cease to exist.

An objection may be raised at this point. Are separatist fundamentalists really acting in relation to the outside world? Indeed, they are. The separatism of the enclave is an important mode of fundamentalism, and it is also a form of fundamentalist interaction with the outside world. This is true in two ways. First, fundamentalists are religious sectarians who build their enclaves with one eye on the threatening enemy. Fundamentalist parents form their children with the goal of strengthening them to resist the enemy's lures; fundamentalist movements recruit their members on the basis of a sophisticated critique of the outside world. Hence fundamentalists calculate the height and strength and constitution of their walls according to their evaluation of the enemy's invasive power. In this sense the enemy helps to determine the strategies of the fundamentalist. Second, fundamentalists look to the future, not to the past. Unlike sectarian separatists such as the Amish, fundamentalists expect the sinful world outside the enclave to be transformed sooner or later. The transformation may come directly at the hands of the true believers, or it may be solely God's doing. Yet even separatist fundamentalists, who would renounce the world and wait upon God, are actors in the world—even if their interaction takes the form of a running commentary on "the signs of the times," that is, on where the world currently stands in its headlong cascade toward oblivion and final redemption. The fundamentalist renunciation of the world is therefore tactical and incomplete.

We have identified four patterns of fundamentalist interaction with the world. They are the *world conqueror,* the *world transformer,* the *world creator,* and the *world renouncer.* Before discussing these patterns in detail, however, we must establish two interpretive principles.

First, over the course of its lifetime a movement is likely to exhibit two, three, or even all four of these patterns. A movement may go into a kind of hibernation, later to re-emerge, reconstituted and fortified for battle. In addition a movement may simultaneously exhibit more than one pattern of relating to the world; we often see two patterns linked together in the complex behavior of fundamentalisms. The world-creating impulse, for example, often accompanies the world-renouncing pattern: a movement simultaneously rejects the external world and turns inward, creating its own world as an alternative to the threatening outside. Times of social or political crisis present the fundamentalist movement with an opportunity, or a danger. If the crisis is seen as an opportunity, the movement may abandon its world-transforming orientation in favor of the more aggressive program of the world conqueror. If the crisis is seen primarily as a danger to the life of the movement, the world-transformer (or the world-conqueror) may retreat to the enclave of the world-creator or world-renouncer. Usually, however, one finds a dominant impulse in the movement *at a particular time in its development*.

Second, the "world" of fundamentalism varies in definition and scope according to how particular fundamentalists understand the concepts of space and time.

In terms of space, the world may be a village or nation-state, rather than the entire globe, the whole of human civilization. In other words, the world is the *immediately significant environment* of the movement in question. To the followers of Khomeini in Tehran in 1978, for example, the world was the nation-state known as Iran. This was the primary environment with which the Iranian Shi'ite radicals were interacting at the time. And their particular form of interaction, at that time, was militant-hegemonic—what we are calling the world-conqueror model. That is, Khomeini's followers focused their fervor on a defined world, and set out to *conquer* that world (rather than *transform* it gradually, or *create* their own alternative world in competition with that world, or *withdraw* from that world as much as possible).

Of course, other "worlds," such as that of the "Great Satan"—the United States—were also invoked in the Iranian Shi'ite ideology of that time. But these were secondary; in terms of their actual program, the operative target, so to speak, was Iran, not the U.S. The immediate purpose for the taking of U.S. hostages in 1979 was not a desire to conquer or otherwise influence the United States, despite the harsh anti-American rhetoric of the captors; rather, the purpose of the episode was to consolidate the revolution in Iran, the primary world of immediate significance for Khomeini's followers. We will be classifying movements according to their actual behavior rather than their professed intent.

As the goals and status of a movement change, of course, the "world" changes, and vice versa. After the Shi'ite movement in Iran came to power, the world of immediate significance expanded to include not only Iran, but other nation-states (especially Iraq), the larger Shi'ite world, and indeed, the whole of the Islamic world, over which Iran sought a transformative influence. In terms of its world of origin, Iran, Khomeini's movement now focused its efforts on transforming the conquered world. The movement changed its strategies to adapt to its changed environment.

In terms of time, the external world, no less than the movement itself, may be seen in historic time, or in messianic time. This makes an enormous difference in how the fundamentalist movement chooses to relate to the world. Historic time is open-ended, plentiful, amenable to a gradualist, transformationist approach to the reconstruction of society. Messianic time is trickier: the end is fast approaching, the enemies are about to be conquered—but who is going to do the conquering? Depending on their answer to this question, fundamentalists acting in messianic expectation may become world-renouncers (i.e., Leave the outside world alone—God will do the conquering) or world-transformers (God expects the true believers to pave His way) or world-conquerors (God establishes His kingdom through the agency of the true believers). In any case, the fundamentalist is also always a world-creator (whatever the condition of the outside world, God is present in the enclave or "world" of the true believer.)

Apocalyptic sects of Judaism, Christianity, or Islam may normally despair of seizing immediate control of society outside the enclave—unless and until the messianic figure arrives, causing an eruption in, or cessation of, historic time. At that point, they may enter a world-conquering phase, as did Gush Emunim at its inception as a radical settler movement. In other cases, however, the expectation of an eschatalogical deliverance seems to intensify in proportion to the distance fundamentalists are from seizing real power in historic time. Haredi Jews do not seek to dominate Palestinian Arabs in the Holy Land. Why try to conquer the world, they reason, if the Messiah is about to arrive to do the work for you?

In sum, the fundamentalists' stance toward the world will depend, first, on their assessment of the outside world; and, second, on the role they think they are supposed to be playing in the divine plan. But whether they operate in historic time or in messianic time, whether the threatening "world" is the village across the river or the powerful nation-state rival, all fundamentalists expect the enemy to be abolished, one way or another, sooner or later. God's world is pure, not pluralist.

There are four ways of abolishing the enemy. First, one may eliminate the enemy altogether. This is the goal of the fundamentalist pattern of behavior we are calling the world conqueror. *The primary strategy of the world conqueror is to assume control of the structures of society which have given life to the enemy.* Once in control of the means of coercion and the resources in a society, the world conqueror is in a position to define and dominate outsiders, eliminating them, or placing them in cultural or political or geographic exile, or converting them forcibly to the cause. World-conquering is usually undertaken by those fundamentalist movements in a position, they feel, to meet these ambitious objectives. Radical, revolutionary fundamentalisms adopt world-conquering ideologies and corresponding organizational structures and programs of action. Ideologically, as we saw in Chapter 16, they place heavy emphasis on dualism and reactive selectivity; organizationally, they feature authoritarian leadership in control of disciplined cadres or militant cells. Theologically, world conquerors make a claim that redemptive action is scheduled to occur at least in part in historic time, not solely in eschatalogical time. If the messiah is to come, the fundamentalists must first prepare the threshing floor.

It is tempting to say that all fundamentalists aspire to be world conquerors. By this way of thinking, fundamentalism is defined as essentially reactive, militant, and anti-pluralist; in its complete expression it must therefore seek to suppress alternative visions and movements within a given society, or world. As we have just noted, however, the world-conquering tendency can be modified even in messianic fundamentalisms, in which the ultimate victory over evil is to come at the hands of the longed-for Messiah or Mahdi. The world-conquering impulse of fundamentalism may also be modified for purely pragmatic reasons as well as theological ones. Even messianic movements acknowledge that they must operate in historic time. And even those fundamentalists who do intend to conquer their world in historic time often find themselves forced to adopt other strategies in order to survive the vicissitudes of history.

Thus *a second means of abolishing the enemy is to reinterpret and influence the structures, institutions, laws and practices of a society,* so that opposing fundamentalism may become more difficult, and so that conditions become more favorable for the conversion or marginalization of the enemy. The world transformer adopts this strategic approach to the fundamentalist problem of pluralism. It shares with the conqueror the ultimate aim of reforming the society in its image, but adopts a variety of accommodating strategies, over a longer period of time, to achieve this end. Ideologically, the movement may selectively relax its boundaries to include some shades of gray, and adjust organizational requirements to this strategy. Legal advocacy, political lobbying, cultural warfare, and missionary work may be emphasized as heavily as militant activism. Civil society rather than the battlefield is the primary arena for fundamentalist interaction with the enemy. (The arena may shift of course, if transformational strategies are frustrated and abandoned for the sword or the bomb.)

The world creator and world renouncer also displace the world-conquering mode. Both devote considerable energies to the building up of the enclave, the demarcation of boundaries, the securing of the niche. The movement's *ultimate* aims may or may not be clearly envisioned or even attainable within history. In both patterns, God is the agent of justice and power; world conquering will be left to the deity. In the meantime, militance, reactivity, and antipluralism will be the preserve of the remnant, the anxious ones awaiting the day of redemption.

The world creator, however, is intentionally in direct competition with the outside world; it seeks to enlarge and replenish its own world to attract others as a clear alternative to the fallen world. *The world-creator strategy, therefore, is to create alternative and encompassing societal structures and institutions.* Missionary work is important, not to transform the structures of the world outside, but to increase the numbers of the enclave. In a certain sense, as we have noted, all fundamentalisms are world-creators: unlike mere traditionalists, they begin by creating enclaves set apart from the world. They may move quickly into world-conquering or world-transforming modes, but they will never entirely abandon their world-creating activity. In other words, a world creator need not be a world conqueror—but a world conqueror will always also be a world creator.

The world renouncer, a relatively rare mode of fundamentalism, seeks purity and self-preservation more than hegemony over fallen outsiders. Ideologically, the world renouncer may be as doctrinaire and rigid as the world conqueror, but the energy is directed inward, to the self-construction of the fundamentalist world in contrast to the threatening outside. Not intent on building a world parallel to the outside world, it concentrates usually on education, domestic life, and religious ritual. *Strategically, the world renouncer relates to the outside world in a complex pattern of dependence and rejection.*

Of course, all fundamentalists, whatever their pattern of relation to the world, seek purity, draw sharp ideological boundaries, value mission work, and want to avoid the evils of the fallen world even as they seek to redeem it. But in different times and circumstances certain ingredients of the fundamentalist recipe are present in greater doses than others.

Structure, Chance, and Choice

We argue that fundamentalist movements adopt these strategies and are otherwise shaped and formed by three sets of causes: (1) structural factors by which we mean long-term contextual conditions and changes; (2) contingent, chance factors; and (3) "human" factors of choice and leadership.

Thus, to begin with contextual causes, these movements arise from and are shaped by different religious settings. In some cases as in Italy or Algeria, there may be a single dominant religion; in others, the United States and India, there may be competing religions. Conflict between religions will affect the goals and programs of fundamentalist movements. The organizational and theological patterns of their host religions also will necessarily influence their organizational and theological characteristics. Outside religion, those factors affecting fundamentalism that shape values and beliefs have the most direct impact. But the larger socioeconomic and international developments can also have powerful, if mostly indirect, effects.

Hence in our exploration of the causes of fundamentalism we begin with the religious sector, then turn to proximate cultural factors such as the educational system, the media, and the condition of the civil society. Then we work our way out to social structure and mobility, ethnicity, economic trends and conjunctures, and politics and public policy. The international environment—war, imperialism, trade, and demonstration effects—may have direct and dramatic consequences, or work indirectly. Finally, we may not neglect the way in which fundamentalist movements "cause" themselves, so to speak, the way in which ideological and programmatic choices interact with organization and tactics, or the constitutive and creative role of leadership in mediating among and drawing the theological, organizational, political, and tactical implications of all of these contextual influences.

CHART 17.1

EXPLAINING ASPECTS OF FUNDAMENTALIST MOVEMENTS

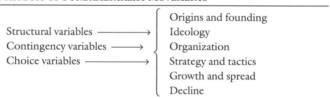

Chart 17.1 tells us that we must describe in each case how our three sets of "independent variables"—structure, contingency, and choice—combine differently in each aspect of a particular fundamentalist movement (the dependent variables). A fundamentalist movement, like any movement, exists and changes in space and time. It is "founded," grows, spreads, develops new programs, changes strategy and tactics, wins and loses elections, succeeds or fails in revolutions, declines, disappears. An explanatory theory of fundamentalism, hence, must disaggregate "movement" into its significant aspects, just as we have disaggregated the "independent variables" into specific structural, contingency, and choice components. Thus we expect that leadership would have a special relationship to the founding of movements, their strategy and tactics, and their decline (often associated with the death of leaders); religious structure and theology would have a large impact on fundamentalist organization and ideology; war, economic crises, and population movements may have a close relationship to growth and spread; and so on.

Long-term structural factors, such as the organization and theology of the host religion, ethnic and religious heterogeneity, the growth and character of the economy, cultural secularization, and the domestic and international political situations, must be understood as necessary but not sufficient causes of fundamentalism. Without such long-term structural changes and conditions (such as secularization), there would be no fundamentalism. But secularization produced liberalism, radicalism, romanticism, and the like, as well as fundamentalism. It was a strong, necessary cause. But even if we take all the structural causes together, they would only tell us that **if** a fundamentalist movement arose in this context it would probably have such and such particular characteristics and geographic and social structural distributions. To turn these potentialities into reality we need human choices—the decisions of leaders, and the needs and demands of members and supporters. These are the *sufficient* causes in the sense that they convert the "human material" and material resources into actual movements.[1]

Even though we may "explain" a fundamentalist movement by exhaustively investigating the long-run structural causes, the short-term chance developments, and the inputs of leadership, we are far from suggesting that we can predict the rise of fundamentalism, or the forms that it takes, or the strategies that it pursues. The impact of structural factors are predictable up to a point. But short-run developments, such as the illness or death of leaders, poor crops, and famine, are less predictable, or not predictable at all; and human factors such as leadership decisions, or popular actions, are responsive and creative actions, and hence unpredictable.

It might have been possible, for example, to forecast the religious characteristics of Iranian Shi'ite fundamentalism by considering traditional Shi'ite doctrine and organization, to take this particular structural factor. But plotting the vulnerability of Iran to a fundamentalist takeover would require that we be able to forecast the illness of the shah and the indecisiveness of the regime; the widespread availability of the tape cassette; changing American policy resulting from the election of Carter, and the like. Taken together, these two sets of factors might have allowed us to predict some kind of revolution in Iran, even some kind of religious movement; but we would need to factor in the Ayatollah Khomeini to produce the contemporary Iranian fundamentalist phenomenon.

Structural Factors

Religion

We begin with religion as one of the long-range deterministic factors. The nature of the host religion out of which fundamentalism arises is perhaps the most important conditioning factor in the explanation of fundamentalism—its theology, its organizational structure, its vitality. Does the host religion have an hierarchical structure as in Catholicism, a semi-hierarchical structure as in Shi'ism, or a congregational one as in Protestantism and Sunni Islam? Or is it a relatively unspecialized, diffuse set of roles and institutions as in Hinduism, Sikhism, and Buddhism? Table 17.1, describing the organization of the host religions of a number of fundamentalist movements, shows most of them to be associated with religions in which authority and legitimacy are concentrated in individual congregations or around individual mosques—in other words, where fundamentalist breakaway is relatively low in cost, where a congregation may simply go fundamentalist, or where new ones may easily be formed. In contrast

TABLE 17.1

ORGANIZATION OF HOST RELIGION

	Diffuse Charismatic	Congregational	Semi-hierarchical	Hierarchical
Christian				
U.S. Protestant		X		
Catholic traditionalist				X
Guatemalan Pentecostal		X		
Comunione e Liberazione				X
Islamic				
Egyptian jamaʻat		X		
Algerian FIS		X		
Gaza Hamas		X		
Iranian Khomeini			X	
Lebanese Shiʻite			X	
Jewish				
Haredi		X		
Habad		X		
Gush Emunim		X		
South Asian				
Hindu RSS	X			
Sikh radicals	X			
Sinhala Buddhist	X			

there are relatively few cases of effective breakaway among Roman Catholics. Organizationally speaking, since the church is the sole source of salvation, great danger is involved in separation from and opposition to the church establishment. For a fundamentalist movement to arise in Shiʻite Islam with its semi-hierarchical structure would require the action of an ayatollah having or mobilizing the support of associates and lower clergy. The relatively centralized Shiʻite organization would lend itself more easily to takeover, as the case of Iran suggests. In the cases of Hinduism and Sikhism, clerical organization tends to be diffuse and/or charismatic, consisting of gurus and their followers, temple priests, and administrators. Hindu and Sikh "fundamentalist" organizations are lay associations and not religious organizations, properly speaking. Among the Sri Lankan Buddhists religious organization consists of monasteries, abbots, and monks stratified according to seniority. Buddhist movements in Sri Lanka are lay extremist groups with some participation by monks.

The theology of the host religion is similarly important in influencing fundamentalist movements. Are its beliefs explicit and coherent, codified in texts as in the case of the Abrahamic religions—in Judaism, Christianity, Islam—and in Sikhism? What are its conceptions of deity, of history, of the religious life? Where there are explicit authoritative texts, it is easier for fundamentalist movements to separate themselves from a compromising, secularizing religious establishment. Religions with a millennial, messianic theology are, with some noteworthy exceptions, particularly susceptible to fundamentalism, since the hope of dramatic redemption is attractive to suffering adherents.

Is the religious context a homogeneous one, or are there significant competing religions? Does religion coincide with ethnolinguistic differences? What is the historic pattern of relations among these ethnoreligious groups? A multireligious, conflictual context is more likely to produce ethnonational-religious militance (as in the cases of Northern Ireland, India, and Sri Lanka) rather than simple religious fundamentalism.

Major short term precipitants in the religious domain include the outbreak of open competition and conflict among religio-ethnic groups as in India and Sri Lanka; major changes of policy on the part of the host religious establishment as in Vatican II; and individual acts of excommunication as in the case of Archbishop Lefebvre. But one should not overlook the impact of what are viewed as revelations, epiphanies, and noumenal events of one kind or another—direct interventions of the divine into human affairs. The alleged miraculous vision of the Virgin Mary in a Coptic church in Egypt in the aftermath of the 1967 war is a case in point. And the vision of the Lord Ram in the Babri Masjid (mosque of Babur) in Ayodhya played a role in its final destruction at the hands of Hindu fundamentalists. The religious Zionists who joined the Gush Emunim in Israel viewed the victory of 1967 and the narrow escape of 1973 as divine signals to move into messianic gear.

Education

The educational system and the media of communication, like religion and in competition with it, are concerned with the shaping of "hearts and minds." The secular schools and universities spread the knowledge and cultivate the analytical skills that challenge and erode religious beliefs. Hence the fundamentalists are in conflict with the educational and scientific establishment, seeking to maintain or establish beachheads, to assert epistemological equality between "creation science" and "secular humanism," to legalize prayer in the schools, and the like.

Changes in government policy toward education may serve as short-term triggers or precipitants for fundamentalist movements. The most dramatic example of such a precipitant is the rapid growth of higher education after Sputnik in the United States, and similar rapid growth in Western Europe and in some parts of the Third World. The sudden increase in the numbers of students, and the formation of new universities and colleges without traditions, contributed to the cultural turmoil of the 1960s, as well as the imbalance of supply and demand in the job market for university graduates in the Islamic world, in India, and after the 1960s, in the West. The cultural revolution, centered on university campuses, was a threat and shock to religious groups, furnishing ammunition to fundamentalists. Generally speaking, the most educated strata of populations are least susceptible to fundamentalism. This is true in India as well as in the United States.

Communication

Long-run trends of media development—the spread of print, the rise of mass-circulation newspapers, the more recent development of the cinema, radio, and television—have changed the mode and quality of the exchange of information and ideas throughout the world. This has had several implications for religion and the rise of fundamentalism. On the one hand these new and powerful media in the hands of the secular world spread the information, knowledge, and moral standards, that threaten religious beliefs and practices. But later generations of religious leaders, particularly the fundamentalists among them, have discovered that they may put the media to their own uses. Thus the rise of televangelism, the use of data banks for direct mailing, and the use of tape cassettes to proselytize are examples of the enhancement of access to potential supporters through these new technologies. The global world of communication and information increases the speed and significance of "demonstration effect." The diffusion of information about ideas and events across national, cultural, and religious boundaries occurs at a dizzying pace. The success of televangelism in the United States, the power of the tape cassette in Iran and elsewhere in the Middle East, the electoral success and suppression of Islamic fundamentalism in Algeria, the destruction of the Babri Masjid in India—all of these developments are quickly registered by movements around the world. The secularizing impact of the media, on the one hand, and the entrance of fundamentalist movements into the struggle for access to these powerful media, on the other, suggests the quandary of these fundamentalist movements as they modernize themselves in special ways in their efforts to resist the larger modernizing trends.

Civil Society

Civil society refers to the social formations between the state on the one hand and family and kinship on the other—voluntary associations and agencies of one kind or another formed around economic, ethnic, religious, local, and other interests and values. The vitality of such associations and their relations to the state are crucial to the understanding of civil society—which is the realm within which fundamentalism arises. It makes a great deal of difference if a society has strong and independent trade unions, civic associations, communications media, and political parties, capable of draining off anxiety and resentment in response to social and economic crises, and converting them into secular politics and public policy. We would fail to understand Islamic movements, for example, if we did not take into account the fact that civil society in Islamic countries has been reduced over the last century by the interventionist state.

Social Structure

Fundamentalist leaders and members are recruited from different parts of the social structure, depending on the structural characteristics of the society, its level of development, degree of urbanization, the pattern of distribution of wealth and income, and differences in patterns of consumption. The social structure creates "fault lines," social "fissures"—anxious and relatively deprived strata that may be drawn to the communitarian, revitalizing, often vindictive appeals of militant religious movements.

In the United States the most significant religious development in the last several decades has been a decline in the membership of the mainline Protestant denominations (e.g., Episcopalian, Presbyterian, Methodist, Lutheran) and the sharp increase in the size of evangelical and Pentecostal denominations. Thus the Southern Baptists increased from around 10 million in 1960 to 15 million in 1990; Pentecostal denominations increased more than fourfold, from under 2 million in 1960 to almost 10 million in 1990; while the Episcopalians dropped from 3.5 million in 1960 to 2.5 million in 1990, and the United Methodists dropped from more than 10 million in 1960 to under 9 million in 1990.[2]

One writer estimates substantial support for the causes supported by the New Christian Right.

> Potential political support for the New Christian Right is sizable. A number of NCR positions are quite popular among the mass public . . . Large proportions of Americans oppose homosexuality and pornography, favor school prayer and private school vouchers, and support sex education emphasizing abstinence. Smaller, but still substantial groups have serious reservations about abortion. . . . While such a coalition of traditionalists would not constitute a majority of the American people, it could easily exceed 30 percent of the population.[3]

In her authoritative study of the Southern Baptist clergy and activist laity in the years of struggle for control of the Southern Baptist Convention (a battle won by the fundamentalists), Nancy Ammerman describes the social differences between these moderates and fundamentalists in the following terms:

> [S]tatus in the denomination and in society appears to have been related to the positions people were taking in the Southern Baptist Convention controversy. Those who had more comfortable lives—from white collar and professional families, with more income, and a professional at the head of household—were more likely to have been found to the left of center in the denomination and to declare themselves moderate. In addition, pastors of larger urban churches . . . were also likely to prefer the moderate side. Those who came from farming and blue collar backgrounds, who had less money, and whose jobs involved them in a more routine sort of work, were more attracted to fundamentalist ways of thinking. Status cannot explain all the differences between the Southern Baptist Convention's left and right wings, but it does appear to explain a good deal.[4]

Ammerman also found education to be a strong predictor.

> There were many well-educated people who were fundamentalists and many moderates who had little schooling. But the differences between the two wings were tangible and real. Almost no pastors on the moderate side had less than a seminary education, while over two-thirds of the pastors on the fundamentalist side had only a college degree or less. Only 17 percent of fundamentalist laity had a bachelor's degree, while over half of the moderate laity had a bachelor's degree or more. Fundamentalist leaders often had blue ribbon educations and could debate the best-educated moderates on their own terms, but fundamentalist followers were at a considerable educational disadvantage compared to their moderate counterparts. Among the many social sources of Southern Baptist division, then, education must be seen as a leading influence.[5]

Ammerman's study also demonstrated that urbanization influenced affiliation with the moderate and fundamentalist wings of the Southern Baptist leadership. "People who grew up in suburbs and small cities were the most likely to adopt a moderate theology, while those who grew up on farms were the least likely to locate left of center. There was, in fact, a direct negative relationship between the size of a person's community of origin and the conservatism of his or her beliefs. People who grew up in cities were simply less conservative than people who grew up in the country."[6]

This marginality to the modern in the sense of social status and education may be characteristic of fundamentalist movements across religious traditions and cultures. For example, Hindu fundamentalists seem to be predominantly recruited from the "cow belt" Hindu traditionalist country; the Sikh Khalistanis are primarily recruited from the more backward western districts of Punjab.

Short-run social structural shocks resulting from recession and unemployment, labor conflicts or strikes, the introduction of foreign workers, or ethnic clashes may produce or sharpen grievances in particular sectors of the society, rendering them susceptible to protest movements, including fundamentalism. The Sephardic-Ashkenazic socioeconomic division among Israeli Jews, as well as the deterioration of Israeli-Palestinian relations, created, with the help of recurrent crises, a ready made soil fertile to the Kach movement of Rabbi Kahane.

Mobility

Major migrations have had important consequences for the development of fundamentalism. For the Jews the depopulation of the Jewish shtetl in Eastern Europe at the turn of the nineteenth century was made possible by emancipation and the Jewish enlightenment, resulting in massive emigration to the larger towns and cities, and to the United States and other countries. The residual shtetl communities and yeshivot reacted to this depopulation by a drawing of lines and a strengthened orthodoxy. A second major Jewish population movement was the large-scale immigration to Israel, the United States, and elsewhere after the Holocaust and the establishment of the Jewish state. This transplanted Jewish fundamentalist movements from their Eastern European origins principally to Israel and the United States.

For Islamic fundamentalism there was the migration of Palestinians after the establishment of the Jewish State, and the large scale recruitment of Muslim guest workers into Western Europe in the 1960s and 1970s. In Italy there was the large-scale movement of southern Italians into the prosperous industrial cities of northern Italy. In the United States there was the movement of southerners into northern cities, the general movement from countryside to city and from city to suburbs which affected recruitment into fundamentalist movements. The mechanism converting the breakup of community, resulting from emigration and settlement in a new culture and society, into potential fundamentalist affiliation is the need to maintain, or reestablish, identity.

Mobility may be either long- or short-term in its impact. For example, Muslim migration into France has been going on ever since World War I, but was largely precipitated in the boom years of the 1960s, and then was terminated after the first oil shock in 1973—74, thus pushing guest workers to become permanent French residents, aggravating their identity problems. Jewish immigration into Palestine took on significant proportions during the 1930s, and then sharply increased after World War II and the formation of the State of Israel. As we have suggested above, many of the haredi communities date from the immigration of Eastern European survivors.

Ethnic-Regional

The ethnic-linguistic-regional composition of a society—its homogeneity or heterogeneity, the distinctiveness of regional divisions, the historical background of relations among ethnic and regional groups—may have important implications for the development of fundamentalism. The subordination and exploitation of one ethnic or regional group by another, and historic ethnic tensions may create grievances in the long term. Violent clashes in the short term may convert these grievances into collective awareness and action. Militant religious movements in a heterogeneous country such as India carry distinct ethnic imprints. In Northern Ireland the Ulster Protestants and the Irish Catholics have been locked for decades in an intractable struggle. (See Chapter 19 for an extended discussion of ethnicity and fundamentalism.)

Economic Development

The economic circumstances of a society—including its level of development and GNP, its natural resources, its rate of growth, and the unevenness of the geographic spread of growth—relate to the emergence and life of fundamentalism in a variety of ways. This is true whether a society is "First World" or Third; whether it contains a growing tertiary sector, as well as an industrial one; and whether it is primarily agricultural and extractive. We do not have to subscribe to the Marxist or "dependencista" view that tends to reduce all religious categories to economic ones, in order to recognize these interactions between economy and religion. We have observed that fundamentalists tend to be recruited from the less developed, less "modern" parts of societies, from the rural population, from the poorer parts of cities, from the less well educated, from social strata relatively deprived in economic and social development and improvement, and the like.

In the short run, recessions, depressions, inflation, strikes, unemployment, and famine may create attitudes and grievances among particular groups in the population, inclining them favorably to fundamentalist arguments, themes, and practices. Contrariwise, the availability of abundant natural resources such as oil may make it possible for some countries to offer opportunities and services to their people that may obviate or blunt the impact of such economic shocks.

Political Characteristics

The authority structure of a state, the legitimacy of its institutions and leadership, the extent to which the state penetrates the society, the level of popular participation, the degree of partisan polarization—all may shape the nature of movements arising in that society. Different kinds of political and constitutional arrangements may be associated with differences in the goals and tactics of fundamentalist movements. Thus in secularized democracies such as the United States, Italy, and India fundamentalist movements operate openly in political and partisan competition. In contemporary India the second largest party, the Bharatiya Janata Party (BJP), dominated by militant Hindu ethnoreligious movements, is seeking to eliminate this secular pluralism. Right-wing Hindu movements have been suppressed in the crises that resulted from the assassinations of Mohandas, Indira, and Rajiv Gandhi, and most recently after the destruction of the Babri Masjid in Ayodhya.

Israel is a semisecular democratic state in which the Orthodox rabbinate and the canon law have privileged positions. Jewish fundamentalist movements, given Israel's electoral system, have the electoral support that enables them to bargain for the extension of Orthodox Jewish regulations into the public law. Algeria and Egypt are secular authoritarian regimes following repressive policies vis-á-vis their fundamentalist oppositions. Iraq and Syria are strong authoritarian, anticlerical regimes in which fundamentalist opposition has to operate underground. Pakistan has a partially clericalized regime which limits the autonomy of secular movements; and Iran is the outstanding example of an authoritarian clerical regime in full control of the state, and following repressive policies against secular movements.

In the short term, revolution, civil war, changes of government, changes in policy, or important judicial decisions may serve as triggers to the formation of movements, or to their later development. The recent fundamentalist explosion in Algeria can be explained by the opening up of the Algerian political system to free elections in 1988, and the capture by skillful fundamentalist leaders of a majority of the voters, alienated by the failure of the Algerian oil economy. In Israel the rise to power of the Likud in 1977 created a political atmosphere supportive of the Greater Israel aspirations of the Gush Emunim. The U.S. Supreme Court's 1973 *Roe v. Wade* decision legalizing abortion nationwide increased the appeal of fundamentalism among conservative Protestants. (See Chapter 19 for an extended discussion of politics and fundamentalism.)

International Environment

We cannot overestimate the importance of Western imperialism in the explanation of fundamentalism in the Third World—in the Middle East, Africa, and South Asia. Commerce and the secular culture of science, technology, and modern industry, appeared in the Third World under the auspices of exploitative, colonialist Western powers. And the independent governments established in these formerly colonial countries continue to bear these neo-colonialist stigmata, long after the departure of the imperial authorities. Thus Third World fundamentalist movements tend to have nationalist and anti-imperialist tendencies in addition to their religious ones.[7] They tend to be parochial and "isolationist" in their relations to the outside world. The lively exchange of goods and ideas implied in open diplomacy, trade, and communication threatens the integrity of their traditions, and opens their members to competing religions, debilitating materialism, and moral corruption. As these movements come closer to power, they are constrained to adopt more open policies vis-á-vis their internal and external political and cultural worlds. A fundamentalist movement has to hedge its isolated approach in order to engage in the coalition making essential to effective politics. Once in power, similar pressures constrain a fundamentalist movement to relate to different societies, cultures, and value systems. Inevitable ambivalence exists in the external and foreign affairs of fundamentalist movements. There are difficulties, perhaps inherent limits, in accumulating power internally and in spreading internationally. Once in power, there are difficulties in the long run in avoiding the compromises and pluralism required by effective coalition making and conduct of foreign policy.

In the short term, the appeals of fundamentalism are influenced by international events that create grievances—wars and their aftermath; terms of trade and global economic fluctuations harming Third World economies; "demonstration effects" such as the Khomeini revolution in Iran that arouse hopes. The 1967 war and the capture of Jerusalem by Israel was an exhilarating moment for Jews as well as for fundamentalist Baptists; it was a deep shock and a mobilizing force among Muslims everywhere.

The logic of our explanatory scheme is that it moves from the more proximate variables of religion, culture, the media, and education, to the more remote, more indirect stimuli and constraints deriving from ethnicity, the economy, the social structure, and the political and international systems. As we have pointed out, our explanatory scheme recognizes the importance of contingency and chance and is open to the significance of human choice and the creativity of leadership. The long-term factors may create a niche for fundamentalist movements. Structural unemployment may, for instance, create a pool of potential recruits. Likewise, people who feel relative deprivation because of inconsistency between status and income may express grievances through a fundamentalist movement; persecuted ethnic groups, dislocated people, victims of war, or migrants looking for identity and community may join them.

The chance factors influence the size and social location of the niche. For example, an area where a riot or a strike has recently galvanized the population, or some part of it, will be fertile recruiting ground. A new media technology such as the tape cassette introduced in Iran in the mid-1970s enabled Khomeini to smuggle his sermons from Iraq and Paris into Iran where they were easily and cheaply duplicated and spread like brushfire. Defeat in war (Egypt and Syria in 1967) or an evident economic failure (Algeria after the second oil bust of 1984–85) damages the legitimacy of the political system, and facilitates recruitment to protest movements, including fundamentalism.

Ideology, Organizational Structure, and Leadership

However important the impact of long- and short-term constraints, the interaction of the components of the movement itself is of substantial significance. The movement has an internal life of its own. A new ideological development calls for and causes organizational changes, and may require new resources. Or organizational changes such as the development of bureaucracy may influence strategic choices and inhibit militance.

We can begin our discussion of the ways in which the environment affects these movements with an analysis of how the environment impacts the resources—manpower, weapons, money, political access—that have the most unambiguous connection with the success of fundamentalist movements. Recruitment of membership is affected by grievances and limited or catalyzed by state repression. Money may come from the state, from the international environment, from philanthropists or from tithing of the ordinary adherents of their own tradition. The Assemblies of God in the U.S. finance Pentecostals in Guatemala; Iran helps the Shi'ites in Lebanon and Iraq; wealthy Jews in the United States and Canada support the haredim; the Iranian Shi'ite opposition under the shah was supported by tithe-paying believers.

The ideology of the movement, both in its affective and cognitive dimensions, may draw on structural and chance factors. The Iranian demonology that described America as the Great Satan with such success was drawn from Shi'ite tradition, while the Khomeini propaganda assimilated faddish expressions of third world critics of Western neo-colonialism such as Franz Fanon's "damned of the earth." The rise of activist messianism in Israel after 1967 was due to the firing of the collective imagination by what appeared to be the result of divine intervention in the Six-Day War. Independent Baptists in the United States use the language of psychology and "pop" psychology as well as sports and military metaphors pervasive in American culture. To illustrate the great importance of structural constraints on fundamentalist organization, consider the hierarchic authoritarian structure of the Catholic church which, in contrast with the decentralized character of Protestant denominations, inhibits the formation of new Catholic religious organizations, particularly those of an egalitarian nature.

As we have suggested, the components of fundamentalist movements—ideology, organization, resources, and leadership—also interact, constrain, and explain each other. Organization and ideology are closely interrelated. The need for boundaries in order to stem slippage from traditional religion is fleshed out in the form of elaborate behavioral requirements such as dress codes, rigor in ritual, and prohibition of intermingling with impious people. These boundaries, however, are first and foremost expressed in theological terms, the movement being the virtuous "remnant" while all the rest of society is the realm of darkness and vice. The transformation of an ideology in the direction of militance affects both organization and resources. Organization becomes compartmentalized and may go partly underground; and new resources must be found—weapons, communications equipment, military specialists. The leadership balance may change, with military professionals gaining the upper hand over ideologists and educators.

Yet resources also shape ideology and organization. Most fundamentalist movements, at least in the earlier phases, lack coercive resources and have little by way of remunerative ones. This contributes to the salience of two ideological properties—election and dualism. The members of such movements are compensated by a notion of their moral superiority over the impious. These two properties are elaborated in organizational terms in the tendency of these movements to be egalitarian, or at least to have as small a hierarchy as possible. A charismatic leader does not create an imbalance within the egalitarian community of the virtuous, because of his inherent superiority, blessed and God-given.

Leadership plays the quintessential creative role in the formation, transformation, and maintenance of fundamentalist movements. Its significance may be elaborated in ideological, organizational, and resource terms, as in the capacity to transform preferences and attitudes through creative ideas, to create and modify organization, to discover and mobilize new resources, and to broker combinations and coalitions, both within the movement and with powers external to it. Leadership is, of course, constrained or stimulated by the long-term trends we have described. A leader may wish to resist and transcend certain latitudinarian trends of his religious denomination in order to ensure the survival of the tradition. But he must still use the language and concepts of the tradition, and reinterpret it in an innovative yet orthodox manner. Such skills as a sense of timing and the ability to use the "right dosage" in response to opportunities that become available due to short-term crises, are important capacities in the leadership of militant movements.

These leadership talents and skills, as well as other qualities that we associate with personality, may be explained, of course, by family background, parental and sibling relations—that is, in terms of individual life history. These background characteristics and experiences help explain why a leader does what he does and is able or constrained to do so. But the explanation of these personality characteristics is quite separate from the explanatory logic of the movement as a whole. Two systems of causation intersect in the recruitment and performance of the fundamentalist leadership, as is true in any movement. The strength, uniqueness, and success of Khomeini consisted in the combination of his scholarly stature, his boldly innovative political theory, his charisma, his down-to-earth provincial homeliness, his mastery of conversational homiletic style, his shrewd understanding of the way the political game was played within Iran, his capacity to broker broad but ever-shifting coalitions. His physical decline in his later years, his ignorance of the larger world, his tendency to nourish grievances and harbor personal hatred (illustrated by his animosity toward Saddam Hussein which needlessly extended the Iraq-Iran war), were qualities that constricted the movement he had created. We do not intend to undertake explanations of these personal characteristics of leaders, but we will call attention to them as they enter into the explanation of the fate of the movements that they lead.

Structural Causes: Secularization

The defining and distinctive structural cause of fundamentalist movements is secularization. As we consider the sweep of fundamentalist movements across nations, cultures, and civilizations, some degree of secularization is present in all of them. Confronted with the threat of secularization, the world of religion responds adaptively or militantly—by assimilating to the values of the secular world, or by mobilizing, usually in part, in opposition to this invasion and to the traitors who compromise with the enemy. Protestant, Catholic, and Jewish haredi fundamentalism fit into this relatively unambiguous cultural category. Perhaps multi-generational Hasidic fundamentalism ought to be viewed under more than one aspect. In its original formation in the eighteenth century, Hasidism was a reaction against the formalism and intellectualism of shtetl religiosity; in other words, it arose out of religious conflict. In its late-nineteenth-century reformulation it took on its strong antisecular character.

Sunni Islamic fundamentalism, while also strongly antisecular, has the added complication of a strong nationalist, anti-Western component. That is, it is caused not only by the threat of modern science and technology to religious tradition and values, but by the fact that these values are carried by powerful alien and exploitative agents such as the United States, her puppet Israel, and their Islamic "lackeys." Shi'ite fundamentalism adds to these enemies its religious competition and enmity with Sunni Islam. Hindu fundamentalism adds to its antisecular, anticolonialist, antireligious antagonism, an ethnic, nativist component.

The objectives of fundamentalist movements are thus shaped by these basic social structural and historic forces. If there are to be fundamentalist movements, these social templates will define their goals and channel their energies. This is a structural and necessary explanation of fundamentalist movements. But it is not a sufficient explanation.

Contingency and Chance

In normal social situations, in the absence of fundamentalist movements there are "inert" templates, lines of cleavage of an economic, social-status, ethnic, religious, or political sort. Typically it takes some precipitant, shock, trigger, to turn these inert potentialities into "live" ones. It might be a depression; a famine; deteriorating economic situations among particular groups; riots over migrant labor; sudden population movements; ethnic clashes; sharp changes in government policy; wars and other signal international events, governmental interventions in education, culture, religion; church decisions, noumenal events, and the like. These shock and trigger factors are contingencies, matters of chance. The Green Revolution accentuates economic inequalities in Punjab. The development of the cassette extends the range of the ayatollah's voice. The 1967 war deepens the feeling of humiliation among the Arabs. A judicial decision in India giving special status to Islamic marriage law provokes mass anti-Islamic reactions among the Hindus.

These chance events have the effect of mobilizing people along these structural lines of cleavage. They may be necessary aspects of explanation; without them there might not be a fundamentalist movement. But they are not the sufficient explanation. For this we must turn to choice—the choices of threatened, aggrieved, and anxious people looking for safety and security; and the choices of their religious leaders offering fundamentalist ideas, organization, and programs to meet these powerful needs.

Choice and Leadership

A movement requires leaders and followers. For the formation and maintenance of a fundamentalist movement, followers must be "prone," susceptible to fundamentalist appeals and tactics. Leadership converts these susceptibilities into commitments, mobilizes these members around particular goals and programs, and makes the decisions regarding interaction with the outside world.

There are different kinds of fundamentalist leaders in terms of their skills and specialization. There are *ideological catalyzers* such as the Hafetz Haim, Rabbi Kook the Elder, C. I. Scofield, J. Gresham Machen, Sayyid Qutb, the Ayatollah Khomeini, V. D. Savarkar, Jarnail Singh Bhindranwale, Archbishop Lefebvre, and others. There are *organizers and coalition makers* like Rabbis Ovadia Joseph and Eliezer Schach, Father Luigi Giussani, the Reverends Frank Norris and Bob Jones, K. B. Hedgewar, and M. S. Golwarkar. In fundamentalist movements, as in any movement, leadership constitutes a very large part of the sufficient causation, effectively inventing and presenting ideas, converting them into action programs, seeking and accumulating resources, devising the formulas for and negotiating the formation of coalitions.

Yet leadership does not operate in a vacuum; there must be a mobilizable mass of potential followers. Often the movement really gets off the ground only when the "trigger" is added. As we have noted, the trigger is a cataclysmic, transformative event either within the movement itself, or, more likely, in the local, national, or international environment external to the movement itself. The trigger may be the predictable consequence of the internal logic of long-term or short-term structures (bread riots may follow a period of economic instability and inadequate production); or it may come out of the blue, the result of unpredictable human freedom (the enfeebled shah of Iran, vulnerable to the entreaties of President Jimmy Carter, chooses not to fire on the Islamic revolutionaries); or it may be a combination of both, with latent trends surfaced and transformed by the inspired free act of a leader (Pope John XXIII, predicted to be a "caretaker pope," convened the Second Vatican Council and transformed the face of world Catholicism by legitimating a reform movement that had been growing within the church for several decades). In any case the trigger creates a new set of circumstances that provides an opening for a fundamentalist movement to expand and assert itself, usually, as we have said, under the guidance of a charismatic and/or authoritarian leader.

But while leadership is of unusual importance in the explanation of fundamentalism, there are cases in which the factor of choice—necessary as it is to all social movements—is expressed not so much through leadership as through the impulses, the knee-jerk behaviors, of groups and masses. Consider, for example, the incandescence of mobs and riots in Ayodhya or Bombay, the massacre at the Golden Temple in Amritsar, the Dry Zone of Sri Lanka, the revolver shots of anonymous assassins.

Having elaborated our explanatory model, in which structure, chance, and choice together determine the fate of fundamentalist movements, we now turn to a demonstration of the model by applying it to specific historical manifestations of fundamentalism.

Notes

1. For a discussion of causation as it is defined in the philosophy of science, see Richard Taylor "Causation," *The Encyclopedia of philosophy* (New York: MacMillan, 1967), vol.2, pp. 56ff.

2. Benton Johnson, "The Denomina-

tions: The Changing Map of Religious America," in Roper Center, *The Public Perspective* (Storrs: University of Connecticut, 1993), pp. 3 ff.; Andrew Greeley, *Religious Change in America* (Cambridge: Harvard University Press, 1989), chapter 3, reports similar denominational trends up to 1985.

3. Ted Jelen and Clyde Wilcox, "The Christian Right in the 1990s" in Roper Center, *Public Perspective*, pp. 10, 11.

4. Nancy Ammerman, *Baptist Battles: Social Change and Religious Conflict in the Southern Baptist Convention* (New Brunswick, N. J.: Rutgers University Press, 1990), p. 132.

5. Ibid., p. 142.

6. Ibid., p. 146

7. See, for example, Mark Juergensmeyer, *The New Cold War? Religious Nationalism Confronts the Secular State* (Berkeley: University of California Press, 1993).

Examining the Cases

Gabriel A. Almond, Emmanuel Sivan, and R. Scott Appleby

To explain fundamentalist movements means to show how structure, chance, and choice combine to determine their formation, growth, and fate—and their shifting patterns of relation to the world. We tallied the frequency with which structure, chance, and choice factors were important in the development of fundamentalist movements in Christian, Jewish, Islamic and South Asian religious traditions. We specified how these factors influenced the emergence, growth and decline of movements, their ideological and organizational characteristics, and their strategies. Each of us was required to make these judgments about the historical experience of those movements with which he was most familiar.

The conclusion of this exercise appear in Tables 18.1 and 18.2. Table 18.1 sums up the frequency with which these factors were cited for all of our fundamentalist and fundamentalist-like cases grouped together. For example, if the host religion had been scored as influential for the origins and founding, the ideology, the organization, the strategy, growth, and decline of all sixteen of our cases, then the category "host religion" would have received a perfect score of 96 (6 x 16). In fact it received roughly half of that number. This was the highest score among the structural variables, with religious context, public policy and civil society next in order of significance. However, leadership looms as by far the most significant factor, receiving a tally of 77 out of a possible score of 96. Table 18. 1 tells us that a fundamentalist movement is shaped by its religious setting—the theological and organizational characteristics of the host religion and competing religions, and the ways in which its own religious establishment adapts to the secularizing policies of the state and to secularizing trends in the civil society. Nevertheless, in every case the formation of these movements required the decisions of leaders.

The second column of Table 18.1 gives the weighted frequency for our three sets of variables. Each factor for each fundamentalist movement was given a score from one

TABLE 18.1

IMPACT OF EXPLANATORY FACTORS IN SIXTEEN FUNDAMENTALIST MOVEMENTS
BY NUMBER AND WEIGHTING OF IMPORTANCE

	Frequency	Weighted Frequency
Structure		
Host religion	47	88
Religious context	38	75
Civil society	37	81
Migration	27	54
Government structure	27	49
Public policy	41	88
Economic trends	31	59
International environment	31	62
Chance		
Endogenous	19	39
Exogenous	18	42
Choice		
Leadership	77	189
Rank and file	26	57
Total possible score	96	288

TABLE 18.2

FACTORS AFFECTING ASPECTS OF FUNDAMENTALISM BY FREQUENCY

	Origins	Ideology	Organization	Strategy	Growth	Decline
Structure						
Host religion	10	16	12	4	1	4
Religious context	12	10	3	7	5	1
Civil society	8	4	6	7	5	1
Migration	13	3	1	3	6	1
Government structure	9	5	5	5	2	1
Public policy	9	1	6	8	10	7
Economic trends	9	1	2	5	10	4
International environment	9	9	3	3	4	3
Chance						
Endogenous	8	1	1	2	4	3
Exogenous	8	1	1	1	4	3
Choice						
Leadership	16	14	12	13	10	12
Rank-and-file	3	1	3	9	7	3

to three, ranging from "some importance" (one) to "important" (two) to "very important" (three). Thus if host religion had received "very important" ratings for all sixteen cases, in all six aspects (3 x 16 x 6), it would have a score of 288. It actually had a score of 88, roughly one third of a perfect score, while leadership had a weighted total score of 189, roughly two thirds of a perfect score. Again religious context, civil society, and public policy had high weighted scores as well.

Considering the impact of these variables on the different aspects of the fundamentalist phenomenon (see table 18.2), we have the striking finding that "leadership" was rated as significant for all aspects—origins, ideology, organization, strategy, growth, and decline—in almost all of our cases. Among the structural variables, host religion was important in the origins, ideology, and organization of these movements; public policy in the origins, strategy, and growth; religious context in the origins and ideology ; economic trends in origins and growth. International environment was of significance in the origins and ideologies of these movements. Migration was very significant in the origins and growth of these movements.

We offer these findings, based on informed judgments, as suggestive rather than as precise numbers and percentages. To demonstrate the findings in another way, we now provide individual case studies, in which cause and effect are returned to their clinical settings. We organize the material around the patterns themselves—world conqueror, world transformer, and so forth—noting the stage in a movement's life at which the pattern appears (For example, the modern Shi'ite movement in Iran is world-conquering *in its time of origin*.)

The reader who wishes to follow a particular movement throughout its life can do so by reading about the movement's various patterns in sequence. In the case of multigenerational U.S. Protestant fundamentalism, for example, the movement emerges in a defensive mode during the last quarter of the nineteenth century, seeking to fend off a particular "enemy," liberalism/modernism, and to transform the emerging worlds of modern science and higher education—that is, to discredit, delegitimate, or otherwise neutralize them—by influencing (rather than revolutionizing) American educational, scientific, and cultural institutions. In a second phase, following the Scopes trial in 1925, fundamentalism enters an explicitly world-renouncing phase, in which the doctrines of biblical inerrancy and premillennial dispensationalism are placed in the service of a separatist ideology and organizational network. In the middle decades of the twentieth century, Christian fundamentalism enters a third phase, a world-creating project, featuring the buildup of alternative schools, media centers, and the like. By the standards of this alternative world the secular world is to be judged. In the late twentieth century, Christian fundamentalism re-emerges as a world-conqueror. It takes on a distinctly political cast in an effort to assume control of the structures of the state, not simply to influence its deliberations (as in the original emergence of the movement) but to reorient it to its transcendent destiny.

World Conqueror

In the world-conqueror pattern we see the most virulent type of fundamentalist movement in terms of the disruption and possible transformation of a previous order. Here everything, or almost everything, is clicking for the emergence of a durable movement: abundant intellectual and theological resources from the host religious tradition; social and economic displacement creating human need that has gone unmet; and, most of all, the leader who combines these elements in an innovative package, often tied to his personal authority and status. These movements are hegemonic and tend to seek to export the revolution, renew the faith and orthodoxy of the tepid believer (or eliminate him or her), and convert the unbeliever. Their ideologies exhibit strong nationalist or theocratic elements. The world, a realm of Satan and darkness, must be overcome if not brought back into the fold. Its institutions, structures, values must be brought under the control of the true believers. Depending on the specific political objectives of the movement, the world may ultimately be conceptualized as the *umma,* or merely Northern Ireland. In either case, it is a "kingdom" or "sacred realm," the borders of which are to be reclaimed and, in some millennial visions, expanded.

Revolutionary Shi'ism in Iran: Origin and Emergence, 1960s and 1970s. The fundamentalist movement itself, as opposed to its precursors in nineteenth- and twentieth-century Iran, emerged in the 1960s and '70s in the coalescing of two long-term trends: a secularization process (built upon the expansion of education and the media) and strains of rapid and unequal socioeconomic development, entailing mass migration (rural to urban) as a result of important demographic growth. The state served as the locomotive of the two processes, vigorously intervening everywhere and further sapping an already enfeebled civil society. In revitalizing civil society, on a plank designed to respond to the challenges of secularization and economic development, the Islamic movement had to take on the state, that is, to get into politics. The ideology that established a cosmological framework for this endeavor was developed when the regime seemed successful and impregnable (in the early 1960s), and gained wide currency when strains and failures accumulated (in the 1970s).

One could already in the 1960s speak of a radical Islamic movement, due to the hierarchical and autonomous nature of the Shi'ite clergy (especially in Iran), which enabled part of the clergy to serve as a ready-made cadre for such a movement. These mullahs were helped in this endeavor by the very existence of a hierarchy, by its self-sufficient economic basis, and by a tradition of circumscribed collaboration with the powers that be (i.e., a long-standing ideological heritage, typically Shi'ite, which privileged the "right of resistance"). None of these three factors exists among Sunnis.

An overpowering leader, Khomeini brought all of this together, while interpreting the heritage creatively. The movement did not have to develop a cadre of laymen (as in the Sunni world, where ulama had been tarred by servile collaboration with the powers-that-be), and the ideological challenge of justifying insurgency was less daunting than the one facing Sunnis.

Iran was oil rich. The socioeconomic strains thus had less to do with a stalling development (though on the eve of the 1979 revolution oil prices declined), than with the unequal (in terms of sectors) and inegalitarian nature of this development. Furthermore, it was molded by an exponential rise in expectations, fueled by the shah's megalomaniacal discourse, as the country became awash with money in 1973–74. The size of the native "profiteering" elites was much larger than in Egypt, for example, and their conspicuous consumption more salient. All this resulted in a severe syndrome of *relative* deprivation. Actual perspectives of decline (in status and income) were relevant merely for the old merchant classes (*bazaari*). In fact, even the "disinherited" lower classes, in whose name Khomeini spoke, had known some material improvement.

If 1973–74 was thus a powerful trigger, so was the onset of the shah's terminal illness sometime later—an illness that made his wielding of power more erratic and less resolute. This, in an autocracy, sent signs of flagging strength throughout the political community. The enfeebled state, harassed by its American patron to observe human rights, watched helplessly as the Islamic movement expanded, drawing the dissatisfied lower-middle and part of the professional urban classes. (The countryside was apathetic or mute.)

Yet the movement could not have maintained that momentum, despite the availability of a cadre of clergy, without Khomeini's hands-on charismatic leadership: as developer of an innovative ideology, buttressed by the aura of his scholarly authority; as a master communicator of this ideology and its application to specific, tangible cases, combining an attractive, homespun provincial (i.e., populist) style with adaptability to technological innovations (e.g., tape cassettes); as coalition builder (with rival Shi'ite top clergy and reformist Shi'ite liberals, with the secular democratic opposition, and even, for a while, with Marxists). Personal leadership, operating through the Shi'ite hierarchy, was the linchpin of the whole endeavor.

Sunni Radical Movements in Egypt: Origins and Emergence, late 1960s. The Egyptian case is paradigmatic of Muslim Brotherhood evolution elsewhere in the Middle East and North Africa. Founded in 1928 by schoolteacher Hasan al-Banna, the movement emerged in a world-transformer mode (the emphasis being on creating a network of Islam-inculcating schools, youth clubs, trade unions and syndicates), but was radicalized into a world-conqueror mode by confrontations with secular Egyptian governments unsympathetic to its Islamization project. (Other elements of the larger movement, like the Samawiyya sect, turned inward, in a world-renouncing mode.) Both orientations continue to exist side by side, although the political activists, journalists, and syndicalists of the "mainstream" Islamic current, no less than the terrorist cells, see and seek an ultimate victory for (their construction of) Islam.

The radicalization, its seeds present in Banna's insistence on involvement in politics, took definitive ideological form only well after his death, and after the movement had suffered as a result of its forays into power politics. (The Brotherhood was bitterly disappointed when the victorious Free Officers under Nasser outlawed it and later imprisoned its leaders.) Interestingly, the radical ideology, developed in the prison writings of Sayyid Qutb, anticipated the actual emergence of the radical movement.

Qutb, influenced by the writings of Pakistani thinker and Jamaat-i-Islami founder Abul Ala Maududi, justified the shift to world conquering by diagnosing a case of *jahiliyya* (pre-Islamic barbarism) infecting Egypt. Organizational shifts following his execution in 1966 mirrored the ideology: *takfir wal hijra* cells (identify and flee the enemy, in order to retaliate against him) sprang up, led by Qutb-inspired charismatic preachers. These charismatic leaders differed on strategy and targets (was all of Egyptian society the enemy, or just the state, or primarily the head of state?) but agreed that the infidels should be vanquished, by violent means if necessary. Qutb's ideology, which justified radicalization and world conquering, was an innovative response, given the absence of strong eschatalogical or religious-polity justifications in the host religion (Sunni Islam being neither as messiah-friendly nor hierarchical/semitheocratic as Shi'ism).

Hamas: Growth and Radicalization, mid 1980s to Present. The movement of Islamic resistance of Palestine, an offshoot of the Muslim Brotherhood in Gaza, also began as an Islamization project. Under the guiding genius of its founder (the crippled Shaykh Ahmed Yassin), however, and goaded by the daring acts of the tiny Islamic Jihad sect, Hamas in the mid-1980s moved from its world-transforming mode to a world-conquering phase. In so doing it assimilated nationalist elements by imitating and competing with the PLO for control of the resistance to Israeli occupation. The Intifada was a trigger for Hamas' rise to prominence in this new mode—a trigger shaped and exploited by the movement's leadership. The Oslo Accord of 1993 left Hamas as the best-organized and most influential obstructionist force in the territories. In its world-conqueror mode Hamas seeks the domination of Israel and hence is reluctant to shift ideologically and organizationally in response to the new facts in the field as of 1994.

Ulster Protestants: Emergence and Growth (the Ian Paisley Era). The Ulster Protestants are an interesting contrast to the North American Protestants in their world-transformer mode, who share the basic religious doctrines and symbolic resources with the Paisleyites. In Ulster, however, the political and social context, determined by the entrenched ethnic conflict between Scot- and English-derived Protestants and Irish Catholics, has dictated strikingly different patterns of mobilization and organization. The Ulster case suggests comparisons, instead, with other ethnonationalist movements that display a completely different religious portfolio (e.g., Sikhs, Sinhala Buddhists, perhaps even Hindutva militants). In each of these cases the "fundamentalist" movement adopts religious symbolism and discourse and strives for dominance of an ethnic opponent who is also constructed in religious terms (i.e., Ulster Protestants versus Irish Catholics, pure Sikhs versus false Sikhs and militant Hindus, Sinhala Buddhists versus Tamil Hindus, and Hindu nationalists versus upwardly mobile Indian Muslims).

In the early nineteenth century the politicization of the Irish and a Catholic church-sponsored nationalist movement mobilized the conservative Presbyterian minority (its origins in Ulster dating back to 1630) to forge an alliance with Anglo-Episcopalians and Scottish Presbyterians, upon whom they subsequently depended for economic and political resources. Steve Bruce points out that Protestantism and Catholicism were not just different religiopolitical traditions in Ulster: each defined itself in opposition to the other, with strict prohibitions on intermarriage, economic cooperation, and other alliances that would transgress strong boundaries and weaken ethnoreligious bonds. In the early twentieth century, however, the religious element of this affiliation was affected by secularizing trends brought on by industrialization; this was especially true of the Presbyterian presence.

This long-term structural factor provides an important set of structural conditions for the rise of fundamentalism, but the sufficient cause for its emergence in the twentieth century was the charismatic leadership of the Reverend Ian Paisley. Here we see a dynamic that social scientists can determine with high levels of accuracy—predictable patterns of social, economic, and political competition between ethnic groups—flavored and to a significant degree shaped by the unpredictable variable of personal choice. Paisley's brilliance has been to make a narrow premillennial sectarian religious discourse serve as a political idiom and rallying cry for Protestant Unionists, people who would not normally be recruits to a fundamentalist movement. (Many of Paisley's followers are not active church participants or born-again Christians.) He has done this by stoking the embers of the centuries-old conflict, while creating ex nihilo two very modern vehicles, one religious (the Free Presbyterian Church, founded in 1951, now with ten thousand members in forty-eight Ulster congregations) and one political (the Democratic Unionist Party, established in 1972). Despite secular trends, Paisley perceived that religion remains a vital part of the Scottish and Anglo-Irish heritages, and he appropriated conservative Protestant ideologies and languages to make sense of their apparently beleaguered position in the north of Ireland and to give purpose to their political agenda, which is dominated by a desire to remain part of the United Kingdom.

From 1921 to 1972 Northern Ireland was governed by a directly elected parliament at Stormont. Protestants enjoyed considerable material and cultural advantages over Catholics, but many were uneasy when Catholics were allowed their own institutions. Catholics could migrate to the republic and teach in southern schools. They had a monopoly in Catholic schools and a legal claim on jobs in state schools. In 1971 Paisley charged the Unionist government with cowardice for not opposing resurgent Irish nationalism and a compromising British government. Since then his Democratic Unionist Party has come to be accepted by other Unionist parties as an equal partner in various campaigns against British government policy. For a time Paisley was the most popular Unionist politician; in the 1984 elections to the European Community parliament, nearly a quarter of a million people—a sixth of the whole electorate—voted for him.

U. S. Protestant Christians: Second Public Emergence, Late 1970s to Present. There was a subtle but decisive theological shift in Protestant fundamentalism in its second emergence as a public force in the United States. The shift, from a strict premillennialist orientation to an operative postmillennialist orientation, had profound ideological and organizational implications; in short, it prepared the way for, and justified, the movement's turn to a new pattern of relating to the world. Premillennialism, the doctrine that the world would sink deeper and deeper into sin until Jesus returned to establish the millennial kingdom of the righteous, had provided the theoretical framework for the previous world-relational patterns of fundamentalism. After 1925, for example, the movement had retreated from the fallen world and established alternative institutions—independent churches, schools, radio stations, clinics, and the like—in the expectation of Christ's imminent return. "I am a fundamentalist," proclaimed the Reverend Jerry Falwell in the 1950s, "and that means that I am a soul-winner and a separatist." The task of the premillennialist was to *renounce* the fallen world of sin, *create* an alternative world of grace in which to win souls, and await the rapture and Jesus' triumphant arrival. Politics was off-limits.

The shift to an operative postmillennialism—the belief that Jesus would come only *after* Bible-believing Christians had prepared the way by inaugurating the era of righteousness on earth—was triggered by the moral and social crises of the 1960s. In establishing the Moral Majority in the late 1970s, Falwell explained that the forces of secular humanism had become so invasive in the 1960s and early 1970s—taking the form of the drug culture, the "new morality," the U.S. Supreme Court decisions (against prayer in public schools and in favor of abortion), and legislation "enacting secular humanism"—that Bible-believers could no longer wait passively for Jesus, but must protect the next generation of Christians by concerted political efforts to "repeal" or "roll back" secular humanism. Although he avoided explicit postmillennial rhetoric on most occasions for fear of scandalizing the old guard,[1] Falwell and his associates in the Religious Roundtable and other Christian Right lobbying groups pushed Protestant fundamentalism toward a new, world-conquering pattern of political activism in reaction to the threatening pluralism of belief and lifestyle that appeared to be overtaking "Judeo-Christian" America.

The first wave of this new political activism, designed to "take back" the courts, schools, and Congress from the secular humanists (and, presumably, to vanquish them or at least diminish their role in public life), was active during the Reagan presidency and followed a strategy of applying pressure at a national level. A second wave, inaugurated by the Reverend Pat Robertson's Christian Coalition in the late 1980s and 1990s, has profited from the lessons of the Moral Majority era, and now focuses its impressive and far more successful political activism on local politics—state assemblies, school boards, state political parties. The goal, however, remains basically the same, and the Christian Right is positioning itself in the 1990s to make a major impact on national politics.

Two aspects of this new world-conquering fundamentalism must be noted. (1) For the activists of the Christian Right, the language of restoration is favored over the language of revolution. The political structures and founding principles of the United States need not be overturned, but merely returned to their philosophical-theological basis in "the Judeo-Christian tradition." This may *seem* like a revolution, the Christian activists say, given how far we Americans have strayed from our divine origins. (2) The theological precision of separatist, Bible-believing fundamentalism in its early stages of origins and growth has given way, ironically, to an internal theological pluralism tied together by political coalitions (the Christian Right) rather than by historic theological and religious distinctions (fundamentalist, Pentecostal, etc.). Robertson, the leader of the Christian Coalition, is a Pentecostal rather than a fundamentalist; he affiliates not only with fundamentalists like Falwell, but also with the "Reconstructionist" Christians led by Gary North and the ideologue Rousas John Rushdoony, who preaches the concept of "theonomy" and would base U.S. law on the Mosaic codes of the Hebrew Bible.

In the world-conquering phase of fundamentalism, ideology and political considerations tend to muffle potentially divisive religious and theological elements.

Sikh Militants: Bhindranwale and After, 1980s to Present. Sikhism is a religion of fourteen million adherents, living mainly in the Punjab in the north of India.[2] The religion originated in the late fifteenth century under the leadership of the Guru Nanak, a member of the Kshatriya (warrior) caste. All ten of the Sikh gurus came from this caste.[3] The Adi Granth, the Sikh holy book, contains sacred documents and hymns composed by the first five gurus and the Bakhta saints; it was revised by the last guru, Gobind, in 1704.[4] The sixth guru, Hargobind, affirmed the inseparability of state and religion and legitimized reliance on the sword in the defense of Sikh interests.

Gobind, after persecutions by the Mughals and the execution of the two preceding gurus, founded the Khalsa (the pure), a fraternity of holy warriors all assuming the common name of Singh (lion). The Khalsa is a "chosen" corps of soldier-saints committed to a rigorous code of abstinence, prayer, and virtue. The number five has a mystical significance in Punjab; the first members of the Khalsa were the five Sikhs whom Gobind baptized and named Singh. The members of the Khalsa commit themselves to the five Ks—*kesa* (unshorn hair), *kangha* (comb), *kacch* (military shorts), *kirpan* (saber), *kara* (bracelet of steel). Unlike Hindus, the Sikhs are monotheists and opposed to image worship. There are some two hundred Sikh temples (gurdwaras) governed by temple priests, custodians, and congregational committees. Yet the Guru role persists in the form of sants, with disciples and followers. Since every Sikh has the right to read scripture, they recognize no priestly caste. There is a general governing body, the Shiromani Gurdwara Prabandhak Committee (SGPC), in Amritsar, the Sikh holy city.

In the power vacuum created by Persian penetration into Punjab in the mid-eighteenth century, the Sikhs were able to establish their own kingdom, which had an autonomous existence until the mid-nineteenth century when the British took the area under their protection. After several Sikh-British wars in the 1840s, the area was assimilated into British India. The Sikhs sided with the British in the Indian mutiny, and were thereafter favored in recruitment into the British army, in government service, and through investment in the development of agriculture in Punjab.

In the partitioning of India in 1947 almost three million Sikhs were forced to leave Pakistan and resettle south of the new border, in less desirable areas vacated by the Muslims. The new government of free India reduced the various privileges that the British had granted to the Sikhs, including special access to the military and civil services. A second aspect of chance was the introduction from the West of the Green Revolution (new, high-yield seeds and agricultural practices) into Punjabi agriculture during the 1960s and 1970s. This enriched many Punjabis, but accentuated Punjab polarization, leaving the western rural regions relatively backward and impoverished. After the partition a strong separatist mood developed among the Sikhs. Their religious party (Shiromani Akali Dal) led the agitation that culminated in the mid-1960s in the division of Punjab into three states, one of which had a Sikh majority. But the division of water rights among the three states left the Sikh Punjab with a major grievance.

The Akali Dal shared political power with the Congress Party in Punjab and controlled the Sikh temples through the SGPC. Sikh agitation, however, led to the formation of a smaller Punjab with a Sikh majority. The Sikh leader of the time, Sant Fateh Singh, used fasts and threats of self-immolation on the roof of the Golden Temple to bring pressure to bear on the Congress authorities.

Indira Gandhi's efforts to play secular bargaining politics with the Sikh leadership ended in tragic failure and catastrophe. In order to offset the extremism of the Akali Dal under the leadership of Sant Harchand Singh Longowal, she supported a new organization, the Khalsa Dal (group of the pure) formed by Jarnail Singh Bhindranwale in the early 1980s. Far from becoming a moderate alternative to the Akali Dal, the Khalsa Dal under Bhindranwale led an increasingly violent tendency into a series of assassinations and arrests. Bhindranwale found support among impoverished and displaced elements among the Jat farmers, and from the All India Sikh Student Federation, mobilized by his second in command, Amrit Singh. Bhindranwale's sermons defined the Sikh enemies as the secularism of the Indian state, the moral decay of urban life, and the threat of Hindu religious nationalism. He advocated the formation of an independent Sikh state (Khalistan) in which state and religion would be combined (*miri-piri*). In this sense he was a world creator; in order to create the world he envisioned, however, the Sikhs must conquer the alien in Punjab, and control the land entirely.

Bhindranwale's followers thus engaged in violence and terrorism. The emergence of the radicalized movement was triggered in 1983 when Bhindranwale and his followers headquartered themselves in the Golden Temple in Amritsar, and accumulated weapons. Longowal also occupied the Golden Temple, and violent skirmishes between the two groups ensued. After months of futile negotiations with both groups, Prime Minister Indira Gandhi sent in the Indian army. After a bloody battle in which the Golden Temple was profaned and damaged, Bhindranwale killed, and more than a thousand lives lost, the occupation and rebellion were terminated. In revenge two of Gandhi's bodyguards who were Sikhs assassinated her. Longowal also was assassinated by Bhindranwale's followers.[5]

The radical Sikh groups—those associated with Bhindranwale and militants among the Akali Dal favoring Khalistan—clearly fulfill the criteria of fundamentalism, more so than other South Asian varieties. At the same time they share with them, as well as with Islamic fundamentalism, a strong ethnonationalist component. Ideologically, Sikh fundamentalism is reactive, first to the Sikh apostates—those who fail to adhere to the five Ks—and second to the secular Indian state and the menacing Hindu nationalists, whom, in the eyes of the Sikhs, the state seems to support. It is selective of the tradition, emphasizing the sixth guru, Hargobind, who justified the sword, and the tenth guru, Gobind Singh, who originated the Khalsa. It stresses moral dualism, outlawing, even condemning to death, "heretics" such as the Niranjiri, or compromisers such as Longowal of the Akali Dal. It attributes absolute and exclusive validity and inerrancy to its scripture, the Granth Sahib. The aspiration to Khalistan—the ultimate Sikh theocracy—has utopian and millennial overtones. Thus there is a strong nation-building as well as religious component in Sikh fundamentalism. Ideologically the miri-piri doctrine of the unity of religion and the state continues to be the central principle of a separate Khalistan. The form of organization is charismatic authoritarian in its sant-disciple version, with the idea of the Khalsa as a group of baptized holy warriors, and of the ultimate domination of the Sikh community by such an elect body. Organizationally, the diffuseness and totalism of the sant-disciple relationship makes for great difficulty and instability in forming organizations and coalitions, and may be the principle reason for the breakdown of communication and resort to violence. Almost all of the Sikh militants come from 10 percent of the Sikh villages in western Punjab, where the Green Revolution has had the least effect. The uneven impact of the rapid agricultural development in Punjab polarized Sikh society. The Sikh militants are subsistence-farmer Jats, marginal small farmers, and depeasantized farm laborers. Support for Sikh extremism also comes from that part of the population forced to leave productive farms in what was to become Pakistan and to occupy inferior properties vacated by the Muslims. The Sikh militants are thus recruited from the least educated, least literate strata of the population. Bhindranwale completed only the first five primary school grades. The Sikh sants have been educated in Sikh seminaries such as the Damdami Taksal.

If we take regional backwardness, economic marginality and downward mobility, minimal and predominantly religious education, low media exposure, and relative absence of civil society, we have a picture of Sikh militancy as drawing on the social sectors and strata least affected by economic benefits, educational opportunity, and civic vitality.

Gush Emunim: Origins and Emergence, 1970s. Starting out as a world-conquering movement, the Gush Emunim also appears in the world-transforming category, because its tactics and ideology change after its initial messianic fervor and it recognizes itself to be involved in a longer struggle for control of "the whole Land of Israel." In its origins the Gush was guided by the authoritative teaching of the Rabbis Kook. The rise of the movement itself is due, however, to an unexpected trigger, the 1967 war. In its miraculous swiftness and in bringing under Israeli control the historical heart of biblical Palestine (i.e., Judea and Samaria), the war struck off a wave of national euphoria and changed the fortunes of a tiny group of Mizrachi youth (Religious Zionists). This hitherto insignificant group, predicated upon the ideology of Rabbi Kook the Elder and led by his son, considered that the redemptive era had already begun with the return of the Jews to Palestine in the 1880s, and was significantly advanced by the establishment of the State of Israel, as a sacralized tool of the messianic endeavor.

This is somewhat similar to the Egyptian case, where ideology was developed long before the movement emerged. The ideology developed in both cases in different (and inauspicious) circumstances and was given its chance when its prognostications suddenly came true. The marginal group of Merkaz Harav yeshiva, headed by Rabbi Kook the Younger, saw its gospel becoming attractive to the sector of religious Zionism and especially to its activist youth movement, Bnei Akiva, which served as a sort of ready-made cadre. The group of young leaders that coalesced around Rabbi Kook the Younger saw the settlement of Judea and Samaria as a way of keeping the divine gift, locking it in so to speak, and hence setting forward the Redemption. This was a religious gloss on the old (secularist) Zionist belief that tilling the Land of Israel is the only way toward true return to Zion.

Yet the 1967 war barely gave the movement visibility; it was not enough to give it scope and prominence. A second trigger, the 1973 semi-defeat, soon endowed it with the latter. The 1973 war goaded the movement into intensive settlement activity, cognizant of the fact that the Redemption was not on "automatic pilot," as could be construed in the six preceding years; setbacks were coming to block, nay even subvert, it; defeatism among Israeli elites (ready for territorial compromise) was liable to magnify the scope of these setbacks. Until 1977 settlements had to be created against the government's will, and that made them all the more attractive for the young Bnei Akiva activists, as a ritual acting out of the struggle between the true-blue Zionism and tired, washed-out defeatists. Still, without the coalition-building abilities of some Gush leaders, the recruitment of these secularist allies (e.g., the Ein Vered circle of the Labor movement) would not have come about. It solidified during the struggle against the evacuation of Sinai in the early 1980s.

Kach: Meir Kahane. This is the story of a double emergence, although the Kach movement is still in its first generation. The first incarnation of Kach, then (late 1960s) called the Jewish Defense League (JDL), represented the response of lower-middle-class Jews in large metropolitan areas, mostly New York, to the rise of black militancy, claims for affirmative action, the surge of insecurity, and the minority drive for empowerment over local education and welfare agencies in the United States. In the same breath it capitalized upon the feelings of marginality and resentment that these Jews, many of them Orthodox and/or newcomers (post-Holocaust), harbored toward the liberal (Conservative and Reform) establishment, which seemed to disregard the interests and sensibilities of their less fortunate brethren. By stressing a bleak view of all Gentiles and a confrontational activist stance toward them, the JDL preached—and practiced—Jewish inclusiveness, empowerment of Jewish have-nots, and a sharp divide between the beleaguered Jewish community and those outside the fold. We said the JDL, but actually one should say Meir Kahane, for the movement was the brainchild of this charismatic rabbi, and he served as its major communicator, strategist, and organizer. (To the above-mentioned themes he would soon add the cause of Soviet Jews.)

When Kahane moved to Israel in 1971, he tried to transplant this brand of ideology cum practice and incorporate it into the context of the Arab-Israeli conflict, endowing the conflict with ethnoreligious (virtually racist) overtones. The transplantation to Israeli soil took more time to accomplish, for Kahane was alien to the indigenous discourse. The movement continued to be a one-man show even in Israel.

Kahane hit his stride only in the late 1970s, when he developed a lingo appealing to the Sephardic residents of the poorer quarters of big cities (and to a lesser extent to Sephardic inhabitants of the new "development towns"). These populations found in him a leader who articulated their tribalistic notions of Jewish ethnicity as well as their age-old suspicions of the Arabs from whose lands they had been chased in the 1950s. Because their ethnic notions differed from those of the Ashkenazic liberal establishment (for which Jewish identity was based upon individual choice), Kahane also expressed their resentment as a marginal sector with a growing sense of relative deprivation (hence his appeal in big cities where poor neighborhoods border on middle-class, liberal ones). The competition between poor Jews and Arabs in the job market (due to the employment of West Bank and Gaza residents) created ethnic friction in the unskilled and semi-skilled categories. This situation lent particular virulence to Kahane's call for exclusion of the Arab—first exclusion from Jewish neighborhoods and businesses, and later from the Land of Israel altogether.

Exclusion (a.k.a. transfer) was presented as a panacea to the Arab-Israeli conflict as well as to daily economic competition. The militant tactics that Kahane inculcated in his young, uneducated groupies, incarnated a "by force alone" and "it is a jungle out there" vision of the Middle East, a vision typical of Jews with origins in Arab countries. All this was couched in religious terms (Kahane was a yeshiva graduate) that rendered it custom-made for the traditionalist bent of Sephardic Jews, a bent quite distinguished from that of the Ashkenazic haves. In this overarching context, the Intifada was a useful, if rather late, trigger, following the trigger of the economic crisis of the early 1980s (the inflation that hit the have-nots hardest).

Sri Lankan Buddhist Extremism: Origins and Emergence, 1956. Theravada Buddhist doctrine was codified in the first century B.C.E., in a canon consisting of three texts, one pertaining to monastic discipline, a second containing the discourses of the Buddha, and the third concerned with higher doctrine. Organization consists of a monastic order (the Sangha) grouped into monasteries and around Buddhist shrines, and educational institutions. The monk (bhikku) commits himself for life to an ascetic, mendicant, and chaste existence, engaged in meditation intended to attain tranquillity and insight. Yet the withdrawal from worldliness was historically balanced in two ways. The monks and the Buddhist schools inculcated a morality drawn from the lives of great Buddhist heroes such as Prince Vessantara and Emperor Asoka—a moral code emphasizing generosity, righteousness, compassion, nonviolence, and similar virtues. In addition, over the centuries individual monasteries acquired substantial landholdings and other properties granted by kings and noblemen; thus they developed "interests" that led to political and policy involvements. And as Buddhism encountered the rituals, beliefs, and practices of other religions such as Hinduism, Islam, and Christianity, it picked up assorted gods, saints, rituals, and liturgies, which were worshiped and practiced alongside the normative disciplines of suffering, renunciation, and deliverance.[6]

For more than four centuries Western imperialism—Portuguese, Dutch, and British—influenced Sri Lankan culture and society. By the mid-nineteenth century the Protestant and Catholic missions had established a near monopoly of the educational system. Christian converts were favored in appointments to government service, and Buddhists were handicapped in other respects. Western religious, cultural, and political ideas and practices threatened the survival of Buddhist culture and institutions. Yet a Buddhist revival began in the late nineteenth century, supported by the American Theosophical Society, an organization that challenged the supremacy of Christianity, claiming that there were superior metaphysical and ethical qualities in Asian religions. Henry Steele Olcott, its president, helped to establish the Buddhist Philosophical Society and encouraged the successful campaigns by Sri Lankan monks and laymen to establish Buddhist schools, to return controls of temples and temple lands to the Buddhist clergy, and to reinstitute Buddhist holidays.

Shortly thereafter, Angārika Dharmapāla sought to create a "Protestant Buddhism." He legitimated religious nationalism by his interpretation of the Māhavaṃsa, a Sinhala Buddhist chronicle, and of stories about King Duṭṭhagāmaṇi, who defeated the Tamils in the second century B.C E. and reestablished Buddhist rule. Dharmapāla formed the Mahabodhi Society of Colombo in 1891 and started a journal that fostered a revivalist, moralistic, and nationalist Buddhism appealing to the educated and urban Sinhala elite.[7]

Dharmapāla died in 1933; four years later, S. W. R. D. Bandaranaike, a member of the Anglicized elite reconverted to Buddhism by the revivalist movements, founded the Sinhala Maha Sabha, a revivalist party that initially played coalition politics. By the 1956 elections, however, Bandaranaike was exploiting an economic downturn and conducting a successful pro-Buddhist, pro-Sinhala campaign. A significant event in the 1956 election was the controversy surrounding *The Betrayal of Buddhism*, a report of the Buddhist Commission of Inquiry, which had been appointed by the All-Ceylon Buddhist Congress of 1953 to investigate what had happened to Buddhism under the British. The report presented in detail the long record of British suppression and discriminatory practices. Celebrations in 1956–57 of the 2,500th birthday of the Buddha kept alive these denunciations of British suppression, and created widespread millennial expectations of the revival of Buddhist glory in terms of the Mahāvaṃsa and the triumphs of King Duṭṭhagāmaṇi.

The government of the victorious Bandaranaike immediately enacted pro-Buddhist legislation. It established a Ministry of Cultural Affairs which took charge of Buddhist shrines and institutions; prepared a new translation of the Buddhist Canon; published a Buddhist Encyclopedia; and upgraded Buddhist colleges. A movement to make Sinhalese the state language ran into the vigorous resistance of the Tamils, and culminated in the language riots of 1957. These bloody clashes inaugurated the tragic confrontation of Buddhist and Tamil extremists which has dominated Sri Lankan politics ever since. Bandaranaike was assassinated soon thereafter by elements in the United Monks' Front.

Sri Lankan development in the twentieth century has been marked by increasing urban and industrial growth, and economic inequality. Much of village community life has broken down as a consequence of the resettlement of population into new towns and the larger cities. Class antagonism, social mobility, and intensely conflictual language and ethnic politics led to extreme political polarization, the acceptance of violence and intimidation as normal instruments of political action, and increasingly authoritarian and coercive government. The two leading Sri Lankan political parties are the United National Party (UNP) and the pro-Buddhist Sri Lanka Freedom Party (SLFP). The UNP has been in the majority for much of the post-World War II period, and under the pressure of Buddhist-Tamil polarization and violence has become increasingly authoritarian and repressive. The Tamils have been represented by the Tamil

United Liberation Front (TULF), favoring a separate Tamil state in the north, but through negotiation and compromise. Yet extremist groups on both sides—the Janata Vimukti Peramuna (JVP, or National Liberation Front), and the Liberation Tigers of the Tamil Eelam (LTTE)—incited much violence and bloodshed during the 1970s and 1980s. A substantial part of the bloodshed was caused by the security forces of the government.[8]

Only in small part can Sri Lankan Buddhist fundamentalism be described as reacting to the characteristics of the host religion. Yet Dharmāpala's authoritarian leadership demanded that Theravada Buddhism rid itself of syncretic accretions—Hindu gods, magic, sorcery, and the like, and return to the Theravada simplicities. As part of his scheme of domination, Dharmapāla focused his attack on the British colonial suppression of Buddhist culture and institutions, and on the Hindu and Islamic threat to Buddhism resulting from the Tamil occupation of the north. Dharmapāla's stress on sober worldly conduct imitated the Victorian English rather than the world-renouncer ideals of Buddhism. And the great stress he placed on nationalism, despite his effort to legitimate it by his interpretation of the Mahāvaṃsa, could not be unambiguously derived from Buddhist doctrine.

Sri Lankan Buddhist fundamentalism thus rests on a basic ideological ambivalence. On the one hand Theravada Buddhism stresses withdrawal from worldly values, including politics. The Four Noble Truths and the Eightfold Path do not include the cultivation of intimidation and violence. Hence, as Gananath Obeyesekere points out in chapter 9, it is difficult to characterize the extreme ethnoreligious nationalism of Sri Lankan Buddhist extremism as "selected" from the Buddhist canon; there is nothing in the canon to legitimate the fierce violence in which the bhikkus themselves have participated. While the Mahāvaṃsa celebrates military prowess in the defeat of the Tamils and accords legitimacy to the Buddhist claim to Sri Lanka, it was reinterpreted by Dharmapāla and later Buddhist leaders to legitimate a much more unequivocal and aggressive nationalism. From this point of view the ideological reactivity and selectivity of Buddhist nationalism shares with Hindu and Islamic fundamentalisms the elements of anti-imperialism and ethnonational preemptiveness.

Other ideological properties of fundamentalism such as Manichaeanism, inerrancy, and millennialism are in some measure applicable to the Buddhist extremists. They view the Tamils, as well as the moderates in their own Buddhist camp, as evil in contrast with their own virtue. The favorite text of the extremists, the Mahavāmsa, is a chronicle, not a doctrine or set of disciplinary rules. The realized Sri Lankan Buddhist millennium would be a Sri Lanka rid of Hindus, Muslims, and Christians, its people living in a Buddhist "kingdom."

None of the organizational examples—Dharmāpala's Mahabodhi Society, the Sinhala Maha Sabha, the SLFP, or the partly underground terrorist JVP—exhibit in an unambiguous way the typical organizational patterns of fundamentalist movements. The notion that the JVP is an elect group, and its tendency to draw sharp boundaries between its members and all others, can as easily be attributed to guerrilla and terrorist activities, as to their religious beliefs. Rigorous codes of behavior are characteristic of the Buddhist monks in their capacities as members of monasteries, and not as members of these organizations. Strong, charismatic leadership is not a characteristic of Sri Lankan Buddhist social and political movements. Leadership, organization, and membership in Sri Lankan Buddhism is more fluid, more populistic, more easily fragmented than other world-conquering movements we have analyzed.

The historic encounter of Sri Lankan Buddhism with Christianity and Hinduism has been of greater significance in the rise of Buddhist fundamentalist extremism. The Hindu Tamil minority in the north, backed by the seventy million Tamils across the twenty-five mile Palk Strait, imparts a degree of paranoia to Buddhist defensiveness. In recent years the emergence of aggressive Hindu nationalism has added fuel to these fears.

Economic growth in Sri Lanka in the last forty years has resulted in a substantial movement of population as industry has grown at the cost of agricultural and village life, new towns have been formed, and people have moved into the cities, particularly Colombo. Increasing income inequality has impaired the sense of community, and unemployment particularly among young men has created potential recruits for guerrilla and terroristic action. Practically all of the civil disturbances in Sri Lanka—the election disturbances and the racial and religious riots—have occurred in settlements in colonization schemes, in the traditionless new market towns, and in Colombo. James Manor attributes Buddhist extremism to the breakdown of traditional village organization, and the rise of modern trading towns and "mass society" urban areas. But Manor also accounts for Sri Lankan violence by noting a thoroughgoing lack of capacity for organization and discipline throughout the whole of Sri Lankan government—central and local—the party system, and individual political parties, as well as the Sri Lankan clergy. Prime ministers cannot control their ministers, and cabinets cannot be counted on to act in concert in the sense of collective responsibility. Ministers cannot count on their officials, and local government, largely ignored by the central government, has little revenue with which to implement policies. Political parties have little organizational substance; they are little more than leaders, and diffuse followings. Buddhist religious organization is similarly fragmented. Individual monasteries move in their own directions, and individual monks have considerable autonomy to engage in whatever religious and political activities they prefer. In a culture such as this, leadership has little capacity to pursue policies effectively, producing rhetoric rather than careful strategy and tactics. And social and political action deteriorates into reactive movements—demonstrations, mobs, and riots.

Thus the international and religious contexts, Sri Lankan economic development, population displacement, and organizational propensities extending throughout Sri Lankan culture are necessary causes of its Buddhist extremism. But chance and contingency have had significant triggering impacts. The intervention of Olcott and the American Theosophical Society gave Dharmapāla the authority and visibility he needed to gain an audience and begin the reversal of British Westernizing and Christianizing policy. The crucial election of 1956 was greatly influenced by the economic distress caused by the decline in world commodity prices and in Sri Lankan exports.

This election of a government on a Sinhala Buddhist platform, followed by provocative legislative measures favoring the establishment of the Sri Lankan language and the Buddhist religion, set that polity on its course of polarization and violence from which it has not yet recovered.[9]

The high incidence of mob violence—the extent to which outcomes in Sri Lankan politics have been shaped by these traumatizing, unpredictable, uncontrollable events—is extraordinary. Sri Lankan Buddhist extremism is a limiting case of weak leadership and strong and chaotic mass action. The leaders who have entered Sri Lankan religious movements and politics since the beginnings of Buddhist revivalism have not been effective ideologists, skilled organizers, or coalition makers. The leaders of the major Sri Lankan political parties have outdone each other in demagogy and in Tamil bashing. Leaders are reluctant to form organizations with explicit divisions of labor, since this deprives them of discretion. Each major party when in opposition challenges the governing party for failing to go far enough in asserting Buddhist redominance. The many Buddhist monks who participate in these extremist movements and activities add another irrational component. Monks are objects of worship in Sri Lankan Buddhism. Despite their inexperience and naivete, their political interventions, which occur on a substantial scale, are not disputed.

Thus we conclude our discussion of the world-conquering pattern with an anomalous case in which political choices and decisions have been frustrated and distorted by anomic violence rather than calculated by strong charismatic/authoritarian leadership. The kind of process those who know Sri Lankan politics describe is a vicious circle of violence feeding on violence, with governments, opposition parties, terrorist movements, and Tamil separatist movements locked together in a tight, irrational embrace.

World Transformer

Movements in the world-transformer mode occupy a niche in society, but they are constrained from hegemonic activity and forced to negotiate their circumstances and transform the environment over time. Leadership may be diffuse, shared by a number of authoritative leaders, mobilizing followers on particular issues; the teachings or fate of any one leader is less important than in the world-conqueror pattern. The community is drawn at times into public confrontation with outsiders; the dominant considerations for the analyst are the character of the host society, the resistance it mounts to fundamentalist movements, and the strategies these movements adopt to increase their influence over society. The organizational structure may be described as an expanding and contracting enclave: it may consist of diffuse organizational networks that may be organized and coordinated in times of mobilization. Movements in this mode exhibit an approach-avoidance pattern of withdrawal from and engagement with the surrounding society. Such a movement may be a religious or ethnic minority with aspirations of achieving a consolidated and multigenerational status.

U. S. Protestant Fundamentalism: First Emergence, 1875–1925. Given the synergy between certain unique features of American political culture on the one hand and the ideological and organizational configurations of nineteenth-century evangelical Protestantism on the other, it would have been rather surprising if fundamentalism, or something very much like it, had not emerged on cue when the new threats posed by liberal religion, secular philosophy, and science triggered a rift between these two powerful modes of public discourse—religion and politics—in the early twentieth century.

By fortifying the wall of separation between church and state while ensuring freedom of religion, the American government had created a cultural environment, marked by religious and ethnic pluralism and religious voluntarism, in which competition between sects was encouraged and social spaces, or niches, for a variety of religious expressions were secured. Evangelical Protestantism further encouraged the splintering and diversification of religious movements and institutions and thereby created a vast network of social sources for old-time religion (e.g., revivalist preachers, Bible institutes, seminaries, strong local congregations, the Princeton School of Theology, etc.). Fundamentalism emerged ready-made from this mix, exploiting the resources at hand while fortifying itself as a unique movement by organizing rapidly around its central ideological principle—separatism—backed by the recently crafted theological doctrines of premillennialism and inerrancy. Early recruits came from disaffected ranks of the pre-existing evangelical network. If the invasion of secularism, especially in the form of liberal religionists who embraced Darwinism and the Higher Criticism of the Bible, initially prompted the fundamentalist reaction, the relative heterogeneity of religion in America made the movement's growth possible.

Over the decades the niches filled by fundamentalism changed and grew. In its first incarnation the movement appeared in Baptist and Presbyterian churches of the northeast; it appealed to newly urbanized middle- and lower-middle-class professionals and laborers, primarily of British and Scottish ancestry, seeking cultural stability and certitude in a time of social and economic dislocation brought on by rapid industrialization. With its specialized lingo, behavioral requirements, exclusivity, and stress on doctrinal uniformity and moral rigor, fundamentalism was for its recruits the functional equivalent of the immigrant enclave. Local pastors and preachers self-consciously created "cultural capital" with which to build a distinct subculture. In weighing the importance of the social sources of fundamentalism, however, most commentators emphasize the central and seemingly independent role of ideology: more than many other protest movements, this one was about religious doctrines, values, and norms, and the motivations of its adherents cannot be understood apart from this integrity of belief (the particulars of which were frozen around the turn of the century). (It may even be argued that the belief system itself outweighs the importance of the individual charismatic preacher who brings it alive on the local level, but this is perhaps a chicken-and-egg argument.) By comparison, social, economic, and educational factors pale in importance. Rural-urban tensions are overplayed in many analyses of the movement's emergence, for even the first generation had adapted to the basic conditions of urban life.

It should be emphasized that the fundamentalist spirit of independence, if not defiance, was in keeping with classic Protestant (especially Baptist) emphases. The come-outers came out of churches that had been on the right course before the infiltration of secularizing agents. The basic organizational structure of fundamentalism is therefore in continuity with the evangelical heritage, but the noncompromising approach proved effective in attracting people beset by fears of assimilation; and as subsequent generations proved, this approach remained appealing in another region, the South, in a time of greater social and economic mobility and prosperity.

Comunione e Liberazione. The Comunione e Liberazione (CL) has an altogether different story from most Catholic reactive movements. Still in its first generation, it is defined by its attempt to formulate a conservative Catholic ideology and strategy of power politics. Unlike Catholic traditionalist movements, CL in its initial emergence offered a blueprint for the future to the young, upscale Italians it sought to recruit. The movement is expert at articulating its ideological principles, social programs, and concrete goals; its organizational structure is a fundamentalist-type blend of political cadre, religious association, and social club. Yet it wavers between attempts to transform society gradually, through the growing prominence of its religious culture, on the one hand, and significant involvement in local and national politics, on the other hand, where it hopes to further its ends more directly.

The movement emerged in Milan as a brilliantly idiosyncratic answer—Father Luigi Giussani's—to the religious declension and political upheaval of postwar Italy. Giussani blended disparate modern ideologies and philosophies. He drew, for example, upon the early-twentieth-century Protestant neo-orthodox theologian Karl Barth to infuse Italian Catholicism with a prophetic realism; and he cited an unlikely existentialist source, Camus, on the priority of grace (and, by Giussani's extension, Catholic sacramentalism) over Protestant scrupulosity to justify moral rigor and severity.

Giussani was a charismatic university and high school teacher in the 1950s and 1960s. He formulated a Christian critique of modern culture, coupled with a political philosophy of "the new Christendom," which Pope John Paul II endorsed as a way to revive moribund Italian (and general European) Catholicism. Giussani's movement grew in the 1960s and 1970s, primarily among university students and young professionals, attracting many who, facing poor employment prospects, were disillusioned with revolutionary radicalism and the moral corruption of Italian society. In CL the intellectual attack on secularization was joined to a political problem and an organizational solution. CL developed programs, implemented through its *scuole* (local chapters of students), and publications devoted to a wide range of social issues, as well as extensive missionary activities. The movement organization also included the Movimento Popolare, an inner core of devoted adherents, and the Compagnia delle Opere, a nonprofit organization founded in 1986 to promote cooperation among Italian companies and institutions for the sake of employing young Catholics. Boundaries are maintained by personal ties (new members adopt a big brother from among those who already belong), daily contacts, frequent devotions, and study groups within the community and by mutual support and elaborate personal networks within secular society, from professors to Christian Democrats.

Although the new Christendom rhetoric suggests theocratic elements, the real transformation CL seeks is cultural, and the political connections are seen as short-term means to a long-term end. This movement now faces the question of whether it can survive its current crisis and develop second-generation leadership.

Pentecostalism in Guatemala. Among the causes for the emergence of the Guatemalan neo-Pentecostals are: (1) the influence of North American missionaries and televangelists such as Bill Bright (Campus Crusade for Christ) and Pat Robertson (CBN), who contributed millions of dollars for media blitzes and short-term, intensive evangelizing; (2) covert political operations and funding designed to strengthen both the budding evangelical movement (seen as a source of "foot soldiers in the advancement of U.S. foreign policy") and right-wing governments; and (3) the decline of the status, fortunes, and influence of the Roman Catholic Church over both the people and powers that be of Guatemala—a decline that backpedaling hierarchs like Archbishop Penados blamed, somewhat disingenuously, on factors 1 and 2 (i.e., the "invasion of the sects" as an imperialist economic and political strategy).

The causes of Catholic decline also lay in the foreign character of the clergy, the unsuitability of its European ideology and religiosity, and the historic and increasingly unpopular Catholic identification with the landed aristocracy and its failed economic policies, which had resulted in undernourishment, slavery, illiteracy, forced migration, crowding, a highly stratified social order, and the exploitation and repression of the masses.

The necessary cause of the rise and growth of the neo-Pentecostal movement was the rapid attempt to transform the structure of the Guatemalan political economy. Within this attempted economic transformation, the short-term trigger for the explosion of the movement in the 1980s was the rise of a born-again retired general, Efraín Ríos Montt, to the presidency of the country.

In these developments the Pentecostal communities played, at most, a passive supporting role. They were not concerned with domination or world conquest as much as with transforming their religious, social, and economic situation from the Catholic, hierarchical model, which seemed to keep them in poverty, to an evangelical, egalitarian, localized, and indigenous form of religious ideology and organization that inspired cultural transformation and the domestication of husbands, the renewing of the nuclear family, and the emergence of small-scale entrepreneurial businesses. Retained in this transformation was a passive approach to political involvement, though it should be noted that Guatemalan evangelicals by and large supported Ríos Montt and, in any case, did not resist him, and turned their backs on the Catholic liberationists who risked their lives to do so.

Hindu Nationalism: Origins and Growth in Staggered Emergences of RSS, VHP, and BJP, 1915 to Present. There are three related fundamentalist-like organizations of national significance in India—Rashtriya Svayamsevak Sangh (RSS, or National Union of Volunteers), the Vishwa Hindu Parishad (VHP, or World Hindu Society), and the Bharatiya Janata Party (BJP, or Indian People's Party). These movements are descended from the Hindu Mahasabha (Hindu Great Council), founded in 1915 in re-action to the formation of the Muslim League. The leading figure in the Mahasabha was V. D. Savarkar, whose book *Hindutva* formulated the doctrinal base of Hindu fundamentalism. Savarkar and his followers affirmed the racial, cultural, and religious superiority of the Hindus. The doctrine of Hindutva has been adopted by the RSS, the VHP, and the BJP.

The RSS was founded in 1925 by Keshav Baliram Hedgewar, a Maharashtrian Brahman reacting to India's long history of domination and exploitation by the Muslims and the British, and to what he viewed as the ineffectiveness of Gandhi's tactics of nonviolence. Hedgewar and his Maharashtrian Brahman successor, M. S. Golwarkar, led the organization from its founding until 1973. The RSS became a highly organized "brotherhood" of militant believers, though its militance subsided somewhat during the decades immediately after the attainment of national independence. Balasaheb Deoras, secretary general and supreme leader since 1973, has restored the militantly activist line that the organization followed prior to the death of Hedgewar in 1940.

The young RSS recruits are required to submit to demanding schedules of indoctrination and physical training. They wear uniforms and carry quarterstaves called *lathis.* They are organized into small troops called *shakhas* and undergo military-like drills, participate in forest encampments, and the like. As of 1990 there were two million such young men, called *svayamsevaks,* organized in twenty-five thousand shakhas, in some eighteen thousand urban and rural centers across the country. The activities of these groups are supervised by three thousand professional organizers—primarily celibate young men. The parallels with Hitler Youth and the Young Communist League are obvious.

The VHP was founded in 1964 at the initiative of the RSS and is led by staff of the RSS. It organizes campaigns carrying the message of Hindutva and Hindu revival to remote corners of India and to the Hindu diaspora overseas. In recent decades it has organized huge religious processions (*yitras*). The VHP is organized at two levels with a "religious assembly" at the center directed by advisory committees made up of leaders from participating religious communities in the regions. It claims to have more than three hundred district units and some three thousand branches spread throughout India. Outside of India it claims to have several thousand branches in twenty-three countries. It reports more than one hundred thousand members, with more than two hundred full-time workers.

The objectives of the VHP are like those of its parent RSS, namely to reaffirm Hindu "values," to bring secularized Indians back to the Hindu fold, and to reclaim the Untouchables to Hinduism, even to the point of eliminating untouchability from Hindu society. The VHP seeks to propagate a modern, coherent, national conception of Hinduism. By a broad definition of Hindu values it seeks to transcend internal differences among Hindus. It downplays differences in religious doctrine and practice and attempts to unite reformism with its own Brahmanical orthodoxy, or more accurately orthopraxis. Hindutva propaganda represents Hinduism as a single all-embracing ethnonational-religious community including Jains, Buddhists, and Sikhs (whether they like it or not). The VHP does not criticize Islamic and Christian theology and ideology as such, but is suspicious of Christians and Muslims because of their foreign origins.

The BJP emerged in 1980 out of the Janata coalition that displaced the Indira Gandhi regime in 1977. Most of the BJP leaders came out of the RSS organization, as was the case with the BJP's predecessor organization, the Jan Sangh. After the election of 1991 the BJP emerged as the leading opposition in the Indian parliament. In its search for votes the BJP has tried to appeal broadly to all Indians, including Sikhs and Muslims. Its various affiliated organizations number more than a hundred, and touch almost every aspect of Indian life. It is what Sigmund Neumann used to call a "party of integration," referring to the chain-link structure of the Fascist, Nazi, and Communist parties of Europe.[10]

These Hindu movements differ from the Abrahamic ones in a number of significant respects. (1) While they are reactive to the growth of the secular, pluralist Indian state, they are also reactive to the competition of Islam and Christianity. There is also an ethnonationalist component—an Aryan, "blood and soil," nativist, preemptive ideology. (2) The RSS and the VHP differ in the way in which they select from Hindu tradition. The RSS emphasizes the Kshatriya military tradition (in its Maharashtrian version). Its central headquarters are still in Nagpur, its capital. The VHP, with its revivalism and inclusive missionary activity, downplays distinct doctrines and reaches out to Untouchables, Tribals, Sikhs, Buddhists, and Jains, excluding only the Muslims and the Christians. In their concern over the possible appeal of Islamic and Christian egalitarianism to the Untouchables, they have attacked caste hierarchy as socially divisive, blocking the kind of social solidarity its leaders believe is necessary for a strong India. (3) These Hindu movements are not enclaves as is the case with Abrahamic fundamentalisms, but rather tend to be revivalist and missionary networks. They view Sikhs, Jains, Buddhists, Tribals, and Untouchables as belonging within the Hindu "community" and argue that most Muslims and Christians are "Hindu by blood," that is, converts to alien religions, though this is explicitly denied by Muslim and Christian leaders. (4) The notion of textual inerrancy is difficult to sustain in view of the large and complex corpus of Sanskritic and traditional Hindu literature of hymns, ritual prescriptions, sagas, philosophical writings, and the like. (5) There is nothing comparable to the "end of days" and the final afterlife as found in Jewish, Christian, and Islamic theology. Modern Hindutva, however, has borrowed from the Abrahamic traditions, an eschatology of ultimate destiny, with Hindutva being realized as the Kingdom of Ram (Ram Rajiya or Ram Rashtriya). Ram is represented as both man and god—imitative of Christianity. This is a synthetic cosmology, an effort to validate a claim to a Hindu version of fundamentalism. (6) The notion of the elect is present, in the larger sense of the ethnoreligious notion of the Aryan race, and in the self-selection of the celibate and highly disciplined staff organizers, trainers, and workers of the RSS and VHP, many of whom are Brahmans or from the other two "twice-born" categories of castes—Kshatriya and Vaishya. There are full-time workers from other lower castes and groups. But this is not the enclave idea of a "returning and loyal remnant." (7) Only the RSS requires specific behaviors and disciplines of its members, the wearing of uniforms, the carrying of the lathi, participation in drill, and the like. Discipline is especially required of the training cadres, some of whom live celibate lives and devote themselves full-time to RSS work. But these propensities pervade the related movements as well.

Hindu fundamentalism appears to be as much a militant nation- and state-building (or rebuilding) movement, as a traditional religion-affirming movement. *Hindutva* defines the geographic, racial, and religious boundaries of Hinduism. It rejects the secular, separated, pluralist state and would replace it with a Hinduized state fully occupying the land within sacred boundaries, and peopled homogeneously by believing and practicing Hindus, however this is defined. The threefold organization of Hindu fundamentalism, with its paramilitary, recruitment and propagandistic groups, and its political party are intended to pursue these various goals. The Hindu movements are "more" than simple militant religious movements struggling against a secularizing state and society, but they are "less" than Abrahamic fundamentalisms in their lack of clear-cut doctrinal content. (The Hindu fundamentalist "doctrine" is in part synthetic and may not go very deep in belief and practice.)

Structural features that contribute to the explanation of Hindu fundamentalism are social aspects such as ethnicity, region, caste, and class. All three Hindu organizations are concentrated in the cities and towns of the tradition-bound "cow belt" of India— the northern states of Maharashtra, Gujarat, Uttar Pradesh—and to a somewhat lesser extent in Bihar and Madhya Pradesh. The leadership and supporters of these movements are recruited primarily from the Brahman, Kshatriya, and Vaishya castes threatened by the anticaste propensities of the secular Indian state. Their favorite deity, Lord Rāma, is very pro-caste. The leadership and membership of these Hindu fundamentalist movements are drawn primarily from the upwardly mobile middle class and lower-middle-class professionals, merchants, and cash-crop farmers, with little penetration among the industrial workers, artisans, subsistence peasants, and agricultural workers.

The educational characteristics of the elite and rank and file of these movements are related to the above social structural features. The full-time professionals of the RSS are at most secondary school graduates. The rank-and-file *svayamsevaks* in large part are illiterate or have some primary school. The VHP elite include graduates primarily from provincial colleges or religious educational institutions. The BJP elite of parliamentarians and state legislators also are college and university graduates, but not from the elite universities such as New Delhi and Bombay. One of the BJP leaders, M. M. Joshi, is a professor of physics at the University of Allahabad. The lower leadership of the party is primarily secondary school-educated. From a social structural point of view, then, the leadership and support of these movements comes from groups fearing marginalization by the modern economy and secular society. Thus their interests lie in the preservation of "traditional Hinduism," the putative ideological opponent of the secular Indian state.

The political structure of India can explain aspects of the organization, ideology, strategy, and tactics of these movements. Under the British brand of imperialism— indirect rule—the Hindu intellectual elites were encouraged to codify and render coherent their complex and variegated Hindu cultural heritage, and to view it on the same level with Christianity, Islam, Buddhism, and Confucianism, as a world religion. Temples, other cultural centers, and monuments were made subject to the protection of the state, and temple officials and priests acquired a quasi-bureaucratic status. Thus the international context laid the ground for the emergence of Hindu fundamentalism by encouraging the development of a relatively coherent Hinduism. Under the pluralist and secular British Raj, Hinduism was one of several religions, the existence and autonomy of which were protected by the state. Independent India continued as a secular, pluralist state, seeking to accord equal protection to all religions and to remove, or at least mitigate, the inequalities of caste. Thus the secular pluralism of the Indian state was a threat to the higher castes in traditional India, producing the fundamentalist movements with their antipluralist, antisecular programs.

Furthermore, the British Raj and the successor Indian state have been governed by the rule of law and freedoms of press, assembly, and organization. This political structure permitted the formation of organizations, recruiting of members, and legal participation in the struggle for power. These arrangements make possible the dual strategy followed by Hindu fundamentalism—the legal contest for control of the national and state governments, attended by considerable success at both levels; and a more threatening revolutionary strategy implied in its preemptive ethnoreligious, nationalist ideology and in the paramilitary structure and tactics of the RSS.

Taken together, these religious, social structural, civil society, political, and international conditions are the necessary causes of Hindu nationalism. They would explain the form nationalist movements would take in the Indian context, assuming that such movements developed. But there was much here that would have to be explained not by necessity but by contingency or chance. The perturbations of international politics (e.g., the impact of the two world wars on Indian internal political development) are contingencies from external arenas. Similarly, the assassinations of Mahatma Gandhi, Indira Gandhi, and Rajiv Gandhi explain the changing leadership chemistry in Indian politics, which in turn helps account for the ups and downs in the growth, spread, and effectiveness of Hindu fundamentalisms.

Structure and contingency create propensities and provide triggers for development and transformations, but they do not determine the specific form that ideas, programs, and institutions take. For these "sufficient" causes of fundamentalist movements we need to factor in the creativity of leaders—the plans, choices, and decisions of individuals, which turn these possibilities into realities.

We distinguish three types of leadership creativity in the Hindu movements—ideological, organizational, and coalitional. The ideological leaders included the Swami Dayananda Sarasvati, founder of the Arya Samaj in 1875 (see below), who played a major role in giving coherence to modern Hinduism. Savarkar wrote the ideological bible of Hindu nationalism *(Hindutva)* while imprisoned by the British for sedition. The key concept of Hindutva was its blending of nationalist and religious sensibilities: "A Hindu regards his land as his fatherland as well as his holyland." K. B. Hedgewar, the founder of the RSS, was an organizational leader who created institutions intended to shape Hindu cultural unity. A Maharashtrian Brahman and medical school graduate, Hedgewar chose a celibate career of nation building. Hindu leadership, according to Hedgewar, was not fascist, but rather guru-like, with the leader as a spiritual guide, planning, implementing, determining policy, and bringing comrades around to his point of view, because of his moral authority. The RSS supplied the leadership of the VHP and the BJP. M. S. Golwarkar, who followed Hedgewar as leader of the RSS in 1940, was long-haired and ascetic. Under his more than three decades of rule, the RSS grew rapidly and proliferated chain-link organizations such as student, labor, and women's groups. He formulated the "five unities" of Hinduism—geography, race, religion, culture, and language, the last in the sense of Sanskrit as the "language of the gods." Golwarkar was both organizer and ideologue.

The contemporary leaders of the Hindu nationalists are coalition builders. Balasaheb Deoras, leader of the RSS, has placed special emphasis on efforts to overcome caste division and to open the movement to the Untouchables, Tribals, Sikhs, Jains, and Buddhists. The VHP was formed during his tenure, out of fear that Hinduism might lose the Untouchables to Islam. In the early 1990s L. K. Advani and A. B. Vajpayee, the president and vice-president, respectively, of the BJP, effectively appealed to a far larger political base that includes Sikhs. The Sikhs were given support by the BJP at the time of the disorders attendant on the Golden Temple riots. The strength of the BJP in the Lok Sabha and the state legislatures could not have been reached without this cross-religious mobilization and dilution of caste norms.

Strong arguments could be made for placing the Hindu variant of fundamentalism in the world-conqueror category, but its circumstances of emergence dictated a transformer pattern. Hindu fundamentalism clearly seeks to "conquer" India and to replace the secularist constitution by a still vaguely defined order based on Hindutva, but it must contend with a secularist government with a considerable military presence and some legitimacy (the degree of which is constantly debated). It must also operate in a setting of cultural and religious pluralism not easily bent to autocratic visions. Thus the Hindu nationalist strategy is diverse, operative on many levels, and long-term in its goals and consequences.

Sikh Militants, immediately prior to the Rise of Bhindranwale and the Golden Temple Massacre. The basic background of the Sikh saga is provided above, in the world-conqueror section. It is important here, however, to underscore that the Sikh activists were not committed to a radical course prior to the implementation of certain Indian government policies. Not least among these was Indira Gandhi's support for what turned out to be the radical elements in a Sikh movement that was moving in a transformationist rather than a revolutionary mode.

But it should be remembered that other government policies—the removal of special privileges accorded to the Sikhs under the British Raj, and the social and economic displacement of farmers in the western region as a result of the Green Revolution—contributed mightily to the polarization in the Sikh community itself. The Sikh religious party, Akali Dal, was pursuing a world-transformer pattern of interaction with the Indian government, hoping to influence its policies by sharing political power with the Congress Party in the Punjab, and by controlling the Sikh temples through the SGPC. But Sikhism as a religion did not exhibit the capacity to move readily from its own religious world to a mode of constant political interaction, and compromise, which is required of the world transformer. Thus its world-transforming stage was relatively brief; it ended when Sant Harchand Singh Longowal, the leader of the Akali Dal in the 1970s, made demands for Sikh autonomy in Punjab. To head off extremism, an attempt that ultimately backfired, Indira Gandhi abandoned the Akali Dal for Bhindranwale and the Khalsa Dal—a case of jumping from the frying pan into the fire.

Sri Lankan Buddhist Extremism: Growth, 1940s. In 1937 Bandaranaike founded the Sinhala Maha Sabha, which brought together a number of Buddhist groups including the supporters of Dharmapāla. Bandaranaike sought to influence and transform Sri Lankan politics, rather than to seize control of it. In 1946 the Sinhala Maha Sabha joined the independence coalition of the UNP. In the mood of national unity after the attainment of Sri Lankan independence, Dharmapāla's version of Buddhist nationalism remained latent while the UNP followed a policy of compromise, western style pluralism, and parliamentarism. As in the Sikh case, however, the Buddhists did not linger long in the transformer mode. By the mid-1950s a series of economic crises resulting from declining world market prices that affected Sri Lankan exports, created substantial dissatisfaction and unrest. The SLFP of Bandaranaike withdrew from the UNP coalition in 1951, and ran a spirited and successful pro-Buddhist, pro-Sinhala campaign in the 1956 election. Bandaranaike's victory was not only associated with the economic downturn of the 1950s but also resulted from a significant rise in world-conquering Sinhala Buddhist nationalism, and a remarkable politicization of the Buddhist religious establishment.

Sunni Movements in Egypt: Origins and First Emergence, Late 1920s-1940s. Hasan al-Banna, the founder of the Muslim Brotherhood, described his mission as a *"salafiyya* [traditional or, literally, ancestral] mission." He described his society as a "Qur'anic, Muhammadan, Islamic society, which follows the way of the Noble Qur'an, takes the path of the Great Prophet, does not deviate from what has come down to us in God's Book, his Messenger's Sunna, and the conduct of the venerable forefathers."[11] According to the Egyptian historian Abdel Azim Ramadan, the name *fundamentalist* appeared in the Egyptian press only upon the rise of militant Islamic groups in the time of Sadat; it was used to distinguish them from the Muslim Brotherhood. "Because they adopted the concepts of *jahiliyya* (pre-Islamic idolatrous society), *al-hakimiyya* (God's sovereignty), and *al-takfir* (branding with infidelity), these groups were considered radical, and thus a part of the modern radical Islamic trend," Ramadan writes, "while the Muslim Brotherhood was largely considered a part of the traditionalist Islamic trend." Banna, a teacher at an elementary school in Ismailia in 1928, challenged religious leaders to defend Islam from the encroachments of the imported, secular, Western colonial culture. The initial goal, Ramadan says, "was merely to hold fast to the basic principles of Islam in the face of obscenity and apostasy." The first steps included the formation of Islamic societies, the publishing of Islamic newspapers, preaching, and providing guidance to the people. "The Muslim Brotherhood was thus a purely religious society, a reformist Islamic movement. Its goal was to bring up youth in accordance with proper Islamic ethics, and to disseminate the merits and purposes of Muhammadan prophecy, including the moral virtues of truthfulness, chastity, and good social relations."[12]

The Brotherhood in its origins thus sought to transform the Egyptian world of Islam by calling its members to reform. Missionary work was paramount; branches of the Brotherhood extended into several cities such as Port Said, Suez, Abu Suwair, and Al-Bahr al-Saghir. Its headquarters was moved to Cairo in October 1932.

The transit to a world-conquering mode was visible even in Banna's original ideology, however, which emphasized the oneness of religion and state, and the need for pan-Islamism in the face of Egyptian nationalism. (The Brotherhood spread quickly outside Egypt, particularly into the Sudan, Syria, and the Maghreb). Banna came to consider noninvolvement in politics an "Islamic crime." The Brotherhood was the first Islamic association to shift its activities from the traditional Islamic centers such as Al-Azhar, the Sufi orders, and the uneducated popular classes, to the secular universities and the educated classes influenced by Western culture. The Brotherhood shifted the responsibility for establishing Islamic government from the religiously educated class to the Westernized class, from the shaykhs to the lawyers, doctors, engineers, pharmacists, and army and police officers. Its political activism soon led to clashes with the Egyptian state and to a radicalization of the movement.

In 1948 Egyptian prime minister Nuqrashi dissolved the organization and detained its most important leaders. Neither he nor Hasan al-Banna survived this initial clash between Islamic fundamentalism and the Egyptian government. The Brotherhood supported the military officers of the July Revolution, but the victorious officers ordered the Brotherhood dissolved on 14 January 1954. In retaliation the Brotherhood attempted to assassinate Abdel Nasser in Alexandria. Its leaders, including Sayyid Qutb, were jailed for terms of five to ten years, and the world-conquering ideology and organizational structure of the Brotherhood jelled in Qutb's jail cell.

Hamas: Origins and Trigger Events. Hamas followed a similar pattern in its origin. It began as an offshoot of the Muslim Brotherhood in Gaza, dedicated to the Islamization of society. After Nasser's repression, the remnants of the movement saw its destiny changed, twice, by external triggers: the Israeli occupation (1967) and the Intifada (1987).

The world-transforming mode lasted beyond the period of Egyptian rule and for the first twenty years of Israeli occupation, as Hamas established clinics, schools, and other social service institutions in the territories. Under the leadership of Shaykh Yassin, however, Hamas later developed a world-conquering mode in competition with the PLO This development was triggered by events in the early 1980s, including the rise of the Islamic Jihad and the example set by Hizbollah in opposing Israel's invasion of Lebanon. On this terrain it had a rival in the form of Islamic Jihad, but that nascent movement was decimated by efficacious Israeli repression. In both the Gaza Strip and parts of the West Bank, the movement, while focusing on a militant core of young males (mostly low and lower-middle class), succeeded in gaining a cross-class support periphery due to an all-out ethnoreligious opposition to the occupier.

World Creator

As in the world-conqueror mode, leadership in the world-creator mode is charismatic, authoritarian, and centralized. But the appeal is to a narrower band of elements within a society; hence social and cultural resources are not vast but very particular. Diverse disaffected segments of society are not immediately attracted to the specialized message and terminology of the movement. The ideology calls for preserving the religious tradition by building it up and/or returning to a state of purity. This pattern of fundamentalism emphasizes the puritanical strand in the religious tradition, the need to avoid corruption from intermingling with outsiders. Accordingly, the stance is defensive rather than offensive or proactive; dualism is high in the origins of the movement. Further, the movement rejects or suppresses nationalist and theocratic elements in the religious tradition; it retrieves those teachings of the tradition that support the inward turn, and it may borrow selectively from the outside. The organization is that of typical enclave: charismatic leader, small hierarchy, egalitarian core. The public impact is middle level, somewhere between the disruptions of the world conqueror and the negligible impact of the world renouncer. In relating to the outside world, a fundamentalist movement may seek political or legal concessions to enable world-creating activities—missionary outreach, religious exemptions—or to safeguard privileges and inhibit encroachment of worlds against which it is competing.

The world creator, for all his defensiveness, may one day find himself strong enough to become a world conqueror or world transformer.

Habad (Lubavitcher Hasidim). Habad was the only Hasidic sect in the early nineteenth century with a relatively small local power basis (in Byelorussia) and a universalistic, pan-Jewish bent in ideology and (to a lesser extent) in organization. It was thus positioned to adapt itself to the new circumstances created by the mass migration of the late nineteenth century, and especially to the disruption created by the Bolshevik Revolution and its aftermath. The revolution cut it from its original power base, exiling the Lubavitcher rebbe to Poland and then (with the advent of World War II) to the United States.

Habad could thus create a centralized worldwide structure, headed by the rebbe and his bureaucracy, which makes ample use of media techniques, controls far-flung local groups, puts them in direct touch with the rebbe (i.e., via satellite), supplies them with indoctrination and information material, appoints and moves around emissaries and organizers. Western economic prosperity and the welfare state were also put to good use.

Yet underlying it all was the twofold ideological innovation introduced by the fifth and sixth rebbes: emphasis upon the oncoming messianic redemption, as an explanation for the Holocaust and other historical disruptions and as a goal for intensive action; and missionary (outreach) action among that majority of the Jewish people won over by the secularist way of life. This missionary activity serves to reaffirm the identity of those who perform it, regardless of how many souls it actually saves. In this work it was helped by the growing goodwill among Jews toward the haredim, in the wake of the decline of the melting-pot ideal and the rise of particularistic identity. Haredim came to be seen as a remnant of a by now idealized shtetl or (in Israel) as carriers of a messianic gospel not unlike the one that erupted in Israel following the 1967 victory.

Discontent with modernity, whether due to the cultural critique of the 1960s or to economic crisis in the 1970s, enlarged the pool of susceptible recruits. Habad's emphasis on the special, innate essence of Jewish identity, inextricably combined with messianism, enjoyed a powerful appeal among Jews in the U.S. due to deteriorating relations with the Black community and even more so among an Israeli public that had become infused with "tribalized" concepts of Jewish ethnicity and was increasingly preoccupied (due to the Arab-Israeli conflict) with the Jewish-Gentile divide. The late rebbe, it should be noted, was a devotee of Greater Israel, an idea much in vogue since the 1967 war. That war is an important trigger for Habad, but not for the rest of the haredim.

Christians in South India. Certain similarities between the south Indian and Guatemalan cases are striking; one may even be tempted to place the Guatemalan case in the world-creator category, were it not for the Pentecostals' support of the regime—the world already in place. In both cases, however, the rise of assertive "fundamentalist-like" forces is very recent and triggered by increased competition for religious loyalties and for social and economic resources, the competition occurring, moreover, among groups that have heretofore been marginalized socially, politically, and economically. In both cases a niche has been created for neo-Pentecostal activists and proselytizers as a result of larger social-religious-economic upheavals, in south India by large-scale campaigns of assertive Hindu nation building by the RSS and the VHP, which claim to represent the interests of the expanding Hindu middle class (newly prosperous entrepreneurs, substantial cash-crop farmers, and urban professional people); and by Islamizing campaigns in the southern states of Tamil Nadu and Kerala, which contain a disproportionately large number of India's fifteen million professing Christians.

In both cases the new Christian forces are so diverse—so eclectic in worship style, ideological particulars, and organizational profiles—that one cannot speak of a unified movement. In south India, in Kerala alone, they include liberation-theology-style Roman Catholic communities led by social justice priests, and hundreds of Pentecostal or "Holy Spirit" churches with some affiliation to the North American denomination the Assemblies of God. In both Guatemala and south India, however, the new Christian activists have adopted a fundamentalist-like awareness that organized fundamentalisms have power as bearers of political and economic resources at times of social upheaval. Each movement thus is groping toward creating a distinctive Christian world—an identifiable subculture and enclave, with borders, existing within a hostile environment. These nascent movements have been influenced by outsiders and by the example of fundamentalisms elsewhere (including, for the south Indian Christians, not only Christian fundamentalism in North America, but Islamic and Hindu radicalism on the subcontinent), but they are nonetheless independent, indigenous movements that are not controlled or funded or inspired in their particulars by foreign missionary organizations.

The important differences between the two cases can be traced to the different long-term structural environments. In India, religious diversity and cultural pluralism are hardly new realities; religious groups of bewildering diversity have shared pilgrimage sites, shrines, and temples, with little apparent regard for confessional boundaries. Yet the presence and pace of religious competition has accelerated sharply, and various strategies, religious communalism being the most significant, seem to have been refined, developed, and fortified in a relatively short time. In the last fifteen to twenty years there has been a growing nationwide sense that everything is up for grabs in the race for communal development resources. (Even the caste system itself, which helped bring order and a certain stability to the pluralism, is challenged by the new Hindutva devotees.)

Whereas in Guatemala the fortunes of the rising Christian movement were largely dictated by the patronage of the state and its ruler, in India the secular state has been opposed to religious communalism (fundamentalism). However, because it has been a relatively weak guardian of the values and principles of the secular constitution—undermining its chances by falling prey to corruption, mismanagement, and ill-advised policies—the state has played into the communalists' hands. In this regard the short-term trigger for the emergence of the new Hindu activism was the twenty-one-month state of emergency imposed by Indira Gandhi, which suspended the constitution and in effect made the state merely another (albeit dominant) player in the civil strife. When the ban was lifted in 1977, there was a sense that, as the state had been discredited in its role as the guarantor of national coherence and order, every community must now look out for its own interests. Something like "fundamentalism" was the blueprint of choice for many of the communities as they reinvented themselves and harnessed the resources of civil society to their ends.

Within the strained demographics of south India, the competition has an economic as well as a spiritual edge. Oil prices rose in the late 1970s, bringing about double-digit inflation just as large hinterland and coastal tracts in the states of Tamil Nadu, Karnataka, and Andhra Pradesh experienced drought and crop failures. This led to waves of short- and long-term migration by displaced cultivators to the packed slum colonies of Madras and other large cities. Such shifts in regional political geography paved the way for violent clashes initiated by self-styled "sons of the soil"—Hindu militants who have organized themselves to resist threats to employment and control of regional political institutions at the hands of "aliens." In Kerala state, to take another example, Christian and Muslim migrant workers returning from the Gulf or from other Arab countries after the collapse of the oil boom in the mid-1980s experienced lengthy unemployment and restricted opportunities, making them prime candidates to join political activist groups organized along religious lines.

Susan Bayly notes that Hindu "fundamentalist" rhetoric, unleashed with a new intensity after 1977, turns on a strategy of portraying the Christian and Muslim "opponents" as both more foreign and more cohesive and monolithic in organization than in fact they are. This has proved, however, to be something of a self-fulfilling prophecy, as various Christian groups have responded to the Hindu-majoritarian rhetoric by taking on their own fundamentalist characteristics: they interpret local disputes as part of a larger pan-regional and pan-Indian conflict; they embrace the literal and political interpretation of scripture and/or the supernatural charismatic authority of individual leaders and spiritual adepts; and, they emphasize corporate identity, promote symbols of "true" Christianity, and repudiate emblems and forms of worship that express common ground with Hindus and Muslims in the same densely populated sacred landscape. "In this shift towards exclusiveness and a strengthening of previously loose and fluid communal boundaries, the fact of interaction, of being spurred to assertive behaviour by the example of others, has been a crucial element in the rise of organized fundamentalism in the southern states."[13]

In accounting for the rise of Christian fundamentalisms, therefore, we may speak of many triggers of the same general type: militant responses to the challenge of other communalists who are claiming sacred sites, as well as economic resources, for their own.

Sikhs, under the Leadership of Sant Fateh Singh, Mid-1960s. Sikhism, as we have seen, moved rapidly from a world-creator orientation to world-conqueror, pausing only briefly in an ill-begotten attempt to transform Punjabi and Indian politics through political power-brokering. The Sikh religion was a "world" unto itself, unaccustomed to the negotiations of identity necessary for political compromise. The Sikh leader of the world-creating stage—Sant Fateh Singh—used fasts and threats of self-immolation on the roof of the Golden Temple to bring pressure to bear on the Congress authorities. He wanted the world outside to conform to the requirements of the Sikh world. Sikh political organization and leadership have distinctive characteristics. The inseparable mix of politics and religion makes bargaining and coalition making highly risky. Hence political leadership as such is confined to authoritative ideologizing; political decisions are sacred acts, made by persons with sacred powers. Pragmatic "cost-benefit bargaining" and coalition making have no legitimate place in the religiopolitical process. Typical means used to attain goals are self-destruction through dramatic fasts or suicides, or through destruction of property or persons. And the predominance of the sant-devotee form of political relationship rules out lower-cost bargaining and compromising as legitimate modes of political action. Moderate politicians are short-lived and constantly in physical danger. World creating, if it gives way in Sikh fundamentalism, yields to the revolutionary radicalism of the Sikh world conqueror.

Sri Lankan Buddhist Extremism: Origins, 1890s-1930s. The world creator, like the world renouncer, may withdraw from the outside world for a time, but the withdrawal is tactical rather than permanent or principled. The case of Angārika Dharmapāla's alliance with the theosophists is exemplary. He withdrew from the alliance when affiliation meant giving up specifically Sri Lankan rituals and holy places. Dharmapāla sought to recreate the world of Sri Lankan Buddhism by ridding it of its syncretic features, inculcating the basics of the Four Noble Truths and the Eightfold Path. In this effort, however, he was influenced by, and imitative of, the outside world, specifically, the world of the Victorian Protestant missionaries. Thus the world he sought to create was a "Protestant Buddhism," a moralistic and ascetic, as well as intensely nationalistic, "updating" of traditional Buddhism. Note that the world he was creating was tailored ultimately to fundamentalist-hegemonic ends; he was a creator of Buddhist nationalism as much as a renewer of Buddhist religion.

Arya Samaj: Pre-RSS. In 1875 Swami Dayananda founded the Arya Samaj, a Hindu religiocultural organization that with the Hindu Mahasabha, was the predecessor of the contemporary Hindu movements, especially the RSS. The Arya Samaj and the Mahasabha were religion-building movements reacting to the competition with codified and organized Islamic and Christian religions. At the same time, as fundamentalist world creators, they were nation-state building movements reacting first against the secular state instituted by the British Raj, and then to the indigenous secular-pluralist state of independent India. The explanation of the mixed character of Hindu fundamentalism hence is in substantial part a clear consequence of the interaction of particular kinds of religious structure in a particular international context. Today the Arya Samaj numbers more than a million members in India and in foreign countries. It supports, primarily in northern India, a network of colleges and schools with Sanskrit-Vedic-Hindu as well as secular curricula. It is especially powerful abroad.

World Renouncer

Movements in the world-renouncer mode often emerge from an existing, long-standing tradition that is modernized abruptly. The leadership is charismatic, authoritarian, renegade, and prophetic—often defining itself and the movement in contrast to tepid, compromising, liberalizing religious leadership that has jeopardized the integrity of the religious tradition. Leaders point to widespread apostasy and marshal resources for apocalyptic battle (or drawn-out conflict, when that hope is disappointed). The ideology is counter-acculturative, with elaborate warnings against selecting from either tradition, which is presented whole (at least rhetorically), or especially from modernity, which is insidious. The true enclave with high walls is the only hope. These movements tend to rank low on the scale of fundamentalist elements, precisely because they are so resistant to adaptation and are niggardly in their sharing with modern processes. Such movements exercise some public impact, for the outside world has to accommodate them; but they are not seeking to transform or conquer outsiders, who are anyway condemned. The world renouncer is a separatist par excellence.

The French Catholic Lefebvrists. The Lefebvrists, whose leader's authority was derived not from personal charisma but from his ecclesial office, are an example of a Catholic traditionalist movement rather than, strictly speaking, a fundamentalist movement. Granted, it did exhibit some of the marks of fundamentalism, such as a strong moral and cosmological dualism, authoritarian leadership, and an inner core of disciplined, elect adherents ("remnants"). Yet its primary appeal was (and is) to a certain type of restorationist Catholic who is nostalgic for the social stability and ethnic privileges of the ancien regime (in Lefebvrist rhetoric, a hallowed time prior to the "unholy trinity" of liberty, equality, and fraternity introduced by the French Revolution and against which Lefebvre constantly railed). This kind of Catholic also longs to return to the time before Holy Mother Church had succumbed to the numbing, differentiating influences of modernism (church differentiated from state, liturgy from social activism, moral reasoning from institutional authority).

Like other forms of nostalgia, the Lefebvrist lament is not accompanied by strategies for change. The "movement" (or organization) looks to the past rather than to the future. When a future is envisioned, it assumes apocalyptic proportions: the vengeance of God is imminent. In terms of their impact upon existing structures, the Lefebvrists began in the 1970s as "bureaucratic insurgents" who sought to restore their place of privilege in church and state. Even when they broke away from the church that had nurtured them, they retained many of its customs, organizational and ideological assumptions, and habits of mind. That they were more bureaucratic than charismatic, more hierarchical than egalitarian, more routinized than ideologically and organizationally dynamic is indicated not only by their limited influence on young people and even middle-aged French Catholics, but also by the slight upsurge in their ranks after their founder died and was replaced by a German bureaucrat. Nationalism is not a strong binding force in this case; it provides no basis for a vital fundamentalist movement, despite the nativist Jean Marie Le Pen's modestly successful attempts to draw upon a traditionalist Catholic base.

Archbishop Lefebvre was ultimately after loftier goals than ridding the world of the Jews and Masons who had corrupted mundane politics; he sought nothing less than the restoration of the one, true church. But his movement withdrew from both church and world, and has not been notably successful in reforming either, preferring instead to concentrate its energies on denunciations and some measure of world building. But the world creation is not a fundamentalist-style competition with the world as much as it is intended to provide a spiritual haven in a fallen world.

Haredi Jews. The haredim's is a story of a double emergence. Leadership was crucial for the movement's take-offs, early in the century and again in midcentury. Leadership set forth an ideology that transcended past internal division (between Hasidim and Misnagdim) and responded to the challenges of victorious Zionism and of the American way of life. Ideologists (such as the Hafetz Haim and the Hazon Ish) were greatly helped by institution builders and coalition makers (such as Rabbi Kahaneman of the Ponovezh yeshiva, or Agudat Yisrael politicians, e.g., J. Rosenheim and I. M. Levin). The genius of the latter (especially the Agudat, established in Poland in 1912 and later moving to the United States and Israel) consisted in maintaining a decentralized structure of "affinity groups" (to borrow a term coined by anthropologist Steve Rayner). Such groups were locally led, but shared ideology, religious practice, major educational institutions, and political affiliation.

The haredim are distinguished from most other fundamentalist movements (except for American Protestants) in being multi-generational. They rely less on new recruits than on old-timers. Their large families "produce" and shape recruits, for the fourth generation, channeling them through *heder,* small yeshiva, great yeshiva, and *kollel* (or *ulpana* for girls). Its totalistic atmosphere, predicated upon clustered residence, facilitates in-marriage, provides employment (beyond years in yeshiva for males; before and throughout marriage for girls). Deferral from Israeli military service provides yet an-

TABLE 18.3

FUNDAMENTALIST PATTERNS OF RELATION TO THE "WORLD" OVER TIME

	World Conqueror	World Transformer	World Creator	World Renouncer
U.S. Protestant				
Origins (1875–1925)	X	XX	X	
Growth (1925–75)			XX	X
Resurgence (1975–)	XX	X	X	
Catholic traditionalist			X	XX
Guatemalan Pentecostal		XX	X	X
Comunione e Liberazione		XX	X	
Islamic Jama'at				
Origins	X	XX	X	
Radicalization	XX	X	X	X
Haredi				
Origins			X	XX
Growth			XX	X
Habad		X	XX	X
Gush Emunim				
Origins	XX		X	
Radicalization	XX	X		
Decline		X		X
Arya Samaj			XX	
Hindu RSS, VHP, BJP				
Origins (1915–25)			XX	
Kingdom of Ram	X	XX	X	
Ayodhya crisis 1992		X	XX	
Sikh radical				
Fateh Singh (1960s)			XX	
Longowal (1970s)		XX		
Bhindranwale (1980s)	XX			
Sinhala Buddhist				
Origins (1890s–1930s)			XX	
Growth (1940s)		XX		
Radicalization (post–1956)	XX			

other incentive (this time negative) for remaining in the fold, and indeed attrition has been brought to a minimum in later generations through the impact of socialization, scholarship, employment, marriage, and army deferral.

While the haredim began as world-renouncers, they always were world-creators as well; and it may even be said that they emphasized this mode above all others when they accepted public monies and privileges from the Israeli government, and shifted in the late 1980s from anti-Zionist to a-Zionist ideology.

Pure world-renouncers are indeed rare among fundamentalisms; the Neturei Karta, a sect within the haredim, probably qualify, as do Islamic sects like the Samawiya of Egypt. Fundamentalism, however, includes a dynamic engagement with the outside world. Even if that engagement takes the form of a renunciation of the outside world, fundamentalists finds that they depend increasingly on that world's resources in order to construct an alternative of their own.

Table 18.3 conveys our conclusions in schematic form with two "X"-marks indicating the dominant pattern at a given time.

TABLE 18.4

EXPLAINING FUNDAMENTALIST TRANSITIONS

	World Creator	World Transformer	World Conqueror	World Renouncer
Structure	Pre–World War II Jewish migration from shtetl function of Aguda and ultra-Orthodox coalition	1875–1925 American Protestant impact of pluralism and congregationalism on development of fundamentalist institutions	1970s Jewish Gush Emunim—in response to 1967 and 1973 wars	1947—Jewish Neturei Karta rejection of Israeli state on literal biblical grounds
Chance	1890s Sri Lankan Buddhism—impact of American Theosophical Society on Dharmapāla	Post–World War II Jewish impact of World War II and Holocaust on Haredi response in the United States and Israel	1970s Iran Shi'ites coincidence of Shah's illness and presidency of Jimmy Carter	
Choice	1875 Hindu founding of Arya Samaj by Swami Dayananda	1950s and 1960s Italian Catholic Father Giussani and formation of Scuole of Comunione e Liberazione	1960s Egyptian Sunnis—Sayyid Qutb advocacy of radical political course for Muslim Brotherhood	1970s French Catholic Archbishop Lefebvre withdraws from Church

In Table 18. 4 we show how structural, chance, and choice variables explain the transition to these four world-relational patterns.

Beginning with structural variables, the world-creator phase of the Jewish haredim—the formation of the Agudat Israel and the coalition of ultra-Orthodox movements—was a response to the depopulation of the shtetl through emigration to the larger cities and to the United States in the nineteenth and twentieth-centuries. The rise of fundamentalist churches and institutions among the American Protestants in the period between the 1870s and the 1920s exemplifies fundamentalism in its world-transformer manifestation, which can be explained in part by the threat of cultural secularization in a pluralist and fragmented religious organizational context. The Gush Emunim's world-conquering phase was a response to the 1967 and 1973 Arab-Israeli wars. The impact of structural variables (the theology of the host religion) in a world-renouncing case is exemplified by the Neturei-Kartei in their withdrawal from allegiance to the Zionist state on the basis of a literal biblical interpretation of pre-Messianic Judaism.

The impact of chance on the emergence of fundamentalism in its world-creator manifestation is exemplified by the influence of the American Theosophical Society on Sri Lanka Buddhist revivalism. Chance causation in the world-transformer form of fundamentalism is exemplified by the impact of the Holocaust on the formation of haredi communities and yeshivot in Israel and the United States. Chance ushering in the world-conquering phase of fundamentalism is exemplified in the coincidence of the Shah's illness and the presidency of Jimmy Carter, which made possible Khomeini's seizure of power in Iran.

There are, of course, many examples of leadership "explaining" the various mani-festations of fundamentalism. Swami Dayananda, for example, was a world creator of Hindu fundamentalism in founding the Arya Samaj in 1875, as was Savarkar in writing *Hindutva* in 1925. The Italian priest, Father Luigi Giussani, was a world transformer in the 1950s and 1960s in establishing the scuole of the Comunione e Liberazione. Among the many leaders who have a major responsibility in the shift to the world-conquering phase, the Egyptian Sunni ideologue, Sayyid Qutb, is a striking example. The classic Shi'ite case, of course, is Ayatollah Khomeini. Finally, a good example of the importance of leadership in a world-renouncing case is the French Archbishop Marcel Lefebvre, who led his small flock out of the Roman Catholic church after the "heresies" of Vatican II.

Table 18.4 is merely suggestive of the complexities of any one fundamentalism's movement from pattern to pattern. Consider the haredim, who emphasized separat-ism and world creation during the inter-war years in Europe, with world-transforming tendencies also evident via Agudat Israel as a political party. Against the threat of "in-fidel" Zionism, the extreme wing split from Agudat Israel in the late 1930s to form the Eda Haredit, an offshoot which combined world-renouncer and world-creator traits. Its nucleus is the Satmar Hasidim, who persist to this day, though the world-creator traits are more prominent in the 1990s due to economic interaction with the Israeli environment. In the United States Satmar separatists accept federal money and even go to court for it (e.g., the Supreme Court case involving the Kiryas Joel school district and special school established for disabled Hasidic children in New York state) but in Israel they do not take money from the Israeli state. In the wake of the Holo-caust, most Hasidic groups in Europe, Israel, and the U.S. passed through a period of world creation in order to reconstitute their identity and network. However, they tended to combine their world-creating efforts with a measure of separatism (i.e. world renouncing). But due to economic prosperity beginning in the late 1950s, they tended especially in Israel to renounce their rigid separatism and manifest world-transformer strategies, hoping against hope to change Israeli society. From anti-Zionism they turned to a-Zionism, participating in Israeli government coalitions and recruiting separatist Israelis from high-status groups as proof that they are able to transform the Israeli society over the long haul through Teshuva (conversion). Whenever their for-tunes ebb, however, they return to their separatist tendencies.

In Islam, the Tablighi Jamaat is like Habad in that is exhibits both world-creating and world-renouncing tendencies simultaneously. The Muslim Brotherhood, by con-trast, began as world creators and moved quickly into the role of world transformers. Extremist groups among them in the 1940s tried their hand at world-conquering but were obliterated by Nasser. When the Brethren turned again to world-conquering in the mid 1960s, they experienced failure and decided to concentrate on world-transforming. On the margins of the phenomenon are tiny sects like the Samawiya, heavily impregnated with Sufism, which conclude that society is completely lost and that the only way out is to renounce the world. Such sects, built around powerful charismatic leaders, exist in Upper Egypt in caves and barely accessible deserts and hilly areas and sometimes also in small town environments. They live completely self-enclosed, recruit sparingly, and limit interaction, including marriage, to group members.

Other movements may pass through a world-renouncer phase. Thus Takfir wa-Hijra in Egypt, having created their own world in the late 1960s and early 1970s, conclude that the external environment was so vile and menacing that the only acceptable response was to emigrate, like the Prophet to caves, hills, and apartments, where they lived as a sort of self-enclosed commune (even assigning female members to marry male members), attempted to be self-sufficient economically, and shared resources. They deemed the larger environment to be infidel/apostate *(takfir)*.

By contrast, the jamaat which proliferated during the 1970s are not world renouncers; they vacillate, according to circumstances, between world-transformer and world-conqueror tendencies. The Qutb ideology is subtle enough to permit such a gamut of interaction. By the mid-1970s, however, some leaders such as Shukri Mustafa thought that they were strong enough to conquer society by force (there was no point of transforming it, for it was too steeped in apostasy). But the 1977 coup failed, and its leaders were executed. The group then split, with many continuing armed underground existence, biding their time. A minority moved back into world-renouncing existence in tiny sects.

We respect the complexity of these movements' changes over time by focusing more narrowly, in chapter 19, on political and ethnic aspects of fundamentalism.

Notes

1. See Susan Harding, "Imagining the Last Days: The Politics of Apocalyptic Language," in Martin E. Marty and R. Scott Appleby, eds., *Accounting for Fundamentalisms* (Chicago: University of Chicago Press, 1994), pp. 57–78.

2. Smaller groups of Sikhs live in Delhi, other parts of India, and in diaspora with large concentrations in the United States, England, and Canada.

3. Nanak was much influenced by the Hindu Bakhti movement, which was monotheistic and opposed to caste, and the Islamic Sufis. He composed hymns and organized community dining and hymn singing, participated in by both Hindus and Muslims. Nanak founded a dynasty which ultimately included ten gurus, each one nominated by the preceding one.

4. The Adi Granth is the sole object of worship in the Sikh ritual. Personified, it is "awakened" in the morning, revered during the day, and put to rest during the night.

5. In the years following the Golden Temple massacre, it has been impossible to eliminate large-scale violence and terrorism in Punjab. Simranjeet Singh Mann, a relatively moderate Sikh leader, has brokered the major factions of the Akali Dal into a loose coalition, in order to arrive at a modus vivendi with the Indian government. The radical "fundamentalists," however, in Bhindranwale's spirit of defiance, will settle for nothing less than Khalistan.

6. These involvements with the world and borrowings from other religions triggered a purist movement among the Buddhist clergy and laity, which James Manor and Gananath Obeyesekere suggest may be more deserving of the fundamentalist label than the extremist ethnonationalist trends, which we are considering here. These "purists" are attempting to rid Sri Lankan Buddhism of Hindu accretions, magical practices, astrology, sorcery, and the like, returning it to the path of the Buddha and the origi-

nal Pali canon. But the purists have been marginalized by the syncretizers on the one hand and by the Buddhist nationalists on the other.

7. Other revivalist and defensive movements formed in these decades were more moderate and less in conflict with classical Theravada Buddhism. These included the Young Men's Buddhist Association (1891) and the All-Ceylon Buddhist Congress (1919).

8. More than fifty thousand Sri Lankans have been killed in these bloody confrontations. In recent years the activities of the JVP have been brought partially under control through killing their known leaders and many of their followers by government troops and special death squads. The JVP continues to operate on a smaller scale. Tamil extremism also has partly subsided. But this politics of savage confrontation has not been replaced by pluralist and parliamentary politics. Given the persistence of Buddhist preemptive nationalism, the weakness of Sri Lankan political and governmental institutions, and the seriousness of Sri Lankan economic and social problems, it would be premature to view the present relative calm as more than an uneasy truce.

9. In 1971 the uprising led by the Maoist People's Liberation Front was triggered by another export crisis, and the serious economic distress and high unemployment resulting from it.

10. As a consequence of the BJP's direct role in the destruction of the Babri Masjid, and of the successive waves of violence throughout India which followed, the Indian government banned RSS and the VHP and made membership in them a criminal offense. The leader of the BJP opposition in the Lok Sabha, L. K. Advani, was put into preventive detention, though he and other arrested BJP leaders were released in early 1993. The governments of the four states ruled by BJP regimes have been suspended and placed under presidential rule under the emergency powers in the Indian constitution.

11. Quoted in Abdel Azim Ramadan, "Fundamentalist Influence in Egypt: The Strategies of the Muslim Brotherhood and the Takfir Groups," in Martin E. Marty and R. Scott Appleby, eds., *Fundamentalisms and the State: Remaking Polities, Economies, and Militance* (Chicago: University of Chicago Press, 1993), pp. 152–183.

12. Ibid.

13. Susan Bayly, "Christians and Competing Fundamentalisms in South Indian Society," in Marty and Appleby, eds., *Accounting for Fundamentalisms*, p. 732.

Politics, Ethnicity, and Fundamentalism

Gabriel A. Almond, Emmanuel Sivan, and R. Scott Appleby

What determines the behavior of fundamentalist movements? As we explained in chapter 17 and described in detail in chapter 18, structure, chance, and choice, taken together, determine the direction a fundamentalist movement will take in its relation to the world. Now let us approach the question in a slightly different way, in an attempt further to clarify our analytical model. Of structure, chance, and choice, policy analysts can be most confident—if *confident* is the word—in their understandings of the structural setting in which a movement exists. We can know whether a host society is democratic or nondemocratic, religiously and ethnically heterogeneous or homogeneous, economically advanced or impeded, and so on. Analyzing or "predicting" contingent events like a war, the illness of a leader, or the eruption of a riot, is a far riskier proposition. This is the case even when the event seems less like a *chance* occurrence (e.g., the election of a pope who surprises everyone by convening Vatican II), and more like a recognizable, if not entirely predictable, outcome of long-term structural tensions (e.g., bread riots, while unpredictable, are hardly a surprise, given long-standing economic mismanagement). Finally, basing an interpretive model in any degree on the *choices* of fundamentalist leaders, with all the vagaries involved therein, requires more boldness than we are able to muster.

Thus we are left with *structures,* and while they do not tell us everything, they do tell us quite a bit about the possibilities open to fundamentalist movements. Among the major conditions influencing the strategy, growth, and decline of fundamentalist movements are the nature of the political regime under which they compete for influence and power, and the ethnic heterogeneity or homogeneity of the society in which they emerge. The regime—whether it is authoritarian or democratic—sets the operating rules of political competition, thereby determining whether the struggle is to be overt or covert, the methods peaceful or violent, and the approach gradualist or integralist. The ethnic character of the society may determine whether a purely religious form of fundamentalism emerges, or whether it is subordinated and intermingled with ethnic and nationalist purposes.

In the preceding chapters we introduced these themes of politics and ethnicity, along with others, in broad theoretical terms. In this chapter we adopt a narrower and sharper focus on political regime and ethnocultural context. We are not setting aside our threefold explanatory logic of structure, chance, and choice. But we argue that the other structural variables are filtered through the political-governmental structure and process. Similarly the cultural identities distributed among the population determine the options available to fundamentalist leaders. If ethnicity and religion are intermingled in the population of a society, what emerges may be a threat not only to the form of government and the content of public policy, but also to the continued membership of minority groups in the national community and the very integrity of the state.

In what follows we elaborate these assertions by examining the strategies, growth, and decline of fundamentalist movements in three structural settings—democratic societies, societies that are nondemocratic, and societies riven by ethnoreligious conflict.

Strategies

By *strategies* we refer to the programmatic means fundamentalists adopt for achieving their goals. The strategies of fundamentalist movements will vary according to their different modes of relating to the world (see chapters 17 and 18), and according to the possibilities available to them in their structural settings.

Non-democratic Structures

By *non-democratic* we mean strong, repressive, centralized governments. Especially in the Islamic world such governments have been expanding pervasively at the expense of civil society—since the end of World War II in most Islamic countries, but since the mid-nineteenth century in Egypt, Algeria, and Muslim India. The media and education are under government control, and the economy, another structural factor, is dominated by the public sector.

This set of circumstances has tended to militate against the rise of an opposition movement, yet some changes in the structure have provided opportunities, notably the development of the private sector in the 1970s. This development was due to a modified international environment: the open-door policy initiated in Egypt after the 1973 war led to a measure of political liberation, and the availability of Saudi money after the oil bonanza led to the funding of various Islamic movements. The decline in the "systemic legitimacy" of the regimes, due to defeat in war (Egypt, 1967) and grave socioeconomic crisis (Algeria, 1988), likewise prepared the terrain.

Two strategies have been devised, by trial and error, in order to deal with this set of circumstances. They may be followed alternately by the same movement or simultaneously (but with no coordination) by different branches of the movement.

The first option is *a combination of world-creator and world-transformer patterns of relation*. The building-up of enclaves comes first in the process, followed by their expansion in a civil society, which needs to be reconstructed after ravages by government. The build up may be facilitated by an opening up of democratic process (a change in government structure), which creates room for maneuver and the possibility of gaining assets in civil society. This path was followed by the Muslim Brotherhood in Egypt under Sadat and Mubarak when they could use the relaxation of the laws on associations and the press as well as the availability of elections in order to garner a growing basis of support. In Iran the Islamic movement used similar opportunities provided by the shah from the late 1960s to the mid-1970s, before turning to the second strategy.

The second strategy option in a nondemocratic structure, adopted when the movement shifts to a world-conqueror mode, consists of *seizing power by violent means*: destabilization by mass demonstrations (Iran, 1978; Tunisia, 1984; Algeria, 1988), assassination (the Egyptian Jama'at murdering Sadat, 1981; their attempts against higher officials and tourists in the 1990s), and open revolt (Syrian radicals in Hama, 1982; Shi'ites in southern Iraq, 1991). Alternatively, the movement may create an alliance with (or infiltrate) a military group that then takes control; this was the case in Sudan in 1989 and in Pakistan under Zia ul-Haq. This process unfolds according to the world-conqueror ideology and organization, as developed above, and is followed whenever the democratic process is either unavailable or seen (in its present guise) as a trap. Government structure, public policy, and control of media and education are the crucial factors in forcing fundamentalist opposition movements in this radical direction.

If the revolutionary movement does not succeed but the movement survives, the transformer pattern tends to be chosen again when control and repression of the movement loosens up.

This should by no means be considered an exclusively Islamic pattern. It does not cover Islamic cases of ethnic domination (see the world-creator pattern), but does include the Pentecostals in Guatemala. The contingency that gave Guatemalan Pentecostals the opportunity to grow in number (from disaffected Catholic ranks) consisted in the rapid attempt of the government to transform the structure of the political economy, very much like in Iran (1962–78) and Egypt (post-1973). The difference was that the Guatemalan evangelicals had available to them a short-term trigger or chance factor—the rise of a born-again retired general, Ríos Montt, to the presidency. Fueled in part by major investments by North American (and Korean) businessmen, the large-scale agricultural and industrial development opened up avenues of opportunity and upward mobility for the lower classes and rural peasants—without, however, providing the necessary educational support and training for the displaced farmers and small-scale entrepreneurs who would make up the bulk of the workforce (and the new recruits for neo-Pentecostal churches). In the 1980s Ríos Montt promoted evangelicalism as an ideology and a cultural force with the potential to provide significant political and social support for the transformation of the economy from small-scale agricultural and entrepreneurial activity to large-scale industrial production.

The evangelical movement, planted by missionaries in the nineteenth century, had developed its own indigenous forms of worship, which combined North American Baptism and Pentecostalism. Yet the boom in the 1980s was the result of Ríos Montt's policies. He surrounded himself with leading Latin American evangelists, supported the burgeoning evangelical media and educational initiatives, and vigorously discredited the Catholic church as standing in the way of moral regeneration and economic development. Membership in Pentecostal churches swelled, reaching about one-third of the population by the end of the decade—the highest such share in Latin America. Thus the Guatemalan evangelicals expanded from congregational enclaves to a world-transformer pattern.

Democratic Structures

In other settings the government structure is democratic (whether centralized or de-centralized), civil society is well developed, the media is free, and education is public-democratic but with some private space. In such cases fundamentalists can raise money in the developed local economy (as is the case with the Protestant and Jewish funda-mentalists in the United States, with Italian Catholics of CL, and others) or venture abroad to other developed countries (as with Israeli haredim collecting money in the United States).

In democratic structures the fundamentalist strategy is predicated upon enclave building and expansion, designed first in order to create a "defensive perimeter" and later as a mode of enlarging the hold over civil society, with the hope of achieving hegemony there. Using the terminology of our four patterns of fundamentalist world relation, we may say that *fundamentalists operating in democratic structures pursue a simultaneous (or consecutive) strategy of world creation and world transformation.* They exploit the freedoms of a liberal society, that is, in two ways: relatively unhin-dered by the government, they carve out social space and amass cultural resources in order to create alternative, oppositional structures and institutions; from this base they attempt to transform the world of the secularized opponent by transferring the values and procedures of their own strongly competitive institutions to the weakened insti-tutions of the larger culture. (When the second phase of this strategy comes to domi-nate the efforts of the fundamentalist movement, we may speak of the movement as a world conqueror, as in the case of second-emergence Protestant Christian fundamen-talism, the political expression of which is now so well-developed that it has emerged as an entity unto itself, known as "the Christian Right.")

The organizational basis for this world-creator—world-transformer strategic mode—that is, the initial manpower resources—consists of traditionalists in the host religion. Action is limited to the hard core in the world-creating enclave phase (from the second to the sixth decade of the twentieth century among U.S. Baptists and har-edim) and even when the movement expands. It seeks lukewarm (or "fallen") believ-ers. This was true of CL as well, targeting as it did nominally Catholic high school and university students in north Italy. Returnees to the faith *(ba'ale teshuva,* as the haredim call them)—that is, former secularists—have media value in the struggle for hegemony (in the United States, Italy, Israel), but their numerical weight is small. And this is true even for the Lubavitcher Hasidim, who have better results among secularists.

It should be stressed that not all movements transcend the enclave phase. The French Lefebvrists, for example, cannot cross this threshold due to the marginality to which they have relegated themselves in their schism from the church, which is still seen as the vehicle of salvation for most traditionalists. They further complicated their position by pitting themselves against a pro-traditionalist, and popular, pope. In the case of the Neturei Karta, (Satmar) extremist haredim in the United States and Israel, staying within the enclave is voluntary: they deem the modern world too dangerous to venture into and expect expansion and hegemony only when normal history ends and the age of Redemption dawns.

The consolidation of the enclave and its expansion are greatly facilitated by economic trends in democratic societies. Paradoxically, the modern economy that endangers the faith (e.g., the boom in the postwar United States, post-Marshall Plan Italy, post-1967 Israel) also creates opportunities to finance the fundamentalist movements: niches for believers in the service economy (e.g., retail electronics, computer programmers), and jobs in the expanding public educational system (e.g., haredi teachers in the National Religious school in Israel). Public policies further help the growth of the movement's own educational (and social) institutions, which is the linchpin of its activity. Such help is given either because of conviction, as under President Reagan, or because of government coalition calculations, as in Israel where the ultra-Orthodox parties (Agudat Yisrael, Shas, Degel ha-Torah) can swing the balance in favor of either of the two big political blocs. A mix of both motivations operated in favor of CL as long as the Christian Democrats were in power in Italy (until 1994).

It is around such economic and political institutions that fundamentalist community building is being pursued in democratic societies. The process is also facilitated by new media technology (audio/videotapes, radio, television, satellites, cellular phones, and the like), which enables people to keep in touch in far-flung places. Negative propaganda against the secular world is therefore possible, with outlets (such as the CBN-TV network) in the global village of media markets wooing eventual recruits outside the social networks of churches and synagogues. Nonetheless, the religious communities themselves serve as the launching pad in the fight for additional social space; they utilize the social mobility of their members, their economic clout, and their access to media.

When the movement enters politics, this is done mostly for defensive reasons, so as to establish a cordon sanitaire for the enclave at either the local or the state level. Later, it may be greatly helped when the general attitude toward religion improves, as was the case in Israel following the euphoria of the 1967 war. Impetus may likewise be provided when the possibility arises of becoming a power broker (the Moral Majority within the U.S. Republican Party in the 1980s; the Christian Coalition in the 1990s).

The role of chance, as opposed to structure, is not substantial with regard to this pattern (except for an exogenous chance such as the Six-Day War modifying the religious context in Israel). Choice, however, plays a vital role, especially at the leadership level, where the cocktail of tactics and strategy is devised and community institution building is initiated. For example, Father Luigi Giussani of Milan, the leader of CL, provided charismatic leadership and concocted an ideology blending neo-Thomist theology and existentialist thought in order to justify mobilization and his critique of modern culture. He also concocted, with the help of efficient deputies, a mix of social programs and a plethora of organizational forms (notably the scuole, the cooperatives, and publishing houses), which attracted, in the 1960s and 1970s, students disillusioned with revolutionary radicalism and with the moral corruption of Italian society. These structures evolved from enclaves into missionary tentacles, extending from social action into politics, through the Movimento Popolare.

In a different context ultra-Orthodox rabbis such as Shlomo Kahaneman in Israel or Aharon Kottler in the United States established a network of modern yeshivot around which the haredi enclave was reconstituted after the mortal blow it received during the Holocaust. The network branched out, in the Israeli case, from the traditional confines of Ashkenazis into the milieu of Oriental Jews. This "world of learners"—comprising long-term (ten to fifteen years' curriculum) yeshiva students, together with their wives (employed in the community) and proliferating children—became a self-regenerating enclave with a broad basis of peripheral support among laypeople *(ba'alei batim)*, many of whom are former yeshiva students now gainfully employed. The parallel political organizations that existed prior to the Holocaust in the Agudat form were greatly expanded and variegated.

Not only in the Jewish and Italian cases, but also in that of U.S. Protestants, members do count. Due to the decentralized, egalitarian nature of the enclave, as well as to the emphasis on action in civil society, the role of the rank and file (their degree of participation, commitment, and initiative) is of import.

The initial impulse in virtually all of these movements is that of dissent and separation. Few are those in which the missionary bent was paramount from the beginning. Even among the Lubavitchers—who are distinguished today by their missionary zeal—this dimension was introduced by the fifth dynastic rebbe in the 1920s. The sole case of missionary zeal from the beginning is that of the Islamic Tabligh.

The Tablighi Jamaat, founded in British India in the 1920s, reacted to the predicament of a particular sector of Islamic society, namely, borderline Muslims who retained many Hindu rituals and customs and were now the object of proselytizing efforts by Hindu groups in northern India. To counter these efforts the Tablighi Jamaat launched a "purification" campaign. It had a populist, cross-class appeal thanks to its emphasis upon learning by doing, its suspicion of learned Islam, and its simple doctrinal principles and minimal and repetitive behavioral requirements. The Tablighi Jamaat's acceptance of modern secular education accounted for its continued appeal in the modernized sectors of post-partition India and Pakistan. Imported to Western Europe in the 1970s, the movement did not change its modus operandi, but its ideology was transmuted by the new context. The basic rituals that the Tablighi Jamaat asked its converts to perform took on a powerful new meaning when acted out in public on the infidel soil of Europe—as a binding declaratory rite of one's identity as Muslim. It determined the way the European environment treated the Muslim person in question, usually a "guest worker." It thus reaffirmed his identity, which may have been not all too deep at the moment the act was first performed.

The Tablighi Jamaat has no enclave, just a loose core of activists who are expected to participate in short-term, intense "missionary tours" and then relapse into the low-intensity daily rhythm of the "purified" convert. In this modus operandi as well as in ideology, it is a glaring exception. All other movements that fit the world-transformer pattern began as a fight for mere survival against heavy odds, including persecution. Even once survival is guaranteed, they must insure themselves against recurrence of such dangers; hence the importance of the enclave as a basis for peripheral activity and as ultimate refuge.

Ethnoreligions Confrontation

In many settings of ethnoreligious confrontation a strong nationalist element is evident: the ethnic and/or religious groups or communities identify their particular heritage, in an exclusive way, with the national identity. Conflict in these cases is not inhibited by the checks and balances of democratic societies. (U.S. Protestant fundamentalists, with their own nativist, nationalist rhetoric claiming special privilege in the "Judeo-Christian" nation, find the rhetoric undermined by a competing discourse of pluralism and by laws and customs proscribing religious exclusivism.)

In cases of ethnic or religious minorities fighting back, the group resents being dominated or marginalized (e.g., Muslims in Afghanistan after the Russian invasion; Palestinians in Gaza and the West Bank, post-1967; Sikhs in India in competition with Hindu nationalism against the background of the decline of the pluralistic Indian state). In other cases, however, a majority group is anxious about the imminent loss of its hegemony. Thus we find Hindutva supporters fearing competition with Islam and Christianity facilitated by the Nehru-established liberal state; Gush Emunim activists perceiving that the defeatism of secular Israeli government may lead to the loss of the "redeemed" territories in the name of the "false slogan" of "refraining from dominating an alien [Palestinian] people"; Ulster Protestants uneasy about the "cowardly" Unionist government, which does not oppose resurgent Irish nationalism and a compromising British attitude.

The common denominator for all the above (as well as others such as the Kach movement and Sri Lankan Buddhist extremism) is that the ethnic group identity comprises powerful religious components, so much so that it is quite difficult to disentangle the nation-building component from the fundamentalist one. In two cases, however, one can clearly state that the latter element has precedence over the former: Hamas, which began as an offshoot of the Muslin Brotherhood in Gaza dedicated to the Islamization of society and only in the mid-1980s became a national resistance; and the Gush Emunim, which had its origins in the mystical-messianic thought of Rabbi Kook the Elder, transmuted into the creed of a yeshiva nucleus (Merkaz Harav) of a religious youth movement (Bnai Akiva), long before the 1967 war made it the standard-bearer of the hard Israeli Right.

The strategy pursued by the majority in cases of ethnic confrontation is three-pronged. First, fundamentalists tend to insist upon sharp external boundaries. As could be expected from an ethnonationalist movement seeking to consolidate a state, emphasis is put on a definite territory, one that has a hallowed character in terms of the host religion. Savarkar, the father of the Hindutva concept, asserted that Hindus had sole legitimate claim to all the lands watered by the sacred Ganges, Brahmaputra, and Indus rivers, and to all the lands stretching from the Himalayas to the confluence of the southern seas at Cape Comorin. The claim is based on many thousand years of continuity in identification, by blood and culturally, with the "holy land" and its "holy waters." Gush Emunim is likewise wedded to the notion of the Great Land of Israel, promised to the Jews by Divine Providence in the Bible and destined to become the theater of Redemption, an age that dawned with the establishment of the State of Israel. (Although the divine boundaries cover lands east of the River Jordan as well, the Gush cut down its aspirations to lands west of the river, controlled in their entirety by the Israeli army after the 1967 war.) The same notion of divine promise and hallowed land were taken over, partly in imitation, by Hamas, for whom the sanctity of the land flows from Al-Quds, the holy city of Jerusalem. In Hamas's charter the claim is pushed even further: Palestine is a *waqf*, a religious endowment, and as such cannot be appropriated, even in part, by non-Muslims.

The second element of this strategy attempts to bolster the sharp external boundaries by a notion of supremacy, electivity, and internal unity of the group the movement wishes to defend. Hindutva disciples affirm the racial, cultural, and religious superiority of the Hindus and the inferiority of all who cannot legitimately make such claims. Internal differences between Hindus are to be transcended, and even the Untouchables are to be reclaimed and fully integrated into a society governed by "Hindu values." (This was, of course, the "Hindu" response to the possibility that two of its competitors, Islam and Christianity would win points for affirming the equality of believers. By the same token it also rejects the secular pluralist state created by Nehru and endeavors to replace it with a Hinduized state, fully occupying the land within sacred boundaries, and peopled homogeneously by believing and practicing Hindus.)

The Sikhs likewise stress their inherent difference with the Hindus. Thus the Sikh ideology notes that the Hindu pagans worship various deities as well as the sun, rivers, trees, and so forth, while the superior Sikhs worship one God and hold in sole reverence their holy book, the Adi Granth (a scripture the Hindus do not possess). And because the sixth guru, Hargobind, posits the inseparability of state and religion, Sikh separatism must find a distinct political expression. The chosen political expression legitimizes reliance on the sword in defense of Sikh interests. Ian Paisley and his Free Presbyterian Church (as well as its political offshoot, the Democratic Unionist Party) resort to Calvinist-derived discourse about the predestination of an elect people, whose chosenness was confirmed in their right religion and their industrious self-sacrificing character. All this serves as an irreducible, sacred basis for nationalist exclusivism. Jewish exclusivism of a different nature was the battle cry of Rabbi Kahane and Kach: the Jews are a chosen people that dwells alone, virtually a race by dint of endogamy (the fight against mixed marriage was a core issue for Kach). In order to maintain the sharp divide between the beleaguered Jewish community and those outside the fold, Kahane preached and practiced Jewish inclusiveness and empowerment of Jewish have-nots (lower-middle class in the United States, Orientals in Israel)—ultimately by the exclusion of competing Arabs from Jewish neighborhoods, and businesses, and eventually from the Land of Israel altogether.

The last and third strategic element follows inexorably: dramatic, at times spectacular, confrontational tactics. We have noted, in the above description of Kach, the interplay of Jewish pride, the "it's a jungle out there" view of the Middle East, and tactics designed to heighten ethnic friction. The belief in the legitimacy of violence undertaken in communal self-defense led the Sikhs, under Bhindranwale and his Khalsa Dal party, to engage in violence and terrorism. The resulting Operation Blue Star and its "theater of cruelty" set off large-scale violence, continuing to this day, which undermined the moderate Sikh party, Akali Dal, which played the political game according to the rules of the pluralist, secular Indian democracy.

In terms of our four world-relational patterns, *we see a combination of the world conqueror and the world creator in the three-pronged strategy of the ethnoreligious fundamentalist.* The ethnoreligious minority—no less than the aggrieved, relatively deprived majority—must sustain and fortify its niche in society to defend itself from alien, penetrating forces; but it also strikes out violently at the enemy, in the absence or weakness or inattention (or calculated policy) of the otherwise restraining state.

In long-term conflicts the gradualist rhythms of the world transformer may eventually appear. The modern media of communication (print, radio, television, cinema) and the institutions of civil society (interest groups, voluntary associations, and informal groups of one kind or another) are the bearers of modernization and secularization, and hence threats to fundamentalist movements. The tactics followed by ethnoreligious minorities or aggrieved majorities is to protect their membership from secular civil society, or from the alien interloper, by forming their own network of interest groups, and to penetrate and use the media for their own purposes.

Civil society and modern media in India, for example, are concentrated in the modern metropolitan and urban areas. In the non-modern sectors where civil society has not had a significant development, the RSS, VHP, and BJP are carrying out a campaign to penetrate or preempt civil society through the formation of their own trade unions, professional associations, sports organizations, pilgrimage centers, and the like; as well as through the proliferation of their own media. Hindu revivalism and fundamentalism have effectively penetrated the cinema. The broadcast of the Rāmāyaṇa in the form of a serial, starting in late January 1987, made a standardized version of the Rāmāyaṇa known and popular among the Indian middle class. It enhanced the knowledge of Ayodhya as Ram's birthplace and therefore as one of the most important places of pilgrimage in Uttar Pradesh.

The VHP shock troops of Hindutva organized aggressive, "in-your-face" campaigns that resembled the world conqueror, however, rather than the world transformer. Led by caravans of trucks (simulating chariots of epic imagination), one such procession marched on Ayodhya in Uttar Pradesh, first to protest and then to destroy the Babri Masjid. The destruction of the mosque, begun as an act of collective nationalist vindication, was transformed by the ecstatically participating Hindutva believers into a high point of religious awakening, directed against the age-old enemy, Islam.

It is amply evident that the crucial factor in ethno-religious confrontation, fundamentalist style, is leadership. Leaders conceive ideology and concoct tactics, all within the confines of the religious context and the nature of the host religion. The role of chance (the 1967 war, the assassination of Indira Gandhi) comes second.

Growth

In the cases covered by democratic and non-democratic settings, a combination of structural factors may be exploited in such a way as to lead to growth of a fundamentalist movement. The coming together of these factors is greatly facilitated by contingency and chance. It could be an endogenous chance (riots that lay bare an economic crisis due to faulty development policy) or an exogenous chance (defeat in war). In either case the legitimacy of the present order is deeply shaken—either just the "performance legitimacy" or, in graver situations, the "systemic legitimacy."

In the case of ethnoreligious conflict, the International Environment (e.g., the Arab-Israeli conflict, the Afghanistan invasion) and government policy (the crisis of the Indian pluralist, secular regime) are the predominant structures that influence growth. Chance occurrences operate here also as a trigger. Consider the road accident in which an Israeli army vehicle killed bystanders in Gaza, leading to the first mass demonstrations of the Intifada; or the appearance of shoulder-held antihelicopter missiles, which gave the Afghan resistance a fighting chance.

Nondemocratic Structures

To see the interplay of structure, contingency, and chance, we look first at two nondemocratic cases, Egypt and Algeria. While a real fundamentalist movement surfaced only in the early 1970s, the nuclei had been formed a decade earlier. They were the product of alarm experienced by hard-core remnants of the embattled Muslim Brotherhood before the success of the secularization drive carried on by the victorious Nasserist regime. Thanks to Sayyid Qutb, the nuclei developed a new ideology in response to the danger that pan-Arab populism constituted to Islam—backed as this populism was by an aggressively interventionist state. Yet the impact of the nuclei was small, whereas the Nasserist regime enjoyed both "systemic legitimacy" and "performance legitimacy."

The 1967 defeat was a short-term trigger that shook both legitimacies and rendered prescient and credible Qutb's critique of the nefarious effects of Nasserism. Moreover, it heightened religious sensitivity among the masses (such as the miraculous appearance of the Virgin Mary in a Coptic church, leading to a huge flow of Muslim pilgrims to this site).

Islamic radicals could now broaden their critique to embrace the long-term social effects of the regime's policies, effects that, though present because of Nasser's policies, became more evident and aggravated under Sadat. These social strains were due to an ever-accelerating demographic explosion (the result of high fertility and a decline in infant mortality caused by preventive medicine), and an exodus from countryside to town and from town to metropolis. Such strains were rendered particularly acute by the expansion of secondary and higher education (from the late 1950s on), which created hordes of diploma-holders with high expectations bred of their presumed proficiencies, facing limited employment opportunities in the (still limited) modern sectors of the economy. Most of these graduates had to make do with poorly remunerated government jobs. Expectations grew even higher following the oil bonanza in the Gulf states in 1973/74, which the Egyptians assumed (wrongly) would have a spillover effect on them; they were further catalyzed by Sadat's "open-door policy" (consisting of privatization, foreign investment, and imports), which created a class of nouveaux riches. The combined effect was to render more acute the relative deprivation felt by the modern lower-middle class. As Nasserism's socioeconomic promise fizzled out, so did its concomitant trait—"progressive"-minded secularism, in a pan-Arab garb. And whereas liberalism had been tainted by collaboration with the corrupt monarchy, a return to old-time religion was virtually inevitable—by default.

Prompted by triggers such as the "bread riots" of 1977, the Jama'at nuclei expanded into a full-fledged movement, with no real modification of Qutb's ideology. The nuclei spawned a plethora of autonomous associations (jama'at), mostly of students (usually of migrant origin) and young professionals employed in the impoverished public sector. All this occurred in a context in which civil society was showing greater vitality.

The Algerian case is similar to the Egyptian one (including the ideology, which is Sunni and inspired by Sayyid Qutb), but differs in two crucial aspects: the extent of the socioeconomic crisis which is far more acute, not just a matter of stalled growth as in Egypt; and the movement developed first as one of pure social protest, with no religious agenda, and was later hijacked by Muslim radicals who transformed it into the Front Islamique du Salut (FIS).

The long-term economic crisis took place in the context of an oil-rich yet densely populated country. It was the end product of an erroneous strategy of development, pursued since 1962, that gambled on the buildup of capital-intensive, know-how-intensive, and labor-extensive industries, while neglecting agriculture and import-substitution (i.e., labor-intensive, light and medium) industries. The resultant unemployment (in a country where the natural growth rate exceeds 4 percent) was "absorbed" by make-work public sector jobs and by subsidies for major staples. This policy could be pursued as long as oil prices were high, for the heavy industries had proven themselves, in the course of the 1970s to be uncompetitive; not only did they not bring in foreign currency, they incurred a spiralling cost in service of the debt.

The crisis was brought to a head by the second decline in oil prices in 1985–86, which halved the state's foreign currency revenues; of the revenues, three-quarters had to be set aside for servicing the debt. Lavish subsidies (for employment, staples, housing) were no longer tenable well before the International Monetary Fund set its stringent conditions for rescheduling the debt. The state was, hence, crippled in its "performance legitimacy" as benefactor, and that at a time when it had barely any "systemic legitimacy" left due to the disappearance (in 1978) of a charismatic president (Boumédienne) and to the erosion of the Front de Liberation National (FLN) governing party's heroic image as leader of the war of liberation (1954–62), due to its long, self-serving and increasingly corrupt monopoly on power.

Triggered by the "couscous riots" of 1988 (following the abolition of subsidies), a huge, yet amorphous, social protest movement spread like brushfire across classes and regions, but was particularly strong in the lower and lower-middle classes in the overcrowded towns. Its spearhead was young unemployed males (of all education levels). Devoid of positive ideological vision and powerful leaders, this movement would be overtaken in the span of less than a year by an ad hoc coalition of Muslim radicals. The latter had shown themselves to be consummate organizers (at the grass-roots level as well as the national level), coalition builders (drawing on various Islamic tendencies), and adept at playing the new electoral game, which had been opened up by concessions granted by the beleaguered regime. Yet perhaps their greatest contribution consisted in endowing the movement with a coherent vision, both positive and negative, an interpretive prism that helped adherents make sense of Algeria's failures during three decades of independence. On the other hand, this interpretive scheme drew up the picture of an alternative moral and political order. The FIS promptly built up its power basis and proceeded to win municipal elections (1990) and then the first round of general elections (1991).

The broad gamut of structural factors operating in the two cases is an urbanization/migration/modernization process, catalyzed by the international environment (e.g., an oil-price hike, economic slump, etc.). The dysfunctions of the process provide fundamentalism with opportunities for growth. It should be noted, however, that fundamentalism does not find itself capable of availing itself of such opportunities in each country thus hit, Syria and Iraq being two notable examples.

The jama'at movement is urban, that is, the product of economic migration (from rural or small towns to city), a phenomenon that also encompasses vertical mobility and educational attainment relative to the host culture. As we shall see, this generalization holds for the democratic setting as well. It is true even for ethnoreligious conflicts, although there the weight of the urbanization/modernization phenomenon is smaller. Only in the Sikh case do we have a movement that is rural and, on top of that, comes from the regions least touched by modernization of the countryside (i.e., by the Green Revolution), and whose members feel relative deprivation because of this very backwardness.

Contingency is present in both the Algerian and Egyptian cases as the culmination of a cumulative process, namely, misguided development policy plus demographic explosion which the government did not stop. In Egypt, however, the chance trigger not only is a direct result of inherent structural problems; it is also present in another guise, "coming out of left field" as it were. That is, the trigger here is the 1967 and 1973 wars, which were not "inevitable" in the same way that economic and demographic problems were inevitable. (And of course, those wars had a different impact on Jewish fundamentalism.)

The basic point is this: short-term catalysts, or triggers, inject urgency into a situation and provide openings for various destabilizing movements, fundamentalisms primary among them in these cases. Among these catalysts in Egypt and Algeria over the past decades were oil-price hikes and sudden drops; Boumédienne's death and the selection of Chadli as successor; the French restrictions on immigration from the mid-1970s on; Nasser's death and Sadat's departure from pan-Arabism and etatism.

All these structural factors are necessary conditions for the growth of fundamentalisms in their various aspects. The sufficient condition was in each case provided by leadership. In the jama'at case this was mostly midlevel leaders who transformed the moralistic critique of a victorious regime (Nasser's) into a moral-cum-socioeconomic critique of a faltering regime (Nasser's in the late 1960s, then Sadat's and Mubarak's). The leadership also knew how to identify resources (e.g., their use of disaffected members of the armed forces; their exploitation of the freedom of expression and association granted by Sadat, and of new media such as tapes) and build coalitions (with the populist Labor Party). Government aggression, though less ferocious than under Nasser, was both a constraint (nipping in the bud many an initiative, deterring potential recruits), and an opportunity used by the fundamentalist leadership in order to point out the true nature of the secularized regime as unjust, morally corrupt, and ultimately relying upon brute force.

The leadership of FIS designed the interpretive scheme offered to a restless public during the crisis year 1988/89—an innovative adaptation of Sayyid Qutb's ideas to the particular Algerian case. The scheme was presented by eloquent media manipulators who appealed to a symbolic capital deeply embedded in Algerian Islam; they likewise drew upon a populist strain, originally generated by the FLN during the struggle against the French, namely, the myth of an inherently united people overcoming all divisions introduced by special interests and various dwarfs, or *sanafir*, which serve as their spokesmen. The myth was given a religious gloss, yet retained its antidemocratic punch.

Institution builders and organizers among the cadres created supple alliances between the myriad of Islamic groups that existed before the crisis or emerged during it. The organizers also integrated the private mosque networks into this alliance.

Democratic Structures

A similar combination of structure, contingency, and leadership obtains when fundamentalist movements in democratic settings seek to expand their niche; but here the openings for fundamentalist growth provided by urbanization and migration are greatly enhanced, not only by new media technology (also available in non-democratic settings), but also by the public policies of the welfare state, which provides a minimum of economic support to would-be social movements in measures such as aid to parochial schools. The interplay may be illustrated by two cases of post-World War II growth of movements that had flourished for a while in the interwar years, then declined, either because of internal factors (in the United States) or because of an unexpected contingency (the Holocaust, liquidating ultra-Orthodox Jewry in Eastern Europe).

After 1925 Protestant fundamentalism in the United States withdrew to its own "enclave" existence. It was, at the same time, an enclave that, as the putative heirs of the Puritans, claimed "insider" status. Resurgent in the 1970s and 1980s, the movement used the Puritan theme as a principle of continuity in order to claim a role in the establishment of the national heritage. The new activism, like the old, saw the state as encroaching upon civil society, but after the 1960s there could be no more ambiguity about the secular (-humanist) character of the state itself, nor about its hegemonic intentions. Thus the Protestant movement entered its own world-conqueror phase.

Despite the theological and religious fragmentation they have experienced as a result of their politicization, American Protestant fundamentalists exhibit a large degree of social cohesion; even as they participate in secular politics, they continue to renew their social base through their schools, publishing houses, and seminaries, with relatively little resistance from the government and the larger American society.

In terms of growth and endurance over time, the multigenerational American Protestant movement is similar to the multigenerational haredi movement.

The haredi Jews had to deal in their first wave with the migration that disrupted the world of the Jewish shtetl of Eastern Europe in the last third of the nineteenth century: migration to large urban centers, driven both by push (persecutions, pogroms) and pull (opportunities in urban economy, the lure of secular secondary and higher education). Age-old communities were disrupted, with all their heavily traditionalist and localized cultural and social networks. Hence the migrants were receptive to new ideologies such as socialism and Zionism. Unlike these new rivals for Jewish loyalty, the haredi movement offered a new ideology with generational continuities. Rather than replace and demolish the Jewish tradition and worldview, haredi Judaism intended to preserve as much of its essence as possible, while adapting it to new circumstances (e.g., by developing a new, universal modus operandi in the practice of *mitzvot* [precepts], instead of the plethora of local customs). The haredim appealed in particular to those migrants who, shocked by cultural discontinuities produced by changes of occupation, residence, and culture, wanted to cling to the anchor of that old-time religion.

The Holocaust wiped out these achievements and made Israel and the United States the two major centers of the Jewish people—two countries where the impact of tradition was less, modernity more advanced, and social mobility easier. In Israel the country also presented a grave theological dilemma. The already-reconverted tradition had to be further transformed in the wake of these twin triggers, the Holocaust and the establishment of the State of Israel. The rebuilding of tradition was carried out on the basis of nuclei existing in both countries, and above all with the help of Holocaust survivors who migrated there. Many of the latter, as in the first wave, found adaptation arduous and disappointments galore. The anchor of reconstructed tradition offered reassurance.

What helped the spread of new-fangled ultra-Orthodoxy were the prosperous economies of the West from the 1950s on, where haredim could find a niche (or rather niches) in the urban market (e.g., the 47th Street Photo chain of electronics shops or the diamond business). They were thus able to sustain a middle-class way of life, based on a work environment that is controlled by the ultra-Orthodox community. The welfare state, which was expanding in this period, contributed in turn by sustaining parochial schools (in the name of pluralism) and through direct aid to needy individuals and families—especially heads of family involved in study. Support also came from the numerous haredim who grew rich in the postwar years. In Israel direct aid to individuals, families, and institutions was expanded due to the haredi role as a swing party in government coalitions. And for this reason young haredi males were offered there an additional incentive: long military deferrals for those who studied from ages eighteen to twenty-nine.

Leadership made all these factors work in unison. It concocted, on solid bases laid down by Agudat Yisrael in the interwar years, an ideology that transcended past internal divisions (between Hasidim and Misnagdim) and developed a coherent answer to the challenge presented by the State of Israel (and, to a lesser degree, to the Holocaust). In the post-World War II era great thinkers (like the Hazon Ish) were rare, however. The major contribution of leadership was rather in institution building (the yeshiva network) and coalition-making between sects and political movements. There developed a centralized structure of locally led groups that share ideology, religious practice, major educational institutions, and political affiliation.

In the haredi Jewish as well as the U.S. Protestant case, the needs of the rank and file—urban isolates from a traditional background—were a necessary condition for movement growth, but leadership response was the sufficient condition for growth.

Ethnoreligious Confrontation

Movements in a setting of ethnoreligious conflict grow when they find a social niche. Kach started to expand in Israel only when Rabbi Kahane tailored his message to the resentment of the Oriental lower classes in big towns, to their feelings of deprivation vis-à-vis middle-class Ashkenazis of secular outlook, economic competition with Arabs for semi-skilled jobs. The common denominator for both resentments was the demand for Arab exclusion in the name of a tribalistic notion of Jewish ethnicity, and prejudices against Gentiles—symbolized by the Arabs (from whose lands the Orientals had been chased).

In India the Hindu nationalists of the RSS, VHP, and BJP attracted members by portraying local Muslims and Christians as an alien and cohesive presence—one that is economically competitive with Hindus. Hindu nationalism thereby found a constituency among the new (and traditional) Hindu middle class and lower-middle class in the "cow belt." These upwardly mobile professionals, merchants, and cash-crop farmers were deeply envious of the Brahman secularized upper class. Despite their own recent achievements, they felt endangered by inflation as well as by Muslim (and Christian) economic rivalry.

In these cases socioeconomic aids to growth were dwarfed by the worsening ethnic conflict, which was a product of the international environment in the case of Israel (the 1967, 1973, and 1982 wars), and of public policy in the Indian case. India has seen the crisis of the secularized secular state founded by Nehru, the inheritor of the British Raj. Hinduism was just one of several religions, the existence and autonomy of which were protected by the state, which guaranteed the rule of law, and freedom of press, assembly, and association. The state of emergency decreed by Indira Gandhi was the trigger that brought this crisis to a head and gave the followers of Hindutva a huge push.

The Arab-Israeli conflict has a differentiated impact upon the growth of three movements, each with its specific social base. The Kach breakthrough into poor neighborhoods was greatly facilitated by the spread of locally initiated terrorism in the occupied territories from the late seventies on and its spillover into Israel proper, which created a climate of fear among the civilian population. Certain car-bomb and knifing incidents in Jerusalem were deftly used by Kahane to mobilize underclass and lower class against the Arab one-fourth of that city's population.

In Gush Emunim the post-1967 euphoria gave the marginal group of the Merkaz Harav yeshiva its first opportunity: its gospel of Redemption became attractive, following the "liberation of Judea and Samaria," to the whole sector of religious Zionism and especially to its youth movement, Bnei Akiva, which served as a sort of ready-made cadre. Bnai Akiva also had distinct social characteristics: Ashkenazic, middle-class, educated yet feeling deprived vis-à-vis the secularized Labor-affiliated middle class (also Ashkenazic), which enjoyed hegemony in society, politics, and culture. But 1967 was just a moment of emergence; most former Bnai Akiva members contented themselves with sympathy to the Merkaz Harav group, for nothing more seemed to be required: after all, God was directing the victorious rise of Redemption. What goaded them into activism was not the 1967 triumph, but the 1973 semi-defeat: it became apparent that Redemption was not on "automatic pilot"; setbacks were about to block, perhaps even subvert, it; and defeatism among Israel's secular elites was liable to magnify the scope of these setbacks. The intense settlement activity—launched in 1974 and sustained until 1977 against the Labor government's will—galvanized the Bnai Akiva sector, in a sort of ritual acting out of the struggle for hegemony. In the atmosphere of soul-searching engendered in Israeli opinion by the 1973 war, the essentially optimistic, combative mood of the Gush, untainted by links to the establishment, was appealing to quite a few secularized Israelis. Movements of an activistic bent saw in the new type of settlement effort the answer to the predicament of secular Zionism, which was perceived as being at the end of its rope.

Hamas is also the product of two distinct phases of the Arab-Israeli conflict. It originated in the ranks of the Muslim Brotherhood in Gaza, persecuted and decimated under Egyptian occupation for its opposition to Nasser. The Israeli occupation in 1967 endowed the Brotherhood with greater freedom for association and expression than under Nasser, at least as long as its members limited themselves to educational and cultural activities. The Brotherhood, now dubbed Mujamma', was determined to avail itself of these opportunities and was not prone to exceed them into the political sphere, given the terrible price it had paid for political agitation under Nasser. A vigorous, well-organized movement took shape, especially among high school and college students, elbowing out its leftist rivals. Saudi and Kuwaiti money was helpful for organizational buildup. The nationalist issue was relegated to a lower plane; the movement limited itself to protest against the occupation, hoping to "deal with it" at a later date, when society is Islamized. Yet this was by no means a moderate movement—as evidenced by the vigilante terror tactics of the Mujamma', designed to punish (or deter) transgressors of religious precepts.

A second shock hit the movement when the Intifada was launched by the radical militants of Islamic Jihad (1987). Taken by surprise, the Mujamma' was torn by internal debates for several months, until it decided to join the Intifada and attempt to take it over. Ideology was completely modified, making the liberation of the Holy Land of Palestine from infidel occupation the most urgent task, the justification being that the occupier also brings in a contaminating and seductive culture, and hence no authentic Islamization is possible as long as the occupation endures. The language became national-Islamic rather than universal-Islamic; organization was likewise overhauled and strict compartmentalization introduced. Recruitment was greatly aided by the "demonstration effect" of heroic acts by members (and by Hizbullah in Lebanon), as well as by the dwindling of employment opportunities in the Gulf for the excess manpower of the Gaza Strip as a result of the decline in oil prices from 1985 on. These two factors help explain the spread of the movement to the West Bank, especially to the southern and more traditionalist part, which was sensitive to the religious idiom with which Hamas couched the strategy of militant resistance.

While the movement had a cross-class support periphery, going back to its Mujamma' days, its hard core came to be constituted by lower-class young males, unemployed or underemployed, especially in situations created by the oil-price slump as well as by the economic crisis in Israel, where a hundred thousand of them were employed. Employment in Israel entailed not only the combination of national and economic domination but also exposure to harassment by military police, a reality that made Palestinians working there a particularly resentful group.

Still, without choice—the choices made by leadership—the opportunities for fundamentalist growth would not have been exploited. Kach was always a one-man show. In the Gush Rabbi Kook the Younger worked out the adaptation of the ideology to the 1973 crisis and incorporated in it a critique of secular Israeli society. A group of young disciples (notably, Hanan Porat, Zvi Katzover, and Daniella Weiss) set itself up as a collective leadership innovating the modus operandi of settlement as the great endeavor of the movement, building bridges to nonreligious nationalists, and organizing the National Religious Party periphery as a support network. In the BJP of India the entry of Hindutva into confrontational politics—including the 1993 Ayodhya campaign—was engineered by L. K. Advani, from a strategy devised earlier in the RSS by Balasaheb Deoras, and from an ideological critique of Indian secularism laid out by M. S. Golwarkar. In Hamas the move from Islamization to Islamic-Palestinian nationalism was spearheaded, and endowed with theological justification, by Shaykh Ahmed Yassin; its implementation in organizational and military terms was left to his younger lieutenants.

The role of chance, as short-term, was important at particular junctions, yet by no means crucial. If the December 1987 road accident had not taken place, some other clash between Israelis and Palestinians would have sparked the Intifada in the tension-laden atmosphere then prevalent in Gaza.

Decline

Movements that rise may decline, for a short or long while, and may or may not rise again. We shall examine the gamut of possibilities in the three settings we have identified.

Non-democratic Structures

Public policy is the most prominent danger to fundamentalist movements in non-democratic societies. By that we mean, above all, policies of repression. President Assad dealt a mortal blow to the Syrian Muslim Brotherhood in the massacre of Hama. Saddam Hussein did the same to the Shi'ite Da'wa first when he executed its cadres in 1980 and then when he ruthlessly put down its revolt in the wake of the Gulf War (1991). More selective but still ferocious repression cut down the wings of the Tunisian Nahda movements (1987–90).

Other regimes use a different but also efficacious dosage: repression against the more extremist elements combined with a buy out of the rest (in the form of government jobs and/or some parliamentary representation following "managed" elections). This is the case in Egypt, Jordan, and Morocco. Repression may be terribly demoralizing for the surviving members, for it creates an atmosphere of "failed prophecy": history does not go the way the enclave believed it should go; the road map it put its trust in appears to be wrong. Compromise with the powers that be after a period of flamboyant speeches (and even acts) may cripple the leaders' credibility. Note the generous-devious gesture of King Hussein of Jordan, who granted amnesty to two Muslim Brotherhood leaders who were found guilty of a plot to topple him.

Dynamics internal to the movement also may contribute to its decline. By its very nature an enclave cannot tolerate internal opposition (which contradicts this ideal of unity cum equality); hence enclaves have trouble negotiating any ideological dispute or competition between powerful leading figures. What may further weaken loyalty to the enclave is the emergence of an evolving hierarchy of leadership due to the growth of the movement, or to demands for specialization brought to bear by the technological requirements of the armed struggle. To put it in Albert O. Hirschman's terms, when loyalty to established leaders, or to a distant hierarchy, is weakened for lack of voice, exit becomes a more likely possibility. This goes against what cognitive dissonance theory would have led us to expect—that hard-core membership would stick it out. Such time- and energy-consuming splits and squabbles, which push activists out of the movement altogether, are the bane of the Egyptian jama'at.

As for the periphery of the fundamentalist movement, it is particularly sensitive to changes in the economic environment (and public policies in this domain). A substantial economic improvement, as in Tunisia in the late 1980s and early 1990s, results in sympathizers dropping out in droves, the very reason for their protest, through the movement, having been greatly attenuated.

Factors of chance may catalyze such peripeties. Bad chemistry between leaders who cannot get along (e.g., Mourou and Ghannushi in Tunisia, Fadlallah and Nasrallah in Lebanon, Chebouti and Layada in Algeria) may produce debilitating splits. Or a key leader may die (or be executed), leaving no worthy successor (Marwan Hadid in Syria, Muhammad Baqir al-Sadr in Iraq, and of course Khomeini). The very dependence of the enclave upon charismatic figures makes it terribly vulnerable in such cases. Moral failures in leaders that are exploited (or provoked) by government agents (as was recently the case in Tunisia) may likewise topple linchpin personalities and undermine the movement's cohesion.

Last but not least, the international environment may create chance occasions for the leaders to make bad tactical decisions, as during the Gulf Crisis of 1990/91, when the Jama'at, the FIS, and Hamas backed Saddam, thus forfeiting vital Saudi financial aid.

Obviously, as in that example, bad choice by the leaders is also involved in the decline of fundamentalist movements. Leaders may decide upon a strategy of confrontation, underestimating the government's ability and readiness to engage in efficacious repression (Syria in 1982, Iraq in 1991). When a movement is involved in terrorism, it may likewise opt for methods that make it lose public sympathy and aid, as when the Egyptian jama'at started to kill tourists (striking at a very key economic sector) or when the Islamic extremists in Algeria started "executing" non-veiled women in 1994.

Democratic Structures

Decline may lurk in too much success too soon, or problems of digestion, one might say. In a democracy it is quite likely that the majority society will coopt the dissenting minority, and even smother it with kindness: financial aid, access to the media and to the educational system. This is not necessarily a Machiavellian ploy but rather the upshot of cultural change in the form of greater acceptance of religion in general. Such an evolution, if bolstered by economic trends, may constitute an even more formidable challenge to the fundamentalist movement: rising levels of affluence in a society may enable fundamentalists to carve out a lucrative niche in the expanding economy. Moreover, the media so ably manipulated by fundamentalist groups may be turned against them; an opportunity becomes a threat. The electronic media may infiltrate every nook and cranny in the enclave.

In the exact moment when the dissenting minority seems to be moving toward ascendancy, rot sets in. The outside boundary weakens and gets fuzzy; greater inequity evolves inside. In Mary Douglas's terms the movement becomes "lower group" and "higher grid"; that is, it begins to lose the tight, clearly bounded, united and egalitarian structure of yore. The upshot is growing bureaucracy, greater distance between leaders and the led, disaffection in the ranks. The rank and file may all the more easily venture out of the movement, for society at large is seductive in its economic possibilities (for individualists) and thus makes dependency on group solidarity less crucial. Paradoxically, because society is no longer starkly opposed to religion as such, it may seem now both culturally less menacing and materially more appealing. High turnover rate is in such situations the harbinger of slow decline.

Alternatively, decline may stem from the host religion, that is, from the tendency of dissenting minorities (here as well as in non-democratic settings) to split over doctrinal issues, a tendency exacerbated by enclave dynamics (intolerance of opposition, clash between charismatic personalities). Whatever the reason, splits may enfeeble enclaves and make them waste energy on infighting rather than directing their fire against outsiders.

As in non-democratic settings, some decline may be precipitated "when prophecy fails." Demoralization may creep in when the majority society shows resilience and does not crumble, and fundamentalist dreams of hegemony are thwarted.

The role of chance in decline appears in the untimely disappearance of leaders like Msgr. Lefebvre and Rabbi Kook the Younger, whose special mix of qualities could not be replaced. Such a loss is all the more sensitive, given the charismatic leader's role in the movement's origins and growth. This is true even when a successor has been preselected and trained, as was the case with Lefebvre's successor. It is certainly truer when no successor was designated, or when a successor was nominated, but in violation of set norms. (The recently deceased Lubavitcher rebbe, for example, designated in his will his secretary, who not only is not a member of the Schneerson family, but lacks charisma.)

Ethnoreligious Confrontation

The movements that come under this heading are all young, so one can only speculate about eventual decline. Because economic dysfunctions catalyzed growth, economic growth may lead to a decline in the appeal of fundamentalist movements. More threat-ening to their well-being may be a political solution (achieved or in process) for the ethnoreligious conflict, which was grist for the fundamentalist mill; once such a solu-tion is found, the hard-core fundamentalists may remain, but the periphery and some rank and file may drop out (as happened to the Gush Emunim in the wake of the Oslo Accord). As in non-democratic settings, recourse to terrorism may isolate the move-ment and/or create splits inside its core (e.g., in Gush Emunim with the discovery of the Jewish underground in the mid-1980s).

Leadership is a sore point in all enclaves. The assassination of Rabbi Kahane led to fragmentation of his movement, which was tarnished by mudslinging between the two factions into which Kach split. In the Gush the demise of Rabbi Kook the Elder did not deal a mortal blow, for he was promptly replaced by a collective leadership, re-spected but not charismatic. This was sufficient to run affairs whenever events were on a steady course according to the messianic road map. But whenever prophecy seemed to run awry (as in the Israeli evacuation of Sinai, the outbreak of the Intifada, and the Oslo Accord), uncertainty and dissension appears at the top, hampering the fortunes of the group. In 1995 one could not yet speak definitively of a decline in Gush Emu-nim, for the international environment may yet again smile upon the Gush if the Pa-lestinian autonomy agreement runs aground.

Conclusion

In this chapter we have applied the explanatory scheme presented in Chapter 17 to fundamentalist movements in different political and ethnic contexts. As we have shown, the political regime and the ethnic context condition the strategies and influ-ence the growth and decline of fundamentalist movements in more direct and impor-tant ways than do other structural variables, however important they may be. Other structural variables such as the international environment and the economy influence fundamentalism indirectly through governmental policies. The ethnic composition of a society divides it into basic identities, and these are even more sharply divided if they combine with religion. Interrelating in complex ways, these structural variables are "turned on and off" by chance events and converted into options by the decisions of leaders.

We suggest a number of conclusions as to how fundamentalism is basically condi-tioned by the nature of the political regime and the ethnonational composition of the society. In authoritarian regimes such as the Islamic ones, the form that the fundamen-talist movements take varies with the coerciveness of the regime. The emergence of fundamentalism in its world-creator/enclave mode is possible in most types of Islamic regimes. In traditional authoritarian regimes such as Saudi Arabia and the Gulf states, fundamentalist movements engaged in anti-Israeli activities have relied on financial and logistical support. But even in these regimes world-conqueror fundamentalists, and most world-transformers as well, encounter suppression. In secular and coercive authoritarian regimes such as Syria and Iraq, efforts on the part of fundamentalist movements to penetrate and transform society encounter extreme coercion, forcing these movements to operate underground to the extent that they operate at all. But it seems impossible to root out these movements in their entirety. Any relaxation finds them rising once again to the surface.

The historical experience of modernizing Islamic regimes suggests a dialectic relationship between government policies and shifting fundamentalist strategies. In the past thirty years there has been a continuous power struggle in which the relaxation of coercive authority leads to rapid changes in fundamentalist patterns of behavior (primarily a move from an enclave-based world-creating separatism to world-conqueror-style bids for power). It does not appear possible to maintain a stable equilibrium in these authoritarian regimes, as the experiences of Iraq, Syria, Saudi Arabia, Egypt, and Algeria attest. If an authoritarian regime relaxes its authority and vigilance, fundamentalists tend to "up the ante" until the regime calculates the cost of suppression as being less than the cost of toleration.

In democratic regimes the emergence of fundamentalist movements from their enclaves is relatively unhindered by the political setting. They have access to, and can seek to transform, the world of politics, civil society, and the media. Even when they take on world-conquering strategies, fundamentalists are constrained by the criminal, civil, and constitutional law, implemented by an independent judiciary. In their transformative and conquering efforts fundamentalists encounter ideological and cultural resistances in a pluralist, secularized society. Furthermore, there is an inherently parochial aspect of fundamentalism which limits its appeal even across religious lines, to say nothing of the resistance found among members of an informed and largely secularized society. In democratic regimes, when fundamentalist movements make their bids for power by bargaining and making coalitions with infidels, fundamentalists' beliefs attenuate and their boundaries become relaxed and diffuse. Thus the dialectic which operates under democratic regimes is different from that of authoritarian regimes. As fundamentalist movements leave their enclaves and seek power and hegemony in a democratic society, they may be penetrated and immobilized by the surrounding culture, which is full of temptations and challenges. In order to avoid this cultural cooptation, fundamentalists periodically withdraw to their enclaves and seek a limited and local influence, until another historic opportunity presents itself.

Where religious fundamentalism is able to tap the power of strong ethnic and/or nationalist commitments it may produce nativist, preemptive ideologies and movements of a very violent sort, provoking responsive violence on the part of the threatened ethnoreligious minorities. Recent South Asian history provides vivid evidence of the virulence of this combination.

Three general findings of the Fundamentalism Project commend themselves as a final conclusion to our discussion.

1. Religious fundamentalist movements are distinct from other religious movements in that they are inherently interactive, reactive, and oppositional—that is, they are inexorably drawn to some form of antagonistic engagement with the world outside the enclave. In other words, fundamentalisms are inevitably political. This judgment can be made perhaps only in the late twentieth century, as we look back on long-term developments in movements that, for a time, seemed to be purely separatist (e.g., U.S. Protestant, haredi Jews). But because they look to the future rather than to the past,

and because they are essentially active in preparation for the future, fundamentalisms cannot resist being caught up in modern bureaucratic and institutional dynamics—the dynamics of change.

2. While they are political in nature, fundamentalist movements are also genuinely religious, which puts them in an analytical category distinct from other social protest movements or political opposition parties. We will fail to understand these movements if we neglect their irreducible religious dimension. The religious dimension manifests itself, among many other ways, in the person of the charismatic leader, whose authoritative interpretation of the religious tradition legitimates his religiopolitical diagnoses and prescriptions, and guides his associates and assistants in setting and implementing policy. Militance, coalition building, "diplomacy"—all of the "ordinary" pursuits of minority political movements—take on unique rhythms and patterns in fundamentalisms, due to their religious character.

3. While all fundamentalisms tend to be hegemonic, their world-conquering impulse is modified in practice in a variety of ways. As political entities fundamentalist movements are often at the mercy of long-term economic, political, and social-structural trends in their host societies. As religious entities they are constrained by the boundaries of the host religion and by their own antitraditional character—that is, their willingness to manipulate the religious tradition and introduce innovation for political rather than strictly spiritual purposes—a propensity that delegitimates the so-called true believers in the eyes of many other believers. Our analysis of the various patterns of world relation and of the diverse factors affecting fundamentalist strategies, growth, and decline demonstrates the complexity of the situation in which fundamentalisms find themselves: authoritarian absolutists in a pluralist world.

In sum, religious fundamentalisms are hegemonic, antipluralist movements that are constrained in their impact by the conflicting demands made upon them by their dual identity as inherently religious and inherently political entities. Despite their various comprehensive blueprints for a "redeemed" society, these movements are not "civilizational," in the sense that Samuel Huntington[1] or S. N. Eisenstadt (in this volume) uses the term. For fundamentalisms are caught in a debilitating paradox. As long as they remain fixed in the enclave culture and mentality that nurture them, fundamentalists are fated to be no more than disruptive and relatively influential dissenting minorities; yet once they exit the enclave, mentally or otherwise, they find that their fundamentalist religious ardor quickly yields to the pragmatic, compromising strategies of a world not of their liking—the impure, very real world outside the enclave.

Notes

1. Samuel P. Huntington, "The Clash of Civilizations," *Foreign Affairs* 72, no. 3 (Summer 1993): 22–49.

CONTRIBUTORS

GABRIEL A. ALMOND is professor of political science, emeritus, at Stanford University and a fellow of the American Academy of Arts and Sciences. He is the author of several classic works on comparative politics, including *A Discipline Divided: Schools and Sects in Political Science* and *The Civic Culture*.

R. SCOTT APPLEBY is director of the Cushwa Center for the Study of American Catholicism and associate professor of history at the University of Notre Dame. From 1988 to 1994 he was associate director of the Fundamentalism Project. He is the author or editor of several books on religious modernisms and fundamentalisms.

GIDEON ARAN is associate professor of sociology and anthropology at Hebrew University, Jerusalem. Aran is the author of several studies of Jewish radicalism in Israel, including *Zealotry: Historical and Sociological Study*, a comparative study of fundamentalisms in the Holy Land.

SAID A. ARJOMAND is professor of sociology at the State University of New York, Stony Brook. He is the editor of *The Political Dimensions of Religion* and the author of several works including *The Turban for the Crown: The Islamic Revolution in Iran* and *The Shadow of God and the Hidden Imam*.

WAYNE C. BOOTH is George M. Pullman Distinguished Service Professor Emeritus in the department of English at the University of Chicago and author of *The Rhetoric of Fiction* and *The Company We Keep: An Ethics of Fiction*.

S. N. EISENSTADT is Rose Isaacs Professor Emeritus of Sociology at the Hebrew University of Jerusalem, where he has been a faculty member since 1946. The recipient of several prizes and honorary doctoral degrees in the social sciences, his many publications include *The Political Systems of Empires* and *Martin Buber on Intersubjectivity and Cultural Creativity*.

ERNEST GELLNER is William Wyse Professor in Social Anthropology at the University of Cambridge, and Fellow of King's College. A Fellow of the British Academy since 1974, he has taught on the faculty of the London School of Economics. Since 1991, he has also been research professor at the Central University at Prague and head of its Centre for the Study of Nationalism. His many publications include *Thought and Change* and *Postmodernism, Reason, and Religion*.

MARK JUERGENSMEYER is professor of sociology at the Santa Barbara campus of the University of California, and chair of the University's system-wide Pacific Rim Research Program. He is author or editor of ten books. His most recent work is *The New Cold War? Religious Nationalism Confronts the Secular State.*

DANIEL H. LEVINE is professor of political science at the University of Michigan. He has published widely on religion, politics, and cultural change in Latin America. His most recent books are *Popular Voices in Latin American Catholicism* and *Constructing Culture and Power in Latin America.*

SAMUEL C. HEILMAN holds the Harold Proshansky Chair in Jewish Studies and Sociology at the Graduate Center and Queens College of the City University of New York. He is the author of *Synagogue Life, The People of the Book, Defenders of the Faith, A Walker in Jerusalem, The Gate Behind the Wall* and (with S. M. Cohen) *Cosmopolitans and Parochials.* He has been a contributor to the other volumes in the fundamentalism series and edited the section on Judaism in *Accounting for Fundamentalisms.*

VALERIE J. HOFFMAN is associate professor in the Program for the Study of Religion at the University of Illinois at Urbana-Champaign. She is the author of *Sufism, Mystics, and Saints in Modern Egypt* and several articles in the areas of Sufism and gender issues in Islam and Egyptian society.

T. N. MADAN is professor of sociology at the Institute of Economic Growth, University of Delhi, India, and author of *Nonrenunciation: Themes and Interpretations of Hindu Culture.*

MARTIN E. MARTY is the Fairfax M. Cone Distinguished Service professor of the History of Modern Christianity at the University of Chicago, the director of the Fundamentalism Project, and a senior editor of *Christian Century.* A fellow of the American Academy of Arts and Sciences, Marty is the author of over forty books, including the four-volume history, *Modern American Religion.*

HARJOT OBEROI holds the chair in Sikh and Punjabi studies and is associate professor in the Department of Asian Studies, University of British Columbia, Vancouver, Canada. He is assistant editor of *Pacific Affairs* and author of *The Construction of Religious Boundaries: Culture, Identity and Diversity in the Sikh Tradition.*

GANANATH OBEYESEKERE is professor of anthropology and director of graduate studies at Princeton University. His most recent book is entitled *The Apotheosis of James Cook: European Mythmaking in the Pacific.*

JAMES L. PEACOCK is Kenan Professor of Anthropology at the University of North Carolina at Chapel Hill and President of the American Anthropological Association. He is author of, among other works, *The Anthropological Lens: Harsh Light and Soft Focus.*

TIM PETTYJOHN is a Ph.D. candidate in the department of anthropology at the University of North Carolina at Chapel Hill.

EMILE F. SAHLIYEH is associate professor of international relations and Middle East politics at the University of North Texas. Among his publications are *The PLO After the Lebanon War* and *Religious Resurgence and Politics in the Contemporary World*. He is currently completing a book entitled *Jordan: Domestic Politics and Foreign Policy* based on data gathered while on a Fulbright in that country during the summers of 1991 and 1992.

EMMANUEL SIVAN is professor of history at Hebrew University, Jerusalem. He is the former editor of the *Jerusalem Quarterly* and author of *Radical Islam,* among several other works on religion and politics in the Middle East.

INDEX